Polanski and Percept

Polanski and Perception

The Psychology of Seeing and the Cinema of Roman Polanski

Davide Caputo

intellect Bristol, UK / Chicago, USA

First published in the UK in 2012 by
Intellect, The Mill, Parnall Road, Fishponds, Bristol, BS16 3JG, UK

First published in the USA in 2012 by
Intellect, The University of Chicago Press, 1427 E. 60th Street,
Chicago, IL 60637, USA

A catalogue record for this book is available from the British Library.

Cover designer: Holly Rose
Cover image: *Repulsion*, 1965, Director: Roman Polanski [COMPTON-TEKLI/ROYAL/ THE KOBAL COLLECTION]
Copy-editor: MPS Technologies
Production manager: Jelena Stanovnik
Typesetting: Planman Technologies

ISBN 978-1-84150-552-7

For Lorna

Table of Contents

Acknowledgements

I must begin by paying respect to Professor Richard L. Gregory, as it was the question of his influence on Polanski's cinema that formed the impetus for this book. Professor Gregory was kind enough to speak with me on a number of occasions as this work took shape; I am very grateful that I had the honour of talking with him directly and listening to his many amusing anecdotes. Sadly, Professor Gregory passed away in May 2010. (For information on Professor Richard L. Gregory's research on perception, see www.richardgregory.org.)

I owe a special debt of gratitude to all those who have reviewed this text, either in whole or in part, and whose suggestions have found their way into the final draft. Thanks to all my friends at the University of Exeter, where this work took its initial shape, in particular to Will Higbee, Song Hwee Lim, Helen Hanson, Don Boyd and, above all, my good friend Susan Hayward, who has seen this project through from its inception and has provided me with much guidance over the years. I would also like to extend my thanks to Mark Shiel at King's College London for his highly useful feedback, as well as the anonymous reviewer for his or her valuable commentary. Thanks also to everyone at Intellect and University of Chicago Press for their assistance, especially Melanie Marshall, Jelena Stanovnik, Alice Gillam, Holly Rose, James Campbell, and the copy editors. I must also acknowledge the support of the Arts and Humanities Research Council (AHRC), the British Board of Film Classification (BBFC) archives in London, and the Bibliothèque du cinema (BiFi) archives in Paris.

I would also like to thank my parents and all my friends and family for their encouragement over the years. Most of all, I want to thank my truly amazing wife, Lorna, without whose loving encouragement this book never would have been written. I love you so much.

Introduction

The young man in Roman Polanski's *Knife in the Water* (1962) lays on the deck of his host's boat and stares at his own index finger. He extends his arm and observes his finger in relation to the boat's mast, which towers over his prone body. In a point of view shot (POV) from the young man's perspective, light floods the frame; both the young man's finger and the mast are in focus. Counter shot. He shuts his eyes, one at a time, alternating rapidly between right and left. Back to the POV. His finger leaps across the screen and back again as he closes each eye. After several seconds of this, the scene ends and is followed by the young man and Andrzej (his host) discussing the relative merits of compasses. The finger-leaping sequence has apparently no bearing on narrative progression, so why bother including it at all?

Perhaps this scene is intended to help us understand something about the superiority of the young man's natural navigational abilities over those of Andrzej, or perhaps it is simply what Bazin calls a 'micro-action' (Bazin, 2004: 90), included to heighten realism; there are undoubtedly many ways of interpreting it, but what I would most like to highlight is that in this scene we have the first explicit allusion to the mechanisms involved in visual perception in a Polanski film. The scene replicates the effects of eliminating stereoscopic vision by (slightly) changing the position from which the boy's hand and mast are filmed, and then cutting between these two shots to suggest that each corresponds to an 'eye' being covered. At least two key issues are called to mind from this rudimentary effect:

1. Attention is drawn to relative size and distance perception; that is, our ability to guess the distance of an object based on size comparison to another object whose size and distance is known. In this case, knowledge of the hand signals how far away the mast is, based on its relative size. Even though both are in plain focus, knowledge of how big the mast should be informs our perception of where it is in relation to the hand, moderated by our (logical) rejection of the possibility that the mast, which we recognise from previous scenes, has shrunk.
2. The (faux) depth effect of the cinematographic image is simultaneously exposed and heightened. Just as the young man does on-screen, we too can reduce the world to 2-D any time we wish by simply covering up an eye and thus eliminating the 3-D effect caused by stereoscopic vision (which, in any case, causes a 'depth effect' that is limited to only about 100 m). Paradoxically, the film's cinematic

> replication of this effect actually encourages us to *overestimate* the parallel between the way we see the cinematographic image (which is flat) and how we see the rest of the world.

Above all, however, with this simple gesture of montage, Polanski invites us to consider the agency of cognition (of the *brain*) in perception, and introduces the concept of *perceptions as hypotheses* into his work.

Whilst extended, inter-film analyses of Polanski's work have tended to focus on biographical elements as a means of engaging with his cinema,[1] shorter academic pieces (far too many to catalogue here) are as diverse in their approach to Polanski's films as the opus itself. Notwithstanding the diversity of the critical work on Polanski, an often-neglected aspect of his cinema is his concern with the functioning of perception and how this is manifested in his film-making; it is this particular authorial hallmark that is the focus of the present analysis of Polanski's cinema. Polanski himself cites the work of the constructivist neuropsychologist Richard L. Gregory (1923–2010) as having had a great influence on his approach to film-making, claiming that Professor Gregory 'lent scientific confirmation' to many of his intuitive beliefs regarding perception, in particular those related to optical illusions (Polanski, 1984: 254–255).

Several critics have mentioned Gregory's influence on Polanski's cinema and their collaboration in the 1970s, but this fact tends to be mentioned only in passing. Other than the interview with Gregory included on a 2003 DVD release of *Repulsion* (cited herein as 'Gregory, 2003'), the effect of Gregory's research on Polanski's work has, for the most part, been overlooked in academic discourse. One important exception, however, is an article by John Orr (1943–2010), promisingly titled 'The Art of Perceiving' (2006), which begins by acknowledging the fact that critics of Polanski's cinema have long neglected the importance of perception in his work. My own research confirms Orr's claim, and I propose that this is likely due to the overemphasis of biographical issues in much of the Polanski-based literature.

Whilst Orr initiates a fruitful discussion on Polanski's fascination with the nature of perception and how he realises its implications at a philosophical level, he too mentions R. L. Gregory only in passing, referring to him as 'Polanski's favourite *philosopher*' (2006: 12, emphasis my own) rather than as a neuropsychologist; this is a mislabelling that is neither disparaging nor entirely inaccurate, but is certainly incomplete. Most importantly, whilst Orr does allude to part of the theoretical basis of Gregory's model of perception ('the nature of perception is at times inseparable from the question of emotion' [12]), there is also much value to be added to this discourse by highlighting how the model of perception to which Gregory is aligned differs from other, and still tenacious, models. It is my intention to carry on Orr's approach to Polanski's cinema by investigating Gregory's model more closely, highlighting how it differs from other theories of perception, and examining the manner in which Polanski's own perceptual discourse engages with these theories.[2]

Approaching a director's cinema via a study of a model of perception does not necessarily mean the total abandonment of what Bordwell refers to as 'Grand Theory' (1996: 3); reading a film via an examination of perceptual psychology, for example, neither excludes nor entails a parallel psychoanalytic reading. And neither does such an approach necessarily reduce itself to the level of purely empirical ('low level') fact finding. What is most interesting about Polanski's active mobilisation of perceptual psychology is indeed the manner in which it enables the reader to simultaneously address two dimensions of the perceptual discourse, each side informing the other. By this I intend:

a) the thematic discourse embedded in these films, both at narrative and aesthetic level, and
b) the actual cognitive experience of the spectator watching these films.

It is my intention to initiate a discussion of Polanski's cinema along these lines, in an approach that I believe is neither low-level empiricism nor Grand Theory, but more in line with what Bordwell calls 'middle-level theory' (1996: 26).

A concern with the working of perception and perceptual 'stability' is not, of course, limited to Polanski's work. An interest in the relative malleability of perception (and reality) is evident in many other directors of his generation and the next, including many 'old masters' like Antonioni (*Blow-Up*, 1966), Coppola (*The Conversation*, 1974) and Kubrick (*The Shining*, 1980, *Eyes Wide Shut*, 1999), as well as 'new masters' such as Lynch (*Lost Highway*, 1997, *Mulholland Drive*, 2001) and Cronenberg (*eXistenZ*, 1999). An analysis of any of these directors' cinema using a methodology similar to that which I employ here would certainly yield interesting results, which I hope this analysis of Polanski's perceptual discourse will encourage.

Although it is beyond the scope of this piece to elaborate on the intricacies of cognitive theory and spectatorship, I hope to at least establish a framework that allows Polanski and Gregory to be incorporated into this wider discourse. The actual degree to which Gregory's research informs Polanski's cinema may be difficult to determine; nevertheless, this book aims to demonstrate that using Gregory's description of the model of indirect and active perception as a 'pathway' through Polanski's films provides a fruitful way of gaining a greater understanding of this director's complex (cinematic) discourse on the nature of perception, which in turn connects to Polanski's grander philosophical concerns, which I shall address in due course.

The structure of this book

The first three chapters of this volume are focused on acquainting the readers with the key concepts that will guide the case studies that make up the rest of this book. In Chapter 1, I provide a brief overview of the early part of Roman Polanski's career. Here I discuss Polanski's educational background, his early shorts, and his first feature, *Knife in the Water*. Whilst this introduction was originally conceived as a means of 'locating' the director within the discourse of national cinema, what soon becomes evident are the many challenges Polanski poses to such a task; hence, the discussion soon veers towards unpicking the intricate notions of transnationalism and nomadism, which I suggest proves a better means of addressing Polanski's work. Emerging from this discussion is Polanski's special interest in visual perception, the issue that ultimately guides this analysis of his films.

Chapter 2 delineates the conceptual framework upon which the forthcoming close readings of Polanski's cinema are based. The majority of this chapter is dedicated to examining the model of indirect/active perception as espoused by the neuropsychologist R. L. Gregory, whom Polanski claims his cinema is greatly influenced by and with whom Polanski has once collaborated. Critical to this discussion is the contrast between 'indirect' and 'direct' theoretical models of perception, the latter strongly argued by the renowned psychologist J. J. Gibson in the form of the (still tenacious) 'ecological' theory of perception. Both of these models are further differentiated from the Gestalt model of perception, and a nuanced distinction is made between active perception and Merleau-Ponty's phenomenology of perception. Also discussed is Sobchack's application of Merleau-Ponty's ideas to cinema in her theory of 'Film's Body', which is carefully distinguished from Polanski's 'tethered camera', a concept that I often employ throughout this book. The remainder of Chapter 2 is composed of series of short discussions intended to highlight the various other concepts that will be utilised in the case studies of Polanski's films that follow. Included are discussions of modernism and postmodernism, the notion of various 'planes' of reality, and the inherently polemical idea of focusing on Polanski himself as an absolute 'author' of this cinema. Finally, a short justification is offered for the decision of grouping the films discussed into two 'trilogies'.

The remainder of the book is dedicated to a series of 'close readings' of Polanski's films, which are primarily impressionistic and technical in nature, but also attempt to locate these works historically when appropriate. Chapters 3–6 are focused on the first set of case studies, namely *Repulsion* (1965), *Rosemary's Baby* (1968) and *The Tenant* (1976), collectively referred to as the 'Apartment Trilogy'. Chapter 3 serves as a specific introduction to the 'Apartment Trilogy', in which all three films are discussed in concert, specifically in regards to the issue of mental illness and how this is dealt with in each of these films. The chapter begins with a description of the polemics surrounding the very existence of schizophrenia in the 1960s, which are discussed in relation to the complex history behind the British Board of Film Classification's rating of *Repulsion*. Several seminal case studies are discussed in terms of the means by which schizophrenia is clinically defined and diagnosed, with particular attention paid to how these diagnostic criteria are represented in Polanski's films. Schizophrenia is then examined in relation to the active model of perception, with the specific purpose of demonstrating how studying non-veridical perception (not only illusions, but the hallucinations indicative of schizophrenia) can shed light on the workings of the perceptual mechanism itself; this discussion is then applied to the analyses of *Repulsion*, *Rosemary's Baby* and *The Tenant*, all of which include increasingly complex portrayals of perceptual crises. Drawing from Neidich's theory of a specifically urban form of psychosis, also included in this chapter is a discussion of the relevance of these films' urban settings, in which the architecture of the living spaces within which these crises occur is related to the physiological structure of the brain.

Chapter 4 is a close reading of *Repulsion* that is guided by the discussions of perception and schizophrenia that have led up to it. In this chapter, the 'two-fold' approach to perception in Polanski's cinema is discussed in detail. Also offered in this chapter are challenges to Goscilo and Wexman's psychoanalytic analyses of *Repulsion*, as well as a discussion of protagonist Carole Ledoux's (gender-based) crisis of self-actualisation, which is argued to both parallel and inform the colouring of her developing psychosis.

Chapter 5 continues the perception-based reading of the Apartment Trilogy and argues that *Rosemary's Baby* marks an evolution in Polanski's treatment of perceptual crises. This chapter sets out to demonstrate the level of ambiguity *Rosemary's Baby* achieves and how readings of this film become increasingly complex the closer one looks at it. The analysis shows how the attempt to 'stabilise' the diegesis proves especially problematic when one tries to identify whether or not Rosemary (Mia Farrow) is suffering from psychosis at all. The film is also examined in the context of feminist history, specifically the emergence of the National Organisation of Women at the time of its setting (1965–1966, two years before the film's release), and, continuing a discussion initiated in the case study of *Repulsion*, draws a parallel between Rosemary's perceptual crisis and the difficulties of female self-actualisation in this period. Also incorporated into this discussion is a (perception-based) reading of *Rosemary's Baby* as a parody of religion.

In Chapter 6, Polanski's enigmatic *The Tenant* is examined in terms of the protagonist's developing schizophrenia and resulting perceptual crises. Close attention is paid to the manner in which Polanski employs profilmic elements in the construction of certain sets as a means of including illusion in the experience of spectatorship in order to represent diegetic hallucination. Also discussed is the manner in which the protagonist's 'feminisation' parallels his developing psychosis, and the various ramifications of this coupling. The chapter concludes with a close reading of the significance of the film's profoundly 'dissatisfying' ending.

Chapters 7–10 deal primarily with *Chinatown* (1974), *Frantic* (1988) and *The Ninth Gate* (1999), referred to collectively as the 'Investigation Trilogy'. In Chapter 7, these films are jointly discussed. The grouping of these works as the 'Investigation Trilogy' is justified in terms of these films' shared evocation of the Oedipal investigation, a narrative framework that is itself greatly concerned with the manner in which the perceptual mechanism engages the outside world. The key issue dealt with in this discussion is Polanski's 'shift' from psychologically intrusive portrayals of (potentially) ill perceiving subjects towards more distant examinations of highly sane perceiving bodies (i.e. the 'investigators'), who nevertheless suffer perceptual crises. Also dealt with in this chapter is the Gordian issue of gender in the two trilogies, namely the connection that is established between psychosis and female or 'feminised' characters in the 'Apartment Trilogy', in contrast to the thoroughly sane male perceivers of the 'Investigation Trilogy'.

Chapter 8 is a dedicated close study of *Chinatown*, in which the previously discussed issue of the 'perceptual crisis' is revisited, but in the form of the cognitive dissonance endured by the film's protagonist. Detective Jake Gittes (Jack Nicholson) faces increasingly perplexing challenges to his well-established conceptual frameworks as he is forced to deal with stimuli, which he is cognitively ill-equipped to handle. Gittes's trajectory is discussed in relation to the Oedipus myth, both in terms of Freud's appropriation of the story as well as the parallels between the myth's and *Chinatown*'s narrative structure, in which the investigator becomes embroiled (and complicit) in the very case he is investigating.

Chapter 9 is made up of case studies of both *Frantic* and *Death and the Maiden* (1994), which are dealt with in relation to each other; as this chapter argues, *Death and the Maiden*, although not included as part of the 'Investigation Trilogy', serves as a thematic 'sequel' to *Frantic* in its dealing with the aftermath of a woman's abduction. In this regard, the Orpheus myth is related to these abduction-based narratives; a further connection is made to the manner in which Paris is portrayed both as a globalised 'safe' space and an Orphean 'hell' in the perceptual crises endured by Walker in *Frantic*. The issue of the 'tethered camera' – a concept used throughout this book – is looked at in great detail through a close dissection of *Frantic*'s opening scenes. Discussed in detail is the importance of perception in both films, but rather than focusing on the representation of perception gone awry as in the Apartment Trilogy, in these films the notion of emotionally fuelled 'hyper-perception' is introduced. Also addressed is the manner in which Gregory's concept of 'perceptions as hypotheses' – a theory in which an identity is established between perception and the scientific method – is made manifest diegetically via inter-character conflict.

In Chapter 10, the 'Investigation Trilogy' case studies conclude with an in-depth examination of *The Ninth Gate*, a film in which Polanski's examination of perceptual and conceptual crises takes a dramatic turn. The 'tethered camera' is again addressed, but this time discussed in pedagogical terms. This chapter also returns to the issue of modernism and postmodernism as it relates to Polanski's cinema, and specifically these films' engagement with perceptual psychology. It is ultimately argued that the (essentially existential) philosophical implications that emerge from the sort of perception theory Polanski engages with indicates that these films are perhaps best understood in terms of their postmodernity, although there are strong elements of both modernism and postmodernism throughout Polanski's cinema. Embedded in this discussion is an exploration of the film's parody of religion, which relates to the similar notion raised in the case study of *Rosemary's Baby*. Finally, the film's particularly enigmatic dénouement is tackled in terms of how Polanski's long engagement with perceptual psychology takes a radical turn with *The Ninth Gate*'s (possibly) supernatural plot twist.

In Chapter 11, I will use an analysis of *The Ghost* (2010) as means of 'tying together' many of the themes dealt with in the preceding case studies. *The Ghost* is especially conducive to such reflection as it serves as a convenient 'bridge' between the films of the Apartment Trilogy and the Investigation Trilogy. I will then conclude my examination of Polanski's cinema in Chapter 12 with a summary of the major points covered in this book, as well as a discussion of what the methodology employed here might add to film studies, in particular cognition-based research into cinematic embodiment.

Notes

1. Typical examples of the biographical approach include Leamings's *Polanski: Filmmaker as Voyeur* (1981), Polanski's own *Roman on Polanski* (1984), and Meikle's *Roman Polanski: Odd Man Out* (2006). However, this trend is showing signs of change – two recent exceptions to the heavily biographical approach are *Roman Polanski: The Cinema of a Cultural Traveller* (Mazierska, 2007) and *Roman Polanski* (Morrison, 2007). (For an extended recap of the Polanski-based literature, see Caputo, 2007).
2. Although Gregory's work is not widely cited in film theory, mine is not the first analysis to bring up his name. Alexander Mackendrick, for example, cites Gregory in his much-revered film-making course (see Mackendrick, 2004: xxviii).

Chapter 1

'Locating' Polanski

Polanski and Poland

Roman Polanski began his career in cinema as a young actor, most notably featuring in Andrzej Wajda's *A Generation* (1955). Wajda's film is credited with starting the Polish Film School, a movement that broke from the Marxist didacticism of Poland's post-war 'socialist realism', in favour of providing a more 'individualised vision' (Ostrowska, 2006: 63) of cinema. Although Polanski's early involvement with Wajda probably accounts for a large part of his early education as a film-maker, Polanski's own cinema, even his early 'Polish' output, sits uncomfortably alongside the Polish School, with his first feature, *Knife in the Water*, marking yet another 'break' in Polish cinema. Whilst Polanski's cinema shares, to varying degrees, Wajda's concern with the plight of the individual, the idea of cinema serving as 'psychotherapist of the Polish audience' (Ostrowska, 2006: 66) was rejected by Polanski. Even Polanski's cycle of schizophrenia-based films (what I refer to as 'The Apartment Trilogy'), although heavily concerned with psychosis, offers no *therapy*. Whilst the Polish School rejected the prescriptive aesthetics of the ideologically didactic post-war Polish cinema, these films were equally defined by their resistance to it. *Knife in the Water*, in contrast, is one of the first examples of truly post-regime Polish cinema.

Nevertheless, Polanski's cinema is certainly influenced by his direct experience of the Polish School, especially in its emphasis on the technical prowess of its film-makers. There are also indications of strong Polish cultural influences on Polanski's work, from Polish romanticism to the Theatre of the Absurd, from Gombrowicz to Grotowski. These influences are often papered-over in the analyses of Polanski's cinema, which tend to identify Polanski as a global entity; as convincingly argued by Mazierska (2007), however, examining the 'Polishness' in Polanski's cinema is indeed informative and not to be entirely overlooked. But the greatest influence on Polanski's early cinema education is, ultimately, *cinema* itself. Whilst studying at Łódź, Polanski was able to access a far greater range of world cinema than would have been possible for even the most passionate Polish cinephile in the mid-1950s, a special privilege that the government afforded film students (Polanski, 1984: 112), along with granting access to otherwise banned texts (if not directly, then through professors who 'carelessly' left these books scattered about classrooms [see Polanski, 1984: 80]). So whilst the influence of distinctly Polish culture on the formation of Polanski's approach to cinema should not be undervalued, it is the influence of *film-makers*, not only Wajda, but globally renowned directors like Carol Reed and Orson Welles, that probably most deeply informed his craft.

The only example of Polanski's early works to employ a specifically Polish set of references is *When Angels Fall* (1959), a film that combines historical events, mythology and the personal recollections of an old woman in order to explore the ways in which all three intermingle and inform the formation of memory. Even without dialogue, the foregrounding of these iconic Polish elements firmly established *Angels* as a 'Polish' text. Polanski anchors the cinematic experience to the vision of an individual: the old woman (a Polish icon in her own right), whose subjective recollection-images we are permitted to observe. Oddly, at times, these 'subjective' images move beyond her (life's) perceptual reach, to an era before her birth. Thus the film transcends its specifically Polish framework to explore the malleability of memory and the influence that popular mythology, and possibly even the state, can have on personal recollections of the past. Here we have the first hint of Polanski's concern with the manner in which perceptions are formed, a concept that dominates much of his cinema.

As Ostrowska writes, 'Polanski's scepticism towards the possibilities of direct access to memory put him in opposition to the exploring of it, the central task of Polish cinema [i.e. the Polish School] at the time' (2006: 66). Nevertheless, the most enduring strength of *Angels* is not specifically its Polish iconography, but its discussion of memory through the superimposition of the woman's vivid recollection-images onto the film's drab actual-image of the men's toilet in which she works. To overemphasise the 'Polishness' of *When Angels Fall* is to miss much of what Polanski is observing about the functioning of human memory and the manner in which each of our concepts of reality are constructed by our individual perceptual mechanisms.

The rest of Polanski's shorts are far more difficult to identify as specifically Polish, although all, save *The Fat and Lean* (1961), were made in Poland during Polanski's time at Łódź. Much of this is simply down to Polanski's tendency of keeping his shorts abstract and dialogue-free.[1] Polanski's preference for dialogue-free shorts, which he nevertheless considered to be the 'correct' language of the short film, suggests a desire to move beyond fixed concepts of nation-, linguistic- or culture- based cinema towards that elusive universal language of the moving picture, that purely visual form of communication cultivated by the likes of Murnau, Chaplin and Griffith that had been all but forsaken after the birth of the talkie:

> Cartoons and documentaries proved that even very short films could tell a convincing story with a beginning and an end, but to do the same with actors required a different approach. Sounds had to be used as punctuation, dialogue kept to a minimum or dispensed with altogether. As far as I was concerned, a realistic theme was out. Though hung up on surrealism, I also wanted to convey a message. The short I aspired to make would have to be poetic and allegorical yet readily comprehensible.
>
> (Polanski, 1984: 132)

In *Knife in the Water*, Polanski manages to retain the allegorical element of his more abstract, silent shorts, but combines symbolic imagery with the realism offered by the inclusion of dialogue, the form he believes should be reserved for the feature film. But as soon as his characters begin to speak, an inextricable link is inevitably forged between language and the nation with which it is associated. Whilst *Knife in the Water* did not fit into the individual-focused Polish School, with its attempts to assume 'the role of "psychotherapist" of the Polish audience' (Ostrowska, 2006: 66) through neorealist-influenced recreations of wartime and post-war Poland, it was certainly not the sort of contemporary social(ist) realism preferred by the state. Polanski's Polish films move beyond a Polish cinema defined by either adherence or resistance to communist ideology. As Wajda himself identified, *Knife in the Water* marked the end of the Polish School, signalling 'the beginning of the new Polish cinema' (in Meikle, 2006: 64), a type of film undefined by the regime; instead, with *Knife in the Water*, Polanski contemporises Polish cinema whilst depoliticising it, offering observations on humanity, but not analysis. The camera does adopt an objective standpoint, but not quite like the neorealist style aped by the Polish School. Polanski's camera 'sees' the unseeable through intra-frame compositions that betray the film's unspoken power struggle and gender relations; analysis, however, is left up to the audience. Polanski's observational stance in *Knife in the Water* would prove to be one of the most enduring aspects of his work; consistent with this 'distance' is Polanski's refusal to become a moralist film-maker, favouring stories that explore the complexities of morality over didactic tales of right and wrong (or those that try to *right* wrongs).

Haltof (2002) makes notes of the 'split' that was beginning to form in the mid-1950s between Poland's established film-makers such as Aleksander Ford and Wanda Jakubowska and the new generation of Łódź graduates influenced by the Italian neorealist films they had the privilege of seeing at university; these graduates were more concerned with individual expression and the 'genuine depiction of national themes' (79) than they were with the Marxist ideology or socialist realism. Coates compares this division to the Polish flag itself, 'torn across, between politics and aesthetics ... between ... "the red and the white"' (2005: 1). The influence of neorealism is evident in Wadja's *A Generation*, a film Haltof argues to be a 'transitional' work that 'heralds the Polish School phenomenon' (79); but even Wadja's film, Haltof argues, is a 'work tainted by political compromise', which still bears the marks of socialist realism and is 'heavily stereotyped' in its re-creation of 'recent Polish history from the communist perspective' (79).

In the early 1960s, a discernable 'third generation' of young Polish film-makers was beginning to make its mark; this group included film-makers such as Janusz Majewski, Henryk Kluba and Roman Polanski, but the most significant contributions to this movement, Haltof suggests, came from Jerzy Skolimowski and, a few years later, Krzysztof Zanussi. Haltof cites Skolimowski's 'new generation trilogy' (*Rysopis* [*Identification Marks: None*, 1965], *Walkower* [*Walkover*, 1965] and *Bariera* [*The Barrier*, 1966]) (125–126), as well as Zanussi's 'Bergmanian' television films *Face to Face* (1968)[2] and *Pass Mark* (1968), and his features *Struktura Kryształu* (*The Structure of Crystals*, 1969) and *Iluminacja* (*Illumination*, 1973) as examples of films that demonstrate the transition towards evermore personalised cinema (Haltof, 2002: 127–128). Polanski's *Knife in the Water*, for which Skolimowski is also credited as a screenwriter, is a film that should be considered as a work of this post-Polish School movement. However, jaded by his experience with the Polish censors, Polanski would leave this 'third generation' to continue his career outside Poland. It would not be until *The Pianist* (2002) that Polanski would return to Poland to make a film, and so he is rightfully considered to be a minor-player in the history of Polish national cinema.

The Gomułka government's censorship policies of the late 1950s and early 1960s had major impact on the cinema of the time; hence, it is worth briefly examining *Knife in the Water*'s own struggle with the authorities in order to gain a better appreciation of the situation Polanski left behind when he opted to continue his career outside the Polish system. A word of caution is perhaps warranted here, as much of the account of Polanski's encounter with the Polish censors I present below is based on Polanski's own testimony, as described in his 1984 autobiography. As Coates (2005) warns, during this time in Polish history, there was both a 'mythical censor' and a 'real one'; he points out that many artists have a 'propensity to recall the more colourful incidents and to colour those that are recalled, his or her primary intention to divert the audience' (75). That said, Coates also concedes that the 'real' censors, namely the government's Script Assessment Committee, the Central Committee and the Politburo, did indeed monitor film projects closely with an eye towards 'nudging' works towards the party line. Coates even directly cites the 'blighting' of Polanski by the First Secretary Gomułka (Coates, 2005: 75–76), who was displeased with *Knife in the Water*, considering it to be irrelevant to Polish society (Polanski, 1984: 170).

Haltof (2002: 102) describes the multiple layers of censoring bodies through which a film project would have to pass, starting with 'The Committee for the Evaluation of Scripts', and then on to the supervision by authorities of the filming process itself and beyond. The key concern was a growing 'Westernisation' of Polish cinema (102), and so the Communist Party sought to regain the levels of control the authorities exerted before the rise of Gomułka and the 'Polish October' of 1956. There are many accounts of how Polish film-makers were harshly dealt with by the authorities, many of which are far worse than that described by Polanski. Many films of the Polish School were 'punished' by the authorities for their 'lack of compliance to the Polish line' (103), such as *Nikt nie wola* (*Nobody is Calling*, Kazimierz Kutz, 1960) and *Koniec nocy* (*The End of Night*, Julian Dziedzina, Pawel Komorowski, Walentyna Maruszewska, 1957), which saw their distribution severely limited, and Aleksander Ford's *Eighth Day of the Week* (1958), which was banned (102–103). Based on examples such as these, it is reasonable to conclude that Polanski's own description of his dealings with the censors is probably not overly 'coloured' by personal animosity.

The script for *Knife in the Water* had originally been rejected by the Polish Ministry of Culture on the grounds that it 'lacked social commitment' (Polanski, 1984: 144). Unable to get funding in Poland, Polanski sought backing in France, where he had recently co-directed *The Fat and Lean* with Jean-Pierre Rousseau (who was added as 'co-director' to avoid funding complications due to Polanski's non-residential status in France). Encouraged by the French producer Rousseau to make a French-language adaptation of the script, Polanski transferred *Knife*'s story to a French setting. In the end, the promise of French funding fell through and Polanski once again pitched the project to the Polish authorities, having 'tinkered with a few scenes' and having added 'some snippets of dialogue designed to impart a trifle more "social commitment"' (Polanski, 1984: 161) to appease the ministry. In this new form, it was finally approved for production.

Knife in the Water's search for funding is telling in that it reveals that the idea itself was not conceived as a specifically Polish story; in fact, what Polish elements the final film does possess are there by way of compromise in order to get funding from the Polish state. The 'social commitment' Polanski refers to can be identified in those lines of dialogue wherein the boy and Andrzej discuss politics. Significantly, Andrzej's politics seem somewhat at odds with his material wealth, and although the (apparent) conflict is complex, Andrzej is presented as abusive and arrogant, and of the three characters it is he who is positioned as the most unlikeable; he is the closest thing to an 'antagonist' the film offers.

The film's most discussed, and perhaps telling, compromises involved Krystyna and Andrzej's car. Andrzej, a representation of the Polish *nomenklatura*, originally drove a Mercedes, but Polanski was 'encouraged' to reshoot using a Peugeot 403 to avoid provoking this emerging (and ideologically inconsistent) class of Warsaw elites, well known for driving around town in their Mercs. The compromise extended only to the exterior shots; Polanski claims that he 'reluctantly left the interiors as they were' (Polanski, 1984: 165), but this continuity mismatch would result in a subtle provocation in its own right, suggesting the true nature of the car to those knowledgeable enough (i.e. the *nomenklatura* themselves) to be able to catch the 'error'.

Although set in Poland and indeed including several Polish references, *Knife in the Water*'s relevance transcends its Mazurian setting through its use of visual style as the agent of communication and Polanski's observations on the dynamics of gender, marital and generational power relations. The film often draws attention towards the physicality of the characters, the camera lingering on all three bodies, highlighting both gender and age differences. We are positioned as voyeurs, connected to no individual character in particular, but nevertheless limited to the collective narrative reach of the triad. The camera inevitably draws our gaze towards not only Krystyna's body (as might be expected), but the men's bodies as well, each man positioned as an icon of visual appeal for his respective generation. Embedded in the film is also a subtle attack on the idea of a prescriptive sense of nationhood, as the bitter conflict between these men, combined with the introduction of taboo homoerotic imagery, serves to undo what Ostrowska identifies as the prevalent Polish notion of 'a male brotherhood tasked to defend the nation' (2006: 69).

Although Polanski avoids outright ideological didacticism in *Knife in the Water*, given the historical context of the time of its release, reading the film as a subtle attack on the regime is certainly valid. What is clearly apparent is the great divide in wealth between Andrzej and the young student in what is a supposedly classless society. The elder Andrzej comes across as the embodiment of the chauvinist, hypocritical and power-hungry state, whose authority is challenged by a new generation, who, whilst seemingly naïve, finally outwits him. Critical to this reading, of course, is the discord between Andrzej's ideological stance and the material reality of his life. No, we are informed, the yacht is not owned by a club, but is his personal possession. Even his Peugeot, whilst not quite the Mercedes Polanski first intended, requires an act of doublethink to be reconciled with communist ideals. Whilst Andrzej's apparent wealth is at odds with his politics, so too is it at odds with his job – a key concern of the Polish critical press. How could a mere sportswriter (not exactly a job fitting of the *nomenklatura*) afford both a foreign car and his own boat? Such discords suggest that there is something more to his character than the one-dimensional social archetype I have outlined above, and raises many questions. Is he lying about his job? Has he inherited the money? Has *she* inherited the money? (Is this what is hinted at by the opening shot of Krystyna driving the car? What about the fact that the boat bears her name?) Such unresolved questions give the film a depth beyond the readings of it as simply a thinly veiled political criticism; it is this type of diegetic 'depth' – that is, the intricate off-screen world that we are made aware of but are never given access to – that Polanski would continue to cultivate throughout his career.

When one begins to dissect *Knife in the Water* it becomes evident that the politically informed elements of the film are merely a part of a series of complex meditations on offer. The way in which the young man's body so often divides the space between Andrzej and Krystyna, the camera's meticulous fetishisation of not only Krystyna's, but also the men's bodies, the complex possible worlds contained by the film's final image, all suggest that to over-'nationalise' the film is to underestimate its scope. By the same token, however, to completely overlook the political climate in which it was made is equally remiss.

According to Polanski, the ministry's reaction to the film was 'generally favourable' (Polanski, 1984: 169), but there was some concern raised by the head of the ministry over the uncertainty of the film's end: 'the idea that an audience should be left to draw their own conclusions about the outcome of the story was an anathema to him: the ending had to be either "positive" or "negative" – preferably the former' (Polanski, 1984: 169). The ending was originally augmented by two more shots of the car framed from increasingly greater distances; by removing these shots, which presumably had the effect of emphasising the non-conclusive ending, the head of the ministry was contented and the film was allowed to pass. The Polish critical press was far less favourable than the ministry, however, with criticism starting even before the film's completion. Polanski recalls an *Ekran* reporter, who, based on what he had seen on a visit to the production set, published an article wherein he expressed his failure to understand how such an intimate film could be relevant to the nation, complaining that Polish taxpayers were being duped by this indulgent young film-maker.[3] Upon its release, the film was panned, in particular due to what was perceived as a lack of realism in terms of the sportswriter's wealth and a general impression of the film's irrelevance to the Polish people. Polanski recalls that many critics were also irked by his own 'cosmopolitan' status as a passport holder, who could hop back and forth between Poland and his native country, France.[4]

Even the Communist Party of Poland's first secretary, Władysław Gomułka, echoed the press's sentiments, calling the film's characters 'neither typical nor relevant to' Polish society as a whole (as quoted by Polanski, 1984: 170). Polanski's own reaction to these kinds of statements would prove prophetic: 'after this sort of official reception I knew I wouldn't be making another film in Poland for a long time to come' (Polanski, 1984: 170). Outside Poland, however, the film was well received, picking up special honours at the 1962 Venice festival and receiving nominations at the 1964 BAFTAs (Best Film) and Academy Awards (Best Foreign Language Film, respectably losing to Fellini's *8½*). A still from *Knife in the Water* was even featured on the cover of *Time* magazine (20 September 1963), behind the banner 'Cinema as an International Art' and the title 'Lovers in Polish Film'. As the cover suggests, *Knife in the Water*, whilst appreciated in the West, was nevertheless recognised abroad by a perceived 'Polishness'. By leaving Poland behind, Polanski was free to pursue his goal of capturing lucid observations of the human experience unburdened by state doctrine; and by mixing the 'nationality' of his productions, he continues to flummox attempts at nation-based readings of his work.

Knife in the Water would prove to be Polanski's only purely 'Polish' feature film, with interference from state officials during production (and its ramifications on the film) leading to his decision to leave Poland. Polanski makes his own feelings regarding the idea of nationhood abundantly clear:

> I am glad I am a nomad. I have always dreamed about leaving [Poland], I have always felt that the significance given by people to borders was ridiculous.
>
> (Polanski in Ostrowska, 2006: 62)

Consistent with Polanski's self-professed nomadism, his next two films, *Repulsion* and *Cul-de-sac* (1966), would both be shot in the United Kingdom (London and Holy Island respectively), using a predominantly British crew and talent, but including a mix of British, American, French and Belgian (albeit, played by French actresses Catherine Deneuve and Yvonne Furneaux) characters. Over the years, his cinema would become increasingly multinational, reflected not only in the filming locations and financing of his productions, but the very subject matter of his films. Once he left Poland, Polanski was no longer bound by an imaginary cultural barrier and would go on to pillage artistic canons and generic conventions from across the world, from Hardy and Shakespeare to American pulp fiction to South American theatre, from schlock horror to slapstick comedy to costume drama, Polanski's cinema almost literally does it all. This 'freedom' is not only transnational, but the kind of freedom that transcends the very concept of 'proprietary' national culture.

The influence of what can be identified as Polish culture (cinematic or otherwise) on Polanski's cinema should not be dismissed, but his resistance to conforming to a 'Polish aesthetic' is evident in both his shorts and *Knife in the Water*; his subsequent departure from the Polish film industry and the lack of explicitly 'Polish' subject matter in his cinema between *Knife in the Water* and *The Pianist* (2002) ensured that Polanski's association to the 'new' Polish Cinema would be limited. I will discuss Polanski in terms of auteur theory in more specific terms later in this chapter, but the key point I wish to emphasise regarding this early period is that Polanski's resistance to prescribed aesthetics, other than those that might constitute the progression of pure cinema, was evident from the start, and this is consistent with his clearly auteurist tendencies; this is not to say, however, that an auteur is *de facto* immune to membership in, or the creation/reinvention of, a cinema concerned with reflecting a nation.[5]

Notwithstanding the notable heterogeneity of Polanski's cinema, both in terms of genre and 'nationality' of production, there remain a number of strong thematic threads that bind much of his work, each film informing the complex discourse that weaves its way through his opus. The present discussion of Polanski's work will endeavour to uncover a number of these repeated motifs, but will focus primarily on an element I have found to be underrepresented in critical analyses of Polanski's cinema; as I have mentioned above, it is Polanski's concern with the working of human perception that I believe provides a novel and fruitful means of engaging with his cinema, and so forms the primary focus of this study.

Deconstructing national identity

It is useful to begin this foray into Polanski's cinema through an attempt (but not necessarily a *successful* one) to 'locate' the director within the wider discourse of national cinema; this is a process that I have already initiated with my discussion of *Knife in the Water*. I will outline some of the useful vocabulary that has emerged from this discourse that may help clarify Polanski's own complex relationship with the issue of national identity as well as his treatment of the often-recurring figure of the 'foreign' national in his films. This meditation on the complexities of national identity above all serves to prime a thought process conducive to dealing with the intricacies of perceptual psychology and how this informs Polanski's cinema, which will immediately follow.

Whilst my approach to Polanski shares the essential assumption of auteur theory, namely that although a film is the product of a collaborative effort, it is 'most likely to be valuable when it is essentially the product of its director' (Caughie, 1981: 9), this analysis does not dwell on Polanski's personal life or the 'biographical legend' (Stachówna, 1994: 34) it has become, which has more than sufficiently been written of elsewhere (see, for example, Mazierska [2005], Meikle [2006], Sandford [2009], Kiernan [1980], Wexman [1985] and Leaming [1981]). I will say only a few words about it here, as the events of his early life may help us understand his attitude towards nationhood and the construction of self-identity.

Polanski was born to a Polish father and a Russian mother in France in 1933, but his family moved to Poland in 1937. It was not until the invasion of Poland in 1939 that a young Polanski became aware of his 'Jewish' identity, a label applied to him by others, notwithstanding the fact that neither he nor his parents were at all religious (Polanski's father was of Jewish origin, as was his maternal grandfather). Polanski managed to avoid the concentration camps that claimed the life of his mother by having his name changed to 'Romek Wolf' and posing as a member of a Catholic family, until he was finally reunited with his father after the war. At the risk of appearing to digress into amateur psychoanalysis, it can be suggested that Polanski's experience of shifting identities highlighted to him the arbitrary nature of what are more commonly considered to be immutable components of identity, such as the genetic innateness of religious affiliation. Although Polanski has never been disparaging about either his Polish or Jewish roots, his autobiography describes a man who openly resists any limits that the imagined community of nation might impose; I refer here not only to the rigid cultural limits set by Poland's post-war regime, but to the very notion that certain artistic texts or styles are somehow the genetic inheritance of those born on a given, politically defined plot of land.

What is perhaps most evident in Polanski's work when observed as a whole is that whilst his films appear to be greatly informed by wide variety of cultural artefacts, his cinema cannot be firmly aligned to one culture or movement in particular; Polanski is neither obliged nor inhibited by his national affiliation. In *The Tragedy of Macbeth* (1971), for example, Polanski does not 'borrow' from the English canon to create a Polish take on Shakespeare, but rather *owns* it, producing a relatively faithful rendition of the story. The result is not a 'Polish' *Macbeth* (in contrast, arguably, to *Throne of Blood* [1957], Kurosawa's 'Japanese' *Macbeth*), but a cinematic interpretation of the stage play text. What is noteworthy in terms of culture clash is not the meeting of British and Polish sensibilities so much as the 'cultural difference' between theatre and cinema. In Polanski's *Macbeth*, the textual becomes subservient to the cinematic. Polanski trims the dialogue as needed, creating a decidedly non-theatrical visual aesthetic, and *showing*, often to shocking effect, what is normally only described on stage.

It is not only cultural lines that Polanski's cinema freely crosses, but also the distinction between 'art house' and 'commercial' cinema. He is by no means alone in this respect, as this crossover between 'art house' sensibilities and commercial appeal is notable in many of cinema's 'old masters', such as Bergman, Antonioni, Wenders, Kubrick and Fellini, all of whom produced works that defied the conventions of classic cinema, but which nevertheless found favour at the box office, both internationally and in their home countries. It is because of the success of these directors' films with audiences beyond the 'art house' that they are so instantly recognisable as 'masters', even by non-cinephiles. The work of these directors can render problematic the conceptual divide that separates 'art cinema' from 'classic cinema', as these films often fuse popular generic frameworks with sensibilities more indicative of 'high culture', none more so than Polanski, whose cinema, I argue, seeks to deliver pleasure at every level.

Of all the directors, it is perhaps with Kubrick that Polanski has most in common, especially the way in which their respective work comfortably resides within the definition of 'art cinema', but without sacrificing commercial ambitions.[6] Whilst Polanski's cinema would never be out of place in an 'art house' cinema, when compared to 'art house' fixtures like Antonioni, Wong Kar-wai, Bergman, Fellini and Lynch, his films have a decidedly more mainstream sensibility, discernable in Polanski's consistent use of stars, the manner in which he embraces generic conventions, and his use of camp and humour. His mainstream ambitions are also evident in his adaptations of literary classics like *Macbeth* and *Tess*, as well as his cinematic rendering of Władysław Szpilman's World War II experience in *The Pianist*, Polanski's most commercially successful film. There is none of the quietness or 'slowness' we often see in Antonioni's or Wong Kar-wai's work, his dialogue is rarely as existentially loaded as Bergman's, he is never as openly confessional as Fellini (there is no *8½* in Polanski's opus), and he is rarely as downright bizarre as Lynch. Polanski shares with these directors a mastery of craft and the desire to manifest grand issues cinematically, but his films are seldom 'difficult' in the way these other directors' work could be described.

In light of this discussion, we should consider Bordwell's (2002) commentary on the emergence of 'art cinema' after World War II, in which he partitions 'classic cinema' from 'art cinema'. By examining Bordwell's means of differentiation between these two types of cinema, the hybridity of Polanski's cinema, which uniformly resists classification, becomes evident. Notwithstanding the heterogeneity of films that he considers to be 'art cinema', Bordwell identifies the primary unifying feature of this category as a slackening of the cause-effect formula of narrative progression and diegetic logic that defines the 'classic cinema', highlighting the unresolved plot lines in Anontioni's *L'Avventura* (1960) by way of example (95). Bordwell suggests that in the 'art cinema', the impetus for narrative progression is instead that of 'realism and authorial expressivity' (95), a combination within which a subtle paradox seems to be embedded.

Whilst Bordwell argues that 'art cinema' is 'realistic' in its use of 'real locations and real problem' and 'psychologically complex characters' (95–96), at the same time 'art cinema' also 'foregrounds the author as a structure in the film's system … a formal component, the overriding intelligence organising the film for our comprehension' (97). It is the authorial voice, then, that 'unifies the text' (97) and frames reality. Bordwell also notes the prevalence of 'technical touches ... and obsessive motifs' (97) of the 'art cinema' director; as I argue further on in this chapter and throughout the forthcoming case studies, Polanski does indeed saturate his cinema with a series of repeated 'technical touches' and 'obsessive motifs', which serve to unify his cinema for the close reader in particular. As I shall discuss over the course of this book, Polanski's cinema also foregrounds psychological complexity, in particular through what I argue to be its direct engagement with perception theory, a trait more often seen in 'Op Art' (i.e. 'Optical Art') and experimental cinema rather than 'commercial' or even 'art house' cinema.

A brief comparison of Antonioni and Polanski is informative in this context. An aspect of Bordwell's (2002) conceptualisation of 'art cinema' shared by Antonioni and Polanski is their mutual championing of ambiguity; but a hallmark of 'art cinema' they do not share is the disregard for cause-and-effect narrative unity. Antonioni's emblematic use of *temps mort* ('dead time') in *L'Avventura* (1960), for example, in which an enigmatic mood is created through the inclusion of a series of scenes that 'have no obvious function in advancing the plot or illuminating the characters' (Salt, 1983: 347) is not an approach often taken by Polanski, who tends to embed more subtle enigmas within apparently 'unified' narratives; however, Polanski often undoes this sort of 'unity' with the manner in which his films are concluded.

Thus, what most strongly aligns Polanski's cinema with the sensibilities of the 'art house' is the level of ambiguity that is embedded in these films, a point that is much discussed in the case studies that follow. Polanski's use of ambiguity is not normally the result of a direct violation of classic cinema's adherence to cause-effect relations, but rather a subtle undermining of the spectator's confidence in his or her own understanding of the diegesis, namely what is and what is not 'real', which is most pronounced in the highly dissatisfying manner in which Polanski tends to end his films. Such dissatisfaction is just the opposite, it could be argued, of the mandate of 'classic cinema' to actively move towards stability. Bordwell sees such ambiguity as a hallmark of the art cinema, and indeed cites the final scene of *Knife in the Water* as an example (99). But Polanski's cinema does not completely forego the cause-effect structure of classic cinema, and nor does it avoid the use of stars nor necessarily privilege passivity over action. Most often, it embraces, even amplifies, popular genres and employs cinematographic and montage techniques specifically designed to engage ('lure in') spectators. In other words, depending on which Bordwellian definition one wishes to apply, Polanski's cinema can be considered as either 'classic' (audience-focused) or 'art' (director-focused) cinema. It is, of course, *both*.

In his history of Polish cinema, Coates (2005) takes issue with Bordwell's nomination of *Knife in the Water* and Wajda's *Ashes and Diamonds* (1958) as 'art cinema'; he argues that whilst Bordwell's classification is not entirely inaccurate, it is, nevertheless, *inadequate*, for it 'designates the mechanism of their Western distribution rather than their essence' (42), by which he is referring to these films' political subtext and their relevance to the Polish political situation at the time of their release. The arguably *covert* functioning of *Knife in the Water* as a critique of the Polish government is a matter of interpretation, but more relevant to the context of Polanski's overall career is the fact that this film's 'art house' credentials put Polanski onto the international stage. However, what ensured Polanski's long-termed status as an internationally renowned director was his ability to combine his 'art house' sensibilities with a Hollywoodian mode of cinema production; it is, after all, the Hollywood style that became the most international.

Polanski's subsequent departure from Poland began his trajectory towards an identification of his work as truly border-crossing. Polanski is by no means unique in this regard, as many film-makers of this kind emerged from his generation, such as Losey, Herzog, Kubrick, Wenders and Bertolucci, all of whom began their careers working within the system of a national cinema, but sought to become unburdened by an over-association with any particular country's need to define itself through its cinema. As Salt (1983) suggests, when dealing with such directors, 'the concept of "national cinema" becomes uselessly vague' (324). Therefore, a variety of terms have been introduced into the discourse surrounding national cinema; or rather, a variety of prefixes have been attached to the 'national' (multi-, inter-, pluri-, trans-, etc.), all of which are to varying degrees useful when discussing postcolonial and diasporic cinema, as well as films that are funded by a variety of globally disparate sources or use crews and other resources that are not easily identifiable in terms of national uniformity.

Nearly all Polanski's films demonstrate such complexity in terms of production and distribution. So given the national boundaries his films cross (production-wise, diegetically, and where they are marketed and shown), the term 'transnational' is definitely an appealing way to refer to Polanski's cinema; but such a statement is applicable to such an enormous number of films (especially when we consider the global hegemony of Hollywood cinema) that it is not especially useful when attempting to identify what makes Polanski's cinema 'special'. In fact, by using what seems to be a term geared towards widening understanding, we risk inadvertently applying conceptual limits to our engagement with Polanski's cinema. As Ezra and Rowden aptly pointed out, the concept of the transnational 'at once transcends the national and presupposes it' (2005: 4). I suggest that in order to more closely consider Polanski's own complex relationship with all things national, we need to look beyond the concept of the transnational and all that it 'presupposes'.

What may prove to be of better use in the analysis of Polanski's work is Higbee's (2007) discussion of 'cinema of transvergence'. A transvergent approach to nationality de-emphasises concepts of identity based on factors of nativity or citizenship, allowing us to move beyond nationhood as an encompassing identity determinant, and hence urging us to consider the constructed nature of the 'national'. Transvergence highlights difference in a fluid, complex and most importantly, non-binary way. Similarly, a key feature that runs throughout Polanski's cinema is a challenge to precisely the kind of epistemological certainty that binary or convergent thinking cultivates. Polanski attacks the certitudes of knowledge in a number of ways, notably through his portrayals of national identity, but also through his challenging of apparently binary concepts such as gender, mental health and morality. Underlining all such discussions, however, is what I argue to be Polanski's primary concern, the functioning of perception, from which all such concepts are derived.

The manner in which Polanski explores the issue of national identity provokes questions about the meaningfulness of terms like 'national' or even 'transnational' and ultimately proposes a more complex way of approaching identity than is offered by (legal) frameworks of nationality or even personal concepts of nationhood. Polanski's films are often populated with émigré characters, whose very status as political/cultural 'other' is, at least subtly, always in question as a possible contributing factor to the turmoil these characters inevitably find themselves facing. Critically, the cause-effect relationship between the characters' 'foreignness' and the obstacles they face is usually not clearly delineated.

Nearly all of Polanski's feature films include major characters that are readily identifiable as 'foreign' to the place in which they reside or find themselves, or contain an ethnic mix in a nationally neutral location, namely the open sea in the cases of *Bitter Moon* (1992) and *Pirates* (1986). What is often difficult to determine, however, is the extent to which these characters' national status actually informs the narrative trajectory of the films. It may be important, partially relevant, or it may even be completely irrelevant; we are left guessing. *Repulsion*, for example, features Belgian sisters Carole and Hélène Ledoux; but however tempting it may be to draw a causal link between Carole's mental disintegration and her diegetic status as a foreign national, *Repulsion* does not allow for such 'neat' conclusions. Similarly, Polanski's portrayal of Polish-Jewish French national Trelkovsky (played by Polanski himself) in *The Tenant* serves to subvert straightforward readings of the film as being a simple critique of French xenophobia. Whilst both films centre on a character's descent into madness, in neither case can the issue of national or cultural 'difference' be categorically assigned as even a contributing factor.

Differences of culture and language are also sometimes explicitly linked to interpersonal conflict, as seen in *Cul-de-sac* and *What?* (1972). Such conflict becomes more explicit in Polanski's later works; it is most pronounced in *The Pianist*, where perceived ethnicity becomes literally a matter of life and death for Szpilman (Adrien Brody). In *Frantic*, the American-in-Paris Dr Richard Walker (Harrison Ford) finds that his linguistic, national and cultural 'stuckness' creates significant obstacles, which turns out to be directly relevant to the narrative's unfolding. The antagonism between the French and Spanish is very much a part of *Pirates*' narrative, as exemplified by 'Frog's' purported motivation for helping (the English) Captain Red. In *Bitter Moon*, there is yet another standoff between America and France, with nationality serving as a major issue of conflict between Oscar and Mimi, and Nigel's 'Britishness' identified as a determinant in his actions (and reactions) on several occasions. In *The Ninth Gate*, on the other hand, Polanski emphasises the unity of the (capitalist) West in a film that spans America and Europe, and in which these cultures intermingle seamlessly and linguistic obstacles are easily overcome.

So, whilst Polanski's films can indeed be considered through a transnational, or even transvergent optic, I ultimately argue it is more useful to consider his cinema along *nomadic* lines. Rather than identifying many of Polanski's characters, or even Polanski himself, as émigré or diasporic subjects, we can instead judge these characters by the degree to which they can be considered as 'nomadic bodies'. By nomadic I do not exclusively refer to Polanski's own shifting domiciles (as far as I am aware, he has been resident in Poland, France, Italy, the United Kingdom, Switzerland and the United States), but more so to the attitude of deterritorialisation that is reflected in his sentiments regarding his own life as well as his cinema, in which he often adopts certain nation-associated aesthetics (often generic) to his own ends, without letting the need for an inherited sense of nationhood interfere. In common with transvergent thought, the key aspect of nomadism is the decentralised subject; the nomad has no coveted 'starting point' to which he or she is physically or psychically anchored and which all other occupied space is relative to. In contrast, the exile or ex-patriot remains (or purports to be) 'connected' to a homeland. With the nomad, previously occupied or traversed places and cultures may well influence the individual's actual cognitive state, but the psychical nomad is not *bound* by such influences as a means of constructing reality. It is in this regard that we can utilise the concept of 'nomadism' also as a means of addressing what appears to be Polanski's cinema's refusal to conform to any particular philosophical ideology or set concepts of morality or ethics.

Polanski's 'psychical' version of nomadism indeed extends beyond the traversal of land and nation, and can be considered in terms of what Deleuze calls *pensée nomade* in his countercultural analysis of Nietzsche (Deleuze, 1977: 142). Mazierska's (2007) identification of Polanski as a 'cultured traveller' is also especially relevant in this context, for her description of both the director and his films echoes Deleuze's notion of nomadic thought. Mazierska acknowledges the multiple countries in which Polanski's cinema has been produced over the years, but this fact alone is not of paramount relevance; it is Polanski's attitude that matters most, the way he 'traverses' cultures without any acknowledgement of barriers. The following quote illustrates Mazierska's point well:

> Curiosity about the cultures encountered through his journeys is accompanied by Polanski's unwillingness to elevate the cultures where his roots lie, namely Jewish, Polish and French, either as locations of the narratives or as the sites of moral norms. On and off

> screen the director distances himself from any type of nationalism, regarding it as the way to overestimate oneself unjustly and consequently underestimating fellow human beings. (2007: 187)

So the idea of Polanski as a 'cultured traveller' represents not only the literal traversal of land, but of concepts as well; it is a freeing of oneself from the conceptual limitations imposed by an overly robust sense of national identity, a 'deep scepticism for such products of culture as religion and political ideology' (Mazierska, 2007: 189). This freedom applies to his artistic influences as well. Mazierska highlights a number of artists with whom Polanski seems to engage in his work, both cinematic and non-cinematic, Polish and non-Polish, Jewish and non-Jewish, etc. These include Alfred Hitchcock, Luis Buñuel, Andrzej Munk, René Magritte and Samuel Beckett, many of whom I will discuss later in more specific terms.

Also strongly represented in Polanski's cinema are characters who themselves embody cultural conflicts, and it is upon these characters that Polanski most often fixes the camera. These are the 'outsiders' who usually become our chief perceptual objects, and sometimes even our perceptual surrogates. But whilst Polanski does indeed include many expatriate bodies in his films, these do not tend to be displaced subjects who 'long for a return to an idealised homeland' (Higbee, 2007: 83), nor do they tend to be elective immigrants abused by an adopted homeland (although in some cases this may be a possible reading, such as *The Tenant*). Rather than a straightforward portrayal of the plight of the foreign national, Polanski favours explorations of states of becoming in which issues of national identity or perceived ethnicity are but possible factors in what are rhizomic, often dissonant, states of being. By including the issue of nation, nationality and nationhood in the frame, Polanski calls attention to the artificial constructs that make up many of the cognitive frameworks that compose one's concept of identity, which in turn, as I shall later discuss, influence perception. In fact, I believe that the recurring presence of the issue of national identity in his cinema is merely symptomatic of Polanski's chief, and far more basic concern with the working of perception, an authorial trace that appears throughout much of his cinema, irrespective of whether or not he is author of the source material upon which a given film is based (thus my auteuristic approach to his cinema, which I shall discuss later). By introducing the spectre of mental illness, Polanski presents a complex ontological sketch in his foregrounding of the unreliability of characters' perceptual abilities. It is Polanski's interest in the way perception works that has perhaps most greatly informed both the thematic content of his films and the manner in which they are presented to the spectator. I propose that by scrutinising the material upon which Polanski's own study of perceptual psychology was based, a novel and informative means by which to engage with his cinema emerges. It is to this conjecture that I will now turn my attention.

Notes

1. Polanski's preference for dialogue-free shorts is also evident in his most recent short, *Cinéma Erotique*, which he made for the 2007 Cannes film festival, as well as his spots for Parisienne, Vanity Fair and for Francesco Vezzoli's fictitious 'Greed' perfume.
2. Not to be confused with Ingmar Bergman's own *Face to Face* (1976).
3. 'For Whom and For What?' read the *Ekran* headline (Polanski, 1984: 165).
4. 'All Polanski has is an international driving license and no film school diploma' (as quoted by Polanski, 1984: 170).
5. One need look no further for evidence than the French New Wave, which sought to invent a new, liberated cinema unbound by studio constraints, and which was more focused on the representation of current social realities, in contrast with the more old-fashioned narratives of the established French cinema (dismissed as '*cinema du papa*'). With its emphasis on the value of a singular creative force (the auteur), the French New Wave, as well as the Auteur Theory of the 1950s that it arguably spawned, can be interpreted as a reactionary movement (see Hayward, 2000: 145). At the same time, however, due to its focus on contemporary society, the French New Wave, like the Polish School, was also greatly concerned with informing a sense of national identity.
6. For a more detailed comparison of Polanski and Kubrick's work, see Morrison (2001).

Chapter 2

Establishing a Conceptual Framework

Professor Richard L. Gregory is best known for his work on the famous case of 'S.B.', a man who became blind at ten months but who regained his sight at the age of fifty after receiving corneal grafts (see Gregory and Wallace, 1974), and his influential book *Eye and Brain: The Psychology of Seeing*, which was first published in 1966. The book represented the findings of years of published research on visual perception, and, now on its fifth edition, continues to this day to be essential reading in the field of psychology. His work reflects the view of the nineteenth-century polymath Hermann von Helmholtz (1821–1894) in its description of an *indirect* and *active* model of perception. Gregory's stance marks a major break from the tenacious *direct realism* model of perception espoused best by the influential psychologist J. J. Gibson (1904–1979) in his theory of *Ecological Perception* (see Gibson, 1979). Gibson's stance echoes that of empiricists like Hume, Berkeley and Locke, for whom perceptions were directly connected to the objects perceived. Whilst Gibson's ecological theory of perception continues to have its disciples,[1] and has even been proposed as a meta-analytical tool for film theory (see Anderson and Anderson, 1996, which I discuss later in this chapter), the basics of the neo-Helmholtzian model of active perception are well established in medical science, and *Eye and Brain* remains a seminal introduction to active perception. Although this analysis of Polanski's cinema is primarily concerned with indirect/active perception, it remains useful to discuss both indirect perception and Gibson's still-tenacious theory of direct perception in parallel, as this will provide a means of better understanding both theories by way of contrast.

J. J. Gibson authored several volumes on the theory of *direct visual perception*, in which the 'common sense' or 'man-on-the-street' (Gibson, 1967: 169) approach to perception is argued most convincingly in modern times. The direct perception model suggests that perception is an unmediated experience that is not dependent on sensation, and one in which information is 'picked up' from the outside world (Gibson, 2002: 77). Gibson's central claim is that the theory of direct perception serves as a 'sophisticated support for the naïve belief in the world of objects and events, and for the simple-minded conviction that our senses give knowledge of it' (Gibson, 1967: 168). Due to this direct connection between perception and the external world, in philosophical discourse it is often referred to as direct (or even 'naïve') *realism*. Gibson's essentially empirical, ecological theory of perception abandons both the mechanical behaviourist view of perception as well as cognitive models in which the brain is positioned as a representational device:

> The act of perceiving is one of becoming aware of the environment or picking up of information about the environment … nothing like a representation of the environment exists in the brain or the mind which could be in greater or lesser correspondence with it – no 'phenomenal' world which reflects or parallels the 'physical' world.
>
> (Gibson in Allen and Otto, 1996: 212)

Direct perception's competing theoretical model has logically been labelled *active perception*, and although this model of perception has only become dominant in recent times (Gregory, 1997a: 2), the basic concept predates von Helmholtz and can be traced back to Plato's cave. Following von Helmholtz, active perception was most vigorously argued by R. L. Gregory and Irvin Rock (see, for example, Rock, 1995 and 1997), both of whom disputed the direct perception model supported by Gibson. Rather than perception being described as a passive experience of 'picking up' information from the world, the model of active perception instead takes a constructivist approach; it theorises that perception is a highly mediated process, in which the brain actively creates perceptions via intelligent problem solving (hypothesising) based on 'unconscious inductive inference from what is signalled and from knowledge of the object world' (Gregory, 1997b: 1121).

When reviewing the pertinent literature on perception, it is important to recognise that theorists often use words such as 'direct/indirect' and 'active/passive' in differing contexts, and so coming to grips with what is meant by these terms can be difficult. For example, some theorists refer to Gibson's theory of direct perception as 'active', but the 'activeness' they refer to is of the eyes themselves (i.e. not the brain), as they physically move to scan the stimuli of a given a scene, 'picking up' information (see, for example, McLellan, 1996: 468–469). Gibson himself also makes reference to a form of 'indirect' perception (or 'awareness', see 1967: 169), but he does not use this term as intended by Gregory. Gibson instead uses 'indirect' as a means of discussing the perception of representational images like photographs, cinema or alphanumeric symbols, but this is a profoundly different level of 'indirectness' compared to von Helmholtz's model of perception I outline here. For Gibson, this form of perception is 'indirect' only due to the nature of the object itself, being, as it is, a representation of a thing and not the thing itself. A simple example of what Gibson means would be the ('indirect') perception of the photo of an apple versus the ('direct') perception of the apple itself. Gibson's, in contrast to Gregory's, use of this term does indeed highlight the central assumption of his ecological theory, namely the passive role of higher cognitive functions in perception.

In the model of active perception espoused by Gregory, on the other hand, the concept of 'indirectness' takes on greater complexity, relating not to the nature of the object of perception, but specifically to the higher cognitive functions involved in the construction of perceptions. In contrast to Gibson, Gregory plays down the role of the senses to 'seek' information, and instead repeatedly stresses the active neurological process of sorting out data and decision making, what he frequently refers to as 'perceptions as hypotheses' (best summarised in Gregory, 1980, but referred to throughout his writings on perception). Inevitably, Gregory's description of the active nature of perception leads to a conceptualisation of perception (in turn, one's experience of reality) that is only *indirectly* connected to the world; by the same token, what Gregory describes as the indirectly connected nature of perceptions to the world should not be confused with descriptions of mental illnesses such as schizophrenia, in which perceptions (hallucinations) become *disconnected* from the world. Conversely, Gibson has perceptions firmly attached to the world itself, which reflects our intuitive way of thinking of our lived experience.

Where Gibson stresses the active nature of sense organs in the 'picking up' of information from the world, Gregory shifts the focus of activity to the brain, which serves to interpret and 'judge' stimuli (Gregory, 1997a: 112); and where Gibson stresses the psychosomatic nature of perception (an act 'not of the mind or of the body but of a living observer' [Gibson, 1979: 239]), Gregory instead emphasises the gap between sense organs and the brain. Direct realism denies the impact of higher cognitive functions in the perceptual process, and instead suggests that the brain is more of a receptacle into which visual information from the outside world is *passively* accepted. Conversely, the indirect/active model of perception proposes that it is the brain, more so than the senses, which is *active* in perception. In turn, active perception stresses the gap between the object of perception and the perceiving subject, who employs prior learning in combination with experience to neurologically construct, to *hypothesise*, a perception of the object.

Central to the model of active perception is the notion that cognitive representation is not composed of images, but is made up purely of cortical electrochemical activity. What differentiates it most from Gibson's direct realism, however, is what Gregory (building on von Helmholtz's model) identifies as an *identity* between perception and the scientific method, describing perception as a process of predictive hypothesisation, in which a hypothesis is generated that may (or may not) 'hit upon truth by producing symbolic structures matching physical reality' (Gregory, 1980: 182). The result of considering perceptions as hypotheses is a model of reality in which perception of the world and the world itself are forever divided by an insurmountable gap. Gibson, on the other hand, demonstrates little regard for this highly subjective 'privatised' model of perception, attacking such notions as potentially solipsistic and futile (Gibson, 1967: 171).

As a matter of great emphasis, Gregory states the shortcomings of comparisons of the visual apparatus to mechanised systems such as the cinematographic device (Gregory, 1997a: 5). Where a photographic or cinematographic image remains substantially connected to its source through a chain of light and chemicals, no such connection, *nor artefact*, exists in the process of visual perception. As Gregory makes clear, it is misleading to utilise a 'pictures-in-the brain' (5) paradigm for the understanding of the way we see, a criticism of active perception that is often made by Gibson.

Light does indeed enter the eye through the iris and is projected onto the retina (much like a camera, yes), causing photoreceptors to react. The retinal image is then electrochemically coded and travels to the brain via the optic nerve (itself arguably a part of the brain). The retina serves as interface 'between the optical projection from objects to the neural-coded signals to the brain' (53), but no light enters the brain, and no *images* are stored as such. The pictures-in-the-brain paradigm, as Gregory points out (in total agreement with Gibson) 'would need a further eye to see *its* picture – another picture, another eye – and so on forever, without getting anywhere' (5). Once this 'pictures-in-the-brain' notion is removed from the discussion, what remains is the question as to how the brain decodes the neurological signals from the retinal image, and what this tells us about the way we understand and interact with the external world; the cognitive process that allows this to happen is far too complex, too abstract a reality, to be described via parallels to the comparatively primitive technologies of photography or cinema.

In his explanation of the idea of 'perceptions as hypotheses', Gregory discusses the effects not only of knowledge of objects and their use, but the profound effect that mental states have on perception. In order to deal with the mass amounts of data flooding in, Gregory's research leads him to describe the brain as acting like a trial court judge, having to determine what is or is not relevant based on experience and understanding of objects (1997a: 112). Our ability to judge is what allows us to identify important or dangerous situations quickly and react accordingly (or even just play games like table tennis). In other words, perception is not total representation, but instead the result of what the brain (not the eye) has deemed necessary to 'see'. In evolutionary terms, the working of this filter is based on what is necessary for survival. It is precisely the limits imposed by this survival instinct that makes even the healthy mind prone to experiencing illusions (a term I shall shortly define properly) and allows heightened emotional states to have an impact on what is seen. Gregory describes the ramifications of the gap between physical reality and our perception of it as follows:

> The fact that perceptions can depart from physically accepted realities of objects has philosophical implications and practical consequences. It tells us that our perceptions are not always, and very likely never, directly related to physical reality.
>
> (Gregory, 1997a: 197)

Like a car suffering from engine trouble, it is often only when things go wrong that we consider the nature of the mechanism. Likewise, Gregory examines a variety of cases of things 'going wrong' as means of understanding the workings of the perceptual apparatus. Gregory is keenly interested in what non-veridical perception tells us about the way we perceive. For Gregory, differentiating between optical *illusions*, such as the Müller-Lyer lines, and *hallucinations* is critical. Whilst both illusions and hallucinations demonstrate the nature of subjective reality, each does so in a different way. Hallucinations were originally defined by Esquirol (1838) simply as 'perception without an object' (in McKenna, 1997: 6), sense-experiences fabricated by the mind independent of the stimuli actually being received. Illusions, on the other hand, are the result of legitimate visual cues that for some reason (accidentally or orchestrated) 'fool' the correctly functioning perceptual apparatus. Whilst the study of illusions helps us understand the evolution of perception, Gregory is also interested in the types of hallucinations experienced by sufferers of schizophrenia, a condition that he describes as a state in which 'the outside world makes little contact with the individual, so that he or she is effectively isolated' (Gregory, 1997a: 199).

Now that I have provided a basic overview of the tenets of active perception (and how these differ from direct perception), it is sensible to return at this point to our engagement with Polanski's cinema. As my discussion progresses, however, I will often return to this topic in order to examine some of the finer points of perception theory in more specific contexts.

Manipulating perception

So great was his interest in Gregory's research, that Polanski reportedly carried *Eye and Brain* around with him on set (Gregory, 2003), with evidence of the influence of this research especially noticeable in Polanski's 'Apartment Trilogy' of *Repulsion*, *Rosemary's Baby* and *The Tenant*. In these three films in particular, Polanski meticulously attempts to represent the distorted perception of a subject suffering a perceptual crisis, at times even employing optical illusions discussed in Gregory's books to reflect diegetic psychosis. In all three films that make up the 'Apartment Trilogy', the protagonists experience severe psychological horrors, located for the most part within the confines of their urban homes. In each of these films, Polanski seems to employ Gregory's research both to direct narrative relevance and as a means of heightening the spectator's engagement with the diegetic reality. Gregory (2003) compares Polanski's approach to film-making to the Venus Flytrap, whereby Polanski uses a variety of neuropsychology-informed techniques to draw us into (to *accept*) the world of these films, and then utilises the same knowledge to *repulse* us at the moment of greatest engagement.

In the 1960s, Polanski established himself as a commercially successful international film-maker of great technical prowess. This was an era of rapid technological development in cinema, some aspects of which Polanski took advantage of, and others of which he did not. The use of colour film stock was now widespread as both Eastman Kodak and Technicolor developed new forms of film with more nuanced colour rendition and improved definition (Salt, 1983: 324–325). Polanski took advantage of both, shooting his first colour film in 1967, *Dance of the Vampires*, using Eastman Kodak's 'Metrocolour' stock, and his second in 1968, *Rosemary's Baby*, with Technicolor.

The Technicolor stock in particular lent itself to the creation of special effects through manipulation in post-production. In *2001: A Space Odyssey* (Kubrick, 1968), released the same year as *Rosemary's Baby* and also shot in Technicolor, Kubrick takes advantage of Technicolor's printing technique by manipulating the three colours matrices to produce a 'false colour' effect to create a special effect for the film's 'trip through space and time' sequence. Salt credits Kubrick with having invented this technique (1983: 325); but, as I discuss in a later case study, in *Rosemary Baby* Polanski also manipulated the stock in post-production to produce a similar effect, in which the matrices of colour seems to come 'unglued'.

There were also several developments in lenses at this time; the most important, Salt suggests, was the advent of the Angenieux zoom lens in 1963. The zoom lens was initially used in European films, such Schlesinger's *Billy Liar* (1963), and Lelouch's *Un Homme et une Femme* (1965), but was also employed in some American films including Brooks' *The Professionals* (1966) and Nichols' *The Graduate* (1967). Whilst the zoom might work well to create a specific effect, its use is highly conspicuous and can work against the establishment of audience engagement, an anathema to the classic Hollywood style with its mandate of seamlessness. As Salt notes, there was a considerable amount of resistance to the use of the zoom lens in Hollywood, which was seen as a 'cheap substitute for a tracking shot' (1983: 335). Polanski's keen awareness of perception and his desire to achieve cinematic perceptual realism precluded the use of the zoom as a shortcut, but he does not put it to 'artistic' use either, preferring instead to work towards 'classic' seamlessness, hence the absence of the conspicuous 'zoom shot' from Polanski's cinema.

Experimentation with lenses of different focal lengths was also becoming more widespread in the 1960s, which corresponded to the increased availability of lenses with focal lengths ranging from 25 mm (wide angle) to 360 mm (extreme telephoto), and everything in-between. In contrast to Polanski, who preferred to minimise distortion in favour of perceptual realism (as I will later discuss, a technique he employed to maximise the effect of distortion when it is actually employed), Antonioni, who also came into international recognition in the 1960s, attempted to achieve an expressive form of 'psychological verisimilitude' (Bordwell, 2002: 99) through his use of colour, camera movement (in particular his use of pans) and zooms, as well as the employment of a range of lenses in films such as *Il Deserto Rosso* (1964) and *Blow-Up* (1966). For example, he employs a 100 mm lens for large part of *Il Deserto Rosso*; instead of attempting to render a 'natural' image, in this film, Antonioni knowingly utilises the 'flattening' effect of the telephoto lens to produce 'near-abstract compositions' (Salt, 1983: 336). In contrast, for the most part, Polanski's use of lenses tends to be more conservative, sticking to a combination of camera placement and lens choice that avoids excessive distortion; as Gregory puts it, this technique serves as a means of keeping the image closer to what the brain expects to see (2003). But there is also evidence, at times subtle and at times pronounced, of both 'telephoto' and 'wide' type lenses in films such as *Chinatown*,

Repulsion, *The Tenant* and *Rosemary's Baby*, as I shall address in due course. But Polanski's 'conservative' use of lenses is no less deliberate or less ambitious than Antonioni's more eclectic choices; the distinction in their individual approaches to psychological realism lies more so in Polanski's attempt to achieve such realism by working within the 'classic' style versus Antonioni's often more abstract sensibilities.

Polanski's goal of exploring cinema's potential to provide the spectator with the semblance of unmediated experience seems to be behind many of his directorial decisions. It is unsurprising, then, to discover that Polanski experimented with 3-D:

> My filmmaking ideal has always been to involve audiences so deeply in what they see that their visual experience approximates living reality. Anything that enhances this 'wraparound' effect – colour, large screens, stereo sound – is an asset. A logical extension of the same idea is 3-D.
>
> (Polanski, 1984: 326)

In the mid-1970s Polanski enlisted Gregory to collaborate on a series of test shots that Polanski hoped would lead to the creation of a convincing 3-D cinematic effect; his aim was to create a type of cinema that would heighten an audience's willingness to devote their minds to the world of the film and let themselves be open to the experiences on offer. The 3-D films made up until that time showed promise, but were ultimately exercises in gimmickry that added little to the 'wraparound effect' Polanski sought.

In an interview I conducted with Professor Gregory in 2008, he explained to me that he and Polanski experimented with a split-frame version of an offset image as a means of reducing the jittering effect caused by dual projection (the standard way to project a 3-D film at the time). Whilst the brain seems capable of compensating for a regular vibration of the frame, which is normal in any 35 mm projection, the 'double jitter' caused by the additional projector proves too difficult for the brain to deal with and is thus distracting. In theory, Polanski and Gregory's split-frame 3-D technique would jitter no more than a conventional film. Ultimately, according to both Gregory (2008) and Polanski (1984), Polanski decided to abandon the project because the 3-D effect they achieved in these experiments was insufficiently convincing; thus, not only would the 'wraparound' effect not be aided, it could potentially be *diminished* due to the audience's awareness of the effect (see Polanski, 1984: 327).[2]

Notwithstanding this failed 3-D experiment, Polanski has used a variety of techniques to move ever closer to the elusive 'wraparound' effect. Polanski reduces his goal of achieving such perceptual realism as follows:

> I'm trying to show on-screen what I see, it's as simple as that. I'm trying only to repeat with the camera as closely as possible what I have seen with my own eyes during the rehearsal of a set-up. Therefore I use the appropriate angle. The angle is determined

> by the distance from which I watch the person. The face seen from the other side of the room is not the same face which is seen across the table.
>
> (Polanski in Thompson, 1995: 9)

Polanski's flippancy aside, to achieve such a goal is anything but 'simple' given the inherent limitations of the cinematographic image or any lens's ('normal' or otherwise) ability to truly replicate the way the human eye deals with light, regardless of how carefully the camera is placed. In *Repulsion*, apart from those images that depict distorted vision, Polanski favours the 'normal' lens (i.e. a 50 mm lens, for 35 mm film) with the camera placed at the same distance from the subject as the nominal observer; in theory, this set-up 'most closely approximates the view of the unaided human eye' (Warren, 2002: 71), and hence is often referred to as 'natural perspective'. The approach is most effective if the spectator sits the same distance from the screen (relative to the size of the screen) as the camera (the invisible diegetic observer) was from the subject (Gregory, 2008). (Luckily, this 'ideal' seating footprint represents most of the centrally located seats of the cinema.)

According to Gregory, Polanski's use of natural perspective creates an image for which the brain need not compensate, and thus we are more readily 'drawn in' to the image as it more closely matches the perspective we expect to see (Gregory, 2003 and 2008).[3] Heightening this effect is Polanski's tendency to favour longer takes and fluid camera movements over rapid editing to cover the action of a sequence. But Polanski also often uses a carefully placed wide-angle lens to represent space more effectively and heighten perceptual ('interior') realism within the overarching diegetic reality, such as the close-ups in *Repulsion*, *Rosemary's Baby* and *The Tenant*, where the distorting effects of lenses are often used to great advantage as a means of reflecting the distorted perception of the schizophrenic[4] subject. For the (presumably) sane spectator, such contrasts are both disquieting and fascinating in that they draw attention to the relative malleability of (our perception of) what we cling to as being essentially immutable external realities. Conversely, if the distorting effects are limited by careful camera placement, Polanski maintains that a wide-angle lens can also serve to heighten the illusion of depth:

> I choose to use wide-angles whenever I want to be aware of the walls around, where I want it to be more three-dimensional. They give a greater sense of a location, and a greater depth of focus.
>
> (Polanski in Thompson, 1995: 9)

Polanski is not bound by any one technique in his quest to achieve what is perhaps best described as perceptual realism, a term effectively defended by Currie (1996), which I will employ often in my case studies to indicate a style of realism in which attempts are made to manipulate perceptions as a means of evoking a specific spectatorial perceptual effect through the manner in which profilmic elements are constructed,[5] creating a representation that, it is hoped, is 'realistic in its recreation of the experience of the real world' (326). Given the framed-nature of the cinematic image and the ever-conspicuous presence of the cinema theatre environment (or, worse, the home-viewing environment), which itself includes one's sense of one's own body within this environment ('proprioception'), it would be a step too far to suggest that true *visual* perceptual realism could ever be achieved within an apparatus that still engages the brain through the sense organs instead of directly.

Cavell (1971) discusses the reproduction of visual stimuli as vastly inferior to the type of perceptual realism achieved by sound reproduction, which has, especially in the four decades since his comment, achieved levels so close to perfection that any difference between the representation of the thing and the thing itself (in this case, sound waves) is often imperceptible to the human listener (19). As Cavell also observes, when it comes to stimuli that appeal to the eye, convincing representation has proved more difficult to achieve: 'if the sense-data from photographs were the same as sense-data of the objects they contain, we couldn't tell a photograph of an object from the object itself' (20). Of course, we can tell the difference, even today. The goal of ever achieving the level of fidelity between representation and 'original' that has been accomplished by sound reproduction (even this term, 'reproduction', indicates remaking of an original rather than a representation of it) remains elusive, greatly due to what seems to be the insurmountable issue of the image's frame and our constant awareness of it due to the means by which the image is presented to the eye. Even with recent developments in digital cinema, screen size (such as IMAX), 'virtual reality' and 3-D taken into account, the representation of the visual image has yet to achieve the 'framelessness' of sound reproduction.

Within the dedicated case studies that follow, I shall discuss Polanski's employment of special optical techniques in his attempts to overcome the natural obstacles to total ('wraparound') engagement with the screen image. How effective these attempts are, and how these techniques have evolved will round out this discussion. It is not my intention, however, to assert that Polanski's efforts are completely successful; whilst I may often refer to the notion of 'perceptual realism' in relation to Polanski's work, I intend this in the sense of 'efforts towards', or, on rare occasions, 'moments of', rather to suggest an absolute achievement of a true 'wraparound' effect. It is the manner in which Polanski makes incremental steps towards this goal that is of most interest, as are the philosophical issues that arise as a result, both those related to the narrative content of the films and those that emerge from a technical analysis of his cinematography (and especially those cases in which the former and the latter are simultaneously present). Notwithstanding the technical prowess and intent of the film-maker or willing suspension of disbelief of the spectator, the hypothetical case in which a spectator truly believes for anything more than a split second that what he or she is witnessing is anything but cinema probably does not exist.

I will soon shift my focus to the application of Gregory's discussion of the theory of active perception to the analysis of several of Polanski's films, but before starting these case studies, allow me to briefly outline a few more key terms and constructs that inform the conceptual framework upon which my overall approach is based.

Polanski's camera and its 'behaviour'

A notion to which I will often make reference to is that which I refer to as Polanski's 'inquiring', but 'tethered', camera. I use such language to indicate a visual style in which we, as spectators, are connected to a single character within the diegesis, rather than roaming through diegetic space to watch action that takes place between a variety of characters. I borrow the concept of the 'tether' from falconry, so as to evoke the image of a lead (albeit, an imaginary one) that connects the camera to this character, but which, like the falcon, allows the camera to move freely within the limits set by its length. By using this metaphor, we can account for the manner in which the camera's narrative, or 'perceptual', reach can sometimes be slightly greater than the character to whom we are tethered, a trope often credited to Hitchcock, but which Polanski also frequently employs to dramatic effect.

Whilst this style is not totally ubiquitous, there are very few examples in Polanski's work in which the camera strays between subjects. The three most notable examples are his 'divided' narratives, *Knife in the Water*, *Cul-de-sac* and *Death and the Maiden*,[6] in which the camera does split its allegiance between several characters. In all three of these films, however, the camera remains limited to the same confined geographical space (the boat, the island, the cabin) as the main characters of the story. But these are the exceptions; far more representative are the major case studies examined in this book, in which the camera indeed remains firmly 'tethered' to a single character.

On a number of occasions, Polanski uses the moment of 'tethering' as a means of opening the film, in which a camera 'floating' through space, often above urban spaces, is reeled in like a falcon (or a fish) to a more limited spatial envelope that shifts only with the movement of the character from whom the tether originates. The establishing of this limit is by no means a hindrance, however, for it is this connection that allows the camera to become part of the narrative trajectory. Examples of this effect are seen at the start of *Rosemary's Baby*, *The Tenant* and *The Ninth Gate*, all of which I will discuss in due course.

The first example of a tethered camera is seen early in Polanski's cinema, in the short *Toothy Grin* (1957), where the camera's superior 'reach' creates dramatic tension by making the spectator aware (just before the protagonist) that the space a man has been spying into is no longer occupied by a naked woman, but by another man brushing his teeth, who then returns the voyeur's gaze with a 'toothy grin' as he peers over the door. Similar moments are played out in Polanski's features. In *Rosemary's Baby*, for example, just as Rosemary secures her door to block her neighbours from entering her flat, we (before her) see a group of them 'creeping' across the hall, already in her home. Another example occurs in *Chinatown*, when we are forced to watch Jake Gittes tell his colleagues a racist, highly sexualised joke as his new client, Mrs Mulwray (Faye Dunaway), lurks, unbeknownst to Jake, just behind him; the 'pain' we experience in this moment nicely parallels what Jake must feel when he turns around.

A related concept also worth introducing here is that of the 'notional observer', an imaginary persona who crosses the gap between diegetic and extra-diegetic (or *afilmic*, see below) space and through whom our spectatorial gaze is controlled; this 'body' observes the action of the film not from an extra-diegetic point of privilege (i.e. behind the fourth wall), but from somewhere *within* the diegetic space. Our vantage point is most often that of a super-voyeur, who, unlike the voyeur in *Toothy Grin*, is (somehow) able to conceal his or her identity from the diegetic characters. It is indeed Polanski's 'voyeuristic' approach that forms the basis of Wexman's (1985) study of Polanski's cinema, but I will refrain from engaging in an analysis of Polanski himself as a perceiving force in this discussion, and instead focus on the experience of spectatorship.

For the most part, Polanski's cinematography aims to enhance sensorial engagement with the cinematic image through the use of naturalistic perspective, but at times this perspective is distorted so as to simulate the perceptual experience of psychologically disturbed subjects whose perceptual mechanisms are becoming increasingly unreliable. Polanski varies his lenses as needed to create subtle variations in perspective for the spectator. Whilst favouring wide angles for the most part, he carefully avoids the distortion the use of these lenses can cause through the employment of calculated camera placements that match the position of his nominal observer for a given scene. The distance between the lens and the actor is crucial to create this type of subtle perceptual effect, which can easily be ruined, for example, by opting for a slightly longer lens and moving the camera closer to the action (a trick often employed by film-makers for convenience) (Pizello, 2000: 40). By the same token, grotesque distortion is not something Polanski completely avoids; but even when such distortion is employed, great care goes into the construction of the shot (in terms of camera placement, choice of lens and *mise-en-scène*) in order to create the exact type of perceptual experience being sought. I will return to the issue of distortion on several occasions, but it is in my case study of *The Tenant* that I will explore it most fully, as it is in this film that Polanski uses both distortion and illusion most effectively.

Polanski employs a variety of means to create perceptual engagement, creating sensorially rich spaces for us to experience. He pays great attention not only to the visible elements of his cinema, but also to the sound design to heighten the sense of 'depth' created by his *mise-en-scène*. By 'depth' I refer not exclusively to the type of perspective achieved by depth of field and/or deep focus, but also the sense that the diegetic space far exceeds the space that is contained by the frame. Polanski also uses a rich tapestry of off-screen sound to extend our understanding of the diegetic space beyond what we see on-screen. In *Rosemary's Baby*, the use of off-screen sound (i.e. the murmuring of the neighbours) is put to direct narrative relevance, but in most cases, traffic noise, the sound of lifts and (Polanski's favourite) the sound of a distant piano, all create a richer understanding of the nature of the fictional world, effectively extending the limits of diegetic space. This 'extension' is particularly relevant in the Apartment Trilogy, in which the barriers that compartmentalise domestic spaces become compromised, and the distinction between 'inside' and 'outside' space is violated to dramatic effect. But even through such use of sound, our access to the stimuli tends to be strictly limited to the perceptual (in this case, aural) reach of the nominal observer 'tethered' to the film's protagonist.

Perceptions as hypotheses and 'philosophical implications'

The central notion of Gregory's *Eye and Brain* is that the brain constructs perception; the 'construction' is representative of the stimuli perceived, but never complete. Reflecting Gregory's thesis, the perceptual experiences of Carole, Rosemary and Trelkovsky illustrate the fact that it is the brain, not the eye, which 'sees' (as I shall discuss in my first three case studies). Whilst using Gregory's research to help decide which lens and camera position will work best to lure us in, Polanski is equally concerned with the philosophical conundrum that results from the kind of neuropsychological research Gregory is associated with; namely, Gregory's question 'how do we know the truth?' (Gregory, 1997a: 194). The ramifications of this question find expression not only in Polanski's films dealing with the issue of mental illness, namely *Repulsion, Rosemary's Baby* and *The Tenant*, but resonate throughout his work, in particular those films in which the diegetic truth of the past remains elusive, like *Bitter Moon* and *Death and the Maiden* (1994), as well as in Polanski's investigation cycle of *Chinatown, Frantic* and *The Ninth Gate* (which I will discuss in my second set of case studies), in which perceptual crises also emerge, not as the result of illness, but from close encounters with concealed reality.

It is admittedly difficult to determine whether by demonstrating the influence of perceptual psychology in his cinema, Polanski is intentionally entering into the perception-based discourse and adopting a specific stance in favour of active perception, or whether he is simply manifesting an interest in perception and exploring the issue cinematically. It is evident that his particular fondness for representing acts of non-veridical perception, as well as his evocation of such perception in the spectator, does indeed align him with active perception over Gibson's ecological model, but I would stop short of claiming Polanski is 'taking sides'. More important in this context is the fact that Polanski's cinema demonstrates how a film-maker can engage with psychological research and apply it both to the manner in which the cinematic image is realised (and received), as well as to direct narrative/thematic relevance, thus (potentially) engaging with the perceptual discourse on-screen. In each of the forthcoming case studies, I shall attempt to identify the various philosophical issues raised by these films. But let us first return to Gregory in order to highlight the tenets of the theory of active perception that are most relevant in terms of their 'philosophical implications'.

The focus of Gregory's description of active perception is to argue the case for a concept of perceptions as hypotheses, and in so doing highlight the gaps that exists between

a) the nature of the object being perceived,
b) the retinal image of the object, and
c) the interpretation of the object at a neurological level.

Gregory sets up an analogy, or rather, an *identity*, between visual perception and the scientific method to help establish a more accurate neurological description. The identity of perception and science remains based in von Helmholtz's concept of perception as a process of predictive hypothesising, in that both perception and science function by generating hypotheses that may (or may not) 'hit upon truth by producing symbolic structures matching physical reality' (Gregory, 1980: 182).

Although Gregory does not elaborate on what the 'philosophical implications' (as he refers to it, 1997a: 197) of the theory of active perception are (which would be, in any case, beyond his remit as a neuropsychologist), it is clear that the theory's stressing of the role of higher cognitive functions, specifically the act of hypothesisation, on the formation of perceptions parallels to a large extent developments in twentieth-century science. In particular, it parallels the growing understanding of quantum physics, which completely overturns common-sense notions of the nature of reality, and which, in a similar vein as active perception, stresses the gap between the intrinsic reality of the world and our capacity to perceive it through calling attention to the agency of the observer to influence what is perceived. However, as if to predict that theorists such as myself would make such a connection, Gregory warns against a potentially solipsistic understanding of active perception that overestimates the parallel between the details of Heisenberg's uncertainty principle and the sort of 'everyday' perception Gregory is primarily concerned with: 'if "deep" physics is accepted, there is a danger of calling all perceptions illusory ... to call all perceptions illusory is not helpful ... so we may accept for reference "kitchen" physics' (Gregory, 2005: 1234).

Notwithstanding the important nuance between the world of quantum mechanics and the 'kitchen' physics of biological human perception, both active perception and the uncertainty principle are premised on the notion that hypothesisation is the basis of perceptions, a distinct shift away from empirical certitudes. I believe that it is this theoretical connection between quantum physics and active perception, namely their mutual emphasis on uncertainty and hypothesisation, which points us towards the far-reaching 'philosophical implications' of the theory of active perception. It is these two terms, 'uncertainty' and 'hypothesisation', that will come up time and again in my analyses of Polanski's cinema, and which will later lead me to the concepts of modernism and postmodernism. Examining Polanski's cinema in this context proves to be an informative means of engaging with both the various strains of philosophical discourse at work in Polanski's cinema, as well as their aesthetics.

I shall discuss Polanski's cinema in relation to modernism and postmodernism in much greater depth in a dedicated section later in this chapter, but it is worth mentioning at this stage of my discussion that active perception's emphasis on uncertainty and hypothesisation is reflected in both (Heisenberg-influenced) post-war existentialism and the ideological ambiguity of works indicative of the 'postmodern condition' (as Lyotard terms it, 1984). Through an examination of the shift from modernism to postmodernism, ideas emerge that help us deal with the complexity of Polanski's cinema, much of which seems to reside on the 'cusp' of modernism and postmodernism. In particular, these concepts help clarify what I believe to be the scope of the 'philosophical implications' of both the theory of active perception and Polanski's own perceptual discourse. But more on this complex issue later.

Although Gregory stresses the Helmholtzian call to consider perception as a representation of reality based on a process of hypothesisation (Gregory, 1980: 181), he warns as well of the falling into the 'pictures-in-the-brain' trap the representational model of perception lends itself to (Gregory, 1997a: 5). Such paradigms of perception are also a chief target of Gibson, who disparages notions of the 'theatre of consciousness' (Gibson, 1979: 239). In this regard, both direct and indirect models of perception depart from the early twentieth-century Gestalt psychology concept of perceptual 'isomorphic mapping', in which electrical brain fields quite literally represent objects according to their properties in terms of shape and even colour. Gregory not only stresses that there is no evidence to support isomorphism (Gregory 1997a: 5), but that we should move away from thinking of perceptual representation as producing a visible artefact in any respect, for, like the oversimplified comparison made by della Porta in the sixteenth century between perception and his protofilmic *camera obscura* (see Gregory, 1997a: 34–35 and Bruno, 2002: 139–140), this would require yet another set of homuncular eyes to see the artefact; to again quote Gregory: 'another picture, another eye – and so on forever, without getting anywhere' (1997a: 5). By renouncing the 'pictures-in-the-brain' paradigm, what therefore remains is a model of perception that is indeed difficult to describe using current language. Although Gregory does make passing reference to 'software' and 'hardware' (Colman and Gregory 1995: xii), he is careful not to draw too close a parallel between perception and information technology.

In the context of Gregory's theory, using the cinematic camera as a model of perception has only limited merit. It is true that both processes are composed of physics and chemistry. At the level of physics, both the eye and the camera use a lens to accept radiant energy. But where in the camera a chemical reaction takes place to inscribe the image into a frame of exposed film, the chemistry of perception is entirely different. When a retinal image is formed from light passing through the lens of the eye, an electrochemical event occurs that stimulates neurological synapses that run along the optic nerve to the brain. Light, Gregory repeatedly stresses, does not pass any further than the eye, and what is transmitted to the brain is not an image but a purely electrochemical impulse or 'action potential' (Colman and Gregory, 1995: xii). In Gregory's model, perception is representation not through the creation of images (like a camera), but through purely neural activity. Vision, and for that matter, all forms of perception (and by extension, the basis of our concept of reality), is not made up of inscribed stimuli, but flashes of synaptic energy.

As Neidich (2003) describes it, subjective reality, both experienced and remembered, 'is no longer [the reality] of the object but of the neuron, and at this … level no things as such appear, only fragmented attributes, surges of brain activity … merely quanta of electrochemical energy discharging along columns and limbs of cortical tissue' (12). Accessing this information (memory) is not a matter of reapplying light to recreate an image and in turn delivering new radiant energy to the eye (or recreating sound wave to be reheard by the ear, etc.), but an entirely different and purely electrochemical process, which, although still not completely understood, is most definitely nothing like cinema.[7] Other than the physics involved in radiant energy passing through a lens, literally everything else about the process is radically different, so much so that there is little to be understood either about human perception or cinematography, or for that matter the perception *of* cinematography, if the analogous nature of the two is overstated. Therefore, according to the model of active perception, cinema cannot be *visual* (a *perceiving* entity), but it can be something *visible* (*perceived*) that causes us to reflect on the nature of vision.

'Film's body', phenomenology and active perception

Although my use of notions such as an 'inquiring' or 'tethered' camera that guides the spectator's gaze or a 'notional observer' embedded (but invisible and ineffectual) in the diegetic world may seem to suggest that I am describing the camera itself as a perceiving 'body', I hasten to emphasise that I use such terms strictly metaphorically. For the sake of clarity, it is important to distinguish my description of the camera's behaviour in Polanski's cinema from the phenomenological ontology of film that Sobchack (1992) delineates in her description of 'film's body', in which she suggests that film (much like a human perceiver) has a dual status of being both a *visible* object (that which can be perceived by another perceiving subjects) and a *visual* entity (a perceiving force in its own right). I make no such claim here, for such a (non-metaphorical) description of film's 'perception' cannot be reconciled with the cognitively active model of indirect perception that guides this analysis of Polanski's work. Sobchack could not be clearer about her literal use of the term 'body'; as she puts it, 'I do not use metaphor … the term *film's body* in this work is meant to be empirical, not metaphorical' (Sobchack, 1992: xviii).[8] My various descriptions of Polanski's meticulous placement of the camera and choice of lens is not meant to suggest that the camera be considered as a *visual* (i.e. seeing, *perceiving*) entity, but rather as a tool used for rendering something *visible*, designed to provoke a specific perceptual effect in the perceiving spectator. In addition, it should be noted here that whilst questions regarding the ontology of cinema are indeed one of many 'philosophical implications' that arise from the present discussion of perception, addressing the specific polemics of this grand issue is not the primary focus of the present work, which is primarily concerned with the analysis of Polanski's cinema. However, as I hope this book demonstrates, Polanski's cinema should indeed be acknowledged in more generalist discussions of embodiment and the ontology of cinema (as is the case in Barker [2009], for example).[9]

Whilst my approach is not guided by a strictly phenomenological conceptualisation of perception, it is evident that most of the basic concerns of perceptual psychology are shared by all strains of phenomenology; for example, both phenomenology and perceptual psychology attempt to describe 'lived-experience' through an examination of perception (and, arguably, to delineate an *ontology* of perception itself), and Merleau-Ponty's focus on embodiment and intentionality is indeed reminiscent of the agency of higher cognitive functions in perception that is stressed by Gregory. But my intention here is not to overcomplicate my analysis of Polanski's cinema through a parallel juxtaposition of the various (and often directly contrasting) 'phenomenologies' of perception argued by the likes of Husserl, Heidegger and Merleau-Ponty; it is, however, worth accessing some of the ideas that emerge from phenomenological discourse and the philosophical ground it shares with existentialism, both of which are relevant when we consider the logical ramifications of the model of active perception argued by Gregory. What is of particular interest in this regard is the intersection of epistemology and ontology at the grand scale, namely that point where the questions of how knowledge is attained eventually spiral out and become questions of the nature of being itself (as McHale suggests, 1986: 60).

Whilst I make no claim to provide a comprehensive 'catalogue' of the philosophical tangents my various analyses can provoke, as my discussions of Polanski's cinema unfold, I will highlight the philosophical questions that I believe to be most recurring in Polanski's work, and how these are nuanced from film to film. It is worth stressing here that the aim of this book is not to delineate a new conceptual framework for addressing the nature of either cinema or perception (or the perception of cinema), but rather to use Gregory's description of active perception to lay a 'pathway' through Polanski's cinema; this means of engaging with Polanski's work proves especially stimulating (and pleasurable), due in great part, of course, to the type of philosophical territory it compels us, the close readers, to traverse.

The theory of active (indirect) perception as a meta-theory for film studies

The primary focus of this work is to engage with Polanski's cinema through an exploration of a theory of perception he has claimed to be influenced by; in other words, my close readings are greatly steered by the desire to discover exactly *how* these films are informed by this particular perceptual theory. The approach proves fruitful, for besides just dealing with the theory of active perception, the pathway this theory forges for us through Polanski's cinema compels the close reader to engage with a number of tertiary issues: scopophilia, 'Oedipal' conflicts, feminist identity crises, modernism and postmodernism – to name but a few concepts the case studies in this book attempt to fold into the greater discourse.

However, whilst this work is firmly intended to function primarily as a novel set of interrelated close readings of Polanski's films, since the methodology employed to create a pathway through this cinema is a theoretical model of perception, it is worth, at least briefly, considering how this theory of perception can contribute to the wider concerns of film studies. So, in this section, I will allow my discussion to 'drift' towards more generalist issues, in particular the developing area of cognitively focused research on cinematic spectatorship.

I will now juxtapose two perceptual meta-theories that have been offered to film studies by members of the Society for Cognitive Studies of the Moving Image (SCSMI), an organisation composed of interdisciplinary researchers who share an interest in 'studying how moving-image media shape and are shaped by human psychological activity'.[10] The comparison of these particular meta-theories is highly opportune in the greater context of this examination of Polanski's cinema, as it corresponds to the juxtaposition of the models of perception I provided earlier, with each approach proving to have its own value to film studies. The first meta-theory, presented by Anderson and Anderson (1996), is based on Gibson's ecological (direct/passive) theory of perception; whereas the second, by Berliner and Cohen (2011), is based on the active model I am primarily concerned with in regards to Polanski.

Anderson and Anderson's approach is essentially rooted in exploiting the commercial potential of cinema by providing a meta-theory to help film-makers increase the global accessibility of their work, and thus increase box-office sales by actively exploiting research into perceptual psychology; as I frequently argue here, both this aim and methodology is reminiscent of Polanski's own approach of combining both philosophical ('high') concerns with commercial ('low') ambitions. Their discussion begins by denying the accuracy of Münsterberg's prediction that 'photoplay' would become the 'domain of the psychologist who analyses the mind'; in actual fact, they point out, at the end of the twentieth century 'psychologists have actually had little effect upon either filmmaking or film theory' (1996: 347). As a response, they attempt to employ Gibson's model of direct perception to make the case for an 'ecological meta-theory' for film spectatorship.

Echoing the sentiments of Gibson, and notwithstanding the status of indirect/active perception as the dominant theoretical model of perception (today, as well as in 1996, the year in which they write), Anderson and Anderson dismiss the concept of representational realism based on von Helmholtz's description of perception as 'unconscious inferences' (Anderson and Anderson, 1996: 353), again bringing to the fore the classic criticism of homuncular 'infinite regress' that active perception is repeatedly confronted with, namely the polemical question of 'who is making the inferences' (353). As I have discussed, Gregory disparages the notion of the 'theatre of the mind' as much as Gibson; I propose that embedded in this sort of dismissal of active perception (which is common) is a confusion regarding the nature of 'representation' the theory of active perception postulates, a confusion that seems to emerge when notions of 'higher cognitive functions' and 'hypothesisation' are muddled with the Gestalt concept of isomorphic mapping, or the ideas of 'representation' and 'illusion' or 'dream' are unduly equalised, which neutralises the semantic distinctiveness of these terms.

The key difference between 'direct'/'passive' and 'indirect'/'active' models of perception is, essentially, a fundamental disagreement as to the extent that higher-level cognition (what Gregory and Rock describe as 'perceptions as hypotheses') is involved in perception. Anderson and Anderson take the position that such a process need not be involved in perception, and go a step further to suggest that their ecological meta-theory allows for the 'development of a theory of perception and, by extension, a theory of film which largely circumvents the problems raised by representation' (1996: 354). It is interesting that this 'ecological meta-theory' focuses so much on the phenomenon of non-veridical perception, illusions in particular, which is an area of research that Gibson himself showed little interest in, but which active perception theorists are greatly focused on. As if to correct a shortcoming on Gibson's behalf, Anderson and Anderson attempt to theorise an explanation for illusions, and in turn cinematic spectatorship, that does not rely on a conceptualisation of perception as dependent on higher cognitive functions. Importantly, they argue that cinema does not 'symbolise' a fictional world, that it is not 'symbolic' because it mimics reality. Let us consider the assumptions embedded in the following illustrative quote:

> If patterns of light reflected from the … screen are processed by the visual system as though they were reflected directly from the surfaces of physical reality, then film theory is in a position to benefit enormously from Gibson's theory of ecological optics.
>
> (1996: 360)

Firstly, the conjecture that begins this quote needs to be challenged. If the information from the light on the screen is perceived in a manner equivalent to 'real world' perception, then *any* model of perception can be argued to be a valuable means of understanding cinematic perception. In any case, it is not clear that this is, or ever could be, the case. It is my conjecture here that short of cinema evolving into the sort of 'holodecks' we see on the later 'Star Trek' series, or a system using a direct cerebral access, something like we see depicted in Cronenberg's *eXistenZ* (1999) or Andy and Lana Wachowski's *The Matrix* (1999), the physiological experience of watching cinema as it is currently known (and I include the early twenty-first century developments in '3-D' and digital media) negates the possibility of establishing such a firm identity between cinematic and non-cinematic perception, due in particular to the dissonant proprioception that inevitably occurs during cinematic spectatorship (namely, the simple awareness of being in a cinema). It must be acknowledged here without reservation that Polanski's goal of achieving a 'wraparound' is never achieved in absolute terms. The chief obstacle to this is the simple fact that the senses work in concert in the construction of perception; during the cinematic experience, only two of the senses, sight and hearing, are engaged, and even these suffer interference from competing stimuli in the cinema environment. An entire arsenal of tools are needed to combat this; Polanski launches his effort towards the 'wraparound' based on an informed knowledge of the working of perception, but it takes all sorts of trickery to even come close to 'fooling' our perceptual mechanism into recognising the cinematic image for anything other than what it really is, even for a moment.

Providing somewhat of a counter to Anderson and Anderson's proposed ecological meta-theory are fellow SCSMI board members Berliner and Cohen (2011), who propose a meta-theory of the classical editing system based on the active model of perception. Their approach is not entirely novel; although not always directly cited, the potentiality for the indirect/active theoretical model of perception to add to approaches to conventional film theory, in particular semiotic, ideological and psychoanalytic approaches, has been explored in several cognitive-based studies of cinematic spectatorship, including the writings and edited volumes by Bordwell over the last two decades (see 1985 and 1996, for example), as well as Levin and Simons (1997), and Brooks and Hochberg (1996a and 1996b). It is upon the 'shoulders' of research such as this that Berliner and Cohen attempt to construct a 'broad model of film perception from sensation to interpretation' (2011: 45).

Berliner and Cohen are more cautious than Anderson and Anderson in their assertion that we perceive cinema the same way we perceive the non-cinematic world; but they consider these experiences 'similar enough' (2011: 44) to draw a direct parallel between general perception and specifically cinematic perception. In contrast to what I argue above, they make no mention of the effect of proprioception on cinematic perception, but this omission makes little difference to their specific study of the parallels between classic 'Hollywoodian' continuity editing and the theoretic model of active perception. Berliner and Cohen propose a 'model of spatial continuity' in which they argue for an empirically testable model of spectatorship, which posits that the tenets of continuity editing are essentially based (although not necessarily intentionally) on the 'same cognitive processes that generate coherence for spectators of the physical world' (2011: 44).

Berliner and Cohen's model is much in line with the description of active/indirect perception presented in this analysis of Polanski's cinema, a model of perception I argue this director has both studied and intentionally employed in his approach to film-making, as well as having manifested many of its key theoretic assumptions diegetically. It is the poverty of the retinal image with which the eye's photoreceptors must deal that Berliner and Cohen point to, asserting that 'unconscious inferences' on the part of the perceiver are critical to accommodate the perceptual system's (evolved) bias for spatial coherence. Thus, a model of spectatorship based on active perception counters the 'common sense' notion that montage is inherently an unnatural means of perception that must be learned by the spectator. As Berliner and Cohen put it, 'common sense is wrong. When we look at our environment, our eyes do not see continuity; they see fragments … Consequently, we sample the environment with our eyes … and reconstruct the total environment with our brain' (49). The connection between active perception and classic editing follows the same logic:

> classic editing and active perception are analogous in that they tend to create discontinuous images that the perceiver later integrates into a continuous space … to produce stimuli that fall within the accommodation ranges for perceptual continuity, *classic editing tends to follow the pattern of active perception.*
>
> (2011: 50, emphasis in original)

For more discontinuous forms of montage, it may well be the case that some 'learning' is involved to come to grips with a particular semantic structure. That being said, as Eisenstein (1992 [1929]) shows, the 'collision' of images has its own type of immediate effect on the spectator; but even the concept of the 'ideogram' reveals the more basic perceptual bias towards continuity, towards unity of not only space, but of concept.

Whilst Berliner and Cohen's cinematic examples are all 'classics' of continuity editing like *The Philadelphia Story* (George Cukor, 1940), they do not shy away from addressing the cinema of Godard and Ozu, two notable examples of directors who have knowingly 'violated' classic conventions of montage, in particular Godard through the 'jump' cut and Ozu though his defiance of the so-called 180 rule. But far from disproving their meta-theory, works such as *Breathless* show that continuity 'rules' are merely guidelines, and that these sorts of 'violations' are indicative both of the fact that 'cognition can accommodate non-classic film stimuli' and that they 'help define the parameters of cognition' (2011: 60).

What Berliner and Cohen's meta-theory does not account for is the philosophical territory upon which the theory of perception they employ treads, which I would argue is, in any case, beyond the remit of their article. But, aside from their mention of *The Matrix*, also missing from their account is a discussion of the possibility of a director putting the tenets of active perception to direct use in his or her cinema, not 'negatively' as in the case of Godard, but through a conscious effort to study the same sort of research that underpins their meta-theory and applying it in his or her craft directly and knowingly, not only in the construction of the shot and decisions about montage, but also using the diegesis as a means of *theorising* perception (although there is certainly scope to consider Godard along these lines). A point to which I often return is that such a goal is the key impetus behind this present analysis of Polanski's cinema, a director who, as much evidence indicates, has directly engaged with both a noted advocate of active perception (Professor R. L. Gregory) and a professional psychiatrist (Dr Stephen Black, as I discuss in Chapter 3).

Polanski and postmodernism

Considering Polanski's cinema in terms of the critical discourse regarding the concepts of 'modernism' and 'postmodernism' provides another useful framework through which to explore Polanski's cinema, and one that helps us reflect on the aforementioned 'philosophical implications' of the theory of active perception alluded to by Gregory. It is therefore worth including these concepts into the fold, for they prove to enhance the discussions that follow.

Writing of Polanski's cinema in 1985, Wexman sets up a qualified framework within which to discuss Polanski in terms of 'modernism': 'To speak of Polanski', she starts her discussion, 'is to speak of modernism. It is also to speak of the limits of modernism, for having embraced modernist principles, he has drawn back from them' (1985: 13). Using Polanski's work to try to identify what, exactly, these 'limits of modernism' are can be a fruitful exercise that helps us come to grips with the meaning of modernism as a theoretical construct, as well as eventually leading us towards the concept of 'postmodernism' in Polanski's work. Although the term 'postmodern' certainly had theoretical currency at the time Wexman was writing (1985), she is wary of employing this term directly. She instead makes mention of it only in footnote, preferring not to engage in what she calls the 'continuing debate' (128) regarding the term. Notwithstanding Wexman's resistance to using the word 'postmodern' directly in her main text, her reference to the fact that Polanski's cinema seems to 'draw back' from modernism suggests that 'postmodernism' may well be the best term in this context.[11]

Wexman was not alone in her hesitation to use the term 'postmodern'; many others theorists have also treated the term with much suspicion, such as Orr (writing in 1993), who makes the point that much of what is referred to as 'postmodern', in particular its use of irony, self-reflection and pastiche, was already present in modernism. Orr warns that the prefix 'post' can be used as a type of intellectual 'shortcut', a label that is used to 'patch over gaps in thinking' or serves as a 'stand in for concept that have yet to be invented' (1993: 1–2). It seems that for both Orr and Wexman, by embracing the 'postness' of 'postmodernism', we risk failing to appreciate the nuances of modernism as a concept. For this reason I use the term here guardedly, and tend to adhere to Calinescu's line of thinking in which the 'postmodern' is addressed not in terms of an artistic tradition or 'world view' in its own right, but rather as a perspective, a way of looking at things that allows us to reflect on modernity and query its multitude of incarnations, as one amongst the many 'faces of modernity' (1987: 279).

Jameson describes the inherent complexity of what he conceptualises as postmodernism as 'not a style, but rather a cultural dominant: a conception which allows for the presence and coexistence of a range of very different, yet subordinate features' (1984: 56). As Calinescu highlights, postmodernism has an 'explicitly interrogative nature … among the faces of modernity postmodernism is perhaps the most quizzical: self-sceptical yet curious, unbelieving yet searching, benevolent yet ironic' (279) – a fitting description for Polanski's cinema, as I shall often highlight in the forthcoming case studies. My intention here is not to discuss the modernism/postmodernism distinction in great detail (although I make frequent reference to theorists who do); I instead hope simply to access some of the concepts that have arisen from this discourse as a means of informing my reading of Polanski's films, which I ultimately suggest can be appreciated as examples of postmodernism.

Jameson (1984) associates the very notion of the auteur whose hallmarks create inter-film connections with a fundamental impulse of high modernism (54, 64–65). If we follow this line of thought, the extraordinary control Polanski exerts over the details of his cinema and the identifiable inter-film discourse that binds his opus are traits that are arguably incompatible with a conceptualisation of his cinema as postmodern. Indeed, a close reading of his work (especially his films from the 1960s to 1980s) could mark him out as a high modernist auteur. But we must resist conceptualisations of the modern and postmodern in such rigid terms, as it is through an examination of the slippages between these concepts that ideas emerge which help us deal with the complexity of Polanski's cinema, much of which seems to reside on the 'cusp' of modernism and postmodernism, and at times includes cinematic manifestations of the transition between these two conditions.

An example of the interplay of modernism and postmodernism in Polanski's cinema can be seen in Trelkovsky's scream at the end of *The Tenant*. The moment is a pastiche of Munch's *The Scream*, a work Jameson associates with the anxiety of high modernism (1984: 61); but the moment is embedded in a film that embraces and celebrates the campiness of the grotesque generic hallmarks of the horror film, a trait more associated with postmodernism. Furthermore, the notion that the sort of anxiety expressed in *The Scream* is exclusively the domain of high modernism is challenged by Huyssen (1990), who argues there is an 'apocalyptic desperate strain' (242) of postmodernism as well. Perhaps what is most relevant to my overall analysis of Polanski's cinema is that exploring the shift from the 'modern' to the 'postmodern' condition allows me to clarify what I believe to be the scope of the 'philosophical implications' of both the theory of indirect perception and Polanski's own perceptual discourse; I argue this to be the same philosophical territory of postmodernism, specifically the strain of existentialism that emerged in the wake of the startling discoveries of quantum physics – an important issue to which I will soon return.

Whilst the continuing overlap of modernism and postmodernism must be acknowledged – there are no clean binaries here – the year 1972 does stand out as a symbolic point of transition. As discussed by Harvey (1989), Charles Jencks humorously marks the exact moment of the transition of modernism to postmodern as 15.32 on 15 July 1972, 'when the Pruitt – Igoe housing development in St. Louis (a prize-winning version of Le Corbusier's "machine for modern living") was dynamited as an uninhabitable environment for the low-income people it housed' (39). This was also the year that Venturi, Brown and Izenour's *Learning from Las Vegas* (1972) was first published, which insisted that 'architects had more to learn from the study of popular and vernacular landscapes … than from the pursuit of some abstract, theoretical, and doctrinal ideals' (40). They identify the 'waning or extinction of the hundred-year-old modernist movement … the final flowering of a high modernist principle' (53) as somewhat earlier than Jencks's (symbolic) date, occurring in the 1950s or early 1960s, at which time the concept of postmodernism begins to serve as the dominant means of theorising cultural behaviour as it moves towards the era of late capitalism. It is impossible, of course, to define an exact barrier between modernism and postmodernism, and the significant overlapping of these 'conditions' both chronologically and in their conceptualisation must be acknowledged; nevertheless, it is interesting to note that Polanski's departure from Poland in the early 1960s parallels the shift identified by Jameson from modernism to postmodernism, a shift that is evident in Polanski's cinema when we compare *Knife in the Water* and *Repulsion*.

According to Jameson, the 'supreme formal feature' of a postmodern work is its 'flatness or depthlessness, a new kind of superficiality in the most literal sense', comparing van Gogh's (high modernist) 'Peasant Shoes' to Andy Warhol's (postmodernist) 'Diamond Dust Shoes' (60) to illustrate his point. The reference to 'superficiality', however, does not necessarily entail that postmodern works are inherently devoid of meaning, for this idea of 'flatness' is also connected to the philosophically complex Platonic notion of the simulacrum, 'the identical copy for which no original has ever existed' (66). Baudrillard picks up on this notion, suggesting that in postmodern culture the object of representation and the representation itself become muddled:

> Abstraction today is no longer that of the map, the double, the mirror or the concept. Simulation is no longer that of a territory, a referential being or a substance. It is the generation by models of a real without origin or reality: a hyperreal … Henceforth, it is the map that precedes the territory.
>
> (Baudrillard, 1983: 2)

I will return to this discussion of Baudrillard, simulacra and the hyperreal in my case study of *The Tenant*, in which I argue that the calculated use of simulacra in the form of filmophanic illusions highlights such 'superficiality' (in the literal sense) as a means of both manipulating the perceptual experience of the spectator and, as I will argue, to cinematically theorise perception as well.

Whilst Polanski's meticulous approach to the craft of film-making, an attitude he inherited from the Polish School, aligns him with what Huyssen calls the 'austere' version of 'high modernism' (1990: 242), he also tends to eschews high modernism's paranoiac fear of 'bad taste' by embracing popular forms, even Camp aesthetics, but creating these works with the meticulous attention to detail of an 'old master'. In this sense Polanski also echoes Calinescu's call for a 'change of the Manichaean definition of aesthetic quality' (1987: 292). A key 'goal' of postmodernism is to render futile the epic battle between 'high' and 'low' culture ('good' vs 'bad' taste) and to imbue this aesthetic dispute with healthy scepticism. Jameson identifies the erosion of this distinction as an important condition of postmodernity (1983: 112), and looks towards aesthetic shifts in architecture as a means of describing his conceptualisation of postmodernism (1984: 54), citing *Learning from Las Vegas* to illustrate the rise of populist aesthetics and the 'effacement … of the older (essentially high-modernist) frontier between high and low culture' (54). Jameson (1984) identifies postmodern architecture as 'grounded in the patronage of multinational business' (57), a parallel he elaborates on in his connection between postmodern cultural behaviour and the rise of the 'late' version of capitalism (1983: 125), a point that I shall soon return to. The changes in architecture permeated other forms of culture as well, as the postmodernists embraced the 'low culture' of the Hollywood B movie, the paperback romance, murder mysteries and science fiction as 'materials they no longer simply "quote", as [modernists] Joyce or Mahler might have done, but incorporate into the very substance [of their works]' (55). Polanski's work has consistently straddled the domain of 'high' and 'low', fusing popular (generic) forms, the use of star-bodies and commercial ambitions with 'deep' existential concerns more often associated with 'high art', although there is none of the direct 'cut and paste' pastiche Jameson connects with postmodernism.

The concept of 'pastiche' is indeed a key element that informs our understanding of postmodernism. Hayward (2000) refers to two modes of postmodernism, a 'mainstream mode', in which pastiche evokes past works, and an 'oppositional mode' that employs parody and irony to express the 'despair at the nothingness of the abyss' (277). In the distinction between these modes, there lies the subtle, but relevant, distinction between pastiche and parody, both of which need also to be distinguished from the mockery of the 'spoof'. Where pastiche literally refers to the 'pasting' together of various elements (which can be done directly or through recreation), parody takes the act of imitation a step further and introduces the concept of exaggeration. But whilst imitation in parody may well be, and usually is, for the purpose of ironic effect, it need not descend into outright mockery, where the intent is to demean the source material.

Polanski's more readily identifiable 'genre films', such as *Rosemary's Baby*, *The Tenant*, *Dance of the Vampires* (1967), *Chinatown* and *The Ninth Gate*, tend to teeter on that fine line between pastiche and parody, seeming to lapse at times into comedy, but never allowing parody to undo the effect of horror or suspense these genres are designed to provide. But these films do not seem to ridicule their sources; rather than demonstrating how ridiculous some generic conventions may be, Polanski tends to amplify these conventions to extract maximum amounts of pleasure from them – a highly postmodern notion. *Dance of the Vampires*, for example, is not so much a spoof of the Hammer horror, but a 'high quality' Hammer-style horror with the 'volume' turned way up.

This emphasis on the importance of pleasure further aligns Polanski's work with the postmodern. As Calinescu suggests, 'enjoyment and complexity go together well in postmodernism' (284), pointing to Eco's *The Name of the Rose* (1983) as a prime example of a postmodern text that contains its complex philosophical and semiotic discourse within a popular form, but without sacrificing the pleasures of genre. I would add that Annaud's cinematic adaptation of *The Name of the Rose* (1986) – a film to which Polanski's own *The Ninth Gate* is clearly greatly indebted to – is also an example of postmodern cinema due to the manner in which Annaud translates Eco's 'pulpy' thriller to the screen.

Here Sontag's (1961) discussion of 'Camp aesthetics' and its 'love of … artifice and exaggeration' (see Sontag, 1994: 96) and inherent antagonism to 'high modernism' proves especially useful, in particular when we consider Polanski's celebratory (as opposed to mockingly antagonistic) use of generic 'stylistic twitches' (to borrow a phrase from Jameson, 1983: 113). Sontag describes the Camp sensibility as one that 'converts the serious into the frivolous' (1994: 97), and indeed Polanski often conceals deep existential concerns, such as those that emerge from the perceptual discourse that guides my analysis of his work, behind Camp theatrics. It is important to acknowledge that Polanski's version of Camp is most definitely 'deliberate', as opposed to what Sontag calls the 'purer' form of 'naïve' Camp. In this light, part of my approach to Polanski is to 'unmask' his cinema, first through an appreciation of the 'campiness' of his work, but then to penetrate this surface to reveal the more serious concerns it conceals. By the same token, this apparent contradiction does not undo the underlying discourse these works contain, for it is the mastery with which these films deliver Camp pleasure that draws us (i.e. the close readers of his work) towards them, and which sustains the multiple viewings of these films that is required to fully engage with the philosophical discourse on offer.

Earlier, I discussed Mazierska's description of Polanski's nomadic eclecticism, in which she describes the director as a 'cultured traveller'. Lyotard discusses such eclecticism in a the context of postmodernity, referring to it as 'the degree zero of contemporary general culture', wherein 'one listens to reggae, watches a western, eats McDonald's food for lunch and local cuisine for dinner, wears Paris perfume in Tokyo and retro clothes in Hong Kong' (1984: 76). It is this sort of eclecticism, namely Polanski's disregard for the invented barriers that partition and ascribe 'genetic' proprietorship to culture in combination with his equal passion for both Camp and 'high' culture, that further aligns Polanski with the postmodern.

Polanski's depictions of the *loss* of personal agency, the 'death' of the subject through the fragmentation of the psyche and perceptual crises, is also highly indicative of the shift towards the postmodern condition, described by Jameson as the death of the 'older bourgeois individual subject' (1983: 115). Active perception, with its rejection of the notion of the 'pictures-in-the-brain' model, adamantly spurns the concept of the 'mind's eye', or a secondary homuncular perceiving self that resides in the mind, bringing into question where the 'I' actually resides and hence rendering problematic the very notion of the 'self'; thusly, active perception stumbles across a 'philosophical implication' in drawing attention to both the 'eye' and 'I' (an unavoidable pun in this context, but one that I shall abuse no further!). The cult of the individual is closely associated with the rise of modernism, what Jameson identifies as a 'bourgeois' notion, which he associates with the 'age of competitive capitalism ... the heyday of the nuclear family and the emergence of the bourgeoisie as the hegemonic social class' (115). Jameson discusses the death of the bourgeois subject and the emergence of postmodernism as 'closely related to the emergence of this new moment of late, consumer or multinational capitalism' (1983: 125), an age of 'corporate capitalism, of the so-called organisational man, of bureaucracies in business as well as in the state' (116).

Notably, Jameson differentiates between two versions of capitalism, the former he calls the 'competitive' version, the 'do it yourself' capitalist spirit that he associates with modernism, and the latter he identifies as the 'corporate' version, in which the spirit of individual agency is eroded by the domination of large corporations, even over the authority of the government. It is this 'new' version of capitalism in particular within which the postmodern condition resides. The shift in what is regarded as 'capitalism' and its impact on the concept of individualism seems to find its way into the subtext of Polanski's cinema, symbolically depicted as the struggle of an individual to assert his or her personal identity as distinct from a swarm of people who seem intent on suppressing it. This struggle is of course most amplified in *Rosemary's Baby* and *The Tenant*, in which the depiction of this battle closely resembles psychosis, leaving open the question as to whether the conflict is truly interpersonal, located entirely within a (fragmented) psyche, or a combination of both.

In *Chinatown* this shift in forms of capitalism is more directly apparent. The film moves back in time to explore an early example of corporate theft of public resources, with businessman Noah Cross's (John Huston) domination of the public water supply inspired by California's real-life Owens Valley 'Water Wars'. The figure of Cross serves as an apt embodiment of the unbridled greed of the 'late' form of corporate capitalism Jameson associates with postmodernism. Gittes, in contrast, serves as an example of the competitive capitalism Jameson connects to modernism, having left the police force in favour of setting up his own private investigation service for his personal financial gain (i.e. Gittes is paid in direct proportion to the work he does, rather than a salary), only to find himself facing a much more complex reality than his epistemological framework can contain.

There is a notable shift in Polanski's cinema that I will be discussing in more detail further on, but which is worth mentioning briefly in this section. The change I refer to is a shift in focus from individual psyches (in films that themselves depict the *destruction* of the psyche) towards more 'distant' films, in which the camera is no longer granted access to this realm. We can draw a parallel here to the similar change from early to late capitalism discussed by Jameson, which he notes as being a shift from the modern to the postmodern condition. *The Tenant* is the film that marks this shift most dramatically, as it is the last of Polanski's films that attempts to depict the subjective perceptual experiences of the main character; but in its tearing to shreds of the protagonist's psyche and its extinguishing of his personal agency, it also represents the last 'gasp' (or 'scream') of psychologically penetrative, individually centred cinema for Polanski, aptly reflecting Jameson's idea of the death of the bourgeois subject in the postmodern condition. After *The Tenant*, no matter how closely the camera follows a character through a diegetic struggle, it is held at bay; the subjective psychological realm of these later characters remains strictly 'off limits' and our knowledge of them is likewise limited.

I do not intend to draw a firm line here between Polanski's 'modern' and 'postmodern' cinema, but simply to indicate the evolutionary process towards postmodernity that actually began very early in Polanski's career. *Repulsion*, *Rosemary's Baby* and *The Tenant* can also be viewed in a postmodern light when we consider the existential paradoxes they present: whilst affirming individual psychology, these films also deconstruct and destroy the psyche, which is finally 'absorbed' by an external social order. I would go a step further to suggest that Polanski's early cinema already bears signs of the shift towards postmodernism, especially in these films' combination of 'high' and 'low' art, and the nearly ubiquitous ambivalence with which both ideology and morality are treated.

Only two of Polanski's early feature films, *Knife in the Water* and *Cul-de-sac*, really stand out as 'high' art (as much as narrative cinema is ever considered as such, that is). But in retrospect, both of these films can be reappraised as 'intermediary' works, early examples of postmodernism in Polanski's cinema, especially considering the high levels of both existential despair and ideological ambivalence each of these films contains. As I discussed in an earlier chapter, *Knife in the Water* was much criticised by Poland's communist government for its lack of 'social commitment' (Polanski, 1984: 161) and its foregrounding of individual concerns. In this sense, *Knife in the Water* can be argued (as Wexman does) to represent a form of modernism. But when we consider the film as a sociological study that deconstructs ideologies and rejects moral didacticism, the 'openness' with which we are left is actually more indicative of the film's postmodernity. In a similar vein, much like Beckett's work, the absurdist colouring of *Cul-de-sac*, as well as Polanski's early silent shorts, also leads to a re-evaluation of these works as postmodern.

So, looking back at the development of Polanski's cinema, we can see played out a trajectory that seems to adhere to Sontag's 'licensing' of 'the flight from the lofty horizons of high culture into the netherlands of pop and camp' (as Huyssen paraphrases Sontag, 1990: 262). Whilst Polanski's cinema seems to start in the realm of 'high' art, it tends to move towards popular genre, as if through his forced foray into genre cinema with *Repulsion* – a project originally treated simply as a means to fund *Cul-de-sac* – Polanski was able to realise his skill at delivering the Camp pleasures of genre. Of Polanski's early cinema, it is in fact *Repulsion*, and not *Knife in the Water* or *Cul-de-sac*, which best predicts the aesthetic direction of his cinematic career. But embedded within these celebrations of decadence and Camp we often find the more serious philosophical concerns associated with 'high' culture, which is why an exploration of the concepts of modernism and postmodernism proves so useful as a means of unpicking Polanski's cinema. But we must also note that as popular tastes changed over the years, Polanski's fondness for certain generic styles caused a shift towards a 'nostalgic mode' as a means by which his cinema is appreciated. Although this was already the case with *Chinatown*, the 'nostalgic mode' of appreciation is particularly true of his later works like *The Ninth Gate* and *The Ghost* (and we could add *Pirates*, *Frantic* and even *Oliver Twist* [2005] to this list), a point to which I will return in the forthcoming case studies.

Ambivalence and ambiguity

I often refer to Polanski's 'moral ambivalence' or 'anti-didacticism', and it is this feature, in parallel with his erosion of the distinction between 'high' and 'low' culture, that perhaps best qualifies his work as postmodern, as well as being the feature that I identify as most revealing of the 'philosophical implications' of both Polanski's cinema and the theory of active perception. But we should be careful here to distinguish between the various 'modes' of postmodernity, in particular that of postmodernity in its 'mainstream', or 'anything goes' mode in which pastiche serves to empty works of meaning, and the 'oppositional' or 'subversive' mode that is more interested in examining this 'emptiness', specifically the way some works seem to provoke us to fret in the face of 'the nothingness of the abyss' (as Hayward puts it, 2000: 277). As Huyssen (1990) argues, however, this 'apocalyptic desperate strain' of postmodernism already existed within the modernist movement.

The Enlightenment project 'took it as axiomatic that there was only one possible answer to any question … that the world could be controlled and rationally ordered if we could only picture and represent it rightly' (Harvey, 1989: 27); as Calinescu (1987) discusses, this axiom was challenged in the post-war period by the indeterminacy of quantum theory, Heisenberg's uncertainty principle in particular, which led to the displacement of the 'clockwork' model of the universe (269), and forced a merger between epistemology and hermeneutics (Calinescu citing Rorty, 271). Harvey identifies the connection of modernity and Enlightenment thought, which 'embraces the idea of progress, and actively sought that break with history and tradition which modernity espoused' (1989: 12). It was this sort of 'optimism' that came under threat in the twentieth century, 'with its death camps and death squads, its militarism and two world wars, its threat of nuclear annihilation and its experience of Hiroshima and Nagasaki' (13), what Harvey calls a choice to 'abandon the Enlightenment project entirely' (14). As Huyssen points out, the 'universal existential *Angst*' that emerged in the wake of World War II 'helped block out and suppress the realities of the fascist past' (1990: 243). It is this angst, in combination with the increased resistance to the strictures of modernism and a growing suspicion of the certitudes of the Enlightenment project, that gave rise to what Lyotard (1984) identified as the 'postmodern condition'. But Huyssen also warns not to consider postmodernism simply as an opposition to modernism (lest we should entangle ourselves once again in a futile binary 'quarrel'), but more so a movement, or condition, 'against a certain austere image of "high modernism"' (242). It is worth noting here that this resistance to the 'austere' effectively differentiates what I am referring to as Polanski's 'postmodernism' from Orr's concept of the 'neo-modernist' strain of cinema that emerged in the 1960s and 1970s from film-makers such as Godard, Antonioni and Bergman, which Orr sees as a return to the 'high modernism' typified by the silent cinema of Murnau, Lang, Dreyer and Eisenstein (see Orr, 1993: 1–34).

It is important not to mistake Polanski's anti-didacticism or moral ambivalence for the 'anything goes' strain of postmodernism, for it is specifically in this ambivalence that the subversiveness of these films lies. In one sense, due to his cinema's emphasis on diegetic 'seamlessness', the highly detailed *mise-en-scène* and the attention paid to micro-details, Polanski presents what Baudry (1992) might refer to as 'complete' or 'closed' worlds through which we are guided by our tethered camera, and so can be argued to be a form of perceptual didacticism; but within these worlds our perceptual abilities are challenged and our conceptual frameworks put under threat, even those that are constructed 'on the go' as we engage with the diegesis. So on the one hand, Polanski's cinema tries to perceptually 'seduce' us, but on the other, the reality of the diegesis we are 'seduced' into engaging with becomes destabilised. Polanski's fondness for undoing binaries and infusing his diegeses with ambiguity is highly visible, for example, in the nebulous portrayal of madness in *Rosemary's Baby* and the slippages of gender in *The Tenant*. Ultimately, Polanski's cinema is *open*.

I must also distinguish my identification of Polanski's cinema as postmodern from the critique of postmodernism as a 'relaxation' of artistic standards. By this I mean to differentiate between 'relaxation' (the 'anything goes' variety of postmodernism) and the value of ambivalence, openness and question-raising to philosophical discourse. The ambiguity that runs through Polanski's cinema is a counter to ideological didacticism, even that which is hegemonically subversive. Lyotard (1984) expressly defines postmodernism as 'incredulity towards metanarratives' (xxiv), a deep scepticism towards the possibility of identifying universal truths and perhaps their very existence. Such relativism destabilises ideology. As Hayward (2000) observes, 'postmodernism rejects meaning in the sense of believing that the world exists as something to be understood and that there is some unifying reality. Ideology becomes distinctively unstable in this environment' (282).

In his examinations of schizophrenic behaviour in particular, Polanski's portrayal of the workings of the perceptual mechanism serves to destabilise the very frameworks within which ideological absolutes are established, namely the way in which we structure our sense of reality. But even his films in which perceiving bodies are portrayed as highly sane individuals, the nature of reality remains elusive. It is this sort of 'pushing' of epistemological questions towards ever more basic queries that McHale suggests causes epistemology to 'tip over' into the domain of ontology (1986: 60), a philosophical transition highly indicative of the shift from the 'modern' to the 'postmodern' condition. To put it another way, pushed to the limit, the ambiguity that envelops Polanski's cinema is that which nudges epistemological concerns into ontological uncertainty or angst.

Polanski as author, Polanski as *auteur*

Throughout this discussion of Polanski's cinema, I often refer to Polanski himself in a manner that seems to suggest he has absolute agency over all of the details that make up these films, including narrative arcs, actors' performances, editing, colour palates, lens choice and the positioning and movement of the camera, in short, total control of the *mise-en-scène*, as if he were a painter working on a canvas, not a film-maker. Such an approach raises (at least) two problematic issues, the first being that it papers-over the vast amount of collaboration that must take place on any endeavour as grandiose as feature film-making, and the second being that by continuously referring to the person of the director himself I risk lapsing into the very type of biographical reading of Polanski's cinema I had hoped to avoid.

Earlier in this chapter, I made reference to the need to justify my approach to Polanski's cinema, which often refers to the director as if he were an absolute authorial force. Such an unqualified assertion is, of course, an exaggeration; however, as I will now explain, it is not without a certain level of validity. By discussing Polanski in terms of the discourse of auteurism that originally emerged from the pages of *Cahiers* in the 1950s, I can qualify what I actually intend when I refer to 'Polanski' in the forthcoming case studies.

In his discussion of auteur theory, Wollen examines the manner in which the concept of the auteur is divided into two 'types'. First, there is the 'total' auteur, that is, the director of his own text unhindered by the pressures of commission. The works of such an auteur possess a semantic dimension that can exist in lieu of a technical one, as core meaning is revealed though the virtue of the director having written the text upon which a film is based, and thus he or she is claimed to be the 'fount' of this meaning. The work of the *metteur en scène*, on the other hand, is primarily concerned with the transposition of an existing text to the screen; but there is still scope for the meaningfulness of films produced in this way to be attributed to the director if he or she is able to exercise complete agency in the realisation of these works. In this case, what is required of the critic is a deductive, intertextual approach in the reading of a director's cinema (Wollen, 1992: 601–603); as Wollen also highlights, the consideration of a *body* of work by a single director is critical, for 'it is only the analysis of the whole *corpus* which permits the moment of synthesis when the critic returns to the individual film' (600).

My approach to Polanski's cinema indeed assumes his status as an auteur, a title Polanski merits whatever 'type' of auteur one has in mind, encompassing all three 'concentric circles' of 'technique … personal style … and interior meaning' that Sarris uses to describe his multifaceted conceptualisation of the auteur (1992: 587). At times, much like Vigo, Fassbinder, Jarmusch or Lynch, Polanski has been the 'total' auteur: director, writer and 'dominant' aesthetic manipulator; but on many other occasions, he has worked on pre-existing sources, but has given cinematic life to these stories through his own particular film-making style, and thus can be considered along the lines of the *metteur en scène*, alongside the directors celebrated by the *Cahiers* group, such as Ford, Hitchcock and Hawks.

But such a partitioning of auteur 'types' risks creating an oversimplified image of the film-making process, which is always a complex web of collaboration between directors and cinematographers, actors, producers, set designers, etc. The extent of this collaboration varies wildly from director to director; where some directors may be credited as both writer and director, their contributions to on-screen performance, editing and cinematography may be limited. On the other hand, a director who takes on a pre-made script may exert high levels of control over even the smallest details of production, and marketing as well. In other words, there is no specific criteria that must be met in order for someone to be credited as 'director'. In the case of Polanski, the personal care taken in the choice of text for adaptation (as I will later argue, choices he seems to make with specific intent), the remarkable amount of control he exerts over his productions, and the level of restrictions he places on his collaborators are the primary reasons it is justifiable, and very nearly completely accurate, to refer to 'Polanski' as the controlling agent of the variety of aesthetic and thematic issues discussed herein, an issue I will return to on several occasions throughout the forthcoming case studies.

Earlier in his career, Polanski normally served as both director and originator of the script, on which he usually worked with Gérard Brach. Beginning with *Rosemary's Baby*, however, Polanski began favouring novels as source material (with some exceptions, such as *What?* and *Frantic*, which he wrote himself), but even when a film is based on an existing novel, Polanski is normally involved in the scriptwriting process. Sarris, himself citing a comment by Godard, notes 'that Visconti had evolved from a *metteur en scène* to an *auteur*, whereas Rossellini has evolved from an *auteur* to a *metteur en scène*' (1992: 587); Polanski can be seen to have followed a similar trajectory as Rosellini, but we must also consider the important intertextual connections between the source material of many of Polanski's adaptation choices and Polanski's own cinema, a point which I address in greater detail below and return to in my discussions of *Rosemary's Baby*, *Death and the Maiden* and *The Ghost*.

Any approach to film criticism that positions the director as a sort of 'quasi-Picasso', that is to say, the exact inverse of the 'quasi-chimpanzee' that Sarris (1992: 587) refers to in his discussion of auteur theory, is inherently problematic given the army of human beings who collaborate on a motion picture; this group of highly skilled people simply cannot be compared to blobs of paint on a palette. But in cases such as Polanski's, where there is ample evidence to suggest a high degree of control over even the smallest details of the films' construction at all levels of production, it is not misleading to discuss elements such as cinematography in terms of directorial intent. By the same token, Polanski has used many high-profile cinematographers as collaborators, including Gilbert Taylor (*Repulsion*, *Cul-de-sac*, *Macbeth*), William A. Fraker (*Rosemary's Baby*), Sven Nykvist (*The Tenant*) and Darius Khondji (*The Ninth Gate*), all known for cultivating their own distinct aesthetic styles.

A key assumption of auteur theory is that of the agency of a director to create a sense of purposefulness, a 'meaningful coherence', both within a film and even intertextually across a body of work; as Sarris asserts, 'this meaningful coherence is more likely when the director dominates the proceedings with skill and purpose' (1976: 246). Polanski's 'domination of proceedings' is remarkable amongst directors, and is much cited by his collaborators. Many of Polanski's actors, including Jack Nicholson, Catherine Deneuve, Johnny Depp and Ewan McGregor, have testified in interviews to Polanski's meticulous directorial style, often highlighting Polanski's tendency to 'act out' scenes as to furnish actors with a model to imitate. In an interview with Francine Stock on BBC Radio 4's *The Film Programme*, Christoph Waltz, much awarded for his acting ability in Tarantino's *Inglourious Basterds* (2009) and who stars in Polanski's *Carnage* (2011), articulates what it is like for an actor to work with the Polanski:

> Christoph Waltz: He is a perfectionist in everything. To have a perfectionist call the shots – literally, call the shots – is, in a way, a very restricting experience …
>
> Francine Stock: So that kind of discipline, those sorts of restrictions … is more apparent when Polanski is directing than other directors?
>
> Christoph Waltz: Yes, because he names every single one of them and nothing escapes him in that respect; or maybe nothing escapes him at all. He lets certain things go because he understands that you cannot impose on everything, but very few things escape his grip. And at the same time he is charming and funny, so you succumb to that, you do not resist it.[12]

Cinematographer Darius Khondji also testifies as to the degree of Polanski's control over the aesthetics of his films. Tellingly, Khondji, one of the most revolutionary cinematographers of modern times (lauded for his work on *Delicatessen* [1991], *Seven* [1995] and *Alien: Resurrection* [1997]), credits Polanski as an influence on his shooting style, calling attention to the director's insistence on using precise camera angles, lenses and focus to achieve his aesthetic goals:

> I'm somehow different since working with Roman … It's not even very clear what I learned from working with him, but I find that I don't line up shots the same way I used to! Roman has very acute, very sharp eyes in terms of things like camera angles … Roman has a very methodical, scrupulous way of filming things – every single detail in the frame is equally important to him … There would be a reason why that particular magazine is over there in that particular place. Everything has not only a visual reason, but a narrative reason.
>
> (Khondji, as quoted in Pizzello, 2000: 39)

A further semantic complication arises in the attribution of narrative content to a film's director when a film has been based on an existing work. Throughout my discussion I will not distinguish between authors of these works and Polanski himself, except for a few cases in which I highlight significant changes Polanski has made from the original texts. I justify any insinuation of Polanski's 'ownership' of these works in the context of this analysis of his films due to the intertextual nature of my discussion; as I am addressing a group (or groups) of Polanski's films, and at times discussing his cinema as a whole, it is relevant to attribute the repetition of motifs and narrative content to Polanski himself simply as the result of his agency in having chosen these particular texts to adapt.

Although there is some suggestion that Polanski has been 'encouraged' to take on certain projects, he has never been a 'hired hand'. He has enjoyed the rare luxury of having personally structured his own opus, a claim few directors can make.[13] There is even strong indication of 'cross pollination' between Polanski's cinema and some of the works he has adapted, in that these texts show signs of having been influenced by Polanski's previous work. Polanski has suggested, for example, that Ira Levin's novel *Rosemary's Baby* was itself influenced by *Repulsion*, which is what attracted him to the idea of adapting the book (Cronin, 2005: 23). More recently, Robert Harris's novel *Pompeii*, which Polanski intended to film in 2007, seemed to be strongly influenced by *Chinatown*. Likewise, Harris's next novel, *The Ghost*, which was written during his collaboration with Polanski on *Pompeii* and was actually filmed by Polanski in 2009 (released in 2010), was equally (if not more so) 'Polanskian' in its subject matter, style and themes. A similar occurrence of possible cross-pollination occurs in *Death and the Maiden*, which I will later discuss as part of my case study of *Frantic*.

Polanski has explained his approach to adaptations as follows:

> When you choose to adapt a novel you find truly interesting, it's vital that you know what you're committing yourself to ... Unless ... you choose a story that you're not really interested in, one that only serves as a pretext to constructing something completely different onscreen. Shakespeare started with mediocre stories and turned them into something extraordinary.
>
> (Delahaye and Narboni, 2005: 26)

There are examples of both these types of adaptations in Polanski's opus. There are films in which he seems to use what is often rather 'pulpy' source material, like Ira Levin's *Rosemary's Baby*, to engage some of his personal concerns (such as the perception theories I am discussing here); and then there are other films that are based on more epic or serious works, like Wladyslaw Szpilman's *The Pianist* or Dickens's *Oliver Twist*, in which the inherent value of a text's subject is itself perhaps more a focus, rather than serving primarily as a springboard for Polanski's intertextual philosophical discourse (although these films arguably do both).

Over half of Polanski's films are in fact based on pre-existing novels or plays,[14] and whilst all of these adaptations stray in some capacity from their origins, for the most part Polanski's adaptations remain faithful to their source material. In *Rosemary's Baby* and *The Tenant*, for example, much of the spoken dialogue in the films is taken directly from the novels. A notable exception is *The Ninth Gate*, which is a radically truncated and re-envisioned version of Arturo Pérez-Reverte's novel *The Dumas Club* (1996), reflected by the fact that it is the only adaptation that does not share its name with the source material.

So whilst it is clear that Polanski's absolute domain over the cinematic artefacts under investigation here should not be overestimated (directing is, of course, famously the art of concession), given the remarkable control that we know Polanski does exert over his productions at all levels, it is useful, and very nearly accurate, to refer to 'Polanski' as shorthand for the authorial entity responsible for all the details discussed herein.

Planes of reality

Given this book's focus on perception, both as represented on-screen and as engaged in by the spectator, throughout the forthcoming discussion it will be necessary to distinguish between various 'planes' of reality. For the sake of expediency, I will employ some of the terminology used by Souriau (1953, as translated in Buckland, 2000: 47–48) to establish a hierarchy of these various 'types' of reality. At the two ends of the spectrum we have *afilmic* reality, which refers to the reality outside of the cinematic experience (i.e. the reality of the 'real world' as we know it), and *diegetic* reality, which refers to the reality of the fiction, complete with its internal sense of what is verifiably true and false (which may or may not equate to afilmic distinctions).

I will include three more 'planes' of reality to nuance these distinctions further. *Profilmic* reality refers to the production of the film, that is, the reality of that which is actually photographed. Discussing the construction of a prop gun, for example, is to examine its profilmic nature, whereas the same object is 'real' diegetically speaking. *Filmophanic* reality refers specifically to the image itself, as it is projected onto the screen. *Spectatorial* reality refers to the audience's perceptual experience of engaging this image; this is the point where afilmic reality (i.e. the physical experience of watching the screen and our awareness of doing it) and diegetic reality meet.

As the 'close readings' that make up the majority of this book are based in a conceptual framework that is heavily informed by perceptual psychology, the experience of the spectator as a perceiving force will be discussed along with Polanski's diegetic representation of acts of perception. Therefore, both spectatorial and profilmic realities will be considered alongside what are purely diegetic forms of reality. Furthermore, given the fact that many of the films under investigation here are heavily concerned with schizophrenic forms of perception, the 'realities' created by the hallucinations and delusions of diseased perceptual mechanisms have to be considered in relation to the 'stable' diegetic reality within which they are nestled; this is a juxtaposition that is often difficult to maintain when these two 'realities' overlap. For the sake of clarity in my analyses, I will often use the term 'diegetically real' to refer to the reality that the film establishes as objective, as a means of contrasting it with that which is hallucinated. As will become evident, however, Polanski creates situations in which this distinction becomes severally muddled.

Polanski's two cinemas

Although Polanski's concern with perceptual psychology is evident in much of his cinema, the manner in which the issue is dealt with has evolved over the years. Many critics have made note of various periods or shifts in Polanski's work, but perhaps the most evident of these can be identified by targeting *The Tenant* and *Tess* (1979) as a kind of transitional moment. Mazierska identifies *Tess* as the point at which '(o)ntological and epistemological ambiguity, which was Polanski's trademark, gradually evaporates from his films and the kingdom of fantasy shrinks' (2007: 88). We can add to Mazierska's discussion by examining Polanski's work in the context of perception theory, in which her classification of these two periods remains useful, in that it identifies a relevant aesthetic change from films that attempt to represent the subjective psychological experience of a character from the 'inside' to films in which access to these cognitive experiences remains elusive, keeping us 'outside' the psychological sphere. We can nuance this shift a step further. The psyches to which we are granted 'access' in these earlier films tend to be in a state of crisis in which these characters' perceptual acuity is seriously questionable. Contrariwise, the crises faced in the later films are not portrayed as the result of psychosis. In other words, when Polanski penetrates the psyches of his characters, these minds tend to be diseased, or at least *possibly* diseased, as I shall discuss. It is along this axis that I have divided my study into two parts: the group of films in which the camera is able to penetrate the psychological sphere of the characters to which it is connected, and those in which it maintains a more observational stance, 'outside' the subjective perceptual experiences of these characters.

Whilst this stylistic shift corresponds to what Mazierska has identified as the two 'halves' of Polanski's cinema, it must be noted that this is a crude distinction. In several films of the 'early' period, the camera remains well outside the psychological realm of the characters it follows; *Chinatown*, for example, is more indicative of the 'later' style, even though it was made before *The Tenant*, which is arguably the most psychologically (or 'fantasy', as Mazierska puts it) focused of all of Polanski's films. Nevertheless, with the exceptions noted, the conditions that define this 'divide' prove particularly relevant to my discussion. The most important distinction that needs to be made between these two groups of films lies in the locus of conflict. Where the psychological films actively represent inner conflicts, what I argue to be *perceptual crises*, the later group keeps this type of conflict concealed from the spectator and instead focuses on interpersonal ('outside') conflict. The particular films I discuss, however, do indeed conceal a perceptual crisis of sorts, but a crisis to which we are not granted direct access.

Whilst Gregory's research is perhaps most directly (and visually) relevant to the films that include psychological penetration, it is also a useful means of addressing many of the thematic elements present in Polanski's later films. Where Polanski's 'psychological' films are primarily concerned with demonstrating the complexity and fallibility of subjective perception, that is to say, that which is *behind* the eyes, these later films also take a look at the complicated situations that occur *in front* of them; this is a shift in focus from *how* we observe ('inside') to *what* we observe ('out there'). Where films like *Rosemary's Baby*, *The Tenant*, *Repulsion* and even *Macbeth* try to demonstrate the effect that heightened emotions and mental illness can have on one's perception of reality (and in turn, draw attention to how one's sense of reality is constructed), films such as *Chinatown*, *Tess*, *Frantic*, *The Ninth Gate*, *The Pianist*, *Oliver Twist* and *The Ghost* position us as observers to the bizarre, capricious and wholly unpredictable twists and turns the events of life can take, challenging the conceptual frameworks upon which the perceptual mechanisms of the characters in these films rely to perceive effectively. The overall theme of uncertainty, of our inability to master the world either through observation or participation, is a binding thread in all these films.

Starting with the next chapter, the rest of this book will focus on two 'sets' of films, which I will (crudely) refer to as the 'Apartment Trilogy' of *Repulsion*, *Rosemary's Baby* and *The Tenant*, and the 'Investigation Trilogy' of *Chinatown*, *Frantic* and *The Ninth Gate*. In addition, *Death and the Maiden* will be discussed in concert with *Frantic* as a means of further exploring some of the fundamental concerns raised in all of these films. I approach Polanski's cinema through these two 'trilogies' as a convenient and fertile means of engaging with the perceptual discourse that develops over the course of Polanski's oeuvre. Whilst my analyses will be primarily informed by what I have argued is the influence of perceptual psychology and its philosophical implications on Polanski's cinema, these will also incorporate what I consider to be the key 'satellite' issues that stem from this basic concern, namely the formation and mutation of identity, which in turn includes Polanski's often polemical representation of gender and nationhood.

This approach is not intended to suggest that these groups of films are true trilogies in the sense of being continuous stories divided into three parts, and nor do I believe there is any deliberate attempt on Polanski's part that these films be considered thematic trilogies in the way intended by Kieślowski in his *Trois Couleurs* (*Bleu, Blanc, Rouge* [1993]) or by von Trier in his *Europe Trilogy* (*The Element of Crime* [1984], *Epidemic* [1987], *Europa* [1991]). The formation of these trilogies is more the result of a specific form of critical reading; the term 'trilogy' is itself merely a term of convenience resulting from the fact that there happen to be three films that share a common trait (a type of setting or narrative thrust, in these cases) that forms the focus of said reading.

Given that Polanski tends to use a series of repeated motifs, what Cappabianca (1997) and Leaming (1981) like to call his 'obsessions', Polanski's work can be studied via other groupings, such as the water films (*Knife in the Water, Cul-de-sac, Chinatown)* or the doppelganger films, an often recurrent motif in Polanski's cinema, which is highly pronounced in one of his latest films, *The Ghost*. My own focus on Polanski's overarching perceptual discourse is best served through the 'apartment' and 'investigation' groupings, which both through their narrative content and aesthetic construction reflect and challenge various aspects of perceptual psychology.

Each of the Apartment Trilogy films presents a scenario in which the possibility of mental illness serves as the chief cause of conflict. Notably, in each of *Repulsion*, *Rosemary's Baby* and *The Tenant*, we are presented with foreign bodies taking up dwellings in large, Western, urban centres. Urbanity indeed proves to be a major motif in Polanski's cinema, often serving as a means of associating cognitive decay with city life by mapping mental landscapes onto urban landscapes. In *Repulsion*, Belgian émigré Carole Ledoux lives in her sister's flat in London; we are told Rosemary Woodhouse in *Rosemary's Baby* is from the Midwestern United States (Omaha, Nebraska) and has moved to New York; and in *The Tenant*, Trelkovsky is a (presumably) Polish-born, but naturalised French citizen, living in Paris.

The spectre of urbanity makes its first appearance in Polanski's short film *The Fat and the Lean* (1961), a master-and-servant scenario. The film concludes with an image of the liberated manservant, played by Polanski himself, dancing off into the frame towards Paris, the city to which Polanski's cinema most often returns. In *The Tenant*, Paris is portrayed as a city in which housing shortages compel a young man to assume the flat of a hospitalised (suicidal) woman in hopes that she will soon perish; and in *Frantic*, for American Richard Walker, Paris turns from a romantic tourist Haven to a stand-in for Hades as its Orphean narrative unfolds. In *The Ninth Gate*, however, Paris is asserted as a global/capitalist space in which America and Europe overlap seamlessly.

In each of *Repulsion*, *Rosemary's Baby* and *The Tenant*, the apartment that is assumed by the protagonist as a dwelling space becomes the site of this character's perceptual breakdown. As I shall argue, Polanski's interest in perceptual psychology and its direct application to his cinematic style is increasingly evident in each of these films. Whilst *Chinatown*, *Frantic* and *The Ninth Gate*, on the other hand, do not penetrate the inner sphere to create the kind of psychological realism seen in *Repulsion*, *Rosemary's Baby* and *The Tenant*, they remain concerned with the same sort of cognitive processes. But rather than examining the perceptual mechanism 'up close' through a depiction of its breakdown, these investigation stories take a step back to observe a high-functioning perceiver encounter perceptual challenges that initiate a series of epistemological crises, often paralleled by moments of serious physical peril. The key difference in these two groups of films is the presence of madness, or a 'malfunction' in the perceptual apparatus. Where Carole Ledoux, Rosemary Woodhouse and Trelkovsky all display psychotic behaviour patterns, there is no indication that Walker, Gittes or Corso (Johnny Depp) are suffering from mental illness in any way. Just the opposite: all three of these *men* (as I shall later discuss, there is a relevant, and rather polemical, gender distinction between these two 'trilogies') are clearly delineated as highly rational. Instead of struggling with mental illness, these 'sane' minds experience cognitive dissonance as they are forced to confront a reality that does not match their concept of the way the world should work.

Notes

1. The International Society for *Ecological Psychology* and their publication Ecological Psychology best summarise Gibson's enduring influence.
2. The recent advent of digital projection has eliminated the type of 'jittering' found with 35 mm projection, and so unsurprisingly 3-D is having a resurgence. Nevertheless, a convincing 3-D image that increases, rather than decreases, engagement remains elusive. Polanski has always been more of a perfectionist than innovator, preferring to fully realise the potential of 'classic' cinema rather than reinvent the medium (Polanski has never, for example, aligned himself with or initiated an aesthetic 'movement'), but it remains to be seen whether or not he will renew his fascination with 3-D given the latest developments.
3. As any good photography book will show, shooting a subject with a telescopic lens at a greater distance could yield a similarly constructed image as shooting the same subject more closely with a normal lens, or even more closely with a wide-angle lens. However, the *perspective* (i.e. the relative size of the subject compared to the background) would be radically different in each image (see Warren, 2002: 73, for example). The normal (50 mm) lens is thought to best approximate the perspective of natural human vision, if the observer was positioned at the same distance from the subject as the camera.
4. Or drugged, or drunk, depending on how one reads the rape sequence in *Rosemary's Baby*.
5. I use the term 'perceptual realism' here to signify a specific form of cinematic 'realism', but the term is more often used to describe a philosophical stance that stresses the existence of objects independent of our perceptions of them. Both direct and indirect theories of perception are forms of realism, although each describes a very different version of the workings of perception. Nevertheless, both direct and indirect theories are distinct from 'idealism', which instead identifies the mental sphere alone as custodian of existence.
6. At the time of writing, Polanski's *Carnage* (2011) had yet to be released; all indications suggest, however, that this film will join the list of 'divided' narratives.
7. We must equally be careful not to overstate the parallel between *digital* cinema and perception, notwithstanding the fact that certain elements of digital 'inscription' seem to account for the discrepancies outlined above. It is true, of course, that in the digital recording of images (moving or still) no actual images are stored in the device. Here the parallel to biological vision seems to stand up better than film, and the fact that the radiant energy that passes through the lens onto a receptive plate (the sensor) is then codified into electrical pulses to be stored as pure data only further justifies the comparison. Indeed, just as Gregory reminds us that there are no 'pictures in the brain', we can equally state that there are no pictures in the hard drive.

   But the parallel between the way the brain deals with vision and the digital camera, whilst compelling, is again superficial. The digital device's entire *raison d'être* is to reproduce the image, onto a screen, to then serve as object of perception to a perceiving body. Whilst the digital device is not literally storing images as images (the way film does), this does not move it much closer to serving as analogy for our visual system, which is not geared to reproduce an image for the proverbial 'mind's eye' that is meant to serve as both perceiving organ and projection room.

8. It is also important not to confuse Sobchack's literal notion of 'film's body' with strains of film theory specifically concerned with the spectator's perceptual relationship with the on-screen corporeal form, such as Shaviro's (1993) use of the term 'Cinematic Body' or Mulvey's (1975) famous discussion of the 'male gaze' and the objectification of women's bodies.
9. The discourse surrounding the ontology of film itself has moved on considerably since Sobchack's discussion of 'film's body'; see, for example, Marks (2000), Sobchack (2004), Rodowick (2007) and Barker (2009). There is also a range of scholarship explicitly dedicated to the general study of cinema and cognition; see, for example, Bordwell (1989), Smith (1995), Carroll (1996), Anderson (1996), Plantinga and Smith (1999) and Grodal (2009).
10. Quote taken from the SCSMI website: scsmi-online.org (accessed 4 April 2011).
11. Rather than distinguishing between modernism and postmodernism, Wexman instead focuses on the influence of the better-understood artistic movements of absurdism and surrealism on Polanski's cinema, a useful approach as Polanski's forays into absurdism in his early silent cinema foreshadow his shift towards examinations of psychosis and perception. As Wexman notes, a clinical study by Litowitz and Newman (1967) relates the 'despair' of the absurdist worldview to 'the minimally developed character structures found in borderline schizophrenics' (Wexman, 1985: 16), a point that greatly informs my first group of case studies. (It is worth noting here that at this time the American Psychiatric Association considered Borderline Personality Disorder a subcategory of schizophrenia, but this is no longer the case.)
12. Broadcast on 6 May 2011.
13. Even Stanley Kubrick, whose control over his own career was very similar to Polanski's, was more-or-less compelled to direct *Spartacus*, a film often omitted from critical analyses of his work as a whole. Polanski has no such film to 'pollute' his opus.
14. Polanski's adaptations: *Rosemary's Baby* (1968, from the novel by Ira Levin), *Macbeth* (1971, from the play by William Shakespeare), *The Tenant* (1976, from the novel by Roland Topor), *Tess* (1979, from the novel by Thomas Hardy), *Bitter Moon* (1992, from the novel *Lunes de Fiel*, by Pascal Bruckner), *Death and the Maiden* (1994, from the play by Ariel Dorfman), *The Ninth Gate* (1999, from the novel *The Dumas Club*, by Arturo Pérez-Reverte), *The Pianist* (2002, from Wladyslaw Szpilman's autobiography), *Oliver Twist* (2005, from the novel by Charles Dickens), *The Ghost* (2010, from the novel by Robert Harris) and *Carnage* (2011, from the play *God of Carnage* by Yasmina Reza).

Chapter 3

Schizophrenia and the City

Illusions, hallucinations and delusions

As a means of priming my discussion of the first of Polanski's 'trilogies' under investigation here, I shall provide a basic overview of the history of the illness called 'schizophrenia', a condition which features prominently (although never explicitly nominated) in a number of Polanski's films. It is beyond the scope of this work to give a detailed account of the research that informs the clinical understanding of schizophrenia, but multiple references are made to seminal volumes that are devoted to the subject. What is outlined below is intended to facilitate a discussion of Polanski's cinema based on the history of the clinical recognition of the illness, the development of its diagnostic criteria, and how the clinical understanding of the illness relates to the theory of active perception. As a means of highlighting some key points that will be addressed in the dedicated case studies that follow, as the discussion of schizophrenia in this chapter develops, I shall indicate which of the Apartment Trilogy films is most relevant to the specific points mentioned.

It is appropriate at this point to distinguish between a number of often colloquially confused terms that we will need to carry on this discussion, namely *illusion*, *hallucination* and *delusion*. Both illusions and hallucinations are non-veridical ('not true') perceptions in that both are perceptions that do not coincide with the objectively measurable characteristics of the stimuli from the outside world that is being perceived. A quick and easy definition that distinguished these terms, however, carries its own difficulties. As Gregory notes, to simply define an illusion as a perception that does not correspond to a concrete physical reality is to assume the existence of an independent, antecedent truth from which a given perception has departed. 'But how do we know the truth?' Gregory rightfully challenges himself (1997a: 194). But such logic becomes quickly self-defeating, as Gregory also hastens to point out:

> To say that all appearances of objects are illusions is no more helpful than to say all experience is a dream. Although logically irrefutable, this drains useful meaning from 'dream' and from 'illusion'. (Similarly, there is little point in saying that everything is beautiful or everything is ugly: perception and language need contrasts to have meaning.)
>
> (Gregory, 1997a: 194)

The 'truth' of the independent existence of objects is not a philosophical conundrum Gregory spends much time wrestling with, and nor will I. And nor does Gregory allow the apparent contradictions of quantum physics (i.e. Heisenberg's Uncertainty Principle) and relativity sway the argument: the issue at hand is the functioning of the human perceptual system within the perceivable world as determined by the limits of our sense organs (such as the small band of visible light that the eye is able to see); we are not discussing perception within the quantum sphere nor at the speed of light, but at the level of 'kitchen physics'. There is plenty to observe, test and discuss within these limits without resorting to philosophies that dismiss the discussion *ab initio*.

Where *illusion* is used to refer to a misinterpretation of a physical reality, a *hallucination* is instead a perception that is auto-generated and not (or only tenuously) linked to external stimuli. Another way of putting it is to consider a hallucination to be a 'perception without an object', as referred to by McKenna (1997: 6), himself citing Esquirol's 1832 definition. McKenna mentions 'abnormal perception' in his list of 'cardinal' symptoms of schizophrenia, in which the use of the term 'abnormal' allows us to differentiate between illusions and hallucinations. Simply put, to experience an illusion is to experience a perception that departs from the physical reality of the external stimulus due to special properties of said stimuli that cause the brain to react in a certain way. So, to experience an illusion is a *normal*, 'correct' perception, an appropriate misrepresentation of the stimuli. On the other hand, a hallucination, which is also a perception that departs from the physical reality of the stimuli, can be entirely self-generated (i.e. not linked at all to external stimuli), and is not due to the type of 'special properties' considered to cause illusions. These are therefore considered to be *abnormal*, the result of an incorrectly functioning perceptual apparatus. The distinction is of course best illustrated via example.

Gregory provides a number of examples of 'normal' illusions that are the result of a combination of special properties in the object of perception and the way the brain reacts to certain stimuli. These include the 'hollow face' illusion (Gregory, 1997a: 207), in which the brain seems to simply refuse to see a concave face and thus forces a (false) convex face to be perceived. The ubiquity of this perceptual experience suggests that such a 'misrepresentation' of the stimuli is normal, that is, a perceptual effect that is the result of a healthy perceptual apparatus. The predominant theory regarding this particular illusion suggests that the special attention the brain pays to faces for the purposes of survival (such as the need to quickly identify a family member who is likely to protect you) causes faces to be processed by the brain in a different way than other stimuli (for animals who rely more on smell for identification, for example, this could be different). Similar evolution-based explanations are offered for most illusions. So normal are such illusions that failure to experience them could actually be a contributing factor to the diagnosis of mental illness. Recently published research, for example, shows that there are many optical illusions, including the 'hollow face' illusion, that are *not* experienced by a significant number of patients diagnosed with schizophrenia (see Bonnemann et al. [2009] and Borsutzky et al. [2002]).

In contrast to illusions, the nature of hallucinations depends completely on the subjective perceptual mechanism of the person experiencing them. Hallucinations need not be visual; stimulus-less perception can mimic any of the senses. A well-known symptom of schizophrenia, the hearing of voices, is classified as an auditory hallucination, for instance. But McKenna also discusses non-verbal auditory hallucinations, including hearing noises ('tapping, scuffling, banging, car engines' 1997: 7) and even music. As the 'reality' of these sounds from the subject's perspective seems as legitimate as a real sound, it is unsurprising that quite logical, albeit incorrect or exaggerated, responses occur. Just as hearing the sound of rainfall through an external door would lead the perceiver to conclude it was raining, so too could hearing footsteps outside a bedroom door in what was thought to be a locked, empty house lead one to conclude a menacing presence was approaching. Polanski's use of sound in the Apartment Trilogy films, *Repulsion* in particular, is highly reminiscent of the above description, a point to which I shall return in the next chapter.

Kraeplin and Bleuler (the first to identify schizophrenia) also make note of subjects experiencing *somatic hallucinations* (Mckenna, 1997: 9), which are various forms of hallucinatory bodily sensations, including the feeling of being touched (identified as *haptic hallucinations*, although the sensations described are passive rather than active) and the feeling of movement (*kinaesthetic hallucinations*). They include sexual sensations in the category of *somatic hallucination*, along with a series of other bizarre (often impossible) bodily sensation. Berrios (1982) importantly makes note of the difficulty of determining the 'relative contributions of hallucination and delusion to the bizarre bodily complaints of schizophrenic patients' (in McKenna, 1997: 9), in which beliefs (such as believing one is pregnant) and somatic hallucinations (feeling something 'kicking' from inside one's body) are completely intertwined; this is a relevant detail to keep in mind when we turn our attention to our close readings of *Rosemary's Baby* and *The Tenant*.

Delusions need to be distinguished from both illusions and hallucinations. A delusion is not a perception linked to the physical senses, but an erroneous *belief*, 'held with fixed, intense conviction; which is incorrigible to argument; and which is out of keeping with the individual's social educational, and cultural background' (McKenna, 1997: 2). McKenna describes delusions as 'fantastic, patently absurd, or at least inherently unlikely' that, as Simms (1988) describes it, are 'justified by the patient in a peculiarly illogical way' (in McKenna, 1997: 2). Whilst DSM IV TR[1] does not define delusion, its use of the term is consistent with this definition. McKenna extends the definition to include a number of subtypes as well as several examples of cases taken from various studies. Amongst these, McKenna highlights *delusions of persecution*, *hypochondriacal delusions*, *delusions of misidentifications*, and, of special interest to all the films of the Apartment Trilogy, *sexual delusions:*

> are by no means uncommon in schizophrenics. Sometimes they are intimately bound up to hallucinatory sensation, for example in genitals; in other cases, however, there are beliefs – *of pregnancy, in a fantasy lover, that one's sex is changing* – which cannot be attributed to abnormal perceptions.
>
> (McKenna, 1997: 4)

The emphasis in the above citation is my own, which I have included as a means of indicating that each of these examples calls to mind at least one of the Apartment Trilogy films (pregnancy: *Rosemary's Baby*, fantasy lover: *Repulsion* and *Rosemary's Baby*, sex changing: *The Tenant*), each of which I will elaborate on in due course.

Also of great relevance to this discussion are *grandiose delusions*, defined as beliefs in irrationally high levels of certain talents (*grandiose ability*), elevated sense of importance (*grandiose identity*), and delusions of a particularly religious nature, such as a patient's belief that he or she is on a special religious mission, or that the patient is indeed a 'divine'/ supernatural being him- or herself (often times God or the Devil). Interestingly, although McKenna never breaches the subject directly, there is no mention of the type of beliefs held by many considered to be strongly religious; millions worldwide profess to believe in virgin-birth, transubstantiation and resurrection, for example. Instead such beliefs seem covered by the caveat of the deluded subject's 'erroneous beliefs' needing to be 'out of keeping with the individual's social educational, and cultural background' (1997: 2).

In the act of diagnosing cardinal symptoms of schizophrenia, drawing a distinction between delusional thought and religious belief is indeed challenging. Nevertheless, in McKenna's summary of the research there are several descriptions of case studies in which religiously coloured behaviours have been classified as delusional. In each case, the references to religious subject matter (the god, prophet, or action) is consistent with, or stems from, the religious practices the patient was closely familiar with; for example, I have not come across any reports of a patient who was a practising Hindu, brought up in a Hindu family and living in a Hindu community who claims the Virgin Mary has asked him to build a shrine to her. Grandiose religious delusions tend to be consistent with the religious experience of the patient in question.

Whilst some religiously coloured delusions are identified as 'grandiose', others, irrespective of how irrational they may be in any other context, are excluded from this definition if they are found to be in keeping with cultural norms. The difficulty in the case of religious delusions is then to identify a precise point where a belief ceases to be a 'normal' religious conviction and crosses the line to become 'grandiose'. Knowledge of the specifics of religious doctrines is therefore of great importance in the diagnosis of schizophrenia. There may be one patient who claims to be the reincarnation of a Prince, another who believes that her car is occupied by evil spirits, and yet another who insists that some wine and bread wafers have literally been transformed into the blood and flesh of a god born to a virgin two thousand years ago; in none of these cases can the belief can be diagnosed as delusional if the subject in question holds it within a framework of a recognised religious doctrine (in these cases: Hinduism, Animism and Catholicism respectively). I shall return to this highly problematic issue in my discussions of (what I argue to be) Polanski's parodic critique of religion in both *Rosemary's Baby* and *The Ninth Gate.*

Schizophrenia and perception

Where illusions such as the hollow face reveal the extent to which learning can influence perception in a healthy brain, delusions and hallucinations indicative of mental illnesses, especially schizophrenia, reveal just how powerful the brain can be in its creation of subjective realities unrelated to external stimuli. Where the healthy brain acts as judge to sort out the meaning of the evidence (stimuli) it has presented to it, it can often be fooled. In cases of schizophrenia, however, the brain not only misjudges stimuli, but generates it outright, causing the sufferer to mistake purely imagined perceptions for those that are based on stimuli actually being received by the sense organs.

In Gregory's discussion of the nature of perception in *Eye and Brain*, the issue of 'malfunctions' in the perceptual mechanism is often raised; and it is through examinations of these malfunctions that much can be learned about how we should define the 'correct' functioning of the perceptual apparatus. To reaffirm a basic point, in this conceptual framework, a distinction is indeed made between 'correctly' and 'incorrectly' functioning perceptual mechanisms. Ever-wary of the model of active perception being accused of solipsism, Gregory stresses that the proposition that perception is an active cognitive process does not inherently suggest the absence of an antecedent reality, nor does it suggest a perpetual dream state; to do so, to identify reality as an illusion, is to render terms such as 'illusion' or 'dream' useless. Instead, Gregory focuses on examining and qualitatively distinguishing between different forms of perception: those that are signalled from external cues (and interpreted), and those that are *not*. Schizophrenia is one of the 'malfunctions' Gregory expresses particular interest in, specifically due to the fact that the behaviour associated with this illness highlights the critical tenets of active perception.

Schneider (1958) established a series of 'first rank' symptoms for schizophrenia to distinguish the relative importance of various observed or reported behaviours. These 'first rank' symptoms are: somatic passivity experiences ('the experience of influences playing on the body'); 'all feelings, impulses (drives), and volitional acts experienced by the patient as the work or influence of others'; thought withdrawal; diffusion of thought; and delusional perception (in McKenna, 1997: 26). For Schneider, a diagnosis of schizophrenia can be made if any one of these symptoms are determined to be manifest in a subject. As Schneider notes, what all of these first rank symptoms have in common is their 'lowering of the barrier between the self and the surrounding world' (27). In common with Schneider, Keefe (1998) similarly refers to a *collapse* of the barrier between the neurological sphere and the outside world, which seem to overlap to the extent that the schizophrenic subject is unable to determine the difference between perceptions that are imagined and those which are connected to external stimuli (142). As I mentioned in the previous chapter, Gregory describes the condition from a different perspective, as one in which the sufferer *loses* contact with the outside world 'so that he or she is effectively isolated' (1997a: 199). Although apparently contradictory, Gregory, Schneider and Keefe are all simply using metaphors to describe the same thing; namely, the subject's inability to differentiate veridical perceptions that are based on external stimuli and non-veridical perceptions that are self-generated, independent of the stimuli that is actually present. There is a connection here between this concept of 'barrier collapse' and the idea of the cinematic 'wraparound effect', which will become increasingly relevant as we examine Polanski's attempts to achieve this goal in his representations of the disturbed perceptions of his protagonists. Polanski seeks to cause a similar 'collapse' on the spectatorial plane, applying a concerted effort to muddle the spectators' sense of the border between afilmic and diegetic reality through active manipulation of their perceptual mechanisms.

An issue that informs my discussion of *Rosemary's Baby* is the effect of intoxicating substances on perception. It should be noted that hallucinogenic states similar to what are thought of as symptomatic of schizophrenia can be generated in subjects through the ingestion of certain drugs, which in turn has initiated much research concerned with seeking a biochemical explanation for the illness. McKenna (1997) identifies the synthesis and use of LSD is the late 1940s as a key starting point for such research, which eventually led to 'dopamine hypothesis' (135), a theory that suggests that the hallucinations typical of schizophrenia are the result of excess brain dopamine. Essentially, such research showed only that the use of drugs known to increase dopamine levels could indeed cause schizophrenia-like psychosis; but the conclusion that excess dopamine is the cause of schizophrenia does not necessarily follow. What is important to note is that whilst certain drug-induced states may *resemble* schizophrenia, this is not to say that they are *causes* of schizophrenia. In fact, the clinical definition of schizophrenia specifically precludes the influence of such drugs. It is therefore relevant to distinguish Polanski's representation of schizophrenic behaviour from other films in which hallucinated, or 'parallel', realities are induced by drug use. In neither *Repulsion* nor *The Tenant* is there any suggestion of drug use, but in the case of *Rosemary's Baby*, a film in which the diagnosis of the protagonist as mentally ill is particularly vexing, drugs may (or *may not*) play a part in Rosemary's perceptual crisis.

In addition to using the vocabulary provided by Gregory, my intention is to utilise DSM's diagnostic criteria and the clinical case studies I have discussed above to enlighten my discussion of these films, especially as to how Polanski uses the representation of schizophrenic behaviour to initiate discourse on perception. By doing so, I hope to illustrate the manner in which Polanski uses profilmic elements to realistically convey the schizophrenic condition, as well as inspire novel readings of these films. Whilst these films share the objective of exposing the relatively malleable nature of perception (and in turn of subjective concepts of reality) with 'trip' films like *Naked Lunch* (Cronenberg, 1991), *A Scanner Darkly* (Linklater, 2006) and *Jacob's Ladder* (Lyne, 1990) (to name but a few), Polanski's cinema does not rely on the intoxicating effects of drugs to explore perception. Polanski's camera keeps the spectator close to the schizophrenic characters, not only making the spectator bear witness to this character's suffering, but also allowing (often forcing) the spectator to experience the same sort of distorted perceptions.

A note on Lacan and 'schizophrenia'

For the sake of clarity, I will restrict my use of the term 'schizophrenia' to its clinical (psychiatric) definition; whilst at times I discuss Lacan, I do not completely subscribe to his understanding of the condition of schizophrenia, which he seems to attribute to retardation of language development, justifying this stance on psychoanalytic terms. That being said, there is value in the connection that Lacan makes between language articulation and the subject's lack of the concept of 'I' to this discussion of schizophrenia as a condition in which the interconnectedness of signifiers becomes fragmented. For Lacan, the schizophrenic state is entered due to a subject's inability to assert his or her autonomous existence, caught between the Imaginary and the Symbolic order due to a failure to achieve a robust sense of 'I' or 'me' (Jameson, 1983: 118–119). In Polanski's cinema, this scenario is played out most dramatically in *The Tenant*, in which Trelkovsky's sense of self (and time) becomes completely fragmented as his identity crisis morphs into an even more terrifying epistemological (and ultimately ontological) crisis.

Deterritorialising mental health

Whilst there is some variation in the way Polanski deals with mental illness across his films, these also differ significantly from many other films that deal with the issue, such as *A Beautiful Mind* (Howard, 2001), *Fight Club* (Fincher, 1999), *Psycho* (Hitchcock, 1960) and *Peeping Tom* (Powell, 1960); this results primarily from Polanski's avoidance of denouements designed to deliver satisfaction through the 're-stitching' of 'torn' diegetic realities, or exposition in which the causes of mental illness are neatly delineated by experts.

It is worth accessing Martin-Jones's (2006) application of Deleuze and Guattari's notion of 'deterritorialisation' and 'reterritorialisation' (see Deleuze, 1986 and 1989, Deleuze and Guattari, 2004) to his discussion of national cinemas, and extending this notion to Polanski's own (as I would suggest) connected method of dealing with perception through representations of mental illness. Martin-Jones introduces his discussion of the national narrative by addressing the early twenty-first century trend towards non-linear narrative structures (films like *Eternal Sunshine of the Spotless Mind* [2004] and *Memento* [2000], for example), highlighting that whilst these narratives are indeed labyrinthine, they are *not* examples of the crystalline time-images discussed by Deleuze due to their 'reterritorialisation' of time at the spectatorial level. In other words, whilst these films seem to 'unstitch' time, great pains are taken so that it can be 're-stitched' in the mind of the spectator as part of the 'gestalt' of the film experience. Time is fragmented, but the pieces are put 'in order' during, or perhaps after, the experience of spectatorship; hence, time is effectively *reterritorialised*, and these films remain within the realm of the movement-image.

Polanski's narrative time structures tend to be extremely linear, unrelenting movement-images (the only possible exception worth mentioning is *The Tenant*, which I will come back to in its case study), but a similar logic can be applied to Polanski's treatment of mental illness and, as I shall discuss in terms of the second set of films I look at, national identity. Both *Peeping Tom* and *Psycho*, for example, seem[2] to *reterritorialise* mental health through the exposition of a doctor who 'explains' the cause of the psychosis. Those moments of 'revelation' (for the spectator) in *A Beautiful Mind* and *Fight Club* serve a similar purpose: that is, to reterritorialise diegetic realities in which the boundaries between what is and what is not real have become muddled (deterritorialised). The attribution of distorted perception to the taking of drugs similarly reterritorialises mental health. What is delivered in all these cases is *satisfaction* through the message that these worlds' departure from order is still framed within a greater order that governs even such aberrations from normality. Polanski is far less generous; he tends to deny us such satisfaction, leaving the causes of mental disorders, and even the question of their very existence, unresolved. The complexity of this form of deterritorialisation markedly increases in both *Rosemary's Baby* and *The Tenant*, but is already present in *Repulsion*, in which, although teased, no satisfactory aetiology is offered for Carole's perceptual breakdown and resulting actions. In these films, psychosis is presented with varying levels of diegetic certainty, ranging from the more clearly defined hallucinations of *Repulsion*, to the ambiguous nature of the neighbours in *The Tenant*, who may or may not be responsible for Trelkovsky's fears and eventual suicide attempt, to the utter uncertainty of the events of *Rosemary's Baby*, in which it is never made clear the extent to which, if at all, Rosemary is imagining the Satanic plot against her.

Cinematic psychosis, the censors and the 'anti-psychiatry' movement of the 1960s and 1970s

The release of both the film *Repulsion* and the book *Eye and Brain* in the mid-1960s came on the cusp of a growing anti-psychiatry movement that challenged not only the diagnostic criteria for schizophrenia, but the condition's very existence. The history of the classification of *Repulsion* is especially interesting not only because it deals with a schizophrenic subject during this time frame (it is certainly not alone in this respect), but in particular due to the backing of the film by the British Board of Film Classification (BBFC), who, after a lengthy investigation and the involvement of an expert, decided the film was a serious (i.e. not exploitative) work that supported clinical claims regarding the syndrome.

According to documentation held in the BBFC dossier[3] for *Repulsion*, whilst the classification board was greatly concerned with the content of this film, specifically its graphic portrayal of sexual violence, correspondence between BBFC official John Trevelyan and executive producer Michael Klinger reveals that it was suspected quite early on that Polanski's film was a serious work of art that intended to deal with mental illness in a realistic manner, although there was great concern regarding the effect it might have on the general public. The BBFC's 'Examiner's Report', which was written several months before shooting began and was based on a reading of the original script (called *Lovelihead* at the time, which was then changed to *The Edge of Darkness* before *Repulsion* was settled on as a title), summarises the BBFC's early feelings about the project:

> What I do not think is that it has got anything which we ought to encourage for the ordinary cinema. It seems to me that any film which came out of this project would be essentially a cinema club piece, not for general distribution. I would be very uneasy about any proposal to get together with the makers in an effort to secure a watered down version which would please us and them: I feel sure that the two aims are incompatible with a subject of this kind … I would strongly urge that our friend Dr Black be asked how this piece strikes him. I should have thought that there was a strong possibility of it sending some uneasily poised personality right round the bend…. There may be some way of showing this sort of diseased mind which will not convey the impression of being itself a diseased work of art: all I can say is that I do not think these people have brought it off…. We have got standards to maintain which are important, not perhaps to the welfare of the intelligentsia who make up the greater part of the club audience, but certainly to the average X cinema audience with its high proportion of older adolescents.
>
> (A.O.F., 23 June 1964)

The BBFC report makes it clear that notwithstanding Polanski's status as an art house wunderkind at the time, his debut British film would certainly not pass the classification board unchallenged. What is also of great interest in this report is the mention of Dr Stephen Black (whom Polanski erroneously refers to as 'Steven Blake' in his autobiography, 1984: 209–210), a psychiatrist and 'friend' of the BBFC, who, based on the recommendation of this report, was enlisted to serve as consultant for the project during the script phase. Black was best known in this period for his research into hypnosis and psychosomatic disorders (see Carstairs, 1970, and Black, 1969), and it is clear from the BBFC dossier that he was well known to the classification board; the same dossier also reveals that Black had recently served as technical advisor to John Huston for the film *Freud* (1962).

In a letter from the BBFC to Dr Black, Trevelyan makes it clear that the young film-maker was eager to make the film as realistic as possible. 'It is very important [to Roman Polanski] that the mental disintegration is one which would be true to the fact, and he was pleased that I should put it to an expert' (letter dated 29 June 1964). According to Trevelyan, Black considered the script to be 'very accurate in psychiatric terms' but strongly recommended (echoing the BBFC's original sentiments) that some amendments should be made in order to ensure the film was not a danger to psychotics. Black's most explicit concern was that the film should not endorse Carole's behaviour in any way. His key recommendations along this line were that 'the girl should not be shown to get happiness and peace from the killings' and that 'it should be very clearly stated that she needed medical help and could have been saved if she had had such help' (letter dated 09 July 1964). It is transparent from these comments that, in sharp contrast to the growing anti-psychiatry movement of the time, Black clearly supported the 'medicalisation' of mental illness and the potential for psychiatry to treat sufferers. In the same letter, Trevelyan reports that Polanski was positive about these suggestions and eager to involve Black in the production of the film, agreeing to 'insert some dialogue before Michael and Hélène go off on their holiday in which Michael suggests that Carole is behaving rather oddly and should see a psychiatrist' (letter dated 23 July 1964).

It is known (reflected in both the BBFC dossier and Polanski's autobiography) that Black's influence resulted in at least one major change to *Repulsion*, a change that demonstrates Polanski's keen willingness to keep this portrayal of mental illness as accurate as possible. A third murder, that of Michael's wife (who has mistaken Carole for her sister), was completely cut. The logic behind this decision was that having Carole kill this woman after she discovers the men's bodies was far too calculated an act for a sufferer of schizophrenia, as well as inconsistent with her delusions regarding men and women. Its inclusion, thrilling as it might have been to audiences (comments in the dossier suggest that Michael's wife attacks Carole with a bottle of Vitriol), would have seriously compromised the film's claim of accuracy in the representation of this form of mental illness.

Black was asked to scrutinise the finished film so that his feedback could inform the board's decision regarding classification and possible cuts. Trevelyan's notes on his reaction are highly informative:

> I took Dr Black with me to Twickenham studios to see Roman Polanski's *Repulsion* since I was anxious to have his advice on whether the picture presented any danger from his professional point of view.

> Dr Black was immensely impressed with the picture, which he considered to be absolutely brilliant. He told me afterwards that his original concern that the effect of the killings on the girl might be dangerous ... was now entirely alleviated by the way in which the picture was made. He did not think the killings had any danger. As to the rape scenes, he was only concerned that it should be clear that these were in the girl's imagination and not in reality. At the present stage of editing this was not entirely clear, and we discussed this with the director and the producer. Dr Black thought that the portrayal of mental illness was remarkably accurate, and that the compassion of the picture justified its portrayal. He saw no reason why from his point of view the picture should not be passed if it was satisfactory to the board in normal censorship terms.
>
> (John Trevelyan, 4 December 1964)

Surprising everyone, Polanski especially (1984: 209–210), the BBFC passed the film without a single cut; according to the information held in the BBFC dossier, this decision was very greatly informed by Black's counsel. As a result, the film would not be relegated exclusively to 'club' viewers as a means of protecting the public at large, as had been originally predicted by the BBFC Examiner. It was allocated an 'X' certificate, which at the time permitted the film to be viewed by anyone over the age of sixteen; from a purely commercial point of view, this classification was hugely advantageous, as it meant that the film could indeed be shown uncut in regular venues, instead of being regulated to a much smaller 'club' audience.

Although Polanski denies having performed extensive research on schizophrenia (Polanski, 1984: 211), we do know that he actively investigated the perception-based research of the time and discovered that his own ideas on the subject were reflected by the work of the neuropsychologist R. L. Gregory, whose *Eye and Brain: The Psychology of Seeing* not only gave scientific confirmation to Polanski's understanding of perception, but indirectly provided further evidence to back up Dr Black's support of *Repulsion*; a film dealing with the breakdown of the higher cognitive functions that indirect/active perception insists are required for the perceptual apparatus to function is indeed a good way to explore this theory of perception cinematically. Polanski was not shy about revealing the film's 'intent'; as he divulges in an interview at the time of the film's release, 'the story is not important: it is a study of madness' (Todd, 1964: 14). As I shall discuss in the next case study, embedded in *Repulsion* are manifestations of the controversy surrounding the diagnosis of schizophrenia at the time of its release. Also included are direct reference to the general public's ignorance and fear of mental illness, illustrated especially well by Hélène's angry reaction to Michael's querying of the stability of Carole's mental state. Another scene that seems to reflect the public at large is the mixed reaction of the neighbours to Carole at the end of the film, one of whom insists on getting her a cure-all brandy. The scene is repeated, to another extreme, in *The Tenant* a decade later.

Far from intending to influence a global debate on mental health, for Polanski and Gérard Brach, *Repulsion* was originally conceived as no more than a means to an end: a sexy horror film that would ensure funding from film producers Michael Klinger and Tony Tenser, noted for their exploitation films such as *Naked as Nature Intended* (1961), *London in the Raw* (1964) and *The Black Torment* (1964). It was hoped that the profits from *Repulsion* would enable them to finance the film they really wanted to make, the artistically ambitious *If Katelbach Comes* (which they would go on to make as their next film, re-titled to the slightly less Beckettian *Cul-de-sac*). Although the pitch for *Repulsion* was pure horror cliché ('a homicidal schizophrenic running amok in her sister's deserted London apartment' [Polanski, 1984: 197]), Polanski was intent on at least investing the cinematic realisation of the story with as much psychological realism as possible (Polanski, 1984: 197).

The notion of a film centred on mental illness was not new at the time of *Repulsion*'s release; it was preceded by high-profile 'psychological' films like *Psycho, Peeping Tom* and *Marnie* (Hitchcock, 1964); each of these films uses intra-diegetic exposition to address the causal factors of their characters' psychological problems. What differentiates the depiction of psychosis in *Repulsion* from these others films, however, is the film's *lack* of diegetic psychoanalysis and the attempt to *represent*, rather than merely include, the perceptual crises experienced by the film's protagonist; these are both qualities the film arguably inherits from Buñuel's *Un chien andalou* (1929), to which *Repulsion* seems to make direct reference in its opening credits.[4] The omission of diegetic psychoanalysis continues with both *Rosemary's Baby* and *The Tenant*; as I shall later discuss, these two films present the issue of the protagonists' psychological struggle with an even greater level of complexity than *Repulsion*.

Polanski returns to the territory of psychosis on a number of occasions over the next ten years, most notably in *Rosemary's Baby* and *The Tenant*, but also in *Macbeth*, a story whose narrative hinges greatly on the developing psychosis of its protagonist. As the next set of case studies deal so explicitly with the issue of mental health, it is relevant to further historicise the Apartment Trilogy films as a whole before beginning the individual close reading of these films, specifically in terms of the polemics in psychiatric circles and the public at large regarding the diagnosis of various forms of psychosis, as well as the ethicality of psychiatric practices at the time. The period I refer to ranges (roughly) from the early 1960s to the mid-1970s, an era that encompasses all three films of this 'trilogy'.

'Anti-psychiatry'

The influence of the anti-psychiatry movement in the public sphere during the time frame of the Apartment Trilogy is perhaps best represented by the popularity of Ken Kesey's novel *One Flew Over the Cuckoo's Nest*, published in 1962, and the massive international success of Milos Forman's multiple-Oscar-winning film version in 1975. It is difficult to determine the exact effect on public opinion of *One Flew Over the Cuckoo's Nest*'s portrayal of the dehumanising effect of the institutionalisation of patients diagnosed with mental illness and its representation of (forced) lobotomy and electro-convulsive therapy, but there is no denying that both the film and novel unequivocally support the conceptualisation of mental health clinics as a form of prison in which patients are held against their will and subjected to procedures they do not agree to.

The era that marks this book's transition from page to screen roughly covers the time frame of Polanski's Apartment Trilogy, which is also the time frame that saw a peak in anti-psychiatry literature. The term was itself coined by Cooper in 1967, but represented a body of commentary from both the United States and the United Kingdom that had been steadily published in the wake of the first English translations of Bleuler's diagnostic criteria for schizophrenia in 1950. Kesey's novel and the subsequent film version are essentially populist echoes of the voices of dissent in clinical circles on both sides of the Atlantic over this period, perhaps best represented by the published works of Szasz (1960, 1971) from the United States and Laing (1960, 1964, 1967) from the United Kingdom, both of whom vigorously challenged the ethics of psychiatric practices at the time, and disputed the very existence of mental illness; schizophrenia was one of their prime targets, which they claimed could best be understood as a psychodynamic or cultural phenomenon.

It is difficult to pinpoint the exact genesis of the backlash against psychiatry that emerged in the early 1960s, but it must be recognised that, in the United States in particular, many highly questionable practices were uncovered that tarnished the reputation of psychiatry in general. Blashfield (1984) identifies one of the most controversial issues as being an increasing 'looseness' with which the diagnosis of schizophrenia in particular was made in the United States, which was likely due to the overestimation of the relevancy of a comment made by Bleuler (1911) regarding latent forms of the condition. As McKenna (1997) comments, in the United States, the 'concept of schizophrenia became so loose that it could be diagnosed in virtually anyone' (74). Likewise, Clare (1976: 133) highlights the 'US-UK Diagnostic Project', a study that demonstrated that US admission rates for schizophrenia were much higher than in the United Kingdom during the 1960s. Whilst there may have been a legitimate variable that might have caused a higher occurrence of the syndrome in New York over London, a more likely hypothesis was that the persistently varying diagnostic criteria between the United States and the United Kingdom, which had already been highlighted by Kramer (1961), was directly responsible for what was probably an over-diagnosis of schizophrenia by American psychiatrists. Findings such as these provided an ethical basis from which the likes of Szasz and Laing could launch an attack on psychiatric practices, as well as challenge the very existence of schizophrenia. Many other studies followed that demonstrated the lack of reliability of American diagnostic techniques (see Cole et al., 1969 and Rosenhan, 1973, for example), all of which gave further credibility to the anti-psychiatry position, whose proponents continued to argue that many of the behaviours identified as indicative of schizophrenia were actually 'better understood in social or cultural terms' (McKenna, 1997: 75) and demanded nothing short of the complete 'abolition of existing psychiatric institutions' (Clare, 1976: 2) on ethical grounds.

A brief overview of Szasz and Laing's positions (which do differ significantly at times) is useful in the context of this analysis of Polanski's cinema, in particular the case studies of the Apartment Trilogy films that follow. In Szasz's unambiguously titled articles and books, including 'The Myth of Mental Illness' (article, 1960 and book, 1974), and *The Manufacture of Madness* (1971), it is fair to say he presents a 'strong' view against psychiatric practices at the time from an American perspective. Szasz repeatedly compares institutional psychiatry to the Inquisition by describing a parallel between the spurious 'diagnostic' techniques of witch hunters to common psychiatric methods of the time:

> A direct line of progression can be traced from the witch's marks to the so-called stigmata of the hysteric, and, most lately, to the signs which schizophrenics are made to reveal through projective psychological testing. Each of these 'diagnostic' findings is used to incriminate the subject – as witch, hysteric, or schizophrenic; each is then used to punish him – by means of theological, medical, or psychiatric sanctions.
>
> (Szasz, 1971: 32–33)

Szasz also points to the labelling at the time of homosexuality as a form of mental illness as evidence of the malleability of what institutional psychiatry considered to be an 'illness', claiming that same sort of specious logic was used to diagnose schizophrenic behaviour as a form of abnormal behaviour (1971: 161). Several decades on, Szasz's point, or at least *half* of it, does indeed seem lucid and history has justified his de-conceptualisation of homosexuality as an illness. (It should be noted, however, that 'homosexuality' was not entirely eliminated as a form of 'sexual orientation disturbance' until the release of DSM III in 1987). The key point that Szasz makes remains clear: the identification of certain behaviours as 'normal' or 'abnormal' is not empirical; it shifts with the ebb and flow of dominant ideological stances.

It should also be noted that Szasz, writing in 2003, attempts to distance himself with the greater anti-psychiatry movement with which he is so often associated. He claims that anti-psychiatry (as represented by Cooper and Laing) is just as fraudulent as psychiatry itself and equally guilty of engaging in the coercive methods Szasz so strongly opposes (2003: xxviii–xxix). Szasz's alternative to psychiatry is based on his efforts to 'recast mental illness and psychiatry from a medical into a linguistic-rhetorical phenomenon' (2003: xxiii), and to ensure that the individual is held fully responsible for his or her actions (thus negating the notion of the 'insanity defence').

Beyond what he considers to be unethical, coercive psychiatric practices, Szasz questions the very basis upon which the identification of behaviours are considered to be symptomatic of the illness 'schizophrenia'. His argument is essentially dualistic, in that he claims the term 'illness' to be exclusively related to 'a bodily disorder whose typical manifestation was an alteration of bodily structure' (1974: 11), a historical definition that can be very difficult to reconcile with conceptualisations of mental illness, schizophrenia in particular, which seems to leave no reliable organic trace (McKenna, 1997: 98). Due to the inherent 'invisibility' of mental illness, Szasz posits that 'whereas in modern medicine new diseases were *discovered*, in modern psychiatry they were *invented*' (12).

Laing proposes an existential-phenomenological (1960: 15) psychodynamic approach to dealing with the types of behaviours associated with schizophrenia, in which the subject's understanding of self in relation to others is analysed, in particular through examinations of the family dynamic as a means of isolating the aetiology of these behaviours and establishing possible methods of treating them. As Clare argues, Laing points to the family dynamic as an outright cause of what psychiatry calls 'schizophrenia' (Clare, 1976: 170), wherein schizophrenia is seen as 'an intelligible and inevitable response by the child to overwhelming interpersonal and social stress, the main source of which is located in the parents' (185). Clare astutely identifies a paradox that emerges from Laing's position by pointing out that 'some critics of psychiatry confuse the situation ... in that they assert that schizophrenia does not exist and that parents are responsible for making their offspring suffer from it' (194). Much like Szasz, there is also a strongly relativistic tone to Laing's argument that challenges what is argued to be institutional psychiatry's unstable method of differentiating 'normal' from 'abnormal' behaviour. Laing echoes a sentiment from Jung to make his point: 'the schizophrenic ceases to be schizophrenic when he meets someone by whom he feels understood. When this happens most of the bizarrerie which is taken as the signs of the disease simply evaporates' (1960: 179–180).

Whilst I by no means argue that Polanski's films take an anti-psychiatry stance (unlike *One Flew Over the Cuckoo's Nest*, which is unabashedly anti-psychiatric, as well as several times more financially successful than Polanski's three 'apartment' films combined), the portrayal of psychosis in *Repulsion*, *Rosemary Baby* and *The Tenant* is in each case a highly nuanced issue; in each film the aetiology of the characters' behaviours (which we are compelled, as spectators, to 'diagnose') is presented in a highly nebulous fashion. The films present a series of 'cardinal' symptoms, but at the same time fail to diegetically validate the absolute veracity of any diagnosis or provide a robust explanation for the origins of these behaviours. Each film, in fact, teases the possibility of psychodynamic causal factors, which, although I ultimately argue against their relevancy, must be acknowledged as present in these works. What I do argue for in the forthcoming case studies, however, is a reading of these films as works that express the psychiatric controversy of the time through the diegesis; I do not mean to imply that the works take a strong stance either way, but rather that they present destabilising spectatorial experiences that compel us to meditate on the question of not only the diagnostic criteria used for the identification of a mental illness, but its very existence.

Apartments, brains and the city

Polanski once commented that *Repulsion* was 'not a Polish subject' (in Ostrowska, 2006: 63), making reference to the fact that the environment that would cultivate the type of solitude needed for such a story did not exist in Poland, or at least, the concept of 'Poland' as he understood it at the time. It is unclear if Polanski believed *Repulsion* to be a specifically 'London' or 'British' subject, but when considering it in the context of his other two 'Apartment' films, it becomes evident that it is the urban, possibly Western, space he was most likely referring to. As my primary focus is on the way in which these films add to an ongoing, inter-film perceptual discourse, a brief discussion on the role of urbanity in these films is certainly warranted here, especially in regards to the concerns of perceptual psychology with both urban space and the cinema; as Fitzmaurice and Shiel observe, the joint-study of cinema and the city is 'archetypal ground for examination of visual and sensory experience, form and style, perception, cognition, and the meaning of the filmic image and the filmic text' (2003: 1).

Cinema and the modern city will forever be co-considered by theorists and historians due to their concurrent emergence in the late nineteenth century. But the connection between cinema and the city is not simply a chronological overlap. It is true that cities provide the milieu for diegeses and that cinemas themselves become integral parts of the architecture of the city; but the intersections run deeper than this. As conceptualised by Virilo, the screen indeed becomes the 'city square' (1991: 25); or, as Bruno puts it, 'the machine of modernity that fabricated the city is also the "fabric" of the film' (21). For Bruno, cinema and the architecture of the modern city are intimately connected in a 'fluid exchange', each informing the other. As Shiel discusses, society and culture are interlinked and 'can only be properly understood ... in their relation to each other' (2001: 4); this concept can then be applied to the unity of cinema – 'the most important cultural form' – and the city – 'the most important form of social organisation' (Shiel, 2001: 1). In addition to functioning in relation to each other, Shiel also recognises that both cinema and the modern city are best understood in terms of the organisation of space, the city as a planned or organically developed (or both) physically partitioned space, and cinema as a spatial (as opposed to exclusively textual, as it is often conceived) form of culture (2001: 5).

The 1960s and 1970s marked an era of increased location shooting, in which mainstream cinema, echoing the neorealists, became increasingly interested in 'a realist examination of contemporary urban environments' (Fitzmaurice and Shiel, 2003: 6).

Polanski's 'city films' reflect this trend, in which he uses the actual streets and landmarks of Paris (*The Tenant*, *Frantic*, *Bitter Moon*, *The Ninth Gate*), New York City (*Rosemary's Baby*) and London (*Repulsion*), but also combines these with intricate, meticulously realistic interiors completely created in the studio. In *The Tenant*, Polanski collaborates with the cinematographer Sven Nykvist and the set designer Pierre Guffroy to create a seamless overlap between 'authentic' locations and highly convincing sets to create Trelkovsky's flat on Rue la Bruyère in Paris's Pigalle district; even many of the externals, in particular the courtyard of the building itself, were completely created in the Épinay studio in order to permit for the film's often complex camera movements.[5]

In his discussion of the 'Chicago School' style of architecture, Strathausen describes the conceptualisation of the city in terms of it being not only a unified space, but also a space of 'startling complexity' (2003: 22) for the individual who resides in it. In cinematic terms, we can juxtapose Strathausen's description of the 'unity' of the 'translucent, organising gaze from above the city' utilised by the floating, 'untethered' camera at the start of *The Tenant* and *Rosemary's Baby*, with the 'complexity' of 'the multiplicity of conflicting perspectives experienced down below' (22). In both films, this 'conflict' and 'multiplicity' is played out through the perceptual crises of a single individual.

Linking the stimuli of the big city to emerging forms of mental distress, Neidich (2003) discusses the 'new perceptual challenges imposed by the new urban environment' (52) (indeed, in this context we can truly refer to a form of 'bourgeois' perception). All three films of the Apartment Trilogy take place in a major urban centre, arguably the capitals of Western civilisation. In each case, the film's protagonist faces a psychological crisis that is played out, for the most part, in a centrally located flat: *Repulsion* in South Kensington, *Rosemary's Baby* in Manhattan's Dakota Building (corner of 72nd and Central Park West, renamed 'The Bramford') and *The Tenant* in the Pigalle district of Paris. In each of these films, the protagonist is identifiably an 'other' in the city in which he or she resides, which seems to reflect Neidich's notion of the 'perceptual challenges' of these vertical, heavily peopled environments as being possibly complicit in these characters' perceptual breakdowns. In a related vein, Strathausen (2003: 28) examines *Man with a Movie Camera* (Vetrov, 1929) and *Berlin, The Symphony of a Great City* (Ruttmann, 1927) to discuss both the new mode of perception that evolved in modern urban spaces and the experience of specifically urban forms of crisis with which it coexists. As Strathausen expresses it, 'the camera literally enables the modern uncanny to come to life in the form of a new cyborg-like being – the metropolis, which threatens to absorb and ultimately replace the very humanity it was meant to benefit' (2003: 20). Although unproven, it is plausible that the idea of urban ('bourgeois') psychosis may indeed be rooted in biology, especially if the proposition that living in large cities (a completely new type of environment relative to the time span of human evolution) requires a perceptually 'evolved' being to deal with the flurry of stimuli one finds in city life. But whether or not the psychoses depicted in these films are the 'fault' of the cities themselves, they at least provide an environment that seems to nurture, as well as reflect, these perceptual crises.

Whilst I do not give much weight to the relevance of these particular cities, neither do I argue that these settings are quite the Deleuzian 'any-space-whatevers'. Unlike Deleuze's description of depersonalised, discontinuous and transitional 'any-spaces', the cavities in the building occupied by the character to whom we are (perceptually) tethered in these films become highly personalised. The densely urban environments in which these apartment stories are set must indeed be considered, at the very least, as 'urban-any-spaces'. Moreover, the way in which these flats are nestled within larger structures, and the manner in which inside and outside (external as well as neighbouring) space interacts is also relevant. In all three films, the flats not only become the site of the protagonists' descent into mental illness, but the structures themselves sometimes become expressionistic manifestations of the characters' interiority. The distinction between the body (and what it contains) and the *mise-en-scène* becomes confused; indeed, the body and its mind sometimes seem to *form* the *mise-en-scène*. Hence, these flats become not just projections of these (intangible) psyches, but material parallels to their degenerating cognitive functions. The flats become not only psyche, but *brain*.

Within the skull (of primates), the brain is further protected by three layers of connective tissue membranes (the meninges) that separate it from the bone of the cranium. Penetrating these layers are the arteries that supply the brain with nutrient-rich blood, the veins that remove depleted blood, and the various links to the central and peripheral nervous system. These connections allow us to receive stimuli from the sense organs and to perform motor functions. The eye is special amongst these organs in its direct connection to the brain, with the retina and optic nerve in particular arguably an extension of the brain itself. It is this detail of the eye and brain anatomy that is most relevant considering the role apartments play in these films, serving, as I claim they do, as projections of intra-cranial space. Reflecting this 'cranial' theme, both *Repulsion* and *The Tenant* include scenes in which the protagonist accidentally bumps his or her head with another character whilst reaching to pick something up. In both cases (in fact, there are *three* such occurrences, as the scene is repeated in *The Tenant*), there is an audible 'crack' that accompanies the contact, stressing the bone-on-bone contact. The image is suggestive of the psychic 'overlap' that occurs in these films, in which both Trelkovsky and Carole suffer interrelated identity and perceptual crises.

Although meant to be protected cavities within larger bodies (like the skull), the apartments in these films are often compromised by nosey, sometimes nefarious, bodies and stimuli from the outside world or adjacent flats. Sometimes these invasions are hallucinatory, sometimes they are real, and sometimes this line is thoroughly blurred. In each film, the borders between apartment and non-apartment space is compromised. Light, for example, enters these cavities not only via windows but also through 'peepholes', as demonstrated by Polanski's frequent use of POV shots through these (distorting) little lenses, which serves to create a sort of *camera obscura* of the flats. Sound also seems to have little respect for the apartments' confines. In *Repulsion*, we hear the lift as Michael (Ian Hendry) leaves the Ledoux flat, a plane flies overhead as Carole and Hélène talk, the bells from the Brompton Oratory across the street routinely invade the flat, and Carole is unable to prevent the sound of her sister's lovemaking from entering her room. Similar auditory invasions are seen in *The Tenant*, where it is Trelkovsky who cannot contain noise within his apartment, to the chagrin of his neighbours (who express their displeasure through the floor/ceiling). In *Rosemary's Baby*, it is the bickering of the Woodhouses' geriatric neighbours, and later the sounds of ominous chanting, that not only passes though the (partitioned) walls into Rosemary's bedroom, but into her dreams as well.

Solid matter also makes its way into these spaces. The first occurrence in *Repulsion* is the (unwanted) presence of Hélène's boyfriend in the flat, who leaves personal artefacts (shaving razor, toothbrush and clothing) lying around. As Carole's mental faculties begin to deteriorate, hands reach out from the walls to grope her, a construction worker with whom she made eye contact 'appears' in her room and rapes her, a courting young man breaks down the door (allowing neighbours to stare into the flat) and an angry landlord lets himself in. Like Carole, both Rosemary and Trelkovsky attempt to keep evil neighbours out by barricading doors with large cupboards (a reoccurring piece of furniture in Polanski's cinema), but the structure of the flat is unable to keep these bodies out (hallucinatory or otherwise). In Rosemary's case, hostile bodies enter through a secret door connecting the Woodhouses' and Castevets' flats.

In both *Rosemary's Baby* and *The Tenant*, the apartments also demonstrate themselves incapable of *containing* solid matter: Rosemary's new friend Terry (Victoria Vetri) falls to her death from the Castavetes' flat, and Trelkovsky himself is ejected *twice* through the window.[6] In each of these films, the flats themselves not only parallel the cognitive degeneration of the characters, but become manifestations of the organ in which cognition resides, the chaos in these spaces reflecting the chaos of the minds (the *brains*) that occupy them. Just as stimuli from the outside world makes contact with the sense organs, which then send messages to the brain, so too are the flats bombarded with stimuli; and just as illness (schizophrenia) corrupts the brain's ability to interpret stimuli effectively, so too do these flats become incapable of maintaining order.

Shonfield (2000) discusses the 'fear of penetration' in *Rosemary's Baby* and *Repulsion* in both sexual and architectural terms, suggesting that these films employ an 'analogy between the interior space of their heroine's bodies, and the interiors of the apartments where they live' (55). As Shonfield postulates it, both of these films display the 'vengeance of the interior' in the aftermath of Brutalism, an architectural movement that attempted to eradicate the distinctiveness of interior space (56). As Shonfield also notes, the physical traumas that occur to the very fabric of Carole's flat have a real-world antecedent, as they are all typical 'constructional failures' of buildings in post-war London, namely 'damp penetration, cracking of internal surfaces, and failure of mastic sealants', all of which 'come under the microscopic eye of Carole's technical inspection' (2000: 57), fuelled and exaggerated, of course, by her schizophrenia.

In Shonfield's view, the issue of the perceptual stability of the protagonists of *Repulsion* and *Rosemary's Baby* is delineated by a clear difference in how each woman engages with her respective interior and exterior spaces. In the context of these films, she defines the 'sane world' as 'the one where … personal edges, bodily and architectural, are firmly in place' (2000: 65). Where both women suffer similar perceptual crises within their apartments – to be specific, the rape each of them endures (plural in Carole's case) – Shonfield argues that the different manner in which these women engage with outside space is the true indicator of their respective mental health. Whilst Carole's hallucinations all take place within the confines of her apartment, her behaviour symptomatic of schizophrenia is evident on the streets of South Kensington as well (68). In contrast with Carole, Shonfield suggests that in Rosemary's case, the streets of Manhattan outside the Bramford (i.e. the Dakota building) are a safe zone; New York is a 'benign city' (70) in which her paranoia subsides, even though she continues to suffer the pain of her difficult pregnancy. For Shonfield, this serves as evidence of Rosemary's sanity; but it must be acknowledged (as Shonfield does, 2000: 70) that the 'benignness' of the city does not last, and ultimately Rosemary's paranoiac behaviour indeed spills out onto the humid streets. As I will discuss in my case study of *Rosemary's Baby*, the issue of Rosemary's mental health is more perplexing than Shonfield estimates; ultimately, I will suggest, the diegetic veracity of Rosemary's perceptual crisis is fundamentally irresolvable for the persistent close reader.

What is created by this apartment-as-brain paradigm is a representation of the brain as an independent, disembodied structure. These flats come to represent the place where cognition, healthy or unhealthy, occurs. They are also positioned as the seat of perceptual *consciousness*, that is, the point from which both external stimuli and the body to which the brain is tethered (to evoke a term I have been using to describe Polanski's camera work) is appreciated. However, as Smith (2009) identifies, the trajectory towards *self-consciousness* goes beyond mere proprioception to include an even more reflective awareness of 'the nature of one's being in the world' (42). A 'fully fledged' state of self-consciousness requires simultaneous awareness of both 'the embodied nature of human existence' and 'the character and limitations of such embodiment' (42); it is the struggle to achieve such double-awareness that is expressed in Polanski's Apartment Trilogy as acute identity crises and even psychosis.

The ability of Polanski's 'apartment dwellers' to effectively associate their material body with their identity is indeed a major issue in each film, a key element of their cognitive breakdown. Such formal thought disorders (associative disturbances) are typical symptoms of schizophrenia. It is difficult to know what to make of the note left behind by Mrs Gardenia in Rosemary and Guy's flat, where she writes, simply, 'I can no longer associate myself', but the crises of identity seen in each film may give us a clue. In both *Repulsion* and *The Tenant*, the (respective) identities of Carole and Trelkovsky are muddled with those of the 'rightful' or former tenants of the flats they occupy. Carole is often identified via her link to her sister (Carole being 'the beautiful younger sister'), or is mistaken outright for her (they, of course, share the name of 'Miss Ledoux'); Trelkovsky instead invades the home of an attempted suicide victim, Simone Choule (herself an isolated brain trapped in a useless body), and he is quite literally transformed into her by the end of the film. In Rosemary's case, it is her problematic pregnancy that serves as the cause of another quite-literal transformation, as not only is her dwelling space invaded, but so too is her body (first by being raped, and then by the growing child that results from it).

Characters' efforts to establish and control personal spaces is in fact often a central conflict in Polanski's cinema: a struggle that quickly assumes existential proportions in the Apartment Trilogy, but is present in other films as well. In *Cul-de-sac*, George's Holy Island castle, evoking Rob Roy and Kafka in equal measure, has its extensive 'moat' compromised daily by the shifting of the tide, resulting in the invasion of his domain. Macbeth's usurpation of the throne is essentially an invasion of another's space (a *bedroom*), which then, like Trelkovsky's invasion of Simone Choule's flat, has its own consequences. Tess's struggle is also directly determined by her attempt, and failure, to establish not only her name but also a structure in which to dwell, a personal space. Similarly, the primary narrative thrust of *Oliver Twist* is the boy's attempt to seek and maintain a home. In *The Pianist*, we return to a highly Polanskian apartment scenario when Szpilman hides out in a flat in the middle of occupied Warsaw, where he is forced to remain completely silent to disguise his presence from (again, highly Polanskian) 'nosey' neighbours. The space is ultimately penetrated in the most extreme fashion imaginable when the walls of the building are blown to pieces, deafening Szpilman with a thorough compromise of the 'sound barrier'.

As I have argued throughout this chapter, whilst they share motifs with a number of Polanski's films, *Repulsion*, *Rosemary's Baby* and *The Tenant* are thematically similar enough to justify a group reading. By the same token, each film addresses the issue of cognitive malfunction differently, complicating the issue further in each successive work. I will now turn my attention towards an analysis of each individual film, and in so doing explore several different aspects of the discourse that binds them.

Notes

1. The American Psychiatric Association's Diagnostic and Statistical Manual for Mental Disorders ('DSM') is the definitive authority for the clinical diagnosis of abnormal behaviour. It is the tool with which diagnoses of mental illness can be made, with each

condition being defined by a list of symptoms, a minimum of which must be present to qualify a set of behaviours for a given diagnosis. The manual is in constant evolution. The version I make reference to here is the fourth edition, text revision ('TR') released in 2000. A new edition, DSM-5, is set for release in 2013.

2. I use the term 'seem' here in acceptance that there are likely many interpretations of these films' epilogues that may well undermine my arguably superficial reading of them.
3. The archival documents I refer to throughout this section are held in a single dossier, BBFC reference: AFF039104.
4. In the opening of *Repulsion* a giant eye fills the screen as the credits run across it. The last credit, Polanski's name, 'cuts' across the eye much like Buñuel himself cuts the eye in *Un chien andalou.*
5. Bibliothèque du Film Archival reference: BAUDROT-GU253-B85.
6. It is interesting to note the recurrence of falling in Polanski's cinema, which is employed in the demise of the 'villains' in both *The Ghost* and *Oliver Twist*, as well as the *threat* of falling, as seen in the roof scrambling scenes in both *Frantic* and *The Pianist*. The fine line Polanski treads between horror and humour is especially evident in the juxtaposition of falls from balconies in his films, played for maximum realistic horror in *The Pianist* in the scene in which a wheelchair-bound man is thrown off an apartment balcony, and for laughs in *Cinéma Erotique*, which makes light of a man's fall from a cinema balcony.

Chapter 4

Repulsion

Running amok in 'Swinging London'

Desperate to raise the funds for their high-concept project *If Katelbach Comes* (what would later become *Cul-de-sac*), Polanski and his writing partner Brach pitched *Repulsion* to producers Klinger and Tenser as a horror film set in the heart of 'Swinging London' (Polanski, 1984: 197). As Brunsdon (2007) notes, the films most often associated with 'Swinging London' are quite a heterogeneous group, varying greatly in tone and style (35). It is therefore fair to identify *Repulsion* as an (early) 'Swinging London' film, along with other iconic works of this era, such as *The Knack … and How to Get It* (Lester, 1965), *Georgy Girl* (Narizzano, 1966), *Darling* (Schlesinger, 1966), *Alfie* (Gilbert, 1966) and *Blow Up* (Antonioni, 1967); but we should not limit our conceptualisation of the film based on this association alone.

In the documentary *Hollywood U.K.* (1993), Richard Lester (director of *The Knack …*) highlights the issue of 'authenticity' as a means of contrasting the 'Swinging London' films from the Northern 'kitchen sink' dramas of the British New Wave that preceded them, such as *A Kind of Loving* (Schlesinger, 1962), *Saturday Night and Sunday Morning* (Reisz, 1960) and *A Taste of Honey* (Richardson, 1961) (see also Brunsdon, 2007: 35). In the philosophical sense, the question of 'authenticity' is essentially one of existential significance; where the modernist characters of the British New Wave openly grapple with their angst, the 'zaniness' of the London cinema that followed is indicative of a more postmodern sensibility, which is not to say, however, that films like *Blow Up* or *Alfie* are any less concerned with 'serious' issues than the New Wave films. *Repulsion*'s chronological position directly between the British New Wave and the emergence of Swinging London is also indicative of the film's hybridity: 'authentic' and modernist in its portrayal of an individual's perceptual crisis (which is an existential crisis as well, as I will later explain), but also visceral and 'pop' in its embracing of the generic tropes of the thriller and the horror film.

Whilst it is not inaccurate to consider *Repulsion* in the greater context of 'Swinging London', it is worth noting that the 'swingingness' of *Repulsion* is, for the most part, a peripheral feature. Colin's iconic car, a Sunbeam, does indeed call to mind the emerging consumeristic youth culture of the 1960s, and the clothes worn by the principals, as well as Carole's bouffant (which takes quite a beating throughout the course of the film) are also highly indicative of the era; but apart from these elements, there is little else in

Repulsion that 'swings'. Apart from the use of an extra-diegetic jazz soundtrack, the music heard from the streets of South Kensington is limited to a trio of aging spoon and banjo players and the ringing of the bells from Brompton Oratory. Whilst Carole works in the 'glamour' business, her clients are all older women, and the pub frequented by Colin and his friends is teaming with geriatrics. The most sexually 'liberated' aspect of the film involves Carole's sister having an affair with an older, married man, but this is not quite the stuff of sexual revolution. The only cultural references are to Chaplin's *The Gold Rush* (1925) and the professional wrestling programme Hélène watches on television.[1] This is hardly the 'Swinging London' Polanski himself was so embedded in.

An element that *Repulsion* does share with many 'Swinging London' films, including *Darling*, *The Knack* and *Smashing Time* (Davis, 1967), is its portrayal of a single, female character who comes to the big city in search of adventure and self-actualisation, which Luckett (2000) contrasts with the 'stasis and confinement' (234) of the men in the British New Wave films. It is perhaps not so much Carole as it is her older sister that fits this description, but notwithstanding Carole's 'difficulties', we should recall that she too has come to London (from abroad, no less) in search of something. On this note, let us begin the perceptual analysis of *Repulsion*.

'Luring us in'

Of all Polanski's works, it is the films of the Apartment Trilogy, namely *Repulsion*, *Rosemary's Baby* and *The Tenant*, which serve as the most overt expression of his fascination with the functioning of perception. It is in these three films that the two-fold manner in which perceptual psychology has influenced Polanski's work is most readily identifiable, informing both (a) the way in which these films are constructed as *objects* to be perceived by the spectator, and (b) the way in which diegetic *acts of perception* are depicted in these films. As I discussed in Chapter 1, Polanski's interest in perception is evident early in his cinema, as demonstrated in *Knife in the Water*'s 'shifting eye' scene. Starting with *Repulsion*, however, Polanski's depiction of the workings of the perceptual mechanism takes on much greater importance, as he employs this 'two-fold' approach to not only depict perceiving bodies, but also to influence the perception of the spectator.

The film combines the use of natural perspective and extended takes, which has the effect of limiting our gaze to what is being observed from the point of view of a notional (but invisible and ineffectual) observer.[2] With the camera placed at the same distance from the action as this voyeur and by using a lens with a principal focal length that approximates the human visual field, the perspective of the human eye at that distance is mimicked. The goal is simply to limit as much as possible the work done by the brain to make sense of the image by furnishing it with the type of perspective that it expects. The contention here is that the way in which both shorter and longer lenses (moving towards 'wide angle' and 'telephoto' respectively) deal with light is sufficiently different from the way we see that the brain is obliged to 'adjust' the image (in the next chapter, I will discuss Polanski's shift to favouring wide-angle lenses, which offer other advantages in terms perceptual realism). The brain is more than capable of making such adjustments, but forcing it to do so involves greater effort and may risk compromising engagement. Conversely, by creating images that correspond to the way we naturally see the world, the brain is more readily willing to 'believe' what it sees (Gregory, 2008). As Gregory (2003) discusses, in *Repulsion*, Polanski sets up a kind of celluloid Venus Flytrap: by using natural perspective, the spectator is slowly lured in, and then, when the time is right, *repulsed* through orchestrated distortion.

Augmenting this 'Flytrap' effect is Polanski's attention to mundane details that seemingly do nothing to advance the plot. The approach often has a sort of 'boredom effect', which is actually one of Polanski's professed objectives: by lulling the spectator into a kind of bored hypnosis, the moment of shock would be greatly amplified. Polanski also uses sound to heighten both our diegetic engagement and, sometimes, even to increase this 'boredom effect' (Polanski, 2003). In *Repulsion*, at times sound and slowness combine to provoke a near-soporific state in the spectator; this is a risky strategy, but in this film the alluring sounds of dripping water, a piano being played off-screen, and even a potato being peeled all serve to draw us in. So even though not much is actually happening in these scenes, we are being (perceptually) primed so that the shocks to come will be more powerful. Polanski reflects on this approach in reference to the scene in which Carole spots (and we spot) her attacker's reflection in the bedroom mirror:

> [A]t the first screening I saw people jumping up from their seats. That gave me great satisfaction and I thought 'it works, we zapped them'. But we can only zap someone when we have lulled them into some kind of peace, when he [*sic*] is almost on the verge of boredom.[3]
>
> (quote from the Polanski interview on the 2003 *Repulsion* DVD commentary, time mark 00:45:21)

Barker (2009: 47–56) offers an alternative, but related, means of approaching *Repulsion* that is worth making note of here, as her analysis of the film is also greatly focused on the means through which Polanski's film first 'lures in' the spectator as a way of heightening 'repulsion' further on. Drawing heavily from Sobchack's insistently non-metaphorical ontology of film as a perceiving 'body' (Sobchack would not use inverted commas, but I do), Barker develops a haptic description of cinematic spectatorship in which she scrutinises the experience of watching *Repulsion* in (visually mediated) 'tactile' terms. Whilst the theory that underpins Barker's phenomenology of cinematic spectatorship is indeed difficult to reconcile with Gregory's description of the theory of active perception, her detailed account of the haptic experience provoked through our perception of the film's 'surfaces' and 'textures' (again, the inverted commas are mine) ultimately adds to what I argue to be Polanski's multifaceted attempt to create a 'wraparound' effect. In addition, Barker's meditations on Carole's crisis of the 'skin' (53–54) and the ontological issues she suggests the film raises are also complementary to a discussion of the 'philosophical implications' (to again cite Gregory, 1997a: 197) raised by the theory of active perception, in particular the attention this theory draws to the point of intersection between philosophical concerns with knowledge and those of the nature of being.

Repulsion's particular concern with visual perception is evident from the opening credit sequence, where a gigantic eye occupies the screen as the credits roll. By (literally) aggrandising the eye in such an extreme manner, a strong suggestion is made as to the importance that the act of seeing will have in the forthcoming film. In contrast to the cinematic convention of locating a narrative via long shot (an approach Polanski himself often uses, as I shall discuss in other case studies), *Repulsion* instead uses an extreme close up to the same effect: this film takes place on the eye of the beholder, and, as I shall discuss, in the organ that lies just behind it. As the camera pulls back, we soon learn that the film centres on Carole Ledoux, a young Belgian émigré living in South Kensington with her older sister, Hélène. She works as a beautician, aiding rich women with their vain attempts to defy the aging process. Carole begins to have trouble at work due to increasingly severe lapses of concentration. Her difficulties continue at home, as she finds the presence of her sister's (married) boyfriend, Michael, in the flat troublesome. She pleads with her sister to spend more time with her, away from *him*, but eventually finds herself alone in the flat when Hélène and Michael set off on holiday to Italy. Isolated, Carole's behaviour becomes increasingly erratic and she eventually departs from reality completely, suffering a number of hallucinogenic episodes that result in the murder of two men: Colin (John Fraser, her suitor) and the landlord of the flat.

By depicting perceptual distortions such as those experienced by Carole, Polanski emphasises Gregory's point about the relative malleability of one's subjective perceptual experience of being in the world. There is an aesthetic shift when the film lapses away from diegetic reality to access Carole's hallucinations; but whilst there is sufficient sensorial evidence to remind the spectator that these sequences are diegetically 'unreal', the shift is often so seamless that we find ourselves, at least briefly, being drawn in by film's depiction of non-veridical perception, which, whilst distorting what is diegetically established as normal perspective, does so with a high degree of psychological realism. We are positioned as observers of her distorted perceptual experiences, but we are also compelled to experience these distortions ourselves through Polanski's manipulation of profilmic elements. Even though we, as spectators, are ultimately able to decipher the difference, it becomes increasingly clear that for Carole, the absolute authenticity of these events cannot be denied, as what she experiences has very serious consequences for her and others.

The camera and its subject

The relationship between Carole and Polanski's camera, and by extension us, is at times complex. For the most part, Polanski's camera sticks to its observational stance rather than breaking up scenes into medium or close shots, or swapping from shot to counter shot. Although this style seems to contradict the 'system of suture' (see Oudart, 1969), Polanski's aim of increasing spectator engagement is similar to that professed by Oudart in his application of Lacan's mirror to the experience of cinematic spectatorship. In *Repulsion*, for example, we are 'sutured' not so much to an on-screen character but to an invisible voyeur who watches Carole. At times the camera seems to adopt Carole's exact POV, but normally it retains its observational stance. For the most part, the camera (and thus the spectator) is tethered to Carole's narrative reach. Here I use the term 'tethered' rather 'bound' to indicate the fact that whilst, for the most part, we experience the film by way of Carole (including the episodes that we can identify as being hallucinatory), we are *not* Carole.

Repulsion, only Polanski's second feature, establishes his preference for the 'tethered' camera technique that would become the norm for the rest of his cinema. It is especially pronounced in the other two 'apartment' films, as well as the investigation films I will later discuss. Even so, at times in *Repulsion* the camera does stray from Carole's narrative reach, following her sister to the door as Carole runs to her room to avoid being seen in her night gown, or even drifting as far as the public house where her friend Colin defends her honour. But these are isolated cases; for most of the film, we are tethered, to varying degrees of intimacy, to her subjective perceptual/narrative reach. We are even allowed to observe the breakdown of her perceptual apparatus; eventually, however, we are forced to abandon her when it ultimately collapses completely. As Orr (2006) observes, Polanski, even more than Hitchcock, 'develops the potentialities of the subject camera without ever lapsing into sentimental or melodramatic forms of empathy' (7); the camera has the ability to watch Carole from various voyeuristic (and male gaze-based) vantage points, and is even privy to what seem to be purely hallucinatory experiences, but it is never permitted to access her internal dialogue or any 'insider' information that might justify her (eventually murderous) behaviour.

The 'distance' offered by the tethered camera is particularly noteworthy in social circumstances. In the scene in which Carole has her lunch interrupted by Colin, the camera stays fixed on a medium two-shot; both characters remain in profile as they sit across the table from each other, with us adopting the view of an observer watching them from the next table. Rather than switching to a shot-countershot formula (the more usual shot combination for conversations like this, and one which Polanski is not adverse to using), Polanski instead holds the two-shot, which prevents us from adopting either character's POV (approximate or otherwise). By doing so, the film avoids the shot-countershot formula as a means of emphasising desire through the close-up. Holding the two-shot allows us to observe rather than being 'sutured' to the gazer (in this case, Colin, as Carole has little interest in gazing at men). The lack of countershot continues throughout the film, with the camera maintaining its observational stance. There is, however, a notable exception. When Michael gazes outside the window at the nuns of Brompton Oratory below, Polanski does indeed use a shot-countershot, just before Michael 'jokes' about being invited to their 'wild parties'. Later, the shot structure is repeated as Carole watches the nuns.

Whilst we do spend most of the film tethered to Carole's narrative reach, we nevertheless remain separate from her. Carole is more the object of our voyeuristic gaze than she is an on-screen surrogate; but there comes a moment when our covert position is compromised, and Carole gazes *back* at us. After having already killed both Colin and the landlord, we see Carole in her sister's room applying make-up and admiring herself in the mirror. Fully made up, she lies on the bed, on her tummy, with a pillow under her hips. At first, it seems as though we are witnessing an autoerotic moment, but as the camera moves in, Carole turns over and the camera literally mounts her. It is at this moment that Carole looks directly at us, as if she has discovered her voyeur. The camera hovers over her as Carole's head fills the frame. Surprisingly, she erupts into a giant smile, seemingly welcoming our presence.

The way in which this image is photographed is of particular interest in terms of Polanski's use of natural perspective. Carole's nose and lips seem disproportionately large, an effect that comes as the result of using of a 'normal' lens at close range, which distorts the dimensions of the face, much like the human eye does at this distance. A more 'flattering' choice would have been to use a 100 mm lens with the camera twice the distance away, which would have filled the frame with Carole's head equally well, but would have 'flattened' her features somewhat, reducing the (quite natural) enlarging effect that occurs with proximity (a trick often employed by photographers to 'enhance' the features of models in close-ups, see Warren, 2002: 69, for example). Polanski's choice to use the normal lens again reflects his preference for natural perspective as a means of drawing us in, even if that means the camera literally mounting the actress.

Representing a perceptual crisis

In addition to speculating regarding the aetiology of Carole's mental state, we are invited to closely study her actions and even experience perceptual distortions similar to those the film suggests she is experiencing; thereby *Repulsion* invites the spectator to reflect on the workings of perception: the 'broken' device sheds light on the nature of the mechanism. It is worth emphasising again the two-fold nature of Polanski's approach, that is, the manner in which he both realistically portrays various acts of perception on-screen (both sane and insane) and uses the same knowledge to influence the spectator's own experience of the film. In other words, it is not enough to depict schizophrenia; the audience must also experience it (albeit, in a microscopic measure).

In *Repulsion*, Polanski's uses both visual and aural aesthetics to draw the distinction between Carole's imaginary realm and the diegetically real, a distinction that does not contradict Gregory's view of the constructed nature of our (or Carole's) perception of reality, as it serves only to stress the difference between hallucinations and healthy perception. It is of great importance to distinguish between what is and what is not diegetically real in *Repulsion*, and foremost to concede that the film does not prevent us as spectators from establishing this binary. In this regard, *Repulsion* is not as ambiguous, or 'difficult' a film as *The Tenant* or *Rosemary's Baby*, both of which far more severely muddle the distinction between the diegetically real and imagined, as I shall discuss at length in the next two case studies.

Polanski is careful to reveal Carole's breakdown slowly, with the film's tension increasing in line with Carole's mental deterioration. As a direct result of this patient approach, the film manages to establish a close bond between the spectator and Carole before we confront the film's darker events. For the first third of the film, we are unaware of the trajectory the film is to take; instead we, through the inquiring camera, observe the minutia of Carole's life, exploring, with her, the spaces she occupies: her place of work, her (sister's) flat, and the streets she walks through to get from one to the other. In the first half of the film, however, rarely are we granted wider views of these spaces, as Carole's head so often occupies the majority of the frame, particularly when she is outside the flat, wandering the streets of South Kensington.

Some initial signs of Carole's illness are present from the outset, such as her vacant gaze in the very first shot, but these are built on so subtly that her descent into madness is nearly seamless. Whilst speaking with her sister, for example, Carole stares off-screen, presumably at the kitchen wall or ceiling, and nonchalantly states that they 'must get this crack mended'. The camera does not comply with our wish to see the crack she is referring to, nor does her sister seem to register what Carole has said. At that moment, we, like Hélène, do not know what to make of this seemingly random statement. It is only in retrospect that we wonder whether the crack was there at all.

Optical distortions are also introduced early, and at first appear to be rather innocent, such as when Carole catches her elongated reflection on the side of a kettle and the 'fish-eye' perspective of the POV shot through the peephole (both shots are repeated in *Rosemary's Baby*, and the latter in *The Tenant*). These distortions can of course be explained by simple physics, but it will not be long before other, more insidious, distortions begin to occupy the frame, generated not by light bouncing off or passing though curved surfaces, but by Carole's own brain. As these emerge, the camera is granted increasing access to Carole's subjective realm, so that we can both witness and, to some extent, *experience* her psychosis.

There is a subtle, but significant, moment early on when Carole, examining herself in a mirror, attempts to wipe away some invisible dirt from her nightgown. The scene is immediately preceded by Carole's accidental discovery of Michael's shaving razor in the bathroom, a startling moment for both her and the spectator, and a scene in which the razor and the shirt (two objects that prove to be highly significant later in the film) are first seen on-screen. From this moment on, the degeneration of Carole's mental state begins to accelerate. More so than those merely 'odd' moments that we witness early in the film, these strange behaviours indicate that something may be seriously wrong with the way she is interpreting the world; and more soon follow. After Carole has comforted co-worker Bridget (Helen Fraser) in their locker room, left alone, Carole sits on a bench and stares aimlessly at the floor as a sunbeam creeps through the small window and casts its light onto the chair in front of her. When Carole notices the beam, she cautiously tries to brush the light off the chair, just as she did with the 'dirt' on her gown.

It is prudent here to access Gregory's discussion of 'visual semantics', which allows us to understand the experience of schizophrenic subjects in terms of a breakdown of their ability to decode stimuli, a failure that can eventually form a chasm between the patient and the world. To illustrate his point, Gregory (1997a) provides the vivid example of the frog that starves to death whilst surrounded by dead flies, 'for although they are edible it does not see them, as they do not move' (8). Gregory is not, or course, suggesting that the frog is ill, but that its perceptual framework for food is determined not only by shape but by movement. It is the animal's steadfast adherence to this framework that will result in its death. Possibly picking up on this very example, Polanski has Carole reverting to a similar state in her flat, where she sits in squalor (another symptom of schizophrenia identified by McKenna, 1997: 38) surrounded by rotting food. She is clearly unaware of the health hazards of the conditions in which she is living, as highlighted by the landlord who promptly throws the decaying rabbit carcass into the bin.[4] Such behaviour becomes increasingly rampant; she writes a letter on a pane of glass, irons Michael's shirt with an unplugged iron, and accidentally stabs a client in the finger with a nail filer; all indications of the missing connection between objects and how they are to be used.

Gregory discusses the process of correct identification of objects in terms of visual syntax and semantics. Like written language, there are *visual* rules (grammar) and meaningfulness of symbols, which are learned over time and stored as perceptual frameworks that are in a constant state of development as we accumulate experience: 'thus we pick up a glass to drink not simply from stimuli, but from knowledge of glasses, and what they may contain' (Gregory, 1997a: 8). One of the key questions examined by Polanski in *Repulsion* is what happens when such learning is lost or becomes confused due to mental illness. Fundamental to what we are referring to as 'sanity' is the ability to correctly identify objects according to their use. Our ability to perceive the nature of an object is based on our ability to access learned schemas that inform us of what certain shapes represent as well as their particular usefulness. Our ability to access and use these perceptual frameworks largely determines our ability to interact with the world. In the case of schizophrenia, such sensory-motor links often go wrong, leading the subject to misinterpret a given set of visual information, and possibly perceive perfectly harmless objects or situations as threatening (or vice-versa).

In the second part of the film, Carole's hallucinations become increasingly intense, and the flat into which she has barricaded herself becomes an ever more bizarre place. One way in which Polanski depicts her distorted perception is by altering the dimensions of this space, sometimes subtly, other times dramatically, to reflect her growing inability to deal with perspective. Besides the uncanny effect the distorted room has on the spectator, Polanski's choice to depict her mental state through perspectival alteration is again in line with a clinically documented symptom of schizophrenia. Chapman and McGhie (1961) identify many schizophrenic patients, especially those in the early stages of the disorder, who experienced *perceptual distortions*, defined in terms of perceived mutations of dimensions, form and distance of objects (103).

There are several shots of Carole staring at the furniture in her bedroom scattered throughout the film, but these become increasingly distorted as her mental state degenerates. After being groped by the invading hands in the corridor, Carole is seen lying on her bed staring at the chandelier above her. Her perceptual struggle is punctuated as the perspective of the shot shifts radically, seemingly causing Carole to float upwards towards the ceiling. Here again the relative size of objects is compromised, illustrating the effect of her schizophrenic state on her grasp of perspectival space. Distortions like this are reminiscent of the deliberately constructed illusions described by Gregory, such as the experience of looking into an occupied 'Ames Room' (see Gregory, 1997a: 186), or, for that matter, entering one yourself. Polanski in fact constructs one of these rooms in *Repulsion*, which can be seen in the first occurrence in which the flat takes on altered dimensions.

I analyse Polanski's use of the Ames Room in detail in my case study of *The Tenant*, but I will start this discussion here, in reference to *Repulsion*. Soon after Carole has killed Colin, she wanders through the flat's corridor, which has now become extremely elongated, towards the bathroom. As she enters the bathroom, we see a severely distorted room in which her body takes on gigantic proportions and the bathtub appears to be much further away than we know it should be, an effect most likely achieved through the construction of an 'Ames'-type set combined with the use of a telephoto lens. Later in the film, after Carole has killed the landlord, she walks into a now greatly enlarged version of the flat's living room. The camera is placed just behind her, so that we are allowed to experience the room over her shoulder, a close approximation of her POV that demonstrates her distorted perception. As we watch Carole turn aimlessly in the centre of the room, we too are tasked to try to make sense of this distorted space. Gregory discusses moments like this in terms of the 'intriguing discrepancies' that emerge when natural perspective meets the distorted vision of the schizophrenic; the changing dimensions of Carol's flat cause (as Gregory phrases it) 'tension between what is signalled to the eye and what you believe should be there' (2003). The contrast is unnerving, but also philosophically stimulating in its emphasising of the relative malleability of our perceptions of the world.

Although much of the focus of this discussion centres on Polanski's exploitation of the eye–brain relationship, his use of sound seems equally informed. Sound is also psychologically relevant in the way it appears to have a conditioning effect on Carole, which is especially notable when she experiences the attack whilst made up as her sister. Just as the camera mounts Carole and her smiling face fills the frame, the sound of bells dominates the soundtrack. In the preceding moments, starting with Carole's rather childish application of lipstick in front of the mirror, the soundtrack was composed entirely of ambient 'silence', punctuated by the barely perceptible sound of a ticking clock. The bells radically shift the mood of the scene, as Carole's smile swiftly disappears. We are repelled backwards as a hand shoots across the frame, grabbing her torso and marking the beginning of another rape.

We have heard these bells before. Early in the film, Michael and Hélène complain about their incessant clanging, joking about what it is, exactly, the nuns from the nearby Oratory are being called to; the bells also accompany Hélène's cries of pleasure when we first overhear her and Michael making love. When Carole imagines she is being raped by the construction worker, the scene immediately cuts to a ringing phone, whose timber and rhythm closely matches the Oratory bells. When the landlord is attacking Carol, those same bells can again be heard ringing. At one point, Hélène comments that these bells sometimes ring at midnight, which suggests that the sound Carole hears is a veridical (i.e. diegetically real) stimulus, which has been superimposed and associated with non-veridical stimuli (the hallucinations). The sound of the bells, paired as it is with these sexual attacks, suggests a Pavlovian connection between the two, the bells themselves seeming to provoke a conditioned response (i.e. Carole's rape hallucination) by way of stimulus coupling. The fact that the bells are also linked to a Catholic source, a male-free sisterhood at that, possibly adds yet another layer of significance. It cannot be determined, however, whether it is an antecedent Catholic association with the bells themselves that triggers Carole's hallucinations, or whether the link between the bells and the rape is purely coincidental; furthermore, we are granted no diegetic 'voice' to clear matters up for us.

McKenna (1997) lists a series of typical affective symptoms related to emotional behaviour, including both 'negative' (passive) and 'positive' (active) symptoms. In Carole's case, her symptoms are greatly 'negative', as exemplified by her withdrawn behaviour both at work and in the company of men. So negative are these symptoms that based on these alone her behaviour could well register on the autistic spectrum.[5] A radical shift eventually occurs when her hallucinations seem to provoke delusions that cause her to overestimate the threat posed by Colin, who then becomes the victim of Carole's extreme reaction (a 'positive' symptom). Colin, much like Michael, may not be the most sympathetic character, but there is nothing to suggest that he is a legitimate threat to Carole's safety, notwithstanding his often-aggressive courting technique. In fact, given the mental and physical state we know that Carole has been reduced to, his breaking down of the flat's door is arguably justified. So whilst we may be ambivalent about Colin, his murder does come as a great shock.

The next murder, however, proves to be far more complicated emotionally, as the landlord is indeed positioned as a real threat to Carole. It is at this point that Carole's delusions of persecution meet a veridical stimulus that confirms this belief. The emotional challenge of this scene, however, is entirely directed at the spectator; we must remember that for Carole, the line that separates the veridical from the non-veridical, rational belief from delusion, has collapsed entirely. Consequently, Carole constructs new conceptual frameworks based on these (hallucinated) experiences. *Beliefs* about the world then emerge, which lead to the diegetically real violence she commits against two men.

It should be noted here that the type of extreme violence *Repulsion* depicts is not representative of the vast majority of sufferers of schizophrenia. That being said, within the range of 'positive' symptoms, McKenna does include the category of *catatonic impulsiveness* (1997: 21), a state in which a normally docile patient suddenly engages in acts of great violence, for which he or she will usually provide simplistic, but irrational, explanations. In instances of *paranoid schizophrenia*, violent behaviour is also not unknown; some patients are compelled to react due to florid delusions of persecution and the hallucinations that often accompany them (38). In Carole's case, her 'reasons' for committing these acts are rational to her. For her, there seems to be little difference between Colin, the landlord, the construction worker and Michael; the absolute veracity of each corporeal presence is firm to her in each case. As observers, however, we are afforded a level of distance that allows us to quite clearly distinguish between what is and is not diegetically real based on the specific aesthetics of these sequences, altered by Polanski's use of visual distortions in the *mise-en-scène* and choice of lenses, as well as the sound design in which an extra-diegetic muting helps us distinguish between the (diegetically) veridical and non-veridical.

Aetiologies of schizophrenia: A family drama?

As the film progresses and Carole's behaviour becomes increasingly dangerous and bizarre, the temptation to speculate as to the cause of her mental illness grows accordingly. The film seems to encourage such speculation by offering several possible, for the most part psychodynamic, aetiologies for her behaviour. The fact that Carole is a foreign body in London, for example, immediately lends itself to readings that connect her 'otherness' to a feeling of victimisation. But whilst she is clearly linguistically accented, her 'foreignness' is not actually emphasised; it is explicitly mentioned only once (by

Colin's friend, jokingly, as a cause of Colin's bad luck romantically), and Carole speaks English without obstacle throughout the film, even with her sister. In other words, I believe that the film offers little to allow us to make sense of her madness though an examination of her transnational experience.

The photo upon which the camera twice lingers (and on which the film ends), on the other hand, provides much fodder for close readers of the film to engage in all manner of psychoanalytic speculation. In Goscilo's (2006) reading of the image, for example, she affirms that young Carole's sight line is fixed on her father (or possibly her uncle), and calls her expression 'a picture of alienated revulsion' (30). She concludes her reading by confidently stating that 'with admirable economy [the photo] establishes her schizophrenia as a result of paternal (or avuncular) rape' (30), but it should be noted that this judgement is not in line with clinical diagnostic criteria and more along the lines of Laing's (1964) (anti-psychiatric) psychodynamic understanding of schizophrenia, which posits that parents are responsible for behaviour patterns such as Carole's.

Wexman (1985) interprets Carole's malaise as stemming from the envy she feels in regard to her sister's ability to both attract men and engage in pleasurable sexual relationships with them, in combination with her own fear of being rejected due to a history of being compared, unfavourably, to Hélène (48–49). Carole's odd behaviour regarding Michael's vest certainly substantiates this reading, oscillating as she does between attraction and repulsion to it. At the peak of her madness, Carole is seen ironing this very vest, with a rather ineffectual (unplugged) iron. At one point, Carole also seems to play-act the role of her sister, by trying on her clothes, and applying her make-up. It is clear that Carole has strong feeling towards her sister and that her emotional state proves to be heavily reliant on the monopolisation of Hélène's attention. We know, for example, that Carole has followed her sister to London and relies on her for shelter. We also know that Carole has trouble making friends; try as she might, for instance, to bond with co-worker Bridget, she is unable to secure a social invitation from her, certainly unaided by the fact that Bridget discovers the rotting carcass of a rabbit in Carole's purse (another of Carole's behaviours that is symptomatic of schizophrenia[6]).

At the risk of undermining my own more general argument regarding the pathogenesis of Carole's condition, I will offer my own psychoanalytic take, itself a variation of Wexman's. Carole's malaise does indeed seem to be connected to her sister, and may well be rooted in her inability to become this other 'Miss Ledoux' due to her own repressed sexuality. Her desire to be in close proximity to females may well be her means of avoiding conforming to the female mould exemplified by her sister, a model of female behaviour that is not just heterosexual, but tailored specifically to fulfil male desire. Importantly, Hélène herself is not portrayed as an 'acceptable' woman in a moralistic sense, but her role as 'other woman' (or even 'whore', from Michael's wife's perspective) is still very much a part of the spectrum of the patriarchical definition of woman; it is Carole's sexuality, not Hélène's, which is outside this framework.

Carole already works in an all-female environment, which affords her a kind of 'protection' (notwithstanding the irony of what her salon is producing), but even her sorority of beauticians cannot protect her completely from the gazes of men as she walks to work through South Kensington. Her own gazing at nuns emphasises that she is not entirely anhedonic, and that she seems to long to join the nuns behind the walls of Brompton Oratory. The chaos that ensues in the flat reflects Carole's inability to join the patriarchical heterosexual framework, to become the other 'Miss Ledoux'. Thus Carole, like Trelkovsky in *The Tenant*, is thrust into the role of 'female impersonator' when she attempts to become her sister, very much in the same sense that Germaine Greer would use this expression a few years later, in her now-famous book *The Female Eunuch*:

> I'm sick of peering at the world through false eyelashes, so everything I see is mixed with a shadow of bought hairs … I'm sick of the Powder Room. I'm sick of pretending that some fatuous male's self-important pronouncements are the objects of my undivided attention … I'm sick of being a transvestite. I refuse to be a female impersonator.
>
> (Greer, 1970: 70)

Carole's identity crisis is very much reflected by her living space, not only in the increasing chaos and squalor within the space itself, but also by the fact that she occupies a flat that is not her own (Carole even has to knock on the door to enter the flat when her sister is home). Just as she cannot assume her 'correct' (prescribed) identity, or even approach the object of her desire (Bridget, her co-worker), she also struggles to establish her 'right' to appropriate a dwelling space and lay down rules therein (i.e. about who can and cannot enter).

For however 'legitimate' any of the above readings of *Repulsion* may be, whilst the film certainly offers nothing to contradict readings such as Wexman's, Goscilo's or my own, it does not explicitly confirm them either. *Repulsion* simply does not allow us to reterritorialise Carole's mental health the way *Psycho*, *Peeping Tom* and even *Shutter Island* (Scorsese, 2010) so neatly do, all of which 'cleanly' link the psychotic behaviour of their protagonists to repressed traumas. It would be difficult to argue that her complex relationship with her sister, or anyone else, was the *cause* of Carole's schizophrenia. As is typical in Polanski's work, truth is elusive. The possibility that Carole is dealing with her own repressed homosexual desire may well be legitimate, but rather than considering this to be the *cause* of her hallucinations, delusions and subsequent actions, the ambiguity of her condition's aetiology prevents us from establishing a reterritorialised view of the illness.

Much in line with the emerging thinking about schizophrenia, Carole's condition is *deterritorialised*, a much grimmer prospect as it prevents the condition from being linked to an identifiable and reliable cause. So, rather than considering the above 'analyses' as pathogenetic, it is more useful to consider them as crises through which her illness finds expression. I would take this argument a step further: far from being a cause of schizophrenia, if we accept the possibility that Carole is struggling with her sexuality, the moments in which Carole attempts to express her desire, specifically in her interactions with Bridget, are those in which her behaviour appears most healthy. This type of behaviour, in fact, seems to be perfectly normal for one with her sexual orientation living in the time and place in which she finds herself.

Whilst the film renders pathogenetic readings of Carole's illness problematic, *Repulsion* does put on-screen a number of behaviours consistent with clinically agreed behavioural symptoms of schizophrenia. But as McKenna clearly establishes, this is a condition that 'shows no obvious signs of having an underlying physical pathology … (n)or has there ever been much to suggest that it is connected in any very direct way with emotional trauma, childhood deprivation, or any of the other vicissitudes of life' (McKenna, 1997: 98). Although a popular theory in the 1940s, the claim that schizophrenia could be linked to abnormal parent–child relations has been widely discredited, as summarised by Hirsch and Leff (1975). That being said, at the time of *Repulsion*'s release, these theories still had some currency (see, for example, Singer and Wynne [1963] and, as discussed previously, Laing [1964]). But *Repulsion*'s inclusion of an *ambiguous* familial back-story seems to reflect the conflict surrounding the aetiology of schizophrenia at the time, rather than take a position itself.

Let us consider again the mysterious photo in this light. Whilst the photo is not proof-positive of childhood abuse, it may at least provide some evidence that Carole's mental illness could stretch back to her childhood. The camera twice lingers on this photo because, mirroring our own desire to reterritorialise the aberrant behaviour we have just witnessed, it seeks to both diagnose Carole's illness and establish a cause. The camera's lingering on the photo indeed encourages us to 'read' this image, but just as in the afilmic psychiatric world, this is not as 'tidy' as it is in the movies; these few shreds of 'evidence' can just as easily be misleading. The photo, after all, is not an 'action' shot but a clearly orchestrated family portrait in which even the dog is forced to pose for the camera. The young girl is clearly not interested in posing, and looks away, out of frame, wearing the vacant expression matched by her adult self throughout the film. It must be added, however, that she is not alone in this behaviour. The photo also features an elderly woman who, like Carole, stares away from the camera; her expressionless gaze shooting in the opposite direction as Carole's.

Without wishing to stray into gratuitous micro-analysis, but simply as a means of demonstrating the ambiguous nature of this photo, I will offer another alternative reading of this image. The most noticeable aspect of this photo, and upon which the camera clearly does draw our attention, is the young girl's diverted gaze. I, for one, do not see the 'revulsion' in young Carole's face that Goscilo makes unquestioning reference to, nor I am sure that her gaze is fixed on the man to her left. Instead, I find the distractedness (i.e. from the task of posing for the camera) of the girl most interesting. Such lack of affect is indeed a cardinal symptom of schizophrenia (as well as autism), as is the onset of symptoms in young adulthood. Judging by Carole's age in the photo, it is likely that she was entering puberty at this time. Although the dramatic events of the film take place over a relatively short period (a week or two, certainly shorter than the one-month period prescribed by the DSM for the diagnosis of schizophrenia), the photo suggests Carole's more subtle symptoms may have existed for some time prior to the starting point of the film, as far back as her childhood.

The inclusion of the elderly woman with an equally distracted gaze also suggests that Carole may not be the lone sufferer in the family, reflecting the genetic component of the disorder's aetiology; and unlike psychodynamic theories, genetic predisposition to schizophrenia has indeed been scientifically substantiated, as originally demonstrated by Kallman (1938) and Slater (1968). Gottesman (1991) provides the most conclusive evidence of the genetic component of schizophrenia by pooling many gene studies and demonstrating a linear growth in the occurrence of schizophrenia when compared to levels of genetic commonalities, identical twins being the highest with near 50 per cent co-occurrence. However, as the twin results most clearly demonstrate, genetics alone are not the *total* cause of the emergence of the condition. Similarly, we cannot deduce from the photo alone that there is an elaborate back-story to Carole's behaviour; but it is worth noting that when Hélène is confronted by Michael's suggestion that Carole should see a doctor, she is extremely sensitive about the topic; it seems as though she has heard this before (shame and denial are, of course, well-known behaviours associated with relatives of sufferers of mental illness).

Towards even more uncertainty

As the theory of active perception stresses, all perceptions, no matter how 'sane', are constructed; and whilst our brains interpret the stimuli from the outside world, there is no artefact of this representation, no *reproduction* of reality *per se*. In other words, our perception of reality is not reality itself; it is never complete, and always 'flawed'. The depiction of Carole's perceptual crisis illustrates the fact that it is the brain, not the eye, which identifies the elements of the external world; in other words, it is the brain, not the eye, which 'sees'. 'Truth', therefore, remains elusive to those who attempt to grasp it through their senses alone. The ramifications of this situation resonate throughout Polanski's work, which, whilst using perception-based research to help decide where best to position the camera and which lens to use, is equally concerned with the philosophical, ultimately existential, conundrum Gregory highlights in his writing on active perception, which finds its expression both on the narrative and aesthetic plane.

Polanski's attention to realistic detail in his representation of schizophrenic behaviour (perceptual and otherwise) in *Repulsion* becomes even more relevant when we consider the (afilmic) social and political realities that surround the fiction, namely the challenges being levied at the very existence of the condition by the anti-psychiatric movement.[7] However, the film never lapses into academic didacticism, and nor does the work demand to be studied, as it functions extremely well as a 'low art' psychological thriller. It does not appear that Polanski's aim in *Repulsion* is to educate us, but rather that he is taking full advantage of what is known about the brain to embroil the spectator into the work in an attempt to find the best way to create a truly unnerving cinematic experience.

Nevertheless, it cannot be denied that *Repulsion* does seem to actively encourage psychoanalytic readings, especially through the camera's enigmatic dwelling on the Ledoux family portrait. However, it also subverts such readings by making *everything* potentially 'readable' but rewarding none of these readings outright, frustrating any would-be Freudian pathogenesis. There is nothing curative in *Repulsion*, nothing to act as a 'warning' for the rest of us. Schizophrenia remains a degenerative illness with no certain aetiology, and for which the 'talking cure' helps little. Ultimately, whilst *Repulsion* does explore the nature of perception, 'clean' psychoanalytic readings are severely obstructed. The more the film is unpicked, the more the final image of the photo seems to mock the very idea that Carole's behaviour could ever be reterritorialised through a psychodynamic explanation; by extension, *Repulsion* arguably also draws a parallel between cinematic close readings of the film that attempt to delineate its absolute 'meaning' and psychoanalytic attempts to 'solve' severe forms of mental illness such as schizophrenia (and many others) by allocating blame to the past actions of the sufferers or those close to them.

I suggest that in *Repulsion*, the deepest source of horror is not the violence perpetrated on or by Carole, but our empathy with her growing alienation from the world; this horror comes from the fear not only that such a thing could happen to us, but the realisation that it may not be something that can be cured or even explained. The same horror is present in both *The Tenant* and *Rosemary's Baby*, where it is not so much the spectre of the supernatural that terrifies (which remains, in any case, unresolved in both films), but rather the characters' inability to 'grasp' the world. Augmenting this horror are the enigmatic endings of the other two 'apartment' films, which serve to similarly upset the spectator's own ability to 'grasp' a stable diegetic reality. In contrast to the next two films under investigation, whilst *Repulsion* shrouds the cause of Carol's condition in mystery, it at least allows us to conclude that Carole was indeed afflicted with *something*, thus permitting us to breathe a (slight) sigh of relief that we are (hopefully) different. Neither *The Tenant* nor *Rosemary's Baby* is so generous, both of which set up even more severe epistemological crises for the films' protagonists as well as the viewer.

Notes

1. Wrestling in the 1960s was not yet the self-knowing postmodern 'entertainment' it would become in the 1980s.
2. When asked a question regarding how he chooses where to place the camera, Polanski replied, 'that's where I would watch the action from' (quoted in Cousins, 2006: 1).
3. I can personally affirm this strategy continues to be effective. At a screening of *Repulsion* at the British Film Institute on 1 April 2010, I watched an entire audience leap from their seats at this very moment, one of many such occasions.
4. The scene is strangely foreshadowed by Colin's earlier criticism of Carole's plate of fish and chips ('You can't eat stuff like that!').
5. The symptoms of autism and schizophrenia often overlap, in particular in children; hence, making an accurate diagnosis can be problematic (see McKenna, 1997: 341–342).
6. *Collecting and Hording*: 'useless items like old newspapers, pieces of stale food, grass, stones, and dead insects are stuffed into pockets and handbags' (McKenna, 1997: 23).
7. See Laing (1964, 1965, 1967) and Szasz (1960, 1971), as discussed in the last chapter.

Chapter 5

Rosemary's Baby

Embracing ambiguity

In *Rosemary's Baby*, the perceptual discourse Polanski initiates with *Repulsion* is continued, and leads ever towards deeper explorations of what Gregory suggests are the 'philosophical implications' of the theory of active perception, which I believe to be predominantly existential in nature. In the process, *Rosemary's Baby* also touches on a variety of relevant psychological and societal issues, most evidently the influence of gender and religious affiliation on identity formation. As in *Repulsion*, Polanski utilises visual aesthetics to both heighten the spectator's engagement with the cinematic image through a careful combination of lenses (this time wider than those used in *Repulsion*) and camera distance, and then provokes in the spectator perceptual effects that simulate the perceptual crises undergone by Rosemary herself by distorting the perspectives that have thus far seduced our brain's sense of diegetic space. *Rosemary's Baby* takes this strategy a step further than *Repulsion* by creating a diegesis in which the line between what we are to believe is real and that which is imagined, dreamed or hallucinated by Rosemary becomes so blurred that our concept of diegetic reality becomes destabilised. We are therefore forced to speculate in order to re-stabilise our personal understanding of the diegesis, but the closer one looks, the more ambiguous it seems to become.

It is the sense of disorientation created in *Rosemary's Baby* that most markedly differentiates it from *Repulsion*, and in turn establishes *Rosemary's Baby* as an evolution in Polanski's perceptual discourse. I consider *Rosemary's Baby* to be a more ambitious film than *Repulsion* due to its more complex and ambiguous treatment of mental health. Notwithstanding having revisited *Rosemary's Baby* on a multitude of occasions over several years, I must admit that I have yet to establish a satisfactory or stable reading; I have therefore given up trying to 'stabilise' it, but instead embrace its ambiguity and the multiple strains of thoughts that emerge from engaging with this film, which is reflected in both the complexity and length of this close reading.

There is a valuable mode of reading *Rosemary's Baby* that is much in line with Gregory's description of the theory of active perception and which warrants a brief introduction. The phenomenon discussed by Gregory that I suggest is most relevant to this discussion of *Rosemary's Baby* (and, looking forward, to *Death and the Maiden* as well) is the multistability of the 'visual ambiguity' (1997a: 205), that is, the carefully constructed optical illusions that highlight the brain's inability to simultaneously see contradictory images within the visual field. Famous examples of 'shifting' visual ambiguities include E. G. Boring's ambiguous figure of the old/young woman and the 'duck-rabbit' illusion, as well as many other basic shapes in which the brain, faced with identical retinal images, is forced to oscillate its perception of said image, perpetually incapable of settling on one as its 'true' representation. Any attempt to 'stabilise' multistable perception is both futile and uncomfortable.

I am not suggesting that *Rosemary's Baby* literally contains such 'trickery' (although profilmic illusions are indeed employed by Polanski at times, as I shall discuss in my case study of *The Tenant*), but that the film as a whole operates as an 'ambiguity' in which competing 'realities', especially those that delineate the difference between the diegetically real and the diegetically hallucinated, perpetually clash in the mind of the spectator, especially the 'close reader', without resolution. Furthermore, it is worth pointing out that this 'clashing' of realities is also highly reminiscent of many works identified as 'postmodern', a label that I believe helps our understanding of *Rosemary's Baby*. As Calinescu puts it, 'in the postmodern view, there simply is no "reality" that might validate … hypotheses, even under ideal conditions' (1987: 305), a quality it inherits from surrealism. Think of Magritte, for example, who was also fond of provoking cognitive dissonance through works such as 'The Treachery of Images' (perhaps better known as '*Ceci n'est pas une pipe*'), 'Empire of Light', 'Carte Blanche' and 'Not to Be Reproduced'.

I propose that the most interesting, perhaps even most 'fruitful', way to approach *Rosemary's Baby* is to follow the Deleuzian ethos of not speaking *about* the film, but rather speaking *with* the film (see Deleuze, 1989: 268). So what I attempt here is not so much a reading of *Rosemary's Baby*, but rather to present an analysis that seeks to *map* the various conflicting ideas that the film provokes. My primary intention in this chapter is to explore the deep ambiguity of this film by often countering my own (and others') readings in the process of discussing them. On this note, I shall begin this case study *Rosemary's Baby*.

The outsiders come in

One of Polanski's most repeated motifs is that of the 'insider' versus 'outsider', often expressed in the form of a character's perceived national otherness. But nationality is rarely an absolute factor in this determination. In *Repulsion*, for example, I have suggested that it is not Carole's Belgian identity that establishes her as an outsider as much as it is her inability to cope with heterosexual social interactions. I will return to this issue in my case studies of *The Tenant*, *Frantic* and *The Ninth Gate*, but it is worth highlighting now that, like *Repulsion*, in each of these films the protagonist is positioned as national 'other' in the context in which 'he' (a problematic pronoun in reference to Trelkovsky) finds himself. But whilst both *The Tenant*'s Trelkovsky and *Frantic*'s Dr Walker are portrayed as 'outsiders', in *The Ninth Gate*, although Corso is an American in Europe, he maintains an 'insider' status, and eventually becomes the *ultimate* insider; but more on that later.

In *Rosemary's Baby* the notion of the national 'other' is nuanced somewhat by the fact that Rosemary and Guy are both immigrants to New York, not from other countries, but from other American cities. Early in the film, they visit their new neighbours, Roman and Minnie Castevet (Sidney Blackmer and Ruth Gordon) for dinner, in which the pleasantries of initial conversation reveal that Guy and Rosemary are from Baltimore and Omaha respectively. Their hosts, on the other hand, are 'authentic' New Yorkers. So Rosemary and Guy, whilst both American, are nevertheless positioned as outsiders in the process of becoming insiders as they carve out a life for themselves in the city. Their task is made more difficult due to the lack of support from greater familial structures in this area, a conspicuous absence that conveniently allows the Castevets to take up this role. For Rosemary, these new 'parents' serve to usurp the place of another surrogate parent, Hutch (Maurice Evans), Rosemary's former landlord.

So in their attempt to achieve 'insider' status, first and foremost, Rosemary and Guy secure an extremely centrally located flat, within walking distance of the theatres in which Guy hopes to work. For Rosemary, the task is now to conform to her role as a young wife, with a view towards motherhood (hence the size of the flat). For Guy, the task is to achieve success in the city as an actor, an occupation with a highly uncertain earning potential. Without some 'initial breaks' (as Roman puts it), Guy will not be able to live up to his 'role' as rent payer for this flat. Guy is well aware that the flat is outside their price range; a fact Rosemary seems blissfully (or wilfully) ignorant of.

In lieu of parental support, Guy initiates his trajectory towards 'insiderness' by adopting the Castevets as parental figures, through whom there seems to be a chance he can get these 'breaks' given Roman's connections in the theatre world. In the process, Hutch is expelled from his role as counsellor to the young couple, and thus Rosemary becomes fully divorced from both her own parents and adopted father figure in order to fully join Guy's new 'family' (further symbolised, of course, by her customary assumption of her husband's surname). But whilst Guy becomes more and more an 'insider', Rosemary's 'outsiderness' becomes increasingly pronounced. It is her Catholic upbringing that proves most relevant in this regard. The religious element of her identity is first highlighted over dinner with the Castevets, when Roman, Minnie and Guy all openly criticise the Pope, who is currently visiting New York. There is also a reference to Guy having played a role in *Luther*, a subtle indication of her husband's protestant affiliation (a possible explanation for Rosemary's alienation from her family; an element of the novel that Polanski leaves ambiguous in the film). Most importantly, it is Guy's lack of a dominant religious framework that differentiates Rosemary from her husband, as well as from the Castevets who show no respect for 'her' Pope. Even though she claims not be a practising member, she is unable to shed the psychological baggage that sustains her (parentally imposed) Catholic identity; thus, an identity crisis is established that seems to greatly inform the perceptual crisis that ensues later in the film.

Rosemary's double status as a Catholic out-of-towner indeed contributes to her being an 'outsider', but both of these elements seem subservient to the more fundamental issue of her *gender* as determinant of her 'outsiderness'. Rosemary is granted opportunities to become an 'insider' through the acceptance of her 'place' as Guy's wife and by conforming to the framework of behaviours he prescribes, but her struggle to establish her own identity seems incompatible with this role. I suggest that Rosemary's perceptual breakdown can be read along the lines of Lacan's much-cited provocation '*la femme n'existe pas*' (1975: 68), which suggests that she is a 'symptom' rather than a being in and of herself, as if the state of being female *de facto* renders one incapable of achieving the highest state of personal achievement, what Maslow refers to as 'self actualisation' (1973: 162). Rosemary's crisis can be seen as a manifestation of this very identity struggle, which is emphasised by the fact that her attempt to become a self-actualised woman in a patriarchal framework is portrayed in the film as an act of madness. Like *Repulsion*, however, there seems to be such great care taken in the realistic portrayal of Rosemary's psychosis, that upon ever-closer analysis one begins to wonder whether such a reading is itself overly superficial. The possibility that these repressed 'stressors' are simply informing, rather than *causing*, schizophrenic behaviour in Rosemary must also be considered in parallel.

Setting the Flytrap

In earlier chapters I have discussed Polanski's strategy of enhancing the spectator's engagement in terms of visual and aural techniques aimed at creating a 'wraparound' effect. In *Rosemary's Baby*, Polanski also plays with generic expectations as a means of heightening engagement, but ever towards that same goal of 'luring' us in so as to make the shocking moments to come that much more effective. Catering to generic convention through colour palette, musical score, performance style and dialogue type serves as an effective 'lure' by establishing a diegetic framework that, at first, meets spectator's expectations. Thus, in a manner analogous to the perceptual realism sought through the use of natural perspective, by setting up particular aesthetic parameters in line with the conventions of a certain genre, the brain can be put at ease.

The initial 'generic lure' in *Rosemary's Baby* does not come by way of the horror genre, but rather by an opening act that is more suggestive of a Hollywood romantic comedy. To help achieve this goal, Polanski originally sought to cast Robert Redford to play the role of Guy Woodhouse (see Polanski, 1984: 251), in what would have been a fundamentally against-type choice. Redford's own star persona (which still persists) would have undoubtedly greatly informed spectators' reading of his character, making his betrayal of Rosemary even more shocking due to the 'betrayal' of spectators' expectations as well.

John Cassavetes instead brought no star baggage to the role,[1] and so the impact that Redford would have had was somewhat diluted.

Mia Farrow, on the other hand, did indeed possess some star power of her own, known at the time for her role on the TV series *Peyton Place*, as well as being the young bride of the American singer and actor Frank Sinatra. Farrow's bubbly innocence, combined with Krzysztof Komeda's title theme, are all suggestive of a city-bound comedy along the lines of Wilder's *The Seven Year Itch* (1955) or *The Apartment* (1960), not quite a satanic nativity play or the story of a young woman's psychotic breakdown. Hence, we are 'seduced' not only by the painstaking details of the *mise-en-scène*, but the film's (*initial*) adherence to misleading generic tropes. Granted, the effect of this strategy is greatly enhanced by a combination of time and place of first viewing and ignorance of the story arch. Given the infamy of the film and its marketing strategy at the time of its release, a spectator without a basic idea of the narrative trajectory would have been rare indeed; but this does not necessarily undo the effect completely, as these opening scenes still maintain an aura of innocence and fun that greatly impact the shocking nature of the second act and the tension of the third.

At a purely visual level, *Rosemary's Baby* marks an advance compared to *Repulsion* both in terms of production value (the 'quality' of the *mise-en-scène* and effects) and cinematography. Having just completed *Dance of the Vampires*, Polanski had direct experience with the wide-screen format and colour stock, but here he moves from 'Metrocolor' (aka Eastmancolor) to the more vivid Technicolor, a stock that Andrew (1979) suggests actively promoted 'a Hollywood notion of colour', which was 'purer than reality' and 'almost whorish' (46) in its artificiality. The use of colour further contributes to Polanski's trick of reinforcing the generic expectation of the Hollywoodian romantic comedy; this is, after all, not only the colour film used by most Hammer films, but the palette of *Gentlemen Prefer Blondes* (Hawkes, 1953). Eventually, however, these same hyperreal tones would be put to a far more insidious use, as the colours become disturbingly saturated, even 'bleeding', during the film's most notorious 'dream' sequence, in which the colour distorts completely, seemingly separating into green, blue and red, as if the three layers of the Technicolor stock have come unglued. Polanski also widens the screen compared to *Repulsion*. Whilst not quite the 2.33:1 of *Dance of the Vampires*, in *Rosemary's Baby*, Polanski opts for a 1.85:1 ratio (compared to *Repulsion*'s more boxy 1.66:1), a format that allows for the extension of the horizontal visual field, but without overly inhibiting the film's ability to convey the 'verticalness' of the urban environment in which the film takes place.

Even more so than *Repulsion*, *Rosemary's Baby*'s tethered camera keeps us close to its protagonist through the use of wide-angle lenses that help create a sense of intimate proximity. Pizzello (2000) argues that the 'primal grip' exerted by Polanski on the audience is greatly down to the director's 'insistence on visual consistency throughout a film' (40). Whilst this is largely the case, Polanski does sometimes intentionally compromise this 'consistency' for dramatic effect. As I have already discussed in reference to *Repulsion*, Polanski mixes natural and distorted perspective to create a 'Venus Flytrap' effect. Richard L. Gregory himself praises Polanski's use of natural perspective in *Repulsion* as a means of 'drawing' the brain into the diegesis (2003), which then allows him to amplify the shock value of the distortions that follow. In *Rosemary's Baby*, Polanski (carefully) takes advantage of the 'exaggerated depth' (Warren, 2002: 71) afforded by the wide angle, using a 25 mm lens for most of the film to simultaneously keep us close to Rosemary and to create a sense of depth *around* her. When distortion is called for, Polanski switches to a more extreme 18mm lens (Pizzello, 2000: 40) to heighten that 'tension' between the eye and brain that occurs when the stimuli that strike the retina differ from what the brain expects to see (Gregory, 2003).

In light of Gregory's comments regarding Polanski's use of natural perspective in *Repulsion*, it is pertinent to stress that Polanski's method of achieving perceptual realism is not limited to the use of a 'normal' (50 mm) lens. But the use of the wide-angle lens carries with it the risk of distortion that could compromise this type of realism (even a 25 mm lens, which falls well short of causing the 'fish eye' effect). Polanski mitigates this risk through informed camera placements, thus allowing for a heightened depth effect without compromising perceptual engagement. As Polanski himself explains it to an interviewer:

> A wide angle distorts only inasmuch as you put the three-dimensional world onto the two-dimensional screen … At a distance of two metres, your face would not be distorted. So it's not the angle that changes the perspective, but the distance.
>
> (Polanski in Thomson, 1995: 9)

So the creation of a sense of on-screen 'depth' is yet another manner in which Polanski attempts to increase perceptual realism and heighten the 'wraparound' effect. Whilst his use of wide-angle lenses serves to augment the depth effect by provoking awareness of the area surrounding the subject, Polanski also uses shot structures and set architecture to create a realistic 3-D effect for which no special glasses are required. A subtle, but effective, example of Polanski's calculated use of depth is his frequent visual references to intra-frame concealed space. In order to access this space, we are encouraged to want to move 'into' the frame; sometimes the camera complies, sometimes not. In *Rosemary's Baby*, an interesting example of this effect occurs in a scene in which cigarette smoke is used to beckon us into this concealed space. After dining with their new neighbours, Rosemary's husband Guy retreats to the parlour with Roman whilst Minnie and Rosemary wash dishes in the kitchen. Rosemary is distracted and peers into the next room whilst Minnie carries on washing. We are granted a countershot to observe what she gazes at, but rather than being shown the source of her interest, we, like her, see only smoke drifting in from the other side of a doorway. What results is a sort of 'negative' effect, that is, the desire to penetrate the space we know is there (i.e. the desire to look around the corner) is augmented by the *denial* of access to it. Furthermore, this denial of access serves to heighten our sense of the extent of diegetic space by encouraging us to think about concealed or out-of-frame space, rather than present a diegesis that is completely contained (and visible) within the frame. Whilst far less technologically complex than using a stereoscopic camera, a 3-D effect is achieved nonetheless, and without the use of distracting gimmickry or special glasses that risk undoing the totalising experience that the film sets out to deliver.

Let us examine another shot that illustrates how this technique is used to differing effect. In the sequence where Guy receives a phone call in which he is offered a starring a role in a theatre production (due, of course, to the original star having come down with an unfortunate bout of spontaneous blindness), Rosemary carefully approaches the room to which he has retreated to take the call. Rather than staring at the doorway, this time the camera seems to obey our desire to look around the doorframe and get a better look at (or perhaps just hear better) what is going on in the room. The camera pans across the hallway to let us look in, as if the cinema audience had changed the angle by collectively tilting their heads to the right. Rosemary then enters frame, reinforcing the fact that the 'view' we are experiencing is not that of Rosemary herself, but still that of our nominal observer to 'whom' she is tethered. She moves directly to the door, her mastery of the space finally allowing us to look in as well.

More than just strengthening the spectator's 'suture' to the film, these types of shots (and there are many – the 'doorway shot' in particular being one of Polanski's favourites) demonstrate the strong bond between visual style and narrative content in Polanski's cinema. In *Rosemary's Baby*, off-screen space is of the utmost relevance, for it is these spaces that hold the answer to the question of whether Rosemary's perceptions are veridical or non-veridical, which is the issue from which the film's tension is largely derived. As we, with only marginally more information than Rosemary herself, try to put the pieces of the puzzle together, it is these above-mentioned off-screen moments that inform our understanding of what has transpired: it must be during their concealed conversation at the dinner party that Roman Castevet planted the seed of the 'unholy pact' in Guy's mind, it must be Roman and Minnie with whom Guy is plotting when he hurries out of the flat (like when he has a sudden 'yen' for ice cream), and so on.

It is only when Rosemary penetrates the wall between the two flats that her epistemological crisis is 'resolved' (a conjecture I will challenge later in this chapter); the appropriation of knowledge, understanding and above all safety is linked to the appropriation of space and the overcoming of physical obstacles (walls, doorways). In line with my introductory discussion of the flats in this trilogy serving to represent 'cranial' spaces, we can interpret these barriers not only as physical impediments to perception (we cannot see through them and sound is heavily muffled), but also as symbols of the insurmountable gap between the subjective, personal (neurological) sphere of perception and the true nature of the external physical reality with which we, and these characters, engage. But whilst we may struggle to overcome this gap (i.e. to 'embrace' reality), to do so risks sacrificing the borders of selfhood. To do so also risks entering the territory of schizophrenia, where the ability to distinguish between veridical perceptions and self-generated, non-veridical perceptions becomes compromised.

Trading places and the oneiric image

Just as in *Repulsion* before it, in *Rosemary's Baby* a flat nestled in a large urban centre, this time the Dakota building in Manhattan, serves as the setting for a perceptual crisis. *Rosemary's Baby* also germinates the seed planted in *Repulsion* regarding psychosis and the appropriation of living space. Where it is Carole's sister, Hélène (and her boyfriend), whose presence dominates *Repulsion's* South Kensington flat, in *Rosemary's Baby* it is the lingering presence of a recently deceased former tenant, the aged Mrs Gardenia, that must be removed from the flat as a first priority in order for Guy and Rosemary to truly claim the space for themselves (a scenario that is repeated in *The Tenant,* as we shall discuss in the next chapter).

The task of redecorating falls to Rosemary, who gives the flat a makeover so extreme that it is no longer recognisable to Mrs Gardenia's old friend and neighbour Minnie. But notwithstanding the changes made to the look of the flat, Rosemary's assumption of Gardenia's space seems to carry with it an assumption of some aspects of her identity as well. The film first establishes a connection, superficially at least, between these two women through the horticultural allusions in their names, 'Gardenia' and 'Rosemary', as if the latter is being cultivated in the former. Rosemary is in fact initiated into the geriatric community of the Bramford (as the Dakota is renamed) by neighbours Minnie and Laura-Louis (Patsy Kelly), who almost literally push their way into Rosemary's living room and establish a knitting circle as if it was still their old friend's flat, sending Rosemary a clear signal of the 'vacant' position she is expected to fill, in spite of her young age.

But it is not only the late Mrs Gardenia to whom Rosemary is connected. Early on Rosemary meets Terry, a young woman of about Rosemary's age who lives with the Castevets. As they do their laundry together, Terry tells Rosemary that Roman and Minnie 'picked [her] up off the sidewalk, literally'. Later, in a scene horribly reminiscent of Terry's comment, Rosemary and Guy find Terry's body splattered on the pavement outside the Bramford. It is at this point that they meet the Castevets for the first time, which initiates their relationship with the old couple. When Minnie and her friend Laura-Louis later come to visit Rosemary (the 'knitting circle' visit), not only is Rosemary positioned to take the role of Mrs Gardenia in their social group, but she is also 'nudged' into Terry's shoes when Minnie gives Rosemary the now-deceased lodger's necklace, an unusual charm filled with 'Tanis root'.

Rosemary's connection to Terry is emphasised on the night of Terry's death in a sequence that establishes the confusing role the oneiric image will play in this film. As Rosemary lies in bed, the camera glides across her face (her eyes wide open) and drifts onto the wall behind her. The wall turns red and morphs into an image of Terry in a pool of blood (her eyes also wide open). We then start to hear murmurs. It has already been established that Rosemary and Guy can hear across this partitioned wall, particularly Minnie with her rather loud voice, whom they have heard bickering with Roman (and even asking him to get her a 'root beer'). Breaking the silence (a 'silence' punctuated by Guy's heavy breathing and the sound of a ticking clock), we hear Minnie say the rather ambiguous phrase 'sometimes I wonder how come you're the leader of anything'. But the stimuli become muddled here, for it does not appear to be Minnie saying these words, but rather an old nun. We return to the bedroom, where we see (and hear) Guy asleep and Rosemary beginning to drift off. There is a thump, and we hear Minnie, but again, it is the nun speaking with Minnie's voice, pointing to a group of men blocking up a window, the damage to which Rosemary seems to know something about.

Here we have the first example in *Rosemary's Baby* of the film's attempt to represent Rosemary's subjective perceptual experiences in a manner that gives our surrogate observer access to diegetically unreal (oneiric, at this point) images. What is particularly noteworthy here is the way in which oneiric imagery (the nuns, the bricklayers; both, interestingly, reminiscent of *Repulsion*), recent memories (Terry's body), and what are likely diegetically veridical stimuli (the murmuring across the wall) mix to such an extent that it is difficult to distinguish between them. The scenario is subsequently repeated (but in a far more extreme manner) in the film's infamous rape scene, the event upon which any interpretation of *Rosemary's Baby* hinges.

'This is no dream; this is really happening!'

In order to best appreciate the complexity of the rape sequence, I propose to address it along several different, but interrelated, axes. Firstly, in line with the primary focus of the rest of this analysis, the sequence shall be examined structurally and aesthetically, with special attention paid to the psychological/perceptual effect of the cinematic techniques employed and the possible readings that emerge from this approach. Secondly, it is useful to acknowledge the various psychoanalytical readings this sequence lends itself to, and how these may actually inform the above-mentioned 'perceptual effect'. Thirdly, it is important to consider the ideological issues raised in this sequence, specifically in the context of the feminist concerns surrounding the film (and for that matter, much of Polanski's work); although the primary focus of this discussion remains the two-fold nature of perception in Polanski's cinema (i.e. the way in which Polanski represents acts of perception and the way the films themselves serve as objects of perception for the spectator), the issue of gender in this film simply cannot be dodged, even in the specific context I propose here. I will therefore take account of some of the feminist criticism of this sequence and the film as a whole; in turn, I will also offer another take on the gender issue in this film.

The step forward that Polanski's perceptual discourse takes in *Rosemary's Baby* is perhaps best exemplified through a comparison of its rape sequence with those in *Repulsion*. My basic contention is that the manner in which *Repulsion* portrays the violation of Carole slightly *reduces* the horror of the rape as it is anchored in a hallucinatory context. The horror is instead mostly derived from witnessing the character to whom we are tethered experience such horrific *hallucinations* due to her increasingly tenuous grasp of reality. As disturbing as the rapes scenes are, in *Repulsion*, we remain quite certain that these events *are not really happening*.

It is significant that in *Repulsion*, the first time we witness Carole being attacked by the construction worker the linearity of time is maintained. There is no indication, for example, that this is a memory, or even a nightmare derived from a memory. It happens in the film's actual-moment, not in flashback, but is nevertheless aesthetically divorced from the diegesis; there is a stylistic shift that signals a 'non-reality' or hallucinatory moment. At a visual level, the lighting is more expressionistic, the close-ups more extreme, and the angles more bizarre than usual. Perhaps even more dramatic in its difference to the film's established aesthetics, however, is the use of sound in these scenes. What is immediately striking about these scenes is the lack of coordination between sound and image, which serves to create a moment of intermodal crisis for the spectator that reflects Carole's own distress. Carole's scream, for example, goes unheard; it is replaced instead by a bizarre wailing that is not readily identifiable, but certainly not of human origin. The normally ubiquitous ambient sounds of the room, the flat and surrounding area (piano lessons from neighbouring flats, the muffled sound of the lift, traffic, planes flying overhead, etc.) are completely absent and the soundtrack is instead dominated by seemingly extra-diegetic noise.

It is precisely this lack of *logical* (i.e. in line with sensory expectations) diegetic sound (on- or off-screen) that allows us to comfortably identify these moments as 'non-realities' or hallucinations within *Repulsion*'s diegetic reality. That is not to say, however, that these scenes are not still repulsive. The fact that we are provoked to process the image and fill-in the sound may well be the very reason these scenes are so disturbing, but due to the inherent safety-net offered by the hallucinatory image, I propose that the deepest horror of *Repulsion* lies not in these particular images, but the realistic portrayal of the way in which Carole has 'lost touch' with reality and the more basic horror this evokes, namely the idea that such a condition is even possible. Keeping this idea in mind, let us now turn our attention back to *Rosemary's Baby*.

As the title suggests, the narrative tension of *Rosemary's Baby* hinges greatly on the rape that takes place in the second act and the strong suggestion that this event is directly responsible for Rosemary's pregnancy. The conventional reading of this scene[2] is that this is a diegetically real event, which indeed causes Rosemary to become pregnant with no less than the Antichrist himself. On closer analysis, however, competing readings emerge that destabilise one's understanding of the diegesis. Where *Repulsion* makes it quite clear that Carole is suffering from some kind of serious mental illness, *Rosemary's Baby* offers no such certainties, whilst at the same time offering just as robust, if not more so, a reflection of the cardinal symptoms of paranoid schizophrenia. The key difference is that in *Rosemary's Baby* we are tethered more firmly to Rosemary than we are to Carole in *Repulsion*, and as a result *Rosemary's Baby* offers little to counter what reason dictates should be a hallucinatory image, such as being raped by the Devil. As spectators, we are encouraged to accept these events as diegetically real, which is not especially difficult once we shift our generic dial to 'horror', a genre in which supernatural activity is commonplace.

A close reading of this scene reveals the extent of its complexity. We are presented with a variety of images, some of which logic tells us must be diegetically non-veridical (i.e. representations of Rosemary's perceptual experiences that are not based on diegetic stimuli), but others of which are more ambiguous. Just as she closes her eyes, there is a cut to an image of Rosemary, still lying on her mattress, floating on water (a lake, or perhaps the ocean). The camera is placed just behind Rosemary's head, approximating her POV without actually adopting it, so that we too can look over her prone body as it undulates on the water. The impact of such a shot not only mimics that sense of nausea that accompanies both seasickness and drunkenness (the 'floating mattress' is no doubt a familiar experience to many of us), but also serves to set up a sensory-motor logic that will be echoed in the events to come. Paralysed by her alcoholic stupor and/or the toxic chocolate mousse ('mouse'), she is unable to physically stabilise herself (vividly demonstrated by her fall in the corridor), and so her perceptual mechanism seems to generate an image that matches her physical state. It is important to remember when unpicking this scene that the rape sequence in *Rosemary's Baby* differs from the one in *Repulsion* due to the fact that it is preceded by a scene in which Rosemary is clearly intoxicated and collapses into bed, an element that seriously challenges our ability to 'read' what happens next.

The scene returns to the bedroom with the camera hovering over Rosemary as she discusses the failure of 'baby night' with Guy. As usual, we remain very closely tethered to Rosemary, with the shot-countershot between her and Guy coming close to, but never matching, either POV directly. What is more significant here, though, is the fact that the camera continues the undulating motion of the previous shot, subtly moving in and out and in turn triggering in the spectator a minor version of that sense of nausea Rosemary is feeling.

The scene, visually but not aurally, then abruptly cuts to Rosemary, new drink in hand, on a yacht mingling with who appear to be the Kennedys. Penetrating Rosemary's psyche further, the camera reveals what seems to be a clear-cut representation of an oneiric-image, suggesting that our notional observer (Polanski's ubiquitous 'inquiring camera') seems to have infiltrated her dream space. At this point, there is no difficulty for the spectator to distinguish between the oneiric and the diegetically real. The camera hovers on its tether around the boat, exploring its surroundings. The image of water is momentarily superimposed in the frame, but fades out quickly as the camera (and what we believe to be a close approximation of Rosemary's oneiric gaze) moves across a map and rests upon the captain, a Kennedy lookalike. As he puts his Captain's hat on, however, he seamlessly (in the cut) 'becomes' Rosemary's friend Hutch in a moment of corporal transposition reminiscent of dream scenarios discussed by Freud (1952: 46). So, thus far, the details of this sequence seem to indicate that Rosemary is not hallucinating, like Carole, but dreaming. However, nothing is straightforward: whilst our judgement that Rosemary is simply dreaming may be greatly informed by the aesthetics of this sequence, the matter is heavily complicated by Rosemary's alcohol consumption and the fact that she may even have been drugged, the latter in particular a possible cause of hallucinatory perception. What we seem to be left with is a melange of images that may have been dreamt, hallucinated, diegetically real or some combination of the three.

A minor digression is in order here to address the difference between hallucinating and dreaming, and furthermore, how this difference is relevant to the discussion at hand. Both dreams and hallucinations share the definition of being non-veridical, objectless perceptions that masquerade as objective representations of antecedent reality, and in cinema both should be considered as diegetically non-veridical. As the dream perception is 'believed' in the oneiric moment, the body is placed into a state of paralysis during REM (rapid eye movement) sleep, so as to avoid what would otherwise be appropriate sensory-motor responses (precisely what 'goes wrong' in sleepwalkers). Upon waking, the dream is either quickly forgotten or recognised for what it was, that is, a non-veridical perception. As a result, the dream does not normally inform future perceptual judgement. A hallucination, on the other hand, remains indistinguishable from reality to the perceiver and thus influences his or her judgement of veridical stimuli, which can in turn lead to the formation of delusions.

In terms of its effect on the spectators' understanding of a diegetic time structure, a dream sequence need not cause a perceptual crisis *per se* (nor, for that matter, does a flashback); when a dream is clearly delineated, or 'framed', as spectators we have little trouble accommodating these types of sequences into the diegesis, as we can, with little effort, categorise what is real, dreamed, hallucinated, a flashback, etc. when the film provides a structural or aesthetic means of distinction. In other words, crisis is averted when we know what-is-what, and when what Deleuze calls the 'actual-image' remains intact.

In *Rosemary's Baby*'s rape sequence, Polanski manages to blur the dividing line not only between hallucination and reality, but the three-way junction that connects non-veridical and veridical stimuli, namely dream, hallucination and reality. The notional observer that guides our gaze becomes so embroiled in this oneiric moment that we are not able (not now, not ever) to satisfactorily determine a sense of diegetic reality that is not directly linked to Rosemary's perceptions. We can be no more sure than Rosemary herself if she is dreaming, hallucinating or whether these perceptions are based on external stimuli; this is an uncertainty that remains until the end of the film.

After the JFK–Hutch body swap, we move below deck where the diegetically real and oneiric again mingle, where Guy begins to remove Rosemary's body suit as she leans back on the lower deck ladder (i.e. her bed). At this point the sequence begins to even more severely muddle the veridical and non-veridical, as we lose the ability to distinguish between what is real, dreamt or hallucinated. The image of Rosemary having her wedding ring removed, for example, is ambiguous, as it could be diegetically real, although we are not sure for what reason it would occur. The image of her being hoisted up to the roof of the Sistine Chapel, on the other hand, *cannot* be diegetically real, so we accept it as dreamed. Likewise, Hutch's cry of 'Typhoon!' is a dream-image, but what of the seemingly random 'Easy, easy. You're holding her too high' that we hear just as Rosemary passes (we pass) under a doorway arch? The images become increasingly bizarre: Rosemary is now warned by a ship-hand steering the yacht ('played' by the Bramford's lift operator) to move below deck, where she finds herself in a dark room in which a large building, what looks like a church, burns in the background. She walks towards a bed, where she lies down, naked, and is surrounded by a number of nude chanting geriatrics.

Amongst the group are a number of characters we recognise. Neighbour Roman Castevet, clad in a black robe and a rather Papal-looking black hat, applies red paint to Rosemary's body. We recognise another neighbour, Laura-Louis, chanting with the crowd, and then Minnie Castevet and Guy, also naked and chanting. At this point there is a verbal exchange between Guy and Minnie that again confounds our diegetic understanding of the scene. 'She's awake, she sees', says Guy to Minnie, who replies 'She don't see. As long as she ate the mouse she can't see nor hear, she's like dead.' (The 'mouse' in question seems to be a reference to Minnie's mispronunciation of 'mousse' in an earlier scene.) Such a blatant reference to the question of Rosemary's consciousness now seriously compromises our reading of this image as 'unreal', and so the horror of the scene becomes accentuated. Rosemary is then bound and raped by Guy, whose face and body, in a manner similar to the dream/reality shifts that occurred at the start of this sequence, are interchanged with that of a monstrous beast. It is here that Rosemary makes the statement that she, and we, will have to grapple with for the remainder of the film: 'This is no dream', she screams. '*This is really happening!*'

The detailed structural analysis of the dream/rape sequence I provide above raises several (ultimately unresolved) questions regarding what is and is not diegetically real in the narrative. I have outlined the basic visual (and to a lesser extent, aural) structure of the sequence in an attempt to detail the manner in which the sequence is presented to the spectator, who is cajoled out of his or her (leaving gender aside, for the moment) 'passive' engagement with the unfolding narrative, towards the more 'active' role needed to decipher the stimuli. I keep the terms 'passive' and 'active' in quotes here to differentiate them from the manner in which the theory of active perception (to which this discussion is wedded) uses these terms, ever mindful of the fact that in its presenting of such ambiguous imagery, the sequence is highly evocative of this model of perception in its call for active engagement, reflecting active perception's insistence that perception, all perception, is a cognitively active act of hypothesisation and judgement. In contrast, cinema in which diegetic reality is portrayed unambiguously, and indeed Polanski's own attempt to create a perceptual 'wraparound' effect, tries to create in the spectator a more 'passive' state, in which the brain relaxes so that the screen image is more readily accepted. Here again we return to the concept of the 'Flytrap', in which the perceptual mechanism is lured into a more relaxed state, but only to set up a startling reminder that this mechanism is actually *never* passive.

Reverence, rape and religion

In the scene that follows the rape sequence, we see Rosemary asleep in her bed and being woken up by Guy. Our real-time analysis of the previous sequence spills over into this scene when we notice that Rosemary is covered by scratch marks, just as she makes reference to 'the dreams [she's] had'. For a moment we are compelled to conclude that whilst much of what we have witnessed was dreamt, some of it did indeed 'really happen'. So at this point the situation seems relatively clear (i.e. Rosemary has been raped by the Devil), until, that is, Guy struts back into the room, and jests, 'Don't yell, I already filed 'em down [*referring to his nails*]. I didn't want to miss baby night.' Rosemary accepts the explanation and speaks no more of her 'dream'. Whilst Guy's statement reintroduces ambiguity, it also furnishes an extremely *unambiguous* element of the diegetic reality – there is no doubt about whether or not Rosemary was raped, merely *how*, and by *whom* (or *what*).

Rosemary offers a rather weak protestation to Guy, but quickly moves on, seemingly accepting the rape as a structural component of their marriage. It is Rosemary's acceptance of marital rape that has earned the film (and Polanski himself) some well-founded accusations of misogyny, such as Haskel's description of Rosemary as 'lobotomised' (Haskell, 1987: 346–347). Mazierska, who ultimately offers a feminist take on Polanski's cinema, concedes that Polanski's portrayal of feminism (and feminists) can be seen to have 'an infantilising effect on men while at the same time failing to empower women' (2007: 129); indeed, in Polanski's cinema it is 'mastery' that remains most elusive for everyone, including the spectator.

It is worth permitting a brief tangential discussion to allow for a historicised interpretation of the 'dream'/rape sequence in *Rosemary's Baby*, which, in turn, opens up a more complex reading of *Rosemary's Baby* as a whole in terms of its treatment of gender. The film echoes some of the most fundamental concerns of the feminist movement of the time, and even some that continue to resonate today. But, as is normally the case with Polanski, instead of resorting to reductive didacticism, these issues are presented in all their frustrating complexity. I do not claim that Polanski's cinema is either pro-feminist or misogynist, but rather that both depictions of misogyny and feminist concerns add to what is an even greater meditation on the perceptual mechanism and how this informs concepts of identity, including gender roles. In parallel, I hope to demonstrate that whilst *Rosemary's Baby* and other of Polanski's films (*Death and the Maiden* in particular, which I will discuss in a later case study) portray misogyny, this does not make the works inherently misogynistic.

A key point that is often confused by close readers of *Rosemary's Baby* concerns the ambiguity regarding the diegetic reality of the rape. Whilst I argue repeatedly that *Rosemary's Baby* in a highly ambiguous film, this is one of the few diegetic elements that is *crystal* clear: Rosemary *has* been raped, either by her husband, the Devil or someone dressed as the Devil. Diegetically speaking, there is no ambiguity about this, but it is a 'fact' that is often overlooked due to the perceptual maelstrom of the sequence. Even critics who have re-evaluated this film in a pro-feminist light have 'fallen' for the trick played by the film and have overlooked a key detail. I believe Mazierska, for example, overestimates the parallel between *Repulsion* and *Rosemary's Baby* in her suggestion that in both of these films the 'rape might only have taken place in the woman's imagination' (2007: 131). Fischer, who devotes her entire article to contextualising *Rosemary's Baby*'s depiction of pregnancy in a feminist framework, refers to the event as a 'warped rape fantasy' that 'mocks woman's "designated" coital stance: passive and undemanding' (1992: 9). She does not, however, put much emphasis on the impact of the *real* rape (and its repression) on Rosemary's mental state, but rather shifts her discussion to addressing Rosemary's own 'fantasy', which Fischer suggests 'evokes the primitive belief that human males are removed from procreation' (9).

When she awakes in the morning, Rosemary is confronted by Guy, who immediately normalises the fact that he has had sex with her whilst she was unconscious. As spectators, we are also distracted. We are so preoccupied with resolving whether or not Rosemary, like Carole, has imagined the sexual attack, that our thoughts are deflected away from the issue of marital rape. The important difference between Rosemary and Carole is that where in *Repulsion* we are reasonably sure that Carole has not actually been raped (in the course of the film, at any rate), in *Rosemary's Baby* it is only the details of the rape that are ambiguous, for it is diegetically certain that she has been raped by someone and this has likely resulted in her pregnancy.

At the risk of lapsing into amateur psychoanalysis, it is worth highlighting the various means by which the rape sequence can be interpreted in a feminist context. It could be argued that as a way of dealing with the fact that she has been raped by her husband (which she accepts as true at the time) and his subsequent attempt to normalise the event, Rosemary psychologically recasts Guy in the role of Satan, an extension of her own guilt for having abandoned Catholicism. Rosemary's religious upbringing is portrayed as a lingering issue, not only in the way that she cannot bring herself to criticise the Pope (notwithstanding her own professed agnosticism) but also in the way that her residual Catholic sense of identity is oneirically emphasised in the images of the nuns who educated Rosemary as a child, as well as the various images of the Vatican and the Pope. The presence of the Kennedys is another indicator of the Catholic 'colouring' of this sequence, especially in that they include Rosemary as an 'insider' on their yacht ('Catholics only'). It is also worth noting that the rape sequence and the suggestion that it results in the impregnation of Rosemary is itself an aggressive parody of the 'immaculate conception', the absolute veracity of which is so heavily emphasised in Catholicism. (Mary, of course, is not asked for her consent to being impregnated, but is simply informed of it.)

It is along these lines that much of the film can (alternatively) be understood. It is her repression of both her marital rape and the greater identity crisis in which she finds herself that fuels Rosemary's hallucinations and delusion, in which the elements that contribute to her crisis are reinterpreted ('recast') by way of Catholic mythology, and in turn represent a regression back to her childhood frameworks of reality. Hence, the ('protestant') husband who rapes her in her sleep is recast as the Devil, and the aged 'big city' neighbours become leaders of a coven of Upper West Side Satanists (much reminiscent of *The Seventh Victim* [M. Robson, 1943]); these are examples of extremely 'Catholicised' distorted beliefs and perceptions indicative of grandiose delusions. It must be emphasised, however, that whilst the attribution of the content of Rosemary's hallucinations and resulting delusions are tied to her upbringing, this is not meant to imply *causation*. The cause of her psychosis remains ambiguous, but the 'colouring' of her crisis does seem to be informed by these childhood experiences and her gendered identity, which are the frameworks into which her distorted perceptual mechanism seems to have retreated as the result of her psychosis.

There are actually an abundance of small 'clues' scattered throughout the film that either effectively counter Rosemary's beliefs (suggesting that she is in fact, delusional) or can be argued to have served as 'source' material for her non-veridical (hallucinatory or oneiric) perceptions and subsequent delusions. Occurrences like the quip that Guy makes when he gets a role due to another actor's tragic ailment ('Hell of a way to get it') and the discussion between Guy and Roman about 'initial breaks' subconsciously unite to suggest a Faustian pact. The name of the root (or mould) in Rosemary's charm, 'Tanis', is a phonetic anagram for Satan. The herbs grown by Mrs Gardenia and Minnie, and even Minnie's jocular rhyme, 'Snips and Snails and Puppy Dog Tails', are all evocative of antiquated notions of witchcraft.

There are many more such tiny examples that could all be argued to 'colour' Rosemary's delusions and non-veridical perceptions, but most significant perhaps is the influence of Hutch, a writer of boys' adventure stories, who relishes in sharing with Rosemary his encyclopaedic knowledge of the Bramford's grizzly past, which seems to be the information that feeds Rosemary's delusions above all. But what are we to make of the appearance of a young Roman Castevet in the witchcraft book[3] Hutch gives Rosemary? In the book, Roman is called Steven Marcato, son of the notorious Bramford witch, Adrian Marcato, killed by a mob outside the building.[4] Rosemary's de-codification of 'Roman Castevet' as being an anagram for 'Steven Marcato' certainly seems to resolve the issue of Rosemary's sanity, but again this 'certainty' does not last long; as both Guy and Dr Sapirstein (Ralph Bellamy) quite reasonably point out, Roman's father may well have been a 'nut', and thus his desire to change his name.

We can also look at Rosemary's crisis of 'self-actualisation' (a higher state of personal 'awareness' than that of *self-consciousness*, which I discussed in Chapter 3) in terms of the transition from childhood to adulthood, in which, according to Maslow's trajectory, the dependence on others to define one's identity is replaced by autonomous identification (see Maslow, 1974). Embroiled in this struggle is of course her role as Guy's wife, which itself entails a prescribed identity to which she must conform; this role is a variation on the conceptual framework with which she was brought up, but is still consistent with the idea of a framework being imposed on her rather than self-generated, positioning the role of wife as similar to that of a child. This element of Rosemary's crisis is actually two-fold: on the one hand, she is forced to reject many of the conceptual frameworks imposed on her by her parents, most obviously that of her Catholic identity, not only in order to meet her husband's 'requirements', but also those of her new environment (as represented by the Castevets); on the other hand, Rosemary is also struggling with her own desire for self-actualisation, a framework of being-in-the-world that is self-determined, not one imposed by either her parents or her husband. Rosemary's own 'schizoid' sense of identity is reflected in the names she considers giving her unborn child. Whilst the 'boy' name remains consistent ('Andy'), there is a new 'girl' name every time she mentions it, changing from Susan to Sara to Jenny.

Notably, Rosemary is supported in this struggle by her group of female friends, who gather around her as her crisis takes hold and physically block her husband from intervening. The scene, which takes place in Rosemary's kitchen, is reminiscent of (or arguably foreshadowed by) the knitting circle we saw earlier, but with a group of younger women replacing the geriatrics. The scene occurs during their party for Rosemary and Guy's 'young' friends, and seems, at least with the luxury of retrospect, to be an allusion to the late 1960s' feminist movement.

Although made in 1968, a year in which New York City saw a series of anti-war protests, there is no indication of these events in *Rosemary's Baby*, as it is notably set two years *prior* to the time of its release, taking place from the summer of 1965 to the summer of 1966. Notwithstanding the chronological proximity of the time of its setting and the time of its filming and release, Polanski claims to have taken great care to 're-create the specific mood and atmosphere of the year in which the action took place' (1984: 249), ensuring that costume design and hair styles (Rosemary's Vidal Sassoon haircut in particular) were all in keeping with the trends of 1965 and 1966. Another touch, the iconic cover of *Time Magazine* that read 'Is God Dead?' (published in April, 1966, the exact time Rosemary visits her doctor) heightens the sense of chronological verisimilitude as well as adding a 'highly topical allusion' (249) to the film. The most relevant historical reference, of course, is the mention of Pope Paul VI's appearance at Yankee Stadium in October 1965, which Rosemary and Guy watch on TV, and which later greatly colours Rosemary's hallucinations. The inclusion of details such as these would leave no doubt in the mind of first-run audiences that the diegesis was not intended to be contemporary, but was deliberately set in the recent past.

Whilst there is no direct mention of politics in the film, the 1963 assassination of John F. Kennedy, a fellow Catholic, is still very much on Rosemary's mind, coming to the fore in her dreams and/or hallucinations (depending on how these perceptions are interpreted). Even more apparent is *Rosemary's Baby*'s focus on the psychological struggle of a young woman, which is also very reflective of the mid-1960s, the short era just after the release of Betty Friedan's *The Feminine Mystique* (1963), but before her founding of the National Organisation of Woman (NOW). In fact, the birth of the child in *Rosemary's Baby* actually takes place on the eve of the official founding of NOW at the end of June, 1966.

A key issue that women such as Friedan were championing at this time was the battle against a patriarchal order that 'forced them into home-bound vicarious lives' (Cullen-DuPont, 2000: 93), arguably the very predicament that Rosemary finds herself in. In contrast to many of the women of the Swinging London films I discussed earlier, Rosemary is not a 'single girl' finding her way (*herself*) in the big city; she has already been there for some time, has found a husband and is now 'settling down' in an aspirational (family) home. Rosemary seems quite contented with her role as a 'house-wife' (with an eye towards motherhood) at the start of the film, but this serenity is soon threatened. Her trajectory towards despair and even psychosis can be read to parallel the psychological stress, even cognitive dissonance, many women of her age must have felt; raised to become a mother and wife, women like Rosemary were now hearing from increasingly vocal social critics like Friedan, who were evolving the agenda put forth by the suffragettes of the generation before (and others) and very publicly denouncing the very framework of the family, as it was conceived, for its inherent subjugation of women. As I discuss below, Rosemary becomes increasingly aware, but perhaps only subconsciously, of a pressure to become self-actualised, an identity crisis that is played out in the form of an interconnected perceptual crisis.

Also highly relevant here is the criticism of the chauvinism in the parturition business offered by Rosemary's friends, an issue that persists to this day. When Rosemary restates these criticisms to Guy, he takes the side of Dr Sapirstein, echoing the misogynistic system of male collusion in the birthing industry, a criticism often raised by the midwifery movement. As Fischer (1992) discusses, it is Minnie Castevet who caricatures the traditional role of the midwife, a figure that is itself historically associated with witchcraft, but which has now been 'reclaimed' by feminists. 'Like the ancient midwife', writes Fischer, 'she must transfer her power to the male physician … who, nonetheless, relies on her expertise' (8). The events of the film prove to further emphasise this critique, especially evident in the scene of forced injection (another rape), and the coarse manner in which Guy and Sapirstein deliver the news of the death of the baby to Rosemary. Sapirstein even echoes the condemnation of home births typical of his field ('At the hospital I would have been able to do something about it – but you wouldn't listen'), and thus places the blame on Rosemary for the death of the child.

Guy's treatment of Rosemary seems remarkably 'old school', especially from a twenty-first century perspective. There is no question whatsoever of Rosemary finding a job, for example, and both her and Guy's roles are clearly delineated by gender. Even the morning after the rape, Guy 'playfully' commands Rosemary to make him breakfast, but there is no doubt that he means it; and when the decision is made to have a baby, it is Guy who allows (indeed, *commands*) Rosemary to get pregnant. Such behaviour, however, would not have been incongruent with the mores of America in the mid-1960s, as at this time neither feminism nor the greater liberal movement had taken hold of the country to the extent that popular mythologies of 'the sixties' might lead us to believe. Whilst musicians like Hendrix, Joplin and The Grateful Dead, and books such as *The Feminine Mystique*, Leary's *The Psychedelic Experience* (1964) and Masters and Johnson's *Human Sexual Response* (1966) may be well remembered today, the 'silent majority', as Nixon famously referred to it in 1969 (Heineman, 2009: 79), was becoming increasingly intolerant of radical new attitudes towards race, war, drugs, sex and women's rights. So whilst America in the 1960s may be remembered for its 'flower power', race-riots, feminism and the anti-war movement, there was also a growing backlash against liberalism because of the increased public awareness of ghetto rioting, marijuana use and violent protesting, which the liberals were perceived to be soft on (Matusow, 2009: xv). The tenacity of this conservative attitude is embedded in the subtext of *Rosemary's Baby*.

Rosemary does try to mount a subtle, but significant, resistance to her prescribed identity; an act that again reflects the embryonic women's movement. There is a covert power struggle between Rosemary and Guy in which she tends to exert her will in whatever small way she can. The scene at the dinner table where they bicker over Minnie's chocolate mousse is a good example of this struggle, where Rosemary 'tricks' Guy into thinking he is getting his way. (It is interesting that the mousse, or 'mouse', would figure so significantly in the following sequence.) But what is perhaps the most explicit example of Rosemary's resistance to Guy's control is her Vidal Sassoon haircut, which she gets in her second trimester. Her new look simultaneously serves as an act of resistance and a visual manifestation of her post-adolescent identity struggle; the haircut is as much androgenising in its rejection of her role as female impersonator as it is infantilising in its reflection of her stunted self-actualisation.

Rosemary's more minor acts of resistance to Guy are eventually replaced by the seemingly impossible task of resisting a much larger version of the patriarchal order. Significantly, Rosemary is completely isolated in this task. She attempts to find support from Dr Hill (Charles Grodin), but is betrayed by another act of male collusion. She tries to call her friend Elise (Emmaline Henry), but her effort is stymied. The image of a heavily pregnant Rosemary walking down a New York street holding a suitcase in the middle of a heat wave punctuates her isolation. Rosemary is forced to utilise whatever weapons she has left in her arsenal. Once captured by Guy and Sapirstein, she resorts to dropping her bag in the lobby of the Bramford, causing the men to scramble to collect the mess. She dashes for the lift and takes hold of the old-fashioned lift controls. The image of the diminutive, although heavily pregnant, Rosemary wrestling with this giant machine, just as the image of her on the street, is highly symbolic of her lone (pre-NOW) struggle against patriarchy.

Having been both invaded and now impregnated, Rosemary has completely lost dominion over her own body to men, including to the 'man' growing inside her. We can push this corporeal motif further: just as we consider the flats she and her fellow Apartment Trilogy protagonists occupy as manifestations of these characters' neurological (or cranial) space, we can also reverse the scenario and consider Rosemary's own body as an occupied living space that is being taken over by a new tenant (an issue I will return to in the next case study, in which *The Tenant*'s Trelkovsky also believes himself to be pregnant).

Another feminist reading of the film's portrayal of Rosemary's psychosis emerges through an exploration of the way in which the film establishes her desire for a self-actualised identity as equivalent to psychosis. In order to assume the role imposed on her, Rosemary is forced into a schizophrenic state; highly elaborate and bizarre hallucinations and delusions are induced by the imposed nature of her identity and her inability to face or even understand her emotional reaction to marital rape. It is possible that Rosemary's inability to rationally face this appropriation of her body is due greatly to the lack of an established linguistic or conceptual framework to deal with such trauma at the time. We should keep in mind that, historically, the idea of 'spousal rape' was considered to be oxymoronic; it was not considered to be a crime in any part of the US until 1976, and it was not until 1993 that it was criminalised in all states (to this day, there are several states that still consider 'spousal rape' to be a lesser form of rape). It is therefore both unfair and unfounded to judge Rosemary's failure to overcome patriarchal control by today's standards, or even those of the year of its release. Lacking a greater framework through which she can comprehend the ills done to her, her conflicted emotions instead find expression through these bizarre delusions. In this sense, Rosemary's experiences in the film serve as manifestation of the truly radical departure from the widely accepted conceptual frameworks that her desire for self-actualisation (even the *idea* of self-actualisation) represents. What *Rosemary's Baby* explores is the idea that within the greater patriarchal conceptual framework, a woman's desire for an identity independent of this order (i.e. an *authentic* identity) is itself schizophrenic, that is to say, the desire for self-actualisation was so dissonant with the established 'reality' that the subject is diagnosed as delusional.

Rosemary's religious crisis also serves as social critique as it connects pre-self-actualised modes of thought with religious belief. The ambiguity surrounding whether or not Rosemary is delusional results in a provocative metaphor for the difficulty in shedding the conceptual frameworks imposed in childhood, especially those that are connected with one's personal sense of identity. Where certain mythical beliefs, such the belief in Father Christmas or the Tooth Fairy, are relatively easy to shed due to the inherent incompatibility of these myths with more dominant conceptual frameworks that are learned both didactically and through direct personal experience (with the laws of physics, for example), the often equally irrational beliefs associated with religious narratives are not as easily shed due greatly to the strongly imposed notion that one's religious affiliation – not one's predisposition to religiosity, but membership to a *specific* doctrine – is somehow *genetically* prescribed. So powerful is this notion that irrational belief structures, most of which would certainly qualify as delusions in any other context, are maintained in the face of a multifaith world in which religious narratives openly contradict each other, and in spite of overwhelming evidence that religious myths are just as spurious as our childhood belief in Father Christmas. Without reservation, I suggest that the portrayal of Satanists in *Rosemary's Baby*, and again later in *The Ninth Gate*, is an unapologetic attack on religion. The fact that Rosemary's inability to truly rid herself of her (parentally imposed) religious conceptual frameworks runs parallel to her inability to become a self-actualised personality (to 'grow up') is further evidence of this work's thinly concealed attack on religion. Catholicism seems to be the prime target here, especially when we consider this witches' coven as a caricature of the Church itself, which in turn reflects the Catholic binary that locks all notions of good and evil within its own narrative.

Reading and rereading the final scene

In *Rosemary's Baby*, diegetic reality, oneiric images and hallucinations are muddled to such an extreme that at times it becomes impossible for either the troubled protagonist or the confused spectator to distinguish between them. Ultimately, these represented acts of perception serve to challenge the very concept of attaining 'certainty' through the senses; they demonstrate the complex nature of perception in *both* the normally functioning and diseased mind, where competing perceptual hypotheses of what is, and what is not, often clash without resolution.

According to horror movie convention, the final scene of *Rosemary's Baby* should be the moment in the film where the various ambiguities are resolved and diegetic stability is re-established, a process which the horror genre tends to exploit to maximise shock value. This is the moment where a killer's identity is revealed, where the protagonist's worst fears are realised, and/or where his or her 'crazy' ideas are proven right. Whilst *Rosemary's Baby* does indeed seem to follow this latter pattern, there are many 'clues' scattered throughout the film and in this scene that suggest such a straightforward reading is in fact not as stable as it might first appear. In fact, the film's ending lends itself to an abundance of readings, all of which fall into two basic 'high-level' categories: either Rosemary is delusional or she is not. Irrespective of which way the last scene is read, however, it is unlikely to yield much satisfaction in terms of re-stabilising the diegesis.

So unsatisfied was writer Ray Bradbury with *Rosemary's Baby*'s ending ('I simply do not believe or accept the ending … Nonsense. Also: balderdash' [Bradbury, 1972: 149]) that he actually felt compelled to publish a new one. Bradbury, an undisputed master of the horror genre, re-envisions the film's ending in which Rosemary flees with the child and takes refuge in a Cathedral, where she begs God to take His 'son' back (reminding us that Satan, too, is God's son). Let us compare this to not only Polanski's ending, but Levin's as well. Levin is far less ambiguous than Polanski regarding the 'nature' of the child, whom he describes in great detail. Levin also describes Rosemary's thoughts when she sees the baby; she contemplates grabbing the child and fleeing, or even jumping through the window with him. Polanski takes the exact opposite strategy, both denying us direct visual access to the child (in contrast with Levin, whose text 'visualises' the child for us) and having Rosemary 'betray' our expectations of her. Where Levin seemingly confirms that the child is a supernatural monster, Polanski denies this certainty. Where Bradbury insists that Rosemary should champion the Christian cause, Polanski has her (either diegetically or as part of an elaborate wish-fulfilling delusion, depending on one's reading of the scene) dismiss what remain of her religious convictions in favour of her natural instinct to mother the child come what may (although, it should be said, the 'Satanic' elements of this scene are still very much consistent with a Catholic conceptual framework).

The vitriolic nature of Bradbury's reaction to the ending of the film highlights just how 'dissatisfying' Polanski's endings tend to be; a quality that sometimes results in a mixed reception of his films. Generic expectations are toyed with, but, as we see in *Rosemary's Baby*, are ultimately sabotaged by narrative swerves that empty the films of 'meaning'. Satisfaction is indeed denied, but in its stead, for those willing, a hunger to explore the minutia of these works (these *worlds*) is ignited; in the process, the close reader engages with the philosophical discourse that these films put forth. We do not simply take on board what Polanski's cinema has to say, but are encouraged, to return to

Deleuze's notion, to 'speak along with' these films, not (just) 'about' them (Deleuze, 1989: 268). It is with this attitude that I approach *Rosemary's Baby*, especially the final scene.

The most common way of understanding this sequence is that which is most generically based. Here we assume that our protagonist cannot possibly be delusional, as convention dictates, and the ending simply confirms that she was right all along, irrespective of how insane her beliefs seemed to others. Two more possibilities stem from the 'high-level' assumption. First, it is of course possible, as Dr Hill himself suggests, that these are 'witches' in name only, but 'witches' who believe in their convictions so strongly that they do indeed pose a legitimate threat. The film actually offers no opposition to this reading, for there is no explicit moment in which the supernatural becomes a diegetic reality. Even the rape scene, in which we see what looks like a beast molesting Rosemary, can be explained by the same logic through which the image is profilmically understood, that is, it is a person dressed as the Devil. Similarly, the question of the appearance of the baby, which we are never shown (the eyes that the scene briefly cuts to are actually an image from the rape scene, not an image of what is in the cot), may well be the result of what these 'maniacs' have literally 'done to him', precisely the words Rosemary cries out when she first sees the child. In this reading, it is of course the witches who are delusional (unless, that is, their religious beliefs are officially 'recognised'), not Rosemary.

But there is a further possibility here, one in which the presence of the supernatural is an established diegetic reality. In this second type of reading, neither Rosemary nor the witches are delusional. The 'supernatural' scenario is actually the most simplistic, even most re-territorialising in terms of mental health in that the presence of a supernatural force (in this case, the Devil) takes the blame for the disruption to what we hold (hope) to be the natural order. In this reading, mental health and perception are re-established as robust elements, which whilst susceptible to interference from supernatural forces, can be protected from this through homage to the 'right' supernatural being. But even following this line, *Rosemary's Baby* does not provide any salvation through exorcism. Sides are chosen, and the Devil wins.

The other 'high level' way that the scene can be understood is one that is more in line with the perceptual discourse that most greatly informs these case studies. If we take up the film's challenge of 'diagnosing' Rosemary's behaviour, we need not be psychiatrists to see that there is much evidence to support an interpretation of her mental state as psychotic, her beliefs as delusional, and her strange perceptions as hallucinatory. Polanski provides little evidence in the film to diegetically confirm the reality of these events, and in fact provides many indications of the opposite, at every step offering alternative, logical explanations to counter Rosemary's 'paranoid' ideas. In terms of the final scene, however, the situation becomes even more complex, for it certainly does appear that these ideas are being diegetically confirmed. The counter-reading here is that at this point the camera, our notional observer, has become so closely connected to Rosemary's own ailing perceptual mechanism that it now 'sees' only through the filter of her psychosis.

Heightening the ambiguity of the film's diegetic reality is the fact that whilst Rosemary's behaviour is indeed highly 'diagnosable' as schizophrenic, the film also presents much evidence to the contrary. Rather than being consistently portrayed as suffering from a distorted perceptual mechanism, Rosemary is often presented as a highly effective perceiver, even a 'hyper perceiver' (a concept that figures greatly in my discussion of the second trilogy). Rosemary frequently notices small details missed by the other (male) characters. It is she that first notices the closet hidden behind Mrs Gardenia's wardrobe (a piece of furniture that figures prominently in many Polanski films, starting with *Two Men and a Wardrobe* [1958]), what would eventually prove to be a 'secret passageway' to the Castevets flat (or, as is also explained, the point at which these two flats used to be connected as a single home in a previous layout of the building). She also notices that Roman's ears are pierced, and that the Castevets seem to have taken down the paintings from their walls when Rosemary and Guy first visit them, which duly reappear in the form of Goya's 'Witches' Sabbath' and an image of a burning Church when Rosemary eventually manages to penetrate the membrane that divides the flats.

Whilst I do argue that embedded in *Rosemary's Baby* is evidence that supports a robust reading that suggests Rosemary is indeed experiencing a perceptual breakdown, it is admittedly difficult to 'diagnose' the nature of her mental illness with any degree of precision. Attempting too detailed a level of categorisation of her condition is in any case inappropriate given the limited information the fiction provides, and for this reason, I will limit my own 'diagnosis' to the cardinal symptoms of schizophrenia and the more general term 'psychosis', without attempting to establish the exact 'sub type' of her condition. Nevertheless, there are several details worth noting in Rosemary's behaviour that substantiate a more clinical attempt to 'stabilise' the film's diegetic reality.

As Fischer (1992) points out, Rosemary's psychosis can be understood as an exaggerated version of the protective stance adopted by women during pregnancy. Here Fischer is citing Leifer's (1980) findings that pregnant women often feel a pronounced sense of 'emotional liability' (9) and a resulting increased anxiety regarding the safety of the child. Whilst such anxiousness was dismissed as hysterical in the past, Leifer suggests that this heightened emotional state serves an evolutionary purpose in the development of the maternal bond (9). It becomes difficult to determine, however, at what point this 'useful' anxiety crosses the line of psychosis, which is precisely the line upon which *Rosemary's Baby* dances.

For the men of *Rosemary's Baby*, however, diagnoses come easily, much like the authoritative voices that re-territorialise psychosis in *Psycho* and *Peeping Tom*. But given what we have seen and our uncertainty as to the veridical nature of these bizarre images, we are not as trusting of these men. Rosemary's husband, Guy, tells her that Dr Sapirstein (her second obstetrician) believes her behaviour and delusions to be the result of 'pre-partum hysteria' (or 'pre-partum crazies', as Guy resorts to calling it). 'Hysteria' is itself a problematic term, as in the 1960s it was considered by some to be a purely female condition (e.g. Guze and Perley, 1963: 960). Whilst one might feel tempted to 'demonise' Sapirstein and dismiss his chauvinist diagnoses outright, it is worth noting that they are not without substance. Incidents of pre-partum psychosis had indeed been recorded around the time of the novel/film (e.g. Cross, Gee and Seymour-Shove, 1968: 686). Rosemary's behaviour is certainly diagnosable as that of a paranoid schizophrenic who takes what she believes to be quite rational action based on irrational beliefs. The fact that Rosemary's delusions have a religious colouring is also consistent with McKenna's (1997) identification of *grandiose religious delusions* (3) as symptomatic of schizophrenia (all the more relevant when one considers the very Catholic portrayal of urban Satanists encountered by Rosemary, and her own conflicting feelings about her religious upbringing) as well as several *sexual delusions* (4), in which both pregnancy and the belief in a 'fantasy lover' are common features.

One possible way of understanding the final scene along these lines (which the film seems to support) is by interpreting it as a sort of *Wunschtraum* ('wish-fulfilment dream') hallucination, which is heavily informed by the delusional conceptual framework Rosemary has cultivated over the course of the film, and which serves as a means for her to reverse the death of her child. Just before Rosemary ventures across to the Castevets' flat, she indeed experiences a 'classic' *Wunschtraum* in which she and her baby are surrounded by friends, and what is possibly Rosemary's family. The paler tones and muted sound in this image are strongly indicative of its non-veridical nature, and we have little trouble accepting it as oneiric.

The scene that follows this oneiric moment, in which Rosemary 'invades' the Castevets' flat, can be interpreted as a hallucinatory image that serves a similar function, but is essentially a wish-fulfilment scenario nestled within the logic of a greater delusion. We should also take note that in the days leading up to this 'invasion', Rosemary deliberately refused to take the pills prescribed to her by Dr Sapirstein, hiding them between the cinder blocks beside her bed. Here we have an inversion of the 'chocolate mouse' scenario, which begs a complex question: is the fact that Rosemary refuses to take her pills responsible for her 'clear' vision, or is it her refusal to take these pills that causes more hallucinations? This query is difficult to answer, but it is important to remember that Rosemary had originally believed that these 'witches' intended to use her baby as a sacrifice in a satanic ritual; identifying this fact allows for a non-conventional reading of the final scene.

By recalling the repressed (non-veridical) memory of being raped by the Devil, Rosemary is able to alter this reality by elevating her child from sacrificial lamb to the Antichrist himself; the scenario is highly reminiscent of Catholic lore in its direct inversion of the Nativity, which is also much in line with the film's savage parody of the 'immaculate conception'. The result of this 'altering' of reality is the fact that the baby is at least *alive*. This sequence has strong symbolic value as well, especially in the context of feminist discourse. To bring her baby back to life, Rosemary must join the patriarchal order represented here not by her husband, but more so by Roman Castevet, who replaces the Pope as the highest patriarch. But whilst Rosemary exacts a small degree of revenge on Guy by spitting in his face, she ultimately does yield to his whim. Seemingly unable to reconcile her role of mother and her resistance to patriarchal control, her maternal instincts force her to succumb to the will of the order.

The trauma of pregnancy or just post-traumatic?

My intention here is not to negate a reading of *Rosemary's Baby* that focuses on the trauma of pregnancy, which, as Fischer demonstrates, is 'fecund' ground for discourse. Having taken such readings into consideration, I wish to suggest that *Rosemary's Baby* may be even more polemical than many have realised. As I have attempted here, through a close reading of *Rosemary's Baby* that accepts the possibility of Rosemary's psychosis, we can interpret the film's trauma not only in the context of the complex psychology of childbearing, but also in terms of its exploration of female identity crises and the aftermath of sexual abuse, in which case the pregnancy and its associated paranoid behaviour serve as a manifestation of the repressed impact of spousal rape. However, if we identify Rosemary's delusions and hallucinations as being the direct result of a repressed personal trauma, we must reconsider the diagnosis of Rosemary's behaviour as *schizophrenic*, and instead consider the possibility that she is experiencing a (schizophrenia-like) *post-traumatic* psychosis.

As identified by Boehnlein and Kinzie (1989), the diagnosis of 'schizophrenia' to those also diagnosed as sufferers of post-traumatic stress disorder is complex and controversial. In such cases, as well as drug-related psychosis (which is also relevant here) expressions such as 'schizophrenia-like' or 'reactive psychosis' are often employed as a means of distinguishing these conditions from schizophrenia, a condition in which a 'cause' is not so readily identifiable. The important distinction in relation to my overall discussion again relates back to the notion of 're-territorialising' mental illness through constructing robust economies of cause-and-effect. My own 'post-traumatic' reading outlined above falls into this category. The chief problem presented by *Rosemary's Baby* is that whilst it furnishes many possible readings, it also subverts attempts to stabilise the diegesis by thwarting efforts at proving the veridicality of Rosemary's perceptions, as well as undermining pathogenetic 'maps' created by readers who accept her perceptions as non-veridical.

Whilst I have outlined the various readings of *Rosemary's Baby* that emerge from a close consideration of the film in the context of the perceptual discourse at play in the Apartment Trilogy, try as I might, I am unable to provide anything resembling a conclusive reading of this complex film. Instead, as I have alluded to above, I believe the highest form of appreciation of *Rosemary's Baby* comes by way of befuddlement; we get the most from this film by embracing its ambiguity and all the frustration it entails. In the next case study I will explore the third of Polanski's apartment/schizophrenia-based films, *The Tenant*, a film whose presentation of psychosis is slightly less ambiguous than *Rosemary's Baby*, but which presents many other puzzling diegetic ambiguities. Looking forward, I will return to the 'unstable' philosophical territory of *Rosemary's Baby* in my discussion of *Death and the Maiden*, which is addressed later as part of the case study of *Frantic*.

Notes

1. If recognised at all, Cassavetes would have been identified as an avant-garde New York director.
2. A reading reflected by the hundreds of plot summaries of *Rosemary's Baby* readily available online and in most of the Polanski-based literature.
3. *All of Them Witches* – a title that sounds like a pronouncement from the Spanish Inquisition or Salem witch hunters, and the very words muttered by Rosemary at the peak of her crisis.
4. 'Outside the Bramford' was also where Terry's body was found. (In a horrible coincidence, twenty-two years after the film's release, this is also where John Lennon was murdered.)

Chapter 6

The Tenant

Paranoid in Paris

The Tenant is not only the last of Polanski's 'Apartment Trilogy', but it is also the last of Polanski's films in which an attempt is made to represent the subjective psychological realm of an individual on-screen. Although released after *Chinatown*, a film that I will later discuss in terms of Polanski's shift towards a more 'distant' form of realism, *The Tenant* marks the end of his cinema's more 'direct' form of psychological realism. As in both *Repulsion* and *Rosemary's Baby*, here Polanski keeps the camera closely tethered to a single subject. The camera follows the inquiring gaze of a nominal (invisible and ineffectual) observer, which ('who') guides the gaze of the spectator through the course of the film; and again, as in both *Repulsion* and *Rosemary's Baby*, *The Tenant*'s 'observer' attempts to access the perceptual experiences of its subject, allowing (at times, forcing) the spectator to share his perceptual crises.

The Tenant established the Apartment Trilogy as a 'tale of three cities', moving the story of urban psychosis from London (*Repulsion*) and New York (*Rosemary's Baby*) to a third major Western metropolis, Paris. It tells the story of Trelkovsky, who, in his desperation to find a living space, finds himself occupying a flat in which the former tenant has left strong traces, or 'haunting signifiers' (as Marciniak puts it, 2000: 6) of her identity. Like Carole in *Repulsion*, Trelkovsky is a more clearly delineated 'accented' persona. The character, played by Polanski himself, is a naturalised French citizen[1]; and whilst Trelkovsky's French is flawless, his (presumably, but not necessarily) Polish heritage is betrayed by his accent[2] and his name.

Just as *Rosemary's Baby* marks an evolution in Polanski's cinematic treatment of psychosis, so too does *The Tenant* furnish a variation on this theme. In *Repulsion*, we bear witness to Carole's developing psychosis, a more or less linear trajectory that results in outright negative catatonia by the end of the film. In *Rosemary's Baby*, the very existence of Rosemary's psychosis is put in doubt and never clarified, so we are robbed of the 'safety net' provided by the more straightforward portrayal of Carole's illness in *Repulsion*. In *The Tenant*, the diegetic reality of Trelkovsky's illness is not as muddled as it is in *Rosemary's Baby*; instead, it is the pathogenesis of his behaviour that becomes questionable as the 'neighbours' are implicated in the trajectory of his crisis, although the extent of their tort or ill-intent remains ambiguous. What differentiates *The Tenant* most dramatically from *Repulsion* is the fact that the power of Trelkovsky's schizophrenia to control his perception and resulting behaviour does not develop entirely linearly, but varies as Trelkovsky puts up a strong fight. Trelkovsky's battle with his illness is manifested most clearly in those moments when he is presented as a double-being: the female/'Simon Choule' masquerade represents his growing schizophrenia, whilst the 'Trelkovsky' voice from within this body manifests his enduring vestiges of sanity.

As in *Rosemary's Baby*, *The Tenant* begins with its protagonist viewing a flat; this time, however, it is not an aspirational high-end apartment, but a much more humble abode (not much more than a room with a sink and a view of the shared toilet, located inconveniently across the courtyard); humble as it may be, even such a flat would have been much sought after in Paris in the mid-1970s. But in spite of its meagre facilities, paying for this flat is still an issue for Trelkovsky, who struggles to keep up with the various deposits and bribes needed to secure it. Also much like *Rosemary's Baby*, the flat becomes available due to the injury and eventual death of its previous tenant, but where Rosemary is assured that Mrs Gardenia did not die in the apartment, the concierge seems to relish in telling Trelkovsky that Simone Choule, the flat's former inhabitant, defenestrated herself (a major Polanskian hallmark that is also present in *Rosemary's Baby*), even nudging him towards the very window she leapt from to get a better look at the damage her body inflicted on the glass eaves below.

Where *Repulsion* was based on an original script written by Polanski and his collaborator Gérard Brach, *The Tenant*, like *Rosemary's Baby*, is based on a novel, this time one written by the surrealist Roland Topor. As I discussed previously, upon first reading *Rosemary's Baby*, Polanski believed that Ira Levin had been influenced by *Repulsion* (see Cronin, 2005: 23); it is possible the same is true in this case. Topor's *The Tenant* was released just after *Repulsion*, and like Levin's *Rosemary's Baby*, it shares much common ground with this film. The major issue of the exploration of a perceptual crisis in an apartment setting is of course the most apparent similarity, but even smaller details, such as the 'accented' protagonist, the nosey neighbours, and even the small dog, are all present in Polanski's *Repulsion*. Topor also includes a detailed description in which Trelkovsky alternatively closes each of his eyes and marvels at the way the objects in his room 'shift' from left to right (Topor, 2006: 115), which is highly reminiscent of the similar scene in *Knife in the Water* discussed in this book's introduction.[3] Granted, it is difficult, even fruitless, to attempt to solve the mystery of 'who-influenced-whom'; it is far more relevant to simply highlight that Roman Polanski, Ira Levin and Roland Topor all seemed to be on the same wavelength, each an artist exploring urban existential angst. The fact that Polanski chose to adapt these works is therefore unsurprising, as they provided (more-or-less) ready-made stories through which his own ongoing perceptual discourse could find cinematic expression.

As a means of opening *The Tenant*, Polanski employs the 'floating' ('untethered') camera he used for the final scene in *Repulsion* and at both the start and the end of *Rosemary's Baby*. The same technique is utilised at the conclusion of *Chinatown* (discussed in the next case study) as a means of disconnecting the nominal observer from protagonist Jake Gittes and recoiling from the carnage it witnesses at the end of the film. Polanski's 'observer' seems now to have made its way to Paris, in search of a new story, a new tethering point. But *The Tenant* begins with the camera exploring not the horizontal plane of a cityscape as it does in *Rosemary's Baby* (and for that matter, Hitchcock's *Psycho*), but rather the vertical intricacies of the organically stacked and interwoven living spaces of a Parisian block of flats. Whilst Polanski often uses elaborate forms of cinematography, *The Tenant*'s opening shot is one of his most complex, and certainly the most self-conscious; this is a quality that is greatly defused, however, by the fact that it occurs during the opening credits, and therefore still within a diegetically ambiguous plane of reality. The shot proves to be only one of *The Tenant*'s several examples of complex cinematography that Polanski created with the help of regular Bergman-collaborator Sven Nykvist in Épinay studio. The other shots, however, whilst perhaps equally intricate, are subtler than the opening scene (insidiously so, as I will discuss further on).

In what is essentially a single, fluid shot, the camera explores the building without regard to gravity, coming across a series of enigmatic images of a man and woman swapping places in various window frames. Upon repeated viewing, it becomes apparent that the camera is actually 'seeing' the narrative as a whole, mapping the events of the film, themselves a repetition of the events that take place *before* the time of the film. The camera finally settles on its tethering point, Trelkovsky, who, much like Guy and Rosemary Woodhouse before him, is house hunting. At this point (i.e. the conclusion of the opening credits), the style shifts to a more conventional form of temporal and spatial unity, as it becomes 'tied down' or 'tethered' to Trelkovsky, thus encouraging an understanding of the film to come as what Deleuze refers to as a stable 'movement-image' (Deleuze, 1986: 2). In the end, however, the temporal unity of this image crumbles. As hinted at in the opening credits, the film ultimately gravitates towards a direct representation of time, a 'crystalline' narrative structure (Coleman, 2005: 59; Deleuze, 1989: 66) in which the realties of time and place (and person) are superimposed to reflect the infinite loop caused by the film's corruption of its previously established 'movement-image', arguably propelling it towards what Deleuze defines as the 'time-image' (Deleuze, 1989: 40) and a subsequent 'crisis' in spectatorship.

Reading ambiguity

Much like *Rosemary's Baby*, *The Tenant* is a rich and complex film-text that lends itself to a wide variety of often-contradictory readings, each of which is as 'robust' as the next due to the crafty ambiguity of the film. Whilst my primary objective here is to demonstrate how Polanski uses carefully constructed profilmic elements to distort the spectator's perception of the screen image, it is useful to draw from Williams's (1982) and Marciniak's (2000) compelling psychoanalytical and sociological readings of *The Tenant* as a means of teasing out my own cognitive/perceptual analysis.

Marciniak (2000) confidently emphasises the relevance of both Trelkovsky and Choule's status as marginalised figures as a means of reading *The Tenant* as an exposé of French xenophobia (and possibly Anti-Semitism), calling the film a 'passionate critique of phobic nationalism' (3). She argues that Trelkovsky's belief that he is being transformed has a diegetically veridical basis due to the frequent associations made by the films' other characters between him and Simone Choule. His neighbours do indeed often evoke her name, nudging Trelkovsky (sometimes literally) towards her behaviours. Monsieur Zy (Melvyn Douglas), for example, points out to Trelkovsky that Simone wore slippers after 10 pm. 'It was much more comfortable for her; and for the neighbours', he hints to Trelkovsky. The barman across the street is perhaps the worst offender in the way he consistently serves Trelkovsky Choule's favourite drink and cigarettes, irrespective of what Trelkovsky orders.

The problem posed by the film, however, is that such occurrences ultimately do not stand firm as 'evidence' of anything. We must consider two important factors here. Firstly, the possibility that the close tether established between the camera and Trelkovsky extends to the montage of the film, not so much in style or pace, but what is and what is not included in the cut. I suggest that the frequency of these 'nudging' associations is not part of any attempt to objectively represent the greater diegetic reality, but form a series of highly subjective, selected images that reflect the preoccupations of the character to whom we are tethered; hence, the occurrences of what appear to be 'nudges' are read as 'proof' of Trelkovsky's fundamental sanity not due to their inherent meaningfulness, but because of their tenacity. Marciniak in fact goes so far as to identify Trelkovsky's perception not as diseased, but highly *attuned*, establishing him as a hyper-perceiver who is punished for recognising and challenging his marginalisation. She argues that Trelkovsky is effectively 'blinded by his own acute perception' (2000: 12), much in line with the horror movie convention in which a protagonist's heightened understanding of the diegetic reality is mistaken for madness, but is ultimately vindicated as having been 'right all along'. But there is no such vindication on offer here.

Based on the complexity and ambiguity of the film, both narratively and visually, we should also take seriously the possibility that Trelkovsky's delusions and hallucinations could in fact be the result of serious mental illness. If this is accepted, schizophrenia is a plausible diagnosis given the symptoms we are privy to, keeping in mind that this is an illness that exists irrespective of the actions of a group of xenophobic geriatrics. The likelihood that Trelkovsky is suffering from some form of mental illness is an important factor that should inform any analysis of *The Tenant*, in particular, perhaps, because of the way this portrayal of psychosis confounds straightforward notions of 'victims' and 'villains'.

For Williams (1981), it is Trelkovsky's guilt over wishing for Choule's death (68) that causes his behaviour. Although Williams concedes that the film robs the spectator of a rational 'voice' within the film that explains the cause of Trelkovsky's condition (66), her attribution of Trelkovsky's delusions and hallucinations to his repressed guilt itself proposes a psychodynamic pathogenesis for Trelkovsky's schizophrenia. Alternatively, if Trelkovsky is indeed diagnosed as schizophrenic, rather than considering the specific details of his delusions and non-veridical perceptions as *causes* of his diseased perceptual mechanism, the various stressors implicit in the situation in which he finds himself can be argued to be informing agents; they are 'loaded' stimuli there to be distorted, exaggerated or even completely misread. This is not to suggest, however, that Trelkovsky's guilt (unconscious or otherwise) and the possibility that the neighbours are xenophobic (at least in its etymological sense of *fear* of difference, rather than its more colloquial use as *hatred* of difference) are irrelevant.

By allowing the spectators access to information slightly beyond Trelkovsky's subjective (and distorted) narrative reach, the film avoids establishing a diegetically certain causal link between either Trelkovsky's guilt or his neighbour's xenophobia and the protagonist's psychotic behaviour. Consequently, the film encourages us to consider the possibility that it is Trelkovsky's schizophrenia, a condition without a certain pathogenesis, that causes these delusions, which are only tenuously connected to diegetic reality. But I argue that it is the spectator's (and critic's) desire to re-territorialise the truly horrific reality of the possible arbitrariness of schizophrenia that provokes us into embracing psychodynamic readings; and whilst the film does indeed seem to support such readings, there is always doubt and ambiguity embedded in the 'reasons' the film furnishes for Trelkovsky's behaviour, rendering any attempt to stabilise this diegesis problematic.

Notwithstanding my call for a more 'clinical' reading of *The Tenant*, it would be admittedly remiss to conclude that Polanski's consistent coupling of marginalised bodies (in particular that of the nationally 'foreign' or 'accented' body, homosexuals, and women) and psychosis is simply arbitrary. As both Williams and Marciniak demonstrate, *The Tenant* rewards readings that make such connections, in turn establishing *The Tenant* as a work capable of generating a huge range of valuable discourse. My own argument regarding Polanski's cinematic presentation of psychosis in this film (and the same holds true of both *Repulsion* and *Rosemary's Baby*) is that any overly conclusive reading risks grafting didactic intent on what is essentially a philosophically (although not entirely visually) open text. With this risk acknowledged, I will not let this stop me from expressing my own understanding of *The Tenant*, a film that I believe augments its horror not only by destabilising its diegesis, but also by rendering problematic the identification of antecedent and/or environmental factors as causes of schizophrenia, as well as by provoking the spectator (in particular the close reader) to reflect on how this syndrome reveals the often counter-intuitive workings of healthy perception.

Using illusion

In the introductory chapter, I delineated a number of 'planes' of cinema-related reality that need to be distinguished from each other in this discussion (afilmic, diegetic, profilmic, filmophanic, spectatorial). Equally, there are also several 'types' of cinematic *realism* that populate film theory, many of which are relevant to this discussion, but none more so than that which can be identified as a cinematic form of psychological, or to be more precise, *perceptual* realism. Keeping this in mind, I will now turn my attention towards the manner in which Polanski orchestrates *mise-en-scène* in some of *The Tenant's* key scenes so as to render the line between representation and 'original' inconsequential. Here I will abandon for a moment my analysis of the diegesis itself and direct my focus specifically to the spectatorial experience of perceiving these scenes.

Helpful in the consideration of perceptual realism and the spectatorial plane of reality is Baudrillard's concept of 'weightlessness' in art, in which each plane of reality upon which a work resides is 'neutralised' to leave only 'pure simulacrum' (1983: 10). In her discussion of simulacrum and the 'replicants' of *Blade Runner* (Scott, 1982), Bruno (1987) engages with Baudrillard's notion of the postmodern as an age of 'simulacra and simulation' (67), in turn addressing the goal of achieving a perpetually 'original' artefact, the 'hyper-real', in which the question of representation is rendered completely moot due to the fact that the work itself is not merely a representation of afilmic or profilmic reality, but rather a reality in and of itself (68). Conversely, the reality of imitation also points to the 'fiction of the real' (67), compelling us to consider the relationship between reality and our perception of it (and in turn the phenomenological pursuit of describing the reality of perception itself). Polanski's own discussion of his desire to achieve a 'wraparound effect' can be understood along these lines, namely his deliberate efforts to construct profilmic illusions that evoke a specific spectatorial perceptual effect, not a representation of something, but an original, and purely cinematic effect 'in the moment'.

Notwithstanding the inherently illusory nature of cinematic simulacra, the cinematographic image remains an object of perception, and so the tenets of active perception are still applicable. Gregory's discussion of the 'intriguing discrepancies' (2003) between knowledge of objects and what is actually seen is often reflected in Polanski's Apartment Trilogy, especially when the nominal observer who directs our gaze seems to be granted 'access' to, or perhaps more accurately, *mimics* the subjective realm of the on-screen perceiver. In *The Tenant*, Gregory's influence is evident in Polanski's use of optical illusion as a means of manifesting Trelkovsky's distorted sense of perspectival space, and it is through this deliberate creation of filmophanic 'phenomenal phenomena' (i.e. illusions, see Gregory, 1997a: 246) that Polanski also manages to introduce non-veridical perceptual experiences into the spectatorial experience (beyond, of course, the inherently non-veridical/illusory nature of cinematic 'movement'). These moments are not merely aesthetic flourishes, however, as they also serve a narrative purpose in that they represent the perceptual distortions experienced by Trelkovsky.

In one scene, the fever-stricken Trelkovsky reaches from his bed for a glass of water, which sits upon a normal looking chair beside him. As he does so, his hand is met by a completely flat surface. We realise that the bottle sitting on the chair is not, as we imagined, a three dimensional object, but rather a *photo* of one.[4] The moment is disturbing not only for Trelkovsky, but for the spectator as well, who has been perceptually duped. It is important to emphasise that whilst we are 'tricked', this is not the same as having a defective perceptual mechanism. Polanski's use of visual illusion in this scene draws attention to the gap between the way we perceive a thing and its own independent reality. Without breaking the fourth wall, Polanski addresses both the nature of the image and our perception of it. The scene effectively achieves a heightened sense of perceptual realism by moving past the retina and engaging the brain directly through its provoking of a non-veridical perception embedded, as it is, within the even greater illusion of the cinematic image itself. The theory of active perception reminds us, however, that we must take care not to confuse our perception of an object with the nature of said object, nor should we conclude that due to the limits of our biology an object's material nature is actually negotiable simply due to the fact that our perception of it can vary.

It is worth recalling here my previous mention of Cavell's comments regarding the photograph and its inability to disguise its own true nature as representation (see opening chapter and Cavell, 1971: 19–20). Polanski seems to be toying with this very concept in this scene through his 'containing' of a photograph within another, and thus achieving, rather fiendishly, exactly the illusion of 'reality' Cavell claims is so elusive (specifically compared to the truly convincing nature of sound reproduction). The craftiness of Polanski's deception here is down to the double-illusion of embedding the photographic illusion within the diegetic plane of reality, thus augmenting the potential for the filmophanic image (i.e. the light as it is reflected off the cinematic screen) to disguise itself, to distract us from our awareness of the greater frame. This is not to claim, however, an absolute victory for the visual 'wraparound' effect tantamount to that which can be achieved by sound, but rather to suggest that here Polanski creates a 'moment' of perceptual realism through this attempt to engage (*manipulate*) the perceptual mechanism directly by taking advantage of its limits.

In his discussion of optical illusion, Gregory pays special attention to the Ames Room, pointing to this bizarre structure as evidence of the ease with which the brain can be fooled into misinterpreting the visual stimuli it has presented to it. The Ames Room's 'distorted room and trapezoid window' (Gregory, 1997a: 186) is specifically designed to provide false depth cues to the brain (via the eye, which is itself indifferent) through the use of exaggerated convergent angles and proportionately smaller-sized objects to give the impression of much greater depth. Viewing the room straight on, it is impossible to see the correct dimensions of the structure, especially if the proportions of the decorations (wallpaper patterns, shape of the windows) are measured (and distorted) specifically to create the effect. Depending on the design of the room, people in it can be made to look shrunken or gigantic, seriously confusing the perceptual expectations of observers. The theory behind the Ames Room illusion is that the brain's knowledge of rooms 'defeats' its knowledge of what the size of the people in the room should be compared to its fixtures or other objects (or people) in the room. The effect proves that depth is experienced not entirely due to the distance of objects stereoscopically viewed, but conceptual understanding of them; our knowledge of the shape of rooms trumps the 'misshaped' structure before us, thus imposing a perception of the structure that corresponds to what we believe a normal room shape should be.

The use of the Ames Room and other forms of perspective tampering in cinema has, of course, a long history. The technique is indeed a hallmark of low-budget monster films, where forced perspective provided a means of presenting what appear to be giants on-screen. Even in the digital age of the early twenty-first century, the rather low-tech method of using misshaped rooms to either enlarge or diminish on-screen bodies still perseveres, used frequently, for example, in both the *Lord of the Rings* and *Harry Potter* series. But the end towards which Polanski employs this device in *The Tenant* is quite different; rather than attempting to convince the spectator of the strange dimensions of certain mythological beings (monsters, half-giants, hobbits, etc.), Polanski unveils the distortions as a way of highlighting the relative malleability of perception, in particular the effect that heightened emotions or outright mental illness can have on how the brain interprets stimuli.

As in *Repulsion*, Polanski uses a type of Ames Room in *The Tenant* to further punctuate Trelkovsky's disturbed mental state. In *The Tenant*, however, the effect is augmented by the fact that Trelkovsky actually enters the room. The room itself was constructed with meticulous attention to precision in collaboration with Polanski's set-designer Pierre Guffroy (1926–2010), based on the specific measurements needed to achieve this 'Ames' effect. In the sequence that immediately follows the 'chair' scene, Trelkovsky enters his flat and walks towards the window, the very trajectory of his eventual (double) defenestration. At first, the room appears to be perfectly normal, just as we have seen it previously (just as we *know* it). Much like the 'chair effect' we saw earlier, however, as Trelkovsky begins to penetrate the space its nature becomes distorted, thus compromising our 'stable' perception of the room by defying our sensory-motor expectations of the objects contained within it. As Trelkovsky walks forward, so too is the camera drawn forward to follow; but with every step his dimensions reduce compared to the objects that surround him, which seem to grow as Trelkovsky is increasingly 'dwarfed' by the room. The time it takes for him to reach the window is likewise extended, reflecting the now-increased length of his path. Considering Trelkovsky's own delusion of his diminishing identity, the 'dwarfing' effect of this scene serves as an apt visual metaphor for how he is being (or believes he is being) 'consumed' by the flat and the residual psychic energy of its former inhabitant.

Before moving on to discuss what the scene may reveal about Trelkovsky's mental state, I will again draw attention to the (extra-diegetic) effect of these scenes on the spectator. To summarise, what I believe to be of interest in these scenes is the manner in which Polanski creates an illusion, effectively an illusion-within-an-illusion, in order to simulate what appears to be a hallucinatory state in the film's protagonist. I am speaking here not so much of the *representation* of psychotic perception, but the use of illusion (beyond the inherently illusory nature of the cinematographic image itself, that is) to create a brief moment of perceptual crisis in the spectator, in which our own sensory expectations come under stress. The type of 'crisis' Polanski attempts to create with such illusions is therefore a combination of *direct cinematic affect* and *affective mimicry*. The term 'direct affect' is normally associated with pronounced cinematic stimuli that provoke an automatic response in the spectator, such as a loud noise or the natural threatening feeling we get when something rushes towards the screen (Plantinga, 2009: 114). The 'distortions' I discuss above are designed to provoke direct affect in the spectator as they elicit a (perceptual) response based on the composition of the image and the movement of the camera, and are constructed specifically with the spectator's perceptual experience in mind (just as a scene of a train rushing towards the camera would be). 'Affective mimicry', on the other hand, refers to the spectator's empathetic response to specifically human elements of the image (Plantinga, 2009: 114–115), and is normally associated with the natural instinct to 'mirror' the emotional state or the bodily movements of the characters we see on-screen (or for that matter, in real life); hence, we may feel sad when we see others weep or tense when we see them cling to the edge of a cliff for dear life. As I have suggested above, the scenes in which Polanski utilises illusions to create a perceptual crisis for the spectator (*direct affect*) also mimic Trelkovsky's state of mind (*affective mimicry*), and thus attempt to elicit a mirroring of his crisis through the evocation of our own.

The difficulty of diagnosis

As is typical in Polanski's cinema, and especially the Apartment Trilogy, the question of what is and what is not diegetically veridical is not clearly delineated, and even those events that are presented as unambiguously non-veridical have an uncertain origin. To reiterate a key point, it is not my intention here to furnish a robust diagnosis of Trelkovsky's condition, and nor do I hope to 'solve' the enigma of the film; by simply *attempting* to diagnose Trelkovsky's condition, however, I hope to demonstrate just how complex this enigma is, and how close engagement with this film stimulates thought on a variety of planes. Along these lines, let us consider the various complications surrounding Trelkovsky's (and our own) more bizarre perceptual experiences. These distorted perceptions, whilst indeed a documented symptom of schizophrenia (Chapman and McGhie, 1961), take place whilst Trelkovsky is in the throes of a high fever, leading us to conclude that he may just be suffering from temporary flu-induced hallucinations rather than a chronic mental illness. The conundrum is similar to that of *Rosemary's Baby*, where the spectator is left unsure if the rape sequence is a diegetic reality buried within a drug- (or alcohol-) induced hallucination, an alcohol-fuelled dream, a psychotic hallucination that conceals the rape of Rosemary by her husband, or some combination of the above. As I have argued in the previous case study, the closer one looks at *Rosemary's Baby* the more difficult this problem is to resolve; a similar statement can be made regarding *The Tenant*.

There is another way to approach these scenes in *The Tenant*, and that is to forego reading them in terms of diegetic realism and instead interpret them purely symbolically. Rather than wrestle with the issue as to whether these distortions of perception are flu-induced *or* the result of degenerative schizophrenia, we can see the image of the shivering Trelkovsky as a physical manifestation (a *hint* to the spectator) of a concealed mental illness, his skyrocketing temperature paralleling his increasingly diseased perceptual mechanism. However it is read, diagnosing Trelkovsky's condition is not straightforward.

Attempts to diagnose Trelkovsky are rendered further problematic due to the camera's own compromised objectivity in these and other scenes. *The Tenant* not only subverts any reading that leads to a clear explanation for either Trelkovsky's or the neighbours' actions, but also causes us to question the reliability of the source of our understanding of this world, namely the accuracy of both Trelkovsky's narrative reach and our notional observer's own ability to perceive this world effectively. For the vast majority of the film we are linked to Trelkovsky's vantage point, not necessarily by direct POV, but by being privileged only to the information that he is privy to. There are some key moments, however, where the camera maximises the limits of its subjective tether and proves itself to be less susceptible to the emotions that seem to cloud Trelkovsky's perception, establishing that his role as our perceptual guide is not absolute. It is only in these precious few moments in which we can be reasonably sure we are freed from the influence of Trelkovsky's subjective perceptions that we can hope to gain some understanding of the diegesis, or even entertain the idea of 'diagnosing' Trelkovsky's condition.

A small but significant example of our nominal observer's ability to 'out perceive' Trelkovsky occurs when he attempts to dispose of a vast quantity of rubbish he has collected from his flat the morning after his house-warming party. As he carries the trash down the stairs, several items fall from the overloaded and seeping bag. He glances at them, but seems to decide that it is better to continue to the rubbish bins outside and return to clean up the mess afterwards. When he does return, a mere thirty-seconds of real-time later, the mess has been cleared up. A mortified Trelkovsky looks about helplessly, wondering who has cleaned up after him.

A few seconds earlier, Trelkovsky spotted the concierge (who ignored his salutation) in her office, so the most likely conclusion for Trelkovsky to make is that *she* must have cleared up the mess on the stairs. For the first time in the film, though, we know better than he. As Trelkovsky was busy stuffing his trash into the bins outside, the camera momentarily pulls away to reveal the concierge glaring at him disapprovingly from her office, indicating to the spectator that she could not have cleared up the rubbish; so where Trelkovsky might speculate that the concierge has cleaned up his mess in an act of passive-aggression, this possibility is negated to us. Perhaps another neighbour? M. Zy? Frustratingly, the net effect of 'out perceiving' Trelkovsky is that we are left even *more* puzzled than he is about this incident.

Toles (1995) offers an interesting interpretation of this stairwell scene, and one that compliments my ongoing discussion on the manner in which the urban domestic structures in the Apartment Trilogy often become physical manifestations of psychological crises. In his analysis of cinematic depictions of humiliation, Toles argues that it is the stairwell itself that has 'repressed' the rubbish, 'so that its final neatness is visually superimposed on a "dirt" that is still there somehow, waiting for a chance to resurface' (7). The image of the overflowing paper bag that is unable to contain the putridity of its contents similarly reflects Trelkovsky's own 'filled-to-bursting inner state' (8). The fact that M. Zy, the obsessively observant, even totalitarian (from Trelkovsky's perspective, at any rate) landlord, comments on neither the leaking bag in Trelkovsky's arms nor the mess Trelkovsky has left on the stairs behind him is truly puzzling. Instead Zy scolds his tenant about the noise that came from his flat the night before; and whilst we may instinctively side with our 'victimised' protagonist, upon reflection, Zy's criticism is arguably quite reasonable, as is his manner, considering the racket Trelkovsky's friends made the night before, and thus (again) undoing any straightforward reading that positions Trelkovsky as a specific target of orchestrated (xenophobic) oppression.

Toles offers that the bag itself acts as a 'surrogate' for Trelkovsky's growing inability to contain his aggression behind his otherwise mild-mannered persona (8). The 'mess' that leaks from the rent onto the carpet in fact foreshadows his later encounter with the ostracised Mme Gaderian (Lila Kedrova), who defecates in front of the doors of all the neighbours who signed the petition to have her evicted. Gaderian exacts a measure of calculated revenge for which Trelkovsky does not have the courage, or is only able to enact in the full thrusts of psychosis.

The conundrum of the disappearing rubbish and the psychoanalytical readings it opens itself up to also draw attention to the complex connection between delusions and hallucinations. It is a relationship that is explored in *The Tenant* through the interrelatedness of Trelkovsky's distorted perceptions and his increasingly paranoid and bizarre beliefs, each seemingly informing and fuelling the other. The clinical designation of *delusional perception* as a symptom of schizophrenia refers to a behaviour in which a patient assigns great personal significance to an observed, often banal, event. The term was originated by Schneider (1949, 1958), but was refined by Koehler (1979), who specifies that the meaningfulness of such distortions is embedded directly in the perception, which suggests a complex intertwining of perception and delusion. McKenna cites the efforts of several psychiatrists (Fish [1962], Hamilton [1984], Mellor [1970], Cooper et al. [1974]) who have, over the years, attempted to clarify this potentially confusing scenario. Critical to the concept of delusional perception is the derivation of meaningfulness from an event by the patient; as McKenna summarises, 'on perceiving a neutral event, a delusional interpretation of it, which is usually elaborate, suddenly crystallizes, dropping, as it were, fully formed into the patient's head' (1997: 29).

In those moments when the camera breaks free from the filter of Trelkovsky's distorted perceptions (whilst still tethered to his spatial reach) and reveals that what Trelkovsky 'sees' is not diegetically veridical, we are reminded of just how dissonant his perceptions have become. As the film progresses and Trelkovsky's perceptions become increasingly distorted, the contrast between the camera's alternating 'vision' becomes more pronounced. When Trelkovsky takes refuge in Stella's (Isabelle Adjani) flat, he sees M. Zy through the peephole (a favourite shot of Polanski's) and hears his voice across the door. Here the small distorting lens indeed reflects a distorted perceptual mechanism, as revealed when the camera manages to extend its tether to the limit to show us a diegetic reality beyond Trelkovsky's perceptual reach: the man outside the door was not M. Zy, but a canvasser of some kind who bears only an extremely superficial resemblance to Trelkovsky's landlord. Trelkovsky's hallucination of the stalking M. Zy then triggers a refinement to his delusional conceptual framework; in a moment that echoes Rosemary's realisation that she has been betrayed by Dr Sapirstein ('All of them. All of them … witches!'), Trelkovsky concludes that Stella too must be one of 'them'.

An even more startling departure from Trelkovsky's perception of the world occurs after he is struck down by a car. Here the camera truly divorces itself from Trelkovsky's vision by contrasting what the film presents as his hallucinations to a more objective view of events, suggesting at this point that not only is Trelkovsky's perception of events unreliable, but completely fabricated. In the sequence in the pharmacy, the camera alternates between Trelkovsky's POV, in which his neighbours, M. Zy and Mme Dioz (Jo Van Fleet) are responsible for hitting him, to a shot of the 'real' culprits, a frazzled elderly couple who again bear only the most superficial resemblance to the people Trelkovsky sees before him. Here again the camera first adopts Trelkovsky's POV and then reveals another 'truth'; this time, the image is not one that is beyond Trelkovsky's perceptual reach, but beyond his perceptual mechanism's ability to interpret stimuli correctly. It is worth noting here that although this sequence is based on one in Topor's novel, Polanski's use of the cinematic medium departs from the text through the inclusion of these 'double visions', an effect that Topor does not achieve on the page.

The rapid alternating in this scene between a representation of Trelkovsky's subjective vision and an objective shot undistorted by the protagonist's schizophrenic perception establishes a state of perceptual multistability in the spectator, and predicts the camera's struggle to 'decide' between adopting or rejecting Trelkovsky's filtered vision of events in the film's climactic scene. As Trelkovsky drags his way back into the building and up the stairs in order to defenestrate himself for the *second* time (a cruel reminder of the film's 'infinite loop'), we are again presented with contradictory images of the neighbours. In one shot we see monsters with forked tongues and beastly eyes who force Trelkovsky to flee back up the stairs and (again) out the window.[5] In the next shot, interrupted only by a reverse shot of the cowering Trelkovsky, we see the same neighbours in a completely different light; whilst they are a disgusted by Trelkovsky's 'odd' appearance, they are nevertheless seriously concerned for his welfare.

By introducing such a high degree of diegetic uncertainty regarding the extent to which Trelkovsky's fears are (veridically) justified, and coupling this ambiguity with filmophanic illusions that render the screen image itself (doubly) non-veridical, we are urged to consider not only the nature of schizophrenic perception, but also the relative malleability of all perception, regardless of how sane the perceptual mechanism. We are constantly forced to consider the insurmountable gap between our perception of the thing and the thing itself, which is the very essence of all representation and arguably the primary concern of art. Let us recall the scenes of misshapen rooms and flattened chairs discussed earlier. Is it wrong, or 'insane', for us to conclude that there is a chair next to Trelkovsky's bed upon which sits a perfectly normal bottle? Or that Trelkovsky's room is full of perfectly ordinary furniture? Looking at the seconds before the moments of visual dissonance reveals no clue as to the 'true' nature of these objects, nor does it matter to the eye and what is transmitted to the brain; the chair and bottle are as real as any other. They are then revealed not to be what we believed them to be (what they had just *been*), not through the use of particularly distorting lenses but by the subversion of sensory-motor expectations regarding the negotiation of perspectival space. We can interpret this to be a reference to the artifice of representation, the 'false reality' of cinema (not just the use of matte backgrounds, or, more recently, CGI, for example, but the inherent 'falseness' of the filmophanic image), but the concept goes much further than this, urging us to consider how the way we perceive affects our perceptions.

Both the distorted dimensions of the room and 'flattened' bedside chair signal Trelkovsky's decreasing ability to perceive effectively, that is, his diminishing capacity to judge the *meaning* of situations (or visual 'semantics', as Gregory refers to it, 1997a: 6). The increasing frequency of his hallucinations parallels his ever-decaying ability to correctly identify the intentions of those around him. Thinking along these lines, *The Tenant* is transformed from a horror film in which an innocent is persecuted by monsters on the outside to a film that (like *Repulsion* and *Rosemary's Baby* before it) derives its lingering horror from its central character's growing isolation from the world. Trelkovsky's 'encounters' with the flattened chair and Ames Room also suggest that he is suffering from hallucinations related to the perception of perspectival space. As discussed earlier, this sort of behaviour has been identified as symptomatic of schizophrenia by Chapman and McGhie (1961), which they have labelled *perceptual distortion*, a perceptual event wherein the subjects experience 'transient alterations in the size, distance, and shape of objects' (103). The impossibly shaped room that Trelkovsky enters is not only an effective way of manifesting this symptom on-screen, but, as I discuss above, the manner in which the shot is executed also causes a similar loss of perspective in the spectator, who is initially 'fooled' by his or her interpretation of the shape of the room. Both the distorted room and the flattened chair sequences cause 'tension between what is signalled to the eye and what you believe should be there' (Gregory, 2003), thus allowing Polanski to utilise optical trickery to mimic a diegetic perceptual crisis; or, to put it another way, he blurs the line between the two types of non-veridical perception by using *illusions* to represent *hallucinations*.

Trelkovsky's perceptual crises are symptomatic of the serious mental illness that he is suffering. His growing paranoia regarding his neighbours, and eventually even Stella, is also indicative of his developing psychosis; but the most notable example of Trelkovsky's delusional state is his increasingly conspicuous donning of Simone Choule's clothing. The 'feminisation' of Trelkovsky is of particular interest to this analysis, as it seems to solidify the connection in Polanski's cinema between women and mental illness, a symbolic and highly provocative gender association that distinguishes Carole, Rosemary and Trelkovsky from the 'sane males' of the Investigation Trilogy. It is important to distinguish Trelkovsky's behaviour from transvestism, which is not (or no longer) considered to be a form of mental illness, but simply a behaviour from which some derive pleasure (sexual or otherwise). Trelkovsky does not seem to be engaging in this crossdressing behaviour for mere pleasure or due to a personal preference, but rather as the result of the profound delusion that he is, in fact, 'becoming' Simone Choule. In this regard, Trelkovsky is not crossdressing at all, but simply wearing the clothes appropriate to the person he believes himself to be in these moments. The most pronounced instance of Trelkovsky's delusional gender shift occurs when he announces (to his mirror image) that he believes himself to be pregnant; the scene is not only eerily reminiscent of *Rosemary's Baby*, but represents the most extreme state of 'feminisation' imaginable, an important issue that I shall discuss in greater detail in the next chapter.

Crystalline dissatisfaction

As I have discussed previously, Polanski's ardent refusal to provide 'satisfaction' in his films' conclusions is not only a narrative hallmark, but reflective of the theoretical discourse at work in his cinema. Dissatisfaction is amply furnished by *The Tenant*'s denouement in various forms. We are frustrated, for example, by the simple fact that the protagonist to whom we have been so closely tethered has been *defeated*, a dissatisfaction compounded by his betrayal of our perceptual trust due to his increasingly diseased perceptual mechanism. As Toles (1995) argues, as spectators we instinctively 'take sides' with the suffering Trelkovsky. We, perhaps inadvertently, may hope that the film will follow a Hollywoodian trajectory, in which Trelkovsky, once pushed to his 'breaking point' will finally retaliate against the oppressors, who are driving him mad, exacting a measured revenge to 'earn a just, violent reprieve for "goodness"' (8), like a peace-loving, hesitant gunslinger. In fact, it takes much for us to betray Trelkovsky and concede that he has probably greatly overestimated his neighbours' level of xenophobia. It is possible that maybe, just maybe, they are merely a part of the orthodox (and yes, *xenophobic*) masses, and not quite Trelkovsky's idea of an organised 'gang of killers' that obliges him to conform or die. In other words, it is not easy to accept that the character to whose perceptual (narrative) reach we have been tethered has become so disconnected from the world that he is rendered effectively isolated.

It is important to remember that even if the diagnosis of Trelkovsky as schizophrenic is accepted, it does not necessarily follow that the *basis* of his delusions is flawed. It is possible that his delusional disposition only exaggerates a situation that is really there, in this way exposing a 'truth' though psychosis, but simultaneously confounding this 'truth' by introducing insurmountable doubt as to its legitimacy, much in line with Polanski's general resistance to didacticism. It is this seemingly insurmountable ambiguity that compels us to consider the existential crisis we must all keep at bay; it is the crisis that results from our isolation from the world of things, that which results from the realisation that our perceptual relationship with the world is cognitively active, and all this entails. But as difficult as this concept is to reconcile with phenomenological experience, we are not necessarily consigned to solipsism; in other words, an acknowledgement of the epistemological ambiguity concerning our perceptual relationship with the 'outside' does not automatically entail a refutation of the independent existence of the world of things.

Just as Trelkovsky's perceptual distortions are represented via the creation of non-veridical filmophanic effects, the horror he feels in this last scene is replicated somewhat by the spectator's own experience of a crisis of the movement-image due to the scene's undoing of the diegesis's temporal unity. *The Tenant* does not present a muddled temporal structure that is eventually re-territorialised or mended either by a 'stitching' of the fragmented pieces of time in the film's denouement or even in the spectator's own mind upon reflection on the film's temporal structure; instead, we are violently thrust back to the confusion of the opening credits by the insanity of the ending, a scene that temporally makes no sense at all and deprives us of even the slightest satisfaction upon our exit from the cinema. In *Repulsion*, a similar effect is achieved through the enigmatic shot of Carole as a child. In *Rosemary's Baby*, it is the utter hopelessness of the ending due to Rosemary's betrayal of our expectations that serves to deflate all satisfaction, irrespective of how one reads the diegetic veridicality of the scene. (As I shall discuss in the following case studies, Polanski's preference for bleak and enigmatic endings is not limited to this trilogy.)

In order to further punctuate Trelkovsky's despair and rob us of the satisfaction that would result from the formation of an inextricable connection between the treatment he receives from his neighbours and his own perceptual breakdown, the film furnishes an 'ending' so enigmatic that the very stability of the movement-image is compromised, forcing us to suppress our own scream of frustration as the lights go up. In fact, the way in which each of the Apartment Trilogy films ends represents a variation of the manner in which a perceptual crisis can climax. In *Repulsion*, Carole is physically overwhelmed by her breakdown and is found unconscious (or possibly dead) under a bed, completely disconnected from the world. The end of *Rosemary Baby*, on the other hand, is far more ambiguous, for whilst we see Rosemary's continued perceptual and physical agency in the diegesis, it is possible to read this scene as being an entirely hallucinogenic episode within the 'legitimate' diegetic reality, in which Rosemary may well be lying in bed. In a moment that is directly paralleled in *The Tenant*, Rosemary 'screams' in horror (actually a silent scream in which an extra-diegetic horn makes a sound more horrifying than her larynx could ever manage) at what she sees in the cot, followed soon after by her cry 'No, it can't be!', a statement that serves well as a rough translation of Trelkovsky's own guttural wail.

The advantage Rosemary has over Trelkovsky is her continued physical influence on this plane of reality (and again, it is uncertain just 'where' this plane is), and so she is able to *choose* to reset her conceptual frameworks by 'joining' the reality in which she finds herself (i.e. accepting the coven's invitation to 'be a mother' to her baby). Trelkovsky has no such agency. His physical paralysis effectively positions him as a pure observer, a spectator unable to effect change on the world. Hence, a fusion occurs between Trelkovsky, the nominal observer who has been tethered to him and us, the spectators. As he screams, the camera penetrates his body, entering the only orifice it can and thus completely nullifying his agency within the diegesis, taking him out of the world and creating of him a ghost; he is present, but isolated from the material world.

As Calinescu (1987) argues, there is an interlocking relationship between the sense of selfhood and time in modernism: 'the personal, subjective, imaginative *dureé*, the private time created by the unfolding of the "self" … [the] identity of time and self constitutes the foundation of modernist culture' (5). Polanski causes this identity to disintegrate, deconstructing the subject through an exploration of perception. The Munch-esque scream Trelkovsky emits when he encounters 'himself' at the end of the film is a visceral reaction to this impossible sight; it signals not only a complete collapse of all conceptual frameworks, including the integrity of time and space, but the *realisation* that this collapse has occurred. It is a form of hell, a worst-case scenario in which Trelkovsky maintains just enough of his rationality to understand the full extent of his predicament. It is implied that he, like Simone, cannot speak; but if he could speak, what would he say upon seeing himself and Stella bump heads and scramble to pick up the oranges 'he' has dropped on the floor?

We can consider Trelkovsky's suicide as an act of epistemological 'self-correction'[6]; but it is not 'Trelkovsky' who he is trying to annihilate, but rather the emergent persona of Simone Choule, which has both destabilised his own sense of identity and seriously confounded his ability to interpret the world. We can therefore identify Trelkovsky's defenestration(s) not as suicide, but a form of homicide. The scream then comes to represent the height of his failure to extinguish Choule, as his actions serve to trap Trelkovsky in her body for 'eternity'. The scream is a final expression of his horror. It is an echo of Trelkovsky's last words before his second defenestration, his great existential affirmation of 'I'm Trelkovsky! Trelkovsky!' *I exist.*

Notes

1. Whereas Polanski is a native of Paris.
2. *The Tenant* was post-synch dubbed in both French and English, with actors speaking whichever language they were more adept at on set, but seemingly with a preference for English when possible. Polanski, for example, spoke English during the filming, but overdubbed his own voice for both the English and French version, the result being that his delivery comes across equally (albeit, only slightly) 'accented' in each version. Considering the Parisian setting, the 'natural' language would be French, but as Polanski oversaw both dubs, and most of the film's original (on-set) performances were delivered in English, either can be considered as 'original' language. That being said, Polanski also overdubbed himself in the Italian version, resulting in a similar 'accented' effect, but it would be difficult to argue that this too should be considered an 'original' language.
3. Virtually identical moments are used by Clouzot in *La prisonnière* (1968) and by Obayashi in *Hausu* (1977), although I cannot say for certain if these are direct references to *Knife in the Water*.
4. Behind-the-scenes photos that reveal the construction of this 'cut out' are held at the Bibliothèque du film in Paris. BiFi reference: PO0024059 and PO0024055.
5. The barman can be seen here menacingly waving a pack of Marlboros, Simone Choule's preferred cigarettes, at Trelkovsky, in what is a truly unnerving blend of horror and absurdist comedy.
6. This notion is much reminiscent of Calinescu's description of the character Ulrich in Thomas Bernhard's *Correction*, whose suicide Calinescu describes as an act of '(self) correction out of existence' (1987: 309).

Chapter 7

Approaching the Investigations

Before shifting my focus to the case studies of a second set of films, what I will be referring to as the 'Investigation Trilogy' of *Chinatown*, *Frantic* and *The Ninth Gate*, it is prudent to first identify and discuss a few of the key issues that will inform my analyses of these works, specifically the manner in which I will contrast this group to the previously discussed Apartment Trilogy. Like the Apartment Trilogy, I argue that the issue of 'indirectness' of perception continues to inform both the narrative content and aesthetic design of the Investigation Trilogy, but the approach Polanski takes in these films differs significantly from that which I have previously discussed. In contrast to the focus on mental illness seen in *Repulsion*, *Rosemary's Baby* and *The Tenant*, in the investigation-based films, the 'illness' is not injected into the perceiver, but out into the world that is being perceived. Furthermore, I will argue that the events of the Investigation Trilogy films reflect the agency of cognition in perception not through intimate dissections of subjective perceptual experiences, but by 'acting out' the basics of the perceptual process in the diegetic interpersonal conflicts of these films, in which diverse characters present competing hypotheses of reality for us to judge.

The legend of Oedipus underscores much of my discussion of the Investigation Trilogy owing to the many ways in which these films all display clear resonances with the trajectory of the Greek hero. Before beginning these case studies, it is therefore pertinent to first provide a brief overview of the various uses of the term 'Oedipal', in which I highlight the fact that reference to the myth itself does not *de facto* allude to either Freud's concept of the 'Oedipus complex' nor Lacan's 'Oedipal trajectory'. In order to integrate this Oedipal discussion into the main focus of this book, I will locate some of the myth's central themes within Polanski's overall perceptual discourse.

Another issue I will address before moving on to the next set of case studies is that of gender in Polanski's cinema. Although Polanski's use of gender is not the specific focus of the present discussion (i.e. neither that of this chapter nor this work as a whole), its relevance is such that it cannot be overlooked and deserves at least brief attention here; so included as well is a short analysis of the role of gender in the Investigation Trilogy, in which I shall also refer back to the Apartment Trilogy. Thereafter will follow my case studies of *Chinatown*, *Frantic* and *The Ninth Gate*, a thematically connected analysis of *Death and the Maiden*, and a chapter dedicated *The Ghost*, a film that, I argue, serves as a 'bridging' work that connects these two 'trilogies'.

Investigating perception

As I have argued in the previous chapter, Polanski's interest in perception, specifically the model of active perception delineated by Gregory, finds its most overt expression in the Apartment Trilogy of *Repulsion*, *Rosemary's Baby* and *The Tenant*. In all three of these films, Polanski uses various aesthetic techniques to attempt to represent the subjective act of perception as engaged in by cinematic subjects to whom we, as spectators, are tethered. What is particularly challenging about these representations is the fact these subjects are undergoing a disturbed, possibly schizophrenic perceptual experience. Polanski's attempt to represent these subjective perceptual acts (or, as I have argued, his attempt to *evoke* similar perceptual states in the viewer) is indeed a type of realism, which I have been referring to as psychological or *perceptual* realism, in which the film is established as 'pure simulacrum' through the orchestration of the experience of spectatorship to provoke perceptual or epistemological states in the audience that mirror that of the diegetic subject, such as the manipulation of perspective in *The Tenant* and *Repulsion*, or the perpetual uncertainty of what is and what is not diegetically real in *Rosemary's Baby*.

Whilst *Chinatown*, *Frantic* and *The Ninth Gate* do not penetrate the inner sphere to create the kind of psychological realism seen in the Apartment Trilogy, they remain concerned with the same sort of cognitive process. Rather than examining the perceptual mechanism 'up close' through a depiction of its breakdown, these investigation stories take a step back to observe a functioning perceiver encounter perceptual challenges that initiate a series of crises (both physical and epistemological). A key difference in these two groups of films is the presence of madness, or a 'malfunction' of the perceptual apparatus. Where Carole Ledoux, Rosemary Woodhouse and Trelkovsky all display behavioural symptoms of schizophrenia, there is no indication that Walker (*Frantic*), Gittes (*Chinatown*) or Corso (*The Ninth Gate*) are suffering from mental illness in any way. Just the opposite: all three characters are clearly delineated as highly rational. Instead, these 'sane' minds are forced to confront a reality that does not match their 'vision' (cognitive schema) of the way the world should work.

In the latter 'half' of his cinema (i.e. post-*Tess*, but including *Chinatown*), Polanski favours a more distant form of realism in which the depiction (or reproduction) of purely subjective psychological states (as seen in the Apartment Trilogy) is excluded. Whilst for the most part remaining closely bound to a single narrative reach, the concern shifts from the subjects' *perceptual* ability (inhibited by mental illness) to the subjects' *conceptual* ability. But this shift in focus should not be mistaken for a major change in Polanski's cinema's overall discourse; as I have discussed, the theory of active perception establishes a firm connection between higher cognitive functioning and perception in its suggestion of 'judgement' being utilised in sensory perception. In other words, the cognitive functions involved in perception are wedded to prior understanding, *conceptions*, of what is being perceived.

Consistent with the more distant form of realism that is indicative of the latter 'half' of his films (although slightly incongruently with the chronological watershed, that is, *Chinatown* comes before *The Tenant*), Polanski's inquiring camera makes no attempt to penetrate the psyche of Gittes, Walker or Corso (as opposed to Carole Ledoux, Trelkovsky and Rosemary Woodhouse), and instead focuses on the complexities of the situation in which they find themselves. The drama of the Apartment Trilogy remains, for the most part, confined to the flats occupied by these films' protagonists. As I have previously discussed, these confined spaces serve as a representation for the brain itself; the conflicts that form the drama are psychological battles with the self, more so than conflicts with others. In the Investigation Trilogy, on the other hand, we are not granted such intimate psychological access. Instead of suffering in their flats, the investigators venture into the world, with the camera trying to keep up with them as they move from space to space (and person to person) in pursuit of knowledge. The worlds these films explore, whilst governed by the whims of individual psyches (i.e. those of the protagonists), are dominated by complex interactions of disparate, but nevertheless connected, subjects, each of whom possesses his or her own complex psychological profile and personal drama.

The Oedipal detective

The use of the motif of the investigation as a means of representing existential crisis finds its origins in antiquity. Sophocles's *Oedipus Rex* (and its two sequels) remains the key text that sets the standard for the existential 'who done it' in which the investigator becomes embroiled into the investigation. As an adjective, the term 'Oedipal' has earned varied connotations, Freud's use of the myth (the 'Oedipus complex') as shorthand for incestuous (maternal) desire being most ubiquitous in the twentieth century. The concept of an 'Oedipal trajectory' is derived from Lacan's description of a subject's overcoming of parental ties towards autonomy and extra-parental relations. The term has been adopted by film theory as a means of describing a classic (Hollywood) formula in which a male protagonist overcomes odds and is rewarded by either being reunited with a woman or finding one. Hayward (2000) refers to this trajectory as a movement *towards* social stability, but points out as well that the crisis may or may not actually be resolved (261). In the Sophoclean sense, the Oedipal trajectory, whilst initiated as a means of re-establishing social stability, ultimately results in further crises, both social and, as I argue, *perceptual*.

Belton (1991) develops Mulvey's (1989: 178–200) observation regarding the structural similarity of psychoanalysis and detective fiction, namely the mandate of each to confront and assimilate seemingly irrational stimuli to produce useful knowledge, to discover (or *conquer*) the truth of what is 'out there'. Essentially, psychoanalysis and detection each involve the assemblage of clues to achieve epistemological satisfaction. As Belton observes, neither Sophocles nor Chandler aims for such satisfaction, but are both more interested in exploring the profoundly dissatisfying possibility that 'through the acquisition of knowledge the limitations of knowledge are discovered' (1991: 937). As the ambiguity with which Polanski typically ends his films demonstrates, he shares with Sophocles and Chandler an aversion to satisfaction as an element of storytelling; as Polanski himself has commented in reference to his various 'hopeless' endings, '(i)f you show your hero triumphant, the audience leaves satisfied. There's nothing more sterile than a state of satisfaction' (Polanski in Ciment, Perez and Tailleur, 2005: 44).

Oedipus Rex brings to the fore the issue of observation as an influencing factor on the observed. In *Oedipus Rex*, the act of investigation itself becomes a variable in what is being investigated, somewhat predicting what quantum physics would eventually discover of the subatomic realm. Heisenberg echoes the Oedipal conundrum in his notion of the 'uncertainty principle', which describes the effect that the act of observation has on the position and speed of subatomic particles. The philosophical implications of Heisenberg's observer effect were tremendous, especially as it applied to what is thought to be the very building blocks of physical reality. It is important to highlight that whilst the uncertainty principle suggests that the act of observation affects that which is being observed, this is due to the fact that light needs to be introduced in order to take this measurement. It is this light that affects the measurement being taken, not the mere fact that someone is observing. Likewise, whilst the theory of active perception stresses the agency of cognition on perception, this is not to imply that observing an object affects its independent nature; unless, that is, the object is somehow aware that it (or he or she) is being observed, in which case, there could well be an 'observer effect'.

Although R. L. Gregory is careful to separate the model of active perception from the 'unobservability' of subatomic particles in the world of quantum physics, there remains a strong parallel between the uncertainty principle's cause–effect relationship between observation and the observed and the active cerebral component of the construction of perceptions described by von Helmholtz and echoed by Gregory. Many of the various philosophical implications that emerge from active perception's acknowledgement of the active component of perception and the 'gap' between the world and our perception of it also emerge from the uncertainty principle; and, if it is not too laboured a connection, these 'implications' are shared by the Oedipus myth as well. In terms of Polanski's cinema, it is the ongoing fascination with the nature of perception that seems to lead his work *towards* the Oedipal, best embodied in his film *Chinatown*, but reflected to varying degrees in his other investigation films, *The Ninth Gate*, *Frantic*, and, as I shall discuss later, *The Ghost*.

Of all Polanski's films, *Chinatown* has most often been considered in an Oedipal framework, normally due to its incestuous subplot; but the structuring principles of *Oedipus Rex* are in fact much utilised by Polanski, most apparent in what I refer to here as the Investigation Trilogy. The manner in which *Chinatown* reveals the limits of knowledge stems from the more basic question of perceptual acuity to which Polanski so often returns; but I do not wish to suggest an absolute identity between the limits of perception and the limits of knowledge, for such a connection reduces the concept of knowledge to being inextricably associated with sensory perceptions of world, thus discounting, for example, understanding of the abstract. Nevertheless, perceptual arrogance (be it self-imposed or institutionally embedded) creates a natural limit to knowledge, as experienced, for example, by Jake Gittes in *Chinatown*.

It is unsurprising that Polanski would gravitate so often to the Oedipal narrative structure as a means of conducting his own perceptual discourse when one considers that the Oedipus legend serves as an early example of a work in which perceptual psychology is reflected in the narrative content of fiction, and one that raises issues that continue to resonate with current debates regarding the nature of the perceptual mechanism. When Oedipus learns the identity of his birth parents and the fact that it is he who is responsible for the plague that afflicts Thebes, he is compelled to put out his own eyes as a means of depriving himself of further knowledge, specifically the ability to look at his offspring, whom he now considers monstrous. In *Chinatown*, it is Evelyn who quite literally has her sight removed by a bullet through the eye so that she too is no longer able to look upon her 'monstrous' offspring. Gittes, on the other hand, whilst initially compelled to gaze upon the scene, performs a symbolic act of self-blinding in his befuddled retreat from Chinatown.

Oedipus Rex's meditation on perception is revealed to be more elaborate, however, when we consider that it is the blind 'seer' who has access to knowledge beyond the perceptual abilities of the sighted. As Polan (2006) points out, in *Chinatown*, 'seeing ... is not necessarily the same thing as understanding' (117). Whilst perhaps not using the same sort of terminology as the neuropsychologists and constructivists, Polan is indeed making reference to the very same 'eye–brain' relationship they are concerned with. Polan, for example, makes reference to understanding as a 'deeper process than mere sensory perception' (118), which echoes the conclusions of research like Gregory's.

Belton makes mention of *Chinatown*'s self-reflective attitude towards cinema, specifically the manner in which the film 'transforms explicit concerns with detection into implicit concerns with the nature of cinema' (1991: 943). By 'the nature of cinema', Belton is referring to the school of psychoanalytic film theory concerned with the spectators' scopophilic drive (as discussed by Metz [1982], for example), but I propose that such concerns are equally well suited to exploring the nature of perception and the various philosophical (and psychological) implications that follow. Where *Repulsion, The Tenant* and *Rosemary's Baby* employ cinematographic methods to represent the subjective distorted visions (hallucinations) of their respective protagonists, *Chinatown* instead focuses on a *mise-en-scène* of observation; the frame is occupied by both observing subject and observed object, the former normally concealed from the latter.

This 'voyeurism' is then doubled: as spectators, we are positioned behind Gittes, rarely adopting his POV, but rather the POV of a voyeur who remains tethered to (but hidden from) Gittes.

The photos in which Hollis Mulwray (Darrell Zwerling) and Katherine (Belinda Palmer) are 'caught' together on the lake in Echo Park, for example, show how preconceptions form perceptions (i.e. Gittes's mistaken reading of the situation as a romantic liaison, in keeping with his role of divorce Private Investigator). Such incidents also serve as signifiers of the active nature of perception at its most basic possible level, that is, the manner in which the brain reads the retinal image. The role that photography plays in the film is as much an indicator of our own ocular *camera obscura* as it is self-reflective of the work's own cinematographic nature. But rather than forming a parallel to the 'directness' of photographic representation (i.e. photochemical exposure of film), *Chinatown* stresses that it is biological perception that is mediated (and often led astray) by the brain.

So, by adopting and adapting the Oedipal narrative, Polanski is able to extend his perceptual discourse beyond the psychological sphere as a means of engaging with sociological and political issues. The Oedipal template does not, of course, exclude psychology, but it does nestle the psychological within a wider, sociological context, connecting the realm of the personal and the social in its examination of the cause–effect relationship of individual action on society. (What is therefore under examination in this structure is *power*, yet another common motif to which Polanski frequently returns.) What Polanski's investigation films have in common with each other, and indeed with the Oedipal myth from which they borrow, is the presence of an epistemological crisis that emerges when existing conceptual frameworks are challenged by novel situations. What these characters encounter are realities that are beyond their perceptual abilities; these realities expose the limits, the *frame*, within which their worlds are constructed, and in turn require each of them to either adapt their preconceptions or suppress elements of what they perceive.

Although the Investigation Trilogy films do not deal with the issue of mental illness, the perceptual discourse initiated by Polanski in the Apartment Trilogy is expanded upon in this set of films. In a manner similar to Mulvey's investigation-psychoanalysis parity (1989: 178), Polanski uses the investigation as a means of further representing the workings, and especially the fallibility, of perception and, in turn, reality-construction. The investigators' collection and deciphering of evidence as a means of knowledge acquisition is indeed analogous to the act of perception (and involves perception) due to the various obstacles that the investigators encounter, as well as the intellectual effort with which these must be overcome. Information is never simply 'picked up' from the world, but needs to be deciphered. In fact, the notion that 'all is not what it seems' is equally applicable to Polanski's investigators themselves, who whilst forced to overcome perceptual biases are also objects for the *spectator* to perceive and comprehend.

In *Oedipus Rex*, an investigation (Oedipus's search for his real parents) brings on the plague. In *Chinatown, Frantic* and *The Ninth Gate*, the effects of investigation are most pronounced by the deaths caused by the investigation itself (most notably in *The Ninth Gate*, where literally everyone connected with the object of investigation, the book, is killed). Like Oedipus, in all three of Polanski's investigation films, the investigator is forced to rethink, to *re-see*, the world as the result of uncomfortable discrepancies between the way he thinks the world works and what is happening around him. In *Chinatown*, Jake Gittes is forced to confront deep-seeded corruption at the highest level of American business, government and law enforcement; in *Frantic*, Walker not only has a piece of his identity 'amputated' with the loss of his wife, but is thrust full-on into the high tension world of global politics; and in *The Ninth Gate*, Dean Corso is also forced to look at a reality beyond his 'percentage' (the answer he gives when he is asked what he 'believes in').

Each of these investigation films conceals a psychological subplot of which the spectator is made aware, but nevertheless remains isolated from. Such isolation of the spectator from the protagonist is far more pronounced in this group of films than in the Apartment Trilogy, in which we are granted access to the psychological (subjective) sphere of the protagonist to whom we are tethered. By these 'psychological subplots' I am referring specifically (but not exclusively) to Jake Gittes's Chinatown complex, the taboo sexual tension between Walker and Michelle (Emmanuelle Seigner) and Corso's shift towards a belief in the supernatural, each of which I will discuss in due course. The presence of these concealed 'subplots' in combination with the ubiquitous lack of satisfying solutions contributes to the hallmark Polanskian effect of leaving the spectator with more questions than answers; it is precisely this effect that most dramatically marks Polanski's departure from the Hollywood formula, notwithstanding most of his films' use of Hollywood star power and his celebratory (although often simultaneously deconstructive) attitude to genre cinema. The 'goal' of these films, in as much as this word is even applicable, is not to resolve problems, but to encourage nuanced thinking through exposing the fallacy of binary moral economies and challenging the assumed benignness of government, big business and religious institutions, all of whom try their hardest to influence our conceptual frameworks on a daily basis. Such a goal is duly complemented by the exploration of perception that weaves its way through Polanski's cinema.

Gender and perception

When juxtaposing the Apartment and Investigation Trilogies, one cannot overlook the role that gender seems to play in each set of films. In all three investigation films, the protagonist takes the form of a white male in his late-thirties to mid-forties.[1] All three appear to be in the prime of their lives, both physically and intellectually. All three are virile, successful, American *men*; in contrast, Carole, Rosemary and Trelkovsky are all either women or highly feminised (i.e. Trelkovsky, who is ultimately transformed into a woman), suffer from both physical and mental illness, are either unemployed or have difficulties in the workplace, and are often bullied by friends, family and colleagues.

Such consistent coupling of madness and femininity no doubt opens these films to the accusation of misogyny, as has been observed by critics in the past (see Haskell, 1987: 346–347, for example). A detailed inter-film analysis of Polanski's cinema shows that such readings are largely superficial, but we must not overlook the fact that Polanski's cinema does indeed often employ gender stereotypes and frequently includes portrayals of (unpunished) misogynistic behaviour as a provocative means of exploring gender roles. It is rare, in fact, to find either condemnation or celebration of any ideological stance in Polanski's cinema, which opens his work up to harsh criticism from both the right and left; the right attacking his moral ambivalence and the often graphic use of sex and violence in his films, and the left his lack of social commitment and use of the individualistic (i.e. highly subjectivised, arguably anti-Marxist) narrative form. But, as I have indicated previously, if there is any consistent ideological stance to be distilled from his cinema as a whole, it is that of ambiguity itself, a profound agnosticism that removes certainty from that which should be most certain: our concept of identity and the very means by which knowledge is attained. Nevertheless, Polanski's cinema is not entirely even-handed; there are 'enemies' that are consistently attacked throughout his work, namely those who abuse power, who are often embodied in the form of wealthy business tycoons, religious leaders or political officials.

Rather than directly challenging gender stereotypes in the Apartment Trilogy, Polanski seems to use the stereotype of gender-based otherness as a means of reflecting the otherness of those characters' perceptual experiences; this is achieved most primitively in *Repulsion*, but is made more complex in *Rosemary's Baby* by positioning Rosemary as fighting against (but defeated by) a plot against her. The coupling of Trelkovsky's increasingly pronounced schizophrenic condition and his re-gendering serves to clarify that Polanski's link of madness and femininity is not a coincidence; in these films they form a parity. Crnković (2004) draws a parallel between Trelkovsky's perceived 'foreignness' and his transformation into a woman, insinuating that his existing marginalisation (as a Pole, as a Jew) was not sufficient, as 'only by becoming a woman can he reach the bottom of victimization'.[2] Indeed, Polanski's use of gender seems to follow the stereotype-based logic that women serve as better representatives of the human condition as they are more emotionally expressive (a strategy much employed in cinema, especially by the likes of Hitchcock, and, more recently, von Trier).

By positioning women in the role of victim, killer or warrior a greater emotional response is elicited from the audiences due to what stereotypes inform us is the female gender's 'inherent' vulnerability. By the same token, in the Investigation Trilogy, it is male impotence that takes centre stage. The effect is similar: by both engaging with and deconstructing stereotypes, the film-maker can manipulate audience's expectations as a means of increasing engagement. The complex, often absurd manner in which these character's perceptual distortions are depicted, as well as the role played by those who surround them (their micro-societies) in the provocation of this madness, does not serve to reinforce the 'place' of woman as the inferior other, but rather to parody such binary gender divisions. In the Investigation Trilogy, Polanski engages in a similar parody, but this time the target is the gender stereotype of the male figure as a sane (sage) perceiver and effecter of change.

Another trilogy

Each of Polanski's investigation films treats the search for knowledge slightly differently. In *Chinatown*, it is established early on that Gittes typically investigates marital infidelity, a 'crime' he seems to understand and is comfortable with. Gittes demonstrates his understanding of the working of infidelity in his initial rejection of the fake Mrs Mulwray's request for his services; he seems to feel that it is more appropriate for men, like Curly (Burt Young), to spy on their cheating wives. When Gittes realises he has been duped (first by an impersonator, and then by his own understanding of the nature of the case he has taken on), he experiences an epistemological crisis that he spends the rest of the film trying (and failing) to overcome. Conversely, the more Gittes investigates, the more complex, more incomprehensible his world becomes, leading him back (both figuratively and literally) to Los Angeles's Chinatown, where he had served as a police officer and where he was advised to do 'as little as possible' by his captain, based on what was believed to be the futility of any attempt to gain control (to understand) this self-contained world. The expression 'Chinatown' (as in 'Forget it Jake; it's Chinatown') thus becomes a byword for the futility of trying to grasp the unknowable.

In Walker and Corso we again have characters in a Polanski film for whom the issue of national identity becomes a factor in the narrative, but the manner in which this is manifested varies somewhat. In *Frantic*, Walker is an American in Paris who is forced to deal not only with his total ignorance of the language, but also with French bureaucracy in a scene that takes us straight back to Trelkovsky's confrontation with Parisian police in *The Tenant*. But just as in *The Tenant*, Polanski refuses to let the spectator conclude that institutional French bigotry is *necessarily* an additional obstacle for the protagonist. When Walker complains that he expects the French 'to take him seriously', he is informed that not only has he been taken seriously, he is in fact receiving preferential treatment (although this is somewhat disguised by their inappropriately jovial demeanour, in Walker's eyes at least). Instead, it is the American Embassy that proves to be far less helpful, diffusing any notion that Walker is being discriminated against by the French, which the scene in the police station initially (seems) to suggest. Nevertheless, whilst Walker's sense of national identity and displacement indeed emerges as a perceptual obstacle, it remains thoroughly unclear as to whether or not this is the result of discrimination. Like Walker, Dean Corso is also an American abroad; but *The Ninth Gate* presents a very different sort of transnational body than *Frantic*. There is no sense of the tragically displaced foreigner seen in Walker. Unlike Walker, Corso is well aware of both local customs and geography. He moves fluidly across both international and European borders (indeed, Europe is a politically different place in *The Ninth Gate*'s 1999 setting than it is in *Frantic*'s 1988). Corso also speaks French effortlessly; and even when his limited Portuguese or Spanish proves insufficient, English takes over seamlessly as *lingua franca*.

In presenting such unclear portrayals of the effects of national, cultural and linguistic otherness, *Frantic*, like *The Tenant* and *Repulsion* in particular, complicates attempts to 'read' the extent of the significance of the protagonist's status as an 'expatriate' in Polanski's cinema. That is not to say, however, that Walker, Carole Ledoux and Trelkovsky are equally disadvantaged; Carole is very much a (relatively) recent immigrant to London, but her command of the language diminishes her otherness greatly in comparison to Walker in Paris. Trelkovsky, on the other hand, is a naturalised French citizen, but it is certainly difficult to avoid interpreting his anxiety towards his neighbours as greatly based on his (and our) assumptions of bigotry and xenophobia. In fact, it is arguably Trelkovsky's identity as 'oppressed other' to which he may be clinging. Walker makes the same assumption, but in both cases, Polanski refuses to let the spectator maintain such notions unchallenged.

Like gender roles and national identity, generic convention is also something Polanski prefers to toy with and deconstruct rather than adhere to. Superficially at least, *Chinatown* is film noir, *Frantic* a thriller, and *The Ninth Gate* a supernatural noir/horror (a subgenre in its own right, with precursors including *The Seventh Victim*, *Alias Nick Beal* [J. Farrow, 1949] and *Angel Heart* [A. Parker, 1987]). In *Chinatown*, marital infidelity specialist private investigator Jake Gittes finds himself embroiled in a murder case connected to mass corruption in the management of Los Angeles's water supply. *Frantic* is the story of the American doctor Richard Walker's attempt to find his wife, who has been abducted in Paris as the result of mistaken identity. Not taken seriously by either the French police or the American embassy, Walker is tasked with finding his wife himself in a city whose geography and language are both unknown to him. In *The Ninth Gate*, New York 'book detective' Dean Corso is hired by the wealthy and eccentric publishing tycoon Boris Balkan to go to Europe and track down the two remaining copies of an ancient and extremely rare volume, *The Nine Gates of the Kingdom of Shadows* (three of which exist, including Balkan's copy), with which he (Balkan) is convinced he will be able to contact the Devil and attain supernatural powers. A shrewd capitalist himself, Corso accepts Balkan's generous remuneration offer notwithstanding what he considers to be an absurd reason for collecting the books.

In all three of these films, the task taken on by the protagonist-cum-detective turns out to be far more difficult than it initially appeared: a simple case of marital infidelity turns into murder and political corruption at the highest level; rather than a kidnapping for money, Sondra Walker's (Betty Buckley) abductors demand a tiny, but highly sophisticated nuclear triggering device of which Walker is inadvertently (and for the majority of film, unknowingly) in possession; and Corso's exploitation of a man with more money than sense results in a multiple body count, which nearly includes his own, as he tracks down a couple of antique books. In each of these films, the men are forced to take on new perceptual challenges and reconsider the realities in which they comfortably reside. Walker is an apolitical American doctor forced to deal with a global nuclear crisis in order to save his wife, and both Corso and Gittes, although already detectives of sorts, are likewise thrust into situations (into *realities*) in which they are not used to operating.

I will now turn my attention to dedicated case studies of each of these films, but this intertextual discourse will continue as these discussions develop.

Notes

1. Although Johnny Depp was slightly younger than this at the time, he was made-up so that his character, Dean Corso, would appear a few years older than Depp himself.
2. No pagination, see: http://www.kinoeye.org/04/05/crnkovic05.php.

Chapter 8

Chinatown

As noted in most analyses of *Chinatown*, the film is inspired by the events of the Owens Valley 'Water Wars' of the early twentieth century. As Walton (2001, see below) warns, however, we must be careful not to overestimate the historical veracity of *Chinatown*. The construction of the Los Angeles aqueduct was initiated in 1905 and completed in 1912, designed as a means of transferring water from the Sierra Nevada Mountains to the water-needy residents and farmers of the Los Angeles area. The means by which this water was divided was a matter of great controversy, which led to unrest amongst farmers. The tensions came to a head in 1924 with the bombing of the aqueduct itself.

Chinatown is only loosely based on these events, taking them as inspiration for the greater setting of its plot, but making no claim, directly or indirectly, to be a work that represents this 'water war' (one of many in California's history) faithfully. As Walton notes, *Chinatown* is by no means historically accurate:

> The site of the conflict was moved 200 miles closer to the city, the events were advanced by thirty years to the depression era LA of Raymond Chandler and the story was reconstructed as a murder mystery revolving around conspiratorial land speculation.
>
> (Walton, 2001: 47)

As Walton examines, notwithstanding *Chinatown*'s merely inspirational connection to history, over time, the public 'memory' of the Owens Valley 'Water Wars' became highly influenced by Polanski's film, especially in the context of the renewed disputes over water rights in Los Angeles in the 1980s and 1990s (see Walton, 2001: 47–48).

With the extent of the film's 'historicity' clarified, let us turn our attention to the issue of perception in *Chinatown*. In the previous case studies I have referred several times to the 'perceptual crises' experienced by the protagonists of the 'Apartment Trilogy'. I have proposed that these films lend themselves to readings that suggest that these crises could be symptoms of neurological pathologies that affected the characters' ability to perceive the world effectively and caused their cognitive frameworks to become destabilised. In *Chinatown*, there is little to suggest that the protagonist to whom the spectator is so closely connected ('tethered') is suffering from any such malady, but crises do emerge nonetheless.

The basis of the crisis endured by *Chinatown*'s Jake Gittes is his failure to coalesce sense data into a form that corresponds to his existing conceptual frameworks. Simply put, he cannot force what he encounters into a 'Gittes worldview'-shaped box. Such perceptual challenges can arouse epistemological crises, and eventually lead to even greater existential crises; this trajectory closely matches that which Gregory describes as the 'philosophical implications' of the model of active perception, in which the highly subjective, relatively malleable and often unreliable nature of perception it describes highlights the gap between (a) our perception of the world, and (b) the world's ontology. The challenge that faces Gittes is to address this gap, a task that forms the basic impetus for all investigations. What he discovers is that the gap he believed he had overcome in his role as a marital infidelity detective remains, and thus he is returned to Chinatown, a place where it is better to not take action, to do 'as little as possible', rather than risk consequences that are beyond his perceptual mechanism's predictive abilities.

Mediated perception

Mechanical means of representation play a role in several of Polanski's films. In *Death and the Maiden*, a video camera is employed as a means of validating Dr Miranda's (Ben Kingsley) 'confession'. In *Frantic*, difficulty with understanding a series of messages on an answering machine serves to connect Michelle and Walker. It is seventeenth-century (printed) engravings that are studied and ultimately direct Corso's plight in *The Ninth Gate*, and digitally recorded interviews are utilised by the ghostwriter (Ewan McGregor) in *The Ghost* to write his client's 'autobiography'. In *Chinatown*, technologically mediated forms of perception are ubiquitous, specifically the use of lenses as aids to vision in the form of binoculars, eyeglasses and cameras. The capacity of these devices, and in the case of cameras, *their artefacts*, to facilitate perception and, in turn, the acquisition of knowledge, is one of *Chinatown*'s principle areas of scrutiny. It is the role of these artefacts (photographs) in *Chinatown* that I will examine first.

The relevance of the mechanically/chemically produced representative image in *Chinatown* is made apparent by the film's first post-credit sequence, in which Gittes creates a primitive cinematic device for his client, Curly, consisting of a series of still photos of a man and woman caught on camera. The sexually explicit nature of the photos is certainly evocative of the scopophilic aspect of imagery geared towards the satisfaction of the male gaze; but what follows quickly undoes such assumptions, as it is not pleasure that is delivered to the (*diegetic*) spectator, but rather a painful revelation that his wife is cheating on him. Ironically, perhaps, in the context of *Chinatown*'s overall emphasis on epistemological uncertainty, this opening scene demonstrates the power, indeed the *reliability* of the representation (i.e. an index, not the thing itself) to reveal truth through the camera's capacity to play proxy to a set of eyes and allow the transmission of sight (of *knowledge*) from one individual to the next. The cuckold's uncertainty is now lifted; no doubt remains that his wife is sleeping with another man. Here the pictures do not lie. All that remains is for him to address the situation, to 'correct' her actions and put his world to right. For Curly, this is accomplished by physically beating his wife into submission.

The simplicity of cases like Curly's, where representations ('directly') reveal truth, is in sharp contrast to what Jake Gittes deals with for the rest of the film, in which the relationship between perception and reality becomes increasingly difficult to interpret. Later, Gittes will use his camera, a tool of the trade, to snap shots of Hollis Mulwray in what seem to be compromising extra-marital situations. But it becomes apparent that these mechanically mediated images (photographic or created by way of mirrors or binoculars) do not tell the 'full story', and that Jake has overlooked pertinent details that are right under his nose. In fact, it is only when Jake has his nose *cut* that he begins to gain some appreciation of both the complexity of the case into which he himself has now become embroiled and the fact that his fidelity to his conceptual frameworks may well be compromising his ability to perceive effectively.

So, whilst *Chinatown* initially puts an emphasis on photography as method of constructing (or framing) meaning, the validity of representation as a reliable means of interpreting the world soon comes into question. The same seems true for the extra-diegetic camera's ability to convey reliable, complete information to the spectator. Just as Gittes's own recorded images fail to convey the myriad of complexities of the diegetic world, so too do the images by which Jake Gittes's plight is communicated to the spectator fail to 'contain' the story, and we are soon aware that there is far more occurring off-screen than on.

It is worth emphasising that the form of 'troubled' perception experienced by Gittes is not tantamount to the type of perception I have previously associated with psychosis. *Chinatown* instead demonstrates that a conflict can arise between what the stimuli being perceived (veridically) signal and the conclusions drawn by the perceiver. As Gregory is fond of repeating, perception is a process of *hypothesising*. The generation of hypotheses, however, presupposes knowledge of plausibility (i.e. what can possibly 'be'). Although interpersonal conflict abounds in *Chinatown*, the film's main crisis remains, as with the Apartment Trilogy, a *psychological* conflict; it is an intrapersonal schism between what Gittes is equipped (or *willing*) to perceive and what the stimuli that he encounters 'out there' are actually signalling.

Soon after the episode in which perceptual certainty is delivered to one client via some photos, Gittes is greeted by another client whose very physicality proves misleading. 'Mrs Mulwray' tells the detective that she believes her husband is cheating on her, a type of case Gittes is very familiar with. But we later learn that this woman was not Mrs Mulwray at all, but an impersonator; she is a fleshy representation of the real Mrs Mulwray. The ontology of both the fake Mrs Mulwray and the case Gittes 'solves' prove to be illusory; the perceptual game is afoot.

Jake Gittes's first action once he has accepted the Mulwray 'case' is to track down his client's husband, Hollis Mulwray, whom he finds giving evidence in the Los Angeles council chambers. Our first image of Mulwray is that of a diminished figure in the bottom right hand corner of the screen, his size is dwarfed by the conspicuous use of a telephoto lens that flattens the image so that he attains the dimensions of the comic strip characters that dominate the left half of the frame. I refer to this as 'our' first image, as the camera here demonstrates that whilst it may be tethered to Gittes, its narrative ('perceptual') reach is slightly greater than his. We see that Gittes is sitting on the other side of the room, not looking over the shoulder of the man reading the comics as the first shot and the next might suggest. The camera attempts to appropriate Gittes's gaze, but since he continues to avoid paying attention to the speaker, the camera is torn between respecting Gittes's (distracted) gaze and the official proceedings. The camera and Gittes are realigned when Mulwray assumes the floor. Mulwray protests the construction of a damn that he believes to be unsafe (and thus creating an obstacle for those who would profit from it), but Gittes seems bored. It is not only Gittes's expression, but the juxtaposition and construction of these shots that suggests that Gittes is paying little attention to the courtroom discourse, which he does not see as relevant; at this point, his perceptual focus is still completely informed by his role as infidelity investigator.

As Gittes tracks Hollis Mulwray, hoping to catch him in the act of committing adultery, he often watches him through a lens of some sort, but rather than learning anything, the images conveyed by these devices prove perplexing. He watches Hollis Mulwray walk into a (dry) floodway and discuss something with a small boy on a horse. He then sees him walk on the beach. Is he there to meet his lover? No. He seems more interested in a large pipe. The photographs taken by one of Gittes's employees reveal Hollis Mulwray and another, older, man in heated debate. But their faces are obscured, and the topic of conversation is indiscernible other than a reference to an 'apple core'. Finally, Mulwray is spotted at Echo Park, with who appears to be his lover. 'Echo park … Water again', says Gittes, a prophetic statement of the importance that water will play in this case, and one that reinforces the cliché that *film noir* has a 'Freudian attachment to water' (Schrader, 1986: 236). Gittes manages to shoot a series of photos of Mulwray and the woman, which seem to put his world to right since the situation he is investigating appears to be conforming nicely to the type of infidelity narrative with which he is accustomed. Such conformity is comforting to Gittes, and he is lulled into complacency until he is confronted with the fact that everything he has witnessed, even the original impetus for the investigation, is *not* what it seemed. The scene in which Gittes first encounters the real Mrs Mulwray, in which she looms behind him as he is telling his colleagues a highly 'inappropriate' joke, neatly foreshadows the uncomfortable revelations to come; it is also one of the few moments in which the camera is afforded a greater narrative reach than Gittes himself, serving to provoke unease in the spectators in anticipation of his (pending) embarrassment.

After realising that he has been duped by an imitation Mrs Mulwray (an implausible event from Gittes's perspective), and once Hollis Mulwray turns up dead, Gittes returns to the original locations he had previously followed Mulwray to in order to re-evaluate, *re-see*, what he had previously observed. The key difference now is not the locations themselves, which remain the same (aside from the obvious absence of Mulwray), but Gittes's own mental state. He must now approach the stimuli with an adjusted set of conceptual frameworks; but this proves difficult.

As the film progresses and Gittes becomes evermore aware that the situation in which he finds himself is not simply another divorce case, he also becomes increasingly frustrated with the way in which the epistemological certainty of his world is disintegrating. He is no longer master of his domain, and the sights (and sounds) that now surround him are no longer informative, but perplexing. Taking a cue from Curly's 'curative' technique, Gittes eventually attempts to reclaim command through violence: when confronted with information from Evelyn Mulwray that he is unable to reconcile with his established conceptual frameworks (i.e. the Oedipal 'shock' Gittes experiences when he is confronted with the 'daughter/sister' paradox) he resorts to the primitive technique of slapping her and throwing her across the room in an attempt, quite literally, to beat the truth out of her. Although the violence does seem to extract information, rather than re-establishing Gittes's mastery, the new information in fact highlights the limits of Gittes's understanding and complete lack of mastery.

When Gittes first begins to track Hollis Mulwray, he employs the usual tools of the trade (camera, mirrors, binoculars) to augment and record what he is able to *see*. Indeed, Jake Gittes's reliance on the sense of *sight* as a means of constructing meaning is greatly emphasised. That being said, the information that Gittes lacks is often aural, not visual; and the silent, distant images he collects do more to perplex than inform; but this is sometimes due to his inability to discern what is being *said* (not *done*). Unlike the rather uncoded images Gittes is used to dealing with, the Mulwray case becomes a struggle to decode an abstract order whose semantics Gittes is not privy to. The investigation therefore moves from the concrete (actions) to the symbolic (linguistic representation of actions); it is a shift to a sphere in which the reach of the visual is insufficient.

The perceptual discourse in *Chinatown* is also manifested via the physical displacement of the protagonist. Each of the investigation films deals with the issue of displacement, specifically the link between mastery and familiarity with (or 'belonging' to) occupied space, but each is unique in the way in which the effects of displacement are manifested. In *Chinatown*, it is through frequent reference to Gittes's former job as a police officer stationed in Los Angeles's Chinatown that we are able to locate him in a space of 'non belonging'. It is not until the final few minutes of the film that we are actually transported there, but until that point Chinatown remains a potent off-screen space, as relevant to the diegesis as anything we see in the frame. During Gittes's time in Chinatown, he led a futile existence; he was completely impotent to effect change, embedded, as he was, in an abstract order that he was unable to decode. Consequently, he did 'as little as possible' in order to do the least amount of harm. We eventually learn that Gittes was indeed involved in an incident in which his inability to take correct and timely action led to the death of a woman he loved.

In order to 'correct' his perceptual abilities, Gittes did not learn to 'decode' the world of LA's Chinatown (although he does learn some Chinese, it did not help him penetrate this world), but rather retreated from this environment to return to the more familiar world of (private) marital infidelity investigation, where he thrives to the point of epistemological and perceptual arrogance. In this light, Jake begins the narrative in a different place than either Walker or Corso (based on what we are privy to, that is) in that he has already experienced his identity crisis and believes he has overcome it, only to have to face it once again; hence the allegorical use of 'Chinatown' throughout the film.

Organs in peril

Having learned that water is being dumped nightly into different sections of the (dry) Los Angeles riverbed, Gittes, under the cover of night, investigates the waterworks in hope of discovering the origin of the mysterious flooding. The scene begins with Gittes's negotiation of a fence marked 'No Trespassing' and 'Keep Out'. Almost immediately, a shot rings out and Gittes is forced to take cover in one of the plant's dry drainage canals. As if on cue, water comes rushing from the plant, slamming Gittes's body ignobly into another fence. Soaked and now missing a shoe, he climbs out and tries to retreat back to his car. Before he can, however, he is met with a punch to the gut by Cross's henchman, Claude Mulvihill (Roy Jenson). Another man, dressed in white and small in stature (Gittes calls him a 'midget'), produces a knife and lectures Gittes menacingly about his 'nosiness'. To stress his point, the man inserts the knife onto Gittes's nose as Mulvihill holds him in place. As the man in white informs Gittes that 'nosey fellows … get their noses cut off', he quickly, almost casually, flicks the knife to the right, tearing Gittes's nose open. The ramifications of the incident resonate for the remainder of the film; Gittes is forced to wear a large bandage at first, which (neatly marking the passage of time) is replaced by a smaller one, and eventually an exposed (but quite gruesome) scar is revealed.

Bodily trauma is, of course, a ubiquitous motif seen throughout Polanski's work; these images often serve to dramatically underscore his frequent meditations on the body and identity. In *The Tenant*, Trelkovsky has his entire body traumatised, with the exception of the eyes, which are left intact as to allow for one last cruel visual trauma. Gittes is also not alone in having his nose violated; in *Cul-de-sac*, Dickie is also cut just beneath the nose, as is Oscar by Mimi in *Bitter Moon*; in *Two Men and a Wardrobe*, one of the men has his nose punched (a scene mirrored in *Chinatown*, with Polanski again playing the aggressor), and in *The Ninth Gate*, Green Eyes (Emmanuelle Seigner) also receives a bloodied nose, not from an adversary, but an unintentional elbow from Corso, in a scene that is itself evocative of the unintentional 'injury' caused to Evelyn by Gittes's wildly swinging arm in the last few moments of *Chinatown*.

The nose-cutting in *Chinatown* lends itself to a Lacanian reading in its allusion to castration, a common motif in *film noir* in which female forces often threaten to emasculate the (male) protagonist. But in this scene, it is not an underhanded *femme fatale* that threatens Gittes's male-mastery, but rather a diminutive, nameless man, played of course by Polanski himself. Rather than focusing on the nose-cutting as *symbolic* of castration, however, I propose a far more superficial reading in the context of my overall discussion. Considering *Chinatown*'s discourse on perception, it is not the phallus that is of towering importance, but the sense organs. By molesting Gittes's nose, the threat to perception is even more menacing than that of castration; next time, it is threatened, it will be the removal of the entire organ, leaving Gittes not sexually impotent, but *perceptually* limited.

The violence here is not threatened or implied; it is literal, and compounded by the further threat of total nasal amputation. Notwithstanding the man-with-knife's (as he is credited) seemingly metaphorical threat relating to 'nosiness', there remains a strongly *literal* aspect in his assault on a sense organ. As it turns out, it is sight, not smell, which proves most deadly in *Chinatown*, as manifested by the bullet that permanently does away with Evelyn's ('flawed') eye. Just as in *Oedipus*, eyes are the body parts that are most violently assaulted. When Hollis Mulwray's corpse is discovered, his eyes bulge unnaturally from their sockets, emphasising a connection between his perceptual acuity and his death. Most severe, however, is the way Evelyn is killed, having her eye shot out completely, as if the flaw on her iris served as a homing device for the stray bullet. Katherine Cross's eyes also 'bulge' as she takes in the horrific image of her mutilated mother/sister's cycloptic death mask, and are promptly covered by her father/grandfather's (monstrous) hand; a hand that at first seems to protect Katherine, but transforms into a grasping talon as he pulls her towards him.

Hearing and understanding

One of the means by which *Chinatown* elaborates Polanski's ongoing concern with perception is by introducing the complexities of language into the discourse. It is not only Gittes's perception of *visual* stimuli that proves challenging, but his ability to comprehend linguistic stimuli is taxed as well. When conversations are monitored, words become muddled and nonsensical due to interference; the highly relevant name of Cross's secret society, 'Albecore', for example, is (over)heard as the irrelevant 'apple core'.

Straightforward language barriers also cause problems, but unexpectedly prove to be revelatory in the end.

Gittes's several encounters with Evelyn Mulwray's entirely Chinese staff are also somewhat suggestive that he is returning to the sphere of uncertainty referred to as 'Chinatown'. His seemingly banal exchange of pleasantries with Mulwray's gardener proves most revealing. Whilst tending to the fishpond, the gardener (casually) tells Gittes that the salt water is 'very bad for the "glass"'. What at first seems to be a silly phonetic joke that highlights the difficulty many non-native English speakers have with the pronunciation of 'L' and 'R' turns out to be a key moment of revelation for Gittes, pointing not only to a possible reason for the presence of salt water in Hollis Mulwray's lungs, but also nudging Gittes towards the discovery of the (broken) glasses in the water; the pond is indeed 'bad for the glass'.

Jake Gittes's verbal exchange with the gardener unifies a series of key elements not only related to the case that Gittes is working on, but the issues the film is itself confronting. In particular, it manages to encompass the interplay between the auditory and visual sensory systems. Importantly, both what is heard (what the gardener says) and what is seen (the broken glasses) convey meaning. The words uttered by the gardener obtain significance beyond what seems to be intended by the object itself (i.e. the words, *sound waves*, produced by the gardener); Gittes hears these words (sound waves) and de-codifies one at first as 'glass', then translates this to the more probable 'grass' (an act of hypothesisation), but then back again to '*glass*'. The glasses themselves are also metonymic in that they serve as indicators, 'pointing' towards murder. But even so, the glasses must be interpreted, for they are not representations of an absent 'thing'; they are a *signpost* for murder.

In one of the most interesting visual metaphors in *Chinatown*, the gardener reaches into the pond whilst de-weeding it. Galperin describes the moment as a literal 'breaking of the plane of reflection' (1987: 1158), but the image also conveys the more nuanced concept with which active perception deals, namely that of the insurmountable gap between object and perception. Gittes will eventually reach through the light-refracting medium (the water) within which the object is concealed to literally grasp the case's most important clue, a symbol of sight itself. But the object's importance is not obvious at the time of its discovery; whilst Gittes's reaching into the pond may trigger thoughts of reaching across the 'perceptual gap' for those so inclined, the image is not inherently clear. The glasses may be an important clue, but Gittes has not quite picked the proverbial apple of knowledge. The glasses are, after all, broken.

As Jake Gittes discovers, the glasses are bifocals, an apt symbol for the multiple layering of 'realities' in *Chinatown*. The plague of *Chinatown* is not just a lack of water; it can also be identified as the wave of incongruent stimuli with which the perceiver, namely Gittes, must grapple. The bifocals also call to mind the various constructed illusions, those multistable perceptions/'visual ambiguities' (Gregory, 1997a: 205) I discussed in my case study of *Rosemary's Baby*, that highlight the brain's inability to simultaneously see contradictory images that defy well-established perceptual frameworks, notwithstanding their coexistence in the visual field. (This sort of contradiction is best embodied, perhaps, by the ironic occurrence of a man drowning in a drought.)

One of the most disturbing images in any Polanski film occurs when Gittes, imitating the cuckolded Curly's method of 'putting things right', beats Evelyn as means of getting the 'truth' out of her. The scene is highly problematic, as would be the case for any scene in which a male protagonist, with whom we are meant to sympathise, inflicts violence on a woman. The fact that the genre and era is permissive of such violence hardly seems relevant, and certainly does not make the act forgivable. Polanski's use of inter-gender violence is of course nothing new; but such violence normally takes the form of rape-revenge scenarios (real and/or imagined) as seen in *Repulsion, Rosemary's Baby, Tess* and *Death and the Maiden*. Unlike these films, however, *Chinatown* runs the risk of normalising Gittes's actions (in spite of the period setting). As offensive as the scene may be, it remains a powerful manifestation of Gittes's growing state of crisis.

The scene in which Gittes beats Evelyn is preceded by another scene in which Gittes and Evelyn share a different sort of physical exchange. After making love, it is Gittes who reveals to Evelyn details of his past, specifically his experience as a police officer stationed in Chinatown, in which he inadvertently caused someone's death. The scene concludes, however, with Evelyn denying a reciprocal self-revelation when questioned about a distressing call that causes her to dash away. Gittes follows her and learns that Evelyn is attending to the very woman his team of investigators had identified as Hollis Mulwray's mistress. Believing Evelyn to be holding her captive, Gittes demands information from Evelyn, who refuses. He resorts to beating her into submission, which results in her blurting out the phrase that, like the cracked bifocals, proves to be a highly revelatory element in the case. 'She is my daughter and my sister', a seemingly contradictory statement, or 'linguistic ambiguity' that is in fact true and represents (at least) half of the motivation behind Hollis Mulwray's murder.

Just as Gittes is forced to re-evaluate the visual and aural stimuli he encounters beyond his conceptual framework, so too is he challenged semantically. The seeming paradox with which Gittes is now faced presents a direct affront to these frameworks; this time, however, the challenge does not take place in the type of sensory context I have discussed thus far, but at the level of the higher cognitive function involved in semantic comprehension, where one's 'daughter' and 'sister' cannot be the same person. When Gittes attacks Evelyn, he is attempting to bridge a perceptual gap by physically striking her, the 'object' that holds the knowledge he needs; but rather than forcing Evelyn to admit what his 'divorce private investigator' conceptual framework is telling him must be true, he is faced with a series of words that highlight the *limits* of the framework into which he retreated after his personal 'Chinatown' tragedy, and thus the limits of his ability to perceive and comprehend the world[1] are exposed. As Coates (2006) discusses, there is indeed a connection in *Chinatown* between the moments of linguistic misunderstandings and those of cognitive revelation: 'In *Chinatown*, key words are knotted with others to create a hallucination of clues to a hidden trauma' (106). Gittes's own struggle to piece together the now shattered reality into which he has retreated is confounded, as reflected by his difficulty with accessing what seem to be simplistic units of (linguistic/symbolic) meaning, such as the overlap of 'grass' and 'glass', or the novel unity of the normally exclusive terms 'daughter' and 'sister'.

Perception, *noir* and the Oedipus myth

Just as Sophocles is assumed to have utilised the ancient Oedipal myth as a means of conducting contemporary social criticism through drama (McGinnis, 1975: 250), so too has *Chinatown* been read as a nostalgic postmodern homage to the hard-boiled films of the 1940s, in which the depiction of corruption reflects not only the era the film evokes (Jameson, 1983: 116), but also the era in which it was made. Zimmerman, for example, himself writing in 1974, calls *Chinatown* a 'Watergate with real water' (74). Whilst Polanski's themes tend to be philosophically 'grand' in their evocation of existential conundrums (as I have suggested, through engagement with perceptual psychology), this is not to imply that his work is immune from direct, contemporary commentary hidden within genre cinema. But the film's enduring relevance suggests that the significance of its focus on perception in both the institutional and personal/familial sphere is greater than its function as critique of a specific political event.

The interpretation of *Chinatown* as an Oedipal text has taken various forms, but whilst many readings of the film have made the parallel, there is also risk of exaggerating the parity. Morrison (2007) rightly encourages us to reconsider the adjective 'Oedipal' in *Chinatown* beyond the Freudian connotation, particularly because the film mirrors the Sophoclean text's emphasis on the 'destructive, not curative' (81) investigation into Los Angeles's 'diseased polity' (79). Where Freud emphasises the exposure of incestuous desire as a means of healing a fractured psychology, neither *Oedipus Rex* nor *Chinatown* provides such solace in its complex, pessimistically fatalistic narrative. Nevertheless, whilst not quite a retelling of the myth, variations on elements of the *Oedipus* story are indeed present throughout *Chinatown*'s narrative, identifiably scattered amongst its characters.

McGinnis (1975) emphasises *Chinatown*'s debt to Sophocles's adaptation of the Oedipus myth primarily in terms of its shared political concern and 'wasteland motif' (249). Like the Theban plague, the cause of Los Angeles's drought is due to its incest-committing 'ruler', Noah Cross. But where Oedipus is impotent in the face of fate, Noah Cross's infliction of a drought on his people is quite calculated. In *Chinatown*, 'fate' comes as the result of wielding power. Reflecting this reversal is the nature of Cross's incestuous crime: rather than unknowingly (or subconsciously) bedding his mother, Cross intentionally mates with his daughter to produce another daughter (not sons, as in *Oedipus Rex*), with whom, it is insinuated, he will continue his incestuous congress. In *Chinatown*, it is the act of investigation that eventually results in the death of Evelyn Mulwray and the delivery of her sister/daughter into the hands of the monster (the 'plague') from which she was being protected. Furthermore, it is not only the physical presence of Noah Cross from which Katherine Cross is being guarded, but the *knowledge* of her genetic aetiology.

The connection between perceptual acuity, knowledge and power is embodied in Noah Cross, whose character revisits the territory of *Citizen Kane* in its exploration of corrupt power structures and the authorities' ability to manipulate perception; as Kane himself puts it, people will believe what he 'tells them to believe'. The character of Charles Foster Kane is itself a pastiche of publisher William Randolph Hearst, who, like Kane, uses his control of the media to seek election. A sceptical, or at least complex, treatment of authority figures is also common feature in post-war *film noir*. The move towards doubtful, 'dark cinema' was already present on the eve of war in films such as *You Only Live Once* (Lang, 1937) and *The Roaring Twenties* (Walsh, 1939); and the first cinema that would be identified as *noir* actually emerged in the midst of the war, including *The Maltese Falcon* (Huston,[2] 1941), *The Glass Key* (Heisler, 1942), *Laura* (Preminger, 1944), *Farewell, My Lovely* (aka *Murder, My Sweet*, Dmytryk, 1944) and *Double Indemnity* (Wilder, 1944).

The worldview presented in these 'dark' films contradicted the Allied Forces' need to encourage patriotism and binary thinking in wartime (Schrader, 1986: 231). Above all, Allied propaganda needed to encourage the absolute belief in the inherent 'goodness' of the Forces and the 'evil' of the Axis. Hence, the fledgling cinema movement that would later be identified by the French as *film noir* was stifled (but not extinguish) during the war. As Schrader highlights, the nuance of post-war *noir* challenged the absolutes of wartime propaganda, reflecting a 'delayed reaction to the [depression of the] thirties' (230) put on hold by the war, and the 'disillusionment of many soldiers, small businessmen and housewife/factory employees' (231–232), which in turn resulted in a critical eye being cast upon the very fabric of American society. Popular post-war *noir* such as *Cornered* (Dmytryk, 1945), *Dead Reckoning* (Cromwell, 1947) and *The Blue Dahlia* (Marshall, 1946) both reflected and encouraged America's renewed scepticism.

Chinatown joins a list of sceptical, arguably even cynical American conspiracy thrillers made in the 1970s, including *Klute* (Pakula, 1971), *Night Moves* (Penn, 1975) and *The Parallax View* (Pakula, 1974), as well as *noir* remakes like *The Long Goodbye* (Altman, 1973) and *Farewell, My Lovely* (Richards, 1975). In the spirit of this revival of cinematic scepticism, *Chinatown* sheds doubt on the assumed benevolence of authority in the Watergate era, and through its explicit focus on the perceptual mechanism and representational devices (the photograph), the film calls attention to the *institutionalisation of perception*, that is, the manner in which authoritative structures (religion, the government, media) use tenacity to 'shape' our perception through the construction of conceptual frameworks, such as the inherent benevolence of those in power. In this respect, Gittes's investigation (like Oedipus's) becomes a form of phenomenological research in that Gittes is forced to reflect on those aspects of his lived (*perceptual*) experience 'lost to our reflective knowledge through habituation and/or institutionalisation' (Sobchack, 1992: 28). The 'lost', or overlooked, element is not only knowledge of facts, but the understanding of the process and structures involved in perception, including the influence of institutions in the construction of conceptual frameworks. Hollis Mulwray's opposition to Cross's plan to build what is clearly a highly dangerous damn is essentially an informed challenge to a flawed, even immoral, conceptual framework; he is denouncing the naked emperor, for which he is killed.

As wielder of knowledge/power, Cross has nothing to investigate; in this regard, Cross differs from Oedipus, who yields power in name but is ignorant of his own nature. The task of investigation falls on private detective Jake Gittes, a (late-arriving) spectator to the Cross–Mulwray scenario, who must, through the use of his sense organs and higher cognitive functions, engage with this world. The investigation leads not to understanding in the curative (Freudian) sense, however, but rather highlights Jake's impotence, ignorance and arrogance. The investigation has an entirely negative effect, as it is Gittes who inadvertently delivers Katherine Cross into the eager hands of her father/grandfather by causing the death of her protective mother/sister.

As per the Oedipus myth, in *Chinatown*, the very act of investigation influences that which is being investigated. But where the Oedipus myth presents a fatalistic paradox, *Chinatown* does not so much ponder the existence of free will as confront the fact that the battle against evil is often futile. Polanski's cinema rarely partitions the world into 'good' and 'evil', and normally when his films appear to do so, these distinctions are either deconstructed or their diegetic reality becomes questionable (as seen in *The Tenant* and *Rosemary's Baby*, in which the 'evil' nature of the neighbours remains uncertain). Instead, one of the most dominant trends in Polanski's cinema is the exploration of moral ambiguity, laying challenges to notions of certainty whenever possible, often by way of the sort of perceptual crises under investigation here. Whilst Cross is indeed given the chance to defend himself ('most people never have to face the fact that at the right time and right place, they're capable of anything'), he is one of the few unambiguously 'evil' characters in Polanski's cinema (joined only by Bill Sykes[3] in *Oliver Twist* and most of the Nazis in *The Pianist*).

McGinnis relates Gittes to the portrayal of Oedipus as a man 'blinded' by success, forced against his will to face up to a reality that does not match his preconceptions (1975: 250). But 'success' is probably not the best descriptor for Jake Gittes, PI, for it is profound *failure* on Gittes's part that provokes his (perceptual) retreat into the reliable world of private detection, a role which hard-boiled lore informs us is not quite the height of PI success. McGinnis also cites Heilman's reading of Oedipus as a man who has been failed by recourse to 'pure reason' (1975: 250); for Gittes this is equally the case if the notion of 'pure reason' is strictly confined to that which is compliant with his own conceptual frameworks.

Back to Chinatown

It is in *Chinatown*'s troubling final scene that the film's narrative threads and philosophical discourse most dramatically collide. The sequence takes place in Los Angeles's Chinatown, which although providing the film's title remains up to this point an off-screen space. For the majority of the film, 'Chinatown' is indeed more a word than a place; it is an utterance that represents a tragic episode in Jake Gittes's life in which he inadvertently caused the death of a woman he loved. In the film's finale, the word is made material/spatial when Gittes is forced back to Chinatown in all its actuality. This final sequence is worth examining in detail; for it is through a close reading of the finale that key elements emerge that underline (I will stop short of saying 'clarify') the overall philosophical discourse of the film. I will address this sequence by both describing the various events that actually take place (which are more complex than many critics have noticed) and addressing its particular aesthetics.

The Chinatown finale (by 'Chinatown' I am referring here to the diegetic place, as opposed to the name of the film) is immediately preceded by Jake's confrontation with Noah Cross, in which his suspicions regarding Cross's complicity in Mulwray's death are confirmed and the perversity of Cross's overall 'game plan' is hinted at. For the second time in the film, Gittes has a sense organ threatened; not his nose this time, but his ear, as Cross's henchman Claude Mulvihill inserts his pistol into Gittes's auricle, forcing him to lead Cross to Evelyn. The sequence then begins with Gittes's arrival in Chinatown, Cross and Mulvihill in tow, the latter of whom keeps his right hand firmly gripped on the gun in his jacket pocket. Gittes find his two 'associates', Walsh and Duffy, to have already been handcuffed by police lieutenant Escobar (Perry Lopez), Gittes's former colleague on the force, who promptly places Gittes under arrest as well. Escobar is unmoved by Gittes's denouncement of Cross, and proceeds to have him handcuffed to the other officer.

The above scene is filmed in a single shot, with a handheld camera held in close proximity to the actors using a wide-angle lens (as per the rest of the film) and a short focal length. At the moment in which Gittes is handcuffed to the police officer, the camera disconnects from Gittes and shifts its focus to Cross's gaze. The camera quickly appropriates Cross's line of sight, which reveals Katherine Mulwray (his daughter/granddaughter) being accompanied to a car. As Evelyn rushes in to block his approach, the camera shifts its attention to her. Unlike the majority of the film thus far, in which the camera remains firmly tethered to Gittes, the camera seems no longer able to maintain its connection to a single character and has some difficulty containing its subjects in the frame; the chaos that is ensuing on-screen is further accentuated by the movement of the handheld camera. As Evelyn draws her pistol and points it at her father the camera momentarily adopts her POV, but is unable to maintain it as she climbs into the car and finally shoots her father in the arm. As she drives off with Katherine (her daughter/sister), we are left behind.

The camera then jumps one hundred and eighty degrees to reveal Escobar firing two shots straight into the air. Next to Escobar is Gittes, still handcuffed to the other police officer. Evelyn ignores the warnings and continues to drive away. As the camera frames him in a medium shot, Escobar fires a bullet towards the car, clearly aiming at its tyres. Before he can fire another shot, however, Gittes grabs Escobar's arm, blocking him from firing again. As a result, the officer to whom Jake is handcuffed is forced to draw his own gun in Escobar's stead. He shoots three times, quickly, but the angle at which he fires is significantly higher than Escobar's; he does *not* seem to be aiming at the tyres as Escobar had been. It is the third of these bullets, it seems, that manages to make contact with the car; or rather, its driver. Gittes, Cross and the police (followed by the camera) race to see what has happened; Katherine Cross is in a hysterical state, and Evelyn Mulwray is draped over the steering wheel, motionless. As Jake opens the car door, the gruesome image of Evelyn face is revealed: in the place of one of her eyes is a large hole.

Unsure where to focus its attention, the camera sways back and forth struggling to maintain a subject in the frame. It momentarily rests on Cross, who wraps his arm around Katherine and covers her eyes, urging her not to look. The camera swings back to Jake, whose own facial scar, which had in the sequence thus far been concealed by shadows, is now highly visible. With the death of Evelyn, Gittes finds history repeating itself in Chinatown. When Jake realises what has just happened, the expression on his face is not so much one of horror (which the situation would certainly merit), but one of blank befuddlement; it is an expression that does 'as little as possible'. As Gittes mutters this Chinatown mantra, the camera rapidly swings back to Escobar; it is a quick sweep that allows for a truly seamless cut to another shot, taken by a camera perched on a crane. Walsh tells Jake to 'forget it … it's Chinatown', and the men walk away. The camera retreats in the other direction and ascends above the street, above Chinatown, and away from the subject to whom it had been tethered.

I am compelled to highlight, especially as it is so often overlooked in critical analyses of this scene, the fact that Gittes is positioned as complicit in the death of Evelyn Mulwray due to his own actions, as well-intentioned as they might have been. By blocking Escobar, who seems to be aiming for the car's tyres, Gittes causes the second officer to fire. Unlike Escobar, this officer seems to fire with the intent to kill. The fact that Gittes is himself physically connected (handcuffed) to the man who kills Evelyn aptly symbolises Gittes's complicity in her death. Indeed, Evelyn's fate is the culmination of a series of events that lead her to Chinatown, which are arguably initiated by *Gittes's* decision to stray from his perceptual comfort zone into the intricate and overwhelmingly complex world of corrupt politics and taboo sexuality.

Retreating from *Chinatown*

As spectators of *Chinatown*, we (with very few exceptions) are consistently bound to Gittes's subjective reach; but the film does not opt for the sort of extreme (visual) subjectivity found in films like *Lady in the Lake* (Montgomery, 1947) and *Dark Passage* (Davies, 1947). Likewise, we are never granted access to Gittes via the type of voice-over narration often used in *film noir*; in fact, the few shots in *Chinatown* that can be considered as POVs are all mediated by way of instrumentation such as cameras (and the photographs they produce), binoculars and mirrors. As I have discussed in all of the previous case studies, representing (and replicating) intimate cognitive experience is certainly not something Polanski is adverse to. Although it was released before *The Tenant*, in which the depiction of purely subjective perceptions is central, *Chinatown* predicts a shift in Polanski's cinema towards a more distant form of realism in which perceptual processes remain concealed.

Whilst adhering to some generic conventions, *Chinatown* also eschews just as many, something that is consistent with Polanski's typical approach to genre. What is most readily apparent about *Chinatown*, of course, is the fact that it is shot in colour (Technicolour), but I do not mean to suggest that this fact is inherently against the *noir* grain, as countless neo-noir's shot in colour have proved. A trait that differentiates *Chinatown* from much of *film noir* is its lack of camera angles or lighting indicative of the expressionist influence on many *noir* classics. Although there is very little 'noir' in *Chinatown* (*Chinatown* is, for the most part, a very *bright* film), its sense of ambiguity remains rich. Where the dark corners of *film noir* remind us that our perception of the world is limited, by reflecting on the overlooked (habitualised/institusionalised) aspects of perception, *Chinatown* highlights that it is not only the absence of light that inhibits perception. In fact, it is the most brightly lit scenes in *Chinatown* that are the most misleading.

Davis (1990) collectively describes the 'hard-boiled' novels and *film noir* set in Los Angeles as the 'great anti-myth' (37), identifying these works as counters to the social mythology of the 'Land of Sunshine' and the utopian ambitions of its urban planning strategies. The Los Angeles of *noir* (and the novels upon which these films are based) is a place of paradox: it is both Heaven and Hell (18), or a mask of Heaven *concealing* Hell. Davis summarises this contrast in LA noir as 'a fantastic convergence of American "tough guy realism", Weimar expressionism, and existential Marxism – all focused on unmasking a "bright, guilty place" (Welles) called Los Angeles' (18). It is this intra-film juxtaposition of sunlight-drenched sequences with scenes that employ more typical, expressionistic use of shadows through which Los Angeles *noirs*, such as *Double Indemnity* (Wilder, 1944), *The Postman Always Rings Twice* (Garnett, 1946), *Nobody Lives Forever* (Negulesco, 1946) and *Chinatown*, both evoke and deconstruct the myth of the Southern California.

'Knowability' in *Chinatown* is emphasised in its classic, seamless montage style as well, which encourages the spectator to accept his or her perception of the diegetic realm as complete. Gradually, however, *Chinatown* begins to undo this assumption, mirroring Gittes's perceptual crisis in the spectator. As Orr (2006) observes, *Chinatown*'s 'continuity editing presents us with a knowable world even when true knowledge evades us' (5); but *Chinatown* does not present knowledge as something worth having. For Gittes, the greatest obstacle to effective perception (I use the term 'effective' in the context of solving the Mulwray case) is not darkness or ambient noise, but a non-reflective attitude towards his conceptual and perceptual frameworks; it is a sort of arrogance that is mirrored in Gittes's *faux*-phallic bravado in the first half of the film. Gittes's (the film's) trajectory is not so much one of overcoming obstacles to achieve a goal as it is towards the (moot) realisation that this world is too complex to perceive. The implications of such a proposition are vast, but that which finds greatest resonance with the rest of Polanski's cinema is the 'noirish' realisation that (a) either there is no intelligence orchestrating the world, whose machinations can be 'discovered' through investigation, or (b) if there is such a force, it is not necessarily benevolent, defeat-able or comprehensible.

As is typically the case in Polanski's cinema, in *Chinatown* there is no attempt to 'objectify' reality beyond the narrative reach of one character. Reality is framed, as it must be, but presented to us (roughly) just as it is presented to Gittes. The 'clues' are collected by Gittes, but he has no better understanding of them than the spectator. Neither the revelation of the cause of Mulwray's death nor the nature of Evelyn's relationship with her father is something Jake 'solves'; rather, contrary to what he is accustomed to as a private investigator, he has reality thrust upon him. In *Chinatown*, the 'real' is everywhere, right under Gittes's (damaged) nose; nevertheless, gaining understanding of it is not curative in the psychoanalytic sense.

At the risk of lapsing into a Lacanian digression, by the 'real' in *Chinatown* I am referring not only to the shocking revelations of the story, but rather the allusions to those cognitive functions at work that inhibit us from reflecting on the nature of these very mechanisms. Gittes is challenged to overcome the limits of his perceptual and conceptual frameworks, those both institutionally and self-imposed. Judging by his expression at the end of the film, it does not seem he is successful. It is difficult indeed to argue in favour of the usefulness of introspection, for, as *Chinatown* seems to suggest, engaging in such phenomenological research is not necessarily a path to well-being. When Gittes first faced 'Chinatown', his reaction was to eschew his (salaried) life of public service with the police force in favour of self-employment. Gittes's auto-'privatisation' allowed him to operate within the limited conceptual framework of the more predictable, *controllable*, reality of infidelity detection. Both Gittes's facial expression and his retreat from the frame at the end of the film suggest that this time around is no different from the last. He is condemned to repeat this fate and is better off doing 'as little as possible'. As if sharing Gittes's sense of complicity, the camera retreats as well, away from *Chinatown* and all its discontent.

Notes

1. Gittes's constant failing to comprehend (master) the elements of this case position him as what Belton describes as a 'burnt out Marlowe' (1991: 942) figure. The fact that Gittes resorts to violence also betrays a lack of 'cool' seen in Marlowe, whose own perceptual abilities are well honed. Even Gittes's role as a divorce PI evokes thoughts of Marlowe, namely his disdain for the type of divorce work that Gittes has been forced to take on.
2. In what is perhaps a direct nod to its debt to classic *noir*, Polanski casts John Huston as Noah Cross in *Chinatown*.
3. *sic*, spelled 'Sikes' by Dickens.

Chapter 9

A Tale of Two Doctors: *Frantic* and *Death and the Maiden*

As I discussed in the last case study, in the latter 'half' (i.e. post-*Tess*, but including *Chinatown*) of Polanski's cinema, his perceptual discourse shifts from a focus on unhealthy perceptual mechanisms towards more 'distant' observations of sane perceivers, who nevertheless face both perceptual and conceptual challenges. The change can be described as a shift from a concern with the representation (even attempted replication) of subjective psychological states, what I have referred to previously as *perceptual realism,* towards a more distant, observational stance in the second half of his opus, in which access to individual psyches remains elusive.

By taking this 'step back', Polanski expands his ongoing exploration of the philosophical ramifications of perceptual psychology (specifically the theory of active perception) to include the examination of the effect of stress, institutionalisation and self-imposed perceptual frameworks on what is considered to be perfectly sane perception. Moreover, the parallel nature of the higher cognitive functions involved in conceptualisation and those involved in sensory perception is further explored through non-psychologically 'intrusive' narratives in which ruptures nevertheless occur to interrelated perceptual and conceptual frameworks. Notably, Polanski also continues his discourse on perception by sometimes playing out the tenets of a theory of perception through inter-character exchanges, symbolically spreading elements of the cognitive process of perception amongst different subjects. So, it does not seem that Polanski has abandoned his concern with psychological subjectivity in these later films, but rather that he changes his methodology in order to nuance the overall discourse.

Both mirroring and furthering this trend towards a more complex exploration of perception is a more direct approach to the issue of national identity. Where *Chinatown* explores the effect of a (self-imposed) limited cognitive framework, in *Frantic*, the framework of national identity comes to the fore in a more explicit manner than in any other Polanski film to this point. Whilst much of Polanski's work includes recognisably transnational characters, in no film before *Frantic* is a protagonist's national 'otherness' so *explicitly* depicted as an obstacle.[1] In *Repulsion* and *The Tenant*, xenophobic attitudes towards Carole and Trelkovsky are hinted at, but these perceptions are so entwined with these characters' psychoses that it is difficult to identify the diegetic truth of these attitudes. In *Frantic*, Walker's 'Americaness' is a high-profile element in the film's narrative progression, as well as an informing agent in the film's visual aesthetics. As Polanski has himself remarked, an 'American gaze' guides *Frantic* (as quoted in De Baecque and

Jousse, 2005: 151); but this comment begs the question as to how, exactly, a concept of national identity can inform a 'gaze', a question which I will attempt to address in this chapter.

Later in this chapter, I will also turn my attention to *Death and the Maiden*. I have chosen to deal with this film in relation to *Frantic*, for there appears to be an overlap of perception-related motifs in these two films, released within a few years of each other (separated only by *Bitter Moon*). Without wishing to overcomplicate the make-shift concept of 'trilogies' I have employed as a means of grouping Polanski's films in a meaningful way, I will add only that whilst *Frantic* is rightly considered as a 'quest' or 'investigation' film, there is also a relevant sideways link between it and *Death and the Maiden*, in that they both deal with an Orphean crisis: a husband losing and attempting to reclaim his wife. *Death and the Maiden* can even be read as a sort of thematic 'sequel' to *Frantic*, in that through its own focus on the imprisonment of one character by another, it also deals with the psychological (i.e. post-traumatic) impact of kidnapping. Even more relevant to my overall approach, however, is *Death and the Maiden*'s concern with the reliability of the perceptual mechanism and its role in the creation of memory, especially when the perceiver is deprived of one of the senses (in this case, sight). *Frantic* and *Death and the Maiden* also deal with the influence of emotional states on a subject's perceptual abilities. The heightened emotional state of both *Frantic*'s Walker and *Death and the Maiden*'s Paulina (Sigourney Weaver) introduces doubt as to the reliability of their respective cognitive 'readings' of situations, but the exploration of the effect of emotions on perception is further complicated when we consider, as both of these films suggest, the possibility that it is these heightened emotional states that actually *enable* Walker and Paulina to perceive even more effectively than normal.

Frantic's 'research question' and establishing a subjective tether

Frantic begins with the image of Sondra Walker and her husband, Dr Richard Walker, in the back of a cab making their way into Paris from Roissy. Sondra, jetlagged, rests her head on Richard's torso, causing their bodies to overlap in the frame. She wakes up and asks her (also exhausted) husband if he 'knows where [he] is'. 'No, it's changed too much', replies Dr Walker, who appears to be too jetlagged to recognise anything. With these simple lines of dialogue (the film's first), their identity as Americans and the notion of the perceptual obstacle are swiftly introduced.

After an incident with a flat tyre on the motorway (to which I will shortly return), the Walkers find themselves in a new cab in a more central part of town, where Dr Richard Walker reluctantly affirms that he does indeed now recognise this place as Paris (unsurprising, as a reverse shot reveals the Eiffel Tower just down the road – once the dustmen get out of the way, that is). The taxi drops the Walkers off near Opera

Garnier, on rue Scribe, where they check into Le Grand Hotel. They are given a tour of the room's various facilities, after which they squabble over the fact that Richard has been requested to attend a lunch meeting that day, notwithstanding the fact that the Walkers have intentionally arrived a full day earlier than his conference required. Breakfast is ordered, the children are called (although Richard has some trouble with the phone) and their bags arrive. As Richard speaks to his daughter, Sondra struggles to open a suitcase in the background. The phone is then handed over to Sondra, and Richard attempts to open the suitcase. The camera now becomes more interested in Richard's struggle to open the case and abandons the phone conversation altogether. It is not their suitcase. As Richard calls TWA to report the error, the camera shifts its focus to Sondra in the shower.

The time dedicated to these banal quotidian events is not (just) an embracing of the type of narratively superfluous detail celebrated by Bazin as realism, but rather a generic marker of the thriller, in which the spectator is lulled into a state of near-boredom just as something is about to occur. The formula is in fact already teased in the opening sequence, where after a lingering two-shot on the post-flight pair of somnambulists, the cab that carries them violently veers off the road. It is here that we first expect the narrative trajectory to begin; it seems to be just the type of chance occurrence (a flat tyre) that could initiate a series of events making up the rest of the thriller. But Polanski subverts the formula; the flat tyre may foreshadow impeding doom, but the fact that it becomes a non-event serves more to draw our expectations *away* from known generic conventions until they are later reinstated to maximum effect. In other words, the red herring of the flat tyre impedes assumptions about the significance of the suitcase mix-up. Both the tyre and the initial suitcase sequences are examples of what Gregory (2003) calls the 'Venus Flytrap' effect in Polanski's cinema. In these examples, however, the effect is not achieved solely by visual aesthetics intended to create a sense of perceptual realism, but by playing on generic convention as another means of 'luring' in the spectator and then manipulating their expectations.

Having already been 'fooled' by the tyre incident, when Richard Walker takes his wife's place in the shower, the spectator cannot be sure what to expect. In fact, like Walker, we do not even know what *has* occurred when it actually *does* occur. It is at this point that Polanski's camera establishes its customary tether to a single subjective narrative reach, namely that of Dr Richard Walker. To reiterate a point I have made in previous chapters, I use the term 'tether' to account for the slight advantage the camera's (our) view sometimes has over the subject to which it is bound. We are not limited exclusively to Walker's POV (approximate or direct), but rather to that of a notional observer connected (*tethered*) to Walker. In this very scene, we are seemingly locked in the shower with him; but as he concentrates on lathering up, we are able to look past him at the events transpiring in the other room. Frustratingly, this slight advantage proves to be of very little epistemological use to us as spectators, as our connection to Walker inhibits our sensory reach. We can see that Sondra is talking on the phone and is attempting to communicate with Walker, but it is difficult to make out what is going on as both Walker's head and the increasingly foggy shower door impede our sight. She says something to him, but we, like Walker, cannot hear her over the noise of the shower (and his singing).

In what is seemingly an attempt to get a better view of the other room, the camera inches closer to the shower door. It is unable, however, to go any further as it seems to have reached the length of its tether. Seemingly exasperated, we (not Walker, who is now facing the other way) see her pick up an item of clothing from an open suitcase, mutter something, walk out of frame, and then drag the suitcase (the one she *has* been able to open) out of frame as well. As if desperate to see more, the camera moves closer and closer to Sondra's previous position, but is blocked by the shower door. It can go no further, regardless of how compelled the spectator may be to see, or at least hear, what is happening around the corner. Both the spectator and Walker will spend the remainder of the film trying to make sense of what has transpired; we are now tasked to derive *meaning* from what we have just perceived.

Emotion and hyper-perception

Walker's attempt to find his wife is essentially a *perceptual* quest that serves to magnify the basic premise of the theory of active perception, specifically in its repeated depiction of competing hypotheses presented to and by Walker and those who are caught up in his investigation (some helpful, some not). The basis for these predictive hypotheses is determined through the employment of *a priori* concepts and deductive reasoning, in which the 'laws' of the characters' worldview are applied to make sense of a set of stimuli. My contention is that Polanski's depiction of the relative malleability of perception finds expression in *Frantic* not through the representation of diseased cognitive processes (as seen in his cycle of films dealing with psychosis), but through scenarios in which equally probable (and therefore *valid*) hypotheses presented by various characters compete, with each theory presenting a plausible 'perception' that fills in the gaps left due to the poverty of the original stimuli.

In order to accomplish the task of finding his wife, there are several perceptual obstacles that Walker must deal with. First and foremost is the most superficial problem, Walker's jetlag, which not only causes him to fall asleep at inopportune moments (as he waits for Sondra in their room, and then again in the lobby as the hotel manager is summoned), but may also interfere with his reasoning abilities and thus his capacity to comprehend stimuli effectively. Offsetting this effect, however, is the fact that Walker's increasing desperation and frustration seem to cause a surge of adrenaline; rather than nodding off, Walker becomes increasingly aggressive. The initial effect of the jetlag is not only overcome, but the stress of the situation and Walker's (quite accurate) sense of isolation may actually serve to sharpen his senses, thus allowing him to pick up on small details missed by others.

Gregory (1997a) acknowledges the connection of emotional states and perception, indicating that not only can our emotions be affected by what we perceive, but also that our very ability to perceive effectively can be influenced by our emotional state. Gregory does not, however, hypothesise at any length as to how this two-way connection can best be understood, but he is quick to differentiate the effect of emotional states on perception from illusions. Gregory clarifies that illusions are *systematic* 'phenomenal phenomena', which are either *physical* or *cognitive* in nature.[2] In contrast, Gregory points to the non-systematic effect that strong emotional states can have in the creation of *hallucinations*, which are defined as perceptions that are fabricated by the brain independent of (or inconsistent with) external stimuli (1997a: 244). What Gregory does not account for, and what Polanski seems to be exploring, is the possibility that strong emotional states could also *heighten* perceptual ability. In this regard, it seems as though in both *Frantic* and *Death and the Maiden*, Polanski extends his perceptual discourse beyond explorations of hindered perception and *damaged* psyches (in which perception and reality become completely estranged) to include the concept of *hyper-perception*.

Whilst Walker may enter a state of hyper-perception caused by emotional distress, his heightened perceptual abilities are only effective within pre-existing cognitive frameworks, in particular those related to the visual perception of non-abstract sensorial stimuli. In parallel, his ability to apply logic, to *judge*, the meaning of stimuli is also heightened, in turn increasing the overall acuity of both 'halves' of the perceptual mechanism, that is, the reception of sensorial stimuli and the cognitive functions involved in the construction of the perception of them. For all of Walker's newfound 'super powers', however, his perceptual abilities are also stymied by obstacles that he simply cannot overcome alone, namely those perceptual challenges that require him to access conceptual frameworks that he does not possess. Whilst Walker's visual acuity may be high, this does not help him read in French, and nor would fine-tuned hearing help him understand it when spoken.

An indicative example of the process of acute sensory information deciphering is played out in *Frantic* when Walker discovers his wife's bracelet. Still suffering from jetlag and facing a completely novel set of stimuli (the Parisian alley the 'Wino' leads him to), Walker is able to spot a small bracelet amongst the cobbles; it is a seemingly impossible task, especially as he did not even know it was a bracelet he was looking for. Complicating the scene further is the fact that Walker is being fed information about his wife by a man whose own sobriety, and by extension the reliability of his perceptual abilities, is seriously questionable. It is also indicated by the 'Wino' (as he is credited) that it was not he who witnessed Sondra's abduction, but some of his friends (likely Winos as well), '*[qui ont] vu la scène*'. A further layer of ambiguity is arguably added by Walker's complete inability to understand French and the Wino's limited English, but a more optimistic reading would suggest that Walker is lucky that this vagrant is able to speak English at all, far better in fact than any of the 'respectable' Parisians approached by Walker beforehand (as we shall see, it is Paris's marginals who prove most helpful to Walker), not to mention infinitely superior to Walker's complete lack of French. Nevertheless, the obstacle is there.

The argument that Walker has with the American authorities is a good example of how *Frantic* uses an interpersonal conflict to depict the role that higher cognitive functions play in perception to make up for the poverty of sensory information. The Embassy employees question the validity of Walker's kidnapping theory, due undoubtedly to much experience with frantic tourists in the past. They, just as the hotel security chief, suggest that Sondra has not been kidnapped, but has simply abandoned her husband for a French lover. The scenario contests what Walker holds fast as being the nature (the *reality*) of his wife, and so the meaning he attributes to the images, both seen and described, differs greatly from that which is proposed by the embassy men. When Walker presents the bracelet to the Embassy officials, its significance is debated; it is *judged* based on its own physical properties (i.e. it is a bracelet with Sondra's name on it) and the context in which it was found (i.e. amongst the cobbles, its latch broken). At the risk of inverting a metaphor, it appears that the cognitive 'trial' described by Gregory (1997a: 112) is played out in *Frantic* between Walker and the embassy men, each of whom hypothesises plausible (and therefore valid) interpretations of stimuli.

It is important to highlight that Walker is not an investigator by choice, but is nevertheless thrust into the role of investigator due to what he considers to be inadequate measures taken by both the French police, who he does not believe are taking him seriously due to his national identity (although they claim otherwise), and the American officials in Paris, who claim they are inhibited from taking action due to international accords. The fact that Walker liaises with authorities, but ultimately works independently of them in the solving of this case positions him, like Gittes, as a private investigator. And like Gittes, the difficult case Walker takes on is based on self-interest rather than remuneration. It is again worth recalling the detectives of popular culture that have carried on the Oedipal tradition. It is indeed his level of personal engagement that aligns Walker, like Gittes, to the hard-boiled detective. As Žižek argues in his discussion of Phillip Marlowe, a defining characteristic of the hard-boiled investigator is that he himself is 'caught up in the circuit', his 'involvement defin[ing] his very subjective position' (1991: 61, arguably making Oedipus the first of the 'hard-boiled'). But Walker's personal involvement not only initiates his investigation, it also triggers his augmented perception. We can therefore contrast Walker to Sherlock Holmes, for example, whose perceptual acuity is unlinked to his emotional state. So whilst Walker's occupation (physician) does position him as a man well-used to the application of deductive reasoning, it is emotional stress that seems most responsible for his hyper-perception, a state that contrasts Walker from what Žižek identifies as Holmes's version of 'bourgeois scientific rational[ism]' (1991: 49) or omniscient 'infallibility' (57).

Walker as Orpheus

Where *Chinatown*'s investigation is motivated by Gittes's desire to put right an epistemological 'wrong' (i.e. he has been fooled), *Frantic*'s Dr Walker has a much more tangible problem in the kidnapping of his wife. In *Frantic*, Polanski provides a physical embodiment of a character's search for meaning through a portrayal of love unparalleled in the rest of his cinema, which more typically depicts treachery in relation to marriage. I have used the word 'love', but for Walker it may be just as valid to speak instead of 'identity', as in *Frantic*, these two concepts are literally intertwined. The interconnectedness of Richard and Sondra Walker is established not only through the frequent references to their union by their children, friends and colleagues, but visually in the opening and closing scenes of the film in which they are physically interlocked in the back seat of a taxi cab. What I propose is that Walker's crisis is also an identity crisis that begins with the removal of his wife; it is an 'amputation' akin to the removal of a limb or an organ without which one cannot survive (to echo the sentiment of *The Tenant*'s dismemberment soliloquy). Walker is frantic not just about securing his wife's safety, but also about maintaining his own, now fractured, identity.

As a means of expressing the emotional drive behind Walker's quest, in addition to including elements of the Oedipal detective story (complete with the trigger for a nuclear 'plague', *unknowingly* in Walker's possession), Polanski's also utilises the Orpheus myth as a narrative framework (as observed by Feeney, 2006: 133). Like Orpheus, out of pure devotion, Walker is forced to recover his wife from the clutches of devils. Standing in for Hades are Paris's labyrinthine alleys, nightclubs and even rooftops (a sacred Parisian space); it is a city revered for its beauty, but which is quickly transformed into Hell when Walker is forced out of *globalised* spaces in search of his wife. At one point, Walker also finds himself in a nightclub called 'A Touch of Class', run and populated by members of Paris's North African community, an alien space even for Parisian Michelle. At this point Walker is located several 'circles' (to evoke Dante) beneath the global 'over-world'. In *Frantic*, Hell is represented not as a place of physical torture, but rather one of displacement and perceptual crisis.

In a role evocative of that played by Virgil in Dante's *Inferno*, guiding Walker through this Hell is Michelle, who, for her own (financially motivated) reasons is forced to become involved in the search for Sondra. Michelle's role is complex; she acts as perceptual guide to Walker, helping him navigate both the Parisian landscape and French language, but she is also a demonic agent in her own right. As Belton (1991) discusses, there is a traditional division of gender in the hard-boiled detective fiction in which the male detective is positioned as a patriarchal force attempting to attain knowledge, which is held by women, through mastery of language, which women control. 'From the perspective of patriarchy', Belton writes, 'the source of mystery in the genre – that which defies the rationalizing power of the detective figure – is woman, who uses language deceitfully' (1991: 939). We have already seen Polanski's coupling of women and ambiguous language in *Chinatown*, and again in *Frantic* it is a woman who holds the reins of language. Michelle, however, does not so much 'defy' Walker's quest for knowledge as facilitate it by serving as translator. Nevertheless, Walker is forced to both intimidate and bribe Michelle to compel her to take on this role, and her superior linguistic ability (she is French, but also speaks English without problem) allows her to both adopt (especially through her clothes and make-up) and deconstruct her role as *femme fatale*. Michelle does indeed eventually double-cross Walker with her last minute bargaining for the triggering device, but ultimately it is *she*, not Walker, who (like Evelyn Mulwray in *Chinatown*) takes a bullet.

A little digression on the use of music in *Frantic* is warranted here. Further complicating Michelle's role is the manner in which she is associated with Walker's daughter through their mutual fondness of the Grace Jones song 'Strange', which we hear playing in the background when Walker speaks to his daughter on the phone, as well as in Michelle's car. The same song is heard yet again playing in the 'A Touch of Class' nightclub. The repetition of this track effectively forms an aural bridge across the Atlantic, as well as managing to unify the ethnic space of the nightclub with the wider world, something pop music seems able to do effortlessly (especially transnational artists like Grace Jones). The song itself reflects as well the atmosphere of the film as a whole in its hybrid musical style, its shifting between French and English, and its *noir*ish imagery of a stranger in the night.

It is also worth highlighting the connection drawn between Michelle and Walker's daughter, which by alluding to the incestuous relationship dealt with in *Chinatown* heightens the taboo of the desire between Michelle and Walker. In the last act of the film, starting with their visit to 'A Touch of Class', Michelle dons the same red dress Walker's wife was wearing when she was kidnapped and is transformed, briefly, from guide to temptress. In a purely physical act of communication performed by Michelle to the ubiquitous Grace Jones song, she offers Walker the chance to abandon his wife to the devils and assume her, a much younger and more nubile woman, as his mate in Sondra's stead.

Frantic in context

A brief discussion of the historic moment within which *Frantic* takes place (sometime between 1987 and 1988) may help clarify the very specific tensions this film reflects, in particular those regarding the threat of nuclear proliferation, the challenges to conservatism in the US and globalisation and postcolonial racial integration in France. The greatest global fear at this time was undoubtedly the threat of nuclear war. So pronounced was this threat in the mid-1980s, that US president Reagan and Soviet General Secretary Gorbachev were compelled to engage in a series of disarmament talks that resulted in the Intermediate-Range Nuclear Forces Treaty (INF) of 1987

(Wittner, 2003: 369–405). However, the INF treaty could not alleviate fear of Arab or Muslim states acquiring materials to create nuclear weapons, a threat particularly felt by Israel after the Palestinian uprising of 1987 (Kam, 2003: 360), just prior to the time of the film; these are the specific fears that *Frantic* alludes to in its inclusion of a hidden nuclear triggering device and the Arab characters who seek it.

From a specifically French perspective, the presence of Arab characters also reflects the tensions within France related to its colonial and postcolonial relationship with North Africa, in particular its former colony Algeria and the increasing demography in France of French citizens of Algerian descent (by the 1980s, many were third generation French-Algerians). The complexities of (ongoing) Algerian–French tensions, far more intricate than a binary conceptualisation of the situation as a 'culture clash' would suggest, cannot be dealt with here; however, it is at least worth noting that by the 1980s France and Algeria had become bound into the 'postcolonial predicament that unites Algeria and France into a single transpolitical space' (Silverstein, 2004: 2). In *Frantic*, we see signs of the division of 'ethnic' space in Paris; this is not only evident in the partitioning of the Arab kidnappers with nuclear ambitions from the 'white' victims, but is also woven into the fabric of the city itself, which conceals 'Arab spaces' like the nightclub visited (*investigated*) by Walker and Michelle. On the other hand, a more 'integrated' version of Paris is portrayed in another nightclub, the 'Blue Parrot', in which Walker first spots Michelle.

As discussed by Kellner and Ryan (1988), *Frantic* also takes place in an era that was showing signs of a waning 'conservative hegemony' in the US and a corresponding decrease of the sway of Ronald Reagan on the American people, due in part to the tarnishing of his reputation at this time by the Iran arms-for-hostages and Contra-supply scandals (263). Kellner and Ryan highlight the link between Hollywood cinema in 1986 and 1987 and the prevailing political mood; their claim is that the weakened status of conservatism combined with growing scepticism regarding the validity of increased American militarism (which was widely perceived as imperialism) contributed to the end of the era of the do-it-all cinematic 'hero' typified by *Rambo* (1985) (297). The 'hero' of *Frantic* is indicative of this demise; the difference is palpable, for example, when we compare the desperate Dr Richard Walker, who scrambles around Paris looking for his wife, and John Rambo, who puts history right by blasting his way through Vietnam, years after the end of the war, to save American POWs. As Kellner and Ryan suggest, 'in 1987, more people desired help from the government than ever before' (297); what we see in Walker is a man in dire need of help, but who does not get it from his own government until they perceive a threat to their own institutions, that is, when the problem of an individual citizen is elevated to the problem of the nation itself. (It should be noted, of course, that Reagan's vice-president George Bush would go on to win the election in late 1988, gaining 422 electoral seats over Democratic representative Dukakis's 111; this is a fact that should put Kellner and Ryan's assertions regarding the extent of the 'liberalisation' of the US in 1987–1988 into some perspective.)

Whilst the domination of American conservatism was coming under scrutiny, in 1987–1988 France was not exactly a socialist utopia itself. Even though Mitterrand and his socialist party maintained power, their reluctance to adopt neo-liberal polices and prioritise the market would result in the loss of the legislative elections in 1986. The gains made in the cabinet by Chirac and his conservative party resulted in a schizophrenic period of 'cohabitation' between President Mitterrand and (the prescribed) Prime Minister Chirac between 1986 and 1988, the very period in which *Frantic* is set. As the result of a more potent conservative voice in government, as well as the adoption of the Single European Act in 1986, the French government was forced to come to terms with globalisation and to somehow reconcile its traditionally republican (more socialist) sensibilities with neo-liberalism (Price, 1993: 389). As I discuss later in this chapter, this shift from socialism to globalism and neo-liberalism forms part of the subtext of *Frantic*, manifested in the character of Michelle and the skills she develops (both financial and linguistic) in her own struggle for survival.

Hell and globalised spaces

It is by addressing the concept of 'globalised space' that I mentioned earlier that we can perhaps best understand what Polanski intends by his comment that *Frantic* is guided by an 'American gaze'. In the scene described at the beginning of this chapter, Walker is unable to recognise Paris as he is driven into town from the airport; this is unsurprising, as Paris's peripheral motorways are hardly part of the tourist trail. Luckily for the Walkers, they are protected by the taxicab, a global space in its own right (the *back seat* of the cab, at any rate), which transports them through this alien terrain. But the breakdown of the first cab signals the fragility of the membrane between global (friendly) and alien (hostile) space. It is important to emphasise that Walker is not displaced merely because he is in Paris, but rather because he has found himself in a situation that is incongruent with his personal faculties and the space (and class) he occupies, which takes him to areas of Paris he would never have otherwise visited and forces him into linguistic situations he is ill-prepared to handle. The departure from global space into (non-touristic) Parisian space both augments and parallels the crisis of the loss of his wife and the many challenges to his perceptual frameworks this entails.

An interesting juxtaposition of spaces takes place early in the film as Walker begins to look for his wife beyond the confines of the quintessentially global space of the five-star hotel. The hotel serves as an oasis for Walker; it is a space where he knows how to operate, and in which people not only speak English but are also incredibly helpful. The hotel is not quite an 'any-space whatever' in the Deleuzian sense, but a *global* space (and by this I mean a western/capitalist standard of 'global') that stands apart from its physical location. It would be difficult indeed, for example, to determine from the shots of the hotel alone that Walker was in Paris without gazing out of the room's window. In the first part of the film, Walker stays within global space. Two taxis serve as bridge between the airport and the five-star hotel; but when Walker moves from the hotel to the outside streets, he begins to encounter increasingly severe perceptual challenges, both in his capacity as perceiving subject and his presentation of himself as object for others to perceive. In the flower shop, he cannot make himself understood and is forced to retreat. He enters a café where the noise and hubbub are a sharp contrast to the hotel lobby's relative calm. By leaving the hotel, Walker takes his first real step into a dimension of foreign stimuli.

As a honeymooning tourist or medical convention attendee in Paris, Walker is perfectly at home, occupying the global spaces of airports, hotels and conference centres. But on this trip to Paris, Walker ends up as neither (second) honeymooner nor convention goer, and is forced to navigate spaces in which his status, abilities and (thus) *identity* are severely compromised and challenged. On the other hand, Walker does manage to employ some aspects of his personal cognitive frameworks, specifically those derived from the capitalist structures he is accustomed to, in which money, above all other factors, motivates people to come to his aid. It is money, of course, that ultimately convinces Michelle to join Walker. Luckily, money is something Walker has a relatively high supply of, notwithstanding his claim to the American authorities that he is not 'rich'.

Whilst Walker's chief perceptual crises are caused by his departure from global space, it is the truly global threat of nuclear annihilation that is behind the abduction of his wife in the first place; but the political element that emerges in the film's third act proves to be as alien a world to Walker as the back streets of Paris. And whilst the terrorist threat is a serious issue for the American authorities, the threat posed by the triggering device in his possession is not Walker's primary concern, which remains that of recovering his wife safely, even if that means putting millions of lives at risk. In its inclusion of such an unlikely grandiose subplot, *Frantic* portrays yet another type of 'space', that of international political conflict; it is not a physical space, but rather a world that operates under a different set of realities than the one occupied by the Walkers, who, as Richard Walker himself points out, 'don't even vote anymore'. The world of politics similarly forms the backdrop of *Death and the Maiden*, to which I will presently turn my attention. In contrast to *Frantic*, however, *Death and the Maiden*'s couple, Paulina and Gerardo Escobar (Stuart Wilson), live in a country (unnamed) where the right to vote has only recently been achieved, due in great part to the efforts of the Escobars and the revolutionary party to which they belong.

The aftermath of abduction: *Death and the Maiden*

There is an odd narrative overlap that signals a connection between *Frantic* and *Death and the Maiden*. Both films include a situation in which a car journey is interrupted by a flat tyre. On both occasions, the tyre cannot be replaced due to the spare tyre being flat as well. Whilst this particular scenario (the double-flat) may well be present in other works of fiction (although I am not aware of any), it is sufficiently odd an event (compared to running out of petrol, for example) that its repeated presence in Polanski's cinema is at least conspicuous. As I have already suggested, in *Frantic* the scene proves not to have any bearing on the narrative thrust of the film, although its inclusion does serve to create a heightened sense of peril (in line with generic expectation) and, as I have argued, hints at the fragility of the borders between what are global and alien spaces for Walker.

In *Death and the Maiden*, on the other hand, the 'scene' does not even occur on-screen; rather, it is recounted by Gerardo Escobar (Paulina's husband) upon his late arrival at home. In contrast to *Frantic*, however, even though we do not witness this scene, the occurrence does indeed prove to be highly relevant to *Death and the Maiden*'s narrative thrust. Remarkably, what seems in *Death and the Maiden* to be a subtle reference back to *Frantic* is actually present in Ariel Dorfman's original stage-play, *La Muerte y la Doncella*, itself published in 1990, two years after *Frantic*'s release. Intentional or not, the overlap is *there*, signalling a connection between the films. We cannot, of course, rule out the possibility that Dorfman may actually be citing *Frantic*; Polanski has himself suggested (as quoted in Delahaye and Narboni, 2005: 23) that such double-intertexuality has occurred before, in reference to the possible influence of *Repulsion* on Ira Levin's novel *Rosemary's Baby*, and a similar argument could be made for the influence of the rape scene in *Rosemary's Baby* on the way Dorfman has Paulina describe her own rape.

Besides the coincidence of both films' inclusion of (double) flat tyres, *Frantic* and *Death and the Maiden* each employ the Orphean motif of a woman being forcibly removed from her husband; but where *Frantic* deals with the abduction of a wife and her husband's attempt to recover her, *Death and the Maiden* instead serves to carry on this story in its dealing with not only the abduction's emotional aftermath, but specifically the abductee's rape-revenge trajectory from passive victim to active abductor (and perhaps even rapist, as Paulina admits contemplating). Both films also share political overtones related to their respective abductions; for the Walkers it is a case of mistaken identity, but the abduction of Paulina and her subsequent torture is described as a far more targeted political act. The imprisonment (and 'trial') of Miranda, on the other hand, which of course drives *Death and the Maiden*'s narrative, is only accidental in as much as it is initiated by a truly incredible coincidence (i.e. Paulina's former captor stopping to help her husband on the side of the road). Whilst Miranda's 'trial' is indeed thought of as a highly political act by Gerardo, who worries how their actions will be perceived by the outside world and how this might compromise his own political aspirations, Paulina is much less concerned with the 'movement', and acts out of a deeply held need for justice (or revenge) that she hopes will recalibrate her unstable emotional state. *Frantic* and *Death and the Maiden* also differ greatly in their portrayals of their male characters. Richard Walker and Gerardo Escobar are similarly cast as highly competent professionals (a physician and a lawyer respectfully), but where Gerardo's professional and personal ethics are highly politically charged, Richard is firmly apolitical, caring about nothing besides the preservation of his familial order. Also, where Richard Walker resists the temptations of his guide, it is made explicit in an argument that Gerardo was significantly less 'Orphean' in his devotion, abandoning Paulina for another woman whilst she was imprisoned.

Sensory deprivation

Death and the Maiden marks the return of Polanski's cinema to the depiction of a woman's perceptual crisis. Like Carole Ledoux and Rosemary Woodhouse, Paulina Escobar's ability to perceive effectively is put into doubt by the distinct possibility of the presence of mental illness. In *Death and the Maiden*, it is a form of post-traumatic psychosis with schizophrenia-like symptoms; as I discussed in my case study of *Rosemary's Baby*, Boehnlein and Kinzie (1989) have identified what are referred to as 'schizophrenia-like' symptoms associated with patients who have suffered severely traumatic experiences. Although not directly cited in Polanski's film, in Dorfman's stage-play, Dr Miranda verbally 'diagnoses' Paulina as a 'prototypical schizoid' (1990: 27). Nevertheless, in the film version, the question of Paulina's sanity is often (euphemistically) alluded to. In this regard, we must separate Paulina from the group of *male* perceiving subjects I discuss throughout this second set of case studies (Jake Gittes, Richard Walker and Dean Corso), all of whom encounter some sort of perceptual or conceptual crisis, but none of whom ever has his sanity questioned. In *Death and the Maiden*, it is also a man, Gerardo, who is positioned as the sane perceiver forced to resolve an ambiguity. Through Paulina, however, *Death and the Maiden* contributes several other layers of complexity to Polanski's ongoing perceptual discourse, in particular the issues of sensory deprivation and the long-term effect of torture on a woman's ability to both perceive effectively during the trauma itself and reliably access what is stored of these perceptions to judge the meaning of stimuli years later. In fact, the fount of conflict in *Death and the Maiden*'s narrative is not just Paulina's exertion of power over Dr Miranda, but specifically the question of Paulina's perceptual acuity. Abducted and imprisoned by this unnamed country's previous political regime, Paulina was bound, tortured and raped (as mentioned earlier, a described occurrence that strongly echoes the rape scene of *Rosemary's Baby*). Blindfolded, she was never able to see the men who committed these acts. But her other senses were not inhibited: she could feel them, smell them and hear them; in particular, one 'doctor' who had a penchant for quoting *Nietzsche* and playing Schubert whilst torturing her.

Just as in *Frantic*, the possibility of hyper-perception forms an important part of *Death and the Maiden*'s overall discourse, adding to it the concept of sensory deprivation as a means of *augmenting* other forms of sensory perception. As Paulina argues, whilst she was deprived of her sight in the torture chamber, due to her highly receptive state, she received sufficient (intermodal) data from her olfactory and auditory senses to be able to identify Miranda by his scent and voice alone, as positively as if she had seen him. In his film adaptation, Polanski elects to remain faithful to Dorfman's stage-play by not portraying Paulina's torture by any means other than diegetic verbal exposition, namely Paulina's conversations with Gerardo and Miranda in which details of her imprisonment are revealed. So just as Gerardo is forced to pass judgement on testimony alone, so too is the spectator denied any cinematic image that may confirm or deny what Paulina says, and just as Paulina is denied access to the visual stimuli that would have informed her judgement, so too are we, as spectators, deprived of a flashback designed to stabilise our own sense of what is and what is not diegetically true. Hence, the possibility that Paulina is suffering from ('schizophrenia-like') post-traumatic psychosis remains a valid hypothesis throughout the film, for both Gerardo and the spectator.

Gerardo's doubtful reaction as to the reliability of Paulina's perceptual claims highlights the special privilege humans afford to sight amongst their senses as the most reliable epistemological tool. At the very least, the scepticism with which Paulina's claims are received highlights the dictatorship of visual perception; but it may also suggest something more. Her claim that she is able to recognise the doctor notwithstanding being blindfolded raises the question of her augmented perceptual abilities, which are not only elevated due to emotional stress, but perhaps also due to the removal of her sight, which might allow the brain to more effectively identify and decode auditory stimuli specifically *because* the senses are not working in concert.

Competing hypotheses

In *Frantic*, our attention seems deliberately deflected *away* from thoughts about what Sondra Walker may be enduring during her imprisonment (considering the nature of the object her abductors were attempting to recover, we can safely assume her imprisonment was not pleasant); our engagement with the film instead relies on our capacity to assume the emotional stress suffered by the character of Dr Walker, to whom we are so closely tethered. In fact, *Frantic* does not address Sondra's plight at all, remaining firmly tethered to Richard Walker's subjective reach. Whilst we are not privy to Sondra's personal experience, Paulina's is recounted in vivid detail. In fact, in *Death and the Maiden* it is the *minute* details of Paulina's imprisonment (although never shown) that are most critical to the narrative's progression (i.e. Miranda's fate at the hands of the Escobars). Also in contrast to *Frantic*, in *Death and the Maiden*, the camera is not tethered exclusively to any of the film's three characters; nor, however, does it stray from their collective, overlapping narrative reach.

The 'group tethering' style utilised by *Death and the Maiden*, which is itself reminiscent of the technique used in *Knife in the Water*, serves to de-emphasise the type of locked spectator–surrogate relationship Polanski's cinema almost always encourages. As two of the three characters are presenting radically different versions of the truth, by avoiding a tight subjective connection, the film further hinders the spectator's ability to establish a reliable, *stable*, diegetic truth, especially in terms of that which is related to the past and to which we are not given direct visual access. In other words, Polanski's camera neither corroborates nor denies Paulina's memory cinematically; we are left to sort out what is or is not true based solely on the testimony offered by Paulina and Miranda (and to some extent, Gerardo). Like *Frantic*, it is in this context of 'competing testimonies' that I believe *Death and the Maiden* serves to develop Polanski's cinematic engagement with perceptual psychology.

Gregory (1980) delineates not merely an analogous relationship between the process of sensory perception and the cognitive act of hypothesising, but affirms a positive identity between the two, that is to say, to perceive is to hypothesise. The process of hypothesisation begins with the application of deductive reasoning to attribute meaning to observed phenomena. Importantly, we do not speak of 'truth' in relation to hypotheses, but rather validity. So where a predictive hypothesis may well have a high degree of (testable) validity, this does not necessarily make it *true* in terms of what is objectively measurable. The problem for perception arises when more than one predictive hypothesis immediately comes to the fore in relation to a particular stimulus. As I have discussed previously, Gregory is fond of highlighting multistable perception in the form of 'visual ambiguities', special images designed to make the brain struggle with competing and (frustratingly so) *equally valid* hypotheses, shifting from one to the next without resolve. It is by studying these types of illusions in particular that the role that conceptual frameworks play on the way we perceive is made most evident: arrows moving in certain directions inform our perception of length; faces cannot be concave; an object cannot be more than one thing at a time; and so on. In *Frantic*, Polanski manifests this process in scenarios in which different characters present competing hypotheses to explain the bits of evidence compiled by Walker in his investigation, with each individual hypothesising according to personal experience. Ultimately, it was Walker's hypothesis that proved most reliable in *Frantic*, resulting in the resolution of the ambiguity. In *Death and the Maiden*, the task proves to be even more of a challenge.

In Ariel Dorfman's stage-play, Polanski found a text in which Gregory's perception/hypothesis identity is played out to an extreme. Polanski's film version respects the enclosed setting of the stage play, utilising the ease of location changes allowed by cinema only three times: in the short scene in which Paulina steals Miranda's car and pushes it over a cliff; the climax in which Miranda finally offers a convincing confession on the edge of the same cliff; and the bookending scenes that take place in the concert hall (a scene that is also present in the play). Crucially, Polanski follows the play's lead by not resorting to flashbacks to portray Paulina's recounting of her torture visually, a directorial choice much in line with Polanski's own tendency at this stage in his cinema to avoid portrayals of subjective psychological states. So whilst *Death and the Maiden* shares similar thematic concerns with *Rashômon* (1950), for example, it does not employ cinematic means to represent competing hypotheses as famously utilised in Kurosawa's film (itself also a recounting of a rape story).[3]

Although it does not attempt to visually represent subjective perception, what *Death and the Maiden* does have in common with Polanski's Apartment Trilogy is its enclosed setting. However, this time it is not an apartment nestled amongst other apartments in a major urban setting, but rather a secluded cabin, in which the approach of any foreign body (i.e. anyone but Gerardo and Paulina) is met with extreme suspicion, as demonstrated at the start of the film by Paulina's reaction to the approach of Miranda's (instead of Gerardo's) car. Like the apartments, however, the cabin also serves as a manifestation of the psyche; the cabin itself stands in for the enclosed chamber in which the brain resides, secluded from the world not only by its remote location but also cut off from its electrical means of communication by a storm. Within this chamber, a perceptual crisis is played out, not through the representation of a psychological (cognitive) breakdown as in the apartment films (although Paulina is arguably suffering from one as well), but manifested by the roles played by each character, none of whose own psyche is represented visually.

The moment in which this perceptual scenario is initiated (and, for the spectator, when Paulina's actions in the film thus far start to make any sense) occurs when Gerardo is awoken by the stereo playing a tape of Schubert's 'Der Tod und das Mädchen'. As Gerardo enters the living room he is positioned in the centre of the frame, forming a triangle with Paulina screen-right (holding a gun) and Miranda screen-left (gagged and tied to a chair). The scene is ambiguous from Gerardo's perspective; whilst there is no question of his visual acuity (he wears glasses, but there is no doubt that he *sees* what is before him as accurately as any sane perceiver would be able to), its meaning is elusive to him. By the same token, it is wrong to assume that he has no framework upon which to reach his own hypothesis; after all, he knows of Paulina's history, and there have been other occurrences in the past when she has mistakenly 'identified' her former captor. Earlier, Gerardo acknowledges Paulina's potential for instability and erratic behaviour when he attributed her theft of Miranda's car to her emotional state. So when Gerardo sees Paulina pointing a gun at a gagged and bound Miranda, he must take this knowledge into account before judging what the image before him 'means'. Gerardo's first conclusion is that Paulina is suffering a (post-traumatic) psychotic episode, a hypothesis to which he is initially wed, but which is challenged as more information surfaces.

Although our subjective tether is extended to three characters, irrespective of what we may feel about him, it is the character of Gerardo with whom we are most closely aligned, due simply to the fact that we share with him the role of judge in this make-shift courtroom. It is ultimately he (being promoted, as it were, from lawyer to judge) who has to decide between competing accounts of reality, each of which has its own merits. Initially, it does seem incredible that by sheer chance the very doctor who tortured Paulina would be the one to save Gerardo on the road side and show up at Paulina's home all those years later. Paulina asks Gerardo (and us) to believe the hypothesis that this man was her torturer based on the evidence that she is able to recognise his smell and voice. Given the combination of the incredible improbability of the coincidence, the fact that Paulina cannot identify the man visually, and the confounding influence of what Gerardo sees to be her unstable emotional state on her perceptual abilities to begin with, the possibility that Paulina might be right is initially dismissed. Paulina's testimony would have to be convincing indeed to sway Gerardo's judgement; and as the film progresses, many details *do* emerge that make Gerardo question what he assumed to be Miranda's innocence. Throughout the film, the 'reality' of Miranda's guilt and innocence changes. Like a visual ambiguity, as we attempt to grasp the truth of the situation we enter into a cognitive state of multistability; the truth 'shifts' uncomfortably back-and-forth from 'guilty' to 'not guilty' as new, often small, details emerge. It is only when we leave the cabin and move to the cliff-side that it appears that Gerardo (and we) are delivered conclusive evidence of his guilt. But even then, this evidence is not 'beyond a reasonable doubt'.

In *Death and the Maiden*'s climactic scene, Miranda is held over the same cliff Paulina previously used to dispose of his car. Facing what must have appeared to be certain death, Miranda offers one more confession to Paulina in an attempt to save his own life. But this time, his confession does not seem to be a rehearsed performance based on information fed to him by her husband. This time, he includes details that Paulina herself did not even know, providing an account of events that finally seems to convince Paulina that he is making a truthful confession. Upon close analysis of Miranda's speech, however, it becomes apparent that there is still no information offered here that Miranda could not simply have made-up in an attempt to give Paulina what he judged she wanted to hear. There is simply no confirmation, diegetically or even logically, that what he is saying is necessarily true. What I believe really makes this speech so believable is, in fact, not what he says or even how he says it, but rather the melodramatic extra-diegetic scoring of the scene, which is especially conspicuous considering the film's predominant use of diegetic music. Ultimately, then, as is so often the case in Polanski's cinema, the closer we scrutinise and reflect on the diegesis, the more we are denied a sense of stable diegetic truth.

Circles of dissatisfaction

Both *Frantic* and *Death and the Maiden* are bookended by visual echoes, but the effect is different in each film. At the end of *Frantic*, we again see the Walkers in the back seat of a taxi as they make their way back to the airport. In contrast to *Chinatown*, whose 'full circle' finale returns Gittes to the location he fled before the start of the film's timeframe, *Frantic*'s circularity is visually explicit, right down to the two-shot of the intertwined Walkers in the back seat of the taxi and the POV shot of the Parisian dustmen. But for Walker, the return (literally, a return to America) is most welcome, as it 'annihilates' (as Cappabianca's puts it, 1997: 26) his separation from his wife, parenthesising the events of the film. In *Frantic*, the 'Orphean' Walker survives his journey to Hell and brings his 'Eurydice' back from the dead, sacrificing his guide in her stead. So, in contrast to the Orpheus myth, *Frantic*'s full-circle return to the over-world (the world his perceptual mechanism is equipped to deal with) represents the accomplishment of the protagonist's goal, not its failure; but it comes at a significant price.

In *Death and the Maiden*, the film begins and ends with an image of Paulina and Gerardo Escobar at a Schubert recital; but this return to the concert hall is not a 'rondo' in the sense of the scene being a repeated occurrence of an event, which is how the device is used in most of Polanski's circular films. That is to say, the scene we see at the end of the film is a return to the same concert we saw at the start of the film. Time has been suspended, with the events of the film all taking place before this actual-image. Arguably, then, the events that make up the bulk of the film exist in relation to this framing scene. Can we consider, then, the film as a flashback? Or recollection-image? And if so, *whose*?

Furthermore, what are we to make of Miranda's presence (with his family, no less) in the concert hall? Is this a confirmation of his (remorseless) culpability? If his confession at the film's climax was invented as a last-ditch attempt at survival, why did he not have the Escobars arrested? Beyond confirming that Miranda did not throw himself off the cliff as the shot at the conclusion of the previous scene may have suggested, the inclusion of Miranda's presence in the concert hall suggests that he did not seek retribution for his imprisonment, as he maintained he would have done. But what does this prove? Is it not also possible he may have had sympathy for Paulina and chosen to not press charges? Could the look on the Escobars' faces not be one of fear of being held to account for their actions? In my own experience, the more one revisits this film, the less likely one is able to establish a stable interpretation of the series of glances shot across the hall between Paulina and Miranda, and then Miranda and Gerardo. Truth, for them and for us, remains unstable, like those visual ambiguities perception theorists are so fond of showing us. *Satisfaction*, yet again, remains elusive.

Notes

1. The 'Americaness' of Nancy (Sydne Rome) in *What?* is arguably a major obstacle for this character as well.
2. By physical, Gregory is referring to illusions caused by disruptions to radiant stimuli that occur before reaching the eye, or *physiological* disruptions that occur on the retina itself.

In contrast, *cognitive* illusions are caused by the 'erroneous' application of knowledge/rules to interpret stimuli (see Gregory, 1997a: 248).

3. An interesting twist on the flashback is instead offered in *Bitter Moon*, the film that is sandwiched by *Frantic* and *Death and the Maiden* and in which the bulk of the narrative takes the form of a visualisation of a recounted story. Ultimately, however, doubt is cast onto the validity of the details of this testimony, and thus the diegetic truth of what we have seen in the extended flashbacks is also questionable.

Chapter 10

The Ninth Gate

You all know me, gentlemen, but hitherto you've known me only on one side.
The Double: A Petersburg Poem (Dostoevsky, 1950: 156)

In collaboration with Darius Khondji, celebrated for his use of colour chiaroscuro in *Seven* (1995), Polanski returns to the world of the 'hard-boiled' detective in the *fin-de-siècle* supernatural noir called *The Ninth Gate*. More so than *Chinatown*, *The Ninth Gate* is rigorously generic in its visual style, opting not for Technicolor to create its rich palate, but taking advantage of French lab Eclair's 'Noir en Colour' (NEC) printing process to create the subtlety of shading that, in the 1940s and 1950s, could only be achieved with black and white film stock and with meticulous attention to lighting (see Peterson and Place, 2004: 66). According to Khondji (in Pizello, 2000: 39), the use of darkness in *The Ninth Gate* was much inspired by Welles's (black and white) *Touch of Evil* (1958), which served as a touchstone for the film's palette.

As Naremore makes clear, achieving an absolute definition of the 'style' of *film noir* is difficult given the heterogeneity of the works included in this category (1998: 168), but given the 'retro' register I argue is being appealed to in *Chinatown* and *The Ninth Gate*, it must be acknowledged that, stereotypically at least, there are a number of stylistic characteristics critics agree are indicative of a *noir* sensibility. Naremore summarises the dominant aesthetic attributes of *noir* as the use of 'low key lighting, unbalanced compositions, vertiginous angles, night-for-night exteriors, extreme deep focus, and wide-angle lenses' (167), but these are not 'criteria'; it is not obligatory for a film to include all these elements to be considered *film noir*. For example, *The Ninth Gate* does not employ deep focus, but instead uses carefully calibrated shallow focus to deny the spectator perceptual access to that which is beyond the perceptual reach of the protagonist, creating a similarly 'limiting' perceptual effect as that which is achieved through the use of shadows in deep-focused compositions. Whilst the film is not above manipulating light as a means conveying thematic concerns or visually representing the psychology of the on-screen figures, the camera work rarely lapses into the type of stylistic excess that draws attention to its presence. The film does not, for example, contain any unnatural angles (save for the moments at the start and end of the film when we are 'untethered'). Such conspicuous camera positions are certainly effective in *Touch of Evil*, which uses an unlikely combination of highly naturalised dialogue and heavily expressionistic lighting and camera placement. Although much indebted to this film in other ways, *The Ninth Gate* keeps its dialogue crisp and stagy, and whilst its use of perspective is not warped to evoke an emotional effect, the tethered camera is so concerned with representing its falconer's natural vision that it is actually prone to inheriting his visual impairments as well.

Whilst *The Ninth Gates*'s performance style and script is greatly out of step with the era of its release (its dialogue, for example, lacks the naturalism to which its contemporary viewers were so accustomed, which may account for its initially cold critical reception), the film sits proudly in the tradition of the 'supernatural noir', alongside films like *Alias Nick Beal* (John Farrow, 1949) and *Angel Heart* (Alan Parker, 1987), as well as bibliophilic thrillers like *Inferno* (Dario Argento, 1980), *The Saragossa Manuscript* (Wojciech Has, 1965) and, above-all, *The Name of the Rose* (Annaud, 1986), the film to which *The Ninth Gate* is perhaps most directly indebted (unsurprisingly so, considering that *Rose*'s screenplay was written by the regular-Polanski collaborator Gérard Brach).

Like *Chinatown*'s Jake Gittes, and in the great tradition of the *noir* investigator, the narrative thrust of the film is fuelled by an investigation for which the detective is, at least initially, ill equipped. Corso takes what seems to be a straightforward case by a client who 'pays well'. Soon enough, however, Corso realises that he, like Gittes, has been duped and has become embroiled in a case far more complex than he had imagined it would be. His first reaction is to bail out, but when offered a much larger sum of money ('Add a zero', Balkan tells him), Corso is persuaded to carry on. Eventually, however, Corso rejects the cash prize in favour of the very treasure sought by his employer-cum-adversary.

An inquiring camera in search of a tether

Throughout the previous case studies, I have often used the concept of the 'tether' to describe Polanski's cinematographic style of keeping the camera closely linked to a single character's subjective narrative reach, whilst at the same time maintaining its stance as a notional observer, whose own perception is sometimes affected by the psychological state of the character to whom it is 'tethered'. In *The Ninth Gate*, the tether is again in place, and is so firmly attached to Corso that it sometimes inherits his myopia.

Polanski's tendency to both depict acts of perception and mimic these acts in the spectator's own perceptual experience is again central in *The Ninth Gate*, in which our tether to Corso extends to the natural limits of his (flawed) eyesight. On several occasions, the camera adopts Corso's direct POV, in turn relying on his corrective lenses; so when he loses his glasses, we too lose focus, when he uses a magnifying glass or loupe, we too are privy to a magnified image. Polanski's preference of framing objects (including people) in medium to close shots and heavy employment of shallow focus also creates a myopic effect that simulates Corso's own perceptual reach. We are limited to examining only what is readily visible (i.e. in focus), rather than exploring the frame in the manner permitted by deep focus.

It is also worth discussing this notional observer in control of the camera in term of its 'personality', since our gaze is so often a slave to its whims. It is important to emphasise, however, that whilst I do risk over-anthropomorphising the camera through such an analogy, my reference to an 'observer' and its 'personality' is intended precisely as an *analogy*, not an identity as delineated by Sobchack's (1992) discussion of 'film's body' (as I discussed in Chapter 1). One of the most dominant aesthetic tropes of Polanski's cinema is what can perhaps best be described as his camera's 'inquiring' sensibility, an adjective that Paulus (2007) uses in reference to Renoir and Rossellini to describe a camera 'that finds dramatic space instead of creating it, that explores instead of orders, that stands along the characters instead of imposing a view of them' (64). The inquiring camera does not necessarily master space; it may well struggle to deal with all the stimuli on offer. Polanski's camera tends to be confident in its stance, but its inquisitiveness is often stymied by doors, walls and corners, and, above all, the subjective narrative reach of the protagonist to whom it is tethered.

It is useful to briefly tap into pedagogical discourse to elaborate on the significance of the term 'inquiry' in the context of Polanski's cinema and its ongoing perceptual discourse. As an educational technique, 'Inquiry-Based Learning' refers to an educational approach that emerged from the constructivist theory of learning espoused by Piaget, Bruner, Vygotsky and Dewey, which itself is much in line with Gregory's own research findings on the way in which the brain actively interprets stimuli and constructs perceptions. The aim of the Inquiry Based-Learning method is to develop independent learning skills through the application of its particular approach to education (Bullard et al., 2008), which, in contrast to more conventional didactic methods, focuses more on the development of reasoning skills than the reproduction of facts (and ideology). The extent to which teachers mediate the learning process in the Inquiry Method varies, ranging from *open* to *guided*. Where *open* implies low levels of teacher involvement (the extreme opposite of 'closed' didacticism), *guided* insinuates higher levels of teacher support in the independent learning trajectory.

Discussing education in such terms, the parallels to cinema become increasingly clear. Broadly speaking, the classic Hollywood model is 'closed'. Its structure leans towards didacticism through the use of the close-up and the shot-countershot formula, as well as through its tendency of minimising moral ambiguity and weaving ideological absolutes into the narrative. Conversely, the type of realism offered by the *profondeur de champ* style of cinematography championed by Bazin necessitates a greater level of openness, both in the way ideology is presented as well as the way in which the frame is occupied and the camera moved, allowing for independent inquiry into both the space offered on-screen and the nuances of the issues being dealt with. Here lies the most relevant parallel between the Inquiry-Based learning system and Polanski's cinema, that is, their mutual emphasis on question raising and independent learning.

We can make a further distinction between forms of cinematic inquiry, each of which can enhance realism in its own way. The freedom of the spectator's eyes to examine the totality of the frame in a long-take in deep-focus is a form of 'openness'. The roaming camera, on the other hand, can enhance verisimilitude in the revelation of detail and strengthen the spectator's engagement with the diegetic world; it is a suture to the film, as opposed to the inherent didacticism of being overly sutured to an on-screen body's worldview. Both of these types of cinematography can be considered as types of inquiry, be they *open* (deep focus) or *guided* (roaming), the latter of which is closest to the 'personality' of Polanski's 'inquiring camera', or perhaps more accurately, the camera that encourages *us* to inquire. It is also relevant to note here that Bazin, as Williams puts it, succumbs to 'the lingering misconception that the human eye as a lenticular system possesses extreme depth of field' (1980: 199). Arguably, then, the deeply focused image with great depth of field is an image in opposition with what the 'brain would expect to see' (to again quote Gregory, 2003). With the inquiring camera, on the other hand, focus varies greatly, more in line with the servomechanism of the ocular lens itself; the 'price' to be paid, of course, is that we must yield our gaze to that of the nominal observer.

Where the 'openness' of the deep-focus/long take aesthetic gives the impression of visual freedom, Polanski tends to prefer establishing perceptual realism through not only the use of illusion (as seen in *The Tenant*) and natural (even myopic) focal lengths, but also through the blatant imposition of perceptual *limits*, seemingly designed to frustrate our gaze. The verisimilitude of these diegetic worlds (i.e. the extent to which we 'believe' in them) is heightened not by what we see, but often by what we are made to *want* to see, but are then denied seeing, reminding us that what we are privy to is *not* the totality of this plane of reality. Polanski uses a variety of means by which off-screen space is suggested, from framing choices that stimulate us to look around the corner (but deny us the ability to do so) to narrative content that emphasises off-screen action beyond the reach of the camera.

Although our gaze is highly mediated in *The Ninth Gate*, the imagery through which we are guided is most often presented as highly ambiguous, effectively forcing us to take notice of details but leaving it up to us to make sense of them. The images remain steeped in mystery, which both the spectator and Corso are tasked to uncover. For however guided our inquiry is through these diegetic worlds, it remains a question-raising pedagogy that encourages us to hypothesise, rather than being ideologically didactic. And whilst Polanski's carefully constructed shots are often designed to manipulate (or upset) our perceptual mechanism, the overall effect remains that of cultivating doubt in the reliability of our perceptions, rather than creating certainties or delivering simplistic satisfaction.

The enigmatic prologue

An excellent example of a cinematic version of guided inquiry occurs in *The Ninth Gate*'s opening sequence, the construction of which the cinematographer Darius Khondji fully attributes to Polanski:

> That opening scene is pure Roman … (h)e lined up the whole scene without any [narrative] interference or compromise. For me, that shot is very representative of Roman's sensibility. His filmmaking is beautiful and classical, but at the same time, it's twisted!
>
> (Darius Khondji, as quoted in Pizzello, 2000: 38)

The first image after the opening titles is a wide shot of the inside of an ornately decorated library/study. In the centre of the frame an elderly man writes at his desk. The shot remains static for a moment. We are permitted to (openly) examine the contents of the frame, complete with the various depth cues suggested by the *mise-en-scène*. But soon the camera begins to move, shifting slowly to the left, revealing a stool that had previously been out of frame. The camera moves towards the stool, creating a medium shot. It slowly tilts up to reveal a noose. The camera then follows the man as he seals his letter and walks towards the stool. It lingers on his slippers, which bear the initials A. T. The man climbs onto the stool and fixes the noose around his neck. The camera remains fixed on his feet as he kicks the stool away, watching them shake wildly and then come to rest, suspended in mid-air (in mid-*frame*).

Rather than moralising the moment of suicide, the camera simply observes, of all things, the man's feet. The scene of Andrew Telfer's (Willy Holt) hanging does not seem designed to evoke the feeling of *being* hanged in the spectator, which could have been more effectively conveyed by focusing on Telfer's neck and facial expression, but rather accentuates the experience of *watching* someone hang by focusing on this small detail. The camera is in fact more concerned with the *mechanics* of the act: it examines the stool-and-noose hanging apparatus, the chandelier to which it is fixed, and the details of the feet and monogrammed slippers, first walking, then kicking away the stool, and then still. The approach serves to accurately convey the exact moment of death, whilst protecting us from the gruesomeness of the act; at the same time, however, we are forced to form our own image of the 'upper half' of the shot. Even though the man's expression is not shown, attention to such micro-details increases the audience's sense of being 'present' in the room. It is worth pointing out that the initials on the man's slippers are also shared with Aristide Torchia, the author (or 'co-author') of the book that serves as the film's MacGuffin. As these initials play such a significant role in the film to come, their inclusion on the slippers appears to be an invitation to consider Telfer as a sort of 'co-author' of the film itself, his suicide serving to sever the tether between himself and the camera, thus initiating the narrative trajectory of the film. With Telfer dead, the camera is now obliged to seek out Corso.

After watching Telfer hang himself, the camera then moves away, tracking along the floor, over the desk (over the letter, which it is powerless to open), and across rows of packed shelves until homing in on a gap between two books. There is a book missing. The camera continues to move forward, penetrating the gap (eerily reminiscent of the gap in Trelkovsky's teeth, a space that the camera also penetrates in *The Tenant*). The rest of the credits roll towards us as the camera moves forward through a series of (nine) doors. After a burst of white light, the frame is filled with a New York cityscape (much like of *Rosemary's Baby*'s opening shot). The camera then pulls back, through a window frame and into a room in which it finds its new tethering point: the film's protagonist, book-detective Dean Corso.

What we see in the opening scene is a form of visually guided diegetic inquiry in which the camera, our notional observer, mediates our gaze to draw our attention to specific diegetic details. But these details remain enigmatic. Rather than simply delineating the meaning of what is shown, the aim seems more to stimulate thought (and provoke interest) than explain ('teach') what is happening onscreen. The technique perseveres for the remainder of the film, although once a new tether is established to Corso, the camera's independent wandering becomes more limited. We begin to trust Corso to act as our perceptual guide, via the tethered camera that tends to follow his gaze (and thus guides ours). Eventually, however, this trust is broken and the camera is again abandoned.

Once the camera 'lands' on Corso, he becomes the means through which our 'notional observer' is able to reunite itself with the missing book; this is an obsession we inherit not necessarily from Telfer, Balkan or even Corso, but the camera itself. Just as it does with Gittes and Walker, the camera often trails Corso from behind, keeping us limited, within the degree of tolerance allowed by the invisible tether, to Corso's subjective narrative reach. We are not, however, privy to Corso's thought process; but we *are* sometimes connected to Corso's *ability* to see. When he receives a blow to the head from Liana Telfer (Lena Olin), the observing eye of the camera is likewise injured; before passing out itself (i.e. fading to black), it goes out of focus and forms an image of a quadruple-eyed Corso (admittedly, an image more reminiscent of Loony Tunes-style ultra-violence than *film noir*). Later, when Corso is studying the engravings in Baroness Kessler's (played by Hammer alumnus Barbara Jefford) copy of the *Nine Gates*, he receives another blow to the head; this time the camera adopts his direct POV and collapses onto the desk (as it happens, onto the image of man about to be struck from behind with a mace).

Another sane male

As I have previously discussed in reference to both *Chinatown* and *Frantic*, in Polanski's cinema the male characters who are positioned as investigators face challenges that create confusion for both their perceptual and (often by extension) the conceptual frameworks that make up their concept of reality. Never, however, is the mental health of these men questioned, which is in sharp contrast to the way female protagonists are often portrayed in Polanski's cinema. Both Carole Ledoux's and Rosemary Woodhouse's relationship with reality is put into serious doubt in *Repulsion* and *Rosemary's Baby*; as we see in *The Tenant*, Trelkovsky's increasingly estranged relationship with reality runs exactly parallel with his gender transformation; and whilst Paulina Escobar's perceptual acuity in *Death and the Maiden* is arguably vindicated, the spectator's uncertainty as to her mental state introduces doubt regarding her perceptual judgement, which forms the central ambiguity of the film (an ambiguity, I argue, which is never resolved).

Polanski's division of madness and sanity is not, however, as clear-cut as my crude gender division might suggest. It is worth highlighting once again that whilst Polanski presents a series of female (or 'femalised') characters whose behaviour seems meticulously designed to fulfil various DSM[1] checklists for psychotic disorders, the diegetic truth as to the pathogenesis of their psychoses is always problematic, and in some cases (*Rosemary's Baby* and *Death and the Maiden* in particular), the accuracy of the diagnosis of mental illness is openly doubted within the diegesis itself. Even in *Repulsion*, the closest thing to a 'straightforward' portrayal of mental illness in Polanski's cinema, there are subtle suggestions that Carole's mental state may be the result of mistreatment by men rather than an innate psychopathological condition. All the same, it cannot be denied that the *spectre* of mental illness is always associated with female bodies, most explicitly highlighted in *The Tenant* through the blatant coupling of increasingly schizophrenic behaviour with a male-to-female gender transformation.

In *The Ninth Gate*, Corso joins Gittes and Walker on Polanski's team of sane male investigators, with Polanski's gender-sanity divide being even further punctuated by Corso's general attitude towards women. In *Chinatown*, in keeping with his era, Gittes's sexism is quite overt. Although more subtle, Corso also demonstrates a deeply rooted form of sexism that has survived well into the twenty-first century, and which finds expression in the way he deals with the female characters of the film, who are positioned as either perilous sexual objects or maternal, post-sexual forces; these are the two 'types' of women that Corso attempts to manage with his 'superior' intellect. His attempt to swoon Baroness Kessler is particularly indicative of his condescension, reminiscent of his treatment of the 'mugs' he swindles when we first meet him. (In contrast to Kessler, however, Corso *does* fear her secretary, a highly phallic, imposing woman.) Most revealing is the glaring inconsistency he demonstrates in the revelation of information about his case. Where he openly reveals his employer's identity to Bernie the book-dealer (James Russo) and *Nine Gate*'s owner Fargas (Jack Taylor), he refuses to do so to either Liana Telfer or Baroness Kessler, who are told this information is 'confidential' (it does not take Kessler long, however, to guess it is Balkan).

But Polanski does not allow Corso's sexism to go unchecked. Like *Frantic*, *The Ninth Gate* also includes a female variation of Dante's Virgil in the form of Green Eyes. Calling to mind her role as Michelle in *Frantic*, Green Eyes is played by Emmanuelle Seigner. Unlike Michelle, however, who is enlisted (nearly by force) by Walker to help him find his wife, it is Green Eyes who follows Corso, guiding him towards his goal, and even helping him redefine the goal itself. And so, ultimately, Corso's sexist cognitive framework comes under serious stress, as it proves to be a female body, Green Eyes, who both saves Corso through physical intervention and eventually expands the framework in which his perceptual mechanism operates, seemingly allowing him to embrace a novel version of reality outside the confines of his (Holmes-esque) rational materialism.

Notably, in *The Ninth Gate*, Paris does not stand in for a perceptual Hell the way it does in *Frantic*, but rather a version of Hell as seen from one of its own dark angels, who is making his way to its inner circle to engage in communion with the Devil him(her?) self. In the process, both the very notion of Hell and the persona of Satan are similarly deconstructed, both materially and in the context of religious mythology. Furthermore, a novel twist is introduced to the concept of the 'male/sane' perceiver in the film's final act, in which the central ambiguity of the film seems to be, for Corso if not for us, resolved.

Forging and breaking the tether

Like Gittes, Corso is already an investigator of sorts, a 'book detective', whose job it is to track down valuable collectables for bibliophiles, or, as is the case in *The Ninth Gate*, verify their legitimacy. And like both Walker and Gittes, Corso also finds himself involved in an investigation that stretches his perceptual abilities. He does not, however, face the type of linguistic or cultural obstacles faced by Walker (and to some extent, Gittes). Whilst not quite a polyglot, Corso is far from an English-language monolingual; he speaks French without difficulty and although he speaks neither Spanish nor Portuguese fluently, he manages quite well in both. There is no indication that these languages pose a significant perceptual obstacle to Corso the way that French does to Walker or Chinese (or even a Chinese *accent*) does to Gittes. Corso also moves easily across borders, both those that are politically defined as well as the less visible confine that divides the global space of commerce and tourism from more 'local', rural spaces.

As Morrison (2001) notes, Corso's trajectory throughout the film represents the fluidity of national space in the new transnational, borderless, but *dying*, Europe (44). But in contrast to Morrison's identification of *The Ninth Gate*'s representation of 'multiple identities and shifting forms of contemporary Europe' (2007: 43), I hasten to highlight that these 'multiple identities' are all embedded within a capitalist framework, a status-quo so universally accepted that (as recent market events have shown) any criticism of it immediately relegates one to the political fringe. *The Ninth Gate*'s bibliophiles serve as apt representatives of the death of 'old' Europe at the hands of globalisation. As Fargas says of his decrepit home in Sintra, 'old families are like ancient civilizations: they wither and die'. He has been forced to sell most of his book collection simply to maintain his home at the most basic level, but, as he is unwilling to sell his most prized possession, Torchia's *Nine Gates of the Kingdom of Shadows* (worth at least one million dollars), he is condemned (literally) to death. Much like Fargas, Liana Telfer (née de St Martin) is a member of a penniless noble (this time French) family. Her solution, however, was to save her château by marrying a rich American and refurbishing her family home with his money (not to mention using it to hold Satanic orgies for millionaires to 'indulge their jaded sexual appetites'). Even Friede Kessler, owner of the third book, is referred to as 'Baroness', suggestive of her own noble (most likely Austrian or German) lineage.

Whilst I will stop short of calling Corso a truly nomadic body, his 'anchoring' in America seems to be only a matter of convenience. We learn that he is of Italian heritage, and that his residence (not much of 'home', really) is on that island between America and Europe called Manhattan (to paraphrase Spalding Gray). Corso represents not a national identity but the lack of relevancy of such a concept to global bodies in globalised spaces. Furthermore, the seamless manner in which he moves outside of what is normally regarded as globalised space is arguably suggestive of the encroachment (or invasion) of the global onto the local, in Europe in particular. After all, it is not so shocking that Corso can move so easily between these worlds in pursuit of what is a purely capitalist venture (or at least *starts out to be*, as I will move on to later). As a transnational force, Corso is in fact more 'Coca-Cola' than 'Starbucks' or 'McDonalds' due to his ability to blend into even the most 'local' of markets, where he is able to gain help from tavern owners and even travel on the back of livestock transport and logging lorries as naturally as he uses first class air and rail travel.

Although the representation of globalisation is not the focus of the present discussion of Polanski's work, it is worth taking note of the appearances of various brands like Shell and Coca-Cola in the film. Whilst the conspicuous presence of these brands arguably punctuates the increasingly globalised European landscape the film seems to be exploring, the reality is that these brands are present in the film as the result of paid product placement.[2] There is a certain irony, then, that even Europe's auteur cinema is subject to the same effects of globalisation the film weaves into its own discourse. The use of the global star Johnny Depp is also arguably part of this same trend towards globalisation, as it is his name, far more than Polanski's, which ensures the marketability of the film. That being said, Polanski has never been averse to using stars and has always done so extremely effectively (it would be difficult to argue, for instance, that Depp and Ford are not perfectly cast in their respective roles).

Comparing *Frantic*'s Richard Walker to *The Ninth Gate*'s Dean Corso is an effective way of exploring Corso's character, and is worth pursuing a little more here before moving on. Most obviously, of course, both Walker and Corso are American men who find themselves in Paris on business trips, staying at 'global' hotels in which they each enlist the help of hotel staff for their investigation. In contrast to Walker, however, Corso's relationship with the hotel employees is long established and financially lubricated (notably with Francs, a neat time-stamp marking the film's *fin-de-siècle* setting). Walker, who also has to spend cash to get what he wants, tends to fumble with the currency and is not always sure when pulling out the cash is appropriate; this is a mistake Corso never makes. When Corso strays away from English-friendly global spaces, language does not prove to be as much as an obstacle as it does for Walker (who is actually quite lucky so many key players in his quest speak English at all).

Unlike Walker, Corso does not suffer from a sense of national displacement. Whilst he too holds an American passport (both he and Walker flash their passports on-screen, just as Trelkovsky has his identity papers examined), Corso's legal identity has little bearing on the effectiveness of his attempt to master his environment; it is the *nature* of the investigation Corso struggles with. Where Walker manages to achieve his primary objective (finding his wife), he makes no attempt to penetrate the 'bigger' reality (nuclear warfare) into which he has unwittingly been entangled. Corso, on the other hand, does both. Finally, whilst our impression of Walker's psychology is unwavering (with only the subtlest hint that he may be considering the temptation offered by Michelle), Corso's persona conceals a profound interior shift that permits him to master the world he is investigating in a manner more extreme than we may have believed possible. Like Oedipus, in *The Ninth Gate* it proves to be the investigator himself who is the key to the resolution of the mystery. Also in contrast to Walker, Corso is not compelled to raise his perceptual game by emotion; however, he does face the most difficult type of perceptual obstacle possible, namely a set of stimuli that pose a serious affront to his most basic (rational-materialist) cognitive framework. It is Corso's rational belief in materialism that is ultimately most challenged in *The Ninth Gate*. As he attempts to make sense out of the mystery into which he has become embroiled, his existing cognitive frameworks prove insufficient and require an overhaul more radical than any Polanski film has portrayed thus far.

As the embodiment of 'pure' capitalism (i.e. the 'modernist' version described by Jameson [1983: 115–116]), Corso never finds himself in the position of 'other' as he traverses both the Atlantic and Europe. As such, he does not seem to suffer the perceptual obstacles that might emerge from culturally specific conceptual frameworks. Corso demonstrates that the capitalist framework, which is his self-professed fundamental belief, is the greatest asset to true transnationalism. Throughout the film, Corso engages in a number of financial transactions (normally associated with the purchase of alcohol or tipping hotel staff), indicating the ease with which he operates as an inter- (i.e. 'between') national body, who can function anywhere as long as the laws of commerce are observed. His job, whilst superficially may seem to be that of someone with a great passion for literature and history, actually reflects Corso's profoundly rooted (do-it-yourself) capitalist ethos, entailing, as it does, the *commodification* of historic (even fetishised) objects. Corso collects books not for the knowledge they contain, but for their monetary value. He has found his niche in the market; he meets the needs of bibliophiles for money, but he is not a true bibliophile himself.

Whilst Corso is a materialist in the philosophical sense (i.e. subscribing to a matter-based ontology of the world), he does not seem 'materialistic' in the sense of seeking fulfilment through the purchase and consumption of goods (he seems perfectly content with cigarettes, alcohol and the odd microwaveable meal). The question that emerges is whether Corso's sensibilities, in particular his cognitive frameworks, can be considered as 'bourgeois'. He is perhaps better understood as an evolution of bourgeois sensibilities in which money itself, that which was intended to represent access to material things, is fetishised over the things themselves. In terms of the 'material conditions' (to cite Marx and Engel, see 1998: 71) of Corso's job, he does not, of course, produce anything of worth but serves entirely as a middleman, generating currency for himself by taking a percentage of that which is owned by others. The 'product' of his labour is the result of imposing what is essentially a type of sales tax on the transfer of property; his specialty happens to be books, his reward is money ('What else?' as Corso tells Liana Telfer). And for Corso, it seems as though it is money for the sake of money, not what it can buy (ironic, given materialism's emphasis on the reality of the tangible). It is difficult to imagine, for example, what exactly Corso would do with all the money he stands to make from Balkan.

Corso's highly self-absorbed, self-serving personality is in fact much in line with the description of the 'true nature of man' as defined by Anton LaVey (1992); this is an unsurprising connection since LaVey is the infamous founder of the so-called Church of Satan, the sect that may well have served as inspiration for the 'look' of Liana Telfer's 'Order of the Silver Serpent'. Notwithstanding the Church of Satan's penchant for Camp theatrics, LaVey always maintained that the Satan figure to whom they pay homage is purely symbolic; the core of his ideology is not that of begging a supernatural being for gifts, but rather embracing the 'true nature' of man, doing for oneself, and becoming self-actualised (very much in the sense intended by Maslow, as discussed in my case study of *Rosemary's Baby*). LaVey's take on the 'true nature' of man and achieving equality with God resonates strongly with the events of *The Ninth Gate*:

> Man is a selfish creature. Everything in life is a selfish act. Man is not concerned with helping others, yet he wants others to believe he is … the first rule of the prideful is to make an exhibition of piety and charity, with a Goodguy Badge to pin to his lapel. Man cannot progress one step further towards his own godhood until he removes that Goodguy Badge.
>
> (LaVey, 1992: 20)

> Don't advertise. … Never, under any conditions, go around proclaiming yourself to be the Devil. Others must recognise you as such … Always harbour some doubt, even about yourself. The booby hatches are filled with megalomaniacs who are cocksure of their own omnipotence. … Be aware of your own mortality. … You must be perceptive enough to see things as they really are, not how you might have been taught by others who stand to gain from your ignorance. … Be merciful … but cruel if you're pissed off.
>
> (LaVey, 1992: 66–67)

It is indeed Corso, far more than Balkan, Telfer or Kessler, who most embodies LaVey's ethos.

At times, Corso also comes across as the bibliophile's version of Indiana Jones (also a transnational presence, played, of course, by Harrison Ford, a.k.a. Dr Richard Walker), but he is actually more of an Indiana Jones *villain* than Jones himself. His ambitions are far more self-serving than Indy's honourable pursuit of archaeological artefacts; it is hard to imagine, for example, Corso proclaiming that the *Nine Gates* 'belongs in a museum', as Indy does of an artefact (a *religious* artefact at that) in *The Last Crusade* (1989). He is, nevertheless, our 'hero'. We witness, and are, in fact, invited to take great pleasure from Corso's 'thoroughly unscrupulous' (as a fellow book appraiser puts it) swindling of a stroke-victim's ignorant son and his wife out of a first edition *Don Quixote*. There is no pity offered for the silly rich as Corso assumes the role of Capitalist Robin Hood, who steals from the rich and gives to *himself*. We are not invited to pity the victims at all. Quite the opposite; however ruthless, Corso remains endearing. He is a scamp, not a scoundrel, through whom we are encouraged to indulge our own (monetary) fantasies.

In line with Corso's embodiment of the capitalist spirit is his relentless forward trajectory and his lack of a diegetically explained personal history. Unlike Jake Gittes, for example, Dean Corso has no back-story. Information regarding his past is scarce, limited only to what is referred to as his 'reputation'. But we get to know Corso quickly enough by way of the various comments made about him by other characters. Witkin (Allen Garfield), another 'book detective', calls him an 'unscrupulous vulture' and a 'double-dealing, money grubbing bastard'. Bernie, a dealer and the closest thing to a friend Corso has, tells us nothing of Corso's past, and is not spared from Corso's financial ruthlessness (and nor is Bernie's death particularly mourned, as the film's score, Wojciech Kilar's memorably bouncy 'Corso's theme', punctuates when Corso is forced to negotiate Bernie's hanged body to get to the 'stashed' book). Balkan, a long-time client, awkwardly attempts to get to know Corso better, but is rebuked. He refers to Corso as 'one of those lean, hungry, restless types that put the wind up Julius Caesar' (in contrast to Witkin, however, one suspects that Balkan intends this description as a compliment). If Corso is known to anyone else, it is only by reputation.

Ancients, moderns and postmoderns

The negation of history is not only a modernist concept, for it also informs the postmodern condition, albeit in a different way. Hayward (2000) discusses the postmodern in terms of its 'lack': '[the postmodern] rejects history, and because it has none of its own – only that of others – the postmodern stands eternally fixed in a series of presents ... ahistorical' (276). It is worth distinguishing here, a subtle, but significant difference, between what Lukács (1963) discusses as modernism's 'negation' of history and Hayward's notion of the postmodern's 'ahistoricity'. The modern nullifies past aesthetic and philosophical (and ideological) tradition through its emphasis, even fetishisation, of novelty, but it inevitably remains connected to the past through this very oppositional attitude, trapped in a relative state of being in need of constant updating. As Harvey terms it, 'modernity … not only entails a ruthless break with any or all preceding historical conditions, but is characterised by a never-ending process of internal ruptures and fragmentations within itself' (1989: 12).

Where modernity simultaneously rejects and claims superiority over the 'ancients' (a reference to the Académie Française's *Querelle des Anciens et des Modernes*), the postmodern, in contrast, seems to destroy the relativity between the past and present, and so the concept of 'ancient' versus 'modern', as well as the notion of one being superior to the other, is rendered meaningless. The postmodern is 'ahistorical' in the sense that it resides outside history, creating a temporal 'bubble' within which the modern notion of the linear trajectory of time becomes fragmented. But even though the postmodern may lack (or 'reject') a sense of its own history, it does not negate or nullify the past in the modernist sense; the postmodern continues to engage past traditions and discourse. It resides outside history, but observes it nonetheless. Lacking modernism's neophilia, the postmodern is free to utilise fragments of the past at will to form an ahistorical semantic framework in which postmodern works can communicate through various forms of citation (both in the form of pastiche and parody). It is postmodernism's ahistoricity that affords works the freedom to engage the past without becoming ensnared in the 'quarrels' of the relativistic ancient–modern binary.

The distinction between modernism's 'negation' of the past and postmodernism's ahistoricity proves useful in this analysis of *The Ninth Gate*, both to the appreciation of it as a postmodern work and our understanding of the characters it contains. *The Ninth Gate* includes several embodiments of the ancient–modern conflict; but whilst the film contains *depictions* of modernity, the manner in which it puts this ancient–modern conflict on display (through a religious parody, I argue) ultimately helps establish *The Ninth Gate* as a postmodern work. To begin with, the character of Corso can indeed be understood in terms of his 'modernity' in the sense intended by Lukács. He is a man with a reputation but not really a past. Corso's relentless forward trajectory and apparent lack of retrospection differentiates him from the bibliophiles for whom he works for (and against), many of whom have personal and family histories, evidence of which the film shows us through anecdotes (Kessler), old houses (Fargas and Liana Telfer) or even postcards (Balkan). In contrast, Corso is aligned most tightly with the mysterious Green Eyes, who proves to outdo even Corso in her tunnel vision and what seems to be a complete lack of personal psychology. It is she, after all, who scolds Corso when he engages in even the most minor reflection on Fargas's death. 'He's dead, who cares?' she tells him. Move on. Move forward.

Corso has no past, and thus embodies not only the ethos of modern capitalism, but also its sub-ethos of frontierism. He is a shark, a relentlessly forward-moving and forward-looking beast, immune to the past. Lukács discusses this sort of character in terms of the 'negation of history' in modernist literature, which he explains as taking two forms, firstly in terms of the hero's trajectory through the narrative, which is tightly bound 'within the limits of his [*sic*] own experience' (1963: 21), uninfluenced by a 'pre-existing reality' (21). The other form this 'negation' takes is the hero's own lack of personal history; 'he' is a being that is 'thrown into the world' (21). Uninformed by a past, this hero's state of being reflects modernism's emphasis on novelty, even neophilia. So in this regard, we can consider Corso (and, as I shall discuss in the next chapter, *The Ghost*'s nameless protagonist) as an embodiment of this specific notion of 'modernity', which differentiates him somewhat from Gittes, for example, the effects of whose past is often referenced and is evidently under active suppression in *Chinatown*.

But we cannot overlook the fact that whilst Corso is not given a back-story to 'deepen' our understanding of his character, his persona is highly informed by his reputation, at least diegetically to other characters. 'Reputation' serves also to inform the spectator's understanding of Corso if the film connects with the viewer at a 'retro' or 'nostalgic' level, namely through its evocation of the various cinematic personas that Corso seems to be channelling: hard-boiled detectives like Phillip Marlowe and Mike Hammer, as well as (parodically) Indiana Jones; and thus we cross over into a more postmodern conceptualisation of Corso and the film as a whole. Corso's involvement with antique books is interesting in this regard, as it reflects postmodernism's 'lack' of its own history and tendency to appropriate the history of others (i.e. past movements and aesthetics) for its own use.

In contrast to Gittes and Walker, Corso's superior perceptual ability is indeed the result of a highly stable, unemotional ('cool') and thoroughly sane psyche, whose relationship with reality is beyond reproach, aligning him also to the (modernist) Holmes-esque model of hyper-perception, steeped in bourgeois rationalism. Upon closer analysis, however, it emerges that Corso is really a subtle deconstruction of the *noir* archetype, but perhaps just short of the 'oppositional' force that Hayward (2000) associates with postmodern parody (277). Corso's lack of psychological 'entanglements' also allows him, at least seemingly, to avoid the types of emotional perceptual obstacles faced by Gittes and Walker. The only obstacle in which Corso becomes seriously entangled is that which is posed by his own adherence to certain bourgeois conceptual frameworks; an obstacle that, seemingly, he is eventually able to overcome. Unbeknownst to the spectator, Corso ultimately reconsiders some of his most basic rationalist frameworks and enters a truly 'postmodern condition'. The transition is aptly symbolised by his penetration of the frame, the act though which he abandons the spectator; and so Corso renounces his role as object of our perception by escaping the diegesis itself.

Polanski's embedding of an existential discourse within *The Ninth Gate*'s celebration of decadent, even camp, generic fixtures is highly reminiscent of that erosion between 'high' art and commercial forms that Jameson (1983: 112) points to as a key hallmark of postmodernism. Where *Chinatown* takes place in a world before *film noir*, *The Ninth Gate* demonstrates a more self-conscious mode of postmodernity, presenting a diegesis in which cinematic citations flow seamlessly in conversation. Where such references remain extra-diegetic in *Chinatown*, *The Ninth Gate* takes place in world in which *noir* has left its mark. When the widowed Liana Telfer visits Corso at home, the scene is a virtual replay of Neff's encounter with Phyllis Dietrichson, so much so that both Corso and Telfer acknowledge the generic reference, one amongst many peppered throughout the film.[3] Rather than 'breaking the fourth wall' and rendering the scene overly self-conscious, the matter-of-fact manner in which the *Double Indemnity*-esque encounter is treated actually diffuses what would otherwise be an obvious generic riff. *The Ninth Gate* is indeed at ease with its postmodernity; but its awareness of *film noir* does not stop it from being one.

Corso's trajectory through the film can also be seen to parallel the transition from the modern to the postmodern condition, especially when we look closely at *The Ninth Gate*'s use of Camp dramatics to observe an ancient–modern quarrel and deconstruct religious epistemologies. Corso seems to 'rise above' the highly Christianity-informed version of Satanism embodied by the 'Order of the Serpent', and also moves beyond Balkan's still-relativistic criticism of their rituals, towards a postmodern, even post-religious condition. Calinescu describes part of the Baudelairean notion of modernity in which the artist is caught up in the exploration of the dichotomy of good and evil that exists within us all, one side pulling us towards God, the other towards Satan (1987: 53–54). The parodic nature of the presentation of this conflict in both *Rosemary's Baby* and *The Ninth Gate*, as well as the general ambivalence with which good and evil are treated, are both steps beyond what Baudelaire describes, and are perhaps best understood as indications of a postmodern condition.

The conflict between the Satanists and Christianity, and indeed that between the Satanists themselves, echoes the battle of 'ancients' and 'moderns', the latter thinking themselves superior to the former, but with these terms slipping ever forward in time to create perpetually updated versions of both 'modern' and 'ancient'. The first battle is played out far before the time of the diegesis, in 1666, by the (co-)author of the film's MacGuffin (the much sought-after book *The Nine Gates of the Kingdom of Shadows*), who is burnt at the stake for betraying the ruling Church. His legacy is carried on by the 'Order of the Silver Serpent', members of which align themselves with the Devil as a means of increasing their wealth. But even within this order, splinters emerge, with both Baroness Kessler (an owner of one of three rare copies of the *Nine Gates*) and Boris Balkan rejecting the group's approach; it is Balkan in particular who believes his understanding of the text to be superior to that of the order members. Balkan rejects what he sees as an 'ancient' version of Devil worship in favour of his more informed, 'modern' version, which itself turns out to be hokum.

There is another comparison to be made here between Corso and Balkan, which further demonstrates the shift away from the modern–ancient divide towards the postmodern condition. As I have discussed above, Corso can be described as 'modern' due to his lack of personal history; the same is true of Balkan, who like Corso, is an isolated individual within the diegesis and not connected to an old family, unlike fellow bibliophiles Liana Telfer (St Martin), Fargas and Baroness Kessler. The connection between Corso and Balkan is emphasised by their growing physical similarity. After his violent struggle with Liana's henchman on the bank of Seine, Corso replaces his eyeglasses with a new pair with much thicker rims. Whilst we can take this as an indicator of a shift in his way of perceiving (new glasses, 'new sight'), we should not overlook the fact that these new specs are very similar to the distinctive glasses worn by Balkan. Corso's new glasses heightening an already significant resemblance between the two, as does their similar hairstyle, in particular Corso's ever-greying temple 'wings'. It is not so much that Corso has adopted Balkan's way of seeing, however, but that he *outdoes* him; by operating outside the ancient–modern framework that Balkan is still enslaved by, Corso transcends both his own bourgeois rationalism and Balkan's misguided desire to win an intra-theological debate. And so, in the end, it is Corso, not Balkan, who becomes the Devil's favourite.

Exposing cognitive frameworks

In spite of Corso's naturally occurring myopia, he is positioned, as is the tradition for fictional detectives, as a hyper-perceiver. In what is perhaps Polanski's most basic representations of hyper-perception, Corso plays a game of Satanic spot-the-difference as he compares the three copies of the *Nine Gates*. He soon notices what others have been unable to, even those who have devoted their lives to studying the book. There are subtle variations in the woodcarvings; the different versions are signed not by 'AT' (Aristide Torchia, the book's author), but rather 'LCF'. Corso initially smirks at the Cenzina brothers' (both played by José López Rodero, with one brother voiced by Polanski) suggestion that LCF stands for none other than Lucifer himself. His reaction aptly reflects Corso's fundamental rational-materialist cognitive framework, the very framework that is imperilled by the riddle of the *Nine Gates* and is at the root of his perceptual crisis.

A brief note on Corso's alcohol consumption: although he is constantly drinking, he is never noticeably drunk, a good indication of a lifetime of alcohol abuse. He drinks in literally every scene in the film in which having a drink is physically possible. The very first time we see Corso (in the midst of a swindle), he has a drink in hand. As soon as he arrives at Bernie's shop, he pours himself a drink. He drinks at home, on planes, on trains, in bars and in his hotel room. And whilst he never seems intoxicated, it is more likely that he is actually in a *constant* state of mild inebriation. Like his glasses, his excessive alcohol consumption filters the world and helps maintain Corso's bourgeois cognitive frameworks, but it is these very frameworks that he eventually transcends when he finally 'sobers up'.

A self-professed 'non-believer', Corso is forced to divorce this cognitive framework from its association with the highly passionate, often silly[4] 'believers' like Balkan, willing to do anything to resolve the riddle the book contains, as well as those who, like Liana Telfer, have convinced themselves that their success is due to membership in a Satanic order and use their beliefs as an excuse for engaging in periodic orgies. *The Ninth Gate*'s other bibliophiles embody different forms of belief. Whilst Fargas, like Corso, professes himself to be a non-believer, he is not interested in the monetary value of the *Nine Gates*, as he strongly affirms to Corso. His passion is truly that of the bibliophile, a passion for the physical presence of these special books. Unlike Corso, Fargas does not see dollar signs as he admires an expertly crafted binding. We also learn that Liana's husband, Andrew Telfer, was a non-believer as well. Baroness Kessler, on the other hand, is a believer, more in line with Balkan's sensibilities but not quite as childish. Like Balkan, the Baroness applies academic rigour as a means of both justifying her belief in the Devil and making profit from it. But like the printing-mogul Balkan, Kessler's primary concern is the pursuit of her theology, the attainment of monetary gain serving primarily to fund this activity. When asked about *his* beliefs, Corso simply responds that he 'believes in [his] percentage', a statement that efficiently represents both his steadfast rational materialism and his embodiment of modernist capitalism.

The frequent attacks on religious institutions in Polanski's cinema are another feature of his work that can be argued to be connected to Polanski's concern with perceptual psychology. By making this association, I echo Berger's (1967) conceptualisation of religion as 'word-building', or an intellectual infrastructure that provides robust conceptual frameworks through which its devotees can effectively engage with the world and live their lives (and afterlives), and I suggest that Polanski's exploration of the truly tenuous nature of our perception of the world through his explorations of how we perceive serves, above all, to undo any such 'robustness' in favour of ambiguity. By putting on display how we perceive the world, both in madness and sanity, the artificial basis upon which institutions, both religious and political (sometimes both simultaneously), build 'worlds' is exposed. Such exposé finds its most playful expression in *Rosemary's Baby* and *The Ninth Gate*, in which Devil worship is portrayed in a manner to maximise its absurdity. I do believe that the humorous tone of the scene in *Rosemary's Baby* in which the geriatrics toast the 'year one' and shout 'Hail Satan' is intentional; such scenes are played for both horror and laughs, as is the Satanic sermon in *The Ninth Gate*, where horrific humour is manifest both in Liana

Telfer's recitation from the *Nine Gates* and Balkan's hypocritical 'mumbo jumbo' rant. Balkan's strangling of Liana and the subsequent 'boo' he delivers to the crowd likewise delivers tremendous Camp pleasure (for those so inclined). Moreover, I propose that these scenes are not only satires of Satanism, but *all religions* (in particular, perhaps, Catholicism, whose mythology greatly informs these versions of Satanism).

As I have discussed previously, due to the tenacious influence of religion on society, the process of diagnosing schizophrenia can be hindered by the ambiguity surrounding which beliefs can be classified as 'delusions' and which beliefs are exempt from this classification due to their concordance with an institutionally acknowledged religious faith (see McKenna, 1997: 2). A vicious semantic circle can result, as both 'delusion' and 'faith' are defined as non-rational beliefs held in the absence of evidence. A patient who claims to believe (truly *believe*) in the legitimacy of the Catholic ritual of transubstantiation, that is, the transformation of wine into blood (one of Catholicism's defining beliefs) should be treated differently, for example, to one who believes in someone's power to transform *blood* into to *wine*. What differentiates delusions from religious beliefs is the latter's cultural historicity and the confirmation of the veracity of these beliefs comes not from evidence, but from 'infallible' authority figures who purport to have 'inside information' (as Balkan puts it) that allows them access to knowledge elusive to the masses. Such authority figures are much lampooned in Polanski's cinema, which often challenges the spectator to juxtapose 'ridiculous' and 'legitimate' forms of belief.

For Rosemary, the confrontation with the (big city) Devil worshippers can be read as a manifestation of her deeply rooted Catholic guilt, a conceptual framework she has attempted to reject but which nevertheless finds expression through dreams, psychotic hallucinations and paranoia. In *The Ninth Gate*, we witness dissension amongst the coven's ranks, with Balkan playing the part of a sort of 'Satanic Luther' to Liana's Holy Roman Emperor (only to find that his 'true' appreciation of the master's will to be as full of 'mumbo jumbo' as he accuses Liana's ritual of being). Once again, it is Anton LaVey's brand of atheistic Satanism that proves to be most legitimised by *The Ninth Gate*, as it embraces the etymological definition of 'Satan' as 'adversary'. For LaVey, Satanism is not religion but anti-religion; it is non-conformity and resistance to institutionalised perception (1992: 9). Hence, it is Corso who best embodies LaVey's ideal Satanist; it is Corso, not Balkan, who is able to circumvent prescriptive conceptual frameworks and penetrate the Ninth Gate.

Although Polanski's cinema normally defuses any straightforward diegetic truth regarding the existence of the supernatural, *The Ninth Gate* joins *Dance of the Vampires* in the presentation of diegetically unambiguous supernatural activity. (As I have alluded to in previous chapters, the presence of the supernatural in the Apartment Trilogy is never diegetically 'confirmed', as the supernatural is presented in the context of dreams or hallucinations typical of schizophrenia.) But the identification of Green Eyes as an unambiguously supernatural figure is not entirely without obstacle, more so for Corso than the spectator, as he is not privy to what seems to be her uncanny ability to float on air. There are two moments in the film when Green Eyes seems able to fly, or at least briefly suspend the laws of gravity. The first occurs on the bank of the Seine as she rushes to Corso's aid as Liana Telfer's henchman is attacking him. Rather than negotiate the steps that allow pedestrian access to the river-level paths (ubiquitous along the various 'Quai' streets on the Seine), she is able is glide effortlessly down to the bank side, reminiscent of the type of wire work popular in many Kung Fu films. Later, as Corso is attempting to prevent Balkan from murdering Liana Telfer, Green Eyes again floats down from the hall's upper balcony just in time to restrain him.

The camera angles and editing in both sequences make clear that Corso's line of vision is either blocked or he has his back turned to her at these moments, so he does not witness these two seemingly supernatural acts. It is the camera, and by extension, the spectator, who sees Green Eyes 'float' (the camera again allowing us access to slightly more information than the protagonist to whom it is tethered). In fact, on the occasions in which the suspension of gravity might be very useful, Green Eyes does not take advantage of her abilities if Corso is watching. A perfect example of this is the way she scales up the drain pipe to grant Corso access to Fargas's house; whilst she is certainly amazingly nimble, there is nothing remotely supernatural about her climbing skills. The same can be said about her fighting abilities; she seems to be a highly accomplished martial artist rather than a woman with superhuman powers. And when Corso inadvertently backhands her, her nose bleeds just as anyone's would. So whilst the spectator may have already judged Green Eyes as a supernatural being, Corso has little evidence to draw the same conclusion; but this 'advantage' over Corso proves insignificant when compared to the psychological transformation Corso is undergoing, which is entirely concealed from the spectator.

Corso's perceptual 'shift'

In order to draw our attention to the front-line of perception, Polanski often frames characters' eyes in close-up. *Repulsion* and *Rosemary's Baby* in particular include several memorable close-ups of eyes. *The Ninth Gate* similarly includes a series of tight shots that draw our attention to Corso's companion's piercing emerald eyes. In *Chinatown*, corrective lenses are utilised to alter the camera's 'vision', as well as serving as highly valuable clues in the investigation. Corso's eyeglasses take on special significance as well. Unlike Gittes, Corso suffers from myopia, to correct which he depends on his glasses. His ability to perceive effectively does not appear hampered by any form of mental illness, but rather a simple case of an elongated eyeball that distorts the retinal image.

Polanski's inquiring camera keeps us closer to Corso not only by limiting itself to Corso's narrative (perceptual) reach, but also by replicating his gaze through the combination of wide angle lenses and short focal lengths, forgoing the 'openness' of depth of field in favour of a more directed visual aesthetic that parallels Corso's subjective vision. There are times when the camera even adopts his direct POV, notably when he is not wearing his glasses, resulting in an out-of-focus image for both Corso and the spectator, thus emphasising his need for corrective lenses. Although this effect may seem rather primitive in light of the complexities of perception that Polanski seems to be addressing, Corso's ability to see, or rather, his *way* of seeing, becomes increasingly nuanced as the film progresses.

Just as Jake Gittes is forced to reconsider his interpretation of reality after he meets the 'real' Mrs Mulwray, Corso is also required to re-evaluate his own 'perspective' on things, and again, as in *Chinatown*, a pair of broken glasses becomes an indicator of a shift in the way things are 'seen'. As in *Chinatown*, Polanski is semantically playful in his treatment of 'glass', foreshadowing Corso's destruction of his own *eye*glasses with an image of a broken *drinking* glass at Fargas's home (the same glass Corso earlier called 'handsome'), upon which Corso also steps. We are well aware of the extent to which Corso relies on these glasses to correct his (physiological) visual impairment, and so the image of Corso in his tattered specs is both absurd and alarming, especially in that it calls to mind Evelyn Mulwray's 'cycloptic death mask' at the end of *Chinatown*. The image of Corso's broken glasses also serves as a kind of extra-diegetic 'hint' that his mode of perception, namely the 'filter' through which he perceives the world, is changing.

Whilst we are closely tethered to Corso and his narrative reach throughout the film and at times even inherit some of his visual impairments, the psychological processes underpinning his behaviour remain elusive. For most of the film, our inability to 'read' Corso's psychology does not seem to be an obstacle to our engagement with his character. The events of the film to which we are privy conspire to delineate a clear enough description of his persona. We know of his reputation as a ruthless book dealer from his interaction with other characters, and we know that he is an excessive drinker (almost certainly an alcoholic) and chain smoker, so much so that any Marlowe-esque 'coolness' is undone by the frequency and fervour of his consumption. Ultimately, however, our key assumptions about Corso are proven wrong. That is not to say these assumptions are unfounded, but rather that Corso undergoes a major transformation to which we are not privy. Unlike Gittes, rather than remaining dumbstruck by the perceptual and conceptual ambiguities he encounters, Corso undergoes a transformation unique in Polanski's cinema (rivalled, depending on one's reading, only by Rosemary at the end of *Rosemary's Baby*); he reinvents his entire concept of reality and seems to achieve a level of perceptual acuity that even the camera cannot match.

Orr (2006) discusses *The Ninth's Gate*'s 'double register in the realm of perceiving' (17), in what is essentially a reference to the spectator's task to both adopt Corso's subjective perceptions as well as take on the endeavour of perceiving Corso himself as an object to be judged. Whilst Orr rightly identifies Corso's transformation as a 'slow burn' (17) (a term I would apply equally to Carole Ledoux and Rosemary Woodhouse, but perhaps less so to Trelkovsky, whose descent into madness is more jarring), there is, as I have mentioned above, at least a subtle hint that Corso's 'frameworks' are changing, literally represented by a pair of broken 'frames'.

Corso is referred to as a 'wolf in sheep's clothing' by Baroness Kessler, an astute observation that predicts Corso's eventual betrayal of the spectator (our 'untethering'). Cinematographer Darius Khondji confirms (in Pizello, 2000: 46) that Polanski's decision to 'half-light' Corso throughout the film was a calculated means of subtly expressing his eventual transformation, highlighting the fact that there is much about his character that will remain concealed from us, notwithstanding the tether that connects us to him. And so, in an attempt to create a strong visual means of communicating the 'split' in his personality, Corso is almost always shot from a side angle, with some, if not most, of his face concealed by darkness.

Corso's shift eventually destroys the tether that connects the spectator to the protagonist. It is not necessarily the case that we do not understand his motivation, for having followed him so closely over the course of the film, we, as spectators, may well have developed the same obsession. As I have suggested earlier, it is an obsession that we assume from the camera itself and which guides its (our) gaze throughout the film. Our own obsession with solving the enigma of the *Nine Gates* in fact mirrors the manner in which Corso has inherited the obsession of his employer, as Balkan himself points out to Corso in their final confrontation. In a scene that elegantly reflects this double-transference, Corso interrupts Balkan just as he is about to initiate what Balkan believes will be a ritual that will put him in contact with the Devil. The two men tussle to gain control of the gun Corso has pointed at Balkan, which results in Corso falling through the loose timber that makes up the flooring in the decrepit castle. Corso becomes trapped from the chest up, producing for Balkan an ideal (diegetic) audience of one. A friend, or rather the man whom Balkan would like to have as his friend, Corso is the one person who can truly appreciate the 'greatness' of what Balkan believes he is about to accomplish ('equality with God'). Balkan creates of Corso an immobilised spectator in front of whom he is able to establish himself as an observed object, in front of whom he can *perform.*[5]

So, for a brief moment, we are united with Corso as pure spectators; we are paralysed perceiving subjects observing Balkan, who, in the best tradition of the generic villainous archetype, so desires to impress our 'hero'. Corso, however, soon realises his ability to affect that which he observes. He convinces Balkan to immolate himself as a demonstration of the success of his ritual. As Corso calculates, Balkan's bravado backfires. Corso manages to wriggle free (whilst we, of course, remain immobilised in front of the screen) and puts Balkan out of his misery, but not before collecting the much-valued woodcut-prints needed for the ritual. We then watch as Corso seemingly achieves what Balkan was unable to: he solves the riddle of the *Nine Gates*. Corso, unlike Balkan (or *Chinatown*'s Gittes), *wins*.

The enigmatic denouement: A 'shift' for Polanski?

Just after Balkan's self-immolation and Corso's escape from the burning tower, Corso again comes face-to-face with his mysterious 'guardian angel', whom he finds waiting for him in Balkan's Land Rover. She surprises him by removing his glasses and staring deeply into his eyes. Something is happening between them; but exactly what it is remains a mystery to us. Their fixed gaze becomes even more intense, and morphs into copulation outside the still-burning tower. But this is not a love scene; it is a moment of communication. Their eyes remain fixed as their respective gazes shoot directly out of the screen, but whilst their gazes may be directed at us, they are not *for* us. Corso's act of copulation with Green Eyes is an act of (orgasmic) catharsis, freeing him from the perceptual confines of his most basic conceptual framework. The time has come for Corso to 'sober up'.

The sex scene is directly evocative of *Rosemary's Baby*, which also contains a scene of mortal–demonic copulation. In *Rosemary's Baby*, the scene takes place with a Church burning in the background, in *The Ninth Gate* it is in front of a burning tower. Corso, like Rosemary, is pinned down by a more powerful being and is filmed in close up, the camera literally mounted on top of both Depp and Farrow respectively. The reverse shot adopts a POV in both cases, with particular attention focused on the eyes of the being 'on top', whose bizarre hues dominate the image: emerald green in *The Ninth Gate*, bright red in *Rosemary's Baby*. In *The Ninth Gate*, however, it is not a case of the Devil raping a restrained woman (an image also suggested in *Death and the Maiden*), but a *man* willingly embracing the Devil. And where Rosemary's encounter with the Devil *provokes* a perceptual crisis, for Corso, it serves to resolve one. Thus, *The Ninth Gate* elaborates on both the Biblical 'apple' and Milton's deconstructive portrayal of Lucifer in 'Paradise Lost', simultaneously emphasising the fallen angel's 'humanity' and association with knowledge. In this regard, the film is strangely optimistic, as Corso is *saved* by the Devil, not through a Faustian pact, but by opening his eyes to a reality beyond the material in what is effectively an inversion of the Eden myth.

In *The Ninth Gate*, it is not that Corso's perceptual ability is compromised, but rather that he has attained knowledge of reality superior to that of the spectator, and so we are abandoned as he enters the 'Ninth Gate'. At the end of the film, the camera does not simply drift away as in *Chinatown* and *Rosemary's Baby*, but, as is the case in *The Tenant*, it is seemingly destroyed. In *The Tenant*, the camera's penetration of Trelkovsky's screaming mouth mirrors the film's attempt to penetrate the workings of Trelkovsky's subjective perceptual mechanism, to *become* Trelkovsky; this proves fruitless, however, as it only manages to be devoured, destroying the image and leaving only darkness. In *The Ninth Gate*, on the other hand, it is not darkness that destroys our tether to Corso, but a flash of bright light that illuminates what, for the most part, is such a darkly lit film. But for us, this is a burst of light that wipes the frame clean, illuminating precisely *nothing*. Corso walks away from the camera, down the path into the frame, in a shot reminiscent of *Chinatown*'s famous crane-shot closing; this time, however, it is not we who abandon the protagonist, but the protagonist who abandons *us*.

The image of Corso being devoured by this bright light is perplexing indeed, and alienating not only for spectators who view this film in isolation, but especially so for those of us who attempt to follow the perceptual discourse embedded in Polanski's cinema. What are we to make of what seems to be a such a diegetically unambiguous supernatural image? Does the fact that Corso's rational materialism seems to be proved 'wrong' undo a strictly materialist reading of Polanski's cinema? Is this image, as Kubrick was fond of saying of *The Shining*,[6] 'optimistic' in that it suggests the possibility of eternal life?

As is so often the case with Polanski's cinema, the film's enigmatic final image is open to many interpretations, but I will venture one nonetheless. I believe that Corso's trajectory towards the resolution (and eventual penetration) of the 'Ninth Gate' is not a voyage initiated by psychological deterioration, but rather a cathartic journey towards intellectual clarity. In the final image of *The Ninth Gate*, Corso seems to be rewarded for his efforts. As he walks into the frame, he abandons his role as *object* of perception (in particular to us, the spectators) to become *pure subject*, effectively bridging the gap between the (unrepresentable) neurological sphere of perception and that of the world of objects as he penetrates the screen. Unfortunately for us, we are not worthy of such a step and are thus cast aside. 'You can't come with me', Balkan tells Corso when he first attempts the ritual. In the end, this is what Corso tells *us* as we are left blinded by an explosion of light. In typical Polanskian style, we are rewarded for our investment in Corso by alienation and disappointment. Yet again, Polanski delivers only dissatisfaction[7] – the only type of satisfaction that lasts.

Notes

1. *Diagnostic and Statistical Manual of Mental Disorders* (DSM), as mentioned in Chapter 3.
2. As documentation stored in the Polanski archive at the Cinémathèque française Bibliothèque du film reveals. Ref: BAUDROT-GU121 to BAUDROT-GU126.
3. CORSO: This has happened before someplace. LIANA: I know. In the movies. CORSO: And she had an automatic in her stocking. LIANA: No automatic.

   Another example is the smouldering cigarette Corso finds in Telfer's hotel room, a citation from *Kiss Me Deadly*, elements of which are also prominent in both *Chinatown* and *Frantic*. Even Balkan's self-immolation recalls the disaster that befalls Gabrielle (and the world) in *Kiss Me Deadly*'s final scene, which bestows supernatural overtones onto the destructive power of science.
4. Polanski lets us know just how pathetic a figure Balkan really is quite early on. The security for both lift access to his library and the library door itself is '666'.

5. Corso's paralysis calls to mind the image of the wheelchair-bound father we saw at the start of the film. Whilst he is physically incapacitated, his ability to perceive seems unhindered, especially when it comes to the value of his book collection. But his uncooperative body will not let him act, he is a trapped perceiver, a *spectator*, being acted upon but unable to take action. We have seen this represented before in Polanski's cinema in the form of the rape scene in *Rosemary's Baby* and the one recounted in *Death and the Maiden*.
6. As reported by Jack Nicholson in the documentary film *Stanley Kubrick: A Life in Pictures* (Jan Harlan, 2001).
7. Roger Ebert's rather negative review of *The Ninth Gate* aptly sums up the 'dissatisfaction' critics felt about this film: 'while at the end I didn't yearn for spectacular special effects, I did wish for spectacular information – something awesome, not just a fade to white.' (see Ebert, 2000, Chicago Sun website: http://rogerebert.suntimes.com/apps/pbcs.dll/article?AID=/20000310/REVIEWS/3100302/1023, accessed 15 January 2010.)

Chapter 11

The Ghost: A Bridge Between Trilogies

Throughout the previous chapters, I have related my discussion of the active theory of perception to the high levels of anti-didacticism, ambiguity and ambivalence nestled within some of Polanski's most commercial genre cinema, as well as the 'dissatisfying' manner in which these films tend to conclude. As a result, finding a way to 'wrap up' discussions of these works proves problematic; the same holds true for my analysis as a whole. I will therefore attempt to weave a summary of my key observations of Polanski's cinema through an analysis of *The Ghost*,[1] a work that serves as a convenient bridge between the two sets of case studies that I deal with in this book.

But first, a minor caveat is in order here to critique my own gravitation towards 'neatness', especially in my treatment of *The Ghost* as a meta-text in which many scenes, plot devices and lines of dialogue are evocative of prior Polanski films. Whilst *The Ghost* serves well as means of tying up *my own* discussion of perceptual psychology and Polanski's cinema, I make no claim that it is a work consciously designed as a means of tying up *Polanski's* (cinematic) perceptual discourse.

A camera again in search of a tethering point

I have often employed the notion of a 'tethered camera' and the related concept of the 'nominal observer' as a means of guiding my analyses of Polanski's cinema; this approach is again helpful to my analysis of *The Ghost*, a film that is keenly aware of its use of the Polanskian tether. In a manner highly reminiscent of several of Polanski's films (*Rosemary's Baby*, *The Tenant* and *The Ninth Gate* in particular), *The Ghost* starts with a 'camera in search of a tethering point'. The film opens with a series of maritime images. It is a stormy night on the sea. A giant ferry fills the screen, from which cars drive off after docking. There are also a few human beings in this sequence, but they are faceless entities who guide the cars off the ferry; these bodies are as much a part of the machinery as the ship's own articulated 'mouth'.

The camera finally settles on one vehicle, which remains immobile as the others disembark. The ferry now empty, this vehicle becomes the centre of the camera's attention; it even 'vocalises' (by way of its alarm) as it is forcibly removed by another machine. The camera jumps to the shore and finds its rightful (human) master, who lies facedown on the dark beach. So, just as in *The Ninth Gate*, the camera in *The Ghost* is left abandoned within the opening few minutes, and is forced to seek out a new tethering point. It hops across the Atlantic to find the dead man's replacement, to whom it attaches itself until it is again abandoned at the end of the film.

In *The Ghost*, the tether is so closely bound to the film's protagonist that it seems as though the notional observer that has guided our gaze throughout Polanski's cinema has now become manifest in the form of this 'ghostwriter' (as I am forced to refer to *The Ghost*'s protagonist, played by Ewan McGregor). But, as we soon realise, the character who most dictates the narrative thrust of the film is not the ghostwriter at all; the story of the film is primarily that of former British Prime Minister Adam Lang (Pierce Brosnan). We access Lang's story through this ghostwriter whose primary task is to observe Lang, and, in a sense, *become* him; this is essentially the task of the nominal observer I have so often discussed in my analyses of Polanski's cinema. The task is also that of the camera itself, whose gaze this 'observer' controls, which in turn guides, and sometimes tricks, the gaze of the spectator.

The ghostwriter's task of penetrating Lang's psyche is the burden carried by the nominal observer/camera in both the Apartment and Investigation trilogies, a task which it manages more effectively in *Repulsion, Rosemary's Baby* and *The Tenant* than it does in *Chinatown, Frantic* and *The Ninth Gate*, where it is held at bay. The ghostwriter himself remains a blank slate upon which we can graft our own psychology. He is neither schizophrenic nor hyper-perceiver, but rather a thoroughly normal perceiver, even quite awkward in the world in which he finds himself (as most of us might be). He is positioned as a nearly 'pure' perceptual surrogate for the spectator: appropriately anonymous, virtually psychology-free and even a bit androgynous (something McGregor himself brings to the role).

Meta-text, novelty and nostalgia

Notwithstanding *The Ghost*'s contemporary settings and many allusions to real-world political personas and events, it still seems to be an 'old fashioned' film (as remarked by numerous critics upon its release); its style is nostalgic for a certain type of cinema now nearly extinct. *The Ghost*'s 'old fashionedness' is particularly evident in the subtle, slowness of the build-up of tension, a style often referred to as 'Hitchcockian', but I would suggest that Polanski is himself also deserving of having his name 'adjectivised' in this regard. What I believe to be most 'retro' about *The Ghost* is the patience and attention to detail through which the story is cinematically told and the gripping atmosphere it manages to achieve through these means, an approach that is increasingly out of keeping with the current Hollywoodian trend of ever-decreasing average shot lengths and reliance on montage to 'create' performances in the editing room (although it should be noted that Polanski's own average shot lengths have steadily decreased over the years as well).

The Ghost is not only nostalgic for a more patient, 'classical' version of the thriller, but, for those who are able to recognise it, the film's many intertextual references also elicit nostalgia for Polanski's own cinema (for us 'close readers' of his work, at any rate). As I have discussed previously in reference to *Rosemary's Baby*, *The Tenant* and *Death and the Maiden*, the texts that Polanski has chosen to adapt often seem themselves to be informed by very Polanskian motifs. The same is true of *The Ghost*, a film based on a novel by Robert Harris, but which nevertheless serves as a highly 'meta' Polanski film through its catalogue of allusions to Polanski's oeuvre, as many early criticisms of the film have picked up on (see, for example, Horne, 2010: 39). Harris and Polanski began working together in 2007, collaborating on a screenplay for a big-budget adaptation of Harris's novel *Pompeii*, which was eventually halted due to complications caused by an actors' strike at the time, in which many of the stars Polanski had hoped to cast were participating. Although Harris had already begun writing *The Ghost*, he finished the thriller whilst working with Polanski on *Pompeii* and offered it to him as an alternative to the shelved project.

It is difficult to determine how much influence Polanski had on Harris's writing of *The Ghost*, but it is undeniable that, like Levin's *Rosemary's Baby*, Topor's *The Tenant* and even Dorfman's *Death and the Maiden*, many Polanskian motifs are readily evident in the original text. As Harris himself concedes, 'the novel is a classic Polanski film ... You couldn't really have put something together that was more Polanski-esque.'[2] *The Ghost* contains several elements already seen in many of the films I have discussed in this book, making it an interesting hybridisation of the narrative motifs presented in both sets of films that I have focused on. Its rich set of intertextual elements proves to be of great use to my present discussion, as *The Ghost* conveniently serves as a connecting text between the two 'trilogies'; it combines the intimate identity crises and existential concerns seen in the Apartment Trilogy with the grandiose political and societal conflicts more prominent in the Investigation Trilogy.

The issue of 'living space' is also once again highly significant to the narrative. Like Walker and Corso, the ghostwriter occupies a series of hotels, although these are not quite the five-star establishments seen in *Frantic* and *The Ninth Gate*; and just as in the Apartment Trilogy, the subject to whom we are tethered finds himself occupying an abode in which traces of the former tenant still seem to 'haunt' the space. In a scene directly evocative of *The Tenant*, Amelia Bly (Kim Cattrall), Lang's assistant, guides the ghostwriter around (the deceased) McAra's room, informing him that he will now be sleeping there rather than the hotel.

Just as Trelkovsky discovers the remnants of Simone Choule's clothes scattered about the flat and in the wardrobe, so too is the ghostwriter unnerved when he comes across McAra's personal effects: suits, underwear and even a pair of slippers (recalling both Trelkovsky's discovery of Choule's sock and M. Zy's suggestion that he don slippers whilst at home). Demonstrating once again Polanski's fondness for using large pieces of furniture as key elements of *mise-enscène*, a wardrobe proves to be a highly relevant object, for it is here, hidden under a drawer, that the ghostwriter discovers the secret message left to him by his predecessor. (It is worth noting that both the discovery of McAra's slippers and the documents being concealed in a wardrobe are details absent from Harris's novel.) The 'double occupancy' theme is pushed a step further in *The Ghost* than it is in *The Tenant*. Not only does the ghostwriter find himself a foreign body occupying another's 'rightful' space, but this space is itself in a greater building that does not belong to those who occupy it. It is a situation that creates a sort of 'Matryoshka doll' of occupancy when visualised, an image that reflects the iterations of identity transference and the issue of the decentralised nature of the subject at play in the film.

Also present in *The Ghost* is a central character who is identified to some degree by his national 'otherness'. As is typical in Polanski's cinema, the nature of this 'otherness' and its relevance to the conflict in the narrative is a highly nuanced issue. Where *Repulsion*, *The Tenant* and *Frantic* (as well as *What?* and *The Pianist*) emphasise, to varying degrees, the relevance of the national or racial 'otherness' of the character to whom we are tethered, nationality in *The Ghost*, whilst often referred to, serves more to emphasise unity than difference. It is the *unity* (although under duress) of the United States and the United Kingdom that is most greatly stressed, especially in the geography of the film's primary setting. The island, like that of *Cul-de-sac* and the boats of *Knife in the Water* and *Bitter Moon*, is a liminal space, an 'interzone' in which the Langs take refuge; it is a 'between' space in which the United Kingdom and the United States overlap, as exemplified by the fact that the island is quite literally positioned between the United States mainland and the United Kingdom, accessible only by ferry.

Both the house and the island itself are essentially minimalist, 'nowhere' (or 'between') spaces, in which these characters, particularly ex-Prime Minister Adam Lang, hide. The island is constantly overcast or rainy, all colours that may be indicative of its own identity are drained away. It is composed of barren roads, non-descript woods and windy, decidedly *grey* beaches. The Rhinehart compound, in which the Langs reside, is also minimalist in its own, more orchestrated way. It is made up of right angles and cold, empty surfaces. The walls are adorned by starkly anti-realist canvasses that challenge perceptual frameworks, punctuating the fact that as restrictive as the island may be, its very liminality also affords it a degree of perceptual freedom, serving as a minimalist void in which conceptual frameworks are laid bare to be re-examined.

The spectre of global capitalism and its impact on the production of art is also shown to be a powerful agent in the creation of Lang's official memoirs. There is no pretence that the 'work' being produced is anything other than a commodity; the ghostwriter wins the contract based exclusively on his appeal to the publisher's desire for profit. In this light, the ghostwriter comes very much from the mould of *The Ninth Gate*'s Corso. Like Corso, he is a man without any apparent interiority that needs 'expressing'[3]; he is motivated entirely by profit (for profit's sake), and, whilst working within the world of books, he is not a bibliophile. Corso and the ghostwriter do indeed seem to have much in common, such as the nearly identical layout of their flats, the iconic satchels worn by both men, their hard drinking (the ghostwriter, like Corso, drinks in almost every scene in which it is physically possible), their jet-lagged state (shared as well by *Frantic*'s Walker), and, especially, the fetish each develops for a book: the much caressed, leather bound *Nine Gates* for Corso and McAra's manuscript for the ghostwriter (it is more a stack of paper than a 'book', but it is fetishised nonetheless).

The character of the ghostwriter slots in well with the 'investigators' of *Chinatown*, *Frantic* and *The Ninth Gate*, in that he is yet another 'sane male', who is challenged by a reality beyond what his conceptual frameworks are used to dealing with; but the bibliophilic element of both *The Ninth Gate* and *The Ghost* also connects Corso and the ghostwriter to Rosemary, for she too becomes obsessed with a book on witchcraft, given to her by her friend Hutch from beyond the grave. In all three films, 'the book' is effectively destroyed, either torn to shreds and burned (*The Ninth Gate*), thrown away (*Rosemary's Baby*) or exploded into a cloud of scattered paper, floating down a London street (*The Ghost*). And in all three cases, the information 'officially' contained in these books becomes secondary to key bits of hidden and highly revelatory information. In *The Ninth Gate* and *The Ghost*, the books are both reduced to a series of pages. In *Rosemary's Baby*, it is only one page, upon which a name is underlined, that really 'matters'.

Rosemary, Corso and the ghostwriter are all tasked to 'solve' a riddle buried within the text (and pictures) of a fetishised book; it is a task each of them takes up reluctantly, but eventually manages to solve. But where Corso conceals the solution from us, the ghostwriter is more generous, 'publishing' (much like Rosemary does with her Scrabble tiles) his findings on-screen. But the ghostwriter's discovery that Ruth Lang (Olivia Williams) is a CIA operative is in no way curative; precisely nothing is 'put to right'. The moment of (faux) satisfaction that takes place as the ghostwriter rather arrogantly raises his glass to Ruth near the end of the film proves fleeting, and we are again resigned to leaving a Polanski movie perplexed, *dissatisfied*. Where Corso penetrates the frame and leaves us behind in a burst of light, the ghostwriter (literally) exits screen right, not only from the frame but the film as well, as we realise his discovery of the secret of McAra's book was all for nought. This time, we are left not with a burst of light that wipes clean the frame, but a burst of white paper that equally well blocks further access to the diegesis.

Like Gittes, Walker and Corso before him, the ghostwriter is tasked to solve a mystery that his conceptual frameworks are ill-equipped to handle. In my case studies of *Chinatown*, *Frantic* and *The Ninth Gate*, I have discussed such crises in terms of the connection between active perception and cognitive dissonance, that is, how the discord between the investigator's pre-existing conceptual frameworks and the complex realities in which they find themselves shows a different version of the perceptual crises explored in the Apartment Trilogy. All of these crises in turn reflect the theory of active perception, which stresses the dissonance (the 'gap') between the nature of an object and our perception of it, created due to the manner (the *process*) by which it is perceived. For the ghostwriter, the challenge is again to perceive in a realm for which his conceptual frameworks are not adequate, to overcome an epistemological crisis in which the societal leader, who wielded the wand of power, is revealed to be nothing more than an unremarkable and deeply flawed person, himself a puppet under the control of others, who are *themselves* deeply flawed.

Whilst I may make much of the 'Polanskiness' of *The Ghost*, it is equally important to highlight a few key features that are completely new to Polanski's cinema. To begin with, *The Ghost* is the first time Polanski has directly explored the artistic process itself as a narrative device, that is, using the *creation* of a piece of narrative literature (in the guise of an autobiography) as the primary plot focus of a film. *Bitter Moon* does flirt with this idea in the way its primary narrative is formed through the telling of a story (how much of which is actually true remains ambiguous), but *The Ghost* deals explicitly with the creation of an artistic artefact, namely, the writing of a book. The 'method of construction' (considering the approach taken, it is perhaps too generous to refer to it as an 'artistic process') used to create this particular book is also of particular interest, especially in its focus on the act of 'ghosting' an autobiography, with a surrogate writing in another's voice.[4] Considering what I argue to be Polanski's ongoing interest with the workings of perception, it is difficult not to find a parallel between the 'looseness' with which reality is treated in the writing of the autobiography and the manner in which reality is constructed through the (cognitive) act of perception. Calinescu's (1987) sentiment regarding the relationship between the writing of fiction and the 'fiction' of reality is pertinent here, especially as it again brings us back to perceptual psychology. He raises the query as to how literature, and to this I would add cinema, can be called a 'representation of reality' when 'reality itself turns out to be shot with fiction through and through' (Calinescu, 1987: 299).

Another significant novelty for Polanski is *The Ghost*'s direct focus on a present-day political situation, specifically the role played by the United Kingdom's government, led by Prime Minister Tony Blair, in the American-led invasions of Afghanistan in 2001 ('Operation Enduring Freedom') and Iraq in 2003 ('Operation Iraqi Freedom') as retaliation for the terrorist attacks in the United States on 11 September 2001, as well as the (ongoing) effects of these actions, particularly the emerging evidence of United States-sanctioned use of torture and British acquiescence. Notwithstanding its pretence of a 'veil', it is nearly impossible, for most western spectators, at any rate, to miss the Lang–Blair connection. Whilst *The Pianist* is of course directly concerned with a real *historical* event, the only other of Polanski's films to include political commentary so relevant to the time of its release is *Chinatown*, a film inspired (albeit loosely) by two scandals, the Owens Valley 'Water Wars' and (arguably) Watergate, which was coming to a climax the very summer of *Chinatown*'s release.[5] Like *Chinatown*, *The Ghost* also deals directly with the political impact of corporate capitalism, but shifts from a concern with corporate control of a critical public amenity to the influence of big business on war and the use of torture in its obvious reference to the sway of Halliburton (renamed 'Hatherton' in the film) on the Bush administration, and, by extension, the Blair government as well.

The Ghost is in fact far bolder and more transparent than *Chinatown* in its reflection of real-world events. Where *Chinatown*'s period setting requires of the spectator a certain degree of 'decoding' to tune in to its political commentary, *The Ghost*'s veil over its parody of public personas is remarkably thin, not only in its reference to the Blairs, but its symbolic portrayal of the long-standing identity crisis of the United Kingdom itself, caught between its allegiance to the United States and its position in Europe. But in spite of *Chinatown*'s political relevance at the time of its release, the fundamental ethical conundrums it puts into play continue to resonate, even for a generation for whom 'Watergate' (or at least '-gate') has been reduced to nothing more than a suffix denoting scandal, its etymology on the verge of being forgotten from the common consciousness. In a similar vein, *The Ghost*'s application of what at the time of its release appears to be a pointless veil may well prove to ensure the film's relevance for years to come, with the Blair connection possibly being reduced to a footnote in the criticism that will emerge in the future (much as I have treated the Watergate connection in my analysis of *Chinatown*). As the years pass, it may be interesting to note whether *The Ghost* has a similar effect to that discussed by Walton (see 2001: 47) regarding the effect on public memory that *Chinatown* had on perceptions of the Owens Valley affair it was inspired by. Lang's speeches could indeed be muddled with Blair's own various defences of US policy and the ethics of his actions, and the role Cherie Blair played in the her husband's actions could equally be confused with Ruth Lang's agency in the film. But given *The Ghost*'s limited success when compared to *Chinatown* (Polanski's second highest-grossing film, after *The Pianist*, but most likely seen by far more people), it is unlikely to have the same sort of 'historical' effect. Nevertheless, its specific reflection of the Zeitgeist is undeniable, as is evident in the presence of technology and how it is used (noticeably missing in *The Ninth Gate*, for example), as well as the Homeland Security Advisory System (i.e. the 'terror' colour-coded alerts) used by the United States between 2003 and 2011 (as seen on the island), and the increased security seen when the ghostwriter visits the London headquarters of Rhinehart Publishing (in contrast to what we see at Balkan Press in New York, which is visited by Corso in *The Ninth Gate* in 1999).

Notwithstanding *The Ghost*'s multiple references to the 2001 invasion of Afghanistan, the 2003 invasion of Iraq and the use of government-sanctioned torture (a controversy that continues to the day of writing), as is typical for Polanski's cinema, the film avoids taking a clear 'stance' on these issues; rather than seeking to impose an ideological message, the film opts for nuance and ambiguity as it renders an already ethically murky scenario even more complex. Lang's 'two lines at the airport' speech, for example, goes unchallenged, destabilising any 'left leaning' assumptions regarding the film's political position. In fact, it is easy to see how Lang's speech could lead to accusations of what Huyssen warns to be postmodernism's 'assumed total collusion with neo conservatism' (1990: 252), especially if the scene is looked at in isolation. Equally, however, in the scene immediately preceding Lang's speech, the assertion by Rycart (Robert Pugh) that the ghostwriter is now 'working for the good guys' also rings hollow.

This lack of resolution in Polanski's cinema regarding both morality and even the establishment of a stable diegetic reality can be described as 'schizoid' in its own right. This 'schizoid' state is arguably in line with Orr's (1993) observation of the 'danger' of postmodern cinema, which, through its ideological emptiness, lends itself to contradictory readings that can be adopted by the spectator in line with his or her own ideological stance (12). The same could be argued about the ideological ambivalence in Polanski's cinema, but I would suggest that Polanski's manner of compromising diegetic stability and deconstructing moral certitudes also has the effect of challenging the very frameworks upon which these ideological, and we can extend this to further to *epistemological*, certitudes are based.

What I ultimately mean to suggest is that *The Ghost*'s most important mask is not the one it places over the face of the Blairs, but rather the mask that is created by the grandiose political overtones of the plot, which serves (at the time of its release, at least) to deflect attention away from its more intimate examination of personal epistemologies and their fragility. As in many Polanski films, Orr's (2006) suggestion of a 'double register' (17) is again called for to access what is perhaps the most provocative aspect of *The Ghost*. Through its political criticism, *The Ghost*, like *Chinatown*, raises a set of probing existential questions; it is to this plane of thought to which I will now turn my attention.

Encore une fois, 'la femme n'existe pas'

> He was brilliant at making speeches and I'm so terrible.
>
> (Ruth Lang)

The issue of a specifically female identity crisis is returned to in *The Ghost*, in a manner again very reminiscent of the Lacanian quip '*la femme n'existe pas*' (Lacan, 1975: 68) I referred to earlier in my discussion of *Rosemary's Baby*. Whilst the ghostwriter suffers from his own crisis as his conceptual frameworks are systematically dismantled, he is not alone. Ruth Lang also suffers an identity crisis, which turns out to be one of the key elements of the 'mystery' the ghostwriter wrestles with.

It is indeed worth contrasting Ruth's crisis to Rosemary's, for whilst superficially similar in some ways, it also differs significantly and ultimately represents an evolution in Polanski's treatment of a specifically female form of subjectivity. It is misleading, however, to suggest that this comparison functions directly along gender lines. In fact, Ruth not only represents a fully self-realised ('actualised') identity, but a person who wields power over the formation of her husband's identity (calling to mind the marital power relations of *Macbeth*). But it proves too simplistic to suggest that Ruth is simply an 'evil' or 'overlooked' female, forced to the background because of her gender as her husband takes the credit (or *blame*) for her actions and ideas. After all, we learn that Adam Lang was already a member of the party when he met Ruth. The picture that eventually emerges is not a masquerade that positions Adam Lang as Ruth's (and the CIA's) puppet, but rather a *collaboration*; it is a symbiotic relationship in which both parties contribute to create a third 'body', that is, Lang's political persona (the very persona the ghostwriter is tasked to 'become').

We can identify (at least) three planes of feminist thought upon which Ruth's character can be read. The most 'basic' feminist reading simply follows the logic of '*la femme n'existe pas*', in which we attribute Ruth's consignment to the background as *de facto* due to male oppression. The second reading is a more nuanced, but still an essentially feminist, version of the first, in which this woman's 'non existence' is not the result of oppression, but one of personal *choice*; a choice, however, still located within a framework of the fight for gender equality. Lastly, the film also lends itself to an entirely post-feminist reading, in which the Langs' genders are completely irrelevant to their interpersonal dynamic. The challenge that is presented to the spectator, then, is to work out if Ruth's consignment to the background is a calculated decision due to her personal unwillingness (or inability) to present herself as a political figure or whether she is indeed held back by a still-patriarchical system that will not accept her 'type' of woman in politics.

I propose a post-feminist approach here. I suggest that the identity crisis played out in the film is not necessarily due to Ruth's suffering at the hands of patriarchical repression, but rather a mutual crisis caused by the formation of this 'inter-being' who resides in Adam's body, but is as much Ruth's as his; this is a scenario that is played out again in the relationship between Lang and the ghostwriter, which becomes increasingly complicated when we reflect on the components that make up the persona he is meant to be 'ghosting'. Such slippages of identity are again highly reminiscent of *The Tenant*, but in *The Ghost* the identity crisis is played out within, and between, people who are presented as sane perceiving subjects.

Ghosting and the family drama

An interesting picture emerges when we map the connections that tie the main characters of *The Ghost* together, the complexity of which comes to the fore when we consider the various incidents of 'ghosting' upon which the film is based. First of all, there is a doubling of McAra, Lang's original ghostwriter, which occurs when the new ghostwriter is selected and is tasked to take McAra's place. But understanding who-is-ghosting-whom becomes increasingly difficult as we learn more about Lang and those who surround him. We soon realise that the ghostwriter has become entangled in a network of 'ghosts' that serves to decentralise the subject of the book he is tasked with writing. We learn that Lang himself, the man being 'played' by the ghostwriter as he writes his 'auto'-biography, is playing a role, effectively reciting the lines 'ghostwritten' by his wife. Furthermore, we learn that even Ruth's actions are being 'written' by the CIA.

The ghostwriter's attempts to connect with Lang are unsuccessful, as the persona he seeks (i.e. the persona he is effectively attempting to *become*) proves elusive. Like the metaphorical onion (or 'Matryoshka', as I referred to earlier), as he peels the layers off 'Lang', he is left with nothing at the centre, a void around which the constituting agents of the Lang persona orbit. The film's portrayal of the decentralisation and inaccessibility of the 'real' Lang is a return to Polanski's recurrent theme of decentralised, fragmented psyches and slippages of identity, elegantly symbolised by the film's final image of the pages making up Lang's memoirs 'decentralised' by the wind. But a paradox emerges here, for whilst this 'void' is also reminiscent of quantum physics' existentially loaded proposition that the very building blocks of matter may well be 'nothing' (whatever that is), the notion of the 'perceptual gap' also presupposes an identifiable 'I' from which (from *whom*) the world is separated. In Polanski's cinema, not only is perception unreliable, but the integrity of the perceiving body's identity is itself compromised.

So whose story, exactly, is the ghostwriter ghostwriting? Allowing ourselves a momentary lapse into some amateur psychoanalysis of the quasi-familial unit that emerges in *The Ghost* proves helpful in unpicking this conundrum (although this also requires an abandonment of the 'post-feminist' approach I mention above). The ghostwriter's relationship with the Langs establishes a sort of impromptu familial structure, in which the ghostwriter becomes intertwined in the Langs' psychodynamic interplay. Pushing this analogy a bit further, in addition to reading the rapport between the ghostwriter and the Langs as symbolic of the individual family unit, we can also see this 'unit' as a representation of the greater societal 'family' in which we are all embroiled, 'children' to the *pater familias* of government. It is through this structure that an Oedipal scenario is again played out in Polanski's cinema.

The architecture of the Oedipal unit is established with Ruth and Adam Lang in the parental roles; the ghostwriter's role is that of the child, his epistemological trajectory being essentially that of the move towards self-actualisation, a journey that depends on the deconstruction of parental figures in which the authoritative persona collapses and is revealed to be fallible, even weak. It was, of course, Ruth's idea to employ the ghostwriter, and thus she takes responsibility for his 'birth' into the Lang dynamic (aptly confined to the island). And like a new mother, she 'presents' him to her husband, who is taken aback when this (younger) man introduces himself as 'your *[Lang's]* ghost', in effect signalling Lang's death. And so the Oedipal scenario emerges, with the ghostwriter both confronting the 'father' and bedding his wife, the 'mother'. The 'father' is eventually killed, and whilst not directly murdered by the hand of the 'son', the ghostwriter is indeed implicated in Lang's death by the police ('you're the prime suspect', the detective informs the ghostwriter).

What is also of interest in *The Ghost*'s Oedipal scenario is the subtext of the overlap between the characters, creating both an image of an *inter*personal conflict as well as serving as a manifestation of an *intra*-personal conflict. As I have discussed above, there is much made of the overlapping of characters within the film, not only between Adam Lang and his ghostwriter (with the ghostwriter literally wearing Lang's clothes at one point), but between Adam and Ruth Lang, and in turn also between Ruth and the ghostwriter, whose bodies merge within the frame on a number of occasions (reminiscent of the intertwined Walkers in *Frantic*): on the beach as Ruth guides the ghostwriter back to the compound; in their sexual encounter; and even in their matching brown bathrobes, which creates an image in which it is indeed difficult to separate one body from the other.

Although this discussion of *The Ghost*'s Oedipal scenario may at first appear tangential to the perceptual discourse that has guided this analysis of Polanski's cinema, it does lead us back to the issue of the epistemological crisis, the point that I believe serves as the key connection between perceptual psychology, the Investigation Trilogy and Polanski's portrayals of female self-actualisation as a form of mental illness. In all these cases, it is *knowledge* that proves most threatening to cognitive stability, especially when new knowledge clashes with existing conceptual frameworks. These incidents of cognitive dissonance help expose the manner in which both conceptual frameworks (our beliefs about the world) and perceptual frameworks (the means by which sensory data is made sense of, that is, how we recognise an object for what it is) are not only interlocking processes, but are likely the *same* process, a process of *hypothesisation* (as Gregory persistently argues).

It is the 'revelatory moment', such as that most shocking moment of discovery experienced by Oedipus and his inheritors, that I argue best reflects the most profound philosophical implication of perceptual psychology, in particular the theory of active perception. Through its stressing of the powerful role of individual cognitive agency in the creation of perception via hypothesisation (including 'proprioception', our perception of our own bodies), the theory of active perception ultimately reveals our isolation from the world, but without necessarily advocating outright solipsism. This isolation is highly evident in those who suffer from mental illnesses like schizophrenia, but which is merely concealed (*must* be concealed) by the healthy perceptual mechanism.

Notes

1. The film was released worldwide under two English-language titles, *The Ghost* and *The Ghostwriter*, depending on the territory. For the sake of consistency, I use the title of the UK release, *The Ghost*.

2. Harris interviewed on BBC Radio 4's *The Film Programme*, broadcast 16 April 2010.
3. All traces of the ghostwriter's own personal history that Harris included in the novel are duly omitted by Polanski.
4. A moment of reflection, however, reveals that this is not actually the *first* time a Polanski film features a writing team: although not the focus of the film's plot, the Cenzina brothers in *The Ninth Gate* do revel in telling Corso the story about Aristide Torchia's secret 'illustrious collaborator' in the creation of a book that is ghostwritten by Satan himself.
5. As I discussed in its case study, writing in 1974 Zimmerman calls *Chinatown* a 'Watergate with real water' (74).

Chapter 12

Concluding Remarks

The aim stated at the start of this investigation of Polanski's cinema was to engage with a set of his films through an exploration of a theory of perception that the film-maker himself claims to have been greatly influenced by. To do so, my strategy was to prepare both the reader and myself by exploring the theory of active perception as espoused by the now-late neuropsychologist R. L. Gregory, whom Polanski specifically nominates as an influence in his autobiography, and with whom he even collaborated. By then contrasting the theory of indirect ('active') perception with the competing, and still tenacious, model of direct ('passive') perception, I was able to begin a discussion of Polanski's cinema guided by this perceptual line of discourse. Rather than attempting to deal with all of Polanski's films, I elected to address his cinema through case studies grouped, roughly, into two 'trilogies' that I believe best embody Polanski's interest in perceptual psychology, namely the 'Apartment Trilogy' of *Repulsion*, *Rosemary's Baby* and *The Tenant*, and the 'Investigation Trilogy' of *Chinatown*, *Frantic* and *The Ninth Gate*. Where I argued that this first group of films deals with the workings of perception through explorations of psychosis, the second group marks a shift towards more 'distant' studies of highly sane perceivers, who are confronted with severe perceptual challenges that spiral into epistemological, and ultimately ontological, crises.

By employing this methodology, I hoped to contribute to the type of scholarship that attempts to move the discussion of Polanski's cinema beyond biographical analyses obsessed with folding the more sensational aspects of Polanski's personal life into close readings of his work; but this is a difficult task, given Polanski's continuing high profile in the public realm, and on many occasions I have undoubtedly been guilty of associating the persona of the director too closely with his works and the discourse they provoke. At times, I am also undoubtedly guilty of crediting too many aesthetic and narrative details to the sole personal agency of Polanski himself, without clarifying the degree of collaboration at work in such decisions. That being said, given the countless reports from his collaborators regarding the remarkable amount of control exerted by Polanski over even the smallest details of production, if any current film-maker deserves to be called the absolute 'author' of (at least) all things cinematic in the films for which he or she is credited as 'director', it is probably Polanski.

The choice to approach Polanski's cinema with a methodology based in perceptual psychology was not intended as a dismissal of conventional film theory. For example, a perception-based close reading of a film does not negate the relevance of either psychoanalytical or philosophical approaches, as I hope the case studies in this book demonstrate. The main advantage of using a perception-based approach as a 'way in' to Polanski's cinema is that it allows for a detailed investigation into the manner in which the director's interest in psychological research is manifested in his cinema both diegetically and in his film-making technique; moreover, it compels the close reader in particular to reflect on the theorisation of perception at play in these films.

On many occasion I have discussed the *malleability* of perception, only to later establish a seeming contradiction by turning my discussion to the *rigidity* of perception. In fact, each of these aspects of perception represents an extreme on the spectrum: from mental illness, such as schizophrenia, in which perceptual frameworks become fragmented and unreliable, to what I have referred to as a sort of perceptual 'arrogance', in which conceptual frameworks become so rigid that the basis upon which they were constructed (which is not always sound) is forgotten or ignored, thus causing a different sort of perceptual crisis. It is worth making note as well of active perception's stressing of the interconnectedness of conceptual and perceptual frameworks, which Polanski's films often explore. Such reciprocity is reflected in Grodal's (2009) concept of 'bioculturalism', in which he refutes both strong culturalism (the notion that the human mind is a 'blank slate' upon which culture is inscribed) and strong biologism (the idea that all human behaviour can be explained in purely biological terms). Gregory does indeed stress the relative malleability of perception, which inevitably leads towards considerations of the source and stability of conceptual frameworks; but like the idea of bioculturalism, the theory of active perception calls for neither strong culturalism nor strong biologism, for it too is greatly concerned with the interplay of (long-term) evolutionary processes and (short-term) learned perceptual behaviour.

As Polanski's engagement with perceptual psychology develops, it moves beyond a primary concern with the manner in which the perceptual mechanism functions towards an increasing preoccupation with what Gregory identifies as the 'philosophical implications' of active perception, which reflect the existential concerns that emerged post-war in the wake of totalitarianism, fascism, mass genocide, the atomic bomb and the entrance of quantum physics' ever-perplexing 'uncertainty principle' into public discourse. It is this angst that matured and evolved into what is now commonly referred to as the 'postmodern condition', in which even the bourgeois division of 'high' and 'low' culture collapses, the very concept of 'ideology' becomes unstable, and perceptual certitudes are so vigorously challenged that questions of epistemology are quickly transformed into ontological crises. It is along these lines that I have argued that Polanski's films can be appreciated as works that reflect the postmodern condition, in which an intersection is established between 'permanent' meaning (such as the concern with the nature of perception) and 'transient' meaning (such as the specific political and social commentary expressed through pastiche of current events and political figures).[1]

Whilst it is evident that Polanski is fascinated with the workings of perception, this seems to be symptomatic of a broader concern with the basic issue of identity and its inevitable connection to existential crises. So whilst Polanski's cinema often draws attention to the perceptual apparatus, either through the representation (and sometimes through the *evocation*) of disturbed or aberrant perceptual experiences or by 'playing out' the perception-as-hypothesis model on-screen through inter-character conflict, what is also of great relevance is the question of the 'location' of the perceiver him- or herself. Polanski often renders ambiguous what should be straightforward certitudes like nationality, profession, (perceived) ethnicity and even gender; these are all 'facts' that make up one's concept of identity, but it is the stability of these 'facts' that is so often undermined in Polanski's cinema.

In my analysis of *The Ghost*, I discussed the concept of the decentralised 'inter-being', a notion that resonates as well in films that I discussed in other chapters. In *Rosemary's Baby*, Guy 'shifts' between human and demonic forms; neighbour 'Roman Castevet' is also 'Steven Marcato'; and Rosemary herself becomes a 'double being' as her corporeal space becomes compromised as her baby grows inside her. More overtly dramatic is the Trelkovsky–Choule overlapping in *The Tenant*, in which the two identities become inseparable. Identities become uncertain as the borders between distinct psyches break down. With these slippages of identity comes the proposition of the overlapping of diverse psyches, even a challenge to the distinctness of the psyche itself. But here lies the basest fiction, for such overlapping is pure fantasy (at best) or pure psychotic delusion (at worse), for ultimately we *are* locked in our own psychic cage. As Polanski so often demonstrates, the notion that subjective synaptic realms of perception can overlap is highly uncanny; it is a source of both fascination and horror.

I have argued that, to a certain extent, Polanski's cinema is itself a theorising force as it serves as a forum for the great perceptual debate. But what has not been much discussed in this analysis of Polanski's films are the various changes that have taken place to the cinematic medium itself and how these have affected Polanski's work. Whilst it may seem as though Polanski's cinema has been immune from advances in digital technology – he has yet to, for example, embrace the digital camera – it would be greatly remiss to overlook Polanski's use of CGI in *Oliver Twist* and *The Ghost*, which is employed so seamlessly in these films that many will undoubtedly be surprised to read they contained any digital effects at all.[2] Possibilities for new threads of analysis connected to the line of discourse introduced here may indeed emerge depending on the technology Polanski employs on his forthcoming projects. Whilst Polanski once experimented (with Gregory's help) with 3-D in the 1970s, he has thus far avoided the twenty-first century version of this technology. Perhaps some recent 3-D films by fellow 'old masters', Werner Herzog's *Cave of Forgotten Dreams* (2010), Wim Wenders' *Pina* (2011) and Martin Scorsese's *Hugo* (2011), may inspire Polanski to try his hand at achieving the 3-D 'wraparound' effect once more.

I have argued that the manner in which Polanski's cinema actively engages with perceptual psychology positions his films not only as objects that can be examined in general terms regarding the way we perceive them, but also as works that call attention to the higher cognitive functions involved in perception. I have also suggested that these films arguably even participate in the theorising of perception itself, which potentially extends the value of this approach beyond the study of Polanski's cinema to the wider area of cognitive film studies.

Writing in 1915, Hugo Münsterberg ventured that cinema ('photoplay') would become, above any other art form, 'the domain of psychologists that analysed the mind' (quoted in Anderson and Anderson, 1996: 347). Nearly a century on, the incorporation of cognitive research into film theory is becoming increasingly relevant, especially considering recent developments in digital projection and 3-D cinema, in which a strong grasp of perceptual psychology is critical to the creation of novel cinematic technologies that aspire to be more than mere gimmickry and truly encourage cognitive engagement. The SCSMI, for example, is a strong advocate for such research and continues to argue for the increased incorporation of cognitive psychology into film studies. As I discussed in Chapter 2, the contrasting meta-theories for cinematic spectatorship proposed by (SCSMI members) Anderson and Anderson (1996) and Berliner and Cohen (2011) demonstrate that the debates of perceptual theorists in the field of psychology can (and should) be the debates of film theorists as well.

It is important to again emphasise that whilst I have engaged with perceptual psychology and psychiatric research throughout my close readings of Polanski's films, what I have furnished here is not the type of scholarship that is primarily concerned with exploring cognition and cinematic spectatorship in general terms, nor has this work argued for a particular ontology of cinema itself; I hope only to have demonstrated how the theory of active perception as delineated by R. L. Gregory can be used as a means of guiding thought through the greater philosophical discourse taking place both within Polanski's films and intertextually across his cinema. Nevertheless, I believe that my particular approach to Polanski's work does demonstrate that his cinema is particularly suited to being examined in the context of more general, cognition-based theorising on spectatorship and cinematic 'embodiment', as in Polanski's cinema we have an example of an authorial force who has quite knowingly mobilised psychological research in a conscious effort to nuance and manipulate the spectatorial experience.

I will conclude this study of Polanski's cinema with a few more words about pleasure, which is a key concept when considering the value of close reading and extended (auteuristic) studies that focus on a single film-maker, two approaches to film analysis that this book clearly champions. For me, exploiting Gregory's writings on perception to lay a 'pathway' through Polanski's cinema has proved to be a useful way of engaging with these works; the primary intent of this approach was not, however, to furnish a definitive reading of these films, but rather to 'unstitch' Polanski's cinema and provoke further thought on a number of different issues. To put it another way, I hope to have nudged Polanskian discourse towards a mode of critical analysis that follows Deleuze's recommendation to talk less *about* cinema and start talking *with* cinema (Deleuze, 1989: 268), or, if I can be so bold as to nuance Deleuze's notion a bit further, to *think* with cinema. In this respect, we can reflect upon Polanski's various efforts to utilise the full potential of cinema and tease from it all the forms of pleasure it can yield. We can appreciate Polanski's films not just for the ephemeral pleasures granted by the manner in which these stories are so expertly told, but also for the access to the more 'permanent' pleasure these works bestow through close readings and reflection on both the complexities of the diegeses and the philosophical conundrums they challenge us with; this latter type of pleasure is that which is derived from what I have referred to as the ubiquitous 'dissatisfaction' delivered by Polanski's work, which, paradoxically, is probably the only means through which lasting pleasure can be achieved.

In Polanski's cinema we have a series of films that not only compel us to think about pleasure, but also invite us to take pleasure in thinking; this balance is achieved by combining an engagement with perceptual psychology with the creation of rich diegetic worlds, the amplification and deconstruction of generic conventions, the deliberate employment of Camp, and the use of compelling stories and storytelling techniques. Such qualities are critical, for it is the pleasure that comes from the dissection of these works that sustains the multiple viewings required of the sort of close readings I have offered here; it is through such detailed inter- and intra-film analysis that the philosophical discourse at play in these works can be best appreciated. But beyond simply identifying a strain of discourse, such as the perceptual concerns I have based my analyses on, we are also compelled to engage with these issues directly, to struggle with these ideas and their implications just as we struggle with the complex diegetic realities that contain them.

In Polanski's cinema, as diegeses become destabilised, so do the certitudes of identity and ideology. Generic fixtures lure us in and are milked for pleasure, but we are also betrayed by them when plot swerves deconstruct these narrative frameworks. Mysteries are presented, but Sherlockian trajectories are usurped by the uncertainty principle. The reliability of our higher cognitive functions' capacity to reveal the world of things is challenged. We are left not with solutions or truth, but with clashing hypotheses. Robust realities are not re-stitched, but unravelled; and thus satisfaction is consistently denied. But it is through this dissatisfaction that Polanski's films transcend their role of delivering visceral pleasure; these are the struggles, I argue, through which an even higher order of pleasure is accessed.

Notes

1. I borrow the notion of 'permanent' and 'transient' forms of meaning from Grodal (2009: 20–21, 205–228), who associates the former with the ambitions of 'high art', and the latter with those of 'low art'.
2. A 'green screen' CGI effect was used to create many of the Dickensian backgrounds in *Oliver Twist*, which was shot in the Czech Republic; in *The Ghost*, the same technique is used to create most of the exteriors as seen through the large glass windows of the house on Martha's Vineyard, recreated on the north German coast.

Roman Polanski Filmography

Shorts

Bicycle (1955, Poland)
Toothy Grin (1957, Poland)
Break Up the Dance (1957, Poland)
Murder (1957, Poland)
Two Men and a Wardrobe (1958, Poland)
The Lamp (1959, Poland)
When Angels Fall (1959, Poland)
The Fat and the Lean (1961, France)
Mammals (1962, Poland)
River of Diamonds, segment in *The World's Most Beautiful Swindlers* (1964, France, Italy, Japan, Netherlands)
Cinéma Erotique, segment in *To Each His Own Cinema* (2007, France)

Feature Films

Knife in the Water (1962, Poland)
Cinematography: Jerzy Lipman
Writers: Roman Polanski, Jakub Goldberg and Jerzy Skolimowski

Repulsion (1965, UK)
Cinematography: Gilbert Taylor
Writers: Roman Polanski, Gérard Brach and David Stone

Cul-de-sac (1966, UK)
Cinematography: Gilbert Taylor
Writers: Roman Polanski and Gérard Brach

Dance of the Vampires (1967, UK, USA)
Cinematography: Douglas Slocombe
Writers: Roman Polanski and Gérard Brach

Rosemary's Baby (1968, USA)
Cinematography: William A. Fraker
Writers: Ira Levin and Roman Polanski

Macbeth (1971, UK, USA)
Cinematography: Gilbert Taylor
Writers: William Shakespeare, Roman Polanski and Kenneth Tynan

What? (1972, Italy, Germany, France)
Cinematography: Marcello Gatti and Giuseppe Ruzzolini
Writers: Roman Polanski and Gérard Brach

Chinatown (1974, USA)
Cinematography: John A. Alonzo
Writers: Robert Towne and Roman Polanski

The Tenant (1976, France)
Cinematography: Sven Nykvist
Writers: Roland Topor, Roman Polanski and Gérard Brach

Tess (1979, France, UK)
Cinematography: Ghislain Cloquet and Geoffrey Unsworth
Writers: Thomas Hardy, Roman Polanski, Gérard Brach and John Brownjohn

Pirates (1986, Tunisia, Spain)
Cinematography: Witold Sobocinski
Writers: Roman Polanski, Gérard Brach and John Brownjohn

Frantic (1988, USA)
Cinematography: Witold Sobocinski
Writers: Roman Polanski and Gérard Brach, Robert Towne and Jeff Gross

Bitter Moon (1992, France, USA, UK)
Cinematography: Tonino Delli Colli
Writers: Pascal Bruckner, Roman Polanski, Gérard Brach, John Brownjohn and Jeff Gross

Death and the Maiden (1994, UK, USA, France)
Cinematography: Tonino Delli Colli
Writers: Ariel Dorfman and Rafael Yglesias

The Ninth Gate (1999, Spain, France, Germany, USA)
Cinematography: Darius Khondji
Writers: Roman Polanski, Arturo Pérez-Reverte, John Brownjohn and Enrique Urbizu

The Pianist (2002, France, Poland, Germany, UK, USA, Switzerland)
Cinematography: Pawel Edelman
Writers: Ronald Harwood and Wladyslaw Szpilman

Oliver Twist (2005, UK, Czech Republic, Italy, France)
Cinematography: Pawel Edelman
Writers: Charles Dickens and Ronald Harwood

The Ghost (2010, France, Germany, UK)
Cinematography: Pawel Edelman
Writers: Roman Polanski and Robert Harris

Carnage (2011, France, Germany, Poland)
Cinematography: Pawel Edelman
Writers: Roman Polanski and Yasmina Reza

Bibliography

Allen, B. S. and Otto, R. G. (1996) 'Media as Lived Environments: The Ecological Psychology of Educational Technology', in D. H. Jonassen (ed.) *Handbook of Research for Educational Communications and Technology*, New York: Simon and Schuster Macmillan, pp. 199–225.

Anderson, J. (1996) *The Reality of Illusion: An Ecological Approach to Cognitive Film Theory*, Carbondale: Southern Illinois University Press.

Anderson, B. and Anderson, J. (1996) 'The Case for Ecological Metatheory', in D. Bordwell and N. Carroll (eds) *Post-Theory: Reconstructing Film Studies*, Madison: University of Wisconsin Press, pp. 347–367.

Andrew, D. (1979) 'The Postwar Struggle for Color', *Cinema Journal*, vol. 18, no. 2, pp. 41–52.

Barker, J. (2009) *The Tactile Eye: Touch and the Cinematic Experience*, Berkeley: University of California Press.

Baudrillard, J. (1983) *Simulations*, Los Angeles: Semiotext(e).

Baudry, J. L. (1992) 'The Apparatus: Metapsychological Approaches to the Impression of Reality in the Cinema', in L. Braudy, M. Cohen and G. Mast (eds), *Film Theory and Criticism Introductory Readings*, Oxford: Oxford University Press, pp. 690–707.

Bazin, A. (2004) *What is Cinema? Volume 2*, Berkley: University of California Press.

Bell, D. (1976) *The Cultural Contradictions of Capitalism*, New York: Basic Books.

Belton, J. (1991) 'Language, Oedipus, and *Chinatown*', *MLN (Modern Language Notes)*, vol. 106, no. 5, pp. 933–950.

Berger, P. (1967) *The Sacred Canopy: Elements of a Sociological Theory of Religion*, New York: Anchor Books.

Berliner, T. and Cohen, D. J. (2011) 'The Illusion of Continuity: Active Perception and the Classical Editing System', *Journal of Film and Video*, vol. 63, no. 1, pp. 44–63.

Black, S. (1969) *Mind and Body*, London: Kimber.

Blashfield, R. K. (1984) *The Classification of Psychopathology: Neo-Kraepelinian and Quantitative Approaches*, New York: Plenum.

Bleuler, E. (1911) *Dementia Praecox or the Group of Schizophrenias*, New York: International University Press.

Boehnlein, J. J. and Kinzie, J. D. (1989) 'Post-Traumatic Psychosis Among Cambodian Refugees', *Journal of Traumatic Stress*, vol. 2, no. 2, pp. 185–198.

Bonnemann, C., Dietrich, D. E., Dillo, W., Dima, D., Emrich. H. M., Lanfermann, H. and Roiser, J. P. (2009) 'Understanding Why Patients with Schizophrenia Do Not Perceive the Hollow-Mask Illusion Using Dynamic Causal Modelling', *NeuroImage*, no. 46, pp. 1180–1186.

Bordwell, D. (1985) *Narration in the Fiction Film*, Madison: University of Wisconsin.
———. (1989) *Making Meaning*, Cambridge, MA: Harvard University Press.
———. (1996) 'Contemporary Film Studies and the Vicissitudes of Grand Theory', in D. Bordwell and N. Carroll (eds) *Post-Theory: Reconstructing Film Studies*, Madison: University of Wisconsin Press, pp. 3–34.
———. (2002) 'The Art Cinema as a Mode of Film Practice', in C. Fowler (ed.) *European Cinema Reader*, London: Routledge, pp. 94–102.
Borsutzky, M., Emrich, H. M., Huber, T. J., Leweke, F. M., Schneider, U. and Seifert, J. (2002) 'Reduced Binocular Depth Inversion in Schizophrenic Patients', *Schizophrenia Research*, vol. 53, no. 1, pp. 101–108.
Bradbury, R. (1972) 'A New Ending to *Rosemary's Baby*', in R. Huss and T. J. Ross (eds) *Focus on Horror Film*, Englewood Cliffs, NJ: Prentice Hall, pp. 149–151.
Brooks, V. and Hochberg, J. (1996a) 'The Perception of Motion Pictures', *Cognitive Ecology: Handbook of Perception and Cognition*, in E. C. Carterette and M. P. Freiman (eds) New York: Academic Press, pp. 205–292.
———. (1996b) 'Movies in the Mind's Eye', in D. Bordwell and N. Carroll (eds) *Post-Theory: Reconstructing Film Studies*, Madison: University of Wisconsin Press, pp. 368–387.
Brown, D., Izenour, S. and Venturi, R. (1972) *Learning from Las Vegas*, Cambridge, MA: MIT Press.
Bruno, G. (1987) 'Ramble City: Postmodernism and *Blade Runner*', *October*, vol. 41 (Summer, 1987), pp. 61–74.
———. (2002) *Atlas of Emotion*, New York: Verso.
Brunsdon, C. (2007) *London in Cinema*, London: British Film Institute.
Buckland, W. (2000) *The Cognitive Semiotics of Film*, Cambridge: Cambridge University Press.
Bullard, J., Keiffer, A., Ray, W., Roberts, C. and Spronken-Smith, R. (2008) 'Where Might Sand Dunes be on Mars? Engaging Students Through Inquiry-Based Learning in Geography', *Journal of Geography in Higher Education*, vol. 32, no. 1, pp. 71–86.
Calinescu, M. (1987) *Five Faces of Modernity*, Durham: Duke University Press.
Cappabianca, A. (1997) *Roman Polanski*, Genova: Le Mani.
Caputo, D. (2007) 'Book Review: *Roman Polanski: The Cinema of a Cultured Traveller*', *Film International*, vol. 5, no. 24, pp. 124–125.
Carroll, N. (1996) *Theorizing the Moving Image*, Cambridge: Cambridge University Press.
Carstairs, G. M. (1970) 'Review of *Mind and Body* by Stephen Black', *The British Journal of Psychiatry*, 117, pp. 102.
Cavell, S. (1971) *The World Viewed (Enlarged Edition)*, Cambridge, MA: Harvard University Press.
Caughie, J. (1981) *Theories of Authorship*, London: Routledge.
Chapman, J. and Mcghie, A. (1961) 'Disorders of Attention and Perception in Early Schizophrenia', *British Journal of Medical Psychology*, no. 34, pp. 103–106.
Ciment, M., Perez, M. and Tailleur, R. (2005) 'Interview with Roman Polanski', in P. Cronin (ed.) *Roman Polanski Interviews*, Mississippi: University Press of Mississippi, pp. 31–46.

Clare, A. (1976) *Psychiatry in Dissent*, London: Tavistock Publications.

Coates, P. (2005) *The Red and the White: The Cinema of People's Poland*, London: Wallflower Press.

———. (2006) '*Cul-de-sac* in Context: Absurd Authorship and Sexuality', in J. Orr and E. Ostrowska (eds) *The Cinema of Roman Polanski: Dark Spaces of the World*, London: Wallflower Press, pp. 92–107.

Cole, J. O., Katz, M. M. and Lowery, H. A. (1969) 'Studies of the Diagnostic Process: The Influence of Symptom Perception, Past Experience and Ethnic Background on Diagnostic Decisions', *American Journal of Psychiatry*, vol. 125, pp. 109–119.

Coleman, F. (2005) 'Crystal', in A. Parr (ed.) *The Deleuze Dictionary*, New York: Columbia University Press, pp. 59–60.

Colman, A. and Gregory, R. L. (1995) *Sensation and Perception*, London: Longman.

Cooper, D. (1967) *Psychiatry and Anti-Psychiatry*, London: Tavistock Publications.

Cooper, J. E., Sartorius, N. and Wing, J. K. (1974) *The Measurement and Classification of Psychiatric Symptoms*, Cambridge: Cambridge University Press.

Cousins, M. (2006) 'Polanski's Fourth Wall Aesthetic', in J. Orr and E. Ostrowska (eds) *The Cinema of Roman Polanski: Dark Spaces of the World*, London: Wallflower Press, pp. 1–3.

Crnković, G. P. (2004) 'From the Eye to the Hand: The Victim's Double Vision in the Films of Roman Polanski', *Kinoeye*, vol. 4, no. 5 (no pagination, see: <www.kinoeye.org/04/05/crnkovic05.php>, accessed 7 November 2009).

Cronin, P. (2005) *Roman Polanski Interviews*, Mississippi: University of Mississippi Press.

Cross, A. P., Gee, D. J. and Seymour-Shove, R. (1968) 'Schizophrenia During Pregnancy Associated with Injury to Foetus in Utero', *British Medical Journal*, vol. 1, no. 16, pp. 686–687.

Cullen-Dupont, K. (2000) *Encyclopaedia of Women's History in America*, New York: Infobase Publishing.

Currie, G. (1996) 'Film, Reality, and Illusion', in D. Bordwell and N. Carroll (eds) *Post-Theory: Reconstructing Film Studies*, Madison: University of Wisconsin Press, pp. 325–344.

Davis, M. (1990) *City of Quartz*, London: Random House.

De Baecque, A. and Jousse, T. (2005) 'Interview with Roman Polanski', in P. Cronin, *Roman Polanski Interviews*, Mississippi: University Press of Mississippi, pp. 146–153.

Delahaye, M and Narboni, J. (2005) 'Interview with Roman Polanski', in P. Cronin, *Roman Polanski Interviews*, Mississippi, University Press of Mississippi, pp. 13–30.

Deleuze, G. (1977) 'Nomad Thought', in D. B. Allison (ed.) *The New Nietzsche*, Cambridge, MA: The MIT Press, pp. 142–149.

———. (1986) *Cinema 1: The Movement Image*, London: The Athlone Press.

———. (1989) *Cinema 2: The Time Image*, London: The Athlone Press.

Deleuze, G. and Guattari, F. (2004) *A Thousand Plateaus: Capitalism and Schizophrenia*, London and New York: Continuum.

Dostoevsky, F. (1950) *The Double: A Petersburg Poem*, in F. Dostoevsky, *The Eternal Husband and Other Stories*, London: Henderson and Spalding.

Dorfman, A. (1996) *Death and the Maiden (La Muerte y la Doncella)*, London: Nick Hern Books.

Eco, U. (1983) *The Name of the Rose*, Orlando: Harcourt Brace and Company.
Eisenstein, S. (1992 [1929]) in L. Braudy, M. Cohen and G. Mast (eds) *Film Theory and Criticism Introductory Readings*, New York and Oxford: Oxford University Press, pp. 127–154.
Engel, F. and Marx, K. (1998) *The Communist Manifesto: A Modern Edition*, London: Verso.
Ezra, E. and Rowden, T. (2005) 'What is Transnational Cinema', in E. Ezra and T. Rowden (eds) *Transnational Cinema: The Film Reader*, London and New York: Routledge, pp. 1–12.
Feeney, F. X. (2006) *Roman Polanski*, Köln: Taschen.
Fischer, L. (1992) 'Birth Traumas: Parturition and Horror in *Rosemary's Baby*', *Cinema Journal*, vol. 31, no. 3, pp. 3–18.
Fish, F. G. (1962) *Schizophrenia*, Bristol: Wright.
Fitzmaurice, T. and Shiel, M. (2003) 'Introduction', in T. Fitzmaurice and M. Shiel (eds) *Screening the City*, London: Verso, pp. 1–10.
Friedan, B. (1963) *The Feminine Mystique*, US: W.W. Norton and Company.
Freud, S. (1952) *On Dreams*, US: W. W. Norton and Company.
Gallafent, E. (1992) 'Echo Park: Film Noir in the Seventies', in I. Cameron (ed.) *The Movie Book of Film Noir*, London: Studio Vista, pp. 254–266.
Galperin, W. (1987) '"Bad for the Glass": Representation and Filmic Deconstruction in *Chinatown* and *Chan is Missing*', *MLN (Modern Language Notes)*, vol. 102, no. 5, pp. 1151–1170.
Gibson, J. J. (1967) 'New Reasons for Realism', *Synthese*, vol. 17, no. 2, pp. 162–172.
———. (1979) *The Ecological Approach to Visual Perception*, Boston: Houghton Mifflin.
———. (2002) 'A Theory of Direct Visual Perception', in A. Noe and E. Thomas (eds) *Vision and Mind: Selected Readings in the Philosophy of Perception*, Cambridge, MA: MIT Press, pp. 77–91.
Goscilo, H. (2006) 'Polanski's Existential Body – As Somebody, Nobody and Anybody', in J. Orr and E. Ostrowska (eds) *The Cinema of Roman Polanski: Dark Spaces of the World*, London: Wallflower Press, pp. 22–37.
Gottesman, I. I. (1991) *Schizophrenia Genesis*, New York: Freeman.
Greer, G. (1970) *The Female Eunuch*, London: MacGibbon and Kee Ltd.
Gregory, R. L. and Wallace, J. G. (1974) 'Recovery from Early Blindness: A Case Study', in R. L. Gregory (ed.) *Concepts and Mechanisms of Perception*, London: Duckworth, pp. 65–129.
Gregory, R. L. (1980) 'Perceptions as Hypotheses', *Philosophical Transactions of the Royal Society: Biological Sciences*, vol. 290, no. 1038, pp. 181–197.
———. (1997a) *Eye and Brain: The Psychology of Seeing*, Princeton: Princeton University Press.
———. (1997b) 'Knowledge in Perception and Illusion', *Philosophical Transactions of the Royal Society: Biological Sciences*, vol. 352, no. 1358, pp. 1121–1127.
———. (2003) 'Eye and Brain Audio Interview', *Repulsion* DVD, Anchor Bay Home Entertainment.
———. (2005) 'Knowledge for Vision: Vision for Knowledge', *Philosophical Transactions of the Royal Society: Biological Sciences*, vol. 360, no. 1458, pp. 1231–1251.

———. (2008) Interview conducted by Davide Caputo, 17 June 2008 (unpublished).
Grodal, T. (2009) *Embodied Visions*, Oxford: Oxford University Press.
Guze, S. and Perley, M. (1963) 'Observations on the Natural History of Hysteria', *The American Journal of Psychiatry*, no. 119, pp. 960–965.
Haltof, M. (2002) *Polish National Cinema*, Oxford: Berghahn Books.
Hamilton, M. (1984) *Fish's Schizophrenia*, Bristol: Wright.
Harris, R. (2007) *The Ghost*, London: Random House.
Harvey, D. (1989) *The Condition of Postmodernity*, Oxford: Blackwell.
Haskell, M. (1987) *From Reverence to Rape*, Chicago: University of Chicago Press.
Hayward, S. (2000) *Cinema Studies: The Key Concepts*, London: Routledge.
Heineman, K. (2009) 'The Silent Majority', in M. Hall (ed.) *Perspectives in American History: Vietnam War Era*, Santa Barbara: ABC-CLIO, pp. 79–98.
Higbee, W. (2007) 'Beyond the (Trans)national: Towards a Cinema of Transvergence in Postcolonial and Diasporic Francophone Cinema(s)', *Studies in French Cinema*, vol. 7, no. 2, pp. 79–91.
Hirsch, S. R. and Leff, J. P. (1975) *Abnormalities in the Parents of Schizophrenics*, Oxford: Oxford University Press.
Horne, P. (2010) 'The Man Who Wasn't There', *Sight and Sound*, May 2010, pp. 38–41.
Horsley, J. (2009) *The Secret Life of Movies*, Jefferson, NC: Mcfarland.
Huyssen, A. (1990) 'Mapping the Postmodern', in L. J. Nicholson (ed.) *Feminism/Postmodernism*, New York: Routledge, pp. 234–277.
Jameson, F. (1983) 'Postmodernism and Consumer Society', in H. Foster (ed.) *Postmodern Culture*, London: Bay Press, pp. 111–125.
———. (1984) 'Postmodernism, or The Cultural Logic of Late Capitalism', *New Left Review*, no. 146 (July–August, 1984), pp. 53–92.
Kallman, F. J. (1938) *The Genetics of Schizophrenia*, New York: Augustin.
Kam, E. (2003) 'Conceptualising Security in Israel', in H. G. Brauch, P. H. Liotta, A. Marquina, P. F. Rogers and M. Selim (eds) *Security and Environment in the Mediterranean*, New York: Springer, pp. 356–366.
Keefe, R. (1998) 'The Neurobiology of Disturbances of the Self: Autonoetic Agnosia in Schizophrenia', in X. Amador and S. David (eds) *Insight and Psychosis*, Oxford: Oxford University Press, pp. 142–173.
Kellner, D. and Ryan, M (1988) *Camera Politica*, Bloomington: Indiana University Press.
Kiernan, T. (1980) *Repulsion: The Life and Times of Roman Polanski*, London: New English Library.
Koehler, K. (1979) 'First Rank Symptoms of Schizophrenia: Questions Concerning Clinical Boundaries', *British Journal of Psychiatry*, no. 131, pp. 236–248.
Kramer, M. (1961) 'Some Problems for International Research Suggested by Observations on Differences in First Admission Rates to the Mental Hospitals of England and Wales and the United States', *Proceeding of the Third World Congress of Psychiatry*, vol. 3, pp. 153–160.
Lacan, J. (1975) *Le Séminaire Livre XX Encore*, Paris: Seuil.

Laing, R. D. (1960) *The Divided Self*, London: Tavistock Publications.
———. (1964) *Sanity, Madness and the Family*, London: Tavistock Publications.
———. (1967) *The Politics of Experience*, Harmondsworth: Penguin.
Lavey, A. S. (1992) *The Devil's Notebook*, Los Angeles: Feral House.
Lawton, A. M. (1981) 'The Double: A Dostoevskian Theme in Polanski', *Literature/Film Quarterly*, vol. 9, no. 2, pp. 121–129.
Leaming, B. (1981) *Polanski: The Filmmaker as Voyeur*, New York: Simon and Schuster.
Leifer, M. (1980) *Psychological Effects of Motherhood: A Study of First Pregnancy*, New York: Praeger Special Studies.
Leven, J. (1996) *The Double (Director's 2nd Draft)*, Mandalay Entertainment. Held in the Roman Polanski archive at Le Bibliothèque du Film, Paris. Archive reference: SBG 171–172 B59.
Levin, D. T. and Simons, D. J. (1997) 'Failure to Detect Changes to Attended Objects in Motion Pictures', *Psychonomic Bulletin and Review*, vol. 4.4, pp. 501–506.
Litowitz, N. S. and Newman, K. M. (1967) 'Borderline Personality and the Theatre of the Absurd', *Archives of General Psychiatry*, vol. 16, no. 3, pp. 268–280.
Luckett, M. (2000) 'Travel and Mobility: Femininity and National Identity in Swinging London Films', in J. Ashby and A. Higson (eds) *British Cinema: Past and Present*, London: Routledge, pp. 233–246.
Lukács, G. (1963) *The Meaning of Contemporary Realism*, London: Merlin Press.
Lyotard, J. (1984) *The Postmodern Condition: A Report on Knowledge*, Manchester: University Press.
Mackendrick, A. (2004) *On Filmmaking*, New York: Faber and Faber.
Marciniak, K. (2000) 'Cinematic Exile: Performing the Foreign Body Onscreen in Roman Polanski's *The Tenant*', *Camera Obscura*, 43 (vol. 15, no. 1), pp. 1–43.
Marks, L. (2000) *The Skin of the Film: Intercultural Cinema, Embodiment, and the Senses*, Durham: Duke University Press.
Martin-Jones, D. (2006) *Deleuze, Cinema, and National Identity*, Edinburgh: Edinburgh University Press.
Maslow, A. H. (1973) *On Dominance, Self-Esteem, and Self-Actualization*, Monterey: Thomson Brooks/Cole.
Matusow, A. (2009) *The Unraveling of America*, Athens, GA: The University of Georgia Press.
Mazierska, E. (2005) 'The Autobiographical Effect in the Cinema of Roman Polanski', *Film Criticism*, vol. 29, no. 3, pp. 28–45.
———. (2007) *Roman Polanski: The Cinema of a Cultured Traveller*, New York: I.B. Tauris.
McGinnis, W. D. (1975) '*Chinatown*: Roman Polanski's Contemporary Oedipus Story', *Literature/Film Quarterly*, vol. 3, no. 3, pp. 249–251.
McHale, B. (1986) 'Change of Dominant from Modernist to Postmodernist Writing', in H. Bertens and D. Fokkema (eds) *Approaching Postmodernism*, Amsterdam and Philadelphia: John Benjamins, pp. 53–79.
McKenna, P. J. (1997) *Schizophrenia and Related Syndromes*, Hove: Psychology Press Ltd.

McLellan, H. (1996) 'Virtual Realities', in D. H. Jonassen (ed.) *Handbook of Research for Educational Communications and Technology*, New York: Simon and Schuster Macmillan, pp. 457–483.

Meikle, D. (2006) *Roman Polanski: Odd Man Out*, Richmond: Reynolds and Hearn Ltd.

Mellor, C. S. (1970) 'First-Rank Symptoms of Schizophrenia', *British Journal of Psychiatry*, 117, pp. 15–23.

Merleau-Ponty, M. (1964) 'Eye and Mind', in J. Edie (ed.) *The Primacy of Perception and Other Essays on Phenomenological Psychology, the Philosophy of Art, History and Politics*, Evanston, IL: Northwestern University Press, pp. 159–192.

———. (1964) *Sense and Non-Sense*, Evanston, IL: Northwestern University Press.

———. (2002) *Phenomenology of Perception*, London: Routledge.

Metz, C. (1982) *Psychoanalysis and Cinema: The Imaginary Signifier*, Bloomington: Indiana University Press.

Morrison, J. (2001) 'The Old Masters: Kubrick, Polanski, and the Late Style in Modern Cinema', *Raritan: A Quarterly Review*, Fall 2001 (vol. 21, no. 2), pp. 29–47.

———. (2007) *Roman Polanski*, Chicago: University of Illinois Press.

Mulvey, L. (1975) 'Visual Pleasure and Narrative Cinema', *Screen*, vol. 16, no. 3, pp. 6–18.

———. (1989) *Visual and Other Pleasures*, Bloomington: Indiana University Press.

Naremore, J. (1998) *More Than Night*, Berkley: University of California Press.

Neidich, W. (2003) *Blow Up: Photography, Cinema and the Brain*, New York: Distributed Art Publishers.

Orr, J. (1993) *Cinema and Modernity*, Cambridge, MA: Polity Press.

———. (2006) 'Polanski: The Art of Perceiving', in J. Orr and E. Ostrowska (eds) *The Cinema of Roman Polanski: Dark Spaces of the World*, London: Wallflower Press, pp. 4–21.

Ostrowska, E. (2006) '*Knife in the Water*: Polanski's Nomadic Discourse Begins', in J. Orr and E. Ostrowska (eds) *The Cinema of Roman Polanski: Dark Spaces of the World*, London: Wallflower Press, pp. 62–75.

Oudart, J-P. (1969) 'Suture (Part 1)', *Cahiers du Cinéma*, 211, April 1969, pp. 36–39.

Paulus, T. (2007) 'View Across the Courtyard: Bazin and the Evolution of Depth Style', *Film International*, vol. 5, no. 6, pp. 63–73.

Peterson, L. and Place, J. (2004) 'Some Visual Motifs in *Film Noir*', in A. Silver and J. Ursini (eds) *Film Noir Reader*, New York: Limelight Editions, pp. 65–76.

Pizzello, C. (2000) 'Satanic Verses', *American Cinematographer*, April 2000, pp. 38–49.

Plantinga, C. and Smith, G. M. (1999) *Passionate Views: Film, Cognition, and Emotion*, Baltimore: The Johns Hopkins University Press.

Plantinga, C. (2009) *Moving Viewers: American Film and the Spectator's Experience*, Berkley: University of California Press.

Polan, D. (2006) '*Chinatown*: Politics as Perspective, Perspective as Politics', in J. Orr and E. Ostrowska (eds) *The Cinema of Roman Polanski: Dark Spaces of the World*, London: Wallflower Press, pp. 108–120.

Polanski, R. (1984) *Roman by Polanski*, New York: Ballantine Books.

———. (2003) 'Director's Commentary', *Repulsion* DVD, Anchor Bay Home Entertainment.

Price, R. (1993) *A Concise History of France*, Cambridge: Cambridge University Press.

Rock, I. (1995) *Perception*, New York: Scientific American Library.

———. (1997) *Indirect Perception*, Cambridge, MA: The MIT Press.

Rodowick, D. N. (2007) *The Virtual Life of Film*, Cambridge, MA: Harvard University Press.

Rosenhan, D. L. (1973) 'On Being Sane in Insane Places', *Science*, vol. 179, pp. 250–258.

Salt, B. (1983) *Film Style and Technology: History and Analysis*, London: Starword.

Sandford, C. (2009) *Polanski*, Basingstoke: Palgrave Macmillan.

Sarris, A. (1976) 'Towards a Theory of Film History', in B. Nichols (ed.) *Movies and Methods (Volume 1)*, Berkley: University of California Press, pp. 237–251.

———. (1992) 'Notes on Auteur Theory in 1962', in L. Braudy, M. Cohen and G. Mast (eds) *Film Theory and Criticism Introductory Readings*, New York and Oxford: Oxford University Press, pp. 585–588.

Schneider, K. (1949) 'The Concept of Delusion', in S. R. Hirsch and M. Shepherd (eds) *Themes and Variations in European Psychiatry*, Bristol: Wright, pp. 33–39.

———. (1958) *Clinical Psychopathology*, New York: Grune and Stratton.

Schrader, P. (1986) 'Notes on *Film Noir*', in B. Grant (ed.) *Film Genre Reader III*, Austin: University of Texas Press, pp. 229–243.

Shaviro, S. (1993) *The Cinematic Body*, Minneapolis: University of Minneapolis Press.

Shiel, M. (2001) 'Cinema and the City in History and Theory', in T. Fitzmaurice and M. Shiel (eds) *Cinema and the City: Film and Urban Societies in a Global Context*, Oxford: Blackwell Publishers Ltd., pp. 1–18.

———. (2003) 'A Nostalgia for Modernity: New York, Los Angeles and American Cinema in the 1970s', in T. Fitzmaurice and M. Shiel (eds) *Screening the City*, London: Verso, pp. 160–179.

Shonfield, K. (2000) *Walls Have Feelings: Architecture, Film and the City*, London: Routledge.

Silverstein, P. (2004) *Algeria in France*, Bloomington: Indiana University Press.

Singer, M. T. and Wynne, L. C. (1963) 'Thought Disorder and Family Relations of Schizophrenics', *Archives of General Psychiatry*, no. 9, pp. 191–196.

Slater, E. (1968) 'A Review of Early Evidence on Genetic Factors in Schizophrenia', in S. S. Ketty and D. Rosenthal (eds) *The Transmission of Schizophrenia*, Oxford: Pergamon, pp. 15–26.

Smith, M. (1995) *Engaging Characters: Fiction, Emotion, and the Cinema*, Oxford: Clarendon Press.

———. (2009) 'Consciousness', in P. Livingston and C. Plantinga (eds) *Routledge Companion to Philosophy and Film*, London: Routledge, pp. 39–51.

Sobchack, V. (1992) *The Address of the Eye: The Phenomenology of Film Experience*, Princeton: Princeton University Press.

———. (2004) *Carnal Thoughts: Embodiment and Moving Image Culture*, Berkeley: University of California Press.

Sontag, S. (1994) 'Notes on Camp', in S. Everett (ed.) *Art Theory and Criticism*, Jefferson, NC: McFarland, pp. 96–109.

Souriau, E. (1953) *L'Univers filmique*. Paris: Flammarion.

Stachówna, G. (1994) *Roman Polański i jego filmy*, Warsaw: PWN.

Stevenson, D. (2007) 'Godard and Bazin', *Film International*, vol. 5, no. 6, pp. 32–40.
Strathausen, C. (2003) 'Uncanny Spaces: The City in Ruttmann and Vetrov', in T. Fitzmaurice and M. Shiel (eds) *Screening the City*, London: Verso, pp. 15–40.
Szasz, T. S. (1960) 'The Myth of Mental Illness', *American Psychologist*, no. 15, pp. 113–118.
———. (1971) *The Manufacture of Madness*, London: Routledge.
———. (1974) *The Myth of Mental Illness*, New York: Harper Perennial.
———. (2003) *The Myth of Mental Illness (50th Anniversary re-issue)*, New York: Harper Perennial.
Thompson, D. (1995) 'I Make Films for Adults', *Sight and Sound*, April 1995, pp. 6–9.
Todd, D. (1964) 'Review of *Repulsion*', *Kinematograph Weekly* (Production Review Supplement), September 24, pp. 14–15.
Toles, G. (1995) 'This May Hurt a Little: The Art of Humiliation in Film', *Film Quarterly*, vol. 48, no. 4, pp. 2–14.
Topor, R. (2006) *The Tenant*, Colorado: Millipede Press Books.
Virilo, P. (1991) *The Lost Dimensions*, New York: Semiotext(e).
Walton, J. (2001) 'Film Mystery as Urban History: The Case of *Chinatown*', in T. Fitzmaurice and M. Shiel (eds) *Cinema and the City: Film and Urban Societies in a Global Context*, Oxford: Blackwell Publishers Ltd., pp. 46–58.
Warren, B. (2002) *Photography*, Albany, NY: Delmar.
Wexman, V. W. (1985) *Roman Polanski*, New York: Twayne Publishers.
Williams, C. (1980) *Realism and the Cinema*, London: Routledge and Kegan Paul Ltd.
Williams, L. (1981) 'Film Madness: The Uncanny Return of the Repressed in Polanski's *The Tenant*', *Cinema Journal*, vol. 20, no. 2, pp. 63–71.
Wittner, L. (2003) *The Struggle Against the Bomb (Vol. 3)*, Stanford, CA: Stanford University Press.
Wollen, P. (1969) *Signs and Meaning in the Cinema*, London: Secker and Warburg/BFI.
———. (1992) 'The Auteur Theory', in L. Baudry, M. Cohen and G. Mast (eds) *Film Theory and Criticism*, Oxford: Oxford University Press, pp. 589–605.
Zimmerman, P. D. (1974) 'Blood and Water', *Newsweek*, July 1, p. 94.
Žižek, S. (1991) *Looking Awry: An Introduction to Jacques Lacan and Popular Culture*, Cambridge, MA: The MIT Press.

Information attained from the following dossiers held by the Bibliothèque du film *(*BiFi*) in Paris have been referenced herein:*

The Ninth Gate
BAUDROT-GU121 to BAUDROT-GU126 (inclusive)

Frantic
BAUDROT-GU82-B39, BAUDROT-GU83-B40, BAUDROT-GU271-B88, BAUDROT-GU272-B88, BAUDROT-GU273-B88, BAUDROT-GU274-B88, BAUDROT-GU275-B88,

BAUDROT-GU276-B89, BAUDROT-GU277-B89, BAUDROT-GU278-B89, BAUDROT-GU279-B89

The Tenant
BAUDROT-GU59-B22, BAUDROT-GU60-B23, BAUDROT-GU252-B85, BAUDROT-GU253-B85, BAUDROT-GU254-B85, BAUDROT-GU377-B111, BAUDROT-GU411-B78, Pierre Guffroy *maquettes* (no reference number), PO0024059, PO0024055

Law's New Boundaries

The consequences of legal Autopoiesis

Edited by
JIŘÍ PŘIBÁŇ
Charles University, The Czech Republic and Cardiff University, UK
DAVID NELKEN
University of Macerata, Italy

Ashgate
DARTMOUTH
Aldershot • Burlington USA • Singapore • Sydney

Published by
Dartmouth Publishing Company
Ashgate Publishing Limited
Gower House
Croft Road
Aldershot
Hampshire GU11 3HR
England

Ashgate Publishing Company
131 Main Street
Burlington, VT 05401-5600 USA

Ashgate website: http://www.ashgate.com

British Library Cataloguing in Publication Data
Law's new boundaries : the consequences of legal
autopoiesis. - (Applied legal philosophy)
1.Autopoiesis 2. Sociological jurisprudence
I. Přibáň, Jiří, 1967- II. Nelken, David
340.1'15

Library of Congress Control Number: 2001091574

ISBN 0 7546 2202 9

Printed and bound in Great Britain by MPG Books Ltd, Bodmin, Cornwall

Contents

List of Contributors

Jean Clam is a CNRS (Centre National de la Recherche Scientifique) senior research fellow (Strasburg, France). He published: *Droit et société chez Niklas Luhmann. La contingence des normes* (1997, Paris, Presses Universitaires de France, with Jean-Luc Gaffard); *Norme, fait, fluctuation. Contributions a une analzse des choix normatifs* (forthcoming in 2001, Geneve, Droz); as well as numerous articles on legal philosophy and systems theory.

Roger Cotterrell is Professor of Legal Theory at Queen Mary and Westfield College, University of London. He is the author of *The Sociology of Law, The Politics of Jurisprudence, Law's Community,* and most recently *Emile Durkheim: Law in a Moral Domain*, a comprehensive critical study of Durkheimian sociology of law.

Peter Fitzpatrick is Anniversary Professor of Law at Birkbeck College in the University of London and has taught at universities in Europe, North America and Papua New Guinea. He has published books on law and social theory, law and racism and imperialism, such as *The Mythology of Modern Law* (Routledge, 1992). Outside the academy, he has been in an international legal practice and was also in the Prime Minister's Office in Papua New Guinea for several years.

Michael King is Professor in the Law Department, Brunel University, Uxbridge, UK. He has published several books and articles on autopoietic theory and its application to decisions concerning children's welfare and children's rights, religion and morality.

Tim Murphy is Professor of Law at the London School of Economics and Political Science. Recent books include *The Oldest Social Science?* (Oxford University Press, 1997) and *Understanding Property Law* (Sweet and Maxwell, 3ed., with Simon Roberts). He is currently engaged in a major project provisionally titled Law and Human Nature.

David Nelken is Distinguished Professor of Sociology and Legal Institutions and Social Change at the University of Macerata, Italy. He is a Trustee of the Law and Society Association (USA) and Vice-President of the Research Committee of Sociology of Law (International Sociological Association). He has recently edited *Law as Communication* (Dartmouth, 1996) and *Adapting Legal Cultures* (Hart Publishing, 2001).

Richard Nobles and **David Schiff** are senior lecturers in the Law Department at the London School of Economics. Apart from numerous individual publications, they have written and researched together extensively on criminal justice, particularly in relation to criminal appeals. They have published the book *Understanding Miscarriages of Justice: Law, the Media and the Inevitability of Crisis* (Oxford University Press, 2000).

Eric W. Orts is Professor of Legal Studies and Director of the Environmental Management Program at the Wharton School of the University of Pennsylvania. He has published numerous articles on environmental law and policy. He is also a co-editor (with Kurt Deketelaere) and contributor of *Environmental Contracts: Comparative Approaches to Regulatory Innovations in the United States and Europe* (Kluwer Law International, forthcoming in 2001).

Jiří Přibáň is Associate Professor of Sociology and Philosophy of Law at the Faculty of Law, Charles University, Prague, and Lecturer at the Cardiff Law School, University of Wales. He publishes in the field of sociology of law, jurisprudence, constitutional law, human rights and post-communist legal systems. He is the author of the book *Dissidents of Law* (forthcoming, 2001). He has edited *The Rule of Law in Central Europe* (Ashgate, 1999, with James Young).

Ralf Rogowski is Reader in Law and Director of the Law and Sociology Programme at the School of Law of the University of Warwick. He publishes in the field EU law, labour law, comparative law and social theory of law. He is the author of *Labour Market Efficiency in the European Union* (1998, with Schomann and Kruppe) and editor resp. co-editor of *Reflexive Labour Law* (1994), *Civil Law* (1996), *European Challenges to Legal Scholarship* (1996), *Constitutional Courts in Comparison* (2000).

Gunther Teubner is Professor of Private Law and Legal Sociology, University Frankfurt and Centennial Visiting Professor, London School of Economics. Reseach fields: social theory of law; comparative studies in private law. Author: *Law as an Autopoietic System* (1993); *Droit et réflexivité* (1994); *Il diritto policontesturale* (1999). Editor/author: *Paradoxes of Self-Reference in the Humanities, Law, and the Social Sciences* (1991); *State, Law, Economy as Autopoietic Systems* (1992); *Environmental Law and Ecological Responsibility* (1995); *Entscheidungsfolgen als Rechtsgründe* (1995); *Global Law Without A State* (1998); *Die Rückgabe des Zwölften Kamels* (2000).

Series Preface

The objective of the Dartmouth Series in Applied Legal Philosophy is to publish work which adopts a theoretical approach to the study of particular areas or aspects of law or deals with general theories of law in a way which focuses on issues of practical moral and political concern in specific legal contexts.

In recent years there has been an encouraging tendency for legal philosophers to utilize detailed knowledge of the substance and practicalities of law and a noteworthy development in the theoretical sophistication of much legal research. The series seeks to encourage these trends and to make available studies in law which are both genuinely philosophical in approach and at the same time based on appropriate legal knowledge and directed towards issues in the criticism and reform of actual laws and legal systems.

The series will include studies of all the main areas of law, presented in a manner which relates to the concerns of specialist legal academics and practitioners. Each book makes an original contribution to an area of legal study while being comprehensible to those engaged in a wide variety of disciplines. Their legal content is principally Anglo-American, but a wide-ranging comparative approach is encouraged and authors are drawn from a variety of jurisdictions.

TOM D. CAMPBELL
Series Editor
The Faculty of Law
The Australian National University

Acknowledgments

We would like to thank Andrew Grubb, Gillian Douglas and all members of the research committee of the Cardiff Law School for their support of the workshop 'Consequences of the Autopoietic Law Theory' held in Cardiff in March 2000. Most of the papers presented at the workshop are edited in this volume. Julia Craske and Linda Mackleworth helped us enormously with the workshop's organisation.

We also would like to thank James Young for initiating the whole idea and Dave Campbell, Michael King and, most of all, Gunther Teubner, for their invaluable help in bringing the project to fruition.

We are most grateful to Kluwer Academic Publishers for their kind permission for the sixth chapter to be reproduced in this collection. It was originally published as an article in *Law and Critique* (vol. 12, issue 1, 2001, pp. 1-32).

1 Introduction

JIŘÍ PŘIBÁŇ AND DAVID NELKEN

A decade ago, theory of autopoietic social systems was still seen by many Anglo-American social and legal scholars as a somewhat obscure and hardly comprehensible doctrine. However, it has now become well-known and currently represents one of the most fertile theoretical areas in social theorising about law.[1] Autopoietic social systems theory has achieved such a status because of its power to formulate old theoretical questions and sociological problems in an innovative way. At the same time, it continues to be a very controversial and sometimes misunderstood theory especially within the English speaking world. The case for putting together a volume which interrogates the theory and seeks to test its applicability to law therefore hardly needs making. In this introduction we will first say something about Niklas Luhmann's development of autopoiesis theory, often neglected in the legal academy in favour of the better known work of Gunther Teubner. We will then summarise the contributions to this volume and formulate some tentative conclusions.

Autopoiesis as a social science paradigm

Although proclaiming a strongly critical attitude to traditional metaphysics and emphasising a 'post-metaphysical' proceduralist and anti-individualist approach, Luhmann's starting point shares some features with the fundamental metaphysical question: Why is there anything at all, rather than nothing? Within the context of sociological theory, Niklas Luhmann addresses a similarly fundamental question: Why and how can we discern, speak about and analyse independent spheres of society and perceive them as autonomous parts, which perform different social functions? Why is there society, rather than nothing?

---

[1]For recent collections on Luhmann's work see e.g. *Acta Sociologica* 1/2000; *Zeitschrift fur Rechtssoziologie* 2000; *Droit et Société* 2000 and Berg, Henk de and Johannes F.K. Schmidt (eds) (2000), *Rezeption und Reflexion. Zur Resonanz der Systemtheorie Niklas Luhmanns auflerhalb der Soziologie*, Frankfurt, Suhrkamp.

Autopoietic social systems theory may be perceived as an attempt to draft a grand theory and sociological paradigm after the disappearance of grand theories. Niklas Luhmann's project did not lack the usual ambitions of grand theories to overcome yet another 'crisis' in social theory. It sought to provide a unifying theoretical perspective and conceptual framework for descriptions and analyses of modern societies at their current stage of development.

Social autopoiesis theory originates in critical elaborations of Talcott Parsons's theory of social systems. The important difference is then a change in understanding the structure/function distinction and Luhmann's emphasis on functionality of different social structures and society as a whole. Talcott Parsons's functional structuralism becomes Niklas Luhmann's structural functionalism. For Luhmann, the structure of commonly shared values, so central to Parsons's systems theory, can no longer integrate contemporary societies. They are too complex and value consensus cannot be achieved in them. Social integrity is maintained by the growing complexity of different social systems and their functions.

Another significant novelty of autopoietic social systems theory is its treatment of a constitutive problem of any social systems theory – the system/environment distinction. Luhmann treats autopoietic systems as normatively closed and cognitively opened to their environment (consisting of other autopoietic social systems) and perceives the very difference between a system and its environment as the most important element of the whole system/environment loop.

Drafting such a grand social theory for post-metaphysical societies and post-metaphysical social science as its reflection, Niklas Luhmann's project immediately reminds us of another great social theorist and great influence on Talcott Parsons's own work – Max Weber. Similarities between Weber and Luhmann's approaches turn out to be persuasive and easily discernible in the field of the sociology of law and bureaucratic organisation. Being also a jurist by university education, Luhmann's first books analysed bureaucratic organisation and the social functions of administration, legislation and public law institutions and resulted in formulating the concept of a complex centreless society, which is radically different from archaic traditional and early modern societies. It achieves stability by its permanent differentiation. The former social hierarchy and priority of some social systems, such as economy or politics, with respect to the rest of society, are replaced by horizontal communication among different social systems and their mutual normative closure.

Similarly, like Weber, Luhmann is also fascinated by the concept of positive law and positivity in its sociological sense. His earlier socio-legal texts, such as *Rechtssoziologie* (1st edition, 1972), deal with the positivity of modern law, its development, constant growth and systemic contribution to the establishment of modern complex societies. They also deal with the relation between law and legal theory and perceive this theory (in the same way as general social theory) as a reflection of social and legal evolution.

In reflecting on the Parsonsian and Weberian background to autopoietic social systems theory, another significant difference and novelty of the autopoiesis paradigm must be addressed here. This is the disappearance of the concept of domination. Luhmann's rejection of the concept of domination and refusal to provide another centralised model of social system is also behind the famous Habermas-Luhmann controversy, which dominated social science and political philosophy discussions in Germany throughout 70s and substantively determined the development of social theory in next two decades. Unlike Habermas, Luhmann does not believe in the 'healing' powers of theory and the ideal of a democratic discourse ('ideal speech pattern') free from political domination. He proposes a different type of theory avoiding the ideological traps of reconstructive social science and building on the reflexivity of social differentiation and the decentralisation of different spheres of social life. Autopoietic systems theory itself is both a pragmatic reflection and part of the evolutionary process of growing complexity and differentiation of contemporary societies.

In this sense, Luhmann's autopoietic social systems theory goes beyond modernity and its trust in democratic procedures, rational public debate and expert knowledge. It overcomes a traditional sociological perspective of society being in crisis and sociologists or social theorists providing rational expert solutions to it. It abandons the possibility to understand and organise contemporary societies from some superior social and paradigmatic position. Autopoiesis theory treats itself as a pragmatic response to the spontaneous evolution of modern societies at the level of knowledge and science. It does not have the status of critical external science with the power to re-constitute and re-organise society. It is rather an outcome of social evolution. As for many postmodernists, the paradigmatic point for Niklas Luhmann and subsequently all adherents of social autopoiesis is that there is no point (for these similarities, see Přibáň, 1998). But it is necessary to take the position of social theory of autopoietic systems in order to provide arguments and paradigmatic background for this paradoxical statement.

Autopoiesis of the legal system?

Paradoxes are an integral part of autopoietic social systems theory. The autopoietic sociology of law and legal theory will serve as good examples, here. Niklas Luhmann use of 'sociological metaphysics' to prove that grand sociological theories are dead finds its echoes in his sociology of law. Luhmann addresses the most typical and common problems of legal positivism in order to provide a radical shift from the legal positivist perspective and its emphasis on legal institutions, rules and organisations as means of social integrity and stability.

According to Luhmann, autopoietic law emerges as a consequence of the process of social evolution and is a part of historical process of modernisation. Modernisation means a shift of social structures and differentiation from segmentary (typical for archaic traditional societies) to functional differentiation (typical for complex modern societies) through system formation (Luhmann, 1995: 423-6). Social variety, flexibility and growth of action possibilities together with growing autonomy of different spheres of social life are typical features of functionally differentiated societies.

For the description of this historical process of structuration of autopoietic social systems, two more concepts, besides the concepts of function, differentiation and system/environment distinction, seem to dominate in Luhmann's theory – *complexity* and *contingency*. One of the most condensed summaries of the achievement of evolutionary level of autopoietic society may be found in the following words:

> [t]he possibilities of the world increase whilst the environment of all other systems increases in complexity and contingency. These can react with increased indifference or with more highly developed forms of adaptation and self-maintenance; but in any case it is in a situation of higher selectivity than before, since it stabilises a choice of further possibilities. Evolution thus generally provides a surplus production of possibilities for the social system, at first 'accidentally', then becoming increasingly structure-dependent and, in today's social systems, partly plannable, so that systems can be selectively maintained by structures and, under these preconditions, improbable arrangements are made probable. The motor and regulator of evolution is the level of complexity between system and environment (Luhmann, 1985: 105).

Reading this paragraph, it is easy to see the richness of Luhmann's popular and seemingly paradoxical statement about the whole being less than the sum of its parts (Luhmann, 1982: xx.). There is no supreme normative framework unifying and integrating contemporary societies. Social integration is secured in the form of systemic reproduction and internal normative frameworks, which are specific and limited to different autopoietic social systems and have a high level of variability and temporability. Being one of a number of autopoietic social systems, law also needs its own procedures and normative framework to secure its maintenance in a complex society. It must set up its own modes of regulation and communication, which will be specifically legal and provide law's social reproduction in such a complex and contingent environment.

This approach to the institutionalisation of modern law in some ways reminds us of Herbert Hart's distinction of primary and secondary rules, the unity of which creates the autonomous legal system (Teubner, 1993: 41). It is specifically the secondary rules which constitute this system and put it in social motion and distinctly autonomous reproduction. But any simple analogy between the legal positivist analysis of a legal system and the theory of autopoietic law as a social system would be very misleading. The first fundamental difference is already entrenched in the concept of positivity. For Luhmann and others, positive law is not limited by organisations or structures (whether courts, legal firms, or other parts of the administration of justice) or actors standing behind the process of legislation and application of legal rules. In other words, law escapes the constraints of professional and power organisations, special training and knowledge. The legal system consists rather of all social communication with some reference to law (Luhmann, 1982: 122).

Understanding the concept of legal system as all social communication about law looks at first as if it is a very broad and unsatisfactorily vague definition. Its advantage, however, is its ability to illustrate the systemic character of law. If the legal system consists of all social communication about law, constraints and selective mechanisms concerning which communications really are about law and which fall outside of law's internal limits turn out to be of primary importance. What allows us to treat law an autonomous part of society and makes it into an autopoietic system?

The emergence of autopoietic law is seen as a historical process of the growth of positive legal rules, regulations and documents. Positivisation of law means growth of the body of law and also changeability of legal regulations. Law needs to set up its own internal programmes and regulations. It becomes more socially autonomous and independent and more legal rules refer back to the dynamics of legal system. Law becomes increasingly self-referential and this process eventually leads to its normative closure, while, at the same time, keeping law cognitively open.

Normative closure and cognitive openness of autopoietic social systems is a central dogma of Niklas Luhman's 'decentred' theory, though one which has been challenged or weakened even by many adherents of the autopoietic social systems theory (see, for instance, Teubner, 1993: ch. 3). The autopoietic concept of normativity radically differs from juristic or legal positivist theory. A juristic view would refer back to organisations and institutions of the legal system and link normativity to security and stability of social action. On the other hand, the autopoietic concept of normativity derives from conditional programming of autopoietic social systems and spontaneous processes of social communication. Conditionally programmed legal systems, based on the logic of 'if...then' can better deal with higher contingency and complexity of world. Instead of securing the normative unity and integration of society, legal norms increasingly provide programmes for coping with complex social change and differentiation.

Another contrast with most juristic approaches lies in the concept of validity. While traditional legal theory usually perceives it in terms of legal hierarchy and (often external) force of law, autopoiesis theory arrives at an account of the circularity of legal validity (Luhmann, 1990: 231). Legal validity derives exclusively neither from legal normativity, nor from any external source of will and political authority. Validity of the legal system also does not depend on the validity of norms and regulations coming from its social environment. It is a permanent circular communication between normative legal rules and legal decisions. Law is the sole judge of whether law itself is lawful or unlawful. Rules can be implemented only by decisions and decisions can be made only because of the existence of normative legal background. Neither the political sovereign's decisions, nor morality, nor the Kelsenian basic norm can be an ultimate source of legal validity, because this is determined by mutual rules/decisions interdependence and dynamic processes of social communication and evolution.

Validity and normativity must be seen as a part of social change and differentiation and not of fundamental social unity. Law does not represent any essential or constitutive social norms. It rather reflects social evolution with all its perturbations and turbulences. It produces norms and rules responding and coping with them.

Law changes social conditions, but, as in all feedback relationships, these conditions condition all future legal changes. Although law operates according to its internal programmes and normative structures, these structures nevertheless can operate only due to the recognition of their social environment and within its constantly changing cognitive limits. The autonomy of autopoietic law means the self-referentiality of law. It is only law that can change law whatever may be political control of legislation. Such control is only part of the law's environment, which cannot change its own modes of operation. For autopoiesis theory law and politics are two distinct functional subsystems of complex autopoietic societies. Autonomy of law cannot then be perceived as a political goal or principle that could be formulated in political slogans of the rule of law, even if it appears in that form. It is a consequence of social evolution and necessity for maintenance of law's social functions in the condition of complexity and contingency. Law establishes its autonomous operations, which re-produce and maintain law's social functions independently on its social environment. Autonomy of law is not therefore a desirable political goal of the modern concept of the rule of law, but rather a consequence of the historical process of social evolution and differentiation of social life. Legal communication becomes *circular* and the autonomous legal system achieves a status of a hyper-cycle consisting of various and more specific closed legal normative communications (Teubner, 1993: 37).

Autopoietic law and the problem of justice

At this stage, the 'idiotic' question must be asked, idiotic in the sense of the idiota, the layman representing the commonsensical perspective unaffected by theoretical or expert knowledge (Gadamer, 1975: 20). This question may be formulated in the following words: when can we start talking about the autopoietic law and how can we tell the difference between legal and non-legal communication?

The autopoietic legal system is a product of social evolution and historical process of differentiation of modern societies. Stability and validity of law ceases to depend upon a higher and more stable order of commonly shared values and principles and depends primarily upon law's capacity to alter and regulate itself. Traditional or natural law sources of validity are replaced by the capacity of legal norms to react and adjust to its changing environment. Conditional programmes and self-regulatory mechanism are therefore introduced as a reaction by law to the inevitable social processes of differentiation and growing complexity. In order to enhance growing social complexity, law must produce a complex set of programmes introducing the self-referential communication. Legal communication is then any communication referring to law and no use of expert knowledge or language is required. The lawyer/client or expert/layman distinction already belongs to the legal system.

Especially in his earlier texts, Luhmann seems to give an extraordinarily powerful role to law in the process of social differentiation and evolution towards the establishment of self-referential autopoietic social systems. Modern law responds to society's need to regulate social action by offering programmes based on concrete regulations which enhance social differentiation rather than basing itself on abstract values and ideological principles.

This perspective can also serve as a sociological explanation for modernity's notion of the rule of law (Luhmann, 1982: 108-9). Legal problem-solving procedures give priority to individual questions and reflect better the growth of variability and individualisation of social action. Conditional programming is an intrinsic part of the modern legal system, which consequently initiates further differentiation of the public sphere and radical separation of the systems of politics, morality, administration and law.

In the context of the evolution of modern societies, the problem of the justice of law looks rather old-fashioned and obscure to Luhmann. Truth and justice, the two most decisive concepts of the western thought, lose their appeal as ultimate standards of human action in the light of new social conditions. Abstract concepts such as truth and justice may perform some symbolic functions, but they cannot determine the factual processes of the autopoietic reproduction of social systems. Legal problem-solving programmes must be much more subtle and refined and have to go beyond the language of justice. In other words, justice loses its referential power and regulatory force in highly complex autopoietic societies (Luhmann, 1982: 120). Law has both to fit its social environment and remain autonomous and the concept of justice fails to make any impact on this primary job of the autopoietic legal system.

According to Luhmann, '... [L]aw is unjust or at least not quite in conformity with the idea of justice ...' (Luhmann, 1990: 235). Naturally such a provocative statement has prompted a number of critical reactions. One such reply may be found in the works of Drucilla Cornell and Michael Rosenfeld. Cornell's critical interpretation of the autopoietic systems theory (criticised by Michael King in this volume) calls for a different reading of the distinctions between justice and law inspired by Derrida's deconstructive approach. She approaches autopoiesis from a normative perspective and refuses to accept the autopoietic 'collapse of prescription into description', respectively justice into law (Cornell, 1992: 1596). Rosenfeld similarly calls for supplementing the horizontalization effect of autopoietic self-referentiality with the lost vertical unity of justice. The law's function is also to provide social unification outside the process of differentiation (Rosenfeld, 1998: 111). Law, according to Rosenfeld, must be integrated in the larger social normative framework, which may be translated by the concept of justice.

Cornell, Rosenfeld and many others read the autopoietic concept of normativity as if it were a by-product of legalism and legal positivism. They call for maintaining the difference between 'is'/horizontal differentiation/law and 'ought to'/vertical unity/justice and often take justice as the ethical obligation, aporia or political urgency beyond law's limits. This enterprise of deconstruction of autopoiesis is, however, rather close to the mainstream concept of the rule of law as a political ideal of liberal democratic political communities (even if it is formulated in a radically different theoretical vocabulary). If it is traditional legal orders which are defined by the idea of ultimate moral values or the idea of natural law, as suggested by Luhmann, then Cornell's or Rosenfeld's views might be taken as yet another attempt to construct the already existing utopia of society constantly strengthening its categorical imperative and radicalising the ethical demands, which is so typical for America (Baudrillard, 1988) and had been the subject of Luhmann's early critique of social theory and ideology.

The consequences of autopoiesis

Under this deliberately open ended title a number of international scholars were invited to a workshop held at Cardiff in the spring of 2000 to reflect on the implications of autopoiesis theory for theorising and reform in the realm of legal theory and sociology in law in general and particular branches of law in particular. This volume, the result of these deliberations, has been divided into two parts which broadly reflect the choice to focus on the theory as such or its application to particular areas of law and social life. But clearly there is no hard and fast line between the parts; theoretical debate over the usefulness of the theory cannot be uninterested in the difference it makes when applied to specific areas of legal life and attempts to apply the theory cannot ignore its theoretical complexities (though they may sometimes try to do so!).

The first part of this book illustrates what is involved in developing – and in criticising – theory of autopoietic social systems. The first two chapters, in different ways, show how the theory, far from being static, is continually being developed and reworked as the implications of its assumptions and claims are thought through. The next two chapters illustrate the type of criticisms which are raised by theorists who are each far from convinced by some basic postulates of the theory- namely the law's relation with other subsystems of society and the problem of law's legitimation. The last chapter in this section offers a critical account of what are seen as some of the major misreadings of autopoiesis theory.

The opening chapter is by Gunther Teubner, the scholar most responsible for spreading the influence of autopoiesis theory in the academic legal world. It represents a characteristically rich and brilliant deployment of the resources of autopoiesis theory in this case as an original approach to the problem of 'alienating justice'. Teubner builds on Luhmann's insight that, whatever it may do in the way of resolving social conflicts, law also uses disputes as a way of reproducing itself. He develops the notion of 'production regimes' and shows how these interrelate with the dynamics of the litigation process. Interestingly, for those who argue that autopoieis theory has no role for power, Teubner seeks to show how the fictions introduced by law are both essential to its contribution to resolving conflicts but can also be seen as 'exploiting' these same conflicts. The following chapter, by Jean Clam, asks what is specific about legal autopoiesis as compared to general autopoiesis of society. In what is admittedly a difficult and complex paper Clam tackles fundamental postulates of Luhmann's thought such as ontology, paradox, meaning and operation (at the editors' request he has also added a glossary of some of these terms). His basic claim is the need to distinguish the characteristic features of basic autopoiesis from those applicable to derivative types of autopoiesis characteristic of law and other social subsystems.

In the following chapter, Roger Cotterrell offers a critique of autopoiesis theory. He acknowledges that the theory has played an important role in recent sociological theorising about law, but he claims that its assumptions are 'misleading and harmful' as guides for the progress of sociology of law. It's reification of lawyers own views about the nature of law (turning their interested world constructions into functionalist necessities), its sharp contrasts between the internal and external points of view, and its dogmatic approach to self-reference all represent a 'fundamental wrong turning'. It is only when its arguments are so qualified (as they sometimes are) so as to lose their novelty value that these risks are avoided but in that case autopoiesis rejoins mainstream sociology of law in requiring careful empirical investigation of the construction of the various and competing perspectives on and ideologies of law in a given social field. Cotterrell is also worried by claims about conflict and crisis which have more to do with the theory's own conceptual postulates than the experience of social actors.

Jiří Přibáň, in his chapter, raises a different criticism of the theory. He examines the way the concept of 'legitimation by procedure' was originally used by Niklas Luhmann, and notes how it was abandoned in his later works. He argues that the increasing focus on the interrelations between the legal system and its social environment does not allow Luhmann to get rid of the problem of legitimacy of law. Přibáň then formulates the issue of law's legitimation as a problem of communication between the inside and outside of the legal system and as a translation of external political *noise* into the legal *order*, which is secured from within the legal system by legitimation fictions of legality.

The closing chapter in this section is by Michael King, who is well known both for his work on popularising autopoiesis theory and for applying it to the realm of family law. In this contribution King is critical of the often ill-informed level of discussion of autopoiesis theory. He argues that much debate rests on mistaken ideas of what Luhmann actually says. He illustrates the strategies of rejection and assimilation and the many misunderstandings which characterise much of the reception of autopoiesis theory especially in Anglo-American thinking and claims that such discussions often tell you more about the authors' own preferred theoretical approach than the one they are supposedly developing or criticising.

The second part of the book offers a series of chapters by scholars who seek to apply the theory to specific topics. The subject areas covered are labour law, environmental law, criminal justice, the reform of the administration of justice, globalism and lex mercatoria and the efficacy of legal transplants.

Ralf Rogowski, in his chapter on reflexive labour law, outlines what is intended to be a faithful application of Luhmann's and Teubner's ideas as applied to the realm of labour law. He discusses, inter alia, the relationship between the autopoietic legal system and the autopoietic industrial relations system, the regulation of self-regulation through collective agreements and employment contracts, and the deregulation of employment protection as a reduction of complexity. Rogowski usefully distinguishes a number of meanings that are given to the overworked concept of 'system' within autopoiesis theory (system as interaction, as network, as social or protest movement, as conflict, as immune system and as a full blown societal system within a functionally differentiated society). He shows how the theory produces a new way of thinking about the classical problem of the relationship between external regulation and processes of self-regulation in labour law. He concludes that law can and should become reflexive by acknowledging the limits of its own constructions of that which it purports to regulate.

In the next chapter Eric Orts addresses the relevance of autopoiesis theory for environmental law. Unlike Rogowski, however, Orts is much more eclectic about his use of the theory to deal with 'the problem' of the environment. Thus he attempts to embrace ideas deriving from Habermas (as Teubner also did in his earlier work) insisting on the need to go beyond a focus on communication to one on what Habermas calls 'communicative action'. Where Luhmann and Teubner are primarily concerned about how to protect the integrity of different subsystem discourses Orts is worried by the dangers of over specialisation and even speaks of autopoeisis itself as being a 'problem'. Orts describes what he considers to be four mistaken ways of responding to threats to the environment, and proposes instead the creation of a 'regulatory ark', purportedly drawing on Luhmann's ideas, which would combine reflexive environmental law, informal regulation and environmental contracts between business and government.

The chapter by Richard Nobles and David Schiff sets out to apply insights derived from autopoiesis theory to the sociological study of criminal justice. Like Orts they specifically seek to show how an autopoietic approach can improve on rival theories. For them its major contribution lies in its capacity to illuminate the meaning of the term 'system' when talking about criminal justice systems, and to do so in relation to the problems of coordination in functionally differentiated society seeking to maintain high levels of social complexity. Another great merit of the theory for them is its focus on communications between different groups of social actors, and the ensuing difficulties of 'translation', rather than conventionally explaining competition and conflict only in terms of the interests of these actors. Indeed they identify autopoiesis as 'the most stable self-referential system of communication in a field'.

In his chapter on 'modernising justice' Tim Murphy examines the extent to which current British reforms of the administration of justice evidence the sort of changes in the relationship between law and other spheres of society which would be expected on the basis of Luhmann's thinking. Murphy argues that Britain is in the middle of a process which is likely to involve a quite significant reconfiguration of the legal infrastructure and thereby indirectly of the law. Murphy points out that, as autopoiesis theory would suggest, government increasingly regulates itself as a means of regulating society, including the way it deals with issues such as gender equality, racism, and above all, efficiency. He notes that government increasingly tries to be more like business, just as business aspires to or is asked to develop features of public governance. The Lord Chancellor's department in particular is seeking to become a Department like any other so as to impose 'performance indicators' for evaluating legal processes. The issue which particularly engages Murphy is the way the emphasis on value for money (VFM) threatens a process of de-differentiation with 'money replacing justice'. He talks of 'the coming of age' pains of the legal system, the trauma of a system in itself coming to communicate with and about itself. Whilst he thinks it important to trace (the unpredictable effects) of these processes of 'mimesis', 'de-differentiation' and 'colonisation' he is unwilling to see these developments as undermining Luhmann's theory that ultimately processes of increasing differentiation are likely to prevail. What his account does demonstrate however is that differentiation needs to be seen as a challenge as much as an acquired achievement.

The last two chapters are both concerned with what autopoiesis theory (as interpreted by Gunther Teubner) tells us about the spread of law from society to society in the current period. In his chapter Peter Fitzpatrick examines what autopoeisis theory has to say about globalism and the 'lex mercatoria'. Certainly, Fitzpatrick concedes, we are witnessing a growth in the volume of global economic transactions. But much that is written about globalisation is unpersuasive and for Fitzpatrick this is true also of the way autopoiesis theory insists, inconsistently, both that global law already exists and that it is only in the process of formation. Taking up the ideas of Derrida, appropriated for other purposes by Teubner, Fitzpatrick stresses the impossibility of postulating the autopoiesis of social systems as if there was nothing external to them to which they relate. On the contrary, he argues that it is essential to work out the 'apposition' which limits and completes all processes and systems.

In the closing chapter of the volume David Nelken examines the way autopoiesis theory has been applied to the explanation and evaluation of legal transplants. In the course of a recent analysis of the likely effects of spreading the German doctrine of 'good faith' throughout the European Union, Gunter Teubner proposed a general substitution of the metaphor of transplants with that of 'irritants'. Teubner's article offers many original insights into the complexities of legal transfer under conditions of advanced social differentiation, mobilising autopoiesis theory so as to offer claims and warnings about law's changing relationship to economic and other spheres. But Nelken identifies three issues which need much more careful attention. In the first place he interrogates the role of metaphors in thinking about legal transfer, queries how far Teubner's alternative metaphor is necessarily superior to that of transplants, and asks about the relationship between this metaphor and autopoietic theorising in general. Secondly, Nelken argues that autopiesis theory does not really allow us to get to grips with differences in legal culture. The theory is more ambiguous than its proponents are prepared to admit about the extent to which law has in fact become unbound from local social and business contexts. Finally, problems are raised about whether Teubner sees himself as using autopoiesis theory mainly as a contribution to social science or more as an intervention in legal reform.

Evaluating the theory

Both the theoretical and the more applied essays in this collection raise matters which require further consideration. At the most fundamental level there are continuing difficulties in understanding and accepting many of the ontological and epistemological presuppositions of autopoiesis theory. On the one hand we have the use of 'scientific' biological and cybernetic ideas and metaphors and hence criticisms of the theory for biological reductionism, misplaced evolutionary parallels etc. On the other hand, there is the equally plausible view that Luhmann is rather part of the post-modern project of undermining ontological claims (a perception also encouraged by Teubner's increasing flirtation with postmodern theorists such as Derrida and Lyotard as compared to his earlier interest in integrating the modernist ideas of Habermas).

What exactly is meant by legal autopoeisis? How does it relate to general autopoiesis of society? Should it be seen as a definite historical stage in the positivisation of law? If so, when did it happen? There is an important disagreement between Luhmann and Teubner over whether autopoiesis should be seen as an 'all or nothing' concept or a matter of degree (and it is easy to see how this causes confusion for those mistakenly tempted to interpret autopoiesis as a version of the idea that law has relative autonomy in relation to the rest of society) (Nelken, 1987).

What is less often discussed is whether the type or degree of autopoiesis is something that can vary in terms of different legal cultures. Orts (in this volume) suggests that China must be considered a society where law is not (yet?) autopoietic. But why just China? There are large differences in the ideal and actual relationship between law, politics and economics even within the Europe Union. Indeed in his arguments about legal transplants Teubner makes much of significant differences in the relationship between law and the economy as between Germany and the UK (see Nelken, in this volume for criticism of the attempt to reconcile this with the assumptions of autopoiesis theory). We also need to ask how far it is possible to formulate a theory of the 'fit' between law and society in a way that is free of any given legal culture. Teubner's first theoretical departure came in the idea of 'reflexive law' crafted as a departure from Selznick and Nonet's work on responsive law in Berkeley. This could well be justified as an understandable reaction by someone from a continental 'state and law' tradition to the American and common law assumptions built into their concept of responsive law.

For those used to middle range socio-legal research many of the claims made by autopoiesis theory can seem dogmatic, or even deliberately overstated for effect. It is difficult sometimes to know what is essential to the theory and what, by contrast, is open to empirical verification or disproof. What exactly is meant by law being cognitively open and normatively closed? What is the substantive point in insisting that whatever the external influences on law it is ultimately law that changes the law? Are either of these claims matters for empirical testing? What about the argument that subsystems and discourses can never do more than reconstruct each other in their own terms? This seems more testable (especially if we are allowed to sample documents and opinions produced by the human agents behind such discourses). But in practice as the theory has been developed ways have regularly been found to overcome such assumptions of radical incommensurability (for example through the development of concepts such as 'structural coupling', 'interference' etc.).

In considering the attempts in this volume to apply the theory in the course of sociological research into specific areas of law the main problem to emerge is that of knowing when such efforts are consistent with the theory. If it is to be faithful to the theory should research focus on subsystems and discourses or can it also discuss groups and individuals? Is 'meaning' a property of systems or social groups? It is only if we have an answer to these questions that we can decide if, for example, proposals in this collection to identify different 'interpretative communities' in the world of criminal justice, or to encourage contracts between 'government and business', have anything to do with the theory of autopoietic social systems. The problem is complicated by the way some work by Teubner shows unexpected willingness to classify social actors as is commonly done within mainstream sociology of law. A recent paper on regulation by Paterson and Teubner, for example, argues for the need to distinguish the perceptions of legislators, regulators, inspectors and engineers (Paterson and Teubner, 1998). But is this a warrant to include all empirical sociology of regulation within the ambit of autopoietic theory?

A final set of issues (which by no means exhausts the range of topics relevant to the evaluation of autopoiesis theory) concern the normative bite, if any, of the theory. Some criticise autopoiesis theory for not having a politics or ethics. Others accuse it of having a reprehensible politics and ethics (especially by shifting attention from agent responsibility to system constraints.) For King autopoiesis theory is not about 'improving things'- and this is liberatory given the heavily policy driven of most work in socio-legal studies. But Orts is convinced that autopoiesis theory can be used to develop a better response to environmental problems (more controversially he also describes autopoiesis itself as a 'problem') - and the same emancipatory hopes characterise some of the other chapters.

Is Luhmann's work in fact value free? Could it be? In his chapter Murphy concedes, that, at a minimum, buried in Luhmann's work there are 'crypto-normativities' in favour of what it takes to ensure ever-greater functional differentiation and social complexity. A more explicit move by Luhmann (and Teubner) is to point to sociological 'facts' as an argument which dooms the success of particular recommendations; this is seen for example in the way Luhmann dismisses Habermas's recommendations on how to reduce domination.

This question of normative implications is also another example of significant divergence between Luhmann and Teubner. Where Luhmann took a stand against adopting autopoiesis theory for use in argument within the legal subsystem Teubner shows no such reluctance. In deploying the theory Teubner tends to focus on the need to respect the integrity of different subsystems (this could be seen as a natural progression from his earlier concern about 'juridification'- or what Habermas called law's 'colonisation of the life world'). But there may be a danger that an exclusive emphasis on this one problem can obscure other equally important ones (and make it impossible to ask whether it could sometimes even be acceptable to show disrespect so as to deal with other problems).

It is important to stress that the questions and difficulties mentioned here should not be taken as sufficient reason to reject autopoiesis theory. On the contrary, the highest compliment that can be paid to any theory is the effort to think it through and, if necessary, reformulate its claims in the course of applying it to specific problems. Anglo American sociology of law, for all its strengths in middle range theorising, has nothing to match the breadth, originality and versatility of the synthesis offered by theorists such as Luhmann and Teubner. Given that autopoiesis theory, like any important theory, is already a synthesis of different approaches, there may also be room for greater rapprochement between autopoiesis theory and mainstream sociology of law. In any case we hope that this collection will help illustrate the sweep of the theory and makes it possible for there to be more considered reflection on the value and feasibility of such a goal.

References

Acta Sociologica, 1/2000.

Baudrillard, J. (1988), *America,* Verso, London.

Berg, de H. and J. F. K. Schmidt (eds), (2000), *Rezeption und Reflexion. Zur Resonanz der Systemtheorie Niklas Luhmanns auflerhalb der Soziologie*, Suhrkamp, Frankfurt.

Cornell, D. (1992), 'The Relevance of Time to the Relationship Between the Philosophy of the Limit and Systems Theory', 13 *Cardozo Law Review,* pp. 1579-1603.

Droit et Societé, 2000.

Gadamer, H.G. (1975), *Truth and Method,* Sheed and Ward, London.

Luhmann, N. (1972), *Rechtssoziologie*, W-deutscher Verlag, Opladen.

Luhmann, N. (1982), *The Differentiation of Society*, Columbia University Press, New York.

Luhmann, N. (1985), *A Sociological Theory of Law*, Routledge, London.

Luhmann, N. (1990), *Essays on Self-Reference*, Columbia University Press, New York.

Luhmann, N. (1995), *Social Systems*, Stanford University Press, Stanford, Cal.

Nelken, D. (1987), 'Changing Paradigms in the Sociology of Law,' in G. Teubner (ed.), *Autopoietic Law: A New Approach to Law and Society*, De Gruyter, Berlin, pp. 191-217.

Paterson, J. and Teubner, G. (1998) 'Changing Maps: Empirical Legal Autopoiesis', 7 *Social and Legal Studies*, pp. 451-486.

Přibáň, J. (1998), 'Doing What Comes Naturally, or a Walk on the Wild Side?: Remarks on Stanley Fish's Antifoundationalist Concept of Law, its Closure and Force', 9 *Law and Critique*, pp. 249-270.

Rosenfeld, M. (1998), *Just Interpretations: Law between Ethics and Politics*, University of California Press, Berkeley, Cal.

Teubner, G. (1993), *Law as an Autopoietic System*, Blackwell, Oxford.

Zeitschrift fur Rechtssoziologie, 2000.

PART I:

THEORISING AUTOPOIETIC LAW

2 Alienating Justice: On the Surplus Value of the Twelfth Camel

GUNTHER TEUBNER

Consequences of legal autopoiesis

An old wealthy bedouin sheikh wrote his will and divided his fortune, a large herd of camels, among his three sons. Achmed, the eldest son, was to inherit the first half of the fortune, Ali, the second son, should get a fourth, Benjamin, the youngest son, a sixth. When the father died, unfortunately only eleven camels were remaining. Achmed, of course, demanded six of them and was at once contested by his brothers. Finally, when everything broke down, they turned to the khadi. He decided: 'I offer you one of my camels. Return it to me, Allah willing, as soon as possible'. Now, with 12 camels, the division was easy. Achmed got his half, 6 camels, Ali got a fourth, 3 camels, Benjamin a sixth, 2 camels. And indeed, the twelfth camel was left over which they kept and fed very well and happily returned to the khadi.

On various occasions, Jean-Pierre Dupuy and Niklas Luhmann, in their debates on self-organisation and autopoiesis had retold this old story in order to shed light on the internal paradoxes of the law, on the problematic relation of law to itself (Dupuy, 1988; Luhmann, 2000b; for a general discussion of legal autopoiesis, see King and Schutz, 1994; Baxter, 1998).[1] In the dazzling light of the desert – at the same site, where Derrida observes the violence of law's self-foundation, where Kelsen had seen the *Grundnorm,* and Hart the basic rule of recognition – they see the khadi's twelfth camel grazing at a green place. But they quarrel whether the site is an oasis or a Fata Morgana. For them the twelfth camel is not a symbol

[1]For further reflections on this theme, see the contributions in the special issues on Niklas Luhmann, *Zeitschrift fur Rechtssoziologie* 2000 and *Droit et Société* 2000 (forthcoming).

representing something else, rather it performs itself the symbolic operations of law. It is the localized self-reference of the legal system which ends in the interplay of paralysing paradoxes and liberating moves.

I would like to continue this debate on the consequences of legal autopoiesis, but shift the focus from law's internal self-reference to the external relations of law to society: What is the social surplus value of the twelfth camel? This raises intricate issues of mapping social conflicts in law: How realistic is the image of the judge's camel? At the same time the problematic relation between the legal decision and its grounds comes up. Does the judge's camel filter produce only a smokescreen which hides something else or does it produce good legal arguments which determine or justify sufficiently the final decision? Finally, questions of justice are at stake. Is the twelfth camel a satisfying conflict resolution and/or does it justice to the customs and manners of the bedouin society?

Conflict alienation

The twelfth camel refutes a basic assumption which unites diverse strands in the sociological critique of law, from Ehrlich and the realist school, via normative thinkers like Hayek and Habermas to recent entrepreneurs in deconstruction. What they have in common is to criticize law's estrangement from its social and human origins, its violent abstraction from the relation between ego and alter, and to ask for law's return to what they see as its roots: social norms, spontaneous rules, community standards, discursive rationality, or deconstructive justice. Most drastic is Christie's formula of law as expropriation of conflict (Christie, 1977). Law is systematically unable to understand social conflicts and to resolve them adequately. The reason is that law's formalising violence via legal procedures and conceptualisations expropriates conflicts from their proper context of social and moral understandings of the parties. The new formula is: Expropriate the expropriators! Give the conflict back to the people! With this suggestive slogan Christie expresses the wide-spread uneasiness about law's ability to resolve conflicts: non-responsive, inhuman, irrational, (non-em)pathetic...

The twelfth camel, in contrast, celebrates law's expropriation. It transforms law's original sin into its primary virtue. Indeed, by reconstructing a social conflict under highly artificial procedural conditions and with the help of a highly artificial language, the law expropriates, alienates, displaces, disseminates, falsifies the original conflict. But, witness the twelfth camel, this is the legal proprium. The law does not all develop sufficiently profound empathy to understand the original social conflicts out there; instead, it transforms them into technical legal questions. And it constructs them in such a way that they can be answered by its procedural and conceptual means. As a consequence, the *quaestio juris* has very little or virtually nothing to do with the original social conflict (Galtung, 1965). The khadi's camel is different from the sheikh's camels. Legal cases do not - and are not supposed to - map social conflicts. Law has not developed any adequate understanding of their causes, their meaning to the conflicting parties, their perspectives of acceptable solutions, their social consequences. As the debate over alternatives to the legal system has rightly shown, the law is by no means particularly suited for solving disputes among people satisfactorily to all concerned (Fitzpatrick, 1992). Mediation, arbitration and settlement do much more justice to the nature of conflicts, their causes and the needs of the people at dispute. Accordingly, one could in conflicts very well do without the law. In short, law falsifies the realities of the conflict and produces decisions that are based on self-produced fictions.

The alienating effect is a historical variable, not a universal attribute of law. Many legal orders rely heavily on the communal character of their procedures and rules, reflecting the dominant religious and political orientation of their societies. Alienation by law is the result of a specific historical configuration. On the other hand it has not been institutionalised by intentional planning and rational design. There was no political decision to build a legal machinery in order to alienate conflicts. The key to legal alienation is a phenomenon called re-entry (Spencer Brown, 1972: 56f., 69ff.; Luhmann, 1993a; Luhmann, 1997: 179ff.; Esposito, 1993). The thesis of this article is that conflict alienation is the typical by-product of a double closure of law which in its turn is created by the re-entry of legal distinctions into themselves.

Court judgements, legislative acts, but also contracts and standardisation acts are decisions that are distinguished from other economic or political decisions by the fact that they transfer the symbol of legal validity from one normative proposition to another. Transfer of validity on the basis of the binary code legal/illegal takes place exclusively in recursive chains of court judgements, legislative and contractual acts. This is the (in)famous primary closure of law: operational closure by concatenation of legal acts (Teubner, 1993a: ch. 2-4; Luhmann, 1987; Luhmann, 1993b: ch. 2). The problematic aspect of this closure has, of course, been identified as empty tautologies, unproductive self-reference and insulation of law from its social environment. Critics of operational closure tend to look for social phenomena that break the boundaries of the law and recommend communal justice (Cotterrell, 1995: ch. 5, 15; for a critique of operational closure, see Kerchove and Ost, 1992). However, legal evolution has taken a different course. Operational closure has not been compensated through a return to close social embeddedness of the law's underlying structures, but paradoxically, through its opposite: through duplicating closure (Foerster, 1981; Luhmann, 2000a: ch.7). Closure of legal operations has become complemented by closure of legal self-observations. The crucial transformation took place when in court litigation, legislation and contracting legal argumentation began to exclude arguments *ad hoc* and *ad hominem* and to refer to specialised legal materials (precedents, rules, principles) in a very specific way. It is the exclusion of arguments which makes it possible that the legal process begins to insulate itself (more or less successfully) against social influences, especially clientelism, kinship, social status, friendship politics (Luhmann, 1993b: 263). 'The artificial reason of law' which Sir Coke invoked against the political interventions of the King makes it autonomous vis-a-vis the immediate validity claims of moral arguments, economic considerations, political expediency and common sense.

Why should artificial reason compensate for primary closure? The reason is 're-entry' of the extra-legal. While legal operations by virtue of their sequentialisation create the boundary between law and non-law, between legal communication and other types of social communication, legal observations begin to use this very distinction legal/non-legal within the symbolic space of the law. This is, to be sure, different from the use of the binary code, legal vs. illegal, which, as we have said, makes primary closure possible. While the distinction legal/illegal constituting the boundary between law and non-law is responsible for operational closure, the re-entry of the distinction law/non-law within the law is responsible for observational closure (Luhmann, 1993b: 67ff., 338ff.). This distinction opens an internal option for legal arguments: either they refer to internal legal operations or they refer[2] to external social operations. Now, in the second aspect lies the compensation for operational closure. Whenever the distinction legal/non-legal (in the sense of extra-legal) re-enters the

[2]Literally: refer to them as internal constructs, not: reach out, participate, constitute etc them.

sequence of legal operations, legal argumentation gains the capacity of distinguishing between norms and facts, between internal legal acts and external social acts, between legal concepts and social interests, between internal reality constructs of the legal process and those of social processes. This is the paradoxical achievement of double closure. While both, rule-producing acts as well as rule-connecting arguments remain in their closed circuit of internal concatenations, legal self-observation by virtue of the internal distinction of self-reference and hetero-reference makes law dependent on its social environment (which is their 'enacted' environment (Weick, 1979; on enaction as an alternative to representation, see Varela, 1992: 235ff.), not their 'real' one, to be sure). And the higher degrees of freedom that internal reconstruction of reality gains, in comparison with one-to-one relations of the external with the internal, increases the chances that re-entry compensates for primary closure.

Re-entry has drastic consequences (Spencer Brown, 1972: 56f., 69ff.). When the distinction between law and non-law is repeated within the law, it creates an epistemic confusion (à la Magritte: 'This is not a pipe') about the reality status of law's hetero-referential observations. The twelfth camel is a camel is a camel, not different from the brothers' eleven camels? Of course, it is a sheer fiction but the khadi needs to maintain the illusion that his camels are real. Result of the re-entry is the creation of an imaginary space within the law which takes itself for reality. The law cannot but create fictions about the outside world but has to treat them as hard-core realities. The twelfth camel lives only in the imaginary space of the law and still, the judge does lend it to the quarrelling brothers where it has astonishing effects. And here lies the reason why legal alienation of social conflicts is inevitable.

Conflict alienation is not just petty theft. To expropriate the parties of their conflict is poorly understood if one sees it exclusively as the usurpation of the social by legal professionals who use their specialised language as an instrument of power (Bourdieu, 1986). Alienating law helps the khadi's camels to be prolific and multiply, more generally, legal alienation increases the varieties of social signification. Estrangement by law expands communal meaning by opening new, strange worlds. There is a striking parallel between art and law: both create a second reality, an imaginary world in which there are living more camels and different camels than in the real world of the desert. In this light, social science critiques of law look like Herr Beckmesser who scorns the great artist Hans Sachs for his lack of realism. They miss the point that the imaginary worlds of art and law make things thinkable that could not have been thought before. This holds true for otherwise unthinkable artificial constructs within the world of legal doctrine. Reconstructing a conflict in the language of legal doctrine, raising the *quaestio juris*, factorising it into a sequence of questions of fact and questions of law, allows for inventing new arguments, new criteria, new rules which would not be possible at all did legal doctrine not exist. Moreover, after prohibition of *deni de justice,* a legal decision to the conflict is guaranteed even if arguments ended in a deadlock. And under certain circumstances, when the twelfth camel is actually walking into the real world of the bedouin society, it may increase the possibilities for action there as well, which may or may not lead out of the paralysis of the social conflict. To be sure, there is no automatism. It is only under rare circumstances that legal alienation becomes more than legal theft. As a re-translation – from a social conflict into a legal issue and from there into a social event – it may, as a happy coincidence, open up new possibilities of action in the social world.

If the camel symbolises the legal proprium, what is it about? The khadi in the story is not helpful in the sense that he interprets the father's will according to higher legal standards that should govern the conflict, nor does he decide according to principles of distributive justice which serve as a refinement of the current social practices of distribution. Instead, he lends them a fiction – and this is the key. The incongruence fiction/reality is decisive. When conflicts in the social world appear non-resolvable then their falsification by law shows its potential. It creates an additional, admittedly unrealistic, artificial, fictitious world out of the issues at stake. Fictionalisation makes conflicts, in a situation of their moral and social undecidability, decidable, at least in the imaginary world of the law.

This turns the usual ideas about the social (in)adequacy of the law on their head. And it opens some different research questions and some different issues for the political agenda. The point is no longer for the law to be responsive to the self-understanding of the parties involved, to broader social norms, moral values, community standards which govern the conflict situation. Just the opposite, the point is to reconstruct the conflict straightforward against common sense. Not assimilation of legal decisions to community standards but their alienation from them makes the surplus value of legal reconstruction visible. The critical situation is when conflicts have become socially, morally, politically and economically non-resolvable and law reconstructs them in an artificial texture of topoi, concepts, constructions. Then they are almost no longer recognisable as social or moral conflicts, but as technical legal questions within an elaborate doctrine. They become decidable only if one uses legal fictions that have no correspondence in the social worlds of the litigants. And the interesting question is then not whether these fictions 'correspond' to the internal complexities of the conflict, but how they come about, into what directions they develop, and whether they have different latent selective affinities to the outside world.

Legal argumentation

Does the contribution of the fictitious camel lie in the fact that it determines or at least justifies the legal decision of the brothers' fight over the heritage of their father? Here we enter the perennial debate between determinacy or non-determinacy of legal argumentation, but 're-entry' suggests a third position. Whenever legal operations via re-entry distinguish between the worlds of law and non-law it creates itself a non-resolvable indeterminacy within the law which cannot be resolved by its normal operations. This pushes the legal process toward differentiating internally two types of legal operations: legal decisions that convey the validity symbol and legal arguments that regulate the relation between redundancy and variety in law (Luhmann, 1995a). Two different chains of legal communication are resulting – a sequence of legal decisions and a sequence of legal arguments – which are closely interrelated but are not able to determine each other. Legal decisions, due to their binding nature, regularly are transformed into new legal arguments but they do not determine the flow of legal reasoning. Legal arguments in their turn are elements of the legal decision, but they neither determine nor do they justify legal decisions.

This goes directly against theorists of rational argumentation in law who rely on the intrinsic force of rational motivation. They make themselves blind to the non-resolvable indeterminacy of law (Habermas, 1996: ch. 5; Günther, 1988: ch. 3, 4). But it goes as well against decisionist and critical theorists of law (Schmitt, 1985; Schmitt, 1986; Kennedy, 1997; Kelman, 1987). They suffer from a similar blindness. While they are right in stressing the unavoidable indeterminacy that cannot be reduced by any legal argument, they offer no adequate understanding of what then legal argumentation is about. How to explain the persistence of legal argumentation practices after realist disenchantment, decisionist demystification and critical trashing? Either they declare legal reasoning a masquerade which serves other purposes, preferably concealing power structures, or they reduce it to the trivial question of anticipating consensus among the legal elites.

The camel's re-entry suggests that legal reasoning never decides a conflict, but achieves nevertheless something decisive. Legal argument is transforming differences, it transforms the original decision alternative into a different one. Legal reasoning is responsible for the alienation of the social conflict. Not more, not less. It does not determine, it does not justify, nor does it hide something else. It just transforms differences but does so drastically. A decision remains necessary, before and after argumentation, but the concrete alternative that has to be decided will be totally different. It is the job of legal reasoning to lure lawyers into a situation where they have to decide a question which differs from the litigants' original question.

Now, what difference does it make, when legal reasoning transforms a conflict between individual actors into a conflict of semantic artefacts of legal doctrine? Is this a reformulation of the time-honoured problematic relation between the particular case which needs to be 'subsumed' under a general rule? Are we looking for a new golden rule, categorical imperative or veil of ignorance? Legal autopoiesis suggests the transformation takes a course quite different from ethical generalisations. One part of the answer is, of course, to invoke law's closure and self-reference. It is the recursive application of legal operations to the results of legal operations that creates the artificial network of concepts, rules and principles. The more elaborate the network becomes over time, the more it moves legal reasoning away from an adequate appreciation of the particularities of the case. The never-ending practices of the equal or unequal treatment is the alienating mechanism. To treat what is equal equally and what is unequal unequally triggers off a self-propelling series of distinctions. It is a generative mechanism, a 'historical machine' as von Foerster (1981) would call it which relentlessly increases complexity in the world of legal fictions. Precedent, 'stare decisis', and treating the equal equally are less interesting here. Rather, it is the deviation from the precedent, the 'distinguishing' and 'overruling', the unequal treatment of what is not equal, which provokes the search for more and more elaborate legal fictions.

But it is only half the alienation story to talk about internal self-reference applying past decisions and rules to new factual situations and producing new rules by this application. The other half of alienating justice is the permanent irritation by co-evolutionary contacts of the law with external social processes that redirects the changes of legal semantics, rules, concepts, principles, doctrines. The typical incongruence of legal rules and doctrines with the particular conflict is due to their co-variation with the change of distant social structures (Teubner, 1993a: ch. 4, 5; Luhmann, 1993b: ch. 12).

There is, of course, great historical variance how the co-evolutionary dynamics is structured in itself. Today, legal and social institutions co-evolve no longer via spontaneous social norms and customary law, but typically via institutionalised production regimes. Production regimes are structural links between autonomous social systems – between law, economy, politics, education, research – but they do not themselves evolve into autopoietic systems with their own elements, structures and boundaries. As forms of structural coupling (Maturana and Varela, 1988: ch. 5), production regimes are mere configurations of quite heterogeneous components, hybrids in the gap which exists between law and society. As such, production regimes are neither functional systems nor formal organisations, nor interactions in the technical sense of systems theory (Luhmann, 1982) but are merely linkage institutions between them (Teubner, 1992).

Production regimes have internal structures of their own that exert pressures on the way how legal rules co-variate with multiple social processes (Hall and Soskice, 1999; Soskice, 1997; Teubner, 1998; Teubner, 2000b). Contrary to a unified social evolution in which there is diffuse environmental pressure of various selectors on social institutions, here within one production regime several operationally closed systems participate which are each disposing of specific evolutionary mechanisms of their own. Each of them follows a different pattern of variation, selection and retention. Result is a multitude of autonomous evolutionary processes within one production regime which in their turn influence each other via mechanisms of co-evolution. There is no unified trajectory of the production regime which would arise from the social environment by virtue of natural selection. Rather, a variety of diverging evolutionary dynamics are going on simultaneously within one regime. Independent evolutionary mechanisms in the autopoietic systems of the law, economy, politics, science, education force their institutions within one production regime to take an idiosyncratic evolutionary path. And the production regime in its turn provides for specific channels of co-evolution which regulate how these evolutionary movements are influencing each other. Thus, legal doctrine cannot follow its own logic which would be dictated by a common-law-type history of accumulating particular conflicts. It is shaped by co-evolutionary forces within the production regime which direct law into a narrow space of compatibility with economic, political and other non-legal institutions.

Thus, production regimes expose the closed network of legal operations to external irritations that take place in contexts very distant from the irritations of individual cases which are brought to the judge. This second source of external irritations creates an independent dynamics which drives the law into an inevitable incongruence of social conflicts and legal criteria for their resolution. For within production regimes, not only a process of gradual adaptation takes place where internally developed rules and doctrines are exposed to external constraints. But various independent machineries of social norm production intrude law's empire from the periphery by transforming social norms into legal rules. With the help of these machineries, heterogeneous particularistic rationalities and their normative claims infiltrate massively the litigation-oriented law which has little control over the influx. The most prolific extra-legal rule-making machines which are driven by the inner logics specialised social domains are installed in various formal organisations, informal networks, processes of standardisation and normalisation which are competing today with the legislative machinery and the contracting mechanism (Teubner, 1997a). The judicial process cannot reject these externally produced rules as alien to litigation. But what it does to these aliens is to 'litigate them through', to juridify them, to convey to them legal validity, to re-interpret them in terms of internal consistency with precedents, statutes and the political constitution, and – last not least – to draw from them criteria which are supposed to resolve the particular conflict.

Thus, conflict alienation has a double effect. It loosens the contact with the particular conflict situation of the litigants and intensifies contact with external production regimes. In a co-evolutionary process where an autonomous and self-referential legal doctrine develops via irritations from external institutions in various production regimes, the resulting normative structures – although, not because they are necessarily 'orthogonal' to the original social conflict – are acting as 'neutral', 'disinterested', 'outside' 'third parties' to judge the individual conflict. The twelfth camel was not born in order to resolve the fight between the brothers; the twelfth camel 'as such' is the product of an alien context, where arithmetical calculations allow the division of otherwise non-divisible numbers. Today, the hiatus between what the particular conflict would require as a satisfying resolution and what a production regime produces as legal rules in co-evolution with other institutions is impressive. What is the interest of litigants fighting for their money to have their case decided according to a new policy twist in anti-trust law? Why should the criterion of allocative efficiency which is applied to a technical question of tort law be a good conflict resolver for compensating somebody who suffered from a car accident? It is not the adequacy to the intricacies of their personal conflict situation, but, if anything, it is the incongruence of perspectives – litigation versus production regime – which allows for deciding the undecidable. The only thing the litigating parties receive for sure is decidability. Forget the criteria.

And what do they pay in return? The energies of the litigants who are desperately striving to win their individual cases are exploited by the argumentation machinery of law for other purposes. They are utilised to fuel the production of distant and abstract rules, concepts and principles which are oriented toward co-evolution in production regimes. By their litigation, the parties are sacrificing time, energy and devotion for the sake of creating future normative structures of distant production regimes. This is how the quarrelling brothers indeed fulfil Allah's will ordering them to return the twelfth camel to the judge. And the khadi makes a good profit from the camel transaction. Alienating justice? There are good reasons to change the title of this article: Exploiting justice.

Production regimes

This turns our perspective around. Exploiting justice: the law exploits people's quarrelsomeness to fuel the production of future norms. The khadi, in his wisdom and generosity, knows how to exploit the brothers when they quarrel about father's heritage. They have to feed the khadi's camel with their conflict resources and have to return it to him well-nourished, well-kept, well-trained, and in much better shape than it was before. Indeed, this is what court litigation does to multiple projections of legal rules which are made in diverse productions regimes. 'Litigating through', as we said before, exposes the rules of the production regimes to the particular conflict, but at the same time creates a considerable surplus value for the production regime itself. It transforms drastically the original meaning of proto-normative structures; it changes the status of diverse social rule projections in contracts, standards, competitive market processes, intra-organisational rules and, of course, legislative statutes. Court litigation is the *via regis* of law to make binding decisions about how to select among competing rule projections and to transfer legal validity to one of them; on this road the law resolves collisions between divergent contractual obligations, different standards and legislative rules; it separates legal rules and principles from mere social norms, political goals, economic expectations that have no legal status; it clarifies ambivalences of meaning in one binding interpretation and creates new controversies of interpretation and thus fuels the dynamics of legal and social institutions within production regimes. It is through court litigation and – one would have to add – through anticipation of court litigation, too, that the production regimes enjoy the fruits of juridification: a considerable difference in clarity, stability and external support of their expectations.

However, the price is alienation, incongruence of perspectives, now the other way around. Court litigation is obstructing the good intentions of production regimes. According to evolutionary economics, a competitive market creates over time, after repeated transactions, transactional and organisational 'routines' which can be called efficient (Nelson and Winter, 1982). However, when these routines are 'tested' in court litigation they become in their turn estranged from their origins. Exposed to the multiple strategies of court litigation, their original market orientation will be contaminated by legal considerations of compensation, of distributive justice, of interest weighing, policy goals and particular aspects of the case at hand. Making them consistent with a multitude of legal topics ruins the economic purity of these routines. And re-litigation which is supposed to make law in the long run economically efficient (Cooter and Komhauser, 1980), only strengthens the deviation from the path of virtue in a positive feedback loop. Off goes efficiency.

Regulatory politics do not fare better. 'Mon code est perdu!' Napoléon broke into tears when he had found out that his famous *code civil* had undergone court litigation and had been changed by the obscure hermeneutics of shifters, sophistic advocates and judges. Contemporary regulatory politics, their definition of political goals, their choice of policy instruments, among them legal rules, their careful strategies of implementation, will be necessarily obstructed when they have to go through the litigious interaction of clients, lawyers and judges. Strategies of policy-formation are replaced by the strategies of winning a legal case. Legal rules change their content when they are transformed from policy instruments into conflict tranquillisers.

Such obstruction of the original 'institutional' orientation of legal rules happens in all types of production regimes. Not only contracting and legislation, but also standardisation, normalisation, market competition, administrative decisions, intra-organisational rule making are suffering from this inverse alienation. Several dynamics can be identified in court litigation that are responsible for obstructing institutional justice: (1) Goal displacement: the original orientation – facilitating technical processes, efficiency enhancing, regulating behaviour, stabilising social institutions – is replaced by one overwhelming orientation: Who wins, who loses? (2) Time horizon: while the institutional perspective tends to stabilise expectations for future action, the litigation perspective is predominantly oriented toward the past. Reconstructing past events in the court room reduces complex normative structures to one *question directrice:* What was the 'right' expectation to govern the singular event? (3) Change of language: While social rules are formulated in the special language of their institutional context, court litigation translates them into the special language of rights: What legal positions do they offer for the litigating parties? (4) Reality construction: While the reality of social rules is dictated by the cognitive mapping of the respective social institution, litigation forces these diverse realities into the two-party-perspective of the legal trial.

The improbability of the arrangement is impressive. Why should this double alienation, the forced unity of highly incongruent perspectives be a stable institutional configuration? Would one not expect that the forces of social differentiation move in and divorce this unhappy marriage among aliens? To be sure, specialised institutions for conflict resolution and rule production have indeed developed within the legal system, but why do litigation and production regimes nevertheless maintain their role as strange attractors to each other? And the forces of strange attraction are increasing in recent developments. International relations where conflict resolution and rule production had been institutionally separated for centuries have been undergoing a gradual process of juridification where increasingly court litigation and production regimes serve as mutual attractors (Higgins, 1997). Similar tendencies can be identified in international markets – witness the juridification of business contracting and international arbitration in the combination of *lex mercatoria* and the gradual transformation of the WTO-bureaucracy into court-like structures where the production regimes simultaneously attract and obstruct conflict management and vice versa (Dezalay and Garth, 1995; Teubner, 1997b).

I see two competing interpretations. One is *Eigenvalues*. Both, conflict resolution through normative expectations and rule-making in production regimes are recursive, self-referential processes that due to their closure in circular processes do not find sufficient stable *Eigenvalues* so that they are desperately searching aliens to find points of stability. While social, economic, political processes do create proto-normative structures by their internal transactions they have difficulties in stabilising them. These volatile structures will be undermined by the very processes that created them, by changes in power constellations, by new market structures, by new social situations. However, when they externalise their products to the law and get them stabilised by the symbol of legal validity, they can avoid this incessant self-destruction. The other way around, a corresponding externalisation takes place in court litigation where the norm-creating dynamics of litigation in order to avoid their self-obstruction refer to external 'authorities', to the legislator, to the contracting parties, to the market, to formal organisations. The returns for alienation consist in relatively stable structures for production regimes and in decision criteria for court litigation.

The other interpretation is a 'lock-in' situation. Once the mutual attraction of litigation and production regimes is established, it develops a path-dependent evolutionary dynamics of its own which drives them deeper and deeper into their obstructive symbiosis and locks them there. Once production regimes are opened to the dynamics of court litigation, there is no chance for saving spaces of legal immunity. Any rule projection bears the risk of being 'litigated through' the courts. And once courts are borrowing their rules from external law-making authorities, they cannot stop parties and their lawyers from drawing into the trial any normative material that has been produced by the officially acknowledged authoritative sources of law.

It is difficult to decide between the two interpretations, *Eigenvalue* and lock-in. Probably, both are true and there are ample opportunities for future empirical research to measure the relative weight of the two explanations. Even more can be expected from future institutional experimentation when it tries to increase the 'rationality' of conflict resolution on the one hand and that of rule-making in production regimes on the other. This could suggest where to draw the line between *Eigenvalue* and lock-in. Knowing the line in its turn will decide about how realistic the chances are of making conflict resolution and rule making in production regimes more responsive to their respective context.

Legal rationality

All this looks like another invisible hand mechanism which transforms strategic intentions into unintended social structures. But it has no benign effects. Does this kind of alienating justice create a 'just and fair' solution to the particular conflict? - No, the conflict is resolved by reference to rules from the alien context of production regimes. Justice by incongruent perspectives, that is all. Does it produce 'just and fair' rules for the production regime? - No, the invisible hand of co-evolution channels social norm projection through the filter of private litigation so that the dynamics of an particular conflict decide about public rules for production regimes. Again, justice by incongruent perspectives. The whole story is basically a matter of blind co-evolution of litigation oriented legal semantics with institution oriented social structures. Co-evolution does not guarantee – rather the opposite, it tends to obstruct – social adequacy of legal concepts in relation to external social institutions. Is here, however, a chance for another re-entry? What if legal argumentation – conscious of its double role - develops systematically social knowledge about production regimes in order to increase the social adequacy of its rules?

A good example to discuss these issues might be constitutional rights and their horizontal effect in non-political contexts (Hunt, 1998; Graber and Teubner, 1998). Recent reports on media intrusion into private lives of people, on violations of public obligations in privatised services, on discriminatory practices in the corporate sector have shown, that constitutional law tends to neglect the crucial role of constitutional rights in the so-called private sphere. Is there something to be expected from a re-entry of social knowledge into legal doctrine?

Social theory, given its engagement with latent structures, claims to see more than legal doctrine does when individuals invoke their constitutional rights in court litigation. Quite apart from the overt effect on winning/losing the case, their latency has to do, sociologists submit, with stabilising social differentiation (Grimm, 1987; Willke, 1975; Luhmann, 1965). In a nutshell, the argument goes like this. Historically, constitutional rights as individual entitlements come about with social differentiation. Their political and legal relevance is tied to the historical emergence of individual spheres of action which is typical for modern societies. Social differentiation creates a variety of spheres of action, individual and non-individual, the autonomy of which is mirrored in complementary constitutional rights. Social differentiation and the emergence of constitutional rights are complementary historical processes. In the expansionist tendencies of the modern state, the historical process of social differentiation threatens to undermine itself. In long lasting political fights, constitutional rights emerge as social counter-institutions protecting social differentiation against its inherent self-destructive tendencies. Individual conflicts between private citizens and administrative bureaucracies are transformed in legal institutional support of political self-restraint.

What happens if such a latency is destroyed and parties, lawyers, and judges become conscious of it and legal arguments are overtly dealing with a different reality of constitutional rights? Then a considerable gap between individual motivation and unintended results comes to the fore. Why should individual actors litigate for the sake of social differentiation? A predictable and recommendable reaction is then to strengthen the link between individual motivation for litigation and social effects of constitutional rights. A heavy particularistic component would have to be added to the formal and general orientation in the conflict resolving rule. The judge would have to inject a strong dose of particularism into the rigid rules of the production regime. The recommendation to bridge the gap is: Create individual rights in the public interest and allow for class actions, associative action and other forms of public litigation.

Another reaction is to refine 'social theories' within constitutional law in order to render rules more adequate to the production regimes involved (Wielsch, 2000: ch. 3). The recommendation is: Import Williamson and/or Luhmann into constitutional argument. Economic institutionalism calls legal doctrine adequate to private governance regimes when it re-interprets particular conflicts as calculations of transaction cost minimization. This would be law's contribution to constitutionalising private governance regimes (Williamson, 1996; Williamson, 1991). Systems theory would suggest something else: to reconstruct particular conflicts between actors in the private sphere as collisions of discourses (Teubner, 1997a; Teubner, 2000a). The consequences for horizontal effects of constitutional rights would be that constitutional rights do not exclusively deal with economic power relations, but curb any media of communication which tend to colonize other sectors of social life. They can no longer be seen as protecting only the individual actor against the repressive power of the state, but would need to be reconstructed as 'discourse rights' against expansive tendencies of social systems. Its normative correlate would be an extension of constitutional rights into the context of private governance regimes (corporations, media organisations, educational institutions, professional associations, quangos, international organisations). This, however, requires a fundamental transformation of the classical model of constitutional rights in all its four elements: individual - state - power - right.

These are two cases of law importing criteria from the social sciences – transaction cost minimisation/collision of discourses – and applying them to individual cases. Clearly, again the criteria would be orthogonal in relation to the particular conflict. But would the incongruence of perspectives not be compensated by a new adequacy of law: developing rules that are suited to efficient market structures or to polycontextural society?

Probably, such an illumination of law by social theory is over-optimistic. It underestimates problems of re-entry. 'Social theories' within the law – with or without subsidies from the social sciences – are nothing but another form of re-entry of the law/non-law distinction into law, but on a different level of abstraction as compared to other re-entries – facts/rules, legal acts/social acts, concepts/interests. Again one faces the inevitable confusion of internal constructs with external reality. There is no way of testing the theories by directly accessing social reality. But also radical constructivism is no practical way out. If law took radical constructivism seriously and incorporated it into ongoing operations it would end in paralysis. Perhaps, what seems to be possible is a tentative and partial self-transparence of the legal re-entry (Luhmann, 2000a: ch. 15). Law, without ever being sure about the adequacy of its reality constructs could experiment with various legal models of social reality. Wait for the result of legal decisions that have experimented with different reality constructs. Resistance of legal communication to legal communication is the only 'reality test' possible.

Legal persons

'Should Camels Have Standing?' Christopher Stone's imaginative claim for trees' rights to which recently Bruno Latour and Michel Serres have lent a certain sociological and philosophical credibility (Stone, 1972; Latour, 1993; Latour, 1998; Serres, 1990) offers a fascinating occasion where law experiments with its assumptions about social reality. Of course, it takes on a different meaning when translated into the language of autopoiesis. Are we moving into the new brave world of deep ecology: Mother Gaia autopoiesis as the new collective actor (Lovelock, 1979)? Or are we travelling back to the medieval times: 'What Was It Like to Try a Rat?' (Ewald, 1995; Amira, 1891). Can natural objects bring legal actions? Is law now exploiting nature itself for the sake of its relentless rule production? These questions change indeed the quantity and quality of legal subjectivity and the law's relationships to the environment. At any rate, the ecological debate has again raised the question as to which 'living' units can rightly claim the status of legal actor.

Autopoiesis reformulates the problem. No longer – what kind of ontological properties (mind, soul, reflexive capacities) does an entity possess in order to 'be' an actor, social legal or otherwise (Luhmann, 2000a: ch. 13)? Instead, two changes occur. Under what conditions does the environing social system, i.e. a closed and autonomous ensemble of recursive communications in which the entity appears, construct the semantic artefact of an 'actor'? It is the surrounding social system – and not the entity itself – that constitutes identity, capacity for action and communication, responsibility, rights and duties, in short: creates the subjectivity of its fictions (Teubner, 1988; Luhmann, 1995b: 198ff.). It does so via attribution. A state becomes a collective actor, not because it has certain natural properties or a specific organisational form. Rather it is the international system of war and peace that constructs its actors and thereby forces ethnic/territorial entities to take on the form of an institutionalised state if they want to participate in international politics (Luhmann, 1998). Similarly, it is the market that constructs firms, otherwise they are nothing but bundles of individual contracts (Teubner, 1993b).

Nomen ossibus inhaeret – once the legal system has abandoned that old prejudice and equipped 'spiritual substances' too with *nomina* by giving them rights of action, then the law can link up to entirely different conflictual dynamics which enhance its production of norms. The invention of the legal person was law's great cultural contribution to the organisational revolution in which attribution of action was expanded from natural people to communicative processes. With the bold idea to attribute legal personality not only to individuals but to mere flows of communications, the law cloned another camel, lent it to society and profited itself greatly from the transaction when society returned the beast. Formal organisations as collective actors are the case in point. Once they were made into legal persons by giving them the right to sue and to be sued, the production of law could exploit the enormous conflict potential of formally organised action for its own rule production, which puts individuals' comparable potential well in the shade (Teubner and Hutter, 2000). 'Why the Haves Come Out Ahead' – under this slogan, legal sociologists have closely studied the great difference in conflict potential between organisations and individuals before the courts (Galanter, 1974; Röhl 1987). But this is only a side-aspect. Certainly, collective actors as a rule have different and frequently better chances of winning; what would be needed instead would be careful empirical study of what the role of organisations to trials means for legal rule production itself in the co-evolution of legal semantics and social structures.

Only human individuals can be actors – this conviction has received a new blow by the ecological movement. But how to identify actors in the new political ecology? Environment protection groups are still the easiest cases of 'new' actors. Future generations? Animal species? Plants? Landscapes? And what about languages? Cultures? The question is whether these new actors in the ecological discourse fighting for their interests and rights are just social movements in the broadest sense who ask for formal recognition as legal actors? Or is the law here linking up with other 'living' processes which would steer its rule production into new directions?

Indeed, the latter would be a consequence of legal autopoiesis. Niklas Luhmann – as well as Bruno Latour and Michel Serres – make us see ecological camels. Does this mean that subjectivity – whether human people, formal organisations, political states or other actors – is simply reduced to their status of legal fictions, communicative artefacts? No, social systems are highly selective in their attribution. They attribute only under one condition: That the soul returns into society. Not really, of course, but again in the ambivalent form of a re-entry, in a double re-entry to be precise. Social systems, before they convey subjectivity to objects – human beings, collectives, spiritual entities, animals, computers – request credible indicators for addressability (Fuchs, 1991; Fuchs, 1997). They attribute subjectivity only under the condition that they have good reasons to presuppose self-referential processes of meaning behind their social addresses and at the same time they request close structural coupling with their communication. Social systems attribute subjectivity only if (1) they presuppose the operation called *Verstehen* behind their communicative artefacts, (2) they presuppose that these artefacts presuppose the same in their partners and (3) the attributing social system itself has developed an internal irritability toward the contributions of those 'subjects'. In their operational closure, social systems do not have access to this self-referential reality of the Other, but they need to be prepared in their internal structures. Not unlike Thomas, they have to be irritated before they believe in the Other's existence. The proof of the pudding is in the irritating.

Formal organisations, for example, become collective actors only when the surrounding social system has good reasons to believe in their invisible self-reference, i.e. a closed self-referential signification process, roles and procedures for collective representation, and when it actually 'feels' irritated by the dynamics of organisational processes. Ethnic entities are recognised as states only when international law is sufficiently irritated by 'overwhelming' evidence that the famous three conditions of statehood – territory, population, actual power structures – are fulfilled. And Latour's ecological actants? Indeed, Latour observes rightly that the historical contribution of the ecological movement is constructing the '*septième cité'*. Extending Boltanski's and Thevenot's mapping of six closed and mutually incompatible discourses of justification (Boltanski and Thévenot, 1991), Latour asserts that the new discourse of political ecology has the potential to develop into a full-fledged new social system, into the 'green city' inhabited by the species of ecological actants.

> Political ecology ... bears on complicated forms of associations between beings: regulations, equipment, consumers, institutions, habits, calves, cows, pigs ... a collective experimentation on the possible associations between things and people ... a network of quasi-objects whose relations of subordination remain uncertain and which thus require a new form of political acitivity adapted to following them (Latour, 1998: 229, 234-5).

However, in the 'parliament of things' only some of Latour's actants, not all of them, have chances of social and legal recognition. Indeed, Latour stresses with good reasons, it is the attribution of autonomy to processes that decides about the actor status. But against Latour (1993), we are, we have been and we remain modern and cannot be otherwise. Angels, temples, gods, oracles that once upon a time had been real subjects of social communication will not be social actors any more, not because they do not exist – who knows – but because modern social systems have lost their irritability toward them. For them the world is no longer populated with

> non-human addresses, with communicative chances which refer to ancestors' spirits, gods, trees, holy shrines, intestines, birds' flight, to all those visible and non-visible phenomena to which dealing with their own self-reference could be presupposed (which includes the potential to deceive, to lie, to trickster, and to express something by silence) (Fuchs, 1996: 120f.).

But ecological entities, socio-technical artefacts, cyborgs, hybrids, networks and other information processing Latourian actants have a real chance of irritating modern society and thus participating in the political ecology.

And the judge's camel? There are signs that the law is beginning to re-engineer its procedural and conceptual machines for producing the new fictitious inhabitants of the seventh *cité*. The inclusion of ecological rights in political constitutions, the gradual juridification of animal rights, the change in legal language from the semantics of 'protection of nature' via 'ecological interests' to 'rights' of living processes, the slow process of granting standing to ecological associations, the expanding conceptualisation of ecological damages are indicators that the law is preparing again to lend a new breed of camels to society (Ogorek, 1999; Godt, 1997; Schmidt, 1996; Pfordten, 1995; Erbel, 1986). 'Actants' and 'mediators' in the emerging ecological discourse need not to dispose of full-fledged legal subjectivity in order to open new political dynamics. Multiple legal distinctions – distinctions between different graduations of legal subjectivity, between mere interests, partial rights and full fledged rights, between limited and full capacity for action, between agency, representation, trust, between individual, several, group, corporate and other forms of collective responsibility – have the potential to confer a carefully delimited legal status to associations of ecological actants. And those real fictions may do their work as actants exclusively in the ecological discourse without necessarily appearing as actors everywhere in society. Legal capacity of action can be selectively attributed in different social contexts. It looks as if the chances were good that the judges' camels will be prolific and will indeed multiply.

References

Amira, K. von (1891), *Thierstrafen und Thierprozesse,* Wagner, Insbruck.

Baxter, H. (1998), 'Autopoiesis and the 'Relative Autonomy' of Law', 19 *Cardozo Law Review*, pp. 1987-2090.

Boltanski, L. and Thévenot, L. (1991), *De la justification. Les économies de la grandeur,* Gallimard, Paris.

Bourdieu, P. (1986), 'La force du droit: Elements pour une sociologie du champ juridique', 43 *Actes de la recherche en sciences sociales*, pp. 3-19.

Christie, N. (1977), 'Conflicts as Property', 17 *The British Journal of Criminology,* pp. 1-15.

Cooter, R. and Kornhauser, L. (1980), 'Can Litigation Improve the Law without the Help of Judges?', 9 *Journal of Legal Studies,* pp. 139-163.

Cotterrell, R. B. (1995), *Law's Community: Legal Theory in Sociological Perspective,* Oxford University Press, Oxford.

Dezalay, Y. and Garth, B. (1995), 'Merchants of Law as Moral Entrepreneurs', 29 *Law & Society Review,* pp. 12-27.
Dupuy, J.P. (1988), 'Totalization and Misrecognition', in P. Dumouchel (ed.), *Violence and Truth,* Stanford University Press, Stanford, pp. 75-100.
Erbel, G. (1986), 'Rechtsschutz für Tiere', 101 *Deutsches Verwaltungsblatt,* pp. 1235-1258.
Esposito, E. (1993), 'Ein zweiwertiger nicht-selbständiger Kalkül', in D. Baecker (ed.), *Kalkül der Form,* Suhrkamp, Frankfurt, pp. 96-111.
Ewald, W. (1995), 'Comparative Jurisprudence (I): What Was It Like to Try a Rat', 143 *University of Pennsylvania Law Review,* pp. 1889-2149.
Fitzpatrick, P. (1992), 'The Impossibility of Popular Justice', 1 *Social & Legal Studies,* pp. 199-215.
Foerster, H. von (1981), *Observing Systems,* Intersystems Publications, Seaside, Cal.
Fuchs, P. (1991), 'Kommunikation mit Computern? Zur Korrektur einer Fragestellung', 29 *Sociologia Internationalis,* pp. 1-30.
Fuchs, P. (1996), 'Die archaische Second-Order-Society: Paralipomena zur Konstruktion der Grenze der Gesellschaft', 2 *Soziale Systeme,* pp. 113-130.
Fuchs, P. (1997), 'Adressabilität als Grundbegriff der soziologischen Systemtheorie', 3 *Soziale Systeme,* pp. 57-79.
Galanter, M. (1974), 'Why the 'Haves' Come Out Ahead: Speculations on the Limits of Legal Change', 9 *Law & Society Review,* pp. 95-160.
Galtung, J. (1965), 'Institutionalized Conflict Resolution: A Theoretical Paradigm', 2 *Journal of Peace Research,* pp. 348-397.
Godt, C. (1997), *Haftung für ökologische Schäden: Verantwortung für Beeinträchtigungen des Allgemeingutes Umwelt durch individualisierende Verletzungshandlungen.* Duncker & Humblot, Berlin.
Graber, C. and Teubner, G. (1998), 'Art and Money: Constitutional Rights in the Private Sphere', 18 *Oxford Journal of Legal Studies*, pp. 61-74.
Grimm, D. (1987), 'Grundrechte und Privatrecht in der bürgerlichen Sozialordnung', in D. Grimm (ed.), *Recht und Staat in der bürgerlichen Gesellschaft,* Suhrkamp, Frankfurt, pp. 192-211.
Günther, K. (1988), *Der Sinn für Angemessenheit: Anwendungsdiskurse in Moral und Recht,* Suhrkamp, Frankfurt.
Habermas, J. (1996), *Between Facts and Norms: Contributions to a Discourse Theory of Law and Democracy,* MIT Press, Cambridge, Mass.
Hall, P. and Soskice, D. (eds.) (2000), *Varieties of Capitalism: The Challenges Facing Contemporary Political Economies,* Wissenschaftszentrum Berlin, Berlin. (forthcoming).
Higgins, R. (1997), 'The Reformation in International Law', in R. Rawlings (ed.), pp. 207-224 in *Law, Society and Economy,* Oxford University Press, Oxford, pp. 207-224.
Hunt, M. (1998), 'The 'Horizontal Effect' of the Human Rights Act', 80 *Public Law,* pp. 423-443.
Kelman, M. (1987), *A Guide to Critical Legal Studies,* Harvard University Press, Cambridge, Mass.
Kennedy, D. (1997), *Critique of Adjudication,* Harvard University Press, Cambridge, Mass.
Kerchove van de, M. and Ost, F. (1992), *Le droit ou les paradoxes du jeu.* Presses Universitaires de France, Paris.
King, M. and Schütz, A. (1994), 'The Ambitious Modesty of Niklas Luhmann', 21 *Journal of Law and Society,* pp. 261-287.

Latour, B. (1993), *We Have Never Been Modern,* Harvester Wheatsheaf, Hemel Hempstead.

Latour, B. (1998), 'To Modernise or to Ecologise? That is the Question', in B. Braun and N. Castree (eds), *Remaking Reality: Nature at the Millenium,* Routledge & Paul, London, pp. 221-242.

Lovelock, J.E. (1979), *Gaia: A New Look at Life on Earth,* Oxford University Press, Oxford.

Luhmann, N. (1965), *Grundrechte als Institution: Ein Beitrag zur politischen Soziologie,* Duncker & Humblot, Berlin.

Luhmann, N. (1982), 'Interaction, Organization, and Society', in N. Luhmann, *The Differentiation of Society,* Columbia University Press, New York, pp. 69-89. G. Teubner (ed.), *Autopoietic Law: A New Approach to Law and Society,* de Gruyter, Berlin, pp. 335-348.

Luhmann, N. (1993a), 'Observing Re-entries', 16 *Graduate Faculty Philosophy Journal,* pp. 485-498.

Luhmann, N. (1993b), *Das Recht der Gesellschaft,* Suhrkamp, Frankfurt.

Luhmann, N. (1995a), 'Legal Argumentation: An Analysis of its Form', 58 *Modern Law Review,* pp. 285-298.

Luhmann, N. (1995b), *Social Systems,* Stanford University Press, Stanford.

Luhmann, N. (1997), *Die Gesellschaft der Gesellschaft,* Suhrkamp, Frankfurt.

Luhmann, N. (1998), 'Der Staat des politischen Systems: Geschichte und Stellung in der Weltgesellschaft' pp. 345-380 in U. Beck (ed.), *Perspektiven der Weltgesellschaft,* Suhrkamp, Frankfurt, pp. 345-380.

Luhmann, N. (2000a), *Organisation und Entscheidung,* Suhrkamp, Frankfurt.

Luhmann, N. (2000b), 'Die Rückgabe des zwölften Kamels: Zum Sinn einer soziologischen Analyse des Rechts', 21 *Zeitschrift für Rechtssoziologie,* (forthcoming).

Maturana, H. and Varela, F. (1988), *Tree of Knowledge: Biological Roots of Human Understanding,* Shambhala, Boston.

Nelson, R. R. and Winter, S.G. (1982), *An Evolutionary Theory of Economic Change,* Harvard University Press, Cambridge, Mass.

Ogorek, R. (1999), 'Recht und Tier: Eine traurige Begegnung', 18 *Rechtshistorisches Journal,* pp. 247-259.

Pfordten von der, D. (1995), 'Die moralische und rechtliche Berücksichtigung von Tieren', in J. Nida-Rümelin and D. v. d. Pfordten (eds), *Ökologische Ethik und Rechtstheorie,* Nomos, Baden-Baden, pp. 231-244.

Röhl, K. (1987), 'Die strukturelle Differenz zwischen Individuum und Organisation oder Brauchen wir ein Sonderprivatrecht für Versicherungen und andere Organisationen?', *Festschrift für Ernst C. Stiefel.* Beck, München, pp. 574-605.

Schmidt, T. B. (1996), *Das Tier - ein Rechtssubjekt? Eine rechtsphilosophische Kritik der Tierrechtsidee,* Roderer, Regensburg.

Schmitt, C. (1985), *Political Theology: Four Chapters on the Concept of Sovereignty,* MIT Press, Cambridge, Mass.

Schmitt, C. (1996), *The Concept of the Political,* University of Chicago Press, Chicago.

Serres, M. (1990), *Le contrat naturel,* Flammarion, Paris.

Soskice, D. (1997), 'Divergent Production Regimes: Coordinated and Uncoordinated Market Economies in the 1980s and 1990s', in H. Kitschelt, P. Lange, G. Marks and J. D. Stephens (eds), *Continuity and Change in Contemporary Capitalism,* Cambridge University Press, Cambridge, pp. 271-289.

Spencer Brown, G. (1972), *Laws of Form,* Julian Press, New York.

Stone, C. D. (1972), 'Should Trees Have Standing? - Toward Legal Rights for Natural Objects' 45 *Southern California Law Review,* pp. 450-467.

Teubner, G. (1988), 'Enterprise Corporatism: New Industrial Policy and the 'Essence' of the Legal Person', 36 *The American Journal of Comparative Law,* pp. 130-155.

Teubner, G. (1992), 'The Two Faces of Janus: Rethinking Legal Pluralism', 13 *Cardozo Law Review,* pp. 1443-14462.

Teubner, G. (1993a), *Law as an Autopoietic System,* Blackwell, Oxford.

Teubner, G. (1993b), 'The Many-Headed Hydra: Networks as Higher-Order Collective Actors', in J. McCahery, S. Picciotto, and C. Scott (eds), *Corporate Control and Accountability,* Clarendon Press, Oxford, pp. 41-60.

Teubner, G. (1997a), 'Altera Pars Audiatur: Law in the Collision of Discourses', in R. Rawlings (ed.), *Law, Society and Economy,* Clarendon Press, Oxford, pp. 149-176.

Teubner, G. (1997b), 'Global Bukowina: Legal Pluralism in the World Society', Teubner, G. (ed.), *Global Law Without A State,* Dartmouth, Aldershot, pp. 3-28.

Teubner, G. (1998), 'Legal Irritants: Good Faith in British Law or How Unifying Law Produces New Divergences', 61 *Modern Law Review,* pp. 11-32.

Teubner, G. (2000a), 'Contracting Worlds: The Invocation of Discourse Rights in Private Governance Regimes', 9 *Social and Legal Studies,* (forthcoming).

Teubner, G. (2000b), 'Idiosyncratic Production Regimes: Co-evolution of Economic and Legal Institutions in the Varieties of Capitalism', in J. Ziman (ed.), *The Evolution of Cultural Entities: Proceedings of the British Academy,* Oxford University Press, Oxford, (forthcoming).

Teubner, G. and Hutter, M. (2000), 'Homo juridicus and homo oeconomicus: Communicative Fictions?', in T. Baums, K. Hopt, and N. Horn (eds), *Corporations, Capital Markets and Business in the Law,* Kluwer, Den Haag, pp. 569-584.

Varela, F. J. (1992), 'Whence Perceptual Meaning? A Cartography of Current Ideas', in F. J. Varela, and J. P. Dupuy (eds), *Understanding Origins: Contemporary Views on the Origin of Life, Mind and Society,* Kluwer, Dordrecht, pp. 235-236.

Weick, K. E. (1979), *The Social Psychology of Organizing,* Addison-Wesley, Reading.

Wielsch, D. (2000), *Freiheit und Funktion: Zur Struktur- und Theoriegeschichte des Rechts der Wirtschaftsgesellschaft,* Nomos, Baden-Baden.

Williamson, O. E. (1991), 'Comparative Economic Organization: The Analysis of Discrete Structural Alternatives', 36 *Administrative Science Quarterly,* pp. 269-296.

Williamson, O. (1996), *The Mechanisms of Governance,* Oxford University Press, Oxford.

Willke, H. (1975), *Stand und Kritik der neueren Grundrechtstheorie: Schritte zu einer normativen Systemtheorie,* Duncker & Humblot, Berlin.

3 The Specific Autopoiesis of Law: Between Derivative Autonomy and Generalised Paradox

JEAN CLAM

General approach

The Luhmannian concept of autopoiesis lends itself to numerous miscomprehensions. Its application to social systems is met with scepticism and critique. Very few are the social scientists – especially outside Germany – who take Luhmann's recasting of sociological general theory seriously and apply its core concepts, especially that of autopoiesis, to their respective fields of research. Moreover, where attempts are made to work earnestly with Luhmann's theory, the results are often not convincing: sociological system research tends to reach an inhibitory level of jargon esoterism as well as to deliver a poor elucidation of the thematised social phenomena. On the whole, the extremely high entry costs of the theory, added to its apparently scanty benefits for empirical research, have clearly discouraging effects on its reception.[1]

What is needed is a constant reworking of Luhmannian theorising in order to further its assimilation within social science. Those who have seriously made the attempt to enter into such a theorising and tried to make sense of it acknowledge the insightfulness, the power and richness of its intellectual accomplishments. In effect, what Luhmann did was simply excessive: he went too far on a path too isolated – and erected a theory too

[1]There is, to my knowledge, no overview of the reception of Luhmann's work. A book on the reception of the latter in the fields beyond sociology is forthcoming (de Berg and Schmidt, 2000). On Luhmann's reception in the various cultural-linguistic spheres, it could be said that the German reception is very lively and thorough, the Anglo-Saxon still very timid and lacking an extensive basis of translated texts, the French almost non-existing – with an slight exception for the theory of law.

elaborate as to be easily followed and understood. The problem with his work is not its deficiencies, but its very proficiency and exceptional inventivity. This fact motivates us to adopt a style of reception which has to combine faithful exposition of the theory with insistent analytical elucidations of its components and articulations. I will follow such a scheme of presentation and interpretation to further the comprehension of the autopoiesis idea within Luhmann's work.

My endeavour is to show the pertinence of the autopoiesis theory as it is applied to law. Therefore, I shall be very careful to clarify its motives and analyse the plausibility of its application to legal phenomena. It seemed to me most suiting for this purpose, as well as objectively necessary, to introduce distinctions into the concept of autopoiesis which were not made by Luhmann himself. A first differentiation should be introduced between autopoiesis in the order of pure operativity (life, consciousness, communication) and those in the order of particular meaning (law, economy, love, ...). A second one should bring forth the particularity of legal autopoiesis when compared to that of other systems. My thesis is that legal autopoiesis is an autopoiesis sui generis and that its specificity is related to the very peculiar figures of its generating paradox.

What is autopoiesis?

Very frequently autopoiesis is perceived as the poorly justified use of a biological metaphor of autonomy and closure and its application to contexts which are exceeded by any presumption of self-production. Such a borrowing from a (questionable) theory of the living seems to be far fetched and inadequate to describe the structure and modi of operation of social systems. It obscures very much the undoubted autonomy of such systems, an autonomy it is precisely designed to elucidate. As a conceptual means intended to underline the differentiation and independent logic of functional subsystems within modern society, it seems so exaggerated as to imperil any sociological analysis. Legal theorists who are ready to acknowledge the highly increased autonomy of the legal system with its impressive conceptual, argumentative, institutional and organisational specialisation are still unwilling to accept the thesis of a self-centred production of the legal exclusively from the self same elements produced by itself. All too evident are common representations, semantic intersections and formal interrelations between the legal system and its various environments. The legal is obviously so profoundly entangled with the ethical and the political as to render any strict conception of its self-production illusory.[2] Autopoiesis appears thus as a highly counter-intuitive, excessive and implausible device for understanding social systems in general and the legal one in particular.

Beyond the violence of biologising and fragmenting the social in a manner as to suppose a self-productive genesis of its components, autopoiesis motivates rejection because of its technicist-cybernetic connotations. The deeply rooted reserves towards any seemingly technicist paradigm are a major liability of systemism as a general theory of social science. The imports of central components of Luhmannian theory from cybernetics and systems theory strengthens the reticence awakened by the terminology and explicit references of the former to both. It adds to the strangeness of the biological metaphor that of an artificialist modelisation of society.[3]

Actually Luhmannian autopoiesis is neither a simple borrowing from biology nor cybernetics. It derives from a cognitivist broadening of the whole of the problematics of reflexivity. It engulfs thus as well artificial intelligent systems as biological ones; as well empirical as transcendental consciousness; as well the social as its constituent systems. This broadening is based on the transformation of theoretical sociology into a sort of proto- or super-theory incorporating the scope of a critique of ontology and the casting of a new differentialist constructivism. It is a theory reflecting itself as such and occurring in itself in the form of a theory of a specific type of observation which has its site within the general system of science and which thematises its social constructions.[4]

Autopoiesis is at the core of such a theory and represents the culmination of its partial breakthroughs. De-ontologisation is not a purely negative concept for Luhmann that could be sustained by revivifying the 'différance' in every meaning and letting its dynamics disrupt the ontological solidity and identity projected in any semantic intention. Luhmannian de-ontologisation is not a deconstructive, but mainly a

---

[2]A prominent critic of Luhmann's biological metaphor is H. Rottleuthner (1987).

[3]The technicist connotation is a dire inhibition of a positive reception for a majority of sociologists still under the shock of the plight of Parsonian systemism.

[4]This raises the problem of a possible point of view from which such a system of production of involutive or 'local truth' (Latour, 1988) could be overlooked and criticised. I have argued (Clam, 2000b) that no such site is given from which such a theory would be falsified, but only other sites on which other theories could be built. The only dominant point of view would be philosophical and would engage a critique of the non-philosophical assumptions upon which Luhmann elaborates a great part of his theory. More precisely, Luhmann borrows pieces of ontology critique by Derrida and works with them as if they were sure results. He supplements these pieces with a whole range of protological borrowings from Spencer Brown which are enormously stimulating, though very problematic philosophically (cf. Clam, 2000a).

constructive theory whose concern is to find ways for a theory of society to be built in a manner as not to be hampered by indirect or rampant re-ontologisation. This is the reason why such a theory is so much attentive to the choice of the numerous pieces of logical, methodological and analytical framing it incorporates. Such efforts are aimed at the projection of society as the space of a flowing construction of reality with no measure of adequacy to anything outside itself and independently of its leading distinctions. The world is given exclusively in such self-referential, self-continent, socially 'operated' distinctions.[5]

It is not the place to enter into the details of the Luhmannian venture to de-ontologise the basis of any description of the world and the projection of human action in it (Clam, 2000a; Clam, 2000b; Clam, 2000c). Luhmann's theory is so penetrating and so thoroughly elaborated that it often leaves behind it the parallel ventures of the philosophies of deconstruction (Habermas, 1988: 411) – while having no pretension at all to deliver any sort of philosophical work. The point I am making here is solely that autopoiesis should be understood as what it is in Luhmann's work: not a simple import from biology or cybernetics to be fitted into a composite theory, but the expression of a much more fundamental transformation of sociological – and more generally scientific – theory as such. This transformation has a prototheoretical (or protological) status that can be elucidated either within a theory of high reflexivity integrating the concepts of distinction and observation (as system generative operations) or within philosophy itself. Autopoiesis expresses the most momentous concept in such transformation bound to obliterate classical action sociology as an ontologising design still working with the supposedly firm identities of subject, action and meaning. Autopoiesis belongs into the project of a radically post-ontological, differentialist theory of society. It crystallises the shift from the '(onto-)logical' to an 'evential' (or 'ergetic') type of thought.[I1][6]

Under 'evential' type of thought I understand a thought where there is no original identity of being and thought and where perplexities of thought do not correlate with impossibilities of being. Thought is not checked by contradiction and paradox, but can be continued within another type of differentialist, highly reflexive recasting of thought and being themselves. Beyond apophantic conceivability and correction there is an operative,

[5]On Luhmann's constructivism and its relation to Derrida's deconstructivism, see Luhmann (1988, 1990 a), Teubner (1999), Staeheli (1997), de Berg and Fraenkel (1995).

[6]The integration of autopoiesis to the post-ontological figure of theory is the most inventive and subtle contribution of Luhmann to this field of thought. The linking of autopoiesis to paradox and to its overcoming is at the core of this contribution.

'actual' continuation of being which can be shown and theorised. There is no identity of being with itself, but only operative differences which are what they are and happen to be when they happen to be. Operation creates worldly facts beyond logical impossibilities, because these are grounded on a principle of self-identity of being blocking the perception of the actually flowing genesis of identity from difference. That means: being is not originary identical with itself because being is what it is as the 'indicated' side of a difference, the positively determined side of a double-sided form in which an unmarked Other (other side) faces and makes possible the delimitation and definition of the marked one.[7] Being is not what it is, but must be 'probabilised' to what it is: at the beginning there is a general 'improbability' out of which being, things, facts, positive states come to pass when they have accomplished a process of probabilisation.[8] Beings are not what they are from eternity and do not conserve this their self-identity indefinitely. Being's advent lies in the effectuation of a distinction, a differentiation from what it is not, and this is an operation, not a given. Being is thus the result of an actually effectuated operation of distinction which is itself contingent and flowing because such a distinction can always be effectuated in another manner and bring forth (differentiate and define) another being. Moreover, once accomplished, the distinction is not maintained in being indefinitely, but must be conserved by regeneration of the original operation of distinction. The self-condensing and self-confirming regeneration of the operation of distinction generates what Luhmann calls a system and is the operation of its autopoiesis.

Contingency and improbability are thus the main categories of evential thought. An 'improbability theorem' (Unwahrscheinlichkeitstheorem) drives the whole conception. It puts being in the perspective of ontology of 'energetic',[9] or more properly 'ergetic' (Clam, 2000d). Overcoming of original contingency and improbability. In effect, not only no being delineating, defining distinction is predestined to be more probable or more efficient than another; not only its continuation is in no way guaranteed once established, but must be actually, actively, operatively assured by continuing condensation of the primary distinction within changing internal and external environments; but the main difficulty is that no distinction is

[7]This recalls the axioms of Spencer Brown's protologic (1969), much reiterated in Luhmann's later work.

[8]I use a non-Luhmannian combination of differentialist (protological) theory with the 'improbability theorem' discussed by Luhmann in earlier works (Luhmann, 1981: 25-34). This combination has here an introductory function and should be much more thoroughly developed, should it become a firm theoretical device.

[9]In the etymological sense of 'actual' (aristotelic energeia), or operative, in Luhmann's terminology.

complete and self-consistent[10] as to be simply processed along repetitive lines of operation. Every distinction is in itself 'paradoxical', that means hampered by the fact that it cannot be completed, closed or unified. No operation, no ergetic unfolding of the distinction brings it to a end, to a point of view where it can oversee itself as a whole and totalise the horizons of its meaning. Luhmann calls this state of affair 'paradox'.

Where ontology put static, extratemporal interrelations between concepts and things, Luhmann puts actual, 'effectual' overcomings of the contingent and improbable. He introduces an actual aspect necessitating the cointroduction of time. Time is thus inherent to his ergetic ontology and evential type of thought. A distinction must be probabilised and this is done within time consuming social processes of communication. All distinctions pertaining to meaning are social processes[11] consuming time in their oscillation from one pole of consistency of the distinction to the other, without ever reaching a definitive appeasement of their tension. This is the reason why Luhmann's prototheoretical considerations do not establish themselves on a philosophical ground, but remain sociological in scope and effect. That means: autopoiesis, paradox and communication should be brought together to be explained in a synthesis in which the *prima facie* purely philosophical dimension of the critique of ontology has to be reread as a (proto-)sociological problematics pertaining to the ways social communication probabilises meaning projections or world interpretations on the ground of a time consuming, operative processing of non totalisable distinctions.

There is still one step to be taken on this very abstract level in order to enter the path leading straight to the problematics of legal autopoiesis and its generating paradoxes. This step has to do with the clarification of the relationship between paradox and autopoiesis. My thesis stresses a point made by Luhmann himself and generalises it: paradox is the generating ground of autopoiesis. Without paradox, there is no autopoiesis. Were distinctions (with their indication of definite being against a background of an unmarked Other to it) complete and consistent, they could come to an end or postulate a telos for their effectuations. Being paradoxical in the sense that their presuppositions involve themselves in any attempt to establish their consistency, this their circularity, added to their own fundamental contingency, makes a circular, non totalisable operative processing necessary. This is autopoiesis: a circular, indefinite operation on

[10]It is in Spencer Brown's logic self-continent, but its self-continence is that which makes it paradoxical.

[11]With the exception of non-communicable meaning whose synthesis play within consciousness.

the ground of an incomplete and contingent structure of being creating factual possibilities beyond logical impossibilities. Paradox designates namely a logical perplexity bringing thought to a paralysing embarrassment. The operation of autopoiesis is a de-paradoxising one, circumventing the logical locking by creating a new space where things are rearranged in a manner that makes the old structure obsolete. Paradox requires thus a displacement and an unfolding of a new dimension through complex operative arrangements: complex chains of operations overcome the inertia of initial contradictions and bring improbable being into existence. Operative complexity is bound to fluctuate in any system without ever coming to an end because the initial contradictions themselves can never be annihilated.

Paradox thus generates autopoiesis, but autopoiesis itself gains from its inception a profile which is to be called, with Luhmann, system. Systems are thus the operative clusters or the effectuation lines of contingent and improbable constructions. Systems of communication are then to be conceived as the sites of probabilisation of inaugural distinctions.

Distinction of types of autopoiesis

Luhmann uses the same figure of exposition to explain the generation of – let us say - global autopoietical systems and those of more particular ones. Thus, he sees communication as an autopoiesis grounded in the paradox of interrelation or interpenetration of a plurality of consciousnesses. It is because two consciousnesses are not able to reach one another that communication becomes functionally possible and meaningful. A consciousness can by no means experience what another is experiencing; consciousnesses are separated monads that cannot merge their contents. This is the starting point for the emergence of communication as an operative system circumventing the paradox of in every point analogical but for each other unreachable beings. Communication does not cancel the paradox of the conjunction of experiences, but it circumvents it by creating a new system which holds in spite and because of the impossibility of conscious conjunction between individual conscious experiences.[12] The new system never achieves the overcoming of the basic impossibility. It remains thus incomplete and paradoxical, structurally open ended and non totalisable.

---

[12]Nassehi (1991: 153) is the author who stressed and generalised most consequently this point. Fuchs (1993: 135) sees in the impossibility at the basis of the emergence of new structures a 'calaytical problem'.

Another example of global autopoiesis is that of consciousness itself which emerges as an overcoming of the paradox of life – the latter being that of the impossibility to reflect its own fundamental self-reference.[13] Consciousness is thus an autopoiesis in its own right emerging in spite and because of the impossibility of full biological self-reference. It circumvents the locking of biological processes at a level of paradoxical self-reference by creating a higher level of operative complexity where biological self-reference is processed, without being annihilated, by means of the emerging autopoiesis of conscious self-reflection. Luhmann sees the emergence of ever-higher autopoiesis as an evolutionary process where each autopoiesis is condition and result of evolution. This evolutionary scheme adds stress to the operativism of the Luhmannian version of system theory. The building of higher synthesis on the ground of locking paradoxes has nothing to do with logical defusion or dialectical reconciliation of contradictions. It is an emergent, wholly contingent and improbable event which brings with it its own type of observation. That means: there is no preconception of the type of objects brought forth by an emergent particular autopoiesis (no prefiguration of consciousness and conscious contents before the emergence of consciousness). Autopoiesis is thus inaugural of the representability (thinkability) of its own synthesis and its own objective correlates.[14]

The same figure of explanation is applied to autopoiesis of systems which I would like to differentiate from these first ones. Thus, the autopoiesis of law is designed along the same principle of emergence 'in spite and because' of a fundamental paradox: 'Recht weil Unrecht'

[13]Luhmann does not elaborate much on the emergence of consciousness out of the paradox of life. At one point Luhmann discusses in a cursory manner the emergence of time and time consciousness out of a sort of presentiment of time at the level of pre-conscious life, namely out of what has been called 'anticipatory reactions' (1990a: 43). The figure of argument which is used here recalls that of the operative circumvention of paradoxity. In effect, in order to reach higher levels of prognosis (allowing higher combinatory levels of operation in general), conscious cognitive systems construct a difference between past and future on which they base the processing of all their operations. Time is thus constructed to trespass a threshold of a reality whose given structure could be changed as to enlarge it and to enrich it with a wide range of new possibilities. This illustrates once more the fact that what is called paradox on the level of basic autopoiesis is not semantical contradiction and oscillation between two irreconcilable poles, but the trespassing of a level of construction of reality towards a higher one. The higher order is a more complex one, i.e. one which is richer in combinatory possibilities.

[14]It is thus thinkable that a paradox which would become acute and visible at a higher level could motivate an operative transcending of communication towards another order, generating a higher level autopoiesis. However, this does not appear at the level of communication itself, but with the emergence of the new system and as its own generating paradox.

(Luhmann, 2000: 23), Luhmann says stressing the paradoxical 'weil' (because). In both cases paradox is the generating principle of autopoiesis. However, looking closely at the second case, one would observe a slight difference between it and the state of affairs described in connection with the purely operative autopoiesis of life, consciousness and communication. In effect, the underlying paradoxes of the latter do not oppose two contradictory values with an express logical impossibility of uniting them in one type of praxis. Communication is grounded in the impossibility of two consciousnesses to communicate by reaching each other's actual experiences, but this impossibility is from the onset an operative, and not a logical one. Whereas autopoietic law is generated by the paradox of law itself which lies not only in the impossibility for law to be realised without its Other, the other side of its defining distinction, namely violence (Gewalt) as unjust lawlessness (Unrecht, iniuria), but in the positive opposition or contradiction between the Same and the Other (Recht, Gewalt). The Other to consciousness is communication but both are not opposed like the contradictory values of justice and injustice or violence.

Thus, one would search in vain for an analogy of the fundamental value opposing paradoxes of autopoietic social systems like law (law, violence), politics (power, non power), economics (scarcity, non scarcity), science (truth, error), ... on the level of the main global autopoiesis. By the same token there is no correspondence on the level of the latter with the characteristic phenomenon of social autopoiesis in which the contradictory values of the fundamental paradox are simultaneously produced in way of the operative effectuation of the particular autopoiesis: the operation of the legal system produces concomitantly both values of law and lawlessness, the operation of the political one its both opposing values, and so on. Further, the de-paradoxisations typical of such systems are not to be found in the other systems: the legal system until late in modern times did cope with its paradox (the entanglement of law and power or violence) by essentialising the idea of law, claiming thus that law could be thought and practised 'in itself' without any reference to its Other and Opposite. Law as an *eidos* could thus be grasped, 'seen' (erschaut) in an pure vision, and the contents of its meaning deduced or unfolded in bodies of law and systems of procedures. It could build the apex of a legal order with its hierarchies of sources and levels of law, sheltered from paradox by its linear and transitive architecture inhibiting the typical circularities of entangled orders. There are no analogues to such de-paradoxising devices in the basic autopoiesis.

Thus what we are tempted to call purely operative, global or basic autopoiesis show a marked difference with the autopoiesis involved in the differentiation, autonomisation and self-referentialisation of social orders. This difference seems to crystallise around the problematics and reference to meaning in both types of autopoiesis. The basic autopoiesis are forward going processes, a sort of blindly operating systems, 'effectuating simply' their specific operations.[15] The constituting reference of two of them (consciousness and communication) to meaning – they are, in Luhmann's theory, meaning processing systems – is actually problematic. In effect, this reference does not elicit the articulation of a paradox around the paradoxical oscillation of the basic meaning involved between two contradictory poles. The generating paradoxes of consciousness and communication do not involve a particular basic semantic dimension whose internal paradox would be generative of autopoiesis as an operative circumvention of such a typical perplexity. The problem of such a theoretical design where meaning systems (Sinnsysteme) operate differently at two different levels is that of the differentiating factors: what determines such a different treatment of what basically remains a multiplicity of autopoiesis of meaning? How is law to be conceived within such a theory: as an autopoiesis that is to be superadded to the basic autopoiesis of communication, or as a particular configuration of the basic one? Why is the meaning processed in the basic autopoiesis not in itself paradoxical as to generate systems with typical value oscillations as is the case with social systems?

The question is not an exegetical one, of interest only for virtuosi of Luhmannianism. It paves the way towards a strong thesis pertaining to the description of differentiated social systems in terms of autopoiesis, in other words to the autopoietisation of social systems within Luhmannian theory; it has in particular a heavy incidence on the particular autopoiesis (more precisely: autopoietisation) of law. In effect, it leads to the consideration of a differentiation between robust, basic autopoiesis and derivative ones (which would only appear, on the ground of the former, under certain circumstances). A special status should then be granted to any autopoiesis – I think in advance of the legal one - that would not fit completely into such a differentiation. My thesis is that such a differentiation is legitimate and in harmony with the general scope of Luhmann's theory; that law, as understood by Luhmann, while differentiated from the basic autopoiesis like any other social system, derogates to some aspects common to the derivative ones: its paradox can be generalised as to engulf the paradoxity of any order of meaning.

---

[15]Luhmann says: 'schlicht durchgeführt' (1990a: 15).

Autopoiesis of meaning

To cope with our present difficulties two Luhmannian concepts are crucial: meaning (Sinn) and observation (Beobachtung). Both concepts are reworked by Luhmann as to deliver a cognitivist broadening of their received, intuitive meaning. Their recasting breaks their roots and links to ordinary as well as received theoretical comprehensions (in common speech or within the frame of classical philosophies of consciousness). Thus, meaning and observation are de-coupled from intentionality which represents the intuitive access to the phenomena they are involved in. Meaning was conceived hitherto by means of the presentification of the experience of meaningful intention (*intendere*) of something in a conscious act. Something has meaning when it means something to me and corresponds to a conscious intention and intuitive fulfilment on my part of what it means. In the cognitivist recasting, meaning is the title for a type of enrichment of cognitive processes (cognitive processes being any calculatory processes straddling subsemantic and semantic dimensions):[16] it is a device of accretion of possibility in a strictly actual process. Actuality, in the cognitivist frame of theory, is a very firm coupling of cognitive and worldly processes allowing things to be just what they are and to correspond to each other along very narrow, one-to-one correspondences. In this rather mechanistic type of co-ordination meaning brings a whole restructuring and opens a 'world' where there was only an environment - to speak with the phenomenologists of the beginning of the century.[17] Meaning is a virtualising device in the sense that it opens a space of continuing reference (Verweisung) in which every point is itself a network of references. Meaning enlarges the channels of worldly being and of the advent of reality. It inaugurates a new dimension in which reality reveals always around its actual givenness a cloud of possibilities – possibilities of its being different of what it is actually. It refers to them to be understood as what it is. Reality is apprehended from its Other, this Other being the thinkable variations of what is actually real. Thus, reality is the actual world at the centre of a variety of alternative, possible worlds which are not

[16]See von Foerster (1993: 110). The question is how far should such a cognitivist broadening go. Should meaning actually straddle the divide of life and consciousness and thus be ascribed to biological processes, these being cognitive-calculatory processes like any others? Luhmann would tend to be restrictive with the concept of meaning as such: he uses the cognitivist broadening of this concept just for the purpose of detaching the problematic of reflexivity from its traditional rootedness in intentionality and intuitive-introspective consciousness. Another problem is raised by the concept of observation.

[17]Heidegger made the distinction between *Welt* and *Umwelt* and referred to the biologist von Uxkuell.

realised, but from which reality has its 'meaning'. Meaning and observation – as the operation of making sense of meaning – enable a givenness of the world on the ground of the difference: actuality/virtuality. They let the actual world appear as a replication of something broader (a 'world form')[18] and not as an alternativeless, immediate, brute being. The difference of actual reality to its Other is the double-sided form of meaning. This is the concept of meaning in its cognitivist understanding with no reference to intuition and intentionality.

Observation is related in Luhmann's theory to meaning: it is a sort of prefiguration of what meaning would bring to full unfolding in the dimensions of consciousness and communication. Observation is however to be found at inferior levels of autopoiesis like those of the synthesis of the living. It designates there the simple operation of discrimination and of focussing, creating facts which provoke reactions in the discriminating organism.[19] It is thus confined to an elementary level of self-reactivity. Whereas, to observe in the dimension of meaning is to set a distinction through the position of a difference between a positively indicated term and its unmarked, non-indicated Other. The basic processing of meaning is observation. Meaning is the difference between the actual and the potential allowing for a type of presence in the world in which distantiation from its narrow actuality is the opening of a space of autonomy and self-centredness. Observation is the processing of such a difference in order to open particular (meaningful) perspectives on the world and to explore them. Meaning and observation are both devices of enlargement of the possible, of creation of autonomous spaces and of distantiation of self-centred processes from the steady going, linear, one-track process of actual reality.

Luhmann's thesis is that consciousness and communication are each in its own right autopoiesis of meaning. Meaning emerges with consciousness as decisive enlargement of the self-reference of life through much wider oscillations of its processes. With the virtualisation of the tracks of reality

---

[18]Weltform. It is Husserl's terminology (Husserl, 1922).

[19]Unlike Maturana who universalises the concept of cognition which comes to be used as a double with that of life, Luhmann (1990a: 53) is ready to concede the operation of observation to life as a sort of 'discriminative focussing' (diskriminierendes Focussieren). Some wordings are ambiguous like that of the study 'Wie ist Bewusstsein an Kommunikation beteiligt?' (1995: 48): 'Erst auf der Ebene des Beobachtens kommt Sinn ins Spiel…'. Whatever the relationship between meaning and observation, what is sure, is that communication necessarily brings forth a new type of observation, namely the second order observation through which first order observation is observed (see 1990a: 56). The linking to meaning in communication transforms thus the very scope of the operation of observation.

effectuation, (conscious) life can distantiate itself further from its environments and enhance its autonomy and closure against the flow of linear determination from the world. Communication opens a still higher level of autonomy for whole systems of communicatively interrelated consciousnesses. These systems are articulated around major meaning dimensions and further their self-reference. With communication emerges the dynamics of the clustering of meaning dimensions to consistent wholes.

Derivative autopoiesis

What I would suggest is to differentiate this framing of autopoiesis on the ground of the fundamental processing of meaning in observation as the only basic and robust type of autopoiesis in the space of meaning systems. That means: I suggest to consider the autopoiesis involved in the self-referentialisation of social systems in modern societies as derivative ones. The reason is that, whereas basic autopoiesis are always structurally circular and purely operatively paradoxical, the derivative ones are evolutionary circular and semantically paradoxical. Consciousness and communication, like life itself, are fully autopoietical from the onset. Their systems enjoy operative closure with their first operation, so to say. The circularity of their operative networks is established with their own emergence as systems which overcome the paradoxes of underlying orders through the opening of new spaces of structuration. There are no possible ambiguities in the attribution of any one of their operations to the adequate system in which it is generated. One cannot confuse an operation of consciousness with an operation of life, or an operation of communication with an operation of consciousness. These basic systems are instances of strict and inflexible autopoiesis. They correspond to its most pure and demanding paradigm.

There is, to be sure, a reductionist posture, inspired by physicalist approaches, which would always tend to reduce communicative processes to conscious ones and conscious ones to biological ones, the end of the trajectory being the reduction of the latter to physico-chemical ones. Such a questioning does not reach the theoretical level of a theory of self-reference and of operative closure. It would have a correspondent in the reduction of all operations of social communication to one sole type which would be economic or political (like in Marxism) leading to a theoretical inflation of the correspondent media of money and power (as in Bourdieu's theory). One could be tempted to link such a reductionist critique of autopoiesis denying systems the necessary autonomy for real, not subordinated self-centredness with a theoretical exploitation of the phenomenon of possible confusions of the systemic location of operations. In effect, it is sometimes difficult to ascribe unambiguously an occurring operation to one of the autopoietic systems of politics, law, economy, science... Intersystemic couplings are sometimes so intricate as to leave very poor a chance to find other than institutional criteria of ascription – which are superficial and non reliable criteria. Ambiguities at this level of the ascription of operations to their relevant systems constitute a major and insuperable challenge of the thesis that social subsystems are strictly autopoietical. Thus, operations occurring within the global autopoiesis of communication are not precisely ascribable to one or the other autopoietic social system, contrasting with the clear cut operative distinctions obtaining between the global autopoiesis.

Another motive of reluctance to accept the autopoiesis thesis is grounded, as we have seen, in a misapprehension of its meaning and scope. Autopoiesis makes too strong demands on intuitive thinking: the representation of a social order which would be fully self-referential and self-productive seems excessive and unjustified. We have reached the point where a line of thought elaborating on Luhmannian systemism in a most sympathetic manner seems to be akin to the same primary rejection of strict autopoiesis. This is a delusive convergence. The differentiation of a basic and derivative level of autopoiesis is not a rejection of the latter. I consider the theory of the operative closure of systems as very sharp and well founded. The autopoiesis of subsystems of communication on the ground of paradoxical premises and of operative closure seems to me also compelling. However, the contrast with the purely operative basic autopoiesis is also compelling and instructive. Thus, the differentiation between both levels of autopoiesis does not amount to an invalidation of the derivative autopoiesis as such. It motivates though to an important qualification of its conception.

Derivative autopoiesis are founded on semantic paradoxes in the sense that their generative matrix is the incompleteness and the fundamental ambiguity of the order of meaning in which they occur. Thus, it is because law and lawlessness or violence are originally and irreducibly entangled, because the idea of law is not sufficient to unfold the whole of law, that law develops into an operative system not able to rest on internal consistency, but obliged to borrow and return virtual 'camels' which help de-paradoxise the system (Luhmann, 2000). This movement of processing and overcoming the originary semantical paradox is the whole operativity of the legal system. The autopoietical character of such a system is founded in the fact that no one non-legal operation can contribute to such a processing of the paradoxity of law. A legal operation must be defined in the terms of such an autopoiesis theory as an operation that contributes to overcome the entanglement of law and lawlessness. The fact of such a contribution bestows on the contributing operation legal character. Thus, every dimension of meaning is fundamentally paradoxical and is operatively organised in a circular manner on the ground of the fundamental paradox. The circle described by the scope of its operations draws the limits of its autopoiesis.

Now this theoretical scheme, which I believe is a faithful rendering and continuing of Luhmannian intentions, raises the problem of the objectivity of fundamental dimensions of meaning (like law, power, scarcity, truth,...) and the objectivity of their paradoxity. What Luhmann does, can in effect be seen as the postulation of a few dimensions of meaning and practice which would be objectively given and objectively paradoxical. This is problematic because it runs against the assumption of a fundamental contingency of meaning. It has, however, an intuitive support in the evidence promoted by every experience we make with such orders of meaning: indeed, in all societies, these dimensions of meaning are given; indeed, any moderately thorough consideration of their semantics suffices to convince us of the fundamental perplexities they involve. However consistent or not with the metatheoretical assumption of contingency, the thesis of the givenness and the paradoxity of these orders must be assessed in relation with the assumption of their autopoietic structuring.

The question is then: if law, politics, science, art, economy, ... are objective, fundamental orders of meaning, are they as objectively and fundamentally paradoxical? Luhmann's exposition of related topics induces such an assumption: premodern, even primitive projections of these orders as highly consistent in themselves and highly consonant with each other – going to the length of postulating an equivalence of their *transcendentalia* – are interpreted by Luhmann as processes of 'invisibilisation' of fundamental paradoxity. Assertions of such internal and global consistency follow paths and use means which Luhmann describes as de-paradoxising devices. Luhmann supposes thus paradoxity as an originary feature of these meaning dimensions ahead of the emergence of the awareness of their paradoxity as such. The paradox does not emerge with its own idea.[20] The deep structure of meaning appears to be in itself (semantically) paradoxical.

The thesis means that myth and mythic etiology, and also philosophy and its argumentative constructions, are modes of understanding and explaining orders of meaning which are unaware of their basic

[20]Classical antiquity circulated a number of paradoxes and enjoyed reflecting upon them. Renaissance Europe cultivated the paradox and made an art of it. However, paradox becomes a central figure of thinking and feeling only in late modernity. A rich material and capital insights on the topic can be found in Luhmann (1990b; 1996).

performance: they do not understand themselves as de-paradoxising devices, creating stories or arguments to defuse central paradoxes of the meaning complexes they tackle. Myth narrates beginnings and explains thus why things are what they are and the way they are. Philosophy – in its ontologic configuration – sees being as an external order that it seeks to represent in its own orders of reasons, mirroring its hierarchical organisation in the hierarchy of its ideas and its deductions. Narrative and logical hierarchy suppose a consistent whole unfolding in a global story or a definite gradation. Being and meaning are not paradoxical in themselves. They just need to be explored in a certain manner to give insight into their organised totality. Certain mythic and philosophic endeavours can thus pretend to reproduce quite exactly in their own genealogic, geometric or dialectical forms the process of being itself: they produce then systematised theogonies (Hesiod), axiomatic-deductive metaphysics (Spinoza), systems of oscillating development of Reason (Hegel). Luhmann sees in hierarchy and deduction a device – one of the most performative – to 'invisibilise' paradoxity and to cope with it both theoretically and practically. This is what is meant, in my exposition of the matter, by the supposition of objective paradoxity.

Let us concede so much for the sake of the argument and look at the consequences of these assumptions on the problematic of autopoiesis. If paradoxity is originary and structurally inherent to the fundamental orders of meaning, then its processing must be operative – in opposition to simply logical. However, Luhmann seems to assume that until the emergence of a particularly paradoxising type of observation (or meaning production) which is that of second order observation (the observation of 'How one observes') the handling of underlying, non thematised paradoxity could still be confined to linear-transitive logic and semantics. The paradox which was not perceived as such was invisibilised by means of onto-logical and semantic constructions which established univocity and consistency, by means mainly of hierarchy and linear transitivity of causes, reasons and arguments, within the partial realms as well as the whole of being. That would mean that meaning and its paradoxity as such do not elicit the emergence of autopoietic systems. They motivate the building of systems of thought and practice which handle paradoxity, but in a way that is not essentially operative. Semantical syntheses are projected which do not rely on constant operative introduction of elements of fluidity.[21] They do not

[21]Operativity as overcoming of a semantically perplexed system by introduction of elements of virtuality and fluidity is best presented by Luhmann (2000) in 'Rückgabe des zwölften Kamels'.

involve an autopoietic processing in order to provide the system with a floating basis as mobile as its own fundamental paradox.[22]

One has thus to distinguish between logical-semantical and systemic-operative coping with paradox. The first does not see paradox as such at the fundament of being but only a difficulty in bringing thought (that is itself) into correspondency with real being it has to represent. Once the propedeutic to pure philosophic reason is accomplished, such a correspondency is established and the true chain maintaining being in its coherence and constituting its totality is unveiled. Being in itself can still inspire astonishment and still appear as enigmatic; however, being's mystery is not linked to its paradoxity but to the marvel of its ultimate order, bringing the whole of being into the unity of a cosmos encompassed by a supercosmical intelligence. The ground for astonishment and infinity lies in the encounter of intelligence with itself: it is a finite intelligence having its specific difficulties to grasp large orders of rationality that gets insight into the working of an infinite one that unifies into one order and logic an infinite multiplicity of beings. By contrast, systemic-operative concepts break with the representationalist framework of theorising, suppose the heterarchy and incompleteness of disjunctive, contingent and flowing orders.

Fully operative de-paradoxisation seems to be reached only when the onto-logical and semantical constructions break down definitively. This initiates the process leading to autopoiesis of social systems of communication. The whole is synchronic with the process of functional differentiation which establishes the main dimensions of meaning as systems of communication banded around the main functions of human social practice. Autopoiesis appears thus as an emergent level on the way from semantical to fully operative de-paradoxisation. It can be seen as a result of evolution. The hypothesis of a progressive emergence of autopoiesis, i.e. the question of the inflexibility versus graduality of autopoiesis, is not decisive here. Such a question is superseded by the corroboration of the thesis that autopoiesis of social communication within functionally differentiated subsystems are derivative, even if their inflexibility can be established. Autopoiesis on the fundament of semantic paradoxes is not originary and contrasts in this respect with the basic autopoiesis of life, consciousness and communication – which are autopoietic *ab initio*, with the emergence of their first operation. Orders of meaningful social practice do not reach operativity until the late emergence of a new and highly improbable type of de-paradoxisation. Autopoiesis

[22] As Luhmann says in an early work (1970: 190).

designates, strictly speaking, the level at which operativity is fully circular.[23]

Let us consider what this means for law and the legal system. Even if legal autopoiesis is inflexible, our results underline the fact that it is not robust. This lack of robustness has an impact on the closure and the globality of the system. It shows the relativity of the assumption that autopoietic law – as any autopoietic system in Luhmann's theory – is a self-substitutive order. It questions the theorem that a legal operation can only be replaced by another legal operation and that no operation referring to law subsists outside of the legal system. The poor robustness of the system means that in spite and because of its full closure and of its internal, coherence enhancing complexity, too much law can still be flowing through non-systemic channels within society. Such an extra-systemic law can take the positive form of partial constructions resting on onto-logical and semantic (in opposition to purely operative) de-paradoxisation; or negatively that of an inflation of systemic law leading to the non application of important portions of it, challenging thus its exclusivity. In both cases, the neutralisation of law is not purely technical and does not involve a type of material impossibility of excluding non-systemic or of non including systemic law. It is not because onto-logical constructions are in-built in the structure and spirit of legal rules that they are technically unavoidable; nor is it because systemic law is materially too complex that it is not equally applied in all its parts. In both cases, the neutralisation of systemic law is based on 'legal' impediments: it is an understanding and a feeling of what law is (Rechtsverständnis and Rechtsgefühl) that provides a living resistance to autopoietisation. Those resources of resistance can cause a regression in the autonomy and the differentiation (i.e. a 'Entdifferenzierung') of law, leading to parallel constructions of legality while autopoiesis is formally still going on. The legal systems of modern totalitarianisms are instances of such reversions of the social substance of law towards non systemic, non purely operative, but intuitive and confusional forms of legal action.

Luhmann's thesis challenged in advance such a conclusion by stressing the correlation of closure on the one side and lack, inadequacy and paradox on the other. Autopoiesis is the more inflexible, closure assertive and fertile, the more complex its fundamental tension is. The derivative character of social autopoiesis questions this correlation between closure and lack. It shows that the improbability and lack of robustness of

[23]The hypothesis of a mixed regime of de-paradoxisation in which logical and semantical modes ally themselves to operative ones would be an expression of a gradual autopoiesis, an option rejected by Luhmann.

autopoiesis does not only enhance its complexity and intelligence, but also vulnerabilises it considerably. Since autopoiesis cannot be originary operative, i.e. cannot concentrate from its first operation on the whole substance of law in it, it is exposed to a type of regression unknown for the basic autopoiesis. The paradoxical fact that incompleteness is precisely the motor of an operative autopoiesis whose principle vector is to handle law as a non totalisable dimension of meaning, is not the whole story with adventitious autopoiesis. This impossibility of concentration of the whole of the systemic meaning production within the system, is something more. Thus, the fact that the autopoiesis of law is not the whole act of law is not only the prime mover of legal autopoiesis, but also its prime destabiliser. It represents a flaw in the drawing of a border between operative inside and environmental outside, suggesting the existence of a further inside at the skirts of the operative reach of the system. When autopoiesis is derivative and adds its structural deficiency to the essential blindness of autopoiesis as such for its environments,[24] there is no guarantee, in the case of an adventitious autopoiesis like that of law, that a considerable amount of legal substance would not escape systemic processing.

There exists, to be sure, always the possibility of a nominal, in fact a tautological definition of autopoietic law. Such a position, and many a Luhmannian text seems to induce it, would amount to a declaration of complete coextensiveness between all communications oriented on the values of the just and the unjust and all the operations of the legal system. Thus, the system would host a multitude of operations which are neither identified nor identifiable within it: no legal institution would recognise such operations as legal, nor are there any formal legal operations (unequivocally belonging to the system) which could be observations of such operations. Such would be the consequence entailed by a nominal-definitory delimitation of the legal by a declaration of coextensiveness of the set of systemic legal operations with the set of all 'legally' oriented operations. The legal is the legal and it is nothing else than what 'is there' in the operation of the legal system. The only definition given of an operation oriented on the values of just and unjust is that it belongs to the legal system and is generated in its autopoiesis. Conversely, the definition of a legal operation is that it is the operation oriented on the values of the just and the unjust. Such a tautology is linked to the fact that the specific

[24]This blindness means that the system only reacts to the irritations that are transmitted to it through its own sensors and its own intersystemic couplings. On the blindness of systems and their insensivity for their own dysfunctions – affecting their capacity for reform -, see the last pieces of the collection of essays published under the title *Politische Planung* (Luhmann, 1971).

legal values of the just and the unjust cannot be specified by any material contents, nor can the quality of an orientation of communication on them be circumscribed by material indications – such material contents or indications being the setting of a specifiable legal categoriality within practical reason (like in Kant's splitted deduction of morality and law within his theory of practical rationality), or the acknowledgement of a specific type or mode of legal intentionality (like in the phenomenology of law).[25] The distinction of both values is the grounding operation of the system and is as contingent and as void of non operative constituents as the system itself.[26]

The problem is that the boundaries of the system itself cannot be specified. They are neither spatial nor material nor formal. They are solely operative. When we speak of the legal system as identifying or not identifying itself we do not mean and cannot mean an instance in the system that would represent it and could determine what belongs to it and what does not. We cannot turn to such an instance to get a layout of the system and its boundaries, because such an instance does not exist. The system brings its boundaries forth in each of its own operations and only when it operates. Its operations condense and confirm, each time they occur, the grounding distinction of the Same and the Other which sets the ground for a delimitation of a systemic inside and an environmental outside. Moreover, the operations of the system are neither centralised nor are they dependant upon defining instances or institutions. The legal system in the sense of autopoietic systems theory has very little to do with the legal system in the current comprehension of an institutionally shaped system in which the state, its administrations, private organisations, professional experts, interested individuals, ... articulate their inputs and organise their decisional competencies in a hierarchical manner. The legal system is the (derivative) autopoiesis of law as the self-continuing, 'autoreferentially criterionless'[27] orientation of communication on the distinction of the just and the unjust.

All these assumptions do not make any difficulty as long as we do not need to work on the hypothesis of an 'excluded inside' or of a systemic substance not engulfed by systemic operations. This is indeed the case as long as we confine ourselves to a type of autopoiesis whose type of operation is in itself definitive of a level of emergence of a new global structure – namely the type of autopoiesis I called basic or purely operative, instantiated in the system building processes of life, consciousness and

---

[25]See Kojève (1994).

[26]On the Luhmannian conception of operativity, see (Clam, 2000 a).

[27]Luhmann speaks of 'kriterienlose Selbstreferenz' (1997: 883).

communication. This is, by contrast, not the case for what we are trying to differentiate as derivative or adventitious autopoiesis. Within the meaning processing of the global and purely operative system of communication as a primary autopoiesis the differentiation of subsystems of meaning and practice is not based on the emergence of global structures, but of semantic-practical distinctions (legal, illegal; true, not true; monetary payment, no monetary payment; ...) which cannot be as strictly actual and tautological as the primary ones (life, consciousness, communication). Hence, the advent of a new problematics which is that of an undifferentiated substance or of systemically non ascribable operations, awaiting differentiation and ascription but never exhausted by them, be their pace the most drastic. Such a substance and such operations grow continuously ahead of any differentiation because they are nothing else than the logical correlates of the constitution and the coding of the systems themselves. They correspond to the always plausible inversion of the systemic codes.

The legal system like any other system operating along derivative autopoietical lines shows a break in its reflexive identification, corresponding to a break in the re-entry of its leading distinction in itself, when it is equated with a global primary structure whose operations are coextensive with all possible elements entering it and originally exhaustive of its possible substance. It seems to be 'blind', unable of reflecting in itself its grounding difference, since it is unable to produce operations capable of observing other operations processing its own distinction. The multitude of legal operations thus cannot be delimited by the system itself, but from a postulated vantage point revealing the 'objective' quality (of the value orientation) of operations.

This recalls similar paradoxes which have earnestly undermined classical theological and philosophical constructions. Thus, the doctrine of the *ecclesia invisibilis* as the communion of the redeemed made it impossible for any instance within the (visible) religious system to determine the own limits of the system. Such a doctrine works with the same type of definitory tautology which makes the whole concept paradoxical. The Church was the communion of the redeemed and there could not be any non-redeemed in the Church nor any redeemed outside of it, whereby the set of the redeemed could not be delimited (because it was thought to be veiled for human knowledge). Such a system can consequently never indicate what it is inclusive or exclusive of. It could not define itself and had to rely on the postulate of a transcendent observation point from which the real constitution of the system could be grasped. The organisation of the system had to rely on signs, indirect indications (like work or business success) to identify itself. This unsure self-identifying system had to cope constantly with delegitimising questionings of its real identity. Its institutions – a sort of insecure nuclear identity – had to devise tests of belongings to the invisible body which were merely indicative but had to be shaped progressively into very stringent criteria of affiliation. This is the constraining trajectory that has been followed by the Christian dissidence that took its departure, with the Reformation, from the principle of the invisibility of the true religious community. Such a trajectory illustrates the paradoxes flowing from the declaration of coextensiveness of religious redemption as ecclesial belongint (system affiliation) with an unascertainable orientation of the redeemed on the faith (fides) in the inscrutable divine justification (non delimitable system extension).

The second example of self-defeating self-identification by way of definitory nominal coextensiveness of a postulated set of constituents with given but unascertainable ones, is that of philosophical definition of historical reason. Modern philosophies of history postulated the coextensiveness of history or the historical process with reason or the unfolding of the rational in human history. Since reason was not a straightforward working principle, but hosted at its core a mechanism of deception (in Hegel's words a *List*), the appearances of historical reason suffered from their own opacity. On the whole, however, one had the certainty of the aim-directedness of the process and could live in the confidence on the positivity of the global outcome. Yet, such rational dogmatics could not cope with the eventuality of a recession of reason from history, because non-reason was not identifiable for reason itself.

To escape such a theoretical stalemate, the autopoietological theory of law must avoid tautological delimitations of the system. Luhmann does avoid it by stressing the re-entry of the founding systemic distinction within the system: the identity of the legal system is an actual operative reflexive one. However, definitory formulations of the systemic operation aiming at a widening of the scope of legality to encompass not only the institutionally visible and semantically highly crystallised constituents of law, induce a vague reference to a general orientation of communication on the central values of the system. Our contention is that all of the substance of the Same (law, Recht) is not encompassed by the derivative autopoietic system and that to have it all included within it, we will have to resort to the same type of tautological delimitations of the system we have exposed and criticised. Thus, if our contention is correct, some of the substance of law remains outside the legal system in a sort of extra-legal legal region.

It is not a slight undertaking to prove such a contention. The way to the proof we have already done was a negative one: we could show the irrelevance and confusing effects of nominal definitions of extension determining the set of systemic elements (something is legal so far as it is an operation of the legal system). We have not yet positively proven that legal substance remains actually outside the system. What we did, however, is to show the adventitiousness of the autopoiesis of law on grounds of the late emergence of its paradoxity and the processing of this paradoxity along lines of systemic autonomisation and autopoietisation. In opposition to basic autopoiesis, derivative autopoiesis has to be reflexively achieved. There belongs to it an effort of restraint, since closure of legal orientation is not an objective process and does not happen *sua sponte*. The system must steer itself, against inertial tendencies of disruption of its closure, autonomy and autopoiesis, very closely to its highest level of self-centred consistency. Law is always permeated by manners of feeling, thinking and acting which fit or do not fit into the present configuration of the system. Orders of meaning tend to fuse into a general intuitivity of the meaningfulness of the world and to promote a sort of holistic, monocontextural orientation. This tendency must be confronted and contained within the derivative autopoiesis of the system.

However, the inertial tendencies (towards a re-monocontexturalisation of legal meaning and its fusion with other – moral, political, etc. – meaning) are not the only one applying. Autopoiesis, one could object, is in any event the expression of the impossibility of intuitive congruence. Meaning must be 'diffracted', de-intuitivised by indirect intention and by enrichment with virtual components lacking from the onset any intuitive fulfilment. Meaning must be prevented from becoming too massive and not mobile enough to make possible such a wide conceivability and practicability of the world. This is precisely what de-paradoxising autopoiesis does. That is why we will have to seek for other sources of tension applying on derivative autopoiesis and preventing them from engulfing the whole substance of their media.

The answer for this series of refining questions lies beyond guesses inspired by classical oppositions of formal and material components, imaginative de-paradoxising formalisations and intuitive, inertial substance. We will have to put to question the whole mechanism of systemic coding within autopoietic systems in order to understand what is flowing inside and what is remaining outside the system and why a part of the excluded is made out of the most authentic substance of the system. In effect, it is when we start to invert the coding of the systems that we become aware of the manner they relate to their systemic substance.

Following Luhmann, systems process the stimulations arising within reach of their systemic sensibility by means of a binary code. The processing concatenates operations along connections of the positive value of the code, whereas the appearance of negative one stops the connection – hampers the connectability (Anschlussfähigkeit) of the operations – and requires the overcoming of the obstacle. Thus, the legal system processes the formal normative expectations within society and connects each of its operations to the following one by means of its binary code (legal, illegal), discriminating the operations that do not fit for its processing as illegal and requiring (legal) procedures to identify and to reprocess them. Each time that a legal operation encounters the negative value of the code, the system rushes to overcome it and to restore processing knitting up series of positively encoded operations. The legal system steps in when illegality shows up and interrupts the flow of its operations. It recognises and works only with legal components reading illegality within communication as a fact that has to be counterfactually rejected and that ought not determine the main course of social expectations. The system must 'legalise' everything in its environment that is destined to have occurrence and relevance in it. While doing this, the coding of social communication with the legal code breaks the undifferentiated ray of communication through its prism into legal and illegal constituents. The entanglement of legality and illegality is structural and has secondarily to do with individual intentionalities to break law. Under conditions of high social complexity such an entanglement becomes ubiquitous, because law is then unable to reach consistency and is subjected to the paradox of a simultaneous production of legality and illegality. This sets the stage for a circular and indefinite operating of the system along its binary code values.

The inversion of the coding can take its cue from exotic designs in which 'systems' are called upon ahead from any occurrence of negative values, whereby the occurrence of the latter calls upon a typified, uneventful, so to say syntactic processing. It is said that traditional medicine in China treat the healthy in order to prevent sickness. It is health that calls upon the medical 'system' to enhance it. When illness occurs, the physician has to step in like insurance and to face a failure of its own performance, to repair it without compensation. The logic behind such a comprehension of engaging a social system is very different from the one we are familiar with.[28]

The paradox of legal coding lies in the redundant structure of legal empowerment: it is rights that give right to rights - and not non-rights. Law grants rights which then function like the grounds on which access to

[28]The matter is very complicated because the medical code in Luhmanns theory is the only one with a negative value (sickness – Krankheit) as positive side of the code (Luhmann 1990a : 183-195). Even with such an inversion the Chinese view remains, in its logic, quite different.

concrete benefits is given or enforced. It is he who is already endowed with rights who can expect and lay claim to their effective fruition. This is actually quite logical. If anybody could claim any right, there would be no chance for establishing any congruence within social expectations. However, there is still a point in bringing this redundancy to the fore, because it is the connection style of the code itself which is revealed thereby and because an inversion of the code awakens us to other possibilities (of seeing and doing things). The stricture of a current connectability (Anschlussfähigkeit) through the positive value of the code sets an inflexible divide between legal and illegal operations as well as between those endowed with rights and those who are not.

Thus, the affiliation to any organised social body (nation, firm, hospital, university, association...) gives a series of rights related to such an affiliation. These rights have to do with, let us say, insurantial coverage of risks undergone while the affiliated member is in formal activity on behalf of the organisation; they have to do with the defrayment of expenses arising in connection with such an activity; they have to do with participation to collective decision making through voting and public expression of opinion, etc. Such rights are obviously rational and functionally indispensable. They logically constitute a coherent set consistent with the whole of law and harmonious with the felt-rightness determining normative expectations.

There is, however, a possibility to turn round such a conception and to approach law from an equally plausible but inverted coding. Such a coding would reverse the logic of cumulative positive connections of legal values and the construction of bright spheres of right where lawfulness is syntax of adjusted rights. Thus, one could start with the consideration that rights are most needed where they are not granted, where people are not or not yet in positions from which they can claim them. One runs often more frequently and more heavy risks during the stage preceding the rights granting affiliation than afterwards. Expenses are often more necessary and more painfully felt in periods of aspirancy to rights than beyond them. Were the legal coding inverted as to connect operations of the legal system through the negative and not the positive value of the operation, the 'topology' of the legal system would be turned round: lack of right, non existence of right and not right or interference with rights would call on the system to act, not by granting rights but by inhibiting the process of self-feeding legal endowment, that means by preventing the encoding of law by right. The legal system would withdraw from the 'syntactical' domain of rights processing into the subsyntactical one beneath the emergence of right, where legal substance flows, unseizably.

Of course, the coding of the legal system as we know and experience it is not blindly stringent and exclusive. On the contrary, one could claim that the system strives all the time to widen the circles of its right-endowments (Berechtigungen) as to include everybody. Universal inclusion is the *telos* of the legal system by means of its coupling with the political system and of its coding by right ascription. The endeavour of the legal system in its function as a secondary coding (Zweitcodierung) of the political one is to go to meet all possible aspirations to right, to discover them, identify them and fulfil them. In this sense, lack of right is present in the complex setting of the legal code in its coupling with the political code. Such a coupling gives the legal system, for sure, a highly expansive and paradoxical dynamics: it has to create rights where there are none, but where there should be or where systemic consistency would require them.[29] However, the inversion of the code is quite a real transformation of the comprehension of the system. It is beyond and outside the system that law is most needed and this means that a depository of legal substance lies outside the system. To encounter more legal substance – a substance not totally engulfed by it –, the system must invert its coding and displace its centre of gravity or its point of observation. Where blanks appeared, dots have to be supplemented and where dots were, blanks have to replace and to erase them. Law would have to disinterest itself from right as such or to consider it the non-interesting, secondary, subordinated domain of its operation. The system is namely what is already sheltered, already within reach of coding. It is screened from the radical risk of being beyond the interference of any coding. The system is the syntax, the open existence and operation 'under the sun' of a recourse. The legal system is rational, manifest, discursive, solar. The confidence in it, which is a moment of its own operation, is so overwhelming that the tensions with its shadow are believed to be deferrable to itself and to be reducible by itself. The inversion of the code would turn the attention of the system to its internal outside (so to say) and to listen sharply to what is beneath right, where legal orientation is effective but not formal.

Autopoietic systems are locally operative, self-centred totalities with no windows opening upon an outside. Luhmann's thesis is that they can only either disintegrate from the inside on their own autopoietical terms, or be destroyed physically from the outside. The analysis of the derivative character of autopoiesis of social communication shows that forces are applying to them from an outside which is consubstantial to them. These

[29]This is partly the object of the research on juridification (Verrechtiluchung) and its paradoxes. Indicative of the interest of the juridical theory for these subjects are Zacher and Teubner (1987) and Teubner (1987).

autopoiesis operate with distinctions that cannot exclude only the Other, but leave some of the Same outside. The fact that they function in spite of this is the expression of the vulnerability of their intelligence and the exposure of their efficiencies.

The specificity of legal autopoiesis

We have seen that neither operative closure nor hyperclosure can protect autopoietic systems of communication from their own adventitiousness. I would like to show now that among the variety of social functions that have reached autopoiesis in the processing of the fundamental dimension of meaning each of them embodies, law has a particular status. My thesis is that a certain generalised comprehension of law delivers a paradigm of each and any projection of meaning and its condensation in a system of social communication. Such a generalised concept of law appears in a very specific type of theoretical reflection, namely what one can call the paradoxology of law. Starting from there, I shall work out the generalised concept and show how a protolegal problematic emerges around any observation (i.e. meaning projection) and its gestures of distinction, separation and exclusion involved in the corroboration of meaning and its condensation to a systemic field of practice.[30]

Luhmann's legal theory and sociology are grounded in the most central assumptions of his general theory. As we have seen, Luhmannian protosociology hosts a broad critique of ontology and an extremely developed post-ontological prototheory of meaning and meaning production. Within the frame of such a theory any objectivity (*quid*) is understood as the correlate of a particular, fundamentally contingent and improbable mode (*quomodo*) of observation.[31] Meaning and its ontologised correlates ('things') are the results of operations of distinction which always belong to an indefinite pool of equally possible alternative distinctions. Because of their fundamental contingency distinctions can be assimilated to decisions. Decisions are operations which enforce separation between the decided and the non decided. They have something to do with power and arbitrariness. Each decision/distinction raises the question of its own legitimacy: by what 'right' is such a distinction to be drawn and not another.

---

[30]A much more detailed exposition of the problem is my 'Die Grundparadoxie des Rechts' (Clam, 2000 d). My angle of approach here is however different.

[31]On this problematic, see the most pregnant exposition of 'Identität – was oder wie?' in Luhmann (1990a: 14-30).

Luhmann shows the way for the generalisation of the concept of law (or right) which associates the elementary operation of any meaning processing with the problematic of right and power. He enlarges the problematic of radical contingency as to engulf both the cognitive and the normative dimension of being and thought and to fuse them into a sole originary dimension. A legitimate distinction would be a true and a right one. Since no distinction can be ultimately legitimated, both truth and right appear as factitious. A pretension to truth must prove its right and finds only the originary violence of an arbitrary distinction. On the other side, any distinction and order have to be distinguished as to their legitimacy. Meaning and order cannot crystallise if they are not 'justified'. The violence at the origin of meaning and order requires the right to conserve them. Right and violence are definitively entangled. This is the most plastic version of the paradox of law. Plato, Pascal and Benjamin have given it a classical expression. Contemporary philosophers and sociologists like Derrida, Bourdieu and Luhmann have taken this expression as a reference for their efforts to cope with the deepening of the paradox under the new conditions of late modern thought and sociality (Clam, 2000d).

If we turn back now to the conception of an autopoiesis of law as we have discussed it, we would have to balance its derivative character with that of the generality of its paradox. The paradox of generalised law is not one among others, but a paradigm of the paradoxity of any order of meaning. Although the generative paradox of the legal system is the one linked to the specialised meaning of law after its differentiation from its universal understanding, its paradox retains something from the fundamental level at which law (specific concept) and right (generalised concept) are entangled. The legal system is built and accomplishes its autopoiesis on the ground of a strong reference to empowerment and justification (rendering the ambiguous German concept of Berechtigung). No other system has such an internal relationship to the most drastic embodiment of contingency, namely violence. The political system is exclusively linked to power and non power as its code values, and does not incorporate the fundamental paradox of just(ified) power. The same applies to all other systems who are all entangled in what appears to be partial paradoxes in difference to the fundamental paradox of law-and-violence.[32] Legal autopoiesis is not only crucial because it is the autopoiesis upon which the normative stability and the congruence of social expectancies come to rest. It is crucial because its operative processes are processes of validation of rights or of 'granting rights' (Berechtigung). All claims to

[32]The differentiation between 'Teilparadoxien' and 'Grundparadoxie' is introduced in Clam (2000d).

legitimisation and validation as general claims to entitlement flow into the legal system to establish an order of precedence between them. The legal system brokers the mass of social expectancies and formalises the dominance of certain meaning projections (Sinnentwürfe) within societies. The judicial process reflects the society wide fluid consenses and is the site where such fluidity is at the same time promoted and contained. What is circulating in the networks and the institutions of the legal system is legal validity as such (Luhmann, 1993: 98, 466). Legal validity, in its turn, embodies the circulation of arguments, as devices to enhance the validity of meaning projections, within social communication in general (Luhmann, 1993: 338-406).

With the 'positivisation of law' (Positivierung des Rechts) achieved in the course of the 19th century, the legal system reaches its operative closure (Luhmann, 1987: 207ff.). This is the reflection of the fact that normativity has ceased definitively to be a 'native' component of meaning as such. Under conditions of metaphysical (onto-logical) thinking, be and ought (Sein and Sollen) were not separable. The gap opened between both by critical thinking liberated nature from teleology, but left the subject (as the free author of a moral practice) under the domination of native normativity. The complete withdrawal of human practice – and thereby of the realm of social expectancies as such – away from such an apriorical validation of a unitary normative-cognitive structure of meaning, led to the autonomisation and priorisation of the cognitive posture in personal and collective world perceptions. It is the time of the advent of values as 'Wertnehmungen' (perceptions of value) existing in parallel with 'Wahrnehmungen' (perceptions of being)[33] and conceived as adjunctions, superadditions to a basic ontological substance. Values are, in such a scheme, structurally supervening moments to an inelastic underlying objectivity. They appear as (culturally) variable constructions and projections of normative meaning upon a universal substrate. Even at the climax of the constructivist questioning of the solidity and universality of such a substrate leading to a relativisation of the validity of exact and experimental science itself, 'valuations' (Wertungen) of human practice (i.e. ethical representations) are still perceived as more relative and more variable than the assumptions of sense perception and the scientific imaging of the physical world.

The asymmetrical weighting of cognitive and normative constructions – even within the post-ontological framing of science and ethos – strengthens the tendency to positivise law and to round off the operative closure of the legal system. That means that the normative components of meaning have

[33]This is the terminology of Max Scheler (1966). Scheler vindicates however an originary apriorical status for 'Wertnehmungen'.

to withdraw from any meaning projection, or have to be formulated explicitly in order to purify social discourses from subreptice (ideological) biases. The counterpart of such a process is the building of specialised ethical discourses and the deepening of the functional differentiation of a normative subsystem. Since morality cannot condense in such a system because of its diffuse discursive character, its fundamental relatedness to inner conviction and its structural repugnance to institutionalisation, the whole of the formalisable normative substance of social communication comes to be concentrated in the legal system – which however, being only derivatively autopoietical, cannot totalise it in its own act.

The legal system assumes the formal transposition of worldly facts, whose cognitive approach can only yield a value free imaging, into normative issues. Worldly facts[34] have an impact on social interests and enter thus communication as facts that make a difference for various individuals and groups. The normative problematics is brought forth with such differing evaluations which will need a specific normative processing. Variant or conflicting evaluations cannot be cognitively equated and decided. They inevitably generate colliding claims seeking formalisation as pretensions to rights and prerogatives as well as to effective realisation by executor entitlements. They are structurally associated with the problematics of the empowering, the 'violent' (legally paradoxical) prevailing of an interpretation over the other. This sharpens the closure of the legal system in the sense that cognitive claims as soon as they impact on social interests have to be formalised and transposed into the conceptuality of law. While no difference (distinction) can make a difference without motivating an interest and impacting thus social communication, no cognitive imaging of worldly facts is indifferent and wholly remote from (paradoxically) legal empowerment. Adding to this that no empowerment can, within the frame of a functionally differentiated society, escape legal positive construction, the conclusion that presses itself upon us is that the legal system with its paradox and its autopoiesis becomes the forum where social communication negotiates the empowering of any socially confirmed representation.

At the post-ontological level of heightened legal positivisation, the closure of the normative sphere approaches its fully circular completion. The premises of positivisation itself, namely the mutual autonomy of the normative and the cognitive spheres undergo questioning and revision. In

---

[34]Such facts can also be facts of communication, i.e. acts of valuation, normative judgments... The observation of normative communication from a cognitive point a view (that is for instance the psychological observation of affective or other valuations) does not make any difficulty.

effect, while on the one side any validity claims, be they cognitive or normative, seem to imply at the end the operation of a paradoxically (generalized) legal prevailing,[35] no normative processing of any such claims can be sheltered from an intensive cognitivisation of all its components. Normative representations are cognitivised in the sense that normative variations occur under the impact of the knowledge the cognitive systems produce and diffuse into social communication. Value free imaging of various objectivities – let's say of biological facts – changes the normative representations and attitudes towards them. Moreover, the inquisitive modes of thinking begin to pervade the normative type of assertion, leading to an undermining of the very normativity of such assertions. In effect, the normative posture is in its very essence a counterfactual maintaining of specific expectancies and meaning projections, in spite of their eventual non-implementation by social action. The non-observation of a norm by an actor does not invalidate it for social action in general, but calls upon precisely that type of posture which we call (with Luhmann) the normative posture.

The new situation is however that of a cognitivisation of the norm itself, of the cognitive revisitation of its terms (what is life – as a biological process – or crime as deviant behaviour...?), the transformation of its categories (retribution as reinsertion and education), the questioning of evidence (denial of difference versus its recognition and promotion...). Such a cognitivisation increases in the domain of law the weight of cognitive types of argument, of expertise in judicial procedures – replacing sometimes informally the judge by the expert – and leads to the emergence of the ethical expert whose mission is, as a 'scientific' expert, the cognitive elucidation of normative issues. At this point operative closure reaches a critical level where the normative as well as the cognitive systems must re-introduce the normative-cognitive distinction into their own processing and thus ground their identity upon the re-entry of their constituting difference. This is in Luhmann's theory the decisive point of operative closure as self-continence of a generative distinction.

The autopoiesis of law is thus launched by the process of positivisation and reveals its full closure with the reflection of the premises of positivisation within the positivised system itself. The autonomy of law is achieved at a first level with the withdrawal of native normativity from worldly factuality. It reaches a paradoxical peak with the revealing of the constructed and socially interested nature of cognitive, in principle value free imaging of 'what is the case' in the world. The legal system, after

[35]In the active transitive sense of: letting prevail.

absorbing the whole formalisable normative substance of social communication, becomes the system answering for the existing interpretation of reality. Such an interpretation necessarily includes and excludes, advantages and disadvantages views, interests, individuals and groups. Law uncovers its own paradox as the entangled ordering of right and violence. Full paradoxical circularity is attained with the awareness that specific normative processing of normative issues relies very heavily upon cognitive elucidation and argument. This second entanglement of cognition and normation brings the operative closure of law to inflexible autopoiesis.

Glossary

Cognitivism: The term is used in a generic sense. It is thus not restricted to any particular concept of cognitive science as such. It designates the general style of thought that does not come to a halt by supposedly ultimate data of experience and understanding, but breaks through them to more elementary calculatory and logico-modal processes. Evidence, consciousness, social bond may well be ultimate givens of intuition and intuitive thought; they are however complex derivative and improbable products of a combination of calculatory or distinctory processes operating on a more profound level and incorporating a number of non intuitive, imaginary or non thinkable components (like imaginary, irrational numbers, falsehood integrating hypotheses, virtualising devices...). Luhmann's theory has a cognitivist scheme, which however is not oriented towards a reduction of the given to strictly calculatory processes, but rather to the reconstruction of the system building processes beyond their intuitive basis. It is directed towards the comprehension of these processes as autopoietical ones born out of the overcoming of fundamental paradoxes by means of virtualising devices.

Meaning: Luhmann's meaning theory is primarily inspired by Edmund Husserl's ideas on the structuration of any intentional-attentional field into a noematic thematic foreground and a background horizon of co-posited passive aperceptions. This horizon is a potential of possibilities of confirmation or invalidation, enrichment or impoverishment, fulfilment or deferment of the noematic theme and the perceptive, optative, acquisitive, scientific... intentions which are directed on it. Such a theoretical disposition entails a close linkage of the theory of meaning with the model categories of possibility, potentiality, virtuality. To say of something that it has a meaning is to say that it is the core of an open series of possibilities, the knot of an open horizon of references to other neighbouring and distant meanings, the kernel of an aura of potential transformations. Meaning is thus both, or as Luhmann says, the unity of the difference of both: the core and the series, the knot and the horizon, the kernel and the aura. This builds the transition towards another theory, the logic of forms developed by George Spencer Brown. The fundamental idea in this logic is once again the structuring of any 'indication' of something along the lines of a 'distinction' between the indicated inside space or state of the form and the 'unmarked' outside of it. The unmarked state has a striking and a very deep similarity with Husserl's intentional and noematic horizon. Both theories posit their primary objects as acts of intending or indicating, that means structurally as events or operations. These events are connected to a series which is as open as its horizon itself. Noematic entities (Husserl), forms (Spencer Brown), systems (Luhmann) are contingent processes whose making (condensation and confirmation) is more improbable than their unmaking (non emergence, dilution). To be complete my presentation must mention two more theories which are build into Luhmann's semantics: the neo-cybernetic theory of observation and Fritz Heider's theory of medium and form. They both represent further elaborations on the structure of bipolar open unity of the definite and the indefinite implying an inexhaustible potential of unceasing new references.

Ontology (also: onto-logy): I use the term ontology in the sense that is given to in post-Heideggerian (or of what one can call post-ontological) philosophising. Ontology in such an understanding is an 'epochal' concept relating to a type of thought that has dominated the whole of western thinking until it could be subverted by a critique that could cast anew the question of being as such. The main principle of ontological thought is the position of an outward Reality which is mirrored by thought in representations that are true when they are in adequacy to it. The fixity, transcendence and order of Reality determine a specific logic of thought and a mode of truth searching. Luhmann's theory stands more decidedly and completely than any other on a post-ontological ground. For it, reality is neither fixed, nor transcendent, nor unitarily ordered; it is processually flowing, contingently dependent upon socially projected distinctions, and its orders are plural, autopoietical and not unifiable (heterarchical). In Luhmann's terminology onto-logical reality corresponds (mainly, but still partially) to what he calls 'onticity': ontic is any state of being that is there as it is. Onticity contrasts with virtuality or potentiality. It is blind for the potencies lying in reality as its possibilities to be other than it is, and to be that on an equally functional level (that means: without losses in terms of what it does or represents). Luhmann tries in a direct contradiction to old European ontology to unearth the dynamics of alternativity, mobility and enrichment of reality through possibility. He plays upon the possible variation of the cognitive distinctions projected upon reality and structuring its understandings. He shows how such enrichments are operating at all levels in our complex societies and tries to reconstruct the logics of virtualisation underlying most of their cognitive and normative orders. All these conversions of the ways of thought are part of a presently observable global convergence towards a de-ontologisation of western culture in all domains of theory and practice.

Operation: This crucial concept of Luhmann's theory of autopoiesis is difficult to understand as long as one still adheres to onto-logical habits of thought. To say it more pregnantly: the emergence of a capacity to think on post-ontological grounds is assessed by the capacity to figure 'beings' as constituted exclusively by operations. The apprenticeship and acquisition of Luhmannian systems theory is nothing else than an exercise in operativist thinking, evacuating all remnants of a world view that understood any being as substance, essence, object. The negation: 'there is nothing in a system but operations' de-substantialises, de-essentialises, in a word de-ontologises any position of being. Operations are acts of distinction (Unterscheidung) connecting to each other in processes whose concatenating continuity maintain the distinction in operation, i.e. maintain the distinguished or indicated object of the process in being. There is no object beside the operation, before or after it. Identity (objective identity) is a derivative entity of active, operative differentiation of a system value (an indicated something) against the background of all non-indicated values constituting the horizon of potentiality of the indicated one.

References

Berg, de H. and Prangel, M. (eds), (1995), *Differenzen. Systemtheorie zwischen Dekonstruktion und Konstruktivismus*, Francke,Tübingen.

Berg, de H. and Schmidt, J.F.K. (eds), (2000), *Rezeption und Reflexion. Zur Resonanz der Systemtheorie Niklas Luhmanns außerhalb der Soziologie*, Suhrkamp, Frankfurt.

Clam, J. (2000 a), 'System's Sole Constituent, the Operation. Clarifying a Central Concept of Luhmannian Theory', in 43 *Acta Sociologica, Special Issue on Niklas Luhmann*, 1/2000, pp. 63-79.

Clam, J. (2000 b), 'Unbegegnete Theorie: Zur Luhmann-Rezeption in der Philosophie', forthcoming in H. de Berg and J. F.K. Schmidt (eds), *Rezeption und Reflexion. Zur Resonanz der Systemtheorie Niklas Luhmanns außerhalb der Soziologie*, Suhrkamp, Frankfurt.

Clam, J. (2000 c), 'Was heißt: Sich an Differenz statt an Identität orientieren? Zur De-ontologisierung in Philosophie und Sozialwissenschaft', forthcoming in J. Weiss (ed.), *Die Daseinsanalytik Martins Heideggers und die Kritik der soziologischen Vernunft,* Konstanzer Universitätsverlag, Konstanz.

Clam, J. (2000 d), 'Die Grundparadoxie des Rechts und ihre Ausfaltung. Beitrag zu einer Analytik des Paradoxen', in G. Teubner (ed.), *Zeitshcrift für Rechtssoziologie, Sonderheft 2000*, (forthcoming).

Foerster von, H. (1993), *Wissen und Gewissen: Versuch einer Brücke*, (edited by Siegried J. Schmidt), Suhrkamp, Frankfurt.

Fuchs, P. (1993), *Moderne Kommunikation: Zur Theorie des operativen Displacements*, Suhrkamp, Frankfurt.

Habermas, J. (1988), *Der philosophische Diskurs der Moderne: Zwölf Vorlesungen*, Suhrkamp, Frankfurt.

Husserl, E. (1922), *Ideen zu einer reinen Phänomenologie und phänomenologischen Philosophie. Allgemeine einführung in die Phänomenologie [Ideen I] (2nd edition)*, Niemeyer, Tübingen.

Kojève, A. (1994), *Esquisse dune phénoménologie du droit*, Gallimard, Paris.

Latour, B. (1988), 'The Politics of Explanation: an Alternative', in S. Woolgar (ed.), *Knowledge and Reflexivity : new frontiers in the sociology of knowledge*, Sage, London, pp.155-176.

Luhmann, N. (1970), *Soziologische Aufklärung 1: Aufsätze zur Theorie sozialer Systeme (6th edition)*,Westdeutscher Verlag, Opladen.

Luhmann, N. (1971), *Politische Planung: Aufsätze zur Soziologie von Politik und Verwaltung*, Westdeutscher Verlag, Opladen.

Luhmann, N. (1981), *Soziologische Aufklärung 3*, Westdeutscher Verlag, Opladen.

Luhmann, N. (1987), *Rechtssoziologie (3rd edition)*, Westdeutscher Verlag, Opladen.

Luhmann, N. (1988), *Erkenntnis als Konstruktion*, Benteli, Bern.

Luhmann, N. (1990a), *Soziologische Aufklärung 5: Konstruktivistische Perpspektiven*, Westdeutscher Verlag, Opladen.

Luhmann, N., (1990b), 'Sthenographie', in N. Luhmann, N. (ed. cum aliis), *Beobachter: Konvergenz der Erkenntnisteorien*, Wilhelm Fink, Munchen, pp. 119-138.

Luhmann, N. (1993), *Das Recht der Gesellschaft*, Suhrkamp, Frankfurt.

Luhmann, N. (1995), *Soziologische Aufklärung 6*, Westdeutscher Verlag, Opladen.

Luhmann, N. (1997), *Die Gesellschaft der Gesellschaft*, Suhrkamp, Frankfurt.

Luhmann, N. (2000), 'Die Rückgabe des zwölften Kamels: Zum Sinn einer soziologischen Analyse des Rechts', in G. Teubner (ed.), *Zeitshcrift für Rechtssoziologie, Sonderheft 2000*, (fortcoming).

Nassehi, A. (1991), *Die Zeit der Gesellschaft*, Westdeutscher Verlag, Opladen.

Rottleuthner, H. (1987), 'Les métaphores biologiques dans la pensée juridique', in *Archives de Philosophie du Droit Tome 31 (Le système juridique)*, Paris, pp. 215- 244.

Scheler, M. (1966), *Der Formalismus in der Ethik und die materiale Wertethik. Neuer Versuch der Grundlegung eines ethischen Personalismus*, 5th. ed., Francke, Bern.

Spencer Brown, G. (1969), *Laws of Form*, Allen and Unwin, London.

Staeheli, U. (1997), *Signifying Failures: A Discourse Theoretical Reading of Niklas Luhmann's System Theory*, PhD Thesis, Essex Aug.

Teubner, G., (ed.), (1987), *Juridification of Social Spheres. A Comparative Analysis in the Areas of Labor, Corporate, Antitrust and Social Welfare Law*, De Gruyter, Berlin.

Teubner, G. (1999), 'Ökonomie der Gabe - Positivität der Gerechtigkeit: Gegenseitige Heimsuchungen von System und *différance*', in A. Koschorke und C. Vismann (eds), *System - Macht - Kultur: Probleme der Systemtheorie,* Berlin Akademie Verlag, Berlin, pp. 199-212.

Weber, M. (1988), 'Die protestantische Ethik und der Geist des Kapitalismus', in M. Weber, *Gesammelte Aufsätze zur Religionssoziologie I*, Mohr, Tübingen, pp. 1-236.

4 The Representation of Law's Autonomy in Autopoiesis Theory

ROGER COTTERRELL

What is at stake in current debates in socio-legal literature about the nature of law's 'autonomy'? The first part of this paper tries to sketch an answer to this question. Then the remainder of the paper will, as its main focus, suggest some strengths and weaknesses of autopoiesis theory's particular effort to portray the autonomy of law as discourse. This theory has stimulated attention to a very important matter - the nature of the discursive structuring of legal doctrine - which modern legal sociology has neglected for too long. Nevertheless, autopoiesis theory has been much criticised. This paper restates some criticisms and tries to extend them. The argument to be developed is that, despite the ambition and power of autopoiesis theory, some of its most important claims about the nature of law as discourse or communicative practice are misleading and even harmful as guides for the progress of socio-legal studies unless qualified to such an extent as to remove much of the theory's distinctiveness.

Debating legal autonomy

The question of how far and in what way law might be 'autonomous' as a normative or discursive field was neglected for a long time in sociology of law. Indeed, legal sociology found space for its own academic existence mainly by denying any interest in identifying this autonomy, implying the insignificance of the matter and leaving it to jurists. Even when Marxist legal theory, imported into social studies of law, postulated law's 'relative autonomy' (Jessop, 1992), the key word was probably 'relative', rather than 'autonomy'. The object was to preserve an idea of law's ultimate explicability in social analysis in terms of something (for example, class or productive relations) other than the distinctive practice lawyers typically understand it to be, and to do this in the face of doubts as to whether such a strategy was really possible in explaining specific legal decisions, doctrines, procedures or institutions.

At the other end of the theoretical spectrum, Durkheimian views treated as self-evident the postulate that law - though having certain (contingent) organisational characteristics - is a branch of morality as social regulation (Cotterrell, 1999), and impossible to consider in isolation from more general and fundamental social phenomena of which it forms part. On this view, characteristics that make law 'autonomous' are merely provisional identifiers of a sociological field. Even Max Weber - focusing strongly on modern law's formal rationality as doctrine - closely linked this, for purposes of sociological analysis, with the broader empirical phenomena of bureaucratic organisation (Gerth and Mills, 1948: 216; Weber, 1978: 975). Certainly, when law was treated in functional terms its functional distinctiveness might be strongly emphasised (Bredemeier, 1962; Parsons, 1977; 174-6). But functional distinctiveness seems a different matter from the normative or discursive autonomy that lawyers often attribute to law.

Thus, despite a focus of classic literature on legal doctrine and lawyers' practices, most legal sociology treated as self-evident that law was to be analysed in terms of something (politics, morality, economics, administrative structure, professionalisation, disputing behaviour, etc.) other than the distinctive discursive features lawyers typically attribute to it. Modern empirical sociology of law, from the mid-twentieth century, established its claim to offer useful knowledge largely by ignoring lawyers' professional learning. It set in place a sharp division of labour to legitimise a field of research entirely its own. Largely avoiding doctrinal concerns, legal sociology mainly focused on law as behaviour. At the extreme, sociology has sometimes been considered as merely seeing its own established disciplinary concerns reflected in law (Ewald, 1995; Cotterrell, 2001).

In fact, the refusal to address most questions about law's discursive autonomy allowed socio-legal studies to achieve much. It enabled socio-legal scholars temporarily to avoid the thickets of jurisprudence, and to use research methods that allowed fresh understandings of legal practices and institutions, radically different from those typical of lawyers. Legal doctrinal debates might collapse in casuistry, circularity or deadlocked rhetoric, or be terminated only by the fiat of judicial or legislative authority. Behavioural researches gave (and continue to give) insights into law, as a mechanism of government and social control, that may be more important, practically and theoretically, than decades of lawyers' doctrinal interpretation.

Yet the very success (and, therefore, increasing ambition) of socio-legal research has now made the old, convenient division of labour between jurists and legal sociologists impossible to sustain. That division depended ultimately on acceptance of some kind of 'internal/external' distinction in legal studies. Typically, the jurist would be the unchallenged 'insider' in the interpretive community of law; the social scientist's role would be as 'outside' observer of behaviour and institutional structures. But as socio-legal research has extended its scope it has begun to insist on the inadequacy of lawyers' typical general understandings of law. The so-called external perspective has refused to stay external; the barbarians have entered the citadel! Social inquiries about law have shown the inadequacy of legal philosophy's perspectives in interpreting contemporary changes in the conditions and character of legal practices and regulation; they have begun to challenge juristic perceptions of law's bases of authority and jurisdiction and of the nature and conditions of its interpretive practices.

To take only a few themes: studies of transnational legal developments raise issues about the location of law's interpretive communities, and of the centres of gravity of legal authority (Dezalay and Garth, 1996; Petersen and Zahle, 1995; La Torre, 1999; Teubner 1997). They portray legal authority, in certain increasingly important contexts, as permanently contested, no longer to be analysed adequately in the terms of traditional jurisprudence. Again, serious questions arise as to what (if anything) legal autonomy should be taken to mean in a world in which state sovereignty is an increasingly problematic concept (MacCormick, 1993; Jackson, 1999) and regulation takes many forms, many of them barely supervised by the state. Regionalism, multiculturalism, separatist movements, devolution, international human rights regimes, proliferating cross-border regulation and transnational financial and economic systems all provoke queries as to how the social context of law is now best to be understood, what law's typical jurisdictional scope is coming to be, and what are the ultimate bases of its authority in the contemporary world (Santos, 1995; Cotterrell, 1998). As will appear, this links with broader issues about the nature of participation and interpretation in law.

Ideas of legal autonomy are closely related to the concept of an internal/external dichotomy. Indeed, insistence on law's autonomy (whatever this might mean), always implies the acceptance of some version of this dichotomy. Legal sociologists content to see themselves as 'outside' observers of law, accepted, at least implicitly, that there was an 'inside' beyond their reach, even if it might be regarded as (relatively or absolutely) insignificant sociologically (Black, 1989).

Many legal philosophers also accept the importance of an internal/external dichotomy. But their use of the dichotomy is usually diametrically opposed to that of the legal sociologist. For legal philosophy, in general, an 'internal' view of law, however that view is defined, is far from insignificant. Indeed, it is often seen as giving access to the centre of legal reality, that which makes law meaningful as a normative or interpretive realm. Thus, an 'external' description cannot capture the reality of law as a social phenomenon unless it somehow incorporates - or combines with - the 'internal' understanding typical of participants in legal reasoning. Some legal philosophers go further: this insiders' world is the entirety of law; law cannot be grasped at all except in terms of its protocols (Dworkin, 1986). Law is thus the possession of a community of interpreters. One must be a part of this world of interpretation, a participant in it, to have any understanding of law's reality. One need not be emotionally or morally committed as an insider, although one might be.

For much contemporary legal philosophy, an internal perspective of some kind is the marker of law's autonomy. It indicates the gateway that must be passed through in order to enter the world of law in some real or full sense. Thus, the Dworkinian interpretive community of law is the community of insiders (judges, legal philosophers, lawyers and - to a somewhat indeterminate extent (Dworkin, 1978: ch. 8; Dworkin, 1985: ch. 4) - ordinary lay citizens) who reason with law and subscribe to the legal system as their universe of practical reason and social evaluation in matters of shared public concerns. For Hartian positivism, the internal view of rules is the view of someone who understands the rules with a critical reflective attitude as guides to conduct. It is the view of players of a game, of people committed to playing by the rules or who, at least, can think about rules as if they have such a commitment to them (Hart, 1994).

The distinction between Hart's and Dworkin's very different views of what it means to be 'inside' law is very significant in considering different ways in which an internal/external dichotomy might be used. Hart's legal theory, concerned with understanding law as a social phenomenon of rules, treats external as well as internal views as necessary to this understanding. The 'external' sociological observer gains and uses important knowledge of law from a behavioural perspective. No doubt this can be combined in complex, variable ways with 'internal' insight into rule-governed practices. For Dworkin, by contrast, understanding law can only be understanding within legal discourse. One must join the discourse in order to comprehend law. For Hart, internal and external perspectives complement each other to constitute complete legal understanding; for Dworkin they are separate, different understandings, hence not necessary to each other. The sociologists (behavioural observers of law) 'have so far been barred from competing' (cf. Honoré, 1987: 32) in the game of legal interpretation (as though they need some permission to do so). On this view, insiders and outsiders simply cannot engage in communication about law. Law's autonomy has become a postulated autonomy of discourse. If law is a closed discourse of some kind, it follows that the internal/external divide is absolute. Either one communicates within this discourse, or not.

Questionable and very important assumptions are, however, being made here. To accept legal autonomy and the related internal/external dichotomy in these terms one must first accept the idea that law is or can be a distinctive discourse. To make this idea rigorous one must specify what is meant by a discourse, what the characteristics of a discourse are, what would define its distinctiveness. One must ask in what sense and under what conditions law is identifiable as a discourse, what must be taken to follow from this and why. One must ask what requires us to accept that it is a single discourse, or that all who participate in law do, indeed, participate in it as a single discourse. Many other questions present themselves.

The point is that they are ultimately empirical questions; questions about how people communicate with each other in relation to the enterprises of government and social control that we term law. Ultimately they are questions about what it means to participate in law (understood as these enterprises), what different ways of participating there can be, and also what social distinctions can be usefully drawn in general and abstract terms between participating and observing. Sociological analysis might lead us to ask, indeed, whether any firm separation is to be drawn between participation and observation. The lawyer participating in courtroom argument, and in a trial process more generally, relies on observation of the behaviour of others (judge, jury, witnesses) in the courtroom as well as a more diffuse general knowledge of typical workings of the legal system (typical behavioural patterns, institutional structures, processes and procedures). No lawyer, or other social actor, can participate without observation, or knowledge founded on other people's observations. Equally, the observer is necessarily in some sense a participant. It is hard to imagine anyone functioning consistently and permanently as a Hartian 'external observer' of legal rules, without any (probably considerable) normative understanding (Shiner, 1992: 149-50; Waluchow, 1994: 27-9). Observation and participation continually intertwine in actual experience. What Michel Van der Kerchove and François Ost (1994: 9) call a 'moderate' external point of view (which necessarily also appreciates the internal view) is surely complemented by a 'moderate' internal point of view which necessarily observes in order to participate.

What is it to participate? Do scholars of Roman law today participate in any sense in a legal system that no longer exists? They may participate mentally no less than do jurists interpreting the rules of their own contemporary legal order. But they are also observers of a legal regime that no longer regulates social action. Do they constitute part of an interpretive community with the long dead jurists of Roman times? Or are they merely observers of history? What, indeed, constitutes membership in an interpretive community? What are the qualifications for membership? Can there be many different qualifications - for example, being a practising judge or lawyer, a citizen living 'under law', a jurist studying a (perhaps defunct) system, a sociologist or historian seeking understanding of legal consciousness?

What, as a practical matter, defines an interpretive community, and defines positions within it? In law, political authority may determine relative status in such a community (for example, giving appellate courts more weight in legal interpretation than lower courts). But so may economic or other power (for example, affecting status between nation states or other corporate actors operating within transnational regimes of commercial law); or intellectual reputation (between judges of the same court, or scholars of the same legal field). How do these and other determinants interrelate in practice? And what determines precedence or relative status between legal interpretive communities where several such communities exist in the same society or social group?

The questions are unending and, in many cases provoked by changes in social experience in a world in which questions about the nature of interpretation, jurisdiction and authority in law are becoming increasingly complex. I list some of them here solely to suggest how deeply problematic is the internal/external dichotomy in relation to legal thought and scholarship (Cotterrell, 1998). Participation and observation of law may require a wide range of variable, shifting perspectives and practices. To speak of these as 'internal' or 'external' is meaningless without specifying: internal or external to what? And there is surely no single 'what'! The same issues make the idea of law's autonomy puzzling. What does it mean to say law is autonomous when law is taken to exist in so many different interpretive settings and sites and when participation in law can take so many forms? Today socio-legal studies can no longer leave lawyers and jurists to theorise about law's autonomy, doing so in a way that may be conservative and at least partially outdated in terms of contemporary legal experience. If law is characterised as a discourse or interpretive practice it is not automatically to be assumed that it is best understood as a unitary discourse or practice: the shared, unchallenged possession of a single interpretive community. Nor does characterising law in this way necessarily tell us anything at all about its purported autonomy.

Nevertheless, despite all complexities, the great power of law as discourse (or rather, as a variety of discourses) has to be clearly recognised. Various theories of legal ideology have strongly emphasised this aspect of law's power. And critical legal studies have built on the advances of some such theories by stressing that law constitutes, through its discursive power, social relations. But theories of legal ideology are not necessarily also theories of legal doctrine or legal interpretation. Something more is needed, which hermeneutic approaches have tried to provide. But these often fail to focus on the sheer diversity of settings, sites and contexts of legal interpretation and discourse, referred to above. More empirically oriented studies of institutional practices are required to identify this diversity. And these studies have to overcome, in one way or another, the old analytical distinctions between participation and observation which, for reasons given earlier, are often unhelpful if the diversity of legal experience is to be recognised.

Autopoietic law?

On one view, all of this leads to autopoiesis theory, which has rightly been regarded as among the most important recent theoretical developments relevant to legal sociology. But it is interesting that autopoiesis theory seems to have entered legal scholarship much more as a response to a perceived weakness of legal sociology than as an expression of the increasing power and ambition of the socio-legal enterprise, stressed above. In part this theory responds to claims about misguided, ignorant or inefficient social uses of law (excessive juridification and the 'regulatory trilemma') (Teubner, 1987: 21-7). In part, it claims also to remedy a purported inability of legal sociology to predict and explain regulatory failure or the unanticipated consequences of regulatory activities (the long-recognised 'social limits of law') (see, for instance, Allott, 1980; Pennock and Chapman, 1974).

In addressing these matters, autopoiesis theory presupposes a very different agenda for socio-legal studies from that suggested above. I have presented socio-legal scholarship as needing to engage with legal discourse to take further legal sociology's insights which have already added much to those of juristic legal scholarship but now highlight the need for new theories of law in a changing world of jurisdiction, legal interpretation and legal authority. By contrast, autopoiesis theory presumes a legal sociology on the defensive, that must atone for its predictive and analytical failures by finally paying obeisance to law's discursive power.

Certainly autopoiesis theory applied in socio-legal studies is very important because of what it attempts. It takes extremely seriously the problem of characterising what lawyers may think of as law's autonomy. It reinterprets the internal/external dichotomy in law as a matter of social practice and theorises this in a manner more sophisticated than anything to be found in the modern literature of legal philosophy.

Yet I think that autopoiesis theory suffers from opposite faults from those of the older legal sociology. The latter often paid insufficient attention to the character of legal doctrine and so disabled itself from confronting directly jurists' understandings of law. Not only that, but it failed to understand much of the central social reality of law which resides in its discursive presentation and cognitive ordering of the social world. By contrast, autopoiesis theory tends to *reify* lawyers' (and other orthodox) understandings of law, including, above all, the idea of law's discursive autonomy, the internal/external dichotomy and the metaphor of system as applied to law. Each of these it interprets in a certain way, but treats them largely as givens for social scientific understanding of law, as well as givens of legal experience.

In what way does the theory tend to reify these matters? Autopoiesis theory always stresses contingency. Matters could be different from the way they are. Nothing is pre-ordained in some way theoretically. The theory does not dictate empirical outcomes but claims to offer a way of understanding them. Nevertheless it focusses attention firmly on certain matters and requires that we approach social research with certain presumptions. Law is not inevitably an autopoietic social system of communication, or a self-observing, self-producing and self-reproducing discourse, but in modern conditions, according to the theory, it tends to become such and *functional necessity drives this tendency*. The possibility of thinking of law's relations with other aspects or fields of social life in terms of influence, interpenetration, interdependence and interaction is not ruled out. But it is firmly marginalised in a theory which is oriented to explaining why such linkages are, in contemporary conditions, increasingly implausible and, ultimately, impossible. Hence the idea of law possessing uniform and powerful characteristics given *by its system-character* becomes a theoretical presumption. And because this presumption (and its theoretical elaboration) is the central contribution that the theory appears to offer for legal analysis, it is hard to displace. Perhaps, indeed, the theory must firmly resist its displacement, because to do otherwise would be to cast fundamental doubt on the theory's practical utility. Hence presumed ideas tend to be reified, becoming for the theory a kind of 'reality' about law, which is then presented as the basis for predictions, policies or strategies, and sometimes as an adequate explanation in itself of certain social consequences of legal interventions.

Autopoiesis theory thus tends to treat as the very basis of its analysis what might otherwise be seen as merely contingent objects of analysis. I mean here (as such objects) especially certain ideological constructions - taken for granted ways of understanding legal phenomena that present themselves as 'reality', irrespective of the diversity, complexity and contradictions of empirical experience. Indeed, these constructions purport to provide self-evidently 'correct' characterisations of this experience. They include ideological constructions about law's functions, the 'blind' unguided character of its evolution, the uniform coding of its decisions as autonomous of politics, economics, etc., or its nature as a normatively closed system. Certainly, these constructions may be of great value for purposes of professional (and other) legitimation. But autopoiesis theory seems to present them as sociological necessities, although it recognises that they are the outcome of historical processes. It sees radical system-differentiation as required functionally to deal with the complexity of modern society. Even more fundamentally, this differentiation is ultimately dictated by the theory's claims about the way in which the communication of meaning in modern society is possible at all.

Yet law's apparent system-differentiation might be treated in other ways. It might be seen, in part - *but only in part*, as an aspect of a contingent, often contested and far from consistent (Posner, 1987; Cotterrell, 1995: ch. 3) professional project of lawyers in particular times and places. In other respects, what appears as the system-differentiation of law might be analysed as an aspect of a more general political development of particular societies, perhaps especially linked with the development of liberalism and individualism. Autopoiesis theory might appear to marginalise the difficult task of explaining such matters empirically because it treats law's autonomy (in a specific sense) as the functionally necessary result of evolutionary processes considered analytically apart from quėstions of human agency (Luhmann, 1986: 112).

What, from a different sociological point of view, needs explanation thus risks becoming, for autopoiesis theory, what is taken for granted. In so far as a project for sociology of law arises from the theory, it is surely that of finding means of adjustment to the situation of law's autopoietic system-differentiation and self-reproduction. But the theory assumes this situation because its conception of the nature and conditions of existence of meaning in systems of communication necessarily predicts such a state of affairs. It assumes law's autonomy as a social fact, rather than as, for example, a political and professional aspiration. But all of this is a matter of controversial theoretical deduction rather than empirically-grounded observation.

Autopoiesis theory is valuable to legal sociology because it presents in the starkest way social presuppositions that underlie a certain kind of extreme view of legal autonomy. It characterises legal autonomy not in terms of normative structure or reasoning as in much legal philosophy but in the dynamic terms of systems of communication. Hence it has promised a means of analysing sociologically - in terms of social processes - characteristics of legal doctrine and its elaboration that are familiar to all Western lawyers. Autopoiesis theory presents law's 'rational strength' (Lawson, 1951) as an effect of the intensity of its communications in a seemingly self-reproducing realm of discourse. Law's cognitive openness allows continual responsiveness to stimuli (economic, cultural, scientific, administrative, etc.) that provoke (but do not determine) the creation of new legal decisions and hence legal ideas. At the same time, using its own binary code of legal/illegal (legally right or wrong), it appears to produce decisions from decisions, normative judgments from normative judgments. On this view, law regulates the processes of its own creation (Kelsen, 1989: 71, 221). But law also may appear to provide the materials for its own creation. Law is produced from law, because existing legal discourse provides normative resources that can be recycled - and, in the process, elaborated in ever more complex and detailed forms - into new normative resources.

For those who inhabit the world of academic law, as well as the world of social science, this imagery of professionalised, sophisticated legal discourse is, at least at a certain level of generality, familiar and realistic. It seems initially accurate in its portrayal of some of the intellectually and morally closed-off worlds of professional legal discourse. For law teachers who have devoted much of their careers to trying to break down law's splendid isolation as an intellectual product and encouraging law students to see ways in which legal knowledge depends upon and can be enriched by knowledge fields often considered 'external' to law, autopoiesis theory seems to confirm the reality of barriers to achieving this. It offers an image of law which suggests that legal strategies will be frequently ineffective in regulating 'other systems' such as the economy, or that law will 'resist' or merely ignore the various kinds of scientific or technical knowledge and practice that may confront it. Where these are brought into the courtroom, in juvenile justice or social welfare contexts, or where law is required to confront the understandings of psychology, biology, economics or other sciences as evidence, autopoiesis theory predicts that law will interpret these understandings in its own ways for its own distinctive purposes, treating them merely as 'irritants' (see, for example, King and Piper, 1995). It may be spurred to decisions of some kind, but not necessarily those that seem reasonable or predictable from the standpoint of practitioners of the sciences in question. Autopoiesis theory dramatises our deep disappointment that more cannot be done with law to effect social regulation, that law is too unresponsive to a world of problems urgently requiring regulatory solutions and that when law does act, the results seem frequently tangential or arbitrary in relation to the problems it purports to address.

Most importantly, perhaps, autopoiesis theory dramatises law's 'system character' in a way that is likely to ring true for many lawyers. Law students who come to law initially expecting it to be full of dramas of human interest, its decisions richly coloured with passion and engagement, soon learn that it is an important part of law's regulatory technique to drain away these elements into dry abstraction. Passionate law is controversial law, thus of doubtful acceptability. Law depends, especially in highly pluralistic, complex and rapidly changing societies, on abstraction; a calculated distancing from its specific human settings. In this way it nurtures its 'objectivity' and so its special authority. Yet it must be stressed that this is a strategic distancing. It is required because legal doctrine must give generalised normative meaning to social institutions and relationships while recognising their particularised significance in the subjective experience of those who participate in them. Legal practice relies on its own abstractions, yet cannot carry them beyond a certain point because law's social meaning, and so its ultimate authority, depends on a great diversity of forms of understanding and evaluation over which it has no final control.

Autopoiesis theory's picture of contemporary positive law's apparent autonomy is, in important respects, plausible. But one must ask: what does the theory offer that goes beyond lawyers' practical observation of typical experiences of reasoning with rules where a degree of communicative precision and predictability in regulatory and adjudicative practice is sought? These experiences certainly promote practical efforts to secure some kind of autonomy of legal reasoning and doctrine. Regrettably, I think that much of what the theory offers beyond this is harmful in so far as it is used to guide socio-legal inquiry. I say regrettably, because I much admire, for example, Gunther Teubner's effort to bring new rigour to sociologically-oriented legal theory and to use this theory, built especially on Niklas Luhmann's work, in legal analysis. This is important not least in relation to the theorisation of transnational law, and some central concerns of current comparative law (Teubner, 1997; Teubner 1998; Ladeur, 1999). In the rest of this paper I shall try to explain where, from the standpoint of a legal sociologist, I think that the harm in autopoiesis theory applied to law most clearly lies.

Autopoiesis as explanation?

As suggested earlier, the theory observes key features of law in an initially persuasive manner. In my view it does not, however, offer substantial sociological explanations of these features. Rather, it provides analytical models of them but then *takes the models as a kind of reality in themselves.*

Thus, law's postulated autonomy is modelled in a complex and sophisticated manner in terms of the capacity of law to observe, constitute and ultimately reproduce itself as a system of communications. But Teubner's important general statement of autopoietic legal theory offers no substantial sociological account of the interplay of forces that give rise to this autonomy in particular times and places (Teubner, 1993: ch. 4).[1] Of course, it is precisely his point that no general sociological explanation of the development of legal autopoiesis is possible. Strictly speaking, legal development is a matter *only* of legal development (significantly he finds support in Alan Watson's profoundly anti-sociological analyses of legal evolution) (Teubner, 1993: 40, 50, 58). Here one must either accept the theory or not. But it is hard to see how, in this context at least, it can offer much help to a sociology of law, viewing law in terms of general social processes.

All that the theory seems prepared to say of these processes in specific terms is that they are processes of communication, and, in the case of law, communication is about legality or illegality, conceived as a binary opposition. In itself, this may not be much help to lawyers' juristic science which has its own sophisticated understandings of what it takes to be institutional processes of legal doctrinal development, and of the complex formulations, gradations and contextualisations of juristic categories of legality or illegality. Indeed, adjudicative and interpretive practice in law might well be seen by many lawyers as focused on a very diverse range of matters often far removed from what autopoiesis theory identifies as law's distinctive binary coding. Lawyers are well aware that the meaning and use of any such coding are themselves matters for permanent interpretation and reinterpretation. If law's binary coding is taken, in some simple sense, as distinctive of legal discourse it might be best understood as a signal (like alternation between a red and green light) provided to influence the actions of enforcement agencies, citizens, etc. If so this can be seen as a functional output, but hardly as adequately characterising or defining the complex discourses of legal practice.[2]

---

[1]What is important for the theory is that evolution is 'blind' and regulated only by 'filter mechanisms' of variation, selection and retention. 'Structural coupling' between systems may (but may not) inspire developments but it seems that the way this comes about will be, in terms of the theory, inexplicable. And contingency is preserved in the idea that functional equivalents are always possible. The possibility of explaining historical development in terms of the play of social forces is recognised but treated as refering to an entirely different level of analysis to be distinguished from the theory's own focus on functional analysis (Teubner, 1993: 50, 51).

[2]Following autopoiesis theory's own claims, the theory could, indeed, have no influence on

The audience for autopoiesis theory is surely intended, therefore, to be legal sociologists or socio-legal scholars. But the theory's explanatory potential, as regards social processes, seems to me to reduce to very little; perhaps even to tautology. Legal communications are about law: the theory seems to revel in its acceptance of law's circularity and self-reference. Law endlessly creates law out of law (even if in response to social stimuli). This is claimed as almost the entire key to its functioning as a social system. Legal sociology (as an enterprise dedicated to explaining this functioning) is surely therefore rendered redundant, having - through autopoiesis theory - achieved its theoretical goal of declaring why this redundancy arises (or at least modelling it analytically). Are we to accept this with enthusiasm or resignation? The answer is not clear.

I think that Teubner, at least, has been determined to resist this outcome. That is surely why he wrestles in such a strange way in Chapter 6 of his major book on autopoiesis theory (Teubner, 1993) with what he presents as the problem of conflict between law and other subsystems of society. Everything written earlier in the book should suggest, as far as I can see, that in this context 'conflict' in any *strict* sense is impossible. There are simply no points of *direct* contact between subsystems. Therefore there cannot be conflict. Law reads an event in its (legal) terms; the economy reads the same event in its own (different) terms. There cannot be conflict because each system sees normatively only in its own way. Each *sees nothing to oppose*. Law reads the economic environment in legal terms; the economy reads the significance of legal regulation in terms of its own coding. Conflict implies the possibility of (unwelcome) influence. But autopoiesis theory denies the possibility of any influence, as such. Interference (as contrasted with influence) is not a matter of conflict because interference is not perceived by the system as something oppositional but merely as an occurrence that may or may not provoke the system to react to the interference. The system decides on its response and this will always be on its own normative terms.

It seems that Teubner very much wants to reintroduce the idea of system-conflict despite the fact that autopoiesis portrays a world of systems that do not conflict because they do not interact. He wants to do so because this is to reintroduce central concerns of legal sociology into the analysis - above all the issue of the 'limits of effective legal action' on which so much of legal sociology has been founded. As an issue (of the uncertain outcome of conflicts) it might be addressed through empirical study, whereas if taken as a given (an aspect of law's systemic nature) it surely needs no further

---

juristic thought or practice. Autopoiesis theory could register here only as a 'perturbation', a perception of external 'noise', when the discourse of law observes what it takes to be that of social science.

empirical examination. I believe that Teubner is deeply committed to the empirical enterprise of legal sociology and sees autopoiesis theory as uniquely suited to present the discursive construction of social reality as the underpinning of law as an empirically-examinable practice.

However, to reintroduce system-conflict, arguments that seem inconsistent with autopoiesis theory are required. Conflict can arise, he suggests, between external descriptions of a system (for example, law's description of the economy), on the one hand, and 'the way in which a system [for example, the economy] actually operates', on the other (Teubner, 1993: 103). But, in a constructivist theory such as autopoiesis theory, what is meant by the way a system *actually operates*? Surely there is no *accessible* objective standpoint from which this can be recognised or determined? The legal system cannot experience any such 'actual operation', nor even the economy's own self-understanding, but only law's own 'legal reading' of its environment. Thus, reference to 'actual economic processes', 'ways in which the surrounding systems actually operate', or 'real operations of the surrounding systems' (Teubner, 1993: 103), seems a kind of sleight of hand in which objective (actual, real) criteria are postulated to serve as common reference points between systems. Yet surely this is fundamentally at odds with the constructivist nature of the theory. There is no objective meaning (surely no 'actuality', or 'reality' in any trans-system sense) but only meaning within and for specific systems of communication.[3]

Teubner uses his analysis of conflict to paint a picture of law potentially in crisis, at risk even of disintegration because of conflict with other systems. There is, as a result of such crises, a 'dramatic increase in the indeterminacy of law' (Teubner, 1993: 105). But, on the one hand, this seems a manufactured crisis in terms of autopoiesis theory, since, as suggested above, the theory does not appear to allow a place for such crises to exist. On the other hand, if we discard the models that autopoiesis theory has set up, it may seem an overblown, sensational portrayal of crisis (Rottleuthner, 1989). From

[3]Luhmann and Teubner have both insisted that a 'materiality continuum' is 'presupposed as a basis of system operations' and has 'real contact' with them. Indeed, system operations are 'founded on' it (Teubner, 1993: 85). Its nature seems mysterious, however. Not only do Teubner and Luhmann disagree fundamentally as to what it includes (Teubner, 1993: 85) but there seems to be no precise explanation of how it operates on systems. Perhaps some theories of ideology might be helpful here. One of their more important insights has been that the nature of 'material reality' is always interpreted in any particular structure of ideological thought (what autopoiesis theory might identify as a discursive system) in ways consistent with that thought. Thus, ideological understandings collapse only when the emotional and intellectual resources that support them fail (Cotterrell, 1995: 7-14). This is a matter, at least in part, of psychological conditions, including especially those relating to personal and group morale.

any standpoint other than that of autopoiesis theory, law's negotiation, absorption, rejection, modification, colonisation of, or adaptation to moral, scientific, economic, historical, political and other evaluations is normal; the stuff of everyday legal experience, which legal sociology has confronted with varying degrees of success since its modern beginnings. This situation is an inevitable recipe for crisis only if we treat law's discourse as 'pure' in some narrow sense - focused on its legal/illegal coding but not on a host of other valuations that are necessary to wise regulation and are, in fact, taken on in much legal decision-making in routine ways. These valuations, in fact, often involve the use of what autopoiesis theory sees as distinctive codes of other systems (efficiency criteria, for example).[4]

Could it be suggested that autopoiesis theory reflects a peculiarly continental conception of law's 'rational strength' as a form of conceptual or doctrinal purity - an all-or-nothing view of law, very different from common law legal thinking? Much Anglophone discussion of the theory has confronted it with the empiricist traditions of the common law world (Nelken, 1987; Lempert, 1987). But a different aspect of common law thought might be invoked here. The tradition of common law 'law-finding' (now admittedly heavily overlaid with a completely different, modern, 'scientific' legal positivism) is to see law deeply rooted in culture, that is, moral experience in some broad all-encompassing sense. Autopoiesis theory flatters much positivist legal philosophy by 'super-autonomising' this positivist philosophy's 'autonomising' portrayals of law. The problem is that such portrayals of law's autonomy make it hard to see how vital as a practical matter law's direct moral links to the various communities of social interaction are. Positivism in this guise does not make these links central to analysis - quite the opposite; hence it risks promoting the false and, indeed, dangerous idea of positive law's adequate self-referentiality and self-reproduction. This idea leaves law a dead-letter morally, rather than (to paraphrase Durkheim) 'an effective [moral] discipline of wills' (Durkheim, 1975: 277). It denies or ignores the rooting of law in the general and diverse moral experience of citizens, which should be the basis of legal sociology's concern with law.

---

[4]This is certainly not to suggest that, typically, all is well in law's relations with its social environment. But the crisis tendencies of law, as I see them, have causes almost diametrically opposed to those that adherents of autopoiesis theory identify. Crises (of law's authority, and respect or support for law), when they arise, are likely to be rooted in the effort to sustain the mirage of positive law as self-validating or self-legitimating, or requiring merely political authority, rather than acknowledging its dependence on moral groundings arising from the specific social (communal) contexts of its historical existence.

Autopoiesis and agency

I have claimed that analysis of law must focus on law's roots in the diverse moral experience of citizens. It follows that, on this view, the motivations of individuals in relation to law and the contexts it regulates are centrally important for legal sociology. It is important to relate law to the subjective meaning which, as Weber (1978: 22-6) emphasised, individuals attach to their actions in social contexts. People relate to each other in terms of very varied motivations - expressing combinations of emotional attachment, common or convergent interests, shared values or beliefs, or common experience of some kind. But it hardly needs to be said that systems have no motivations; nor can they accept responsibility, set projects, or form attachments. Instead, they have (in the view of autopoiesis theory) functions and are repositories of meaning, understood entirely in their own system-terms.

Zenon Bankowski has raised the very important question of how individuals relate to systems (Bankowski, 1996). Strictly speaking, and despite all protestations to the contrary, it seems that, for autopoiesis theory, they do not. The importance of the individual in a system-oriented world is said, by Teubner, to be reinstated by autopoiesis theory (Teubner, 1993: 45) because individuality can itself be thought of in terms of 'psychic systems' that have an existence entirely independent of social systems. Bankowski's critique, however, is that because individuals have no direct access to social systems (psychic systems lending themselves to autopoiesis no less than social systems) it is impossible to see how individuals engage with social systems, including law. 'How, and by what principle, do we attribute bits of communication to human beings' (Bankowski, 1996: 70). In what way then can individuals be responsible for the consequences of social systems? For example, in a contemporary world conscious of the power of impersonal systems, no one can, it seems, be held responsible for 'globalisation' and its burgeoning transnational legal regimes; yet people and organisations strongly promote this system (however characterised), benefit from it, suffer as a result of it, or struggle against it in various ways. It must be stressed that autopoiesis theory in no way denies the significance of responsibility in relation to the consequences of systems. It is rather that there seems no place for serious consideration of this issue in terms of the theory.[5]

[5]Autopoiesis theory can, it seems, postulate the responsibility of social systems, which might be understood as a form of collective responsibility. The implication would be that all who are agents of the system share its responsibility. This idea was suggested to me in discussion. But I find it hard to understand how responsibility, in any usual sense of the word, can be attributed to or accepted by a system of discourse or communication. Responsibility would

John Paterson has replied to Bankowski that autopoiesis theory actually strengthens the individual's situation (Paterson, 1996). From the standpoint of the individual as psychic system, social systems exist as an array of constructs in relation to which specific choices of action may or may not be thematised. Thus, in the fictional illustration provided by Gabriel García Márquez' celebrated story *Chronicle of a Death Foretold* (1996), it is not that the 'honour system' impels the killing of the transgressor of this system. Nor is it that the killers lack individual responsibility or the possibility of personal choice ('the system did it'; 'there was no option'). Rather the choice is one of how the matter should be thematised - as a matter within the honour system (which requires the killing), or within the entirely different terms of the legal system (which prohibits it). Responsibility remains. In terms of autopoiesis the psychic system negotiates its internal adjustments (for example, individuals make sense of their situation and make their decisions) while responding to the 'interference' or 'noise' produced by the various operative social systems, including law.

Surely, however, we learn little from this particular analysis as to how and why individuals thematise situations in particular ways. While it would be possible to analyse 'agency' in terms of the autopoietic requirements of psychic systems this would still not link the agency of individuals - and so issues of motivation or responsibility - to law. Yet law's attributions of responsibility and its claims about the mental states involved in action must involve, to some extent, an effort to 'see inside' what autopoiesis theory calls psychic systems (although the effort is, admittedly, limited by practicalities of evidence and the need for presumptions that can form a basis for general rules). Equally, law is not merely a system waiting to have situations thematised in relation to it. It is continually being constructed and reconstructed as practice and doctrine through the (particularly judicial) effort to understand actions, responsibilities and intentions of individual litigants and to use this understanding to give meaning to public regulation.

It is not difficult to identify the exact point in the logic of autopoietic legal theory where, in my view, it takes its fundamental wrong turning in reifying 'system' in law and effectively excluding agency from its horizon of social explanation. This point arises in answering a basic question: how can the concept of autopoiesis be extended beyond its original biological application (in analysing processes of life - the cell, the central nervous system, etc.) to the analysis of social systems? If systems of organic life may be self-

---

require the system to 'respond' (give an answer or account) to something or someone outside itself, but this would involve a communication process of which, according to the theory, it is not capable.

producing and self-reproducing it is harder to see this as a parallel feature of social systems. Consequently many adherents of autopoiesis theory among natural and social scientists refuse to apply it to social phenomena. Again, while the autopoiesis of living systems might be understood as an all-or-nothing affair, there is no agreement as to how this aspect of autopoiesis applies to social systems (Luhmann apparently sees legal autopoiesis as all-or-nothing; for Teubner it can be a matter of degree) (Teubner, 1993: 27).

The more serious problem, however, is that for social systems, such as law, to be autopoietic their components *must* be distinct from living beings that are themselves analysed as autopoietic systems; otherwise a social system could not be self-producing and self-reproducing, but would be dependent on processes external to itself. For this reason, Teubner must insist that higher-order autopoietic social systems such as law 'can be formed in such a way that emergent unities are constituted which provide their elements' (Teubner, 1993: 29). Crucially, these emergent unities are entirely distinct from living beings. Thus 'communications (not human beings or cognitive systems)' are the elements of social systems (Teubner, 1993: 29). The banishment of living beings, it must be stressed, is an absolutely necessary step in order to apply the theory of autopoiesis to law. The basis of social systems is thus 'not life' (Teubner, 1993: 30). Legal (communicative) acts are the elements of a legal system (Teubner, 1993: 41-2) but the system itself defines the concept of action (Teubner, 1993: 43). In this way the system drags itself into autopoiesis, with human beings as the bearers of communicative acts whose essential nature is (increasingly, as the system moves towards autopoiesis) given by the system itself.

It is of great interest in this context that John Paterson and Gunther Teubner have recently sought to clarify how these ideas can guide empirical socio-legal research (Paterson and Teubner, 1998). Using the example of regulation of the British North Sea Oil industry they show very convincingly the sharp contrasts between discourses of legislators, regulators, operators and engineers. It is, indeed, highly plausible to suggest that different 'codings' or criteria of value or appropriateness apply in each of the identified discourses. Autopoiesis theory offers an interesting framework for conceptualising these discursive contrasts, a set of predictions about the way discourses will relate, and guidance about relatively successful and unsuccessful legal strategies for regulation of the industry.

It seems to me, however, that, in order to provide this impressive illustration of autopoiesis theory's empirical power and to show how it relates to questions of agency some subtle modifications to the idea of 'system' in the theory are being made. Thus, it now appears that the existence of any system (including presumably the system-character of law as a practice of regulation) is not to be assumed but depends on observation of 'concrete interactions in legislative chambers and lobby halls and the technological processes in our implementation field in order to discover the systemicity of our research object' (Paterson and Teubner, 1998: 459). A regulated area might be defined by many systems, 'the exact number being a matter for empirical observation' (Paterson and Teubner, 1998: 471).

On the one hand, therefore, systems are real - one might say they are Durkheimian social facts - and present themselves to empirical observation. One has only to look to see them and then count them up! The concept of system has been reified into an object to be observed. On the other hand, 'system' as the model that provided the entire structure of claims about discursive autonomy, predictions of regulatory effects, prescriptions for regulation and warnings about failure is downgraded to *a mere pattern* that might appear to some indeterminate degree mixed with many others and *with no strong system integrity* of its own. Therefore, the researcher will construct systems by observing and interpreting human actions. But is it unfair to say that what is now offered as guidance and method is little more than legal sociology has worked with - institutional structures, patterns of action, currents of ideology - in empirical research without need of help from autopoiesis theory? What then becomes of 'system'? It exists, like beauty, in the eye of the beholder - no longer a social fact but a way of talking about perceived patterns of action. The powerful claims and predictions disappear when the theory refuses to assume the existence of autopoietic systems in operation, but recognises instead the empirical impossibility of closure, the intermingling of discourses and the empirical specificity of sites and settings of interpretive practice.

Nevertheless, the theory cannot for long, it seems, give up its powerful and dramatic claims - and as soon as they re-enter they defeat any attempt to supply open analytical frameworks that facilitate empirical research rather than close off the need for it. Thus, in the same paper, Paterson and Teubner refer to Boaventura De Sousa Santos' subtle attempt to explain how and why laws 'misread' reality (Santos, 1987), reinterpreting his thesis in terms of autopoiesis theory. This theory shows, they assert, that such a misreading is 'inevitable', indeed that it is 'impossible' to avoid (Paterson and Teubner, 1998: 461). In the face of such unqualified and universal claims, empirical researchers might as well give up, it seems. Nothing much remains to be discovered when conclusions are so definite and sweeping in advance of research.

Conclusion

It is appropriate finally to return to the point from which this paper started. Legal sociology progressed by denying the social significance of certain features of law treated as important by most lawyers - especially law's 'internal' discursive or doctrinal nature. When legal sociology observed law as a system it saw lawyers and administrators dealing with cases in their offices, regulatory agencies making decisions on law enforcement, police on patrol, judges, advocates or legislators at work, citizens making (or failing to make) complaints, and disputes being processed. It identified system, provisionally and for theoretical convenience, in such matters as collective understandings, organisational needs and aims, informal patterns of regular social interaction, and professionalisation strategies - all of these observed in specific empirical settings. Today it is important to stress the key part of law that old-style legal sociology too often left out of account: the social significance of legal doctrine, including the general structures of social understanding which it supports. For myself, I think that the concept of ideology (reformulated in certain ways) still remains useful (though not necessarily sufficient) in doing this. Some other researchers prefer to think in terms of legal culture and use this concept in productive ways.

But it is by no means apparent that we need to think about these matters in the strong systems-terms of autopoiesis theory. The danger is of reifying systems (especially of reifying law's autonomy as a discursive system); treating as a social phenomenon what is best thought of as a model of convergent and interlocking practices and contingently interrelated understandings and perceptions. Whatever may be the case for biological systems (Zolo, 1992: 79), the concept of *social* systems is useful only as a *metaphor*. Social systems (including legal systems) cannot be observed or even experienced as such. What are experienced (and may be metaphorically described in system-terms) are stable patterns of action and understandings, associated with particular groups or social environments, or embodied in organisations, agreements for co-operation or peace, or policies and strategies; co-operating individuals with distinct but interconnected objectives; social hierarchies of power, influence or authority; and relationships between people linked to each other on the basis of shared beliefs or values, mutual affection, or the familiarity of common experience.

In other words, we should think always, in my view, in terms of people[6] and use the concept of social system only as a convenient way of

---

[6]This is not a reification of subjectivity. It presupposes only an empirical recognition that human beings are discrete entities in a way that (without elaborate conceptualisation) social systems are not.

conceptualising sustained convergences of action of individuals, and the varied patterns of organisation of groups. Used in this way 'system' is obviously a concept of great value, probably indispensible in legal and social theory. If the notion of system implies assemblages, relations and unities in phenomena (Van de Kerchove and Ost, 1994: 5-6), its use allows a focus on these matters in interpreting the aims or consequences of social action. The notion of system, in this sense, is, undoubtedly, a device by which lawyers organise practices of legal interpretion, especially when questions of legal validity are being addressed (Raz, 1980: ch. 8).

Instead of reifying the idea of system in law, we should focus on practices and motivations that promote, and make plausible, ideas of law's autonomy, including the radical claims to autonomy that autopoiesis theory highlights. We should also look at, and behind, the various intellectual, moral and professional interests that have been served by advocacy of different versions of the internal/external dichotomy in relation to legal studies or legal practice. Then, perhaps it will become possible to dust off and re-present in fruitful new ways some old insights of sociology of law - dating back as far as Eugen Ehrlich (1975). I include here the insight that being 'inside' or 'outside' regulatory experience is a matter of being inside or outside particular groups;[7] as well as the further insight that there is, realistically speaking, no single group of legal insiders, but that everything depends on perspective. Hence, it is necessary to look at the many different kinds of social groups that, today, are engaged in the interpretation of law or the promotion or invocation of regulation. Some groups (judiciaries, jurists) may claim a monopoly of interpretation; yet they themselves might be seen to be divided into sub-groups in competition. Within the state as an organisation of governmental power there may be a range of groups (for example, sections within judiciaries; specialised administrative or enforcement staffs) seeking in different ways to interpret law, not necessarily in harmony with each other and sometimes in sharp if often unadmitted opposition.

In society at large, where autopoiesis theory sees incommensurable social systems, it might be better to see a host of different interpretive communities relating in various ways to law, perhaps understanding law in different ways. Sociology of law can examine action in such communities; its conditions, motivations and constraints. Perhaps, indeed, the idea of a single, discursively distinctive or normatively unified legal system, which the reification of the idea of system encourages us to treat with great seriousness, ought to be viewed with suspicion in formulating the

[7]But understood as a process in continual flux, not a rigid status; relations are typically with different groups at different times and invariably with several groups simultaneously.

contemporary agendas of legal sociology. Its replacement would be a recognition of a wide and very diverse array of practices, expectations, doctrines, sites and settings of legal interpretation. Such a focus emphasises - as I think the best work in legal sociology has always done - the complexity and contingency of law as a field of experience marked by endless conflict and competition around vested interests, ideals and aspirations. Viewed sociologically, legal authority, jurisdiction and interpretation are always potentially contested - ultimately not the technical preserve of jurists but the site and stake of social conflict or competition.[8]

References

Allott, A. (1980), *The Limits of Law*, Butterworths, London.

Bankowski, Z. (1996), 'How Does It Feel To Be On Your Own? The Person in the Sight of Autopoiesis' in D. Nelken (ed.), *Law as Communication*, Dartmouth, Aldershot, pp. 63-80.

Black, D. (1989), *Sociological Justice*, Oxford University Press, New York.

Bredemeier, H. (1962), 'Law as an Integrative Mechanism' in W. M. Evan (ed.), *Law and Sociology: Exploratory Essays*, Free Press, Glencoe, Ill., pp. 73-88.

Cotterrell, R. (1995), *Law's Community: Legal Theory in Sociological Perspective*, Clarendon Press, Oxford.

Cotterrell, R. (1998), 'Law and Community: A New Relationship?', 51 *Current Legal Problems*, pp. 367-91.

Cotterrell, R. (1999), *Emile Durkheim: Law in a Moral Domain*, Edinburgh University Press, Edinburgh.

Cotterrell, R. (forthcoming in 2001), 'Is There a Logic of Legal Transplants? in D. Nelken (ed.), *Adapting Legal Cultures*, Hart Publishing, Oxford.

Dezalay, Y. and B. G. Garth. (1996), *Dealing in Virtue: International Commercial Arbitration and the Construction of a Transnational Legal Order*, University of Chicago Press, Chicago.

Durkheim, E. (1975), 'Définition du fait morale' in *Textes*, vol 2, Les Éditions de Minuit, Paris, pp. 257-88.

Dworkin, R.M. (1978), *Taking Rights Seriously*, Duckworth, London.

Dworkin, R.M. (1985), *A Matter of Principle*, Harvard University Press, Cambridge, Mass.

Dworkin, R. M. (1986), *Law's Empire*, Fontana, London.

Ehrlich, E. (1975), *Fundamental Principles of the Sociology of Law*, Arno, New York.

Ewald, W. (1995), 'Comparative Jurisprudence II: The Logic of Legal Transplants', 43 *American Journal of Comparative Law*, pp. 489-510.

Gerth, H.H. and Mills, C. W. (eds), (1948), *From Max Weber: Essays in Sociology*, Routledge and Kegan, London.

Hart, H.L.A. (1994), *The Concept of Law*, 2nd edn., Clarendon Press, Oxford.

Honoré, T. (1987), *Making Law Bind*, Clarendon Press, Oxford.

Jackson, R. (ed.), (1999), 'Sovereignty at the Millenium: Special issue', 47 *Political Studies* No 3.

---

[8]I am grateful to the participants in the Cardiff workshop on autopoiesis theory, and especially to Gunther Teubner, Michael King and Zenon Bankowski, for much valuable comment on and criticism of this paper as originally presented.

Jessop, B. 'The Economy, the State and the Law: Theories of Relative Autonomy and Autopoietic Closure', in G. Teubner and A. Febbrajo (eds), (1992), *State, Law and Economy as Autopoietic Systems,* Giuffre, Milano, pp. 187- 263.

Kelsen, H. (1989), *The Pure Theory of Law*, Peter Smith, Gloucester, Mass.

King, M. and Piper, C. (1995), *How the Law Thinks About Children,* 2nd edn., Gower, Aldershot.

La Torre, M. (1999), 'Legal Pluralism as Evolutionary Achievement of Community Law', 12 *Ratio Juris,* pp. 182-95.

Ladeur, K. H. (1999), *The Theory of Autopoiesis as an Approach to a Better Understanding of Postmodern Law: From the Hierarchy of Norms to the Heterarchy of Changing Patterns of Legal Inter-relationships*. EUI Working Paper LAW 99/3, European University Institute, Florence.

Lawson, F. H. (1951), *The Rational Strength of English Law*, Stevens, London.

Lempert, R. (1987), 'The Autonomy of Law: Two Visions Compared', in G. Teubner (ed.), *Autopoietic Law: A New Approach to Law and Society*, de Gruyter, Berlin, pp. 152-190.

Luhmann, N. (1986), 'The Self-Reproduction of Law and Its Limits' in G. Teubner (ed.), *Dilemmas of Law in the Welfare State*, de Gruyter, Berlin, pp. 111-27.

MacCormick, D. N. (1993), 'Beyond the Sovereign State?', 56 *Modern Law Review,* pp. 1-18.

Marquez, G. G. (1996), *Chronicle of a Death Foretold*, Penguin, London.

Nelken, D. (1987), 'Changing Paradigms in the Sociology of Law', in G. Teubner (ed.), *Autopoietic Law: A New Approach to Law and Society*, de Gruyter, Berlin, pp. 191-216.

Parsons, T. (1977), *The Evolution of Societies*, Prentice-Hall, Englewood Cliffs, NJ.

Paterson, J. (1996), 'Who Is Zenon Bankowski Talking To? The Person in the Sight of Autopoiesis' in D. Nelken (ed.), *Law as Communication*, Dartmouth, Aldershot, pp. 81-104.

Paterson, J. and Teubner, G. (1998), 'Changing Maps: Empirical Legal Autopoiesis', 7 *Social and Legal Studies,* pp. 451- 86.

Pennock, J. R. and Chapman, J. W. (eds), (1974), *The Limits of Law,* Lieber-Atherton, New York.

Petersen, H. and Zahle, H. (eds), (1995), *Legal Polycentricity: Consequences of Pluralism in Law*, Dartmouth, Aldershot.

Posner, R. A. (1987), 'The Decline of Law as an Autonomous Discipline: 1962-1987', 100 *Harvard Law Review,* pp. 761-80.

Raz, J. (1980), *The Concept of a Legal System: An Introduction to the Theory of Legal System*, 2nd edn., Clarendon Press, Oxford.

Rottleuthner, H. (1989), 'The Limits of Law: The Myth of a Regulatory Crisis', 17 *International Journal of the Sociology of Law*, pp. 273-85.

Santos, B. de S. (1987), 'Law - A Map of Misreading: Toward a Postmodern Conception of Law', 14 *Journal of Law and Society,* pp. 279-302.

Santos, B. de S. (1995), *Toward a New Common Sense: Law, Science and Politics in the Paradigmatic Transition*, Routledge, London.

Shiner, R. A. (1992), *Norm and Nature: The Movements of Legal Thought*, Clarendon Press, Oxford.

Teubner, G. (1987), 'Juridification - Concepts, Aspects, Limits, Solutions', in G. Teubner (ed.), *Juridification of Social Spheres: A Comparative Analysis in the Areas of Labour, Corporate, Antitrust and Social Welfare Law,* de Gruyter, Berlin, pp. 3-48.

Teubner, G. (1993), *Law as an Autopoietic System*, Blackwell, Oxford.

Teubner, G. (ed.), (1997), *Global Law Without a State*, Dartmouth, Aldershot.

Teubner, G. (1998), 'Legal Irritants: Good Faith in British Law or How Unifying Law Ends Up in New Divergences', 61 *Modern Law Review,* pp. 11-32.

Van der Kerchove, M. and Ost, F. (1994), *Legal System Between Order and Disorder*, Oxford University Press, Oxford.

Waluchow, W.J. (1994), *Inclusive Legal Positivism*, Clarendon Press, Oxford.

Weber, M. (1978), *Economy and Society*, University of California Press, Berkeley.

Zolo, D. 'The Epistemological Status of the Theory of Autopoiesis and Its Applications to the Social Sciences' in G. Teubner and A. Febbrajo (eds), (1992), *State, Law and Economy*, Giuffre, Milano, pp. 67-124.

5 Legitimation Between the Noise of Politics and the Order of Law: A Critique of Autopoietic Rationality

JIŘÍ PŘIBÁŇ

In modern societies, legality originally dominated the relationship of legality and legitimacy. To the sociological, political and jurisprudential question: 'Which political domination and order can claim legitimacy in the modern society?' was given the answer: 'A political domination is legitimate because it is entirely defined in legal terms'. However, the problem of legal legitimacy is almost immediately turned upside down and becomes the problem of legitimate legality. Instead of legality perceived as an instrument for the legitimation of the political order, the problem is referred back to the structures of legality itself, to its own normative background and social effectiveness. It is legality itself that is subject to the test of legitimacy.

Legitimacy as belief in legal fictions?: normative power of legal theory and social contingency

Max Weber always described the form of political domination typical of modern society as legal-rational and conceived legality to be an essential impersonal technique of the organisation of modern political society by means of general and rational rules (Cotterrell, 1983: 81). Nevertheless, Weber never reduced the problem of legitimacy to these legal procedures and rules. According to him, legitimacy, be it charismatic, traditional or legal, always also requires *a belief* (*Glaube*) on the side of those who are to be subjected to this political domination (*Herrschaft*) (Weber, 1978).

It is in Weber that the basic problem of legitimacy in modern societies is given its clearest statement as the tension between the impersonal and rational order of procedures and rules on one side and the belief in this order on the other side. This tension may be formulated as *the tension between the universality of rules and procedures of systemic rationality and the contingency of the belief in these rules and procedures.* In Weber's sociological theory, the problem of legitimacy cannot be reduced to the very popular metaphor of 'the iron cage' of modernity which is mentioned in almost every introduction to sociology. The aspect of a belief in this cage and the power to persuade others about its rightness and necessity to obey it turn out to be of the same importance. Legitimacy is also defined as a capacity of the political will to impose a certain opinion and worldview or ideology. Legitimacy is a matter of imposition (Connolly, 1984: 12).

Such tension is present for instance in the legal theory of Carl Schmitt, who understood it as an unbearable aspect of modernity threatening the stability and unity of the state. Schmitt's concept of the enemy, which is central to his political works, is just a reflection of the contingency of the belief of modern people in the legitimacy of their political order. According to Schmitt, legality as defined by Weber, was too weak and corresponded too much to the liberal values of an open and free discussion. Politics has a polemic nature. It is structured and determined by inconsistency and conflict and the enemy is the source of polemic. Politics is pluriversum, not universum (Schmitt, 1963: 54). The state, on the other hand, is an integrating institution because it subjects political enemies by imposing its supreme will on them. Therefore, the legitimacy by legal normativity formulated by liberal theories of the rule of law system is not possible. Behind any legitimacy, there is a capacity to impose a state decision and apply it. A decision, will (voluntas) and command are integral to legality, which therefore can never be explained purely by the concepts of normativity, rationality (ratio), and formal legislation.

According to Schmitt, a sovereign is defined by its power to impose a state of emergency. Consequently, any state and therefore any legal system are made up by a decision and not by a norm (Schmitt, 1985: 10). No normativity can be treated as a foundation of any legal system, be it conceived in the sense of the norms of natural law and rights or as the basic norm of the democratic rule of law. The foundations of every legal system and all laws are within the sphere of a sovereign decision which is always able to overcome social heterogeneity.

While Weber seeks to generate this belief from the sources of modern rationality and its normative power, which reveals itself in the field of law (and other social fields), Schmitt supports the idea of the closure of the pluralistic world of politics by a state decision. However, even Schmitt is well aware of the contingency and temporality of such a decision. This dilemma is typical of the relation between modern legality and its legitimacy and can be called *the dilemma of normality*. Max Weber kept it in its original double structure, in which the neo-Kantian concepts of impersonal and formal rationality coexist with the Nietzschean concept of will and human action. On the other hand, legal theorists and philosophers usually seek to resolve this dilemma by keeping a paradigmatic contrast between legitimacy and social contingency (Habermas, 1997: 72) and defining normative foundations of legitimate law. The belief in the legitimacy of legal domination must be supported by a rational normative framework. Political power must look for a coalition with reason in order to control belief in the legitimacy of law.

In his analysis of scientific knowledge, Thomas S. Kuhn defined legitimate steps as those steps which corresponded to the rules worked out and imposed by a scientific paradigm (Kuhn, 1970: 10f.). Legitimacy then means normality in the sense of a set of conventions which must be adopted by everyone who wants to communicate and pursue his/her own goals within the framework of a paradigm and a community which has been established by epistemic commitment to this paradigm.

The paradigm of legal science is a reaction to the social need for order and the subordination of human behaviour to the governance of rules. Legal science must therefore create structures of rules and normality within its own paradigm and transform them into the existing structures of the system of positive law. Legal science is to help the system of positive law by creating new ways of communication about it and its social functions. Science supports the functioning of law and the system of positive law, on the other hand, adapts to what legal science says about it. Social normality is thus generated both by social structures of positive law and the paradigmatic structures of legal science.

Legal theory involves both analysis and normative judgments about the system of positive law. Although it pretends to be an analytical and value-free scientific discourse, legal theory seeks to influence the processes of lawmaking and the enforcement of law and thus the construction of legal reality. Legal science creates 'the nature of law'. Legal theory constructs the true nature of law and reflects law's real functions in the modern society. In order to understand the legitimacy of law and political domination, it is necessary to analyse this constructive and reflexive power of modern legal theory.

The construction of scientific discourse about law turns on an ability peculiar to legal science, to construct *fictions*. Scientific discourse about law, the primary function of which is the analysis of positive law, is possible only when these fictions are formulated. The scientific, analytical enterprise of jurisprudence depends upon an artificial construct which must reformulate legal reality in order to make its scientific description possible. The logically pure crystals of legal theory are conceivable only on the basis of a fictitious notion which belongs to the sphere of imagination as it exceeds the limits of analytical thinking.

Legal fictions are ubiquitous in legal communication and may be traced back to Roman law. These fictions, for instance the fiction of a legal person are an internal part of legal logic and pragmatics. However, legal theory as such, in order to fulfil the demands of scientific, independent and true discourse about positive law, must shape itself against the background of some constitutive fictions. These fictions are the general artificial constructs supporting the claim of modern law to be a rational, logically coherent and hierarchical system which operates independently of (and on) other normative orders and social systems.

The main purpose of constitutive fictions in modern, legalist, positivist theory is to set up the paradigmatic conditions for the 'right' answer to the question: 'What is law?'. They have a constitutive and legitimation function within the paradigm of legal science because they are the basis of all analyses and definitions of positive law. This is exactly the function of Hans Kelsen's fiction of the basic norm, Jeremy Bentham's fiction of the political sovereign, or Rudolf Stammler's fiction of the just law.

Legalist fictions are an attempt to establish normality by means of legal positivist discourse. Legitimacy by legality is a restriction of legitimate steps to those defined by the language of law. Normality must be identified with legality. However, this attitude contains the threat that any behaviour proclaimed by the law as illegal will be immediately prosecuted and excluded as illegitimate and therefore pathological and deviant.

The function of legalist fictions is to establish the conditions in which legality, by the means of scientific speculation on the fiction, will pretend to have set up a unified social space. All kinds of human behaviour falling outside its limits will then be declared illegitimate. The complicated nature of social reality is reduced by its 'transcription' into legal concepts. Legalist fictions are an attempt to translate the conflictual nature of politics and social reality into the codified world of legal normality. Their main function is to provide the legal system with a scientific definition and therefore set up the limits of positive law and legitimate human behaviour. It is eventually juristic and legal philosophical arguments that justify the rule of law.

The 'normalisation' function of legalist fictions helps to reduce the complexity of social reality and set up the structures and social communication framework of the system of positive law. Nevertheless, if the legitimate shall be identical with the legal, the criterion of functionality and effectiveness of legality must be accompanied by *the criterion of comprehensibility of law* and individual legal rules. Law must be both accepted and understood. The problem of legitimacy and the belief in what is legitimate reveals the more general criterion of social comprehensibility. This ability to understand and comprehend also makes political community possible. Joseph Raz means exactly this when he considers trust between government and its subjects to have a fundamental importance for any legitimate political order (Raz, 1994). The intrinsic value of political consensus is determined by this trust. Trust is the right basis for government. That the government is governed by reason makes it possible to trust that government and with that trust, it becomes legitimate.

Transformation of legitimacy into legitimation: legitimation by procedure and the disappearance of the centre of the legal system

Legal theory and law as a social system and the expression of systemic rationality cannot, however, provide society and individuals with good political reason for belief in its own legitimacy, which a citizen-layperson can understand and therefore accept. The systemic rationality of law and arguments supplied by legal theory cannot serve as the foundation of comprehensible political arguments. Comprehensibility goes beyond the internal operations of the system.

In contemporary societies, law has become completely incomprehensible from the political perspective. This is the problem formulated in Niklas Luhmann's concept of legitimation by procedure (*Legitimation durch Verfahren*). Unlike Habermas's theory of communicative reason and discourse ethics, which regards the loss of political and civic comprehensibility of law as the cause of the crisis of law's legitimacy, Luhmann's theory of autopoietic social systems admits and in fact enjoys the disappearance of modern human subjects in contemporary social conditions (Přibáň, 1997). According to the autopoietic theory, social systems (including political and legal systems) are determined exclusively by their inner rules and their main criterion has become the criterion of function. Comprehensibility is subjected to functionality.

The theory of autopoietic social systems regards the mutual influence of modern political ideals, values, and legal procedures only as a historical movement which is not characteristic of contemporary social conditions. It defines the legal system as one of the autopoietic systems of a modern complex society, one which has differentiated itself from systems of politics, morals, and economy during the process of historical evolution.

Luhmann's theory of autopoietic law and legitimation by procedure hardly can be seen only as a political product of ideological conservatism. As Habermas himself admits, it can also have a strong critical impact because it assumes that law is independent of the concrete conditions of a political system, or of a given system of morals and economic interests (Habermas, 1997: 47ff.). Autopoietic law develops at the historic moment when the principles of division and limitation of state powers and civil freedoms have become social facts. Legal systems must reflect and regulate those political and cultural facts in constitutional legal documents. Law is systematically ordered and founded on the principle of general legislation. The definition of what is legal and illegal is done exclusively within the complex system of positive legal rules. Legal systems of complex modern societies concentrate on future actions, so that they can reduce growing social complexity and work as one of many social decision-making mechanisms.

Luhmann admits that there is no simple and persuasive answer to the question of the legitimacy of modern law and political domination (Luhmann, 1981: 132). In modern societies, there are nevertheless no sources of legitimation of law that can be sought outside the framework of positive law. Legitimacy of law is a matter of positive law. It is not related to the concept of truth and the correspondence of positive legal systems to it. Modern societies do not require true law, but law enabling social action and decisions (Luhmann, 1969: 24ff.). Theories of natural human rights are only a historical ideology which had meaning for the development and formation of positive law, because it limited the sovereign power of the king by invoking the laws of nature (Luhmann, 1981: 119-21). In contemporary social conditions, natural law and any other transcendent foundations of positive law have lost their formative function.

Due to the growing complexity of the modern social world and its law, individuals cannot make their own judgements about every single legal case or problem. They cannot invoke transcendental principles and values. All they can do is accept certain legal procedures which define and manage legal cases and problems (Luhmann, 1990: 227ff.; Lenoble, 1996: 935-1004). These legal procedures embody modern political ideals and principles, but their acceptance depends purely on their operative capacity, not transcendent value.

Luhmann comes up with a radically different concept of legitimacy which emphasises the moment of social communication and cognitive processes of learning and criticises essentialist approaches to legitimacy.

The legitimacy of any social structure is not formed or determined by values and principles. This structure is legitimated by its power to communicate and inform its subjected elements about its own decision. Instead of legitimation based on transcendentally founded values, procedural legitimation begins to dominate and its main function is to teach subjects to accept systemic processes and procedures (Luhmann, 1969). *The problem of legitimacy becomes the problem of the permanent process of legitimation!*

The whole project of legitimation by procedure shifts the social science perspective on the problem of legitimacy from essentialist to a proceduralist view. The problem of legitimacy changes and becomes the problem of legitimation. This transformation of legitimacy into legitimation and its strict separation from any transcendent values or socially and politically supreme cultural principles makes the autopoietic theory one of the currently most inspiring paradigms.

At the end of the 60s, Luhmann used some schools of German legal theoretical thinking and the common legalist notion of a proceduralist legitimation for the purposes of his own social theory. The central problem is the acceptance of decisions within the existing social system. Procedures must be flexible in order to translate and convince subjects about the necessity to accept a decision. The social function of procedures is to create a general framework of acceptability of decisions, the content of which has not been yet specified.

Luhmann's concept of legitimation by procedure reduces legitimacy to a passive processes of learning and subjecting to the pre-existing procedures and structures of unequal and power determined communication. Acceptance is not conditioned by some qualified consent, such as we have seen is required in Raz's political and legal philosophy (Raz, 1994: 364ff.). This difference must be emphasised especially because Raz and Luhmann both closely connect the problem of legitimacy with cognitive processes of learning (Raz, 1994: 369). Legitimacy is not a matter of fundamental principles and the character of political community, and therefore it exceeds the common legal philosophical discourse (MacCormick, 1978: 55). Acceptance depends on system rationality and inner structures of communication.

Luhmann rejects the idea of consensus derived from the concept of communicative rationality, and also Weber's concept of belief as the condition of the legitimacy of legal domination. The concept of legitimation is reduced to the question of procedures inherent in the autopoietic system of law. Legality becomes the dominant element in the legality-legitimacy relation. This legality is however much more dynamic than the concept of legality formulated by the positivistic legal philosophy and theory, which, unlike autopoietic systems theory, prefers the structural-normative to procedural-dynamic perspective. Although Luhmann defines procedures from a much broader sociological perspective and the main criterion is the functionality of legal procedures, his concept of legitimation sometimes recalls Carl Schmitt's concept of legitimacy by legality.

Luhmann defines legitimacy as a '... general readiness to accept, within certain limits of tolerance, decisions which are still without content...' (Luhmann, 1969: 28, Přibáň, 1997: 337). Legitimacy depends on the processes of learning and an assumption of the acceptability of legal decisions by those who are affected by them. It depends on the social climate (*sozialen Klima*), which institutionalises the acceptance of binding decisions as something taken for granted, and understands it not as a consequence of personal decision but as a consequence of the validity of administrative bureaucratic decisions. Instead of the Habermasian *consensus*, legitimacy remains a matter of passive *consent* with pre-existing procedures. The symbolic level of consensus with all its democratic connotations is transformed into acceptance and learning to anonymous procedures. Instead of the passionate symbols of modern politics, this is a cold legitimation established by cognitive processes of learning which are a technique for securing the acceptance of the anonymous procedures of legality.

Luhmann refuses psychological explanations about the legitimacy of law. The decisive fact, according to Luhmann, is whether the system enables the procedures of learning, that is, whether it enables citizens as subjects of the system to grasp cognitively the normative expectations involved in the autopoietic legal system. Describing the theory of autopoietic systems, one could speak about the process of auto-legitimation of law, or self-legitimation of law (Lempert, 1988).

Luhmann's concept of legitimation by procedure has provoked many criticisms and misunderstandings. It obviously makes a radical break with the common understanding of the problem of legitimacy within the field of social and polititical philosophy working with the concepts of ideology, democracy, democratic political morality or natural human rights.

It is also criticised for its decisionist view, according to which the problem of legitimation is always about arguments and explanations of the decision-making of the powerful. While other theories legitimate decisions from the outside and require democratic procedures and liberal civil rights, the autopoietic theory defines a decision as legitimate when it effectively transmits information to the addressee and makes it possible for the addressee to adapt to commands. This kind of decisionism in fact dismantles the centralist model of political domination, in which the decision-making centre dictates its moves to the subjects. Decision-making processes are not one-sided communication processes and legitimacy in fact grows in the process of communication between a decision-maker and addressee (Luhmann, 1975: 11).

Unlike the common legal positivist critique of natural law, autopoietic systems theory castigates the whole tradition of legal humanism and rejects the notion of a person who, together with other individuals-persons and within generally binding pragmatics, put rules and limits on their own actions, rules articulated around the modern transcendent ideals of freedom, equality and democracy (Cornell, 1992). According to Luhmann, '...[S]tructural changes ... do not require any special "legitimating" principle, *ius eminens*, or super-norm. They are in any event only possible in law...' (Luhmann, 1988: 18). Besides the essentialist concept of legitimacy and broader political and ethical legitimation framework, Luhmann's theory also dismantles the positivist notion of law being a product of sovereign political power. Behind the law, there is only law. This statement can remind Kelsen's concept of the basic norm because it excludes all extra-legal elements from the legal system (Teubner, 1988: 4). Nevertheless, the autopoietic concept of legitimation by procedure goes further because it does not require *any centre* to found the law as a functioning and self-referential system. The autopoietic legal system can be conceptualised without the basic norm or the fiction of the political sovereign deciding finally about the distinction between the legal and illegal. Luhmann's concept of law can hardly be seen as primarily coercive (Tamanaha, 1997; Rosenfeld, 1998). The sovereign political power is only an element of the environment of the autopoietic legal system and therefore cannot directly influence its procedures and structure.

It would be a fundamental mistake to simplify the interpretation of the autopoietic systems theory and take it as just one of many theoretical fields in current legalist science. One of the facts that make this theory different is the way it employs the concept of *contingency*. While the legal positivists usually understand law in its direct opposition to the contingency existing in modern society and define it as a system of hierarchical social and political integration, the autopoietic systems theory has chosen the opposite perspective. Law is defined as a structure of expectations of a contingent nature (Luhmann, 1985). Modern society as a whole is complex and contingent. There is no hierarchical order in it, but only contingent mutual relations between different social systems. Such a society cannot be held together by some ideological framework, or ruled and determined in its development from just one centre of the political power. The concept of legitimation by procedure confirms the autonomy of law in relation to politics. Politics is law's environment and therefore cannot be its legitimation foundation.

Autopoiesis dismantles the popular notion of society as a system ruled from one centre. The command centre has disappeared because every procedure becomes such a small command centre which seeks to establish communication and the functioning of different elements of a social system. In a society consisting of different autopoietic social systems, there is no sovereign norm or procedure. Instead of this organising master centre, a social system is united and strengthened by its differentiation. Flexibility and differentiation have become the most decisive characteristics of the system.

The master discourse is impossible in any social system including law, in spite of the fact that lawyers and legal scholars conceive of modern legal science as a supreme science about law and the sovereign standing behind the creation and application of law (Schutz, 1994). Society and its law go through a process of their horizontalization (Murphy, 1997: 163). Borders between social systems are not borders between superior and inferior subsystems of modern society. They are horizontal borders which make it possible to distinguish one social system from another. These systems cannot be explained one by another. Law cannot be explained by politics or economics. Law can be explained only from law. The normative closure of autopoietic systems makes them independent of their environment.

The process of the horizontalization of law helps to isolate and separate the 'sovereign' vocabularies of political and moral discourse from the problem of the legitimacy of law. All essentialist and foundationalist attempts to legitimate law by reference to the universal validity of the external discursive framework only make it harder to understand law in the plurality and variability of its social functions, in its flexibility and ability to respond to the growing contingency of our social world (Teubner, 1992). The relation between legality and legitimacy cannot be a relation of superiority and inferiority. Autopoietic theory correctly analysed the fact that the universal acceptance of anything is impossible and indeed unthinkable in contemporary social conditions. Although we might have universal demands for legitimate law, their universality is immediately dissolved on contact with social reality.

The derivation of the legitimacy of law from a 'higher order of norms and principles' which ignores the inner mechanisms of legality is abandoned by the autopoietic systems theory (Luhmann, 1995: 317). The reasons for this are the facts about the actual functioning of contemporary law, which can seemingly operate without ethical or fundamental political legitimation. Values and virtues of democracy or human rights and freedoms do not have a primary impact on the functioning and therefore the legitimacy of law. Law is enforced in society independent on those values, which belong to the political system. The process of the legal system's differentiation and the expansion of its regulations into different social spheres make it also legitimate. Consequently, the matter of legitimacy must become a matter of social facticity.

Legitimation between the noise of politics and the order of law

In his later works, Luhmann paid little attention to the topic of legitimacy. In the 90s, he completely separated legitimacy from legality and understood the former as a problem of the political, not the legal, system. The problems of the sovereignty of the people, democratic decision-making, and human rights belong to politics. They do not determine the legal system's operations. They are law's environment. Such, as it were, legal-political problems must be understood as a structural coupling between two different social systems. The political system must incorporate into its own operations the demand for the legitimate expression of a political will by democratic procedures within the limits of civil freedoms. The legal system must incorporate into its own operations the legal expression of this will in the form of the constitution and laws. The legality-legitimacy relation copies the system-environment relation.

The theory of autopoietic law contains the problem of the legitimation of law within the sphere of the positive legal system where it is a matter of the procedures supporting the system's self-reproduction. The main shortcoming of such legitimation by procedure is not its decisionist character or its narrow identification of legitimacy with social control. Its main shortcomings are its reduction of legitimation to passive processes of learning procedures and its deliberate exclusion of the social contingency of belief in legitimacy.

Luhmann and others ignore the problem of legitimacy, which is one of the instability and changeability of the acceptance of a legitimate order, such acceptance being a matter of understanding and volitive acts of individuals and groups as social actors. Legitimacy and legitimation cannot be explained only as a matter of compliance with procedures. On the contrary, they can involve the need to break with or destroy legal procedures. The concept of legitimation by procedure focuses on what happens inside the system. It ignores what is different from the system and happens outside its borders. Even within the paradigm of autopoietic systems theory, the problem of legitimacy thus remains a matter of normality. Everything that is outside the system is its noise, illegitimate environment and parasite (Luhmann, 1998: 661).

This noise, however, has an extraordinary importance for the problem of legitimacy. If it is impossible to found legitimacy in some kind of universal master discourse or superior social system, this does not mean that legitimacy would have to be defined exclusively in terms of what is normal and functional within the framework of existing social systems.

Legitimation, although its goal always is the stabilisation and normalisation of thought, communication or action, also contains many elements of instability. If legitimacy is normality, the social space of this instability and constant confrontation is the space in which legitimation takes place. System's noise is not only contingent, but also often subversive in respect to what has already been recognized as legitimate and normal.

A parasite is inherent in the problem of legitimacy. Legitimacy is not only a matter of a system's operation expressing social normality. At the same time, it also points to the system's environment, which is not yet described by the language of the system and controlled by its procedures. The problem of legitimacy consequently breaks into two different spaces which must be analysed separately. The first space is already normalised legitimacy. The second space is a plural space of various legitimation strategies, many of which have an openly anti-normative, parasitic or subversive character.

Luhmann's reduction of legitimacy to normal procedure is surprising because autopoietic social systems theory centrally builds on the assumption that difference is the most important part of the whole system-environment relationship. Difference embraces that which is always waiting to be described and grasped by the system and thus contains the open, contingent possibility of social evolution. Legitimation by procedure cannot resolve a tension central to legitimacy, which is the tension between *ratio* and *voluntas* which finds one of its forms in the system-environment loop.

The technical rationality of legal procedures is to isolate legitimacy from the instability of the political world, with the polemic, contradiction and partiality which are the consequences of unorganised expressions of the political will. The legal system has to take political communication, which in all modern societies consists of disputes between the contradictory wishes of individual wills, as its environment. It cannot exist without it. Legitimation is impossible without legal procedures (the principle of the rule of law), but it also must be clear that the whole legitimation strategy is directed beyond the limits of legal system and into its political environment.

Umberto Eco's semiotic theory of the artwork might help us to understand this situation. According to Eco, every work of art must translate disorder into a system of language or conventions in order to be able to convey information (Eco, 1988). Legitimation of law may then be seen as the translation of political forms of information into the organised and systemic language and rules of law.

Legitimacy and the legitimate must have the form of law. Legitimacy is an outcome of the process of legitimation, which belongs already to the context of law and legal system. Legalist fictions are to establish the domain of the law (Teubner, 1993: 3) and prohibit us from leaving the framework of legal procedures or eschewing the language of legality, whenever we are in the legitimation process. The function of every fiction is to transform noise into order and normality as they are defined by the system of positive law. Fictions have a very important legitimating function, because they establish order from noise (Foerster, 1960). The legitimating fictions of legality are to translate the noise of politics into the order of law. Fictions support the movement from pluralistic reality to a legitimate order which is considered normal.

However, the growing contingency of modern world makes the question of what is legitimate a much more difficult problem which exceeds the framework of theoretical arguments, rationality, and fictions of legal science. Because of our experience and acceptance of a particular version of reality, we know that social development could run differently. We know that there are always more possibilities of action than the action taken. Legitimacy is always a product of contingency. It is not derived from the subjection of law to political principles (supported by rationality of legal and political theory), because the only principle in contingent societies is that there is no principle or starting point. Law is politics, but politics is not the foundation of law, and law is not the foundation of politics (Přibáň, 1998). Between law and politics, there is an irreconcilable difference.

Legitimacy must be understood as a legally formulated strategy which has momentarily won in the context of law. Its status nevertheless is always open to question, because, at the same time, there are present many other legitimation strategies inside the legal system which look for their own ways of coming to dominate. This mechanism of legal self-reproduction and self-reference is exactly what makes every law political but it does not mean any simple subjection of law to the political framework.

We may therefore sum up by saying that *legitimacy* is a contingent outcome of the legal definition of a particular social strategy. *Legitimation* is a permanent struggle to obtain this outcome, which does not initially have a legal form and represents what has not been defined, conceptualised and enforced by law, yet.

The law's cult of impersonality and its limits

Legitimation is a permanent struggle for and against legality. It is inseparable from the tension between the legal system and its environment. The environment cannot be understood only as a political space, which penetrates legality from outside and thereby determines the behaviour of the system of positive law.

The complicated nature of the relationship between a system and its environment is nicely reflected in Teubner's distinction between the actual and constructed environment of the system, which must be addressed by the autopoietic theory of law: '...[F]or the theory assumes that, although the environment actually exists, it is inaccessible to the operations of the system. The system can deal only with its own internal construct of the environment...' (Teubner, 1993: 74).

This double character of the legal system's environment raises important problems, the most basic of which is whether the legal system has the capacity to conceptualise the difference between the actual and the constructed environment? Teubner's concept of reflexive law as a system able to interfere and interpenetrate with its environment (if it is at the same ontological level) does not seem to offer a satisfactory answer, because the decision about the environment's ontological status ultimately belongs to the episteme of a particular social system and therefore is an internal construct of the system. It appears that even autopoietic systems theory is confronted by the duality of a system's environment: the first environment being established by the system, while the second one is escaping the language of the system.

As a consequence of its effort to satisfy the idea of justice as formal equality before the law, legality must represent *the cult of impersonality*. In order to become legitimate, law must be without human qualities and, in this sense, inhuman, in order to preserve its functionality. The autonomy of law must be secured by the generality of its internal procedures, which excludes all elements of subjectivity. The only permissible element is the passive capacity of learning and adapting to those procedures, which nevertheless has only an operative meaning.

Coeval with modernity, state power expresses itself in the language of impersonal legality. General legislation codified liberal principles and ideals. Law could legitimate modern politics and state power because it used the most general language and could satisfy the universal aspirations of modern rationality. Its impersonality and power to operate seemingly without qualities made it a very effective strategy of modern state power.

Besides the objectivity of science and the autonomy of art, the universality of law and morality was the main feature of modernity (Habermas, 1987). The universality of law required the development of the internal logic of law able both to assert law's autonomy and represent modern rationality connecting law with science. Modern legality must define its centre and finds it unsurprisingly in Leviathan, this 'mortal god' that is the first and most persuasive picture of the modern legalist fiction of the political sovereign (Hobbes, 1952: 100). God as a power transcending human political society was transformed into a sovereign possessing (almost) divine force in ruling that society (Fitzpatrick, 1992: 73).

Modernity is obsessed with looking for the centre. Legality is also deeply affected by this obsession. All modern political utopias seek to create a 'divine community' which would be governed in a geometrical spirit of regularity. For instance, F.L. Aubry proposed to create an entirely new city corresponding to the spirit of revolutionary France in which logic would prevail over irregularities and impersonal reason secure social transparency. Time has its new beginning, new cities with new centres are founded and modern legality also has to find its own centre. *Legalist fictions are to help to define the centre.* The existence of law is even conditioned by its capacity to identify its own centre, be it the basic norm, the political sovereign, or the principle of the just law. As Peter Fitzpatrick (1992: 86) points out:

> [Law] takes on the impression of the *imago mundi*, affirming the ordered, normal course, often by correcting deviations from that course. The creation and enforcement of any law is a ritual reassertion of the foundational strength and ordering of the centre (cf. Eliade 1965: 20). What is being affirmed is not just a particular order in opposition to disorder but the very being and force of order itself.

The force of the modern law derives from the centre's power to set up its limits by distinguishing between the legal and illegal. Legalist fictions then connect jurisprudence and the modern legal system in order to produce the power of the law's centre. Jurisprudence must establish 'law's truth', that is the truth about what is its part. This truth is obviously different from, for instance, the truth of science, yet it cannot exist without claiming to have a scientific nature (Nelken, 1998). Positive law cannot exist separately from jurisprudence, which both claims a scientific status and performs important functions within the framework of positive law.

The cult of the impersonality of law may be understood as a consequence of modern efforts to establish universally binding law and morality. The concept of the rule of law is the concept of law being the centre of political life subjected to impersonal rational rules and not human arbitrary will. In this sense, Hart's concept of law as the unity of primary and secondary rules is an attempt to bring the rule of law concept to its perfection because it conceives law as a self-regulating system of rules in which the role of political sovereign as an external element of positive law is limited to the minimum (Cotterrell, 1989: 98ff.).

Law should not be an instrument of power. Quite the opposite, every power must enforce the principle of the rule of law. Political power and administration however have an eroding effect on the rule of law principle because it turns out that law and power are rather in a complex relation of horizontal interdependence (Fitzpatrick, 1992: 150, 153) and not in a simple hierarchical relation of law's domination.

On one side, political power and many other spheres of social life are subject to the law and have to accept its language. This development is sometimes referred to as juridification of social reality (Teubner, 1987). Legal procedures organise more and more of social life and adjust to its growing complexity. On the other hand, a consequence of this juridification is the loss of the declared autonomy of the regulative system of law and its transformation into the administration of society which reacts to the demands of social regulation. *The unity and cult of impersonality of law are dismantled.* In order to perform the role of the political centre of modern society, law must incorporate all its elements in the same way as Hobbes's Leviathan did in 17th century. Such incorporation however dismantles law's internal unity because law as a means of regulating social conflict must adapt to the structure of these social conflicts.

A higher social reflexivity of law causes law to become as complicated, incomprehensible and inaccessible as modern society itself. Legitimacy of law is not so much a matter of the symbolic function it had (when it represents the constitutive principles and ideals of state power), but rather of its capacity to reflect and respond to the growing complexity and variability of social reality.

Variability also means contradiction. What is a legitimate solution for some individuals may be entirely illegitimate for others. Legality tries to re-describe the complexity of the world and to offer it its own solutions, but the legal need for generality and universal validity then becomes a problem without any solution.

Modern legality and its internal logic seek to eradicate what cannot be subjected, conceived and calculated in the language of general rules and norms. An Austrian novelist Robert Musil understood that logic as a desire to rule the life itself and compared the logic of law to *ice flowers*, the blossoming of which is in care of lawyers (Musil, 1997: 586, 646-7). Unlike critical legal scholars, Musil would never say that those, whose minds have thawed have overcome falsity and achieved an insight into the right state of things. Thaw brings just the knowledge of contingency and instability of any such flower as the ice logic of law.

The empty form of a rule is the only fabric of our depersonalised world. In this context, Musil's own definition of the 'banality of evil' is not so surprising. In the language of bureaucratic organisations, any order creates a feeling that the moral is impersonal. Bureaucratic consciousness is a consent to and performance of an order, whatever its content may be (Musil, 1997: 696).

Rationality and the logic of our world cannot, however, be demonised in the way it sometimes is in legal and political philosophy. The law's impersonal world may not be opposed to some fundamental order of principles and universal norms. It is impossible to live either without the logic of the law, or in the blind automatism of exclusive subjection to this logic. The impersonal logic of rules and rationality ends up in the world of fantasy. Reason leads to excesses (Musil, 1997: ch. 54). The logic of rules spreads from the centre, shapes a clear fabric of human thinking and acting, but breaks and denies itself at the periphery. The 'luxury of pure rationality' (Musil, 1990) expressed in mathematics is not only a matter of economy and effectiveness. Behind effectiveness, there is passion and pure intellectual fantasy, which may not be programmed in advance as is a machine. Even the purest rationality involves the irrational elements which call for it to exist and function. The periphery of reason and impersonality turns against its centre and foundations. The common logic breaks along a *centre/periphery* distinction and denies itself.

This movement may be detected in law. Legality and its impersonal world of rules, foreseeability, repeatability and security are the absolutely necessary legitimation framework of modern political societies and of law itself. Legal legitimacy creates the centre of legitimation strategies and it is hard to imagine that the state organisation could be legitimated without any reference to legality.

At the same time, the centre of legality, mainly human rights arguments, corrupts the sovereignty of legal discourse and legal legitimacy. Freedom of expression and other human rights involve an ideological plurality which it is impossible to contain within legal language. Legitimation strategies may often be disconnected from legal rules. The legal logic therefore creates a periphery which can be eventually anti-legal.

In contemporary societies, law is decentralized and the common concept of legality as the only source and criterion of legitimacy has vanished. The decentralisation of legality coincides with the dissolution of the sovereign as the central mechanism of modern political society. In post-modern pluralistic societies, law does not have the capacity fully to legitimate political power and its decisions. Legal procedures have only a limited and not a sovereign legitimation force. Legality can never colonize the problem of legitimacy. This distance seems to be eventually more appropriately formulated in Robert Musil's literary irony than in Niklas Luhmann's social theory.

References

Connolly, W. (1984), *Legitimacy and the Modern State*, Blackwell, Oxford.

Cornell, D. (1992), 'The Relevance of Time to the Relationship Between the Philosophy of the Limit and Systems Theory', 13 *Cardozo Law Review*, pp.1579-1603.

Cotterrell, R. (1983), 'Legality and Political Legitimacy in the Sociology of Max Weber', in D. Sugarman (ed.), *Legality, Ideology and the State,* The Academic Press, London.

Cotterrell, R. (1989), *The Politics of Jurisprudence: A Critical Introduction to Legal Philosophy*, Butterworths, London.

Eco, U. (1988), *Opera aperta*, Tascabili Bompiani, Milano.

Eliade, M. (1965), *The Myth of the Eternal Return or, Cosmos and History*, The Princeton University Press, Princeton.

Fitzpatrick, P. (1992), *The Mythology of Modern Law*, Routledge, London.

Foerster von, H. (1960), 'On Self-Organizing Systems and their Environments', in M.C Yovits and S. Cameron (eds), *Self-Organizing Systems*, Pergamon, Oxford.

Habermas, J. (1987), *The Philosohical Discourse of Modernity: twelve lectures*, Polity Press, Cambridge.

Habermas, J. (1997), *Between Facts and Norms: contributions to a discourse theory of law and democracy*, Polity Press, Cambridge.

Hobbes, T. (1952), *Leviathan*, Encyclopaedia Britannica, Chicago.

Kuhn, T.S. (1970), *The Structure of Scientific Revolutions* (Chicago, The University of Chicago Press, Chicago.

Lempert, R. (1988), 'The Autonomy of Law: Two Visions Compared', in G. Teubner (ed.), *Autopoietic Law: A New Approach to Law and Society*, de Gruyter, Berlin, pp. 152-90.

Lenoble, J. (1996), 'Law and Undecidability: A New Vision of the Proceduralization of Law', 17 *Cardozo Law Review*, pp.935-1004.

Luhmann, N. (1969), *Legitimation durch Verfahren,* W-deutscher Verlag, Neuwied.

Luhmann, N. (1975), *Macht,* F. Enke Verlag, Stuttgart.

Luhmann, N. (1981), *Ausdifferenzierung des Rechts*, Suhrkamp Verlag, Frankfurt.

Luhmann, N. (1982), *The Differentiation of Society*, Columbia University Press, New York.

Luhmann, N. (1985), *A Sociological Theory of Law,* Routledge, London.

Luhmann, N. (1988), 'The Unity of the Legal System', in G. Teubner (ed.), *Autopoietic Law: A New Approach to Law and Society*, de Gruyter, Berlin.
Luhmann, N. (1990), *Essays on Self-Reference,* Columbia University Press, New York.
Luhmann, N. (1995), *Das Recht der Gesellschaft*, Suhrkamp, Frankfurt.
Luhmann, N. (1998), *Die Gesellschaft der Gesellschaft*, Suhrkamp, Frankfurt
MacCormick, N. (1978), *Legal Reasoning and Legal Theory*, Clarendon Press, Oxford.
Murphy, W.T. (1997), *The Oldest Social Science?,* Clarendon Press, Oxford.
Musil, R. (1990), *Precision and Soul*, The University of Chicago Press, Chicago.
Musil, R. (1997), *The Man Without Qualities*, Macmillan, London.
Nelken, D. (1988), 'Blinding Insights? The Limits of a Reflexive Sociology of Law', 25 *Journal of Law and Society*, pp. 407-26.
Přibáň, J. (1997), 'Beyond Procedural Legitimation: Legality and Its 'Infictions'', 24 *Journal of Law and Society*, pp. 331-49.
Přibáň, J. (1998), 'Doing What Comes Naturally, or a Walk on the Wild Side?: Remarks on Stanley Fish's Anti-foundationalist Concept of Law, Its Closure and Force', 9 *Law and Critique*, pp. 249-270.
Raz, J. (1994), *Ethics in the Public Domain: essays in the morality of law and politics*, Clarendon Press, Oxford.
Rosenfeld, M. (1998), *Just Interpretations: Law between Ethics and Politics*, University of California Press, Berkeley.
Schmitt, C. (1963), *Begriff des Politischen*, Duncker und Humblot, Berlin.
Schmitt, C. (1985), *Political Theology. Four Chapters on the Concept of Sovereignty*, The Massachussets Institute of Technology Press, Cambridge, Mass.
Schutz, A. (1994), 'Desiring Society: Autopoiesis beyond the Paradigm of Mastership', *Law and Critique*, vol. 5, n.2, pp. 149-64.
Tamanaha, B. (1997), *Realistic Socio-Legal Theory*, Clarendon Press, Oxford.
Teubner, G. (ed.) (1987), *Juridification of Social Spheres: A Comparative Analysis in the Areas of Labor, Corporate, Antitrust and Social Welfare Law*, de Gruyter, Berlin.
Teubner, G. (ed.) (1988), *Autopoietic Law: A New Approach to Law and Society*, de Gruyter, Berlin.
Teubner, G. (1992), 'The Two Faces of Janus: Rethinking Legal Pluralism', *Cardozo Law Review*, vol.13, pp. 1443-1462.
Teubner, G. (1993), *Law as an Atuopoietic Sysem*, Blackwell, Oxford.
Weber, M. (1978), *Economy and Society*, The University of California Press, Berkeley.

6 The Construction and Demolition of the Luhmann Heresy

MICHAEL KING

Foreword

I can remember being a member of a small audience in a very large auditorium at a session of the Law and Society Association's Amsterdam Conference of 1990 at which Niklas Luhmann listened to and answered assessments of his work from members of the Cardozo Law Faculty. After the session, which lasted some three hours, there was an informal reception and opportunity to meet Luhmann. At the coffee urn I found myself chatting with an American law student, who declared herself to be an fervent admirer of Luhmann and said that she was thinking of going up to him to ask a question about law and autopoiesis. When she told me her question - I forget exactly what it was - it was clear to me that she had very little understanding of autopoietic theory. Rather naughtily, I encouraged her to go ahead and put her question to him, as I was intrigued to see how he would respond to such a blatant misinterpretation of his ideas. Shortly after, I caught up with the student and asked her if she had managed to put her question to Luhmann. She told me that 'he was real nice' and that the advice that he had given her was 'to read more'!

On reflection, I am not entirely sure that reading more is sufficient for those who, on the basis of very little reading, are either over-enthused or hyper-critical about autopoiesis. Most of Luhmann's works are, to echo the words of a reviewer of the English translation of *Social Systems,* likely to prove difficult reading for the Anglo-American audience. 'Luhmann's 'flight above the clouds is', this reviewer wrote, 'comparable in conceptual abstraction ... to Spinoza's *Ethics,* Hegel's *Logic* or Foucault's *Archeology of Knowledge*'(Kogler, 1997: 271). In the same vein, an obituary of Luhmann in *Radical Philosophy* identifies as the main reason for 'his remarkable neglect' as,

> the sheer difficulty and complexity of Luhmann's characteristic brand of systems theory ... his theory is pitched at such a high level of abstraction and reflexivity that it is often hard to see its relevance, even to those who are used to more metaphysical bedtime reading (Vandenberghe, 1999).

Far be it from me to suggest that all those Anglo-American scholars, who have passed judgment on autopoietic theory are either dilettantes or intellectual lightweights. While some, as the text of and footnotes to this article will demonstrate, may indeed have put their critical fingers to the keyboard on the basis of very little reading of or engagement with the Luhmannian enterprise, my primary purpose is not to expose poor scholarship or take these writers to task for something of which we have all been guilty at one time or another. Rather, it is to identify through a brief analysis of the various and varied critiques of autopoietic theory the particular difficulties that the theory presents for scholars, whether jurisprudential or sociological, in their attempts to come to grips with its complexities and the ways they find to overcome or circumvent these difficulties. Yet it would be disingenuous of me to suggest that the purpose of this article was purely analytical. As someone who has smarted from the often scathing and dismissive anti-autopoietic attacks that have appeared in English and American journals and books in recent years, it would be overtaxing my powers of self-discipline for me to deny myself entirely the pleasure of answering some of these criticisms.

Those readers who have read the novel, *Pale Fire*, will recall Nabokov's device of running in the notes a commentary which grossly misinterprets the poem in the text, which it is purporting to explain. The commentary is written by a paranoid schizophrenic, Botkin (alias Kinbote), who believes himself to be the exiled king of Zembla. When Shade, the author of the poem *Pale Fire*, is shot dead by an escapee from the Institute for the Criminally Insane, Kinbote believes that he was the intended victim and that the murderer had been sent by the Zemblan extremist government to assassinate him. Throughout his commentary on Shade's poem he reconstructs the poet's heroic couplets in ways which allow him to spin his fantasy about his life as the king, his escape from Zembla and his exile in America. Kinbote is obviously more interested in telling *his* story than in doing literary justice to the poem. I deploy a similar device in this article, but in reverse. I use the main text to set out the accounts of critics of autopoietic theory who, in their attacks on the theory, manage to misstate, misunderstand or misinterpret it and do so in ways which say more about their own theoretical, ideological or moral perspective than about the object of their criticisms. In the notes I refer wherever possible to direct quotations setting out in italicized footnotes what Luhmann and other autopoietic theorists actually wrote on the subject under scrutiny. To add spice to these footnotes, I take the liberty of offering my own reactions to some of these critics and of indicating how near or how far their critical missiles fall from their target. In the main text of this essay, however, my intention is to present an account of the ways in which the theory has been interpreted by different scholars.

An earlier draft of this article ended the last paragraph with the words 'different scholars of the Anglo-American tradition', but on reflection, I recognize that, while there are, of course major differences between the *legal* traditions of common law and civil law countries, one has to be wary of moves to extend distinctions between legal cultures to jurisprudence and social theory (Lempert, 1988). As I suggest later in this article, such distinctions should be seen in the context of attempts by scholars to tackle the complexities of autopoietic theory with its unfamiliar language and concepts. Describing autopoiesis as strange or obscure, *because of* its European origins seems to me to miss the point. Many European writers also have considerable difficulty with the theory (Rottleuhner, 1989a; 1989b). On the opposite side of the coin, one only has to read the work of those (on both sides of the Atlantic and the Channel) who have succeeded in making sense of the theory and relating it to the work of other contemporary thinkers from whatever continent to recognize the rather artificial and constructed nature of this Great Divide.

In an attempt to create some order out of the multitude of comments on autopoietic theory from lawyers, sociologists, philosophers and socio-legal researchers, I have attempted to classify different kinds of critical response and to identify those aspects of autopoietic theory which appear more than any others to draw critical reactions. It is also these aspects of the theory, I would suggest, that cause, the greatest problems of comprehension for Anglo-American scholars. I have, therefore, divided my analysis into the following sections which reflect both these troubling aspects of the theory and the strategies adopted by Anglo-American scholars to deal with them. These sections are: (1) Summary Dismissal (2) Assimilation (3) (Mis)Understanding Closure and (4) (Mis)Attributing Responsibility.

Comments on autopoietic theory

(1) Summary dismissal

Reading some of the more critical accounts of autopoietic theory, one has the distinct impression that their authors see the theory almost as a religious (or diabolical) belief and its adherents as fanatical followers of charismatic, but misguided leaders. This is, of course nothing new. Marxists, Freudians and Darwinians have at one time or another all been cast by their critics in the role of fanatics. It is, however, particularly inappropriate to see autopoietic theorists in this way, as their theoretical stance leads them to see religion as self-referential with no justifiable claim to universality in the modern world.

Very close to this approach is that of autopoiesis as a dogma. Either you choose to accept it or you reject it. At one level this is right! Autopoiesis is a grand theory, a total vision, covering everything in the social world. It is difficult to remain an 'autopoieticist' while at the same time adhering to other social theories as offering equally valid visions of the social world. You cannot pick and mix. At another level it ignores entirely the nature of autopoiesis as a theory about theories (King and Schütz, 1994). In observing other theories observing their environment,it does not dismiss them as wrong or misguided, but points rather to their limitations. Luhmann may be accused of arrogance for the way in which he points out these limitations (for example his account of the 'staggering naivity of Durkheimians, social phenomenologists, action theorist' for being content with and not questioning the existence of 'subjects, intersubjectivity, the social and socially meaningful action') (Luhmann, 1995: xli). On the other hand, nowhere in his writings will you find a claim that autopoiesis is able to lead the way to 'a better society', which is the implicit or explicit message of much social theorising. Furthermore, Luhmann and other autopoietic theorists are bound by their theoretical framework to recognize the limitations of their own theory.

Here, as an example of summary dismissal, is J.W. Harris, an Oxford Professor of Law, in his textbook on *Legal Philosophies* (Harris, 1997) as he advises his student readers that they should abandon the prospect of any dealings with Luhmann's version of reality, where:

> The only legal 'facts' are those which the law itself constructs; and the law has nothing to say about anything outside itself. That is the conclusion reached by Niklas Luhmann in his autopoietic analysis of law - the term 'autopoiesis', borrowed from biology, refers to a self-contained organism which generates and regenerates in isolation from other organisms (Harris, 1997: 251).

On reading the first sentence of Harris' one might be misled into thinking that Harris here may well have grasped one of the fundamental concepts of autopoietic theory, that all systems' communications will refer back to the system, so whatever law is able to communicate about will necessarily be law-related. One problem with Harris' reformulation of autopoietic theory is that he leaves one with the difficulty of knowing what precisely he has in mind when he refers to 'facts' or 'legal facts'. If by legal facts' Harris is referring to information which the law accepts as factual, then Luhmann would clearly agree that the law constructs these as 'facts'. If he means facts about the law, then this is, equally clearly, a misreading of Luhmann, for the capacity to construct such facts is not confined to law.[1] The idea that autopoietic biological systems operate 'in isolation' from other systems is, an invention of Harris; it is not only an inaccurate account of biology, but actually conflicts with the biological definition, since autopoietic systems are indeed dependent upon the existence of an environment which contains other systems.[2]

As for the law having 'nothing to say about anything outside itself', all I can suggest is that Harris has completely misunderstood Luhmann's notion of self-reference. He immediately confirms this impression of misunderstanding by going on to reject autopoiesis in terms which make it abundantly clear that he has grasped nothing of the essence of the theory, but instead is interested only in dismissing it before he 'proceeds' with the important business - his own account of the sociology of law.

---

[1]Luhmann writes in *Social Systems* (1995: 76):

One can speak of 'fact dimension' in relation to ... themes of meaningful communication (in social systems). Facts or themes in this sense can also be persons or groups of persons. The fact dimension is thereby constituted in the meaning that divides the reference structure of what is meant into 'this' and 'something else'. Thus the point of departure for a factual articulation of meaning is a primary disjunction which contrasts something as yet indeterminate to something as yet indeterminate. (emphasis in original)

[2]Maturana (1980: 29) offers the following definition of an autopoietic system:

A dynamic system that is defined as a composite unity as a network of productions that,

a) through their interactions recursively regenerate the network of productions that produce them, and

b) realise this network as a unity in the space in which they exist by constituting and specifying its boundaries as surfaces of cleavage from the background through their preferential interaction within the network, is an autopoietic system.

> There seems to be no way in which the value of this approach can be tested *in its own terms*[3], since presumably all meta-theoretical discourse is also self-referential. *You make an act of faith in favour of autopoiesis and hence reject all other sociology of law, or you refuse to do so and proceed with the rest of this and the next chapter* (Ibid, emphasis added).

On one level this is clearly right. There exists, according to Luhmann, no meta-theory which is not self-referential. The value of the theory cannot, therefore, be judged according to some universal or univocal criteria. Professor Harris, however, in his account of legal philosophies offers no solution to this post-modern predicament, unless it is his own version of legal reasoning and his own undoubted intelligence. What Professor Harris leaves out in his appeal to acts of faith is that 'proceeding' with his chapter may equally be a matter of faith, as there is no way of testing his own exclusive claim to reasonableness, except 'in its own terms'. In his appeal to his readers' better judgement, Harris seems quite unwilling to admit that there is any real choice to be made between what he sees as Luhmann's bizarre ideas and his own totally rational account of the sociology of law. But is this not the one important question that one should decide before 'proceeding', namely which of the two versions, expositions or models of law should be chosen, his or Luhmann's? By giving any credence to autopoietic theory the reader is, according to Harris, engaging in an 'act of faith', and not, therefore, an act of reason. Harris thus ensures that this crucial question is never even asked. This notion that to take autopoiesis seriously is rather like joining some extremist religious sect - to be avoided by all sensible, level-headed people is not untypical of some of the most violent reactions to what is in most cases a very small dose of Luhmann.

Surprisingly perhaps, these 'summary dismissive' critics, for the most part, do not admit to any personal difficulties in understanding the theory or if, exceptionally they do, then any obstacles to understanding are attributed to the obscurity and impenetrability of autopoietic writings, rather than their own deficiencies. All of them appear to have no difficulty in understanding enough of the theory to convince themselves that they thoroughly disapprove of it.

At this point it is worthwhile bringing in Zenon Bankowski who, in an article in *Ratio Juris* (1994) cleverly turns the theory against itself by questioning whether there ever can be an authentic account of what the theory means. He asks what it would mean 'in the theory's own' terms for

---

[3]I take issue with the idea that it is impossible to analyse autopoiesis *in its own terms* in my discussion, later in this essay, of Zenon Bankowski's elaboration of this argument (pp. 129-30).

an autopoietic theorist to say that he had 'completely misunderstood the theory'.

> Our theorist could not understand what I said but merely produce his own version of what I said. Therefore, it's not what I said that is completely wrong but what he said that I said that is wrong i.e as a picture of autopoiesis what I said, in his representation of it, is wrong. That is, it does not correspond to the picture that he has of autopoiesis. Both these pictures are his pictures. How he got to his representation of mine, I don't know and nor can he (Bankowski, 1994: 263).

There are two points to be made here. Firstly, Zenon Bankowski's argument is an interesting one, but it risks casting doubt on the value of all theoretical discussion, since no discussant can be sure that any concept they refer to is understood by listeners (observers) in the same way as he or she intended. It is surely wrong, however, when, as here, it is directed against a specific social theory, where the dimensions and concepts have been defined over and over again by its author(s). It must be legitimate to say that a critic of the theory has mistaken, misinterpreted, misread, misapplied etc. the theory, particularly where that critic gives no specific references and makes no quotations from the theoretical text that he or she is criticizing in order to support their arguments.

Secondly, this strategy of questioning whether understanding autopoiesis 'in it own terms' can have any meaning in the theory's 'own terms' serves two purposes. First, it raises the question as to whether autopoetic theory operates at such a level of generality that it may be interpreted in all kinds of manner, without anyone being able to say which one is right. At the same time, it points out the absurdity of constructivist ideas which rely entirely upon an observer's subjective notions of what consititutes reality. I should just mention in parenthesis here that this seeming absurdity is precisely what Luhmann exposes in his notion of 'paradox', the wonder of it being that society is still able to reconstitute itself through its social subsystems, in spite of the glaring absurdity.

A rather different form of dismissal to that of Harris, or the *reductio ad adsurdum* of total subjectivity of Bankowski is to be found in Anthony Beck's (Beck, 1994) review of Gunther Teubner's book, *Law as an Autopoietic System* (Teubner, 1993). While he admits that the theory may be useful in other spheres, he is quite certain that it has no place in legal theory, because it is a 'phoney' theory in contrast to a 'legitimate' legal theory which for Beck is any theory which 'depends for its success upon securing a fit between the the theoretical terms and the phenomena under consideration'(Beck, 1994: 402).

> Thus its theoretical concepts are those which are generally used in an everyday context, or in a specific technical context, in which they clearly fit the phenomena observed in the context according to the way in which they are habitually used. However, such concepts become 'phoney' when a theorist deploys them as a way of theorizing legal phenomena ... [which] has the effect of obscuring and distorting the phenomena it is now applied to, of misrepresenting them. In other words, the concept becomes an unacknowledged metaphor presented within propositions which claim literal truth.

Later he tells us that:

> The principal concepts in autopoietic theory are 'communications', 'system' and 'autopoiesis'... These principal concepts *are all phoney*. Communications, system and autopoiesis are all notions which fit adequately and serve well in some contexts but do not do so here [that is in relation to the legal system] (Beck, 1994: 409, emphasis added).[4]

One cannot help wondering how Beck is able to draw and apply this distinction in a manner which is not itself self-referential. Who, other than Beck himself (or those applying the distinction he has constructed), can tell us what 'fits the phenomena observed', what 'has the effect of obscuring and distorting ... [or] misrepresenting them'?

The other problem with Beck's criticism is that he appears unable to go behind the generic term, 'communication' in his attack on the theory's applicability to the legal system. If he had done so, he would have discovered that for the legal system 'communications' would include

---

[4]It is interesting from an autopoietic perspective that, in his insistence on labelling theoretical concepts as either 'phoney' or legitimate (non-phoney), Beck employs a distinction in typical binary manner to observe observations about the legal system. Luhmann comments on this form of second order distinction between natural and artificial in *Essays on Self Reference* (Luhmann, 1990b: 139),

The distinction natural/artificial can be utilized in such a way that an observation can interpret as artificial and contingent what the system itself assumes to be natural and necessary. For example, an observer may examine how a system creates the impression of its self-determinations being natural, necessary and lacking functional alternatives. He may then, for example, search for functional equivalents for the notion of God serving to deparadoxize the religious system. To use Heinz von Foerster's (1979) formulation, in this way an observer can see that the observed system cannot see that it is unable to see what it cannot see.

decisions, judgments, pleadings, legal opinions etc., all of which may, in his terms be 'used in an everyday context, or in a specific technical context, in which they clearly fit the phenomena observed in the context according to the way in which they are habitually used', and all of which are seen by the theory as specific legal communications.

It is worth mentioning at this stage that Roger Cotterell (Cotterell, 1992) makes a similar criticism to Beck's complaint that autopoiesis uses concepts to distort 'reality', but he does so in far rather more restrained terms. He criticizes what he sees as the imposition by autopoietic theory of a pre-ordained law/non law distinction. In one of his several discussions of autopoietic theory he writes:-

> it is essential from a professional point of view for the lawyer to be able clearly to distinguish law from non-law... The lawyer needs a test to tell him what materials he can rely upon in legal argument before a court or in devising legal strategies which may one day be tested in litigation. A social science of law, however, while taking full account of these lawyers' tests of 'the legal', must seek not to close off inquiry, before it begins, by conclusively specifying the nature of the object of study in a definition. It relies on 'working models' or open conceptions of law which are adequate to guide inquiry and are constructed solely for that purpose... Open-minded inquiry requires merely provisional concepts... (Cotterell, 1992: 38).

The implication here, of course, is that the unpragmatic, unempirical autopoietic theory 'closes off inquiry' before it begins 'by conclusively specifying the nature of the object of study in a definition'.

What do such summary dismissals of the theory (or at least of its usefulness for the purposes of legal or socio-legal analysis) tell us? That the theory is so riddled with problems that it is not even worth giving it serious consideration; that it represents such a threat to decent folk that even to give it serious attention may expose the reader to untold dangers - best dispose of it once and for all? A more generous interpretation might go something like this: those English and American legal scholars and researchers who reject even the possibility of engaging seriously with autopoietic theory are so thoroughly emersed in an intellectual culture dominated by empirical methodology, liberalism, and humanism that any criteria for success or for having value or usefulness necessarily have to be derived from these traditions. For these scholars, nothing worthy of serious consideration exists beyond these intellectual horizons. Is it surprising that when presented with an account of society which not only deals in unfamiliar, highly abstract notions, such as 'double-contingency, 'time-binding' and 'structural coupling', but in addition seems to turn its back on all those conventional scholarly ambitions of progress through knowledge, truth-revelation and the creation of a better world, they decline the challenge to leap into the chasm that autopoiesis opens up before them? Is it surprising that they prefer to remain on what they experience as firm ground? Whether or not this explanation justifies the summary dismissal that has unfortunately characterized some scholars' response to autopoiesis is not an issue for this article. Nor is this the place to ask why certain of the writers mentioned above reacted with such violence. Suffice it to say that this is only one of the possible strategies open to scholars when they are confronted with ideas which appear as unfamiliar, difficult to understand, and threatening to their own intellectual security. Another, strategy is to transform the unfamiliar in such a way as to assimilate it with or within a familiar conceptual framework. In this way it appears that the author both understands the theory and is ready to undertake a serious analysis of its complexities. Whereas, when put into practice, this analysis often has the effect of simplifying and distorting the theory, sometimes to the point that it is barely recognizable.

(2) Assimilation

Perhaps the most complete example of the assimilation strategy comes from Drucilla Cornell (Cornell, 1995), who sees Luhmannian autopoiesis as 'epistemological constructivism' and, therefore, almost equivalent to Stanley Fish's view of the world for, each, according to Cornell, implicitly relies upon 'the logic of recursivity'(Cornell, 1995: 251-2). What Luhmann offers is

> The newest brand of legal positivism ... [which] goes by the name autopoiesis. But if the name is new, the ultimate project of legal positivism, which is to solve the problem of validity of legal propositions through an appeal to the mechanisms of validation internally generated by an existing legal system, remains the same (Cornell, 1995: 234).

For autopoiesis, law constructs its own reality through its own operations, so that

> The postulation of operational closure explains why systems theory is a form of epistemological constructivism in which reality comes to 'be' only within the recursiveness of the system. The reality of law for

> Luhmann is a normative reality... Normative closure creates the seeming adequation of law and justice (Cornell, 1995: 236).

Cornell's polemicizes against what she sees as Luhmann's abolition of ontology and the displacement of philosophy by sociology - 'We no longer attempt to know Being, only social systems'(Cornell, 1995: 251).[5] Yet this idiosyncratic account of the inherent negativity in autopoietic theory is achieved only through deliberately confusing legal reality with social reality and social reality with total 'reality'. It is then possible for Cornell to claim that for Luhmann there can be no reality outside that constructed through the operation of social systems.[6] Both autopoietic law and autopoietic sociology then come to be seen as imposing a hegemonic vision of social reality within which radical critique cannot exist. In her attempt to turn Luhmann into an 'epistemological constructivist' Cornell attributes to Luhmann the belief that reality is no more than a social construction and that nothing exists outside our (or the system's) own knowledge. In fact Luhmann's account of the relationship between knowledge and the external world is much more complex than Cornell's account suggests. She continues,

> In Luhmann's conception of the legal system's autopoiesis, justice can only be what the legal system defines it to be. The idea of justice as a projected horizon is completely rejected (Cornell, 1995: 241).

> Through autopoietic closure the system becomes the only reality. As such it fills the universe; it becomes a kingdom which reigns over possibility and excludes the dream of a truly different future (Cornell, 1995: 244).

---

[5]For Luhmann anything may become meaningful and so 'real', but at the same time, the absence of a system capable of making certain distinctions results in the absence of reality insofar as meaning based on those distinctions is concerned.

[6]It is interesting to note here that Luhmann rarely use the term 'reality' and nowhere in his writings can one find anything resembling the notion that all reality is a construction and nothing exists outside the reality constructed by social systems. Reality does 'exist', but it is inaccessible and overlaid by the difference between system and environment which, for the system's communications, takes on the status of universal validity.

The difference between system and environment practised by a system presupposes and overlies a continuous reality ... A communicative social system arranges everything in its own communication as either internal or external and practices its own system/environment distinction as something universally valid, insofar as its own communication is concerned. (Luhmann, 1995: 178-9).

> Since we have no transcendental or outside viewpoint, it follows that there can be no social criticism and no critical consciousness. Change can take place only as slow evolution, but not through transformation (Cornell, 1995: 251).[7]

There are clearly differences here in what Cornell and Luhmann understand by 'law'. While Cornell may see herself, justifiably, as a radical critic of 'the law', Luhmann nevertheless would regard her criticism of law as a *legal communication*, that is as communication dealing with law. Luhmann's broad, inclusive notion of 'the legal system' as a system of communications is a difficult one, particularly for lawyers and critics of law who tend to see the legal system as meaning courts, judges, police, judgements, codes, statutes, etc. Cornell's misreading, therefore, is quite understandable. In Luhmann's terms, however, 'social criticism' and 'critical consciousness', where they relate to law, are indeed part of the legal system of communications. However radical or utopian they may be, these viewpoints should not be regarded as transcendental. They may exist as critiques of law, but always within the broad spectrum of legal communications.

Although Cornell is clearly right in stating that for Luhmann there can be no 'transcendental viewpoint', she is just as clearly mistaken in believing that there can be no viewpoint outside law. True, there can be no observation from outside social systems, meaning 'society', but there is nothing to restrict other social systems from observing law, whether from a political, scientific, economic, psychoanalytic or aesthetic viewpoint. Luhmann does not exclude social criticism or critical consciousness. He simply states that they do not occur outside society's communication sub-systems.

---

[7]For Luhmann anything may become meaningful and so 'real', but at the same time, the absence of a system capable of making certain distinctions results in the absence of reality insofar as meaning based on those distinctions is concerned.

Cognitively all reality must be constructed by means of distinctions and, as a result, remains construction ...
The conclusion to be drawn from this is that the connection with the reality of the external world is established by the blind spot of the cognitive operation. Reality is what one does not perceive when one perceives. All of this means that the fruits of the concrete operation of cognition, which issues from the use of distinctions - that is, the proliferation of combinatorial possibilities - is due to an instrument requiring an operational closure specific for the given system. If cognition demands meaning and meaning demands distinction then the final reality must be thought of as devoid of meaning. (Luhmann, 1990b: 76; see also Luhmann, 1986a).

If we now view the world in Cornell's terms, it is not hard to understand how Luhmann's position could be regarded as almost identical with that of Stanley Fish, who maintains that 'what deconstruction or post-modern philosophy more generally has shown us is that all reality, including the self, is socially constructed. This in turn means for Fish that "we" are what our reality makes us. We could not be otherwise' (Cornell, 1995: 251).

Luhmann, however, in direct contrast to Cornell's interpretation of his position, opens up the possibility that reality could be different, making it possible that *we could well be otherwise*[8] and *so could our reality!* -

[8]Everything in Luhmann's vision 'could be otherwise', including (one assumes) the autopoietic nature of social systems in the modern world. Throughout his works he frequently stressed the contingent nature of the social world. For example,

Something is contingent insofar as it is neither necessary nor impossible; it is just what it is (or was or will be), though it could also be otherwise. The concept thus describes something given (something experienced, expected, remembered, fantasized) in the light of its possibly being otherwise; it describes the world as it is given, yet it does not describe the possible in general, but what is otherwise possible from the viewpoint of reality. In this sense, recently it has become customary to speak of the 'possible worlds' of one real lifeworld. The reality of the world is presupposed by the concept of contingency as its first and irreplaceable condition of possibility (Luhmann, 1995: 106).

Double contingency is 'double négation virtuelle' meaning that possibilities of negation can only be retained and stabilized as reciprocally not actualized, but implied possibilities. The doubling of contingencies is possible because this potential is located in subjects and subjects can experience other subjects. The doubling does not double the world and does not construct two separate realms of contingency. The potential is universal for each subject and is an aspect of the meaningful constitution of his encompassing world, so that ego has to identify alter as being another subject in his world and vice versa. Double contingency rests on the fact that contingency is subjective and universal at once (Luhmann, 1976: 509).

Within the world created by operations of this system every concrete item appears as contingent, as something which could be different. Societies, therefore, operate within a paradoxical world, the paradox being the necessity of contingency (Luhmann, 1986b: 7, emphasis added).

The term contingency is intended to express the fact that the possibilities of further experience and action indicated in the horizon of actual experience are just that - possibilities - and might turn out differently than expected, i.e. that these indications might be deceptive... (Luhmann, 1990b: 26, emphasis added).

power is always a matter of social relations in which action could always have been different on both sides of the relation... (Luhmann, 1990c: 156, emphasis added).

although how this alternative state was, or could be, achieved is always uncertain and is likely to remain so. Her misunderstanding of Luhmann's writings allows Cornell to place him fairly and squarely on one side of the predominantly American legal theory debate, the long-running argument between 'the crits' and 'the liberals'. On the one side are those critical theorists who advocate radical change through revolutionizing or reconstituting legal consciousness and thus, legal reality and, on the other, those who maintain that progress is to be achieved through the evolution, development and deployment of well-tried legal principles. Cornell portrays the conservative position, and thus Luhmann's position, as maintaining that 'change can take place only as slow evolution, but not through transformation... [that] there is only evolution, not transformation' (Cornell, 1995: 251) - a liberalism which relieves the individual of responsibility.

I shall take up this issue of autopoiesis and individual responsibility later. In the meantime, let us stay with Anglo-American assimilations and turn to the relation between self-reference and autonomy, which has caused particular problems for Anglo-American scholars. The American socio-legal scholar, Richard Lempert (1998), sees autonomy and autopoiesis as closely related, if not synonymous.

> If the legal system is autopoietically organized it will enjoy the autonomy associated with autopoietic systems regardless of whether and what social functions it fills. It could hardly be otherwise (Lempert, 1998: 154).

While, according to Lempert, Continental legal theorists come from a different tradition, use different methods and present their arguments differently from their Anglo-American counterparts, concern for the notion of legal autonomy, is a constant which unites them - 'two different perspectives *on an idea of legal autonomy*, together with two different sources of inspiration for the two perspectives and the differences in the way that the theories have been advanced.' (Lempert, 1988: 155, emphasis added).

His belief in such a constant leads him to 'construct a theory of legal autonomy rooted in the Anglo-American perspective' and 'then turn to Luhmann's work on autopoiesis to examine ways in which the ideas of autopoiesis accords or conflicts with the theory' (ibid). The problem with Lempert's attempt at comparative jurisprudence is that autopoiesis and the Anglo-American notion of autonomy - which, in Lempert's view, concerns the power to manage one's own affairs free from external constraints and demands - are conceptually so different that there is no basis for comparison and so no reason for believing that it will be possible to identify points of accord and points of conflict between them. Luhmann clearly brings out the incommensurability of the two approaches in his reported response to Lempert's paper, pointing out that, in autopoietic theory

> there can be a simultaneous increase of dependence and independence in system environment relations: the legal system can have more and varied relations with its environment - and to that degree becomes more dependent; however, to the extent that its organization has complexified and powers or self-reproduction increased the system has become more independent of its environment (i.e. becomes better able to deal with external perturbations) (Kennealy, 1988: 363).

Lempert's view of the legal system-environment relationship, however, is 'as a zero sum game between the system and the environment: the more the environment influences law, the less autonomous law becomes' (ibid) is clearly an Americanization of a notion which is both more complex than Lempert's input-output model and, at the same time, not particularly concerned with an observer's account of system power, that is the capacity of each system to manage its own affairs. Rather it is how the system *sees itself and its relationship with its environment* which is of interest to autopoieticists (for a full discussion of this issue see Nelken, 1988).

Contrast Lempert's interpretation of autopoiesis as autonomy with that of another American legal theorist, Arthur Jacobson, who in his Michigan Law Review article, *Autopoietic Law: The New Science of Niklas Luhmann* (Jacobson, 1989) , brings his considerable critical powers and eloquent style to bear on what he maintains is Luhmann's concept of the 'unity of the legal system'. In his efforts to bring autopoietic theory into range of his own overwhelming concerns over the dynamism of the common law and law's relations to 'the individual', he succeeds in producing an elaborately argument both as to why 'autopoietic law' is such an interesting theoretical development and why ultimately certain of Luhmann's ideas should be rejected in favour of his own dynamic view of law. Yet far from analysing autopoietic theory in the terms set out by Luhmann, he proceeds by subjecting his own highly personal interpretations of 'autopoietic law' to his own critical scrutiny. Unfortunately many of these interpretations not only cannot be justified by reference to the original text, but are several light years away from Luhmann's theory. Yet all is done with such eloquence that throughout the reader is led to believe that Jacobson is using Luhmann's ideas as legitimate starting points for his insights and flashes of brilliance. It is assimilation *par excellence* to the extent that one is given the clear impression that Luhmann and Jacobson both share the same assumptions about law and society and the same concerns for the future of the legal system and individuals caught up in that system.

At the start of his article, Jacobson (1989) tells his Michigan Law Review readers why he admires Luhmann's championing of the autonomy of the legal system, but then goes on to explain why he disagrees with his description of the relationship between law morality and politics and to the absence of any reference to 'real individuals' (Jacobson, 1989: 1651-2). Having presented an account of autopoietic law - 'the first image of law drawn from science that comes even close to revealing the secrets of common law's own harsh discipline' (Jacobson, 1989: 1647) - Jacobson sets out the two distinct interests that legal theorists have in this new approach to law.

> The first is the *dynamism* of autopoietic law ... The legal systems of advanced industrial democratic countries generate and transform law in every legal act and communication ... Autopoiesis is a wonderful image for a system dynamically generating and transforming its own elements (emphasis in original).

The second is the unity of the autopoietic law. Referring throughout to page numbers of Luhmann's essay, 'The Unity of the Legal System' (Luhmann, 1988), Jacobson explains that, while law may be 'deeply affected by the political and moral exigencies of administration, modern legal systems claim that they do not 'decompose' to the forces that affect them'.[9]

---

[9]Jacobson refers here to pages 14-15 of Luhmann's article. Luhmann does not, however, mention law on these pages, but is concerned more generally with the nature of autopoietic systems. What he writes is that,

> *An autopoietic system ... constitutes the elements of which it consists through the elements of which it consists. In doing so it sets limits which do not exist in the substructure complexity of the environment of the system.* (Luhmann, 1988: 14).

As for 'decomposing' into the forces that affect them, Luhmann's only mention of decomposing on these pages is in relation to the limitations of action theory as revealed by Parsons' inability to find an answer to 'the constitution of the 'unit act'. He writes:

> *The decomposition of action and the conception of the emergent unity of action based on it was an act which could only be performed by an outside observer. This presents a problem, since the unity did not come from the system itself.* (Luhmann, 1988: 15).

This means that,

> autopoietic law asserts that legal systems can be substantially coherent despite the lack of a single, rationally expressible essence.[10] Autopoiesis proclaims the dynamic substantive coherence - the 'unity' if the legal system in its sustaining control over its own operations[11] The system is autonomous, because it 'can neither derive its operations from its environment nor pass them on to that environment' (Jacobson, 1989: 1649).[12]

There is much that one could write about Jacobson's blatant reconstruction of autopoiesis as set out in this brief extract. In the first place, there is nothing on the pages referred in Luhmann's article (or elsewhere in his writings) to suggest that the legal system is capable of 'sustaining control over its own operations', for Jacobson's idea of control simply has no resonance in Luhmann's theory. Indeed much that goes on in the courts is outside the control of law, but is a reaction of, for example, political, economic or scientific communications. Law's 'control' is always restricted to its own operations, that is to 'its own possiblities of negation'. For Luhmann the legal system is able to declare its own operations legal or illegal,[13] but this does not amount to 'control' in Jacobson's sense of the

---

[10]Jacobson refers here to Luhmann, 1988, (note no. 32) p. 21. Luhmann does not use the words, 'rationally expressible essence' or anything similar on the page referred to by Jacobson. The nearest, he comes, and it is not very near at all, to Jacobson's notion that the legal system has an essence is to point out the circularity in law *'in terms of normativity ... of the relationship between the rule and its application'.*

[11]Jacobson refers here to Luhmann, 1988: 13-14, 18, 23-26.

[12]Jacobson refers here to Luhmann, 1988, p.18. This is a misstatement of what Luhmann wrote. Luhmann is writing on page 18 about 'society' and not about the legal system. Nevertheless, it is the case that the legal system too 'cannot derive its operations from its environment nor pass them on to that environment'. This does not, however, result in 'autonomy' in the way that Jacobson suggests, that is autonomy at the expense of dynamism.

[13]For example, Luhmann (1988: 25) writes:

> *For operative purposes, differentiation is oriented not simply towards the function of law but towards the antithesis of legal/illegal. The legal system must accordingly be understood as the unity of legality and illegality or more precisely as the control by this antithesis of its autopoiesis with the result that every operation of the system must be conditioned by the system itself* (emphasis added).

term.[14] Jacobson misses the crucial point that the unity of the legal system allows law to gain the impression of control, but only at the price of limitating its operations to determining lawfulness and unlawfulness. Secondly, Jacobson criticizes Luhmann's 'construction of autopoietic law' because 'he favors ... the operative unity of modern legal systems and their autonomy from the environment, at the expense of ... the dynamism of these systems' (Jacobson, 1988: 1649). The 'formula, normatively closed and cognitively open' according to Jacobson, 'makes autopoietic law into fancy positivism coupled with covert naturalism'(ibid). Yet, for Luhmann, it is not only possible, but necessary for the legal system to respond to information from its environment in ways that produce new laws, which themselves feed back into the enviroments of other social systems. This could well be interpreted, in Jacobson's terms, as dynamism. Autopoietic law is not, however, 'fancy positivism' and it does not make 'naturalism' any more likely than any other form of law. By 'legal operations', Luhmann is referring to law's production of legal decisions, and not to its 'performance' or results. It is these operations, and not laws, which 'are neither derived from its environment nor exportable to that environment'. They are unique to the legal system. Jacobson has, therefore, completely misinterpreted Luhmann's account of the legal system's unity by reconstructing it within a debate over the dynamism or conservatism of law - but oddly on the opposite side to that chosen by Cornell.

Thirdly, for Jacobson, Luhmann 'treats the legal system as a super-individual'(ibid) which means that 'the real individual, will be missing'(ibid). 'The absence of the real individual leads Luhmann to legal theories that likewise marginalize the individual, namely positivism and naturalism'(ibid). One can only marvel at Jacobson's creativity and weep for poor Luhmann as he watches his attempt to develop a new sociology which removes the individual from the centre of theoretical attention being interpreted as a theory of 'super-individuals'.

But this is not all. Jacobson's idiosyncratic understanding of the theory leads him to maintain that '[t]he legal system can be autopoietic in its own right only if a subsystem - a discrete social system serving a function within another social system - can be autopoietic ... The claim that a legal system is an autopoietic subsystem' according to Jacobson, 'thus stands or falls on Luhmann's ability to distinguish between 'normative' and 'cognitive' and [T]his is an empirical distinction Luhmann cannot validate'. Indeed, '[T]he common law exemplifies the empirical difficulties besetting

---

[14]The only other reference to 'control' in this part of the essay comes on page 15 where, writing of self-referential systems generally, Luhmann states that '*the system, with every operation, controls its <u>own</u> possibilities of negation*' (Emphasis in original).

the distinction'. So, in Jacobson's eyes, an attempt to construct autopoietic law fails and Luhmann descends into 'a mixture of positivism and naturalism'(Jacobson, 1989: 1650). What is particularly interesting, is Jacobson's assertion in the footnotes that 'Luhmann is aware of this problem. See p. 19.' (ibid). Any reader of Jacobson's article with the time and motivation to dig out the Luhmann essay and turn to page 19 would find first of all that what Luhmann wrote was that the differentiation of the legal system is based on the distinguishability of normative and cognitive *expectations*, (emphasis added) that is whether *expectations* are based on norms or experience. This is a very different matter to the difficulties that Jacobson identifies of distinguishing law from facts or norms from knowledge. Moreover, far from recognizing this as a problem, Luhmann asks the question, 'how does this happen?' and then proceeds promptly in the next paragraph to answer that question.

I realise that there is a danger here of the polemicism of my own commentary invading and taking over the main text and I have reached only page 5 of Jacobson's article. I can only apologise and point to my own difficulty in distinguishing between genuine misunderstanding and wilful distortion. Let me just add that, far from attacking Luhmann's theory, much of Jacobson's article is full of praise for what he sees as the autopoietic project. The point is that Jacobson's version of what he calls 'the autopoietic project' bears only a passing resemblance to anything that Luhmann had written, as the following extracts, show.

> As Luhmann sees it, if autopoiesis is a correct description of legal systems in advanced industrial democracies, then law can make good the claim to provide a ... reliable standard for citizens ... to use in their daily interactions. From Luhmann's perspective, if autopoiesis is wrong, then the legal system must seemingly succumb (Jacobson, 1989: 1651).

Where has Luhmann ever entertained the criterion of 'reliable standards for citizens' or the possibility of autopoiesis *being wrong*? Again, where does Luhmann contemplate the idea of the legal system *succumbing*? What in terms of autopoietic theory does this mean?

> The project (Luhmann's) of protecting the legal system from 'non-legal' politics or morality is a false project (Jacobson, 1989: 1652).

When has Luhmann ever been concerned with *protecting the legal system*?

> Autopoiesis too is the science of the individual (Jacobson, 1989: 1653).

Really?

> The intent of the autopoietic paradigm is to account for the power of organisms to control or affect the environments in which they collectively evolve (Jacobson, 1989: 1661).

For Luhmann there is no shared environment or, at least, none that can be recognized collectively as such by social systems. His point is that each system produces its own environment and then reacts to communications from that environment. Any control that a system exercises, therefore, relates to its own environment only and not to some limitless universe.

> My thesis is twofold. First any fully autopoietic legal system must include the individual as such in the self-generating operations of the system.[15] Second, any legal system that puts the individual at the centre must resort to some version (which we can specify) of law as revelation (Jacobson, 1989: 1678).

Luhmann, as we shall see, of course, goes to great lengths to explain why he rejects the individual as his unit of analysis (see below note 18).

Need I go on? Let it be enough for me to say that Jacobson's autopoiesis is not Luhmann's autopoiesis, and that, if from time to time during the course of Jacobson's long article the two fleetingly come close to resembling one another, the illusion is soon dispelled as Jacobson hauls autopoiesis off into yet another flight of fantasy.

(3) (Mis)understanding 'closure'

The idea of normative closure suffers a similar fate as autonomy at the hands of some British and American critics of autopoiesis. Adrian James (James, 1992), for example, denies any possibility that social systems could be closed, because

> it is highly debatable whether any social system can be closed. In particular, it can be argued that law, by its very nature is a *social* institution and the environment in which it exists is a *social* environment.
>
> ... Crucially, law is also closely linked structurally to other key social institutions such as Parliament so that the nature, shape and content of law, ... , are determined of necessity by its parameters, both socially and

[15]But this ignores or does not appreciate the difficulties which Luhmann identifies in his discussion of 'decomposition of action' (Luhmann, 1988, p.15). See above note 9.

> institutional. It can be argued, therefore, that law is inherently an open system which is moulded by its environment, since it must and does change in response to its environment ... (James, 1992, emphasis added).

The trouble is that James, like several other critics of 'closed systems', ignores the essential ingredient of the theory. What Luhmann is writing about is not power relations between people or between individuals and systems, but communications and the distinction between system and environment. Systems create and maintain closure through their ability to distinguish certain kinds of communications as belonging to them and to reject others as being beyond their boundaries. It is this capacity of the legal system, firstly, to recognize some communications as legal communications (Luhmann, 1995: n. 38) and secondly to see itself as the only authority as to what constitutes a 'legal communication' which creates and sustains closure.[16]

Others critics have interpreted normative closure as a denial that professionals from different disciplines are able to understand one another or work together. In an essay on cross-disciplinarity in family justice, the social researcher Mervyn Murch (Murch, 1995) for example, proclaims his disagreement with what he identifies as King and Piper's (King and Piper, 1995) account of the difficulties of effective interprofessional cooperation, caused by autopoietic closure. He writes:

> This paper ... is concerned with the inter-disciplinary mix of law, welfare and child health which infuses the practice and structure of a distinctly hybridized system of justice. In this context I touch on the proposition ... that the autopoietic nature of law makes it particularly difficult for lawyers to collaborate effectively with the health and welfare professionals providing services for children and families. (Murch, 1995: 195).

In fact what King and Piper wrote was of the impossibility of hybrid discourses or, in Luhmann's terms, system of communication - a combination of law and child welfare science. There is no mention of this affecting the ability of lawyers and social workers or child mental health workers to cooperate with one another at an interpersonal or professional

---

[16] *The theory of self-referential systems maintains that systems can differentiate only by self-reference, which is to say, only insofar as systems refer to themselves (be this to elements of the same system, to operations of the same system, or to the unity of the same system in constituting their elements and their elemental operations* (Luhmann, 1995: 9, note n.6).

level. King and Piper stress at some length the difference between psychic (individual) and social systems (King and Piper, 1995: 25-6).

Other criticisms of closure along these same lines point out the impossibility of separating norms from facts and so of establishing empirically the existence of system closure.[17] Michael Freeman, the current author of *Lloyd's Introduction to Jurisprudence* (Freeman, 1994), informs his readers that Luhmann has mistaken the nature of the legal system which, in practice, on occasions adapts to radical normative changes in society (Freeman, 1994: 549). He proceeds to argue his point by demonstrating, with reference to both to American Supreme Court cases and English statutes which 'not infrequently refer to extra-legal norms' (ibid) that law is open to *values* and not just facts. So Luhmann, it seems, has got it badly wrong, at least in so far as the non-codified Anglo-American system is concerned (ibid). Freeman then goes on to anticipate that 'Luhmann's likely response' will be to

> separate facts and norms so that even a statute incorporating an extra-systemic standard can be described within autopoiesis theory. But formalism of this kind distorts - perhaps too high a price to pay to preserve a theory (Freeman, 1994: 548).

Unfortunately, neither Freeman nor the other critics of normative closure whom I have cited, have managed to come to grips with the radical paradigm shift that autopoiesis is attempting. As Tim Murphy, summarising a passage from Teubner's article, 'The Two Faces of Janus' (Teubner, 1992) points out,

> autopoietic theory's first task was to elaborate the notion of operational closure, *in order to overcome the limits of open system's thinking*, while retaining the notion of the distinction between system and environment. This involved 'a fully fledged change of paradigm'. Under this new paradigm, for cognition to be possible, systems must open up their environments not by input output, but by perturbation and structural coupling. In place of the informational output from the environment (from 'outside') which is internally processed, ouputted, and then available in due course as new input through a feedback loop, the new idea is that of using events, perturbations, noise, arising outside the system to create internal order. *'One has to free one's mind of any idea of information transportation'* (Murphy, 1994: 243, emphasis added).

---

[17] See page 17 and 18 above for a discussion of Arthur Jacobson's account of this issue.

These critics' understanding, therefore, of the system-environment relationship or of that between systems is not Luhmann's. To answer Freeman's specific complaint about Luhmann's failure to recognize that the legal system may indeed take in values from its environment, there is no need for Luhmann to attempt the task of separating facts and norms produced by other systems. Both are equally capable of creating perturbations in the legal system's environment to which the system may react through its own normative operations.

Both may enter the legal system only as 'knowledge' of the environment as perceived and interpreted by law, both may be subjected to legal operations and these operations may eventually produce legal communications. The only norms that are available for its own operations are legal norms. Indeed Luhmann's formula, 'cognitively open', can be rather misleading, as was apparent in Arthur Jacobson's reincarnation of autopoiesis, discussed earlier, for law does not have access to 'the environment', but only to *its environment*, so that all knowledge that enters the legal system has already been 'pre-processed' in a way that makes it acceptable as knowledge which law recognizes. To quote Gunther Teubner's celebrated paradox, which apparently 'sent looks of consternation - not to say appoplexy - across the faces of the unbelievers' at a conference in Florence, *'When I say 'open' I mean 'open' in a closed sort of way'* (!) (Kennealy, 1988: 349).

Once again, it is worth emphasing that it is not autopoietic theory *on its own term* that is being criticized by these commentators, but rather an understanding of the theory which has been formulated using concepts from a different paradigm. Autopoiesis is consequently constructed as something quite different from the form in which it was conceptualized by its creators and then its credibility demolished, or subjected to a severe battering for not being up to standard.

(4) Attributing (ir)responsibility

Perhaps the criticism of autopoiesis that has done most damage to its reputation and established its notoriety among some circles concerns the theory's lack of commitment to any moral values. Condemnation of the theory's failure to address intersubjective, ethical issues came originally from Luhmann's long-term, intellectual sparring partner, Jurgen Habermas (Habermas, 1987; Habermas, 1996). He argued that this deficiency effectively disqualifies autopoiesis for consideration as social theory capable of making general statements about meaning and validity and therefore renders it of limited value and applicability (Habermas, 1987: 185, 373; Habermas, 1996: 342). Reading some of the Anglo-American accounts of the theory, one could be forgiven for believing that autopoiesis commits not merely the sin of omission but also that of commission, actively belittling human values and undermining the ideals of a moral society. The moral argument against autopoiesis is cogently presented by Zenon Bankowski in his essay, 'How does it feel to be on your own? The Person in the Sight of Autopoiesis'(Bankowski, 1994). He takes Gunther Teubner to task for suggesting that autopoiesis 'enables there to be both collective and moral responsibility'. Bankowski argues that since Teubner has rejected 'Maturana's view that it is a constitutive feature of a social system that its components are living beings', he cannot claim that human beings exist within social systems. They may be 'bearers of the system' but this makes them merely 'elements in the system' and not human (psychic beings).

> So in fact the theory *assumes* the functional equivalence of the non existence of human beings ... individual responsibility disappears into collective or system responsibility. And that sense of collective responsibility loses any sense of individual responsibility. For the group is responsible, not any individuals (Bankowski, 1994: 259).

He later refers to the Teubner version of autopoiesis (Teubner, 1993) as 'the metaphysical illusion' , 'What are its consequences?', he then asks.

> The self is lost because it becomes the product of that false way of thinking. You don't act and love and hate, it is that illusory constructed self that does so. You no longer act. The self that is the product of the theory that you have constructed to answer the senseless question does ... a judge contradicts himself when he says that he is applying a law but thinks that it ought not to be applied - 'I sentence you to death, but I think that the death penalty is wrong ... What the judge is saying is that in the normative sphere of law you are guilty and deserve to hang ... But we are not talking of the self constructed as judge, condemning an individual constructed as offender. We are talking of one individual causing another to be killed ... It is he as judge, father, moralist, etc that takes the decision and not a bit of him. That would be to accept the metaphysical illusion and lose oneself in a particular normative sphere. Responsibility is evaded because *he* does not decide but the self constructed by the theory of the normative sphere that he has chosen does ... All this does not mean to say that it would be wrong to hang the person. It may be right but that is *your* decision and you cannot evade responsibility by saying that it was not you but you as a judge that took it (Bankowski, 1994: 261-2, emphasis in original).

Roger Cotterrell also takes up this issue of individual responsibility in an essay he wrote for a collection published in Poland in 1993. In his view autopoiesis is guilty of presenting people with the image of 'a world over which individuals have ... lost control' and, by so doing, encouraging them to 'absolve themselves of responsibility, ... for autonomous action' (Cotterrell, 1993: 68).

I have to say that I find this a strange argument. One might just as well condemn astronomy, geology and astro-physics and many other sciences and pseudo-sciences for suggesting that much that happens in the universe is beyond human control, or psychoanalyis, astrology and several religions, for proposing that the behaviour of human beings may be beyond their individual control.

In the same paragraph, however, Cotterrell shifts his ground from that of autopoiesis undermining individual responsibility to the repression, trivialisation and debasement 'in modern conditions' of 'subject-centred reason'. Autopoiesis, it seems, is particularly guilty here because of its reduction of 'the sociological status of the individual theoretically to that of a construct or carrier of various social systems, whose human autonomy is retained *only as a 'psychic system*'' (emphasis added). The words 'only as a psychic system' are crucial to this adaption (some would say 'villainization') of autopoietic theory for ideological objectives. Autopoietic theory, according to this view, describes a contest between the individual and his/her rationality and the chaotic world of social systems, which, like the weather can never be tamed through actions devised by human intelligence. Autopoietic theorists then emphasise the limitations of humanity, the weakness of the individual when, 'only as a psychic system', he or she is faced with the combined forces of social systems.

It is not difficult to see how a superficial reading of some of Luhmann's writings might give this impression. It is also clear that there is an element of assimilation here, particularly to the work of American sociologists, such as Goffman (Goffman, 1968), which describe the phenomenon of institutionalization - the individual and his/her values being swamped by the demands and norms of the organization as well as psychological work on authoritarianism (Milgram, 1974) and self-styled postmodernist sociology which sees modernity as a threat to human values and individual morality (Bauman, 1995). Nevertheless, the attribution of power to systems and the consequent submergence or supression of the individual finds no place in Luhmann's writing. Luhmann's concern is rather to understand how meaning and knowledge come into existence and take on a consensus and air of authority which enables society to exist and the contingent and paradoxical nature of that existence to be hidden from sight in a way that allows for an impression of stability and certainty to prevail at least to the extent that it is possible to communicate and to rely upon communications. In his quest for an answer he rejects any notion that 'man' or 'the individual' is able to take on this task. This does not mean, however, that social systems are the all-powerful forces in the world. It is systems that organize meaning and allow us to observe what would otherwise remain unobservable, but they are always held in check by their own self-referentiality, its limited vision of the world which 'cannot see that it is unable to see what it cannot see' (Luhmann, 1990b: 139) and, therefore, cannot make provision for, or anticipate events in its environment, whether they are produced by nature, human consciousness or other social systems.[18] Luhmann (1995: 186) later identifies '*the requirement of simultaneity*' as a major constraint on the ambitions of social systems. While each system will have its own internal ways of organizing time, creating the present by distinguishing past and future. The system may devise strategies for dealing with events over time - for example, law's device of adjourning cases or reserving judgments. The requirement of simultaneity *'guarantees that the system's and environment's horizons of past and future can be integrated, that is permit themselves to combine with world horizons'*. However, there can be no guarantee that events in the system's environment will order themselves in accordance with the system's notions of time. Far from it. While the system devises its own strategies for reacting to environmental events and ordering them in accordance with its notion of time, '[s]imultaneity of all occurrence', as Luhmann (1998:109), remarks, 'means the *uncontrollability of all occurrence*'.[19]

---

[18] *... the concept 'man' (in the singular!), as a designation for the bearer and guarantor of the unity of knowledge, must be renounced. The reality of cognition is to be found in the current operations of the various autopoietic systems. The unity of a structure of cognition (...) can only lie in the unity of an autopoietic system which reproduces itself with its boundaries, its structures and its elements ... There are now approximately 5 billion psychological systems. It has to be asked which of these 5 billion is intended when a theory of knowledge employing a psychologicl reference system relates concepts such as observation and cognition to consciousness. If no answer is forthcoming, such a theory has to be characterized as practicing socio-communicative observation. And the suggestion would have to be made that it would be better if this practice were reflected upon* (Luhmann, 1990a: 78).

[19] Luhmann (1990b: 185-6) also writes,

no system can advance into the future faster than others and thus lose the simultaneity required for contact with the environment ... The difference between system and

Those who criticise atutopoiesis for its amorality or immorality should be careful to distinguish between two different propositions. On the one side are moral or ethical statements specifically concerned with human responsibility and its limits, whether these simply define individual (or collective responsibility) or go further and prescribe who or what should be held responsible in a variety of situations. On the other side are propositions that were not intended by their authors as ethical or moral statements but which are subsequently interpreted or constructed as such by others. For example, moral philosophers in their writings and clergymen in their sermons make moral statements. Biologists who analyse human behaviour in terms of genetic inheritance do not, although it is always open to the former to interpret their scientific work as having moral implications.

Even a cursory reading of Luhmann and Teubner's accounts of autopoiesis will leave the reader in no doubt that they are both situated on the second side of this divide. Despite Bankowski's (and to a lesser extent, Cotterrell's) determination to see (im)moral imperatives in Teubner's book, *Autopoietic Law*, nowhere in its 158 pages will you find any mention of the conflict between personal responsibility and collective responsibility and nowhere will you find guidance to judges or anyone else on how they should set about explaining their decisions, so as to avoid responsibility for them.[20] Perhaps Bankowski's grievance with Teubner's book come from the absence of any recognition in autopoietic theory of a divine or moral

---

environment can only be established simultaneously. Thus the ongoing linkage between system and environment presupposes a common chronology ...

... Yet temporal autonomy is an indispensable condition for autonomy in questions of fact. If a system always had to react to environmental events the minute they happened, it would have little chance of selecting its mode of reacting.

Above all else, they cannot assume that other systems' notions of time, the distinction of past and future, will correspond with theirs. Any distinction of this kind has to occur within each system.

[20]The closest Teubner comes to an issue of moral conflict is in his discussion of Antigone's disobedience of Creon's law forbidding her from burying her brother. Teubner (1993: 7) remarks,

> *One should not see this purely as a conflict between divine and secular law, but as an insoluble paradox. Antigone maintains that Creon's laying-down of what is legal or illegal is itself illegal.*
>
> *It is at this point that the radical nature of Sophocles' critique of the law becomes clear. It is not, as contemporary critique would have it, individual legal norms, principles or doctrines that lead to antinomies and paradoxes. Rather it is the fact that law itself is based on a fundamental paradox which even alternative versions of a communal law cannot escape.*

law outside the legal system, but within individuals, which enables them to know whether it is right or wrong to disobey the formal law or whether they have taken the right or wrong decision by pronouncing a death sentence?

Luhmann in several of his books and articles tackles the specific issue of morality (e.g. Luhmann, 1993a; Luhmann, 1994), but it always as a sociologist observing the operations of 'the code of the moral' in society and never as moral philosopher or the kind of Durkheimian sociologist who believes that it is possible to discuss social order only in terms of morality or collective consciousness.[21]

Further evidence that what we are dealing with here is not, as Bankowski would have us believe, what autopoiesis says or, the way that autopoiesis would have us behave, but with subjective projections of the sociological theory into the moral sphere, that can be found in the selective way that moral critics of the theory set about their task. For example, if you thumb through the index of the English edition of Luhmann's major work, *Social Systems* (Luhmann, 1995) you will find only one reference to 'responsibility'. On the page referenced Luhmann describes how 'Ever since the second half of the seventeenth century ... the calculation of probability and risk [has] broadened the domain of causalities believed to be valid' (Luhmann, 1995: 387) This, he proposes, has resulted in

> even side-effects, which occur outside of intended effects [being] included ... into the calculations; because moral responsibility is claimed even for them. Responsibility is no longer to be accepted only for 'directing intentions'; it must include the entire future in the perspective of an 'ethics of responsibility' (ibid).[22]

---

[21]Luhmann (1997: 31) put forward his systems theory as a complete departure from Durkheimian sociology with its preoccupation with morality and presents his theory as a new form of sociology.

The answer to the question 'How is social order possible?' can no longer be given with reference to the bare fact of morality or the collective consciousness. Without the reality or relevance of moral questions being denied, such Durkheimian concepts are replaced by concepts such as symbolic generalization, selective or local consensus, the reduction of social complexity, and communication codes.

[22]A more complete account of this aspect of Luhmann's theoretical writings can be found in his book, *Risk: A Sociological Theory* (Luhmann, 1993b). Whether or not you agree with his account, Luhmann, in his writings on risk, at least recognizes these complexities.

Yet one waits in vain for one of the defenders of individual responsibility to seize upon this account by Luhmann and interpret it as a demand for a massive extension of such responsibility. Indeed, the whole issue of attributing responsibility is much more complex, both psychologically and sociologically, than some self-appointed guardians of public morality would have us believe. It is, for example, fashionable to believe that the current increase in opportunities for identifying victims and blaming others for the difficulties or unhappiness they are experiencing necessarily leads to a corresponding increase in responsible social behaviour. Yet as Antze and Lambek (1997) have argued, it could well have the opposite effect by reducing people's willingness to accept any responsibility for *their own* misfortunes.

Conclusion

One thing that I have learnt in writing this article is that the way that and the extent to which difficult and complex ideas become transformed in the hands of interpreters is in itself worthy of a distinct field of study. Hermeneutics, of course, already exists as a 'science of interpretations' but I am not aware of any hermeneutical studies of the transformation of sociological theories. In the socio-legal field, David Nelken's work on comparing legal cultures may go some way to filling this gap, but I would argue that to use 'culture' as the independent variable may, at least where it is social theories that are being reconstructed, be somewhat misleading (King, 1996).

One conclusion might be that the main difficulty faced by many Anglo-American social theorists, when confronted with autopoiesis, arises from their failure to recognise that the theory does not readily fit any formulation with which they are familiar. By the same token, it cannot, without major distortion be placed on one side or the other of ongoing ideological debates, whether political, moral or socio-legal. I would certainly go along with Tim Murphy's commentary (Murphy, 1994) on Teubner's account of the theory in 'The Two Faces of Janus: Rethinking Legal Pluralism' (Teubner, 1992). 'Autopoiesis' he states,

> does not ... challenge the existing organization of society, the distribution of power and resources, or the rightness or authority of the law and legal institutions ... It does not take up cudgels on behalf of the oppressed; it is not a critical-emancipatory theory (Teubner, 1992: 248).

But, as Murphy recognizes, 'it is an attempt to reconceptualize how late modern societies ... work in operational terms.'(ibid). As social theory, it represents a radical departure from existing ideas, 'a fully-fledged change of paradigm'(Teubner, 1992: 1445). In the ideological terms of late 20th Century political thinking, it has nothing to say for or against such issues as human rights, communitarianism, the regulation of corporations or the relief of poverty. What it does is to observe these unfolding phenomena as a result of the contingent operations in the communication of social systems.

Of course, there are those who will argue that there is no such thing as objective science, and still less objective social science, that all is interpretation in which the interpreter's prejudices and predilections need to be made explicit and subjected to critical analysis. The fact that the author may not have been aware of these influences on their ideas is seen as all the more reason to make them explicit. Where Luhmann is concerned, therefore, it is not only 'fair game' and a legitimate act of scholarship, but an unquestionable duty to expose the dangerous anti-progressive, anti-humanist message that lurks behind his false claims for scientific objectivity. According to this view, everything is political, so everything with scientific pretensions *should* be interpreted as political ideology in disguise. Hence, Luhmann's wry description of himself as 'the devil' (King, 1997: viii) and my ironic reference to 'the Luhmann heresy' in the title of this essay. But everything that happens in society may equally be seen in terms of psychology, moral philosophy, economics, religion or law and, yes, in terms of social science - that is, as contributing to a body of knowledge concerning the operation of society. By whose authority does politics attribute to itself this privileged position, if not politics itself? In autopoietic term, therefore, whichever way you turn, you are forced to confront the paradox of self-reference, unless you choose to ignore it altogether.

A second question, needs to be asked of those who see the act of re-interpreting Luhmann's theoretical ideas to expose their ideological dangers as itself representing progress, a way forward leading to a truer, more complete, more valuable or more valid understanding of society. Stanley Fish (Fish, 1989) has already exposed the contradiction in this position in his critique of Stephen Toulmin's essay, 'The Construal of Reality'(Toulmin, 1982). In that essay Toulmin urged scientists to become aware that 'their personal convictions are a function of [their] historical situation and be wary of allowing them to overwhelm [their] judgment'(Fish, 1989, p.437). In addition, he cautions them that when the scientist is about his proper business, he 'must acknowledge and discount his own reactions to and influence on that which he seeks to understand' (Toulmin, p.97). The question that Fish poses is:

> [W]hat enables us to do this? ... how is it that we can suddenly become pure spectators of our own mental operations? If we are already situated in a pregiven structure of interests, how is it that we can simply 'discount' those interests as if they had no weight at all? (Fish, 1989, p.437).

If all rationality is interpretive, why should the rationality of the critics be any less of any interpretation than that of the scientists they are criticizing? What ground have they for believing that they are closer to 'the truth' or 'progress'? Unless there is a plausible answer to this question (and I am not aware of any) then perhaps the best advice that one can give to those who wish to engage with scientific theories is to do so 'scientifically', that is, to repeat Luhmann's advice to the American student: 'Read more'.

None of this should be seen as an assertion of the perfection of autopoietic theory and a refutation of the possiblity of valid criticism. On the contrary, it is quite legitmate to take the theory to task, for example, for its assumption of functional differentiation (Knorr-Cetina, 1992), the overwhelming complexity of its model of society or the deceptive simplicity of the cognitively open/normatively closed dichotomy or of each system's binary coding (Schillmeier, 1999). One could also argue that the theory offers only observation and does not begin to provide a guide to practice or even to ways of understanding the experiences of practice. Moreover, some of the reformulations of the theory that have occurred could possibly be justified on the ground that criticizing autopoiesis presents the observer with a difficult task, because, once within the theory, there is no escape from its relativism and thus no sound way of testing its rightness or wrongness. On the other hand, to state that autopoiesis is 'wrong' from a position outside the theory always lays the critic open to the accusation that he or she is not engaging with the theory, but only with their own (inadequate) observations of the theory.

All this, however, is no excuse for poor scholarship. Criticisms which either ignore the original texts or reconstruct those texts in ways which change or misrepresent their meaning cannot be defended on the ground of relativism or legitmate interpretation. In Nabokov's novel, Kimbote's paranoia and delusions of grandeur may explain his distortions of John Shade's intentions in writing the poem, *Pale Fire*, but they do not justify his poor literary criticism.[23]

---

[23]If one wanted to engage in the kind of word play in which Nabokov (and Kimbote) indulges, one could draw attention to the closeness of Lumann to the English word 'luminary' which has the figurative meaning of 'a source of intellectual light ... a person of

While some of the critics discussed in this essay have clearly made considerable efforts to wrestle with autopoietic theory's difficult and unfamiliar concepts, others have, equally clearly, turned their backs on these concepts, either condemning them to the theoretical garbage can or recycling them in a form which makes them appear familiar, banal and wrong. Students who take these critics seriously may well take the view that it is not worth their while devoting time and effort to understanding the theory, when all they have to do is to quote its summary dismissal or misinterpretation by one or other of the eminent socio-legal scholars quoted in this essay. Yet in doing so they will be turning their backs on one the major achievements in social theory of the last century.[24]

References

Antze, P. and Lambec, M. (1996), *Past Tense: Cultural Escapism, Trauma and Memory* Routledge, New York/London.

Bankowski, Z. (1994), 'How does it feel to be on your own? The Person in the sight of Autopoiesis', 7 *Ratio Juris,* pp. 254-266.

Bauman, Z. (1995), *Life in Fragments*, Blackwell, Oxford.

Beck, A. (1994), 'Is Law and Autopoietic System?', 14 *Oxford Journal of Legal Studies*, pp. 401-418.

Cornell, D. (1995), 'Time, Deconstruction, and the Challenge of Legal Positivism: The Call for Judicial Responsiblity', in J. D. Leonard (ed.), *Legal Studies as Cultural Studies. A reader in (post)modern critical theory* Albany, State University of New York Press, New York, pp. 231-266.

Cotterrell, R. (1992), *The Sociology of Law: An Introduction (2nd edition),* Butterworths, London.

Cotterrell, R. (1993), 'Viewing Legal Discourses Sociologically', in G. Skapska (ed.), *Prawo w Zmieniajacym Si Spólczenstwie* Crakow, Wydawnictwo Adam Marszalek, pp. 55-70.

Fish, S. (1989), *Doing What Comes Naturally*, Clarendon Press, Oxford.

Foerster, H. von. (1981), *Observing Systems*, Intersystems Publications, Seaside, California.

Freeman, M. D. A. (1994), *Lloyd's Introduction to Jursiprudence (6th Edition),* Sweet and Maxwell, London.

Goffman, E. (1968), *Asylums,* Penguin, Harmondsworth.

'light and leading' (Oxford Shorter English Dictionary) , but conveniently, when given its literal meaning of 'source of light' may be used to refer to the morning star and hence to Lucifer (Microsoft Bookshelf - Thesaurus). Luhmann indeed ironically referred to himself as 'the devil' which adds spice to the reference to 'the Luhmann heresy' in the title of this essay. But this nonsense leads us nowhere ....

[24] I should like to thank Anton Schütz, Michael Schillmeier and David Nelken for their helpful comments. I am also grateful to the conveners of and participants at the Cardiff Workshop on 'The Consequences of the Autopoietic Theory of Law', for allowing me the opportunity to develop and present at the Workshop an earlier version of this paper.

Habermas, J. (1987), *The Philosophical Discourse of Modernity. Twelve Lectures*, Polity Press, Oxford.

Habermas, J. (1996), *Between Facts and Norms*, Polity Press, Cambridge.

Harris, J. W. (1997), *Legal Philosophies (second edition)*, Butterworths, London.

Jacobson, A. (1989), 'Autopoietic law: The new science of Niklas Luhmann', 87 *Michigan Law Review*, pp.1647-1689.

James, A. (1992), 'An Open or Shut Case? Law as an autopoietic system', 19 *Journal of Law and Society,* pp.271-283.

Kaganas, F., King, M. and Piper, C. (1995), *Legislating for Harmony. Partnership under the Children Act 1989,* Jessica Kingsley, London.

Kennealy, P. (1988), 'Talking about Autopoiesis - Order from Noise?' in G. Teubner (ed.), *Autopoietic Law: A New Approach to Law and Society*, Walter de Gruyter, Berlin, pp. 349-68.

King, M. (1996), 'Comparing Legal Cultures in the Quest for Law's Identity' in D. Nelken (ed.), *Comparing Legal Cultures* Aldershot, Dartmouth, pp.119-134.

King, M. and Piper, C. (1995), *How the Law Thinks about Children (2nd edition),* Arena, Aldershot.

King, M. and Schütz, A. (1994), 'The Ambitious Modesty of Niklas Luhmann' 23 *Journal of Law and Society*, pp. 261-287.

Knorr-Cetina (1992), 'Zur Unterkomplexität der Differenzierungstheorie' 21 *Zeitschrift für Sociologie*, pp.406-419.

Kogler, H. H. (1997), 'Social Systems' (Review)', 103 *The American Journal of Sociology*, pp. 271-273.

Lempert, R. (1988), 'The Autonomy of Law: Two Visions Compared', in G. Teubner (ed.), *Autopoietic Law: A New Approach to Law and Society,* Walter de Gruyter, Berlin, pp.152-90.

Luhmann, N. (1976), 'Generalised Media and the Problem of Contingency' in J. Loubser, A. Effrat and V. Lidz (eds), *Explorations in General Theory in Social Sciences: Essays in Honour of Talcott Parsons,* New York, pp.507-532.

Luhmann, N. (1977), 'Differentiation of Society', 2 *Canadian Journal of Sociology*, pp.29-54.

Luhmann, N. (1986a), 'The Autopoiesis of Social Systems' in F. Geyer and J. van der Zouwen, (eds), *Sociocybernetic Paradoxes: Observation, Control and Evolution of Self-Steering Systems*, Beverly Hills, London, pp.171-192.

Luhmann, N. (1986b), 'Society, Meaning, Religion - Based on Self-Reference', 46 *Sociological Analysis*, pp.5-20.

Luhmann, N. (1988), 'The Unity of the Legal System' in G. Teubner (ed.), *Autopoietic Law: A New Approach to Law and Society,* Walter de Gruyter, Berlin, pp.12-35.

Luhmann, N. (1990a), 'The Cognitive Program of Constructivism and a Reality that Remains Unknown' in W. Krohn, G. Kuppers and H. Nowotny (eds), *Self-Organization, Portrait of a Scientific Revolution. Sociology of the Sciences Yearbook,* Kluwer, Dodrecht, pp.64-85.

Luhmann, N. (1990b), *Essays on Self Reference (Ch.7),* Columbia University Press, New York.

Luhmann, N. (1990c), *Political Theory in the Welfare State*, Walter de Gruyter, Berlin.

Luhmann, N. (1993a), 'The Code of the Moral' 14 *Cardozo Law Review*, pp.995-1009.

Luhmann, N. (1993b), *Risk: A Sociological Theory*, Aldine de Gruyter, New York.

Luhmann, N. (1994), 'Politicians, and the Higher Amorality of Politics' 11 *Theory, Culture and Society*, pp.25-36.

Luhmann, N. (1995), *Social Systems*, Stanford University Press, Stanford.

Luhmann, N. (1998), *Observations on Modernity*, Stanford University Press, Stanford.

Milgram, S. (1974), *Obedience to Authority: An Experimental View*, Tavistock, London.

Murch, M. (1995), 'The Cross-disciplinary Approach to Family Law - trying to Mix Oil and Water' in A. Bainham and D. Pearl, D. (eds), *The Frontiers of Family Law,* Wiley, Chichester, UK, pp.195-207.

Murphy, W. T. (1994), 'Systems of Systems: Some Issues in the Relationship between Law and Autopoiesis', 5 *Law and Critique*, pp.241-264.

Nelken, D. (1988), 'Changing Paradigms in the Sociology of Law' in G. Teubner (ed.), *Autopoietic Law: A New Approach to Law and Society*, Walter de Gruyter, Berlin, pp.191 217.

Rottleuthner, H. (1989a), 'The Limits of Law - The Myth of a Regulatory Crisis', 17 *International Journal of the Sociology of Law*, pp.273-285.

Rottleuthner, H.(1989b), 'A Purified Sociology of Law: Niklas Luhmann on the Autonomy of the Legal System', 23 *Law and Society Review*, pp. 779-797.

Showalter, E. (1997), *Hystories. Hysterical epidemics and modern culture*, Picador, London.

Teubner, G. (1992), 'The Two Faces of Janus: Rethinking Legal Pluralism', 13 *Cardozo Law Review,* pp.1443-1462.

Teubner, G. (1993), *Law as an Autopoietic System*, Blackwell, Oxford.

Toulmin, S. (1982), 'The Construal of Reality' in W. J. T. Mitchell (ed.), *The Politics of Interpretation,* Chicago

Vandenberghe, F. (1999), 'Niklas Luhmann 1927-1998 Systemic supertheorist of the social', 94 *Radical Philosophy*, see: http://www.ukc.ac.uk/secl/philosophy/rp/.

PART II:

APPLYING AUTOPOIETIC LAW THEORY

7 Autopoiesis and the Natural Environment

ERIC W. ORTS

After a few decades of theoretical development, there are indications that the idea of autopoiesis has begun to enter the lexicon of American legal thought, if not the mainstream. At least anecdotal evidence appears in recent references to the idea in recent issues of the *Harvard Law Review* (Tushnet, 1999: 107-8; Schauer, 1998: 113 n.140; for another recent discussion, see Baxter, 1998). The term is familiar to contemporary German legal academics who work in the sociological tradition of Niklas Luhmann.[1] The conference in Cardiff and the contributions in this book on the 'consequences' of autopoietic theory testify to the theory's influence or at least its recognition across the English Channel. In the United States, however, movement towards thinking along these lines has been halting, and what progress there has been owes in no small part to the influence of Gunther Teubner, who might accurately be dubbed 'the ambassador of autopoiesis' to English-speaking parts of the world (see Teubner, 1983; Teubner, 1993a).

The theory of autopoiesis

The Cardiff conference brought together a number of international legal scholars familiar with the idea of autopoiesis. Even after a few decades of conceptual work and theoretical debate among scholars attracted by the idea, however, considerable danger of misunderstanding remains concerning what various authors mean by the term 'autopoiesis' (Teubner,

[1]Luhmann, who died in 1998, was one of the two leading figures of late twentieth century German legal sociology. For his magnum opus, see Luhmann (1985). For a bibliography of Luhmann's other work available in English, see King and Schutz (1994: 284-5). The other leading German scholar is Jurgen Habermas. For his major work in legal theory, see Habermas (1996).

1993a: 16). This problem is unavoidable given the fact that the idea has migrated from its origin in biology into several different academic disciplines, including law, philosophy, and sociology (Beck, 1994: 403-4). I will not presume to offer an authoritative interpretation here, but in order to try to avoid semantic misunderstanding, I will begin with my own working definition of the idea of autopoiesis.

Autopoiesis, for my purposes here, refers to features of self-reference, self-organization, and reflexive self-production or continual self-reconstruction that an identifiable social system may acquire in the organization of communications around particular 'codes' (or fundamental distinctions) and 'programs' (or routine methods of discussion, argument, and decision making) (Teubner, 1993a: 16-24). The cybernetic or computer-language references to 'codes' and 'programs,' which originate in Luhmann's theory, can be understood as metaphorical. The fundamental insight, which Luhmann derives from sociologists before him such as Emile Durkheim, Max Weber, and Talcott Parsons, can be described roughly as follows. In modern societies, specific systems (or for some theorists, subsystems, reserving the term 'system' to refer to human society as a whole) become organized around key considerations and specialized 'languages.' Law, for example, develops to become organized through discussions, statements, arguments, decisions, and actions concerning whether particular behavior is 'legal' or 'illegal'. Social institutions, including especially courts, but professional bar associations and law schools as well, evolve in modern societies to specialize and, in effect, to assume the job of organizing specialized legal communication and action. Similar specialization and differentiation occurs also in other areas of social life. For example, businesses and economic markets become organized around communications about pricing and production. They calculate consequences of actions in terms of 'profit' and 'loss'. Politics becomes structured according to specialized principles and practices of organized power and its exercise within institutions such as elections and legislatures. One does not need to concur with the details of these descriptions of different social systems to agree with the general proposition of what is called 'systems theory', that modern societies tend to develop specialized institutional 'spheres' that use different 'languages' and 'codes' to address everyday problems and events that human actors in society perceive and discuss when making concrete legal, political, or economic decisions (see, e.g., Habermas, 1996: 80; Walzer, 1984). In a number of differing varieties, 'system theories' of law have become increasingly popular in academic circles in the United States (LoPocki, 1997; Ruhl, 1996; Waldron, 2000).[2]

I believe that the autopoiesis of a system in society refers to characteristics that should be considered as both communications and actions – or what Jurgen Habermas calls 'communicative action' (Habermas, 1984: 94-101, 305, 397-8; Habermas, 1987: 4-5, 62-3, 137-8; Habermas, 1996: 322-6, 354-5). A theory that emphasizes only 'communication' runs the danger of getting caught up in its own language and self-referential concepts without an adequate grounding in an empirical social reality of the actions that really matter to most people in everyday life.[3] In my view, an empirical foundation for autopoietic theory is necessary, and it requires reference to behavioral actions that can be observed as well as communications that can be interpreted. (In this respect, I agree with some previous criticisms of autopoietic theory. See Beck, 1998: 405; Rottleuthner, 1988: 114-27.) The social systems that are most important to study – including law, economic markets, and politics – are important precisely because of the extent to which the communications and actions of these systems affect real people in everyday life. In this respect, Habermas is right to emphasize the importance of 'communicative action' rather than either 'communication' or 'action' only.[4] In a legal system, for example, what matters is not only saying 'legal' or 'illegal' but also having the authority and power to mean it.

It is also important to emphasize that a theory of autopoiesis is not the same as a theory of the 'autonomy' of social systems such as law, economics, or politics. Some American legal scholars have been prone to confusion in this respect (see, e.g., Lempert, 1988: 152-90). Instead,

---

[2]LoPocki (1997) argues for a methodology of 'systems analysis' to apply to law, though he disavows any relation to sociological systems theories such as those advanced by Luhmann or Parsons. Ruhl (1996) advances what he calls a 'dynamic systems theory' of law. Waldron (2000) examines what he calls 'the systematicity of law' and argues that the idea is helpful in jurisprudence.

[3]Teubner, for example, sometimes describes autopoiesis in terms of communications that seem disembodied from social actions, but he also understands law as a 'second-order' system that connects 'legal communications' to 'legal acts' (Teubner, 1993a: 69-70). The latter would be more consistent with Habermas' social theory.

[4]Thus, Luhmann and his followers might be said to overemphasize 'communications' at the expense of 'actions'. Luhmann (1995) refers to 'actions' as 'attributed communications,' but this semantic stretching seems to prove the point. Functionalist approaches in the tradition of Parsons instead seem to overemphasize 'actions' compared with 'communications'.

autopoiesis refers to an empirical observation of the 'relative autonomy' of social systems with respect to each other.[5] As Teubner writes, 'autonomy and autopoiesis' should be understood as 'questions of degree' (Teubner, 1993a: 27).

In modern societies, the operational processes of law, economics, and politics become to some significant extent independent of each other in the sense that the communications and decision-making of the systems do not directly or immediately depend on references to the norms and values of other social systems. This is the meaning of the catch-phrase in autopoietic theory of 'operational closure'. Operational closure means simply that certain organized processes of communication and action become structured independently from other social communications and actions. Different social systems operate according to different normative criteria and with reference to different purposes. At the same time, this relatively autonomous characteristic of 'operational closure' is balanced by the recognition that these systems are 'cognitively open' to other social systems and the general social environment (Teubner, 1993a: 15-6). Cognitive openness means that other social communications and actions *may* be included in the autopoietic communications of any particular system. The essential point is that the systems are not completely open to each other. (As an old aphorism says, it is good to have an 'open mind', but not 'open at both ends'.)

Some Anglo-American critics of autopoietic theory misunderstand the relationship between operational closure and cognitive openness.[6] Part of the confusion may arise from perceiving 'operational closure' to require a strict 'normative closure', that is, a self-referencing of only legal norms in the construction of legal norms. I do not read either Luhmann or Teubner as insisting on such a narrow view of operational normative closure. Instead, with respect to the legal system, the point is that any external norm

[5]For a useful elaboration of this conception of 'relative autonomy,' see Baxter (1998). Lempert glimpses and correctly describes this idea of 'relative autonomy,' but then too narrowly distinguishes it by (1) insisting on reference to 'the law's own standards' rather than the principles or standards recognized by legal institutions and communications within them, and, (2) by following a red herring in the notion of 'the generality of rules' as key to the relative autonomy of law when legal institutions may, just as easily, follow specific rules (Lempert, 1988: 159-61).

[6]For example, both Beck and Lempert make this mistake. Beck (1998: 412, 414) misunderstands that a 'closed system' of law could not be influenced by other 'social values and practices'; Lempert (1988: 173) misunderstands that 'self-referential closure' in a legal system requires reference only to the legal system's 'own norms and values'.

or value (including those from economics, philosophy, or even legal theory itself) is not adopted explicitly within the legal system unless the relatively autonomously operating legal system itself actually decides to include the external norm or value. Then, through the definition of legal communicative action, an 'external' norm or value may become part and parcel of the 'internally' operating norms and values of the legal system.

An interesting problem posed by an autopoietic perspective is how the 'knowledge of the larger world' gets interpreted and processed within specialized social systems. According to autopoietic theory, the longstanding notion of 'differentiation' in modern societies implies the corresponding development of operational methods by which this differentiation occurs and self-reproduces. Specialized 'codes' or 'programs' – including specialized language, principles, and norms – draw on general social knowledge and understandings even as they are interpreted and incorporated into the communications and actions of specialized systems.

For example, the legal system in modern societies develops its own specialized and even ritualized methods of communication about the resolution of legal disputes, the use of statutes, doctrinal interpretation of legal principles, and other topics. Professional lawyers, judges, and academics participate in this specialized and 'operationally closed' process. This does not mean that the legal system is autonomous from other knowledge and understandings outside of the law. In the United States, for example, economic theory has recently had a substantial influence on the development of legal thought, not only among academics but also in many judicial decisions and legislation. Ethical understandings also influence the development of legal concepts. The influence of economics and ethics on the law are two major examples of how law is 'cognitively open' to social knowledge and information outside of the law. (Whether the influence of economic or philosophic rationality on law is 'right' or 'wrong' is another question that must be answered in specific contexts.) The point that autopoietic theory emphasizes is that the influence of other non-legal knowledge is incorporated into legal principles only through the operations of modern legal processes.

Autopoietic theory is therefore not correctly described as a 'new formalism' in which various differentiated social systems are imagined to act autonomously or hermetically sealed off from one another. The theory does not, for example, as some have thought mistakenly, assert the 'independence' of law from society. Instead, autopoietic theory attempts to explain how systems such as 'the legal system' or 'the economic system' become relatively separated from the rest of everyday life and other systems, as well as the empirical extent of this relative systemic autonomy and its implications for social development in general. As Teubner writes, 'a legal system becomes autonomous to the extent that it manages to constitute its components – actions, norms, processes, identity – into self-referential cycles' (Teubner, 1993a: 27).

From this perspective, autopoiesis is correctly understood as an empirical and historical theory of social development. It is important to emphasize the empirical nature of the autopoietic thesis of relative autonomy of social systems. Some theoretical discussions of autopoiesis run the risk of becoming too conceptually creative because they commit the error of assuming rather than demonstrating the actual empirical extent to which particular social and institutional systems have grown to exhibit autopoietic characteristics. Framing autopoiesis as an empirical theory provides a check on the tendency of its theoretical advocates to become too abstract and divorced from the real world of actual everyday practice.

As an historical theory of social development, autopoiesis stands in a close relationship to earlier sociological theories of the gradual division of labor in society (e.g., Durkheim, 1933). Specialization and its economic benefits to social productivity are another major theme of this tradition. As human society has become more successful – at least in terms of the expansion of the number of the individuals that the social economy of our system can support – it has specialized. (For a classic economic account, see Knight, 1921.) Biological cognitive limitations of our hunter-gatherer minds and bodies are overcome collectively through the social specialization of skills, jobs, roles, and (somewhat mechanically) 'functions'.[7]

More than a functional theory of social specialization, however, autopoiesis refers to an historical and evolutionary process of increasing specialization at the level of social systems (or subsystems) (Teubner, 1988: 217-41; see also Teubner, 2000). In other words, autopoietic theory focuses on the social development of specialized institutions, including courts, markets, and political structures. The empirical assumption of the theory of autopoiesis is that certain social institutional systems such as law,

[7]Talcott Parsons is known for his view of social 'functions,' but a strictly functional view of specialization is not necessary for the broader concept advanced here.

economics, and politics become to a significant extent 'codified' or 'formalized' in their operations and, in this sense, relatively autonomous from each other. If this empirical description is accurate, then important implications follow for understanding the operation of these differentiated systems, their strengths and limitations, and the consequences that the phenomenon of autopoietically differentiated systems may have for the overall conditions of society.

In law, for example, specialized styles and even languages of communication develop.[8] Legal procedures, rules of evidence, and the roles of lawyers and judges are part of this systemic specialization. Courts and prisons are social institutions that carry out legally specialized actions. Law schools and bar admission committees train people in the language of the law and 'license' the practice of this specialized communication. Why does law develop in this fashion? Why does it develop into a 'legal system'? The best answer seems to lie in the evolutionary usefulness of social specialization. In general terms, legal specialization is a social benefit. Specialized lawyers can 'know' the law better and focus on developing specialized skills in advising, litigating, law-making, and judging. Of course, the increased social power of this specialized system of law can also be terribly misused – such as by a harsh and tyrannical political state. Broadly, however, the evolution of a specialized legal system tends over time to provide social and economic benefits.

Specialization in the economic realm, specifically in business, seems to follow a similar social and historical rationale of development. The specialized languages of business develop into the mathematical expressions of finance and accounting. The 'codified' or 'formal' focus of business is profit and loss. Again, the differentiation of an economic sphere has resulted in generally positive consequences for society, encouraging greater economic productivity and producing more social wealth. At the same time, as I argue later in this chapter and as other social theorists recognize, there is also the possibility that specialized systems of the economy and law may have counterproductive social and environmental effects that derive partly from the very fact of their otherwise successful

---

[8]Habermas argues that legal language is not particularly specialized from the basic underlying language of its expression (for example, English in the U.S. legal system). But there is at least room to argue that legal language is a specialized type of English language or dialect that employs certain kinds of rules, in addition to basic grammar. In this respect, Luhmann the lawyer seems to have the better argument compared with Habermas, who was not trained as a lawyer.

evolution in becoming highly specialized.[9]

As an empirical matter, then, does autopoiesis exist in modern societies? This is a basic assumption made by some of the participants in the Cardiff conference and their chapters in this book, while others dispute that the empirical fact of autopoiesis has been demonstrated. I agree with the critics that more research is needed to establish with greater precision the extent to which various systems such as law and business have in fact become 'operationally closed' in particular societies. Empirical investigations would also help to illuminate differences between societies with respect to this criteria. To take one example, the legal system of the People's Republic of China does not yet exhibit very strong characteristics of an 'operational closure' or 'relative autonomy' separate from the processes of the political system (Orts, 2001). Progress might be beginning in this direction, particularly in economic law, but the Chinese Communist Party is still too often tempted to put its thumb on the scales of justice, especially in political cases. The empirical situation in China is therefore much different than in Europe and North America where legal systems and 'the rule of law' have become more entrenched, more relatively autonomous, and more 'autopoietic'. Even without formal empirical research to support this view, I think that casual empirical observation of most modern societies supports the general assumption of an emerging 'relative autonomy' and autopoiesis of at least some basic social systems such as law. Granting this empirical assumption – and subject to possible experimental qualification – it then makes sense to consider the second question that is posed by the Cardiff conference: What are the consequences of autopoeisis?

The consequences of autopoiesis for the natural environment

If the general social phenomenon describing the evolution of autopoiesis is accurate, what are the likely consequences for the future of human society? This is a large question, and I will focus on only one smaller but important

[9]As others have discussed, this form of social evolution is complex and in any event is not a variant of Social Darwinism or the like (see, e.g., Teubner, 1988: 47-63). A discussion of the specific nature of this evolution of social systems is beyond the scope of this chapter.

part of it, namely: What are the likely consequences of social autopoiesis with respect to the effects of human behavior on the natural environment?

The short answer is that autopoiesis has had and will likely continue to have unexpectedly detrimental effects on the natural environment. The reason is straightforward. The social effects of human behavior on the natural environment become known to us primarily through the process of science (and sometimes everyday human experience), and science itself has become very highly specialized. Take, for example, the scientific discovery that classes of human-invented chemicals called chloroflourocarbons (CFCs) and hydrochloroflourocarbons (HFCs) have the long-term effect of depleting the stratospheric ozone layer of the Earth's atmosphere. Once this scientific knowledge develops and becomes accepted, then the question shifts to one of social policy (see, e.g., Benedick, 1991). Given scientific knowledge of an environmental threat, how do economic, political, and legal systems respond? The social responses are not automatic precisely because of the 'relative autonomy' of autopoietic systems. The social codes, calculations, and deliberations of law, economics, and politics do not automatically take account of new scientific knowledge about environmental problems without some kind of 'translation' of the issue into the operations of the legal, economic, and political systems (Teubner, 1997: 162-7). If so, then it makes sense to think about how scientific knowledge about environmental problems gets 'translated' (or not) into the differentiated codes and institutional structures of modern society. Understanding this process of intersystemic social translation is needed not only to maximize the chances of survival of the human species (though this is important!), but also to consider how it may be possible to incorporate non-instrumental environmental values into the powerful and somewhat independent processes of other human social institutions.

None other than Niklas Luhmann, whom I will call 'the dean of autopoiesis,' recognizes the gravity of the consequences of autopoietic theory for the natural environment. In *Ecological Communication*, Luhmann first points out that 'the history of reflection on humanity and society this theme – ecology – is not very old'. Only in the last few decades of the twentieth century has 'a rapidly increasing discussion of the ecological conditions of social life and the connection between the social system and its environment' become prominent (Luhmann, 1989: 1). Only recently has modern society – with its differentiated, autopoietically organized systems including law, economics, politics, and science – confronted new ecological problems of a different order of magnitude. In Luhmann's words, these new ecological problems include:

> the increasingly rapid consumption of non-replaceable resources and (even if this would prove beneficial) the increasing dependence on self-produced substitutes, a reduction in the variety of species forming the basis of further biological evolution, the ever-possible development of uncontrollable viruses resistant to medicine, the familiar problem of environmental pollution and not least of all over-population (Luhmann, 1989: 1).

All of these ecological problems are 'themes of social communication', and society-at-large has 'become alarmed as never before'. However, 'the cognitive means for predicting and directing action' on the major ecological issues of our time are lacking because society itself 'not only changes its environment but also undermines the conditions for its own continued existence'. According to Luhmann, massive ecological problems have caught at least sociology 'unprepared theoretically' (Luhmann, 1989: 1). In social theory, the usual focus had been on distinctly social problems, while questions about the effects of human society on the natural environment were left to the 'natural sciences'. But the gravity of current environmental problems makes what Luhmann calls 'sociological abstinence' no longer tenable (Luhmann, 1989: 2). The massive size of the effects of humanity on the natural environment has grown to 'geophysical' proportions akin to those of the continents or oceans (Serres, 1995; Wilson, 1992). As a result, there is a need for theory to move beyond a concern only with the 'social system' to include, in Luhmann's terms, a serious theoretical consideration of 'the unity of the difference of the system of society and its environment' (Luhmann, 1989: 7).

Autopoiesis itself, then, is one of the main problems involved in the environmental crisis facing society today. In other words, autopoiesis itself has serious detrimental consequences for the natural environmental preconditions of human society and other forms of life. The reason is straightforward. 'The primary goal of autopoietic systems', as Luhmann explains, 'is the continuation of autopoiesis without any concern for the environment'. As a result, 'the next step in the process' of the operations of a particular social system is often more important than 'concern for the future' of the natural environment (Luhmann, 1989: 14). The main goals of law and business, for example, will continue to focus on resolving the next case and making the next deal. The macro-level environmental effects of the continued iterations of legal and business decisions are not ordinarily taken into account. Thus there is no doubt, again in Luhmann's words, that 'society itself is guilty' for these new and very large scale environmental problems – but 'we know this already' (Luhmann, 1989: 10). The theoretical problem now is what to do about these problems, taking into consideration the necessarily complex interactions between society and nature.

To begin to take social theory in this new direction, it is instructive to begin with the biological origins of the idea of autopoiesis in the work of Francisco Varela and Humberto Maturana (Maturana and Varela, 1980; Luhmann, 1989: x-xi). They advanced an organic view of 'operational closure' and 'cognitive openness' of autopoietic self-reference and self-reproduction in the biology of life processes and the physiology of knowledge. But it is interesting to think about why and how life evolved to exhibit this feature. One scientific answer to the question is that the biological success of autopoietically organized life – including the complex biological and psychological structure of the human species – have been proven in terms of competitive evolution. In other words, biological autopoiesis has proven to be a successful evolutionary development – or, more precisely, a successful series of evolutionary events – given that many organisms, including the human species, developed successfully along these lines. The question always remains, however, whether previous evolutionary developments will continue to breed future evolutionary success.

Analogies drawn from biological to social autopoiesis are admittedly imperfect, but it is worth considering whether an evolutionary framework is helpful when considering the social development of autopoietically specialized systems such as law, business, politics, and even the natural sciences. (At the same time, one should also be careful in using biological metaphors in legal theory; see, e.g., Rottleuthner, 1988.) Arguably, the development of these relatively autonomous systems have proven to be successful in social evolutionary terms because they have strengthened and enhanced the economic productiveness of societies that have developed in this direction. After centuries of successful expansion, however, autopoiesis today may have begun to yield unintended and potentially very dangerous consequences. One of the most troubling and wide-ranging set of consequences are the unintended detrimental effects that autopoietically organized social systems can have on the natural environment. As Luhmann recognizes, together with many other environmentalists and scientists, the evolution of specialized social systems has led to a potentially serious conflict with the basic underlying preconditions of the human species (as well as other species) in the natural environment. Significant empirical evidence in this respect concerns the overall effect of human social activity on other species. As total human population has increased radically, the number of many other species has seriously declined. As E.O. Wilson and other biologists have pointed out, current era ranks as the 'sixth great extinction' of living species on Earth in geological time. Human activity in the last century has caused the largest extinction of different species of flora and fauna since the cosmological event (probably a comet) that caused the disappearance of the dinosaurs 65 million years ago (Wilson, 1992: 343). Morally, our collective responsibility for the extinctions of other species is important in its own right (see, e.g., Sober, 1995). But evidence of human society's destructive effects on other species also raises the serious question of whether the relatively autonomous systems of human society may not also undermine the biological preconditions for the survival of our own species. In other words, as E.O. Wilson puts it dramatically, 'is humanity suicidal' (Wilson, 1996: 180, 191)?

In terms of autopoietic theory, Wilson's question may be rephrased less directly and perhaps more precisely. The issue is not whether human society collectively intends to kill itself off. The question is rather whether the structure of human society and the operational processes of its relatively autonomous social systems may have the unintended but nevertheless drastic consequences of undermining the natural environmental preconditions of human life. (For a compelling dystopian account of this possibility, see Boyle, 2000.)

This theoretical reformulation into autopoietic terms of the current problems of the effects of human society on the natural environmental is important. An appreciation of social complexity puts environmental problems into a similarly complex theoretical perspective. Given the empirical assumptions of the essential accuracy of an autopoietic account of society discussed above, then at least the easy answers that some commentators offer to address our current environmental situation can be discredited. The harder problems remain - how to adjust or influence current social systems and institutions in order to avert the adverse consequences they otherwise have for the natural environment.

Before getting to the difficult problem of possible solutions, it is first useful to clear some ground by following Luhmann's persuasive arguments against some of the approaches to current environmental problems that are too simplistic. At least four general categories of those who offer the wrong – or at least inadequate or incomplete – answers can be identified.

1. *Naive environmentalists.* Luhmann's first target in *Ecological Communication* are the kind of environmentalists who see and understand the severe environmental consequences of the current organization of modern society, but then simply preach in favor of more 'environmental responsibility' or, like contemporary Luddites, react in a passionate but unreflective fashion to attack 'the system' or 'the corporations' whom they believe to control 'the system'. Earth First! Terrorists or the rioters in Seattle against the World Trade Organization come to mind as examples. This kind of environmentalism is naive because of its failure to recognize the evolutionary success for humanity of the development of specialized and relatively autonomous systems of law, economy, politics, and science. As Luhmann writes, environmental problems 'cannot be solved merely with admonitions and appeals to more environmental consciousness' (Luhmann, 1989: 20-1). The complexity of society must be considered. Naive environmentalism rejects modernity in general, but this strategy is doomed to fail because of its radical implications for human society. If the prescriptions of naive environmentalism were followed and 'the systems' of human society simply dismantled, a new dark age of mass starvation and political anarchy would result. Luhmann therefore justifiably derides much of the ecological literature written in this vein as theoretically naive. In his words,

> Indifference in the choice of words and absence of interest in significant theoretical decisions are two of the most noticeable characteristics of this literature – as if caring about the environment could justify carelessness in the talk about it (Luhmann, 1989: xvii).

One way to read *Ecological Communication* is as a plea for environmental activists to take social theory seriously.

2. *Criminalizing environmental law.* Another basically mistaken strategy is to seek to personalize and even criminalize environmental problems by blaming specific individuals for them. The use of the criminal

law to address environmental problems in the United States and elsewhere is increasing rapidly. (For critical discussion of this phenomenon in the United States, see Herz, 1996; Lazarus, 1994; Schroeder, 1993. Indeed, it sometimes seems that almost everyone in the United States will soon be jailed in an attempt to solve the country's various social problems, including most notably drug abuse.) As Gunther Teubner argues persuasively, using this approach as a primary means to address environmental problems is misplaced (Teubner, 1994). Demonizing particular individuals for the failures of collective social structures and the powerful incentives that they provide to motivate individual behavior does not make sense. Although the criminalization of environmental violations might provide an emotional release for those who want to feel as if society is 'doing something' to address environmental problems, enforcing criminal penalties against those individuals who follow competing social incentives (such as within business organizations) will do little to solve the larger underlying and socially created problems. This is not to say that some intentional crimes – such as an individual purposely poisoning a reservoir used for drinking water – should not carry criminal penalties. The point is rather that the overall scale of current environmental problems cannot be addressed mainly or primarily through criminalizing individual behavior.

3. *Centralized environmental law reform.* A third target for Luhmann are those who promote regulatory reform – usually along the lines advocated by law and economics analysis – as a panacea for environmental problems. This category includes the leading academic variant of proposed reform of environmental law in the United States. This approach has the virtue of arguing that the legal system should be reformed to take into account the fact that businesses tend to act according to economic principles, thus arguing that the 'externalities' of environmental harm should be reduced to actual economic costs through taxes or charges. A problem with this recommended approach, however, is that it requires a centralized administrative state to set up the regulatory system of taxes and charges – adjusting them to yield the best results. But as Teubner argues, following Luhmann, the political state too has become 'decentered' in modern societies (Teubner, 1993b: 553, 556). Therefore, the economic strategies of environmental law reform depend, paradoxically, on a strong state. For Luhmann and Teubner, the multiple development of various autopoietic systems (including legal, economic, and political systems) has

been to weaken each of them relative to one another. In other words, the political system no longer has the power or ability to reform the legal and economic systems successfully from 'above'.

This view distinguishes autopoietic theorists like Luhmann and Teubner from the more politically optimistic Habermas, who seems to retain a faith that an enlightened political state informed by democratic discourse and deliberation can successfully 'steer' the economic and other social systems to avert environmental catastrophe. Autopoietic theory is less sanguine about the possibilities of modern democratic politics. Perhaps partly for this reason, Habermas declares modern systems theory to be plagued by 'a melancholic sense' (Habermas, 1996: 46). But autopoietic theory may nevertheless have the better argument: Although it is often psychologically functional to be optimistic, pessimists may often be more accurate (see Seligman, 1992). Luhmann returns the insult by saying that Habermas is lost in a 'dream of the subject'. For Luhmann, 'the idea that society can determine its own identity in communicative discourse in such a way that this commits the participating subject internally and binds them to the collective identity' no longer works in a modern autopoietically differentiated society (Luhmann, 1989: 133).

4. *The weakness of environmental politics.* The theoretical dispute between Luhmann and Habermas about the potential for the renewal of democratic and deliberative politics as a potential solution to the ecological crisis illuminates a fourth target for Luhmann: politics and politicians. For Luhmann, unlike for Habermas, politics at least in an organized fashion does not look very promising. The difficulty is that 'agreement' must be reached 'that something has to be done' about a particular problem. But to get such an agreement – especially in democracies – 'problems have to become urgent enough so that action can be taken without losing any votes' (Luhmann, 1989: 92). Unfortunately, waiting for this kind of political agreement for some kinds of environmental problems may well come too late.

Averting autopoeietic environmental consequences: sketches for a new ark?

Luhmann's criticisms of many solutions offered by well-meaning environmental scholars and advocates are admirable and often brilliant.

However, he is not so good at coming up with his own suggestions for solutions. Luhmann argues in general terms that 'more complex theoretical tools are needed' to cope with environmental problems, including an improvement of 'the rationality of ecological communication' (Luhmann, 1989: 34, 133-38). He concludes that 'a new environmental ethics' is needed that will become concerned with 'social regulation' (Luhmann, 1989: 139, 142). But these general assertions do not go very far toward recommending theoretical and practical solutions for positive social reform.

Let me suggest, though also only generally and by way of conclusion, several possible directions that the general theoretical and practical project of environmental law reform might take in the future. Some variations of them may prove consistent with the potential constraints of autopoietic social theory.

1. *Reflexive environmental law*. One regulatory approach consistent with the insights of autopoietic theory focuses on encouraging the operations of various social systems other than the legal system itself to take into account environmental considerations and obligations. I have argued elsewhere that some regulatory experiments along these lines have begun (Orts, 1995a; Orts, 1995b). An example is the regulatory encouragement – or even requirement – of environmental management and auditing systems (see also Gunningham, 1997-1998; Rehbinder, 1992; Pezzoli, 2000). In this general approach, the regulator appreciates its own limitations and attempts to design social structures that will encourage self-regulatory processes.

2. *Informational regulation.* Another indirect strategy of law reform that may prove amenable to the autopoietic structures of modern society would focus on the mandatory provision of environmentally relevant information to the public (see Kleinderfer and Orts, 1998; Magat and Viscusi, 1992; Menell, 1995; Tietenberg, 1998; Sunstein, 1999). There are difficulties with this approach in terms of deciding what information to usefully provide or require to be provided. They include quality assurance of accurate data, the danger of information overload, public misinterpretation or overreaction to information, and the possible misuse of public information (such as the misuse of industrial pollution location information by political terrorists). But the basic idea of informational regulation of the environment is to shift the burden of 'regulatory' change to social structures other than (or in addition to) formal legal structures of direct

regulation and enforcement. With accurate and easily interpreted information, for example, environmentally enlightened consumers may exert pressure for environmentally sensitive products and services. Environmental labels or 'eco-labels' are an example (see, e.g., Orts, 1995a: 1246-52; Gesser, 1998; Grodsky, 1993; Kloven, 1998). Suppliers and business customers, as well as nonprofit environmental groups, may also use environmental information to pressure businesses for better environmental performance. Enhanced information about environmental performance may even support new causes of legal action for 'environmental fraud' in cases of misinformation (Orts, 1995b: 787; Morenberg, 1995). Again, as in reflexive regulation, the idea of informational regulation is to empower other social systems as well as the government to exert pressure for environmental improvement.

3. *Environmental contracts.* Lastly, innovations consistent with the insights of autopoietic theory may be found through building 'bridges' to link different social structures together to address common environmental problems. Government regulation, for example, may proceed through 'regulatory contracts' or 'covenants' made with representative business groups and other organizations representing environmental interests (see Orts and Deketelaere, 2001; Rehbinder, 1994). Partnerships between individual businesses and public interest groups might also be possible (Long and Arnold, 1998). For example, a business corporation may agree to enter into an agreement with an environmental group to study and help to solve a particular environmental problem. Or a group of businesses, environmentalists, scientists, and academics may convene to discuss a major problem common to all (such as global climate change) and attempt to reach some common ground on what steps should be taken. In general, the theoretical idea informing experiments with this kind of approach is to make concrete Michel Serres' argument for the paradigm of a 'natural contract' to replace the old-fashioned 'social contract' of government sovereignty and regulatory imperialism (Serres, 1995: 16). Like reflexive or informational regulation, the concept of environmental contracts recognizes the need to communicate across and between different social systems rather than to impose direct regulation of social behavior from a too-weak central state.

Regulatory experiments along these several different lines may begin the task of building the social structure of an ark to survive the environmental challenges that are likely to characterize much of the twenty-first century. Reflexive, informational, and contractual regulations may point in the direction of preserving the advantages modern social organization and its autopoietic structure, while at the same time effectively countering the potentially self-destructive environmental consequences of autopoiesis.

References

Baxter, H. (1998), 'Autopoiesis and the Relative Autonomy of Law', 19 *Cardozo Law Review*, p. 1987.

Beck, A. (1998) 'Is Law an Autopoietic System?', 14 *Oxford Journal of Legal Studies,* p. 401.

Benedick, R.E. (1991), *Ozone Diplomacy: New Directions in Safeguarding the Planet*, Harvard University Press, Cambridge.

Boyle, T.C. (2000), *A Friend of the Earth*, Viking, New York.

Durkheim, E. (1933), *The Division of Labor in Society*, Free Press, Glencoe.

Gesser, A. (1998), 'Canada's Environmental Choice Program: A Model of a 'Trade-Friendly' Eco-Labeling Scheme', 39 *Harvard International Law Journal,* p. 501.

Grodsky, J. A. (1993), 'Certified Green: The Law and Future of Environmental Labeling', 10 *Yale Journal on Regulation,* p. 147.

Gunningham, N. (1997-1998), 'Environmental Management Systems and Community Participation: Rethinking Chemical Industry Regulation', 16 *UCLA Journal of Environmental Law and Policy,* p. 319.

Habermas, J. (1984), *The Theory of Communicative Action (vol. 1): Reason and the Rationalization of Society*, Beacon Press, Boston.

Habermas, J. (1987), *The Theory of Communicative Action (vol. 2): Lifeworld and System*, Beacon Press, Boston.

Habermas, J. (1996), *Between Facts and Norms: Contributions to a Discourse Theory of Law and Democracy*, MIT Press, Cambridge.

Herz, M. (1996), 'Structures of Environmental Criminal Enforcement', 7 *Fordham Environmental Law Journal*, p. 679.

King, M. and A. Schutz, (1994) 'The Ambitious Modesty of Niklas Luhmann', 21 *Journal of Law and Society*, p. 261.

Kleindorfer, P. R. and E. W. Orts, 'Informational Regulation of Environmental Risks', 18 *Risk Analysis*, p. 155.

Kloven, K. M. (1998), 'Eco-Labeling of Sustainably Harvested Wood under the Forest Stewardship Council: Seeing the Forest for the Trees', 48 *Colorado Journal of Environmental Law and Policy*, p. 48.

Knight, F. H. (1921), *Risk, Uncertainty and Profit*, Houghton Mifflin, Boston.

Lazarus, R. J. (1994), 'Assimilating Environmental Protection into Legal Rules and the Problem with Environmental Crime', 29 *Loyola Los Angeles Law Review*, p. 867.

Lempert, R. (1988), 'The Autonomy of Law: Two Visions Compared', in G. Teubner (ed.), *Autopoietic Law: A New Approach to Law and Society*, de Gruyter, Berlin, pp. 152-90.

Long, F.J. and M. Arnold (1998), *The Power of Environmental Partnerships*, Dryden Press.
LoPocki, L. M. (1997), 'The Systems Approach to Law', 82 *Cornell Law Review*, p. 479.
Luhmann, N. (1989), *Ecological Communication*,The University of Chicago Press, Chicago.
Luhmann, N. (1985), *A Sociological Theory of Law*, Routledge and Keegan Paul, London.
Luhmann, N. (1995), *Social Systems*, Stanford University Press, Stanford.
Magat, W. A. and F.K. Viscusi, W.K. (1992), *Informational Approaches to Regulation*, MIT Press, Cambridge.
Maturana, H.R. and F.J. Varela (1980), *Autopoiesis and Cognition: The Realization of the Living*, D. Reidel, Dordrecht.
Menell, P. S. (1995), 'Structuring a Market-Oriented Federal Eco-Information Policy', 54 *Maryland Law Review*, p. 1435.
Morenberg, P. W. (1995), 'Environmental Fraud by Government Contractors: A New Application of the False Claims Act', 22 *Boston College Environmental Affairs Law Review*, p. 625.
Orts, E. W. (1995a), 'Reflexive Environmental Law', 89 *Northwestern University Law Review*, p. 1227.
Orts, E. W. (1995b), 'A Reflexive Model of Environmental Regulation', 5 *Business Ethics Quarterly*, p. 779.
Orts, E. W. and K. Deketelaere (eds) (2001), *Environmental Contracts: Comparative Approaches to Regulatory Innovation in the United States and Europe*. Kluwer Law International, Dordrecht.
Orts, E. W. (2001),'The Rule of Law in China', *Vanderbilt Journal of Transnational Law* [forthcoming].
Parsons, T. (1951), *The Social System*, Free Press, Glencoe.
Pezzoli, K. (2000), 'Environmental Management Systems and Regulatory Innovation', 36 *California Western Law Review*, p. 335.
Rehbinder, E. (1992), 'Reflexive Law and Practice: The Corporate Office for Environmental Protection as an Example', in A. Febbrajo and G. Teubner (eds), *State, Law, and Economy as Autopoietic Systems*, Giuffre, Milan.
Rehbinder, E. (1994), 'Ecological Contracts' in G. Teubner (ed.), *Environmental Law and Ecological Responsibility*, Wiley, London.
Rottleuthner, H. (1988), 'Biological Metaphors in Legal Thought', in G. Teubner (ed.), *Autopoietic Law: A New Approach to Law and Society*, de Gruyter, Berlin.
Ruhl, J. B. (1996), 'Complexity Theory as a Paradigm for the Dynamical Law-and-Society System: A Wake-Up Call for Legal Reductionism and the Modern Administrative State', 45 *Duke Law Journal*, p. 849.
Schauer, F. (1998), 'Principles, Institutions, and the First Amendment', 112 *Harvard Law Review*, p. 84.
Schroeder, C. H. (1993), 'Cool Analysis Versus Moral Outrage in the Development of Federal Environmental Criminal Law', 35 *William & Mary Law Review*, p. 251. Seligman, M.E.P. (1992), *Learned Optimism*, Pocket Books, New York.
Serres, M. (1995), *The Natural Contract*, The University of Michigan Press, Ann Arbor.
Sober, E. (1995), 'Philosophical Problems for Environmentalism', in R. Elliot (ed.) *Environmental Ethics*, Oxford University Press, Oxford.
Sunstein, C. R. (1999), 'Informational Regulation and Informational Standing', 147 *University of Pennsylvania Law Review*, p. 613.

Teubner, G. (1983), 'Substantive and Reflexive Elements Modern Law', 17 *Law & Society Review*, p. 239.

Teubner, G. (1988), 'The Evolution of Autopoietic Law', in G. Teubner (ed.), *Autopoietic Law: A New Approach to Law and Society*, deGruyter, Berlin.

Teubner, G. (1993a), *Law as an Autopoietic System*, Blackwell, Oxford.

Teubner, G. (1993b), 'The 'State' of Private Networks: The Emerging Legal Regime of Polycorporatism in Germany', 1993 *Brigham Young University Law Review*, p. 429.

Teubner, G. (1994), 'The Invisible Cupola: From Causal to Collective Attribution in Ecological Liability', 15 *Cardozo Law Review*, p. 429.

Teubner, G. (1997), 'Altera Pars Audiatur: Law in the Collision of Discourses', in *Law, Society and Economy: Centenary Essays for the London School of Economics and Political Science*.

Teubner, G. (2000), 'Idiosyncratic Production Regimes: Co-Evolution of Economic and Legal Institutions in the Varieties of Capitalism', in *The Evolution of Cultural Entities: Proceedings of the British Academy*, Oxford University Press, Oxford.

Tietenberg, T. (1998), 'Disclosure Strategies for Pollution Control', 11 *Environmental and Resource Economics*, p. 587.

Tushnet, M. (1999), 'Foreword: The New Constitutional Order and the Chastening of Constitutional Aspiration', 113 *Harvard Law Review*, p. 29.

Waldron, J. (2000), ''Transcendental Nonsense' and Systems in the Law', 100 *Columbia Law Review*, p. 16.

Walzer, M. (1983), *Spheres of Justice: A Defense of Pluralism and Equality*, Basic Books, New York.

Wilson, E.O. (1992), *The Diversity of Life*, Harvard University Press, Cambridge.

Wilson, E.O. (1996), *In Search of Nature*, Island Press, Washington, D.C.

8 The Concept of Reflexive Labour Law: Its Theoretical Background and Possible Applications

RALF ROGOWSKI

The chapter aims at highlighting the theoretical background and at discussing possible applications of the concept of reflexive labour law. It introduces the concept by relating it to general discussions in social systems theory and legal theory that focus on developing a new legal theory called reflexive or autopoietic theory of law. In the second part the reflexive law concept is applied in discussing features of modern labour law. These features include the relation of labour law and the autopoietic industrial relations system, the regulation of self-regulation through collective agreements and employment contracts, reflexive elements in the law of labour conflict resolution, and deregulation of employment protection as reduction of complexity.

The theoretical background of reflexive labour law

The concept of reflexive labour law assesses specifically modern aspects of advanced labour law systems. It shares basic assumptions about the legal system with autopoietic legal theory and the concept of reflexive law. A few remarks on these general approaches can provide the background for a discussion of specific aspects of reflexive labour law.

Autopoietic legal theory and the concept of reflexive law

The reflexive law theory, as originally developed by Gunther Teubner, was a response to and continuation of Philippe Nonet's and Philip Selznick's concept of responsive law (Nonet and Selznick, 1978). In his seminal article 'Substantive and Reflexive Elements in Modern Law', published in 1983, Teubner introduced the concept of reflexive legal rationality. He argued that in addition to notions of formal and substantive legal rationality, a complex modern legal system is characterised by reflexive rationality based on aspects of proceduralisation and self-regulation.

The early reflexive law concept, which Teubner developed in collaboration with Helmut Willke, was concerned with legitimation, functions and internal structures of the legal system (see Teubner and Willke, 1984). In fact it was presented as an approach to combine the social theories of Jürgen Habermas and Niklas Luhmann in an analysis of specific modern trends in the legal system like the 'contextual' steering via negotiation systems. Central topics were the external links of the legal system, societal guidance through law (see also Willke, 1992) and in particular the question of legal regulation. The reflexive law concept suggested that particular attention should be paid to the limits of legal regulation and to processes of self-regulation in other social systems.

A shift occurred in the debate with Erhard Blankenburg (see Blankenburg, 1984; and the 'rejoinder' by Teubner, 1984). In response to Blankenburg's positivistic critique that key theoretical assumptions of the reflexive law concept (evolutionism and proceduralism) lacked sufficient empirical grounds, Teubner radicalised the approach. The new focus became the autopoietic nature of the legal system, i.e. the capacity of the legal system to reproduce itself. The core idea relates to Luhmann's somewhat paradoxical concept of an autopoietic social system that, in Luhmann's words, 'constitutes the elements of which it consists through the elements of which it consists' (Luhmann, 1988: 14; see also Luhmann, 1984 and Luhmann, 1997). The discussion embarked on topics like the autonomy and the internal constitution of the legal system and system-specific communications as the basic elements of self-reproduction. The influence of Habermas' theory decreased and Luhmann's systems theory became dominant. Indeed Luhmann himself helped to push the theory in this direction. In a critique of the reflexive law concept he emphasised the vagueness of the concepts autonomy, reflexivity and self-regulation and compared them with the 'rigorously inflexible' concept of autopoiesis (Luhmann, 1985 in German, 1992 in English).

In particular in his collection of essays entitled 'Law as an Autopoietic System' (1989a in German, 1993 in English), Teubner took up the challenge. Although basically accepting Luhmann's theory of autopoietic social systems, Teubner deviated from Luhmann's approach in one crucial aspect. He asked the question that was carefully avoided by Luhmann how the origin, genesis and early history of an autopoietic system can be analysed. Teubner introduced the model of a gradual process in which autopoietic systems are created. He called this the hypercycle in which the system's component's are not just self-referentially constituted but hypercyclically coupled. In relation to the autopoietic nature of law he discussed self-reference, hypercyclical self-closure and self-regulation of the legal system as well as its blind co-evolution with other social systems. The concept of reflexive law became subsumed under the theory of an autopoietic legal system and was largely reduced to a discussion of the regulatory capacities of the legal system. The issues that from now on constituted the core of Teubner's thinking about reflexive law as part of his theory of autopoietic law are indicated in chapter 5 of Law as an Autopoietic System entitled Social Regulation through Reflexive Law. The main topics in this chapter are mutual recognition of autonomy and autopoiesis between social systems, proceduralisation, the limits of legal intervention, constructivist internal models of the external social world, 'interference' of the legal and the economic system through contract and rights, and regulation of self-regulation.

General features of reflexive labour law

The concept of reflexive labour law has been developed along the lines of Teubner's concept of reflexive law and Luhmann's and Teubner's autopoietic systems theory of law (Luhmann, 1993; Teubner, 1989a in German, 1993 in English; see also Teubner, 1988). In our understanding reflexive labour law is both an analytical concept and an object of research (Rogowski and Wilthagen, 1994). It describes a stage in the development of modern labour law when labour law realises its systemic limits with respect to regulation of other social systems. Furthermore, labour law detects at this reflexive stage a source of strength in its capacities for self-regulation.

The concept of functional differentiation can be used to explain the evolution of the modern legal system and the development of the field of labour law. Labour law is the product of differentiation within the legal system and is characterised by specific links with a particular social system, the industrial relations system. In fact it evolves in the beginning of a subsystem of a national legal system, largely in reaction to legal perceptions of the facilitative role of law within industrial and employment relations.

The theory of reflexive labour law offers a new understanding of both the nature and the relation of law and industrial relations. Industrial relations and law are conceived not as systems of action (or collective action) but instead as systems of (collective) communication. Self-reference of their system-specific communications forms the basis of self-reproduction or autopoiesis (see in particular ch. 4 in Luhmann, 1984 in German, 1995 in English). On this basis both systems have developed structures that render autonomy to each system in society. It is the concern with the internal constitution of social systems rather than exchange relations with the social environment which is prevalent in the autopoietic and reflexive theory.

In conceptualising the social systems of 'industrial relations' and 'law' as operationally closed systems of communication, it becomes possible to understand how different communication systems operate with different types of regulation. Furthermore, attention can be directed to the important relationship between modes of external regulation and processes of self-regulation. While labour law forms part of the legal system and is thus constituted by legal communication, collective agreements and collective bargaining belong to the self-regulatory structure of the industrial relations system and are ultimately constituted by industrial relations communication.

Possible applications of reflexive labour law

In the following an attempt is made to use the basic notions of reflexive law and apply them in a discussion of central aspects of modern labour law. I shall address in particular the concept of autopoietic industrial relations as a regulatory object of labour law, the challenge that self-regulation through collective agreements and employment contracts poses for labour law, reflexivity in labour conflict resolution, and deregulation of employment protection as reduction of complexity.

Law and industrial relations

Communications between collective industrial actors constitute the basic elements of the industrial relations system and its centre is the self-reproductive system of collective bargaining. Autopoietic industrial relations create specific institutional structures and procedures for the self-reference of collective communications in autonomous collective bargaining, the structures and procedures which establish a social sphere for new forms of collective communication and collective action. This social sphere and its autopoietic closure are the bases of the independence of the industrial relations system from the economic, the political and the legal systems.

There are several approaches within systems theory that can be used for a more detailed description of autopoietic industrial relations. The general theory of autopoietic social systems offers at least six possibilities to conceptualise industrial relations as a social system. In accordance with Luhmann's distinction of four types of social systems, i.e., interaction system, organisation, social movement and societal subsystem (Luhmann, 1975 in German, 1982 in English; on social, respectively protest movements see Luhmann, 1997: 847-865), industrial relations can be analysed as a social system at any of these levels of sociological analysis. I propose to add two further types of systems which are concerned with the treatment of conflicts either within social systems or within society as a whole. Autopoietic systems theory thus offers the following five possibilities for the characterisation of industrial relations as a social system: (a) industrial relations as a set of interaction systems, (b) as a network system, (c) as a social or protest movement, (d) as a conflict system, (e) as an immune system, and (f) as a full-blown societal system within a functionally differentiated society (for further discussions see Rogowski, 2000a; 2000b).

In my view, the industrial relations system has become a fully-fledged function system within the modern society. In his discussion of the economic system as an autopoietic system, Luhmann has put forward four conditions of a fully-fledged function system (in Chapter 2: Die Wirtschaft der Gesellschaft als autopoietisches System (The economy of society as an autopoietic system) in Luhmann, 1988: 43-90 [51]). These can be applied to industrial relations in the following manner:

- The form and scope of societal differentiation have reached a level that enables autonomous industrial relation systems to develop without being dominated by other function systems.
- The industrial relations system operates with a specific combination of closure and openness with respect to its elementary operations.
- The industrial relations system operates with a binary code (collectively negotiable or non-negotiable) which represents the exclusive function of the system.
- The industrial relations system has achieved a relative prominence in society at large through its ability to regulate labour affairs and to arrange corporatist exchange relations with other function systems in order to further its autonomy.

In assessing the regulation of the industrial relations system by the legal system it is important to analyse the mutual limitations imposed by their respective searches for autonomy. The legal system intervenes according to its legally-shaped view of industrial relations, and the industrial relations system reacts towards the legal system according to its own perception of experiences with the legal system. Both systems are more or less exclusively guided by their internal models of the external world (Teubner, 1989b). Thus, successful regulation through steering an interference of the systems depends largely on mutual internal acknowledgement of the needs of the regulating and the regulated system.

Furthermore, the type of legal regulation of industrial relations depends on the kind of perception of industrial relations in law. The legal system, being itself an autopoietic system, is limited in adopting non-legal world views. In general it only perceives industrial relations as a regulatory object. However, if labour law and its institutions manage to acknowledge the autopoietic nature of the industrial relations system, it can engage in reflexive regulation.

Regulation of self-regulation of collective agreements and employment contracts

The reflexive law concept argues that the main problems of modern law derive from the limits of traditional forms of regulation that impose substantive standards on autopoietic social systems, without reflecting their need for self-reproduction (Luhmann, 1990). The role of law changes in the complex modern society from an authoritative instrument of control into a facilitative instrument of mutual recognition of self-regulation.

The main form of self-regulation in industrial relations is collective bargaining aiming at the conclusion of a collective agreement. Through collective bargaining the industrial relations system fulfils its societal function of providing channels for peaceful interactions between the collective parties. Collective agreements are means by which the industrial relations regulate both important aspects of economic and other social life and their own affairs.

Thus collective agreements have two basic social functions, to paraphrase Otto Kahn-Freund. They are industrial peace treaties and they are sources for terms and conditions of employment, for the distribution of work and for the stability of jobs. Labour law realises this distinction by separating two parts of the collective agreement, the binding contract between the collective parties and the normative rule-making function of the collective agreement which renders it a code and source of law establishing terms and conditions of employment contract (Kahn-Freund, 1986, in particular ch. 6).

The legal regulation of collective bargaining has to be facilitative or auxiliary to be effective. However, this presupposes that labour law acknowledges the societal function of industrial relations. Labour law has the potential to be facilitative as well as destructive for collective bargaining. A good example of the latter destructive potential was the use of labour law in Great Britain in the early 1970s and 1980s. By imposing legal standards that were not consented by the industrial parties national, regional and sectoral collective bargaining was virtually annihilated (see Dickens, 1994). Behind these labour law measures were not only policies hostile towards trade unions but radical neo-classical economic policies that question the need of an industrial relations system altogether.

However, in general so-called collective labour law understands itself as supportive of industrial relations by providing a framework in which collective bargaining can operate effectively. This is particularly true for regulatory bodies that deal with the legal aspects of industrial relations. Labour courts are important labour law institutions that realise the limits of their regulatory capacities by distinguishing types of conflict which are treated in a judicial forum and those which are left to system-specific fora which form part of the self-regulatory mechanisms of the collective bargaining or workplace industrial relations system. This distinction is used in treating employment conflicts which occur in ongoing employment relations in comparison with conflicts resulting from a broken employment relationship. Judicial fora are considered well equipped to handle conflicts after termination of the social relation where the goal is to balance the interests of the parties to the conflict. The judicial forum provides mechanisms for the discussion of the dissolution of the relation independent of the complex web of personal and social aspects of the relationship. The judicial procedure requires a new form of co-operation to match the legal requirements (see Blankenburg et al., 1979; Blankenburg and Rogowski, 1986).

A crucial step in becoming reflexive is the realisation within law that processes of self-regulation within other social systems are best facilitated by low regulating itself. Modern legal systems distinguish between their conflict-resolution function and the regulation of other systems. From an autopoietic point of view the legal system can remain in conflict resolution within its boundaries of self-regulation in applying legal devices (norms, procedures and legal doctrine) whereas the regulation of other social systems requires a sophisticated retranslation of societal needs into legal facilitation. Regulation of other social systems is different because there are no inherent internal guidelines for the legal system to inhibit potentially destructive use of regulations. The legal system has to rely on external sources to assess its impact.

The realisation of the limits of regulatory capacities within labour law can lead to dramatic effects, some of which might be desirable others may be not. When labour law realises that it is used selectively by social actors and within social systems, this can lead to differentiation of forms of regulation within labour law according to different fields of social regulation. In other words, labour law adapts to different ways of self-regulation. However, this can lead to negative outcomes. The system of labour might lose its capacity to influence self-regulation because it overadapts and loses a separate regulatory goal which the social systems needs to be delivered from the external political realm. Furthermore the system of labour law is undermined and loses its unity.

The idea of regulation of self-regulation in labour law is not limited to the relation between law and industrial relations. It can also be applied to the regulation of employment contracts. As Hugh Collins (1999) has recently argued any legal regulation of contracts has to reckon with self-regulation. If contract law wants to be efficient, it has to understand itself as a mechanism of regulating self-regulation. Contract law becomes reflexive regulation when it tries to secure co-operation 'by conferring autonomy upon the parties to demise their own regulation' and 'to express their expectations of the relationship in their own language' (Collins, 1999: 67).

However, the employment contract is a particular regulatory object. It is in general characterised by an imbalance in the distribution of power among the parties. Thus the function of labour law in this instance has to be to counterbalance one-sidedness by insisting on adherence to standards of fairness and non-discrimination (Collins, 1993). Nevertheless the compliance with standards depends on granting autonomy to both parties and on facilitating trust rather than imposing sanctions. For example law can encourage employers to grant employees discretion to define and carry out tasks in exchange for a greater commitment on the side of the employees to obligations of loyalty and professionalism (Collins, 1999: 22).

Reflexive elements in labour conflict resolution

The analyses of developments in labour conflict resolution can contribute to an understanding of labour law as reflexive law. Three mechanisms of labour conflict resolution can be distinguished: arbitration procedures attached to collective bargaining, grievance or dispute procedures in companies and labour courts. Processes in labour courts and in arbitration and company procedures challenge labour law continuously to rethink its role as a regulatory force.

The three mechanisms of labour conflict resolution are embedded in different social systems: arbitration and negotiation procedures are constitutive mechanisms of industrial relations and collective bargaining, and are designed to resolve collective industrial conflicts; grievance procedures and works council dispute procedures are located within organisations, i.e., companies, and deal with conflicts which occur within workplace industrial relations; and labour courts and state conciliation procedures form part of the legal system and deal with judicialised employment conflicts (for further discussion see Rogowski, 1994).

If we look at the evolution of labour courts, their function and position within society can be described as a product of differentiation processes of societal systems. Furthermore, as organisations labour courts are able to operate in different contexts and develop capacities to influence their formation in accordance with self-reproduction purposes. The reflexive law perspective describes these processes as external and internal differentiation and as autonomisation of labour courts.

Differentiation and autonomisation of labour conflict resolution at the judicial level characterise most histories of labour courts in the major European countries. However, labour courts show nationally different trajectories in developing autopoietic organisational structures. Furthermore, labour law historians, as opposed to social historians, often find it difficult to acknowledge that early labour courts were initially institutions of the economic system that had to be transformed from economic to legal institutions.

Autonomisation of labour courts reduces the chances of external intervention in shaping judicial interpretation. If the political system manages to accept a plural judicial system with separate jurisdictions granted to specialized courts, the organising principle becomes the vertical relation of mutual recognition of autonomy. Furthermore, increasing judicial autonomisation means, somewhat paradoxically, that the political system becomes more dependent on labour courts for finding legislative solutions.

With respect to the judicial system in general autonomisation of decision-making changes the relationship of courts and the political system into mutual dependence on the basis of operational closure. The regulation of law through statutes begins in this process to rely on case law. Courts become self-confident in finding own solutions and increasingly demand specific legal changes from the legislator. The hierarchical relationship of courts and legislation transforms into mutual observation of decision-making. Statutory law increasingly is reduced to ex-post endorsement of doctrinal solutions established by case law.

From a comparative perspective (see also Rogowski, 1996) it is necessary to emphasise that the advanced role of the German labour court in creating labour law norms and in maintaining the judicial standards is made possible because of the high degree of organisational judicialisation and internal differentiation of the judicial system. In order to accept the idea of self-regulation in a subsystem or area like labour law, the judicial system must transform itself fundamentally. Its 'nature' has to change from a unitary organisation in which vertical control is exercised at different levels of appeal to a decentralised system comprising of independent judiciaries.

The transformation of the relationship of labour courts and legislation from hierarchical ordering to mutual recognition is intricately linked with internal judicialisation. Professional control over procedures and organisational independence of labour courts are preconditions for autonomisation of decision-making.[1] The lay labour courts in France lack both professional decision-making and independence at the appeal level and are thus largely confined to conflict resolution of single cases.

Their British counterparts are also deficient in this respect. Although common law courts enjoy in general a high degree of independence and can exercise internal control of their jurisdictional basis through precedents, all major common law countries still regard their labour judiciaries as inferior to ordinary courts. The British employment tribunal, the Australian arbitration court, and the American National Labor Relations Board are largely prevented by an undifferentiated national judicial system from transforming into law-making bodies similar to the German labour courts.

Within labour law the regulation of labour conflict resolution is commonly classified as procedural labour law which comprises of a separate body of norms regulating labour court procedure and procedural arrangements arbitration. However, for reflexive labour law this distinction of procedural and substantive labour law remains rather arbitrary. It disguises the use of procedure within substantive labour law, which is of utmost importance for an account of reflexive tendencies in the labour law development.

Labour law understands procedure by definition as a legal concept, both for self-regulation of its own procedures and for the regulation of industrial relations and employment procedures. Legal procedures can be described in sociological terms as episodes in which the procedure itself controls its beginning and end. Legal procedures are distinct from other procedures because they operate throughout the procedure with a high degree of uncertainty about the outcome. A main function of the regulation and

[1]'Organisation' and 'professionalism' create the main conditions for successful judicial decision-making because courts, in comparison with other decision-making bodies, are under the obligation to decide a case and cannot decide not to decide (Luhmann 1993: 310-337).

organisational design of legal procedures is to motivate the parties to become active participants who lose through their involvement grounds for criticism of the outcome. A legal procedure thus absorbs protest (Luhmann, 1969). However, these features often make legal procedures attractive for other social systems that resist substantive regulation but still rely on law as a regulator of procedure. The specific devices of legal procedures for the treatment of conflicts viewed as more successful in solving conflicts in comparison with system-specific alternatives.

The use of legal procedure in the regulation of other social systems can be interpreted as a form of juridification. Teubner and Willke (1984) argue that this type of juridification is in fact a general trend towards proceduralisation, in accordance with the general decline of instrumental law and the disillusion with legal formalisation and materialisation. This proceduralisation is alleged to have penetrated not only the judicial practice but also the rationality structure of law and the development of legal doctrine (see Wiethölter, 1986; Teubner 1986; see also Eder, 1986).

Labour courts are well known to instrumentalize industrial relations procedures for their purposes. In their formative period in the 1970s, British industrial tribunals went beyond mere recognition of industrial self-regulation and actively endorsed dispute procedures for decision-making purposes. The statutory reasonableness test, which was applied to judge the employer's behaviour in dismissal decisions, was linked with concerns with procedural fairness. The Court of Appeal reversed this line of decision-making, thereby arguing that such a direct linkage would lead to formalistic results. In fact, the courts stopped the instrumentalization of company procedures for purposes of judicial decision-making and this can be seen as enhancing the autonomy of industrial relations decision-making. However, the public interest in regulating dismissal according to general standards of justice has largely replaced formal general private law in British unfair dismissal law. Reasons for dismissal related to protected rights in society, e.g. anti-discrimination, trade union membership and activity, protection of pregnancy, are automatically unfair and are specific regulation aimed at general social goals (Collins, 1993).

German labour courts resort to company procedures both in formal and in informal ways. The law requires for all individual dismissal cases to observe the proper works council participation. Informally the labour court uses, in appropriate situations, references to procedures which are required in labour administrations. In the conciliation phase and during conciliation attempts at the hearing, it is standard practice in German labour courts to propose a settlement which fits the procedure at the unemployment agency. In order to secure the dismissed employee the immediate payment of unemployment benefits the court proposes to adopt the agency's procedural requirement of ordinary dismissal, instead of summary dismissal, as terms of the settlement. Thus the employee agrees to the dismissal, and the employer to the transformation of the summary dismissal into an ordinary dismissal with back payment for the notice period. The judges convince the parties in these cases to agree to a settlement because benefits can be achieved from a third party by following certain procedural requirements. Labour courts are, of course, keen on settlements since they relieve the court from finding (and writing!) a decision (see Blankenburg et al. 1979, ch. 6).

Deregulation of employment protection as reduction of complexity

A perennial problem of all function systems in modern societies is internal complexity. Not only the structures of the system tend to increase over time but also the amount of system-specific communications that are available for self-referential or other cyclical relations. In case of the legal system its structural components of legal norms, procedural rules and legal doctrine as well as case law tend to develop in different directions. In addition there is differentiation of the legal system into autonomous subsystems of law like labour law.

The legal field of labour law is confronted with the same problems of legal complexity as the legal system on the whole. There is an increase in statutory and other norms to protect employees, improved access to judicial and other procedures to find redress for rights violations, and a growing labour law doctrine that supports but also complicates decision-making.

The increase of internal legal complexity is usually accompanied by an increase in legal regulation. Thus legal complexity is not just a problem for the legal system but also encountered by those other social systems that are regulated by labour law. These problems have led to the allegation that legal regulation leads to juridification of social regulations.

Internal as well as external complexity constitute unavoidable problems for the modern legal system that nevertheless require adequate responses. If one looks at policies that deal with the complexity of labour law, a prominent strategy is deregulation of labour law and in particular of employment protection.

However, deregulation policies are motivated by different programs or ideologies. A conservative program of deregulating labour law, for example, is usually exclusively concerned with the economic effects of legal rules. It concentrates on 'unburdening business' and the 'needs' of companies. This version of deregulation rests on the neo-classical economic assumption that removing law and lowering levels of employment protection will automatically improve the performance of companies and have a positive impact on the labour market.

A more balanced approach pursues not only economic but also wider social goals in designing deregulation strategies. In many cases these socio-economic goals are directly linked to labour market policies that try to reduce unemployment. Social deregulation operates with a more balanced view of industrial and employment relations. It takes both sides into account and tries to strike a balance between employer demands of reduced levels of protection and the employees' interests to find and keep a secure job (see Rogowski and Schmid, 1998).

There are also cultural aspects underlying some deregulation policies. These relate to changes in general attitudes towards work and commitment, demographic developments and increased female interest in gainful employment. The accompanying type of deregulation tends to focus on flexibility in relation to the forms of employment and reduces barriers and obstacles that limit the use of so-called atypical employment. An increase in female participation rates in the labour market requires to liberalise and indeed to endorse part-time work by removing legal and other (for example social security) obstacles.

Finally deregulation can be motivated directly by legal complexity. This deregulation strategy can be called reflexive deregulation insofar as it is in fact self-regulation of the legal system. Reflexive deregulation balances law's internal requirement for reduction of complexity with wider goals of deregulation in relation to its social environment.

It has to be emphasised that each form of deregulation is more or less a response to legal complexity and is thus engaged in reduction of complexity. Furthermore, in the vast majority of deregulation efforts they are accompanied by re-regulation measures. In fact in a reflexive law perspective deregulation is a predictable event that is almost necessarily leading to new regulation. In any event deregulation is itself a particular form of regulation.

Conclusions

Modern labour law is undoubtedly under strain both as a result of internal developments and external pressures. The theory of reflexive labour law claims that it is able to name the main reasons that explain this situation. Furthermore, by viewing labour law as both reproducing itself and operating within the larger society propositions can be made about conditions for future developments.

Modern society internationalises rapidly. It becomes increasingly difficult for all function systems to confine their operations within national boundaries. It hardly makes sense any longer to talk of national economies. Indeed modern society is already a world society (Luhmann, 1982; Stichweh, 1995). And it is this dimension with which the reflexive and autopoietic law concept fundamentally challenges traditional legal and industrial relations analyses. It becomes increasingly clear that modern labour law and industrial relations operate nowadays in the world society (Rogowski, 1998; Rogowski, 2000a).

Furthermore, there exists already an emerging global labour law. This includes supranational social and employment policy measures adopted by the European Union and international labour standards adopted by international organisations (Bercusson, 1997; Sciarra, 1998). In addition there are social and economic rights and codes of conduct issued by multinational companies.

These measures form part of global law that develops without being backed by a state (Teubner, 1997). Despite considerable confusion about the meaning of globalisation, it seems clear that there is not one trajectory that labour law follows within the world society. It is thus a further feature of reflexive labour law that it observes and compares labour law developments in different parts of the world. The study of global labour law requires a reflexive comparative labour law that is both empirically informed and theoretically astute (see Rogowski, 1998; Twining, 2000).

References

Bercusson, B. (1996), 'Globalizing Labour Law: Transnational Private Regulation and Countervailing Actors in European Labour Law', in G. Teubner (ed.), *Global Law without a State*, Dartmouth, Aldershot, pp. 133-178.

Blankenburg, E. (1984), 'The Poverty of Evolutionism: A Critique of Teubner's Case for 'Reflexive Law'', 18 *Law and Society Review*, pp. 273-289.

Blankenburg, E. and R. Rogowski (1986), 'German Labour Courts and the British Industrial Tribunal System. A Socio-Legal Comparison of Degrees of Judicialisation', 13 *Journal of Law and Society*, pp. 67-92.

Blankenburg, E., S. Schönholz and R. Rogowski (1979), *Zur Soziologie des Arbeitsgerichtsverfahrens. Die Verrechtlichung von Arbeitskonflikten* (Towards a Sociology of Labour Courts. The Legalisation of Labour Conflicts), Luchterhand, Neuwied.

Collins, H. (1993), *Justice in Dismissal. The Law of Termination of Employment*, Clarendon Press, Oxford.

Collins, H. (1999), *Regulating Contracts*, Oxford University Press, Oxford.

Dickens, L. (1994), 'Deregulation and Employment Rights in Great Britain', in R. Rogowski and T. Wilthagen (eds) (1994), *Reflexive Labour Law. Studies in Industrial Relations and Employment Regulation*, Kluwer, Deventer, pp. 225-247.

Eder, K. (1986), 'Prozedurale Rationalität. Moderne Rechtsentwicklung jenseits von formaler Rationalität (Procedural rationality. Modern legal development beyond formal rationality)', 7 *Zeitschrift für Rechtssoziologie*, pp. 1-30.

Kahn-Freund, O. (1986), *Labour and the Law*. Third ed. by P. Davies and M. Freedland, Stevens, London.

Luhmann, N. (1969), *Legitimation durch Verfahren* (Legitimation by procedure), Luchterhand, Neuwied.

Luhmann, N. (1975), 'Interaktion, Organisation, Gesellschaft (Interaction, organisation, society)', in N. Luhmann, *Soziologische Aufklärung* (Sociological enlightenment), Vol. 2., Westdeutscher Verlag, Opladen, pp. 9-20. (English translation: N. Luhmann (1982), 'Interaction, Organization, and Society', in N. Luhmann, *The Differentiation of Society*, Columbia University Press, New York, pp. 69-89).

Luhmann, N. (1982), 'The World Society as a Social System' 8 *International Journal of General Systems,* pp. 131-138. Reprinted in N. Luhmann (1990), *Essays on Self-Reference*, Columbia University Press, New York, pp. 175-190.

Luhmann, N. (1984), *Soziale Systeme*, Suhrkamp, Frankfurt am Main. (English translation:

Luhmann, N. (1995), *Social Systems*, Stanford University Press, Stanford, Cal.

Luhmann, N. (1985), 'Einige Probleme mit 'reflexivem Recht'', 6 *Zeitschrift für Rechtssoziologie*, pp. 1-18. (English translation: Luhmann, N. (1992), 'Some Problems with 'Reflexive Law'', in G. Teubner and A. Febbrajo (eds), *State, Law and Economy as Autopoietic Systems. Regulation and autonomy in a new perspective*, Giuffrè, Milano, pp. 389-415).

Luhmann, N. (1988), 'The Unity of the Legal System', in Teubner, G. (ed.), *Autopoietic Law; A new Approach to Law and Society*,de Gruyter, Berlin, pp.12-35.

Luhmann, N. (1990), 'The Self-reproduction of Law and its Limits', in N. Luhmann, *Essays on Self-Reference*,Columbia University Press, New York, pp. 227-245.

Luhmann, N. (1993), *Das Recht der Gesellschaft* (The law of society), Suhrkamp, Frankfurt am Main.

Luhmann, N. (1997), *Die Gesellschaft der Gesellschaft* (The society of society), Suhrkamp, Frankfurt am Main.

Nonet, P. and P. Selznick (1978), *Law and Society in Transition: Toward Responsive Law*, Harper, New York.

Rogowski, R. (1994), 'Industrial Relations, Labour Conflict Resolution and Reflexive Labour Law', in R. Rogowski and R., T. Wilthagen (eds), *Reflexive Labour Law. Studies in Industrial Relations and Employment Regulation*, Kluwer, Deventer, pp. 53-93.

Rogowski, R. (1996), 'The Art of Mirroring. Comparative Law and Social Theory', in G. Wilson and R. Rogowski (eds), *Challenges to European Legal Scholarship. Anglo-German Legal Essays*, Blackstone, London, pp. 215-232.

Rogowski, R. (1998), 'Autopoietic Industrial Relations and Reflexive Labour Law in the World Society', in T. Wilthagen (ed.), *Advancing Theory in Labour Law and Industrial Relations in a Global Context*, Proceedings of the Royal Netherlands Academy of the Arts and Sciences, Amsterdam et al., North-Holland, pp. 67-82.

Rogowski, R. (2000a), 'Recht und industrielle Beziehungen in Luhmanns Weltgesellschaft', 21 *Zeitschrift für Rechtssoziologie*, pp. 279-292.

Rogowski, R. (2000b), 'Industrial Relations as a Social System', 7 *Industrielle Beziehungen. The German Journal of Industrial Relations*, pp. 97-126.

Rogowski, R. and G. Schmid (1998), 'Reflexive Deregulierung - Ein Ansatz zur Dynamisierung des Arbeitsmarktes (Reflexive deregulation. An approach to make the labour market more dynamic)', in B. Keller and H. Seifert (eds), *Deregulierung am Arbeitsmarkt* (Deregulation at the labour market), VSA, Hamburg, pp. 215-253.

Rogowski, R. and T. Wilthagen (eds) (1994), *Reflexive Labour Law. Studies in Industrial Relations and Employment Regulation*, Kluwer, Deventer.

Sciarra, S. (1998), 'How 'Global' is Labour Law? The Perspective of Social Rights in the European Union', in T. Wilthagen (ed.), *Advancing Theory in Labour Law and Industrial Relations in a Global Context*, Proceedings of the Royal Netherlands Academy of the Arts and Sciences, Ed.. Amsterdam et al., North Holland, pp. 99-116.

Stichweh, R. (1995), 'Zur Theorie der Weltgesellschaft (On the theory of world society)', 1 *Soziale Systeme*, pp. 29-45.

Teubner, G. (1983), 'Substantive and Reflexive Elements in Modern Law', 17 *Law and Society Review*, pp. 239-285.

Teubner, G. (1984), 'Autopoiesis in Law and Society: A Rejoinder to Blankenburg', 18 *Law and Society Review*, pp. 291-301.

Teubner, G. (1986), 'After Legal Instrumentalism? Strategic Models of Post-regulatory Law', in G. Teubner (ed.), *Dilemmas of Law in the Welfare State*. Berlin: de Gruyter, pp. 299-326.

Teubner, G. (ed.) (1988), *Autopoietic Law. A New Approach to Law and Society*, de Gruyter, Berlin.

Teubner, G. (1989a), *Recht als autopoietisches System*, Suhrkamp, Frankfurt am Main. (English translation: G. Teubner (1993), *Law as an Autopoietic System*, Blackwell, Oxford).

Teubner, G. (1989b), 'How the Law Thinks: Toward a Constructivist Epistemology of Law', 23 *Law and Society Review*, pp. 727-757.

Teubner, G. (ed.) (1997), *Global Law without a State*, Dartmouth, Aldershot.

Teubner, G. and H. Willke (1984), 'Kontext und Autonomie. Gesellschaftliche, Selbststeuerung durch reflexives Recht (Context and autonomy. Societal self-steering through reflexive law)', 5 *Zeitschrift für Rechtssoziologie*, pp. 4-35.

Twining, W. (2000), *Globalisation and legal theory*, Butterworths, London.

Wiethölter, R. (1986), Materialization and Proceduralisation in Modern Law, in G. Teubner (ed.), *Dilemmas of Law in the Welfare State*, de Gruyter, Berlin, pp. 221-249.

Willke, H. (1992), 'Societal Guidance through Law?' in G. Teubner and A. Febbrajo (eds), *State, Law and Economy as Autopoietic Systems. Regulation and autonomy in a new perspective*, Giuffrè, Milano, pp. 353-387.

Wilthagen, T. (ed.) (1998), *Advancing Theory in Labour Law and Industrial Relations in a Global Context*, Proceedings of the Royal Netherlands Academy of the Arts and Sciences, Amsterdam et al., North-Holland.

9 Criminal Justice: Autopoietic Insights

RICHARD NOBLES AND DAVID SCHIFF

Introduction

Reference to *the criminal justice system* is embedded in writings concerned with the law in general and criminal law in particular at both the most introductory and the most sophisticated levels. That phrase is used to refer to numerous unifying themes about matters pertaining to criminal law and its operation. Sometimes it is used to situate or contextualize substantive criminal law; sometimes to allude to sequences of events within the criminal process; sometimes to compare, contrast and draw attention to the relationship between criminal law in the books, and law in action. Sometimes, from a functionalist perspective, it is used to highlight the changing identity of institutions that undertake complementary roles, such as the growth alongside the main public policing and prosecution services of private policing and of alternative prosecution authorities. Sometimes it is used to prioritise sentencing practices, on the assumption that the end products of linked processes provide the rationale and unity to what precedes them. Whilst the phrase the criminal justice system refers to many and various things, its ubiquitous use at least acknowledges its apparent meaningfulness and importance to many writers. Perhaps it also acknowledges the suggestion that criminal justice aspects of a legal system can differentiate themselves from other parts of a legal system, its non-criminal elements: civil, administrative, etc.

This is not to say that many of those using the phrase the criminal justice system are entirely comfortable with their uses of it. Some of those who use it have indicated that the word system suggests a level of integration and co-ordination that is in many respects absent. As Ashworth puts it: 'Although many who speak and write about criminal justice tend to refer to 'the criminal justice system', it is widely agreed that it is not a 'system' in the sense of a set of co-ordinated decision-makers … many groups working within criminal justice enjoy considerable discretion, and … are relatively autonomous. None the less, the inappropriateness of the term 'system' should not be allowed to obscure the practical interdependence of the various agencies'. (Ashworth, 1998: 22-3).[1] However, those who are sufficiently sensitive to the unwarranted suggestions of unity conveyed by the word system are likely to be troubled by what to put in its place. How does one identify the overlap of things (interests, institutions, communications) represented by the use of the word system without suggesting a systematic unity? Do words like process avoid the suggestions of unity, or do they introduce in addition unwarranted suggestions of a unity created by a specific set of institutions or interest groups e.g. that criminal justice is organised around criminal legal procedures: pre-trial, trial, appeal.

Beyond the various uses of the phrase the criminal justice system in diverse texts, whether criminological, socio-legal, introductory or more specialised, it also occurs in texts that focus more narrowly on the study of criminal law. Here use of the phrase the criminal justice system breathes life into what might otherwise appear as a sterile and discredited exercise; namely the study of substantive criminal law from a narrow, rule-bound, legal-positivist perspective. That perspective involves reading statutes and cases with a view to finding a consistent and objective interpretation of the conditions that determine criminal illegality. This narrow, rule-bound approach to criminal law assumes that the way to learn about criminal law is to read legal texts containing criminal law source materials, and absorb the way in which others (especially judges) have read such legal texts. However, this seems decidedly less exciting and relevant, less well-grounded or situated than an approach to criminal law organised in terms of criminal justice.[2] The latter approach invites one to look outside of or beyond statutes and cases to find meanings. From this common starting point, different texts go in different directions. Some maintain the focus on doctrine but seek to understand its meaning in terms of the end products of the linked processes where statements of doctrine are made. Thereby the focus is on the interrelations between substantive law and sentencing practice and justifications for punishment. This might lead to analysis of case law in terms of broad philosophical theories such as retributive justice and utilitarianism (general and particular deterrence), or critiques of such

[1]On the other hand there are those who use the idea of criminal justice as a system to describe and explain the mechanisms of co-operation and integration whereby 'The system may … be seen as greater than the sum of its parts.' (Davies, Croal and Tyrer, 1998: 16).

[2]Contrast recent editions of traditional student criminal law texts (Smith, 1999) with more contemporary texts (Lacey and Wells, 1998). For a significant analysis of the underdevelopment of, need for and ability to offer 'irrelation', in the study of criminal justice, between legal doctrine and the effort to contextualise it, see the analysis provided by Nelken (Nelken, 1987).

theories.[3] Others seek to de-emphasise doctrine, to focus on the actions and actors commonly associated with criminal justice (see, for example, Uglow, 1995; Sanders and Young, 2000; Wasik, Gibbons and Redmayne, 1999). Rather than use criminal justice to inform substantive and procedural criminal law, they might jettison formal law in favour of the codes that inform the actual behaviour of prosecutors and police, defendants and defence lawyers, probation and prison officers, informants and victims. Such an approach can lead to the claim that such codes amount to a plurality of laws. And from this position, the codes of actors who come into contact with state law have no intrinsic difference to, superiority over or inferiority to those of clubs, criminal fraternities, vigilantes, or families. Law becomes normativity or, if the focus is function rather than language, social control.

What links all of these approaches to criminal justice and the criminal justice system are the belief that more is better, that there are wider, more informative and thereby superior perspectives. One must look out, or look wider, from a point, or across a whole, although the location of the borders of this whole may lack definition and clarity. What, if anything, could an understanding of autopoiesis bring to the study of this criminal justice system? Is it simply another view of the cathedral, justified by the pluralistic claim that more views are better than less, or can the theory also offer insights into the problematic and the weaknesses of other approaches, thus improving our ability to use them, or even encouraging us to discard some?

This paper asks what it means, from an autopoietic perspective, to address the criminal justice system and what insights follow from this approach. We believe that the theory offers a range of insights that could assist those engaged both in sociological enquiry and radical politics, and would be of particular assistance to those who seek to combine both: using empirical studies of law in action to call for reforms. Much of the form of such empirical research uses a relatively unsophisticated concept of law, which is essentially positivistic. A reasonably pure (or at least clear) understanding of what the law is in the area to be studied provides a standard against which to assess performance and call for change. And, on the basis of such an unsophisticated concept of law, a lot of radical writing in the academic field known as criminal justice is then able to rely on a crude opposition between law in the books, and law in action. As well as potentially informing empirical research into criminal justice, autopoiesis provides a challenge to the praxis of those who hope to use the results of

[3] Such analysis (treating criminal law as a type of moral philosophy) continues to represent a great deal of research, debate and critique, often at a highly sophisticated level (Lacey, 1998; Norrie, 1998).

such research to achieve change. In particular, the theory highlights problems of translation. There is a marked contrast here with much of what constitutes radical legal politics, which, in comparison, relies on an unrefined concept of translation. Radical lawyers seek effective legal rights for suspect communities and persons. But do they pay sufficient attention to the problems of *translating* legal rights into action, given the different systems of communication that operate within the site known as criminal justice?

Our preliminary conclusions on applying autopoietic insights to criminal justice are as follows:

1. The study of criminal justice would be assisted by a more complex concept of law and legality. In particular, one needs an understanding of law that encompasses pluralism without abandoning legality. Autopoiesis provides an understanding of law that accounts for the co-existence of multiple interpretations of what law requires, and explains why situations arise when law is challenged as a normative system.

2. Those seeking to study and reform criminal justice need to take the problems of translation seriously. Approaching criminal justices as a *site* occupied by many communities and their systems of communication, each reflexively communicating back to themselves, would assist them in their task.

Having outlined our conclusions, we will start our analysis by clarifying how we interpret what it means to take an autopoietic approach to the study of criminal justice.

Producing order through differentiated systems of communication

Autopoietic systems theory, as conceived by Luhmann, regards modern society as made up of multiple systems of communication (Luhmann, 1986; for a straightforward introduction, see Mingers, 1995). It provides a radical twist to the Durkheimian orthodoxy that sees modern life as characterised by a developed division of labour. Whereas the orthodox view represents difference in terms of roles, and understands modern society's attempts to overcome difference through its spontaneous construction of mechanisms of interdependence and co-operation, autopoietic systems theory provides new answers to some of the obvious limitations of this approach (Luhmann,

1982).[4] What is the basis of social division, and how, with the consequent fragmentation of experience is co-ordination to be achieved? Co-ordination is made possible, according to this systems theory, by the use of common reductive terms, self-referential communication, and (at the level of discourse) widely shared values. This theory does not deny that different persons may form different understandings of what the communications within a system mean. But it stresses the limitations placed upon interpretation by the need to interpret meanings by reference to pre-existing communications within the same system. Interpretation is restricted, and co-ordination facilitated, by the network of common reductive terms, values and communications. Fragmentation of discourse, and reductive interpretation, produces co-ordination, because those discourses take the form of stable, self-referential, systems of communication. Those that are the most stable can be described as autopoietic (for a more extensive account of the nature of law as self-referential, set out in response to critics of the theory, see Teubner, 1993: ch. 3).

This theory does not claim to solve all problems of interpretation. Rather, it provides both new answers to the differences of interpretation that are the traditional focus of jurisprudence, and invites us to concentrate on different problems of co-ordination. Within the legal system, autopoietic theory is compatible with most of the traditional debates on the nature of legal interpretation. It does not deny hermeneutics; it simply stresses that what counts, as a communication within the legal system requires one to integrate what one wishes to say/argue/claim with existing legal communications. Its self-referential nature and its common task bind legal communication: to establish what is legal, or illegal (Luhmann, 1992a; Luhmann, 1992b). The claim of autopoietic systems theory is simply that restricting what may be communicated and still be law (or medicine, or education, or economy) enables society to exist in a highly differentiated yet co-ordinated form despite the unavoidable need for interpretation. Reductionism through differentiated systems of communication makes complex social life possible. With its limited agenda (how can we have order?) it does not claim to dictate what content that order will or should have.

Autopoiesis prompts the researcher to look for the meaning that actors impose on their actions through their participation in systems of

---

[4]We present this short analysis on the assumption that Luhmann's earlier theorising about modern society, and later development of an appropriate autopoietic theory, is driven by an understanding of modern society in terms of increasing functional differentiation rather than, for example, stratification. For a recent attempt by Luhmann to capture this prerequisite for our understanding of modern society, see his 'Modernity in Contemporary Society' (Luhmann, 1998), and see note 8 below.

communication, and to track changes in meaning through these same processes. With its concentration on meaning, or more particularly meaning-processing, it has been accused of neglecting other explanations for social action, most notably those that seek to provide insights through a focus on interests and culture. The appropriate response is not to claim that an analysis of meaning is the only way to carry out social research. Rather, it is to question whether the meanings of actions could offer important data, and then to challenge those who advocate other methodologies by asking where the meanings of actions can be found, except in language, i.e. in communications. Identifying what action means to actors, and identifying the systems of communications that allow their meanings to be shared by others (objectivity) is only a partial explanation of the world. The meanings that action has for social actors are not the sole determinant of social action. But, on the other hand, asserting that the meaning of action for actors lies in their interests or culture can amount to a refusal to take the analysis of meaning, and the opportunities that this offers for interventions in social life, seriously. One can put this in quite simple terms. The focus of autopoiesis is the meaning processing of communications. One needs to distinguish between the benefits of a focus, and any claim to be a complete explanation. There are investigations that could be assisted by autopoietic insights into the basis of shared communication in modern society.[5]

An autopoietic description of the criminal justice system

Autopoiesis does not locate unity, as expressed by the word system, at the level of criminal justice, but within separate and more definitely structured systems. The unity of the legal aspects of criminal justice can only be found through the separation of law from its environment. The unity of law's participation in criminal justice is established at the level of the legal system: the self-referential system of communications about law that encode experience into the opposition legal/illegal. Criminal justice, within law, is *not* a separate system. Indeed, while lawyers talk of criminal law, we know that its categories and doctrines are parasitic upon other laws: contract, property, etc. Or, if one prefers the approach of Bentham, all of law is coercive (or discoercive), with for example property law being the 'expository matter' (Bentham, 1970: 176-83) that establishes the illegality of theft. Either way, there is no separation. From this perspective, the 'other' material, which informs studies of the

[5]This limited claim, we would argue, does not require us to state a position about the vexed and much debated question of the ability of sociology to offer a valid analysis of legal meaning. See Nelken (1996), especially the discussion of Cotterrell's analysis of this question (Nelken, 1996: 107-28).

criminal justice system, can take a number of forms. It can provide the environment of the legal system: the boundaries created when the legal system encodes events to give them 'legal meaning'. Or it can represent a site of structural coupling between more than one system.[6]

References to the criminal justice system, such as conferences involving lawyers, policemen, probation officers, social workers, economists, politicians, psychologists and sociologists on the criminal justice system or a certain aspect of it, are not references to a single system of communication. Rather, the criminal justice system is the *site* of relatively stable interactions between numerous systems of communication. These systems may share the phrase criminal justice, but they cannot give that phrase the same meanings. This is not, from an autopoietic perspective, a statement that criminal justice is the site of different groups with different interests. Or even that criminal justice is a site of overlapping interests and strong interdependence.[7] Interests may affect communications, but they are not themselves communications. And the focus of social autopoiesis is communications. What kinds of communications are made, self-referentially, from which systems, at the site identified within each system by the words criminal justice? Identifying the kinds of communications made over different periods, and within different areas, of the site known as criminal justice, provides a formal method of classification that may be used to talk about that site.

Approaching criminal justice from an autopoietic perspective, one does not expect to explain the stability of its operations through the common interpretations of its various actors. Nor would one seek to identify the 'balance' of the interests of its constituent groups. Instead, one would regard the site of criminal justice as an arena in which different systems of communication fail to communicate directly with each other, yet coexist.[8]

---

[6]One of the prerequisites referred to in note 5 above is captured in the 'distinction between self-reference and external reference … differentiating internal and external on an operative level is unavoidable' (Luhmann, 1998: 10).

[7]Analysis of the criminal justice system as representing strong interdependence is characteristic of many political initiatives and much 'official' writing about criminal justice (Pullinger, 1985; Feeney, 1985).

[8]The use of modern information technology by agencies operating as part of the criminal process seeks to integrate different parts of that process through the use of common software. Such projects acknowledge the interdependence represented by division of labour, but necessarily suppress the division represented by separate systems of communication. The software will have different meanings in its uses by different actors. If you design common software, which actors is the software talking to and for? See, for example, the Lord Chancellor Department's 'Libra Project'. This is described as 'The beginning of a new approach to integration within criminal justice'. On the basis that 'It is well known that integration problems in criminal justice organisations are widespread' the Project attempts

The site cannot be colonised wholly by any one system. Criminal justice must involve more codification of social life than the opposition legal/illegal. There are other self-referential systems of communication operating in this arena than 'the law'. One needs to identify these other systems of communication, see on what basis they codify their operations and environment, and consider the difficulties of translating the communications of the law into these different systems of communication. For example, one might wish to examine the relevance of psychology to criminal aspects of mental health to see how psychological theories are 'misread' by law to facilitate the various levels of criminal insanity or reduced criminal responsibility. Alternatively, one might wish to look into mental health to consider the extent to which the encoding which takes place is by reference to legality (the legal system), or health (the medical system). Identifying the self-referential nature of (mis) translation, and mapping alternative systems of communications, are both useful insights into the workings of the criminal justice system.

Let us take a wide-ranging example. Among the concerns of those who seek a radical agenda for reforming criminal justice, one of the most challenging tasks is to identify the manner in which the police communicate.[9] Empirical studies point to the interests of the police, their self-perception, culture, and the importance of attitudes within the lower ranks described evocatively, if obtusely, as 'canteen culture'.[10] Autopoiesis

---

to integrate 'today's disparate criminal justice systems into a single seamless, electronic system – an information highway for the nation's criminal justice organisations with one common database.' (www.government.co.uk/public_sector/jus&safety/libra.htm)

[9]For a historically and empirically informed account of 'the reality of police practice' that particularly addresses the dynamic role of legally informed communications incorporating the 'principles of liberal constitutionalism' in police practice, see Choongh, 1997. Choongh's focus is those cases investigated by the police that are never likely to reach the courts. Namely 'a self-contained policing system which makes use of a legal canopy to subordinate sections of society viewed as anti-police and innately criminal' (Choongh, 1997: 40). For a theoretically informed account (although not one informed by autopoiesis) of the role of 'law' in policing, see Dixon, 1997. Dixon's work demonstrates the flexibility of 'the law' in policing practices: 'not as having some fixed essence, but as an adaptable set of practices, discourses, techniques, and modes of regulation' (Dixon, 1997: 318). The substantial difficulties of researching how the police communicate are fully addressed by Young in his insider's anthropology of the police. He concludes that 'policing remains a highly visible yet carefully concealed business, which at one and the same time is perhaps the most symbolically apparent of the systems of social control, but carefully keeps many of its practices hidden from scrutiny' (Young, 1991: 395).

[10]This phrase is commonly used in empirical studies of police behaviour. It suggests both a laddish/male/macho culture, and the presence of an informal alternative set of values/culture/ system(s) of communication to that officially recorded and espoused. However, it is a phrase that often camouflages what it represents (see, for example, Waddington, 1999). Waddington's account has been criticised by Hodgson (1999).

takes such studies seriously, but asks the following question: how do the police communicate within criminal justice? Is policing best understood as a system, in which the police constitute themselves as an autonomous body through a differentiated system of communication? Or are the police best understood as fragmented individuals involved in a variety of systems of communication, in which they must make self-referential communications and achieve translations (never direct) into other areas of communication? Those who desire reform, but who deny the problems (and opportunities) of differentiated systems of communication look to changing the interests of the police by changing personnel or imposing sanctions. But reforming the police cannot start from the premise of an over-night removal of existing personnel. And sanctions move us into problems of effectiveness with, as history repeatedly demonstrates, inevitable elements of regulatory failure.[11]

An autopoietic approach to policing would start with the difficulties and opportunities provided by mistranslation. Consider first the difficulties. Forum in which police and other actors speak to each other (committees, conferences, political agendas, legislative changes, etc.) are to be viewed sensitively as places where mistranslation is likely to occur. This mistranslation is not simply a consequence of separate interests, or distrust. Consider, for example, a conference we recently attended on misconduct by and accountability in the police.[12] Lawyers and senior policemen, in about equal numbers attended this conference. The chairs and speakers were, in almost all cases, lawyers, academic or professional. The agenda was the lawyers' demands for more rights for suspects. In many of the sessions the policemen had nothing to say. This was not simply a function of hostility or distrust. From speaking to police officers in between the sessions it became evident that they had a great deal to say, about the lawyers' agenda, but no way of speaking about it in the same terms as the lawyers. So, for example, if asked whether proposals being advocated at the conference were 'workable', or could be combined with 'good policing', the officers became quite vocal. There was even mistranslation at the level of the conference's general theme. The police came to the conference expecting to talk about the problems of preventing misconduct by the police, on the assumption

---

Hodgson's paper makes a serious attempt at exploring the problematic relationship between empirical research on criminal justice and jurisprudence.

[11]Regulatory failure is of particular relevance to the exercise of police powers and their supervision. For an empirically informed account of the existing regime of powers and safeguards and the likelihood of its regulatory effectiveness or failure, see Bottomley et al., 1991, especially ch. VII 'The Impact and Implications of PACE: Summary and Conclusions'.

[12]Organised by the Mannheim Centre for Criminology, LSE, London, 6 Sept. 1999. See the newspaper article introducing the conference by Graham Smith, one of the organisers of the conference, 'Hounding the Bad Cops' *The Guardian* 30 June 1999.

that their work could be divided into a correct and incorrect way to behave, with the central problem being corruption (identifying bad police officers, and what conditions produce them). The lawyers, from the perception that due process and suspects' rights are currently inadequate, discussed the inappropriateness of much police conduct, rendering the concept of corruption otiose.[13] Our conclusion from the experience of this conference is not that translation would have resulted in an overall consensus between police and lawyers. It is simply that understanding the specialised and differentiated systems of communication that were present at this conference might have facilitated the formulation of proposals that had purchase. Perfect (direct) translation is impossible between languages. But an awareness of the possibilities of mistranslation and the need to convey the 'sense' of one language into another (always an art) could improve the quality of the interface. It may even increase the ability of reformers to intervene strategically in a different area of social life/communication.

A non-autopoietic interpretation of our conference experience might account for mistranslation as a consequence of divergent interests and values. From the perspective of policemen, with their commitments to authority and order rather than legality, and their canteen culture interpretation of what constitutes good order, different meanings to the words: 'police corruption' are given than those represented in the communications of lawyers with their interests and commitments to legality. What if anything is the difference between these two kinds of explanation for the different meanings that are represented by different interests rather than different systems of communication? The answer lies in the order of enquiry. For autopoiesis meaning is not located in interests or group values, but in systems of communication. An autopoietic approach would seek to identify the systems of communication that enable policemen to communicate to each other that an arrest was 'good', whether or not it is thought to be legal or illegal. Such an analysis answers the question: what do policemen mean by a 'good' arrest. A non-autopoietic and logically a second question is: why do they communicate in this way? The answer to this second question (which looks to causality rather than meaning) might well be expressed in terms of interests and values.

The claim that interests and values provide a better basis for the analysis of police communications than a theory which focuses on the meaning of communications may represent a recognition of the difficulties of locating meaning in communication. In our police example, the location of legal meanings by reference to a legal system's system of communication is far

[13]One of the consequences of this mistranslation was the apparent conflict at the conference between one senior lawyer and one senior policeman – 'Lawrence lawyer in police racism clash' (Nick Hopkins) *The Guardian* 7 Sept. 1999.

less difficult than identifying the systems of communication that allow policemen to meaningfully communicate potentially illegal arrests as 'good'. It may simply be easier to attribute non-legal meanings on the basis of interests and values, rather than to trace the communication systems that make such meanings possible. But it is misleading to do so particularly if one recognises that the courts may later ratify as legal many of the meanings attributed by the police to their actions. Indeed, as Choongh claims: 'For much of this century the response of the courts to police illegality has been marked by capitulation to police demands and practices' (Choongh, 1997: 16). Attributing meanings through interests and values rather than tracing them through systems of communication ends up with a short hand - legal meanings can be translated into police meanings if one remembers the factors that cause the difference (respect for authority, order, etc.). But this is not the same thing as finding out what events *actually mean* to the police. If the latter task is taken seriously, and successfully, one should end up with a richer and more developed understanding of police meanings than a set of perspectives, interests and values.

If the first insight offered by autopoiesis is that criminal justice can be usefully studied as a site of interfacing systems of communication, then the second insight comes from the claim that the unity of each system comes only from the self-referential nature of that system's communications. This may assist those, of which there are many, who adopt a law in action approach to the criminal justice system. Much of the writing in this field uses the idea of a gap between law in action, and that in the books, or between law and other normative codes. The concept of a 'gap' is somewhat enigmatic. It acknowledges that appellate case law (the source of much law in the books) bears a tenuous link to practices within criminal justice. But it does not squarely address the question of what *residual* link might lie between the two. If the law in the textbooks bears so little resemblance to that on the street, should one not simply study practices, or local norms, and ignore the textbooks? Before adopting this conclusion, it may be useful to consider an autopoietic answer to understanding the relationship between law in textbooks, and law on the street, in the police station, or even in the courts.[14]

Autopoiesis does not depend on the universality of meaning of law set out in textbooks. There may be an apparent objectivity in such law,

[14]Detailed studies of what actually happens in the criminal courts have consistently demonstrated that they fail to achieve what the rules (substantive and procedural) require of them. This certainly applies in the lower courts (Carlen, 1976; Rock, 1993), but also in the higher courts (McBarnet, 1981). For a succinct statement of the limitations of the law in the books/law in action dichotomy, see Nelken, 1987: 150-1.

produced through a constructionist epistemology, within the confines of a particular interpretative community. Indeed Stanley Fish has argued that objective meanings, and ideas of appropriate linguistic strategies, become established when identifiable communities are initiated into common understandings of the purpose of practice, and the practice of purpose (Fish, 1989: 356-71). The initiation of law students into the practice of reading legal texts will, he claims, create such a community. But from this perspective there is no unity in law since the interpretative community of lawyers (and law students) is not the same as that of the police. Thus if law is the prerogative of the former then those who study the police in action may study non-law, or perhaps another system of law. But, if the unity of a legal system is found in the self-referential nature of the communications within that system, then the relationship between the law of lawyers, and that of the police, can be given a different interpretation. Both form part of the legal system, since they both encode experience using the code legal/illegal, and carrying out such codification, they both refer back to the same system of communication. Policemen who speak about the legal system know that they are referring to statutes and case law, or to textbooks (Blackstone's Criminal Practice, Moriaty's Police Law) which codify the same sources. These same sources are involved when police officers, in their frustration with legality, and with lawyers, use what they refer to ironically as the 'Ways and Means Act' (Reiner, 1994: 712-4). Here they are acknowledging that their actions are not legal. Such ironical references are both an application of the binary code legal/illegal to acknowledge the illegality of what they have done and an assertion of the appropriateness of their actions by reference to some other system of communication. Thus police officers who adopt the 'Ways and Means Act' successfully communicate to their fellows that they have stepped outside the authority given to them under the UK legal system i.e. in deviating from that system, they have applied its coding to their own actions.

From this autopoietic perspective the gap between law in the books and law in action needs to be replaced by an understanding of the diversity of legal communications. There is a differentiated system of communications that is understood in our society as law. While this system is not restricted to state law, nevertheless state law forms an important part of that system of communication. A differentiated system for the pronouncement of legality has been achieved. Communications about normativity that make no reference to the communications of legality that circulate in our society have great difficulty in being understood, by speaker or audience, as legal communications. In the arena of criminal justice, one may talk of police norms as 'law', but this obscures the common understanding of the police and lawyers of what constitutes the law, and non-law. The fact that police officers may have different understandings of their powers of arrest from that of lawyers does not prevent the police's pronouncements on it from being legal communications. But this can be distinguished from a police officer's claim to have 'bent the law', or an ironical reference to the non-existent 'Ways and Means Act', which constitute admissions that the police norms are not part of the legal system.[15]

Autopoiesis can avoid a move from frustration with the limitations of textbook law to an abandonment of law and legality as useful classifications. It can also reduce the apparently informative, but actually vacuous, opposition between law in the books, and law in action. The 'gap' between these two is obvious - action and normativity at any site are never synonymous with textbook law. But how is the local site to be described and assessed. The gap may lead to a pluralism, whereby local practices and standards are described as 'local law'. Formal law is simply part of that local law, or perhaps a rival to it. Alternatively, textbook law may still be understood as law, and local practices and standards as deviations from it. With such an approach, one may (if committed to textbook law) seek to find ways to narrow the gap. Both approaches suffer from the reification of textbook law as something more really law, or state law, or 'academically' law, than what occurs on the ground.

Autopoiesis can offer a more sophisticated way of describing and assessing these factors than the concept of a gap. The inevitability of the gap can lead us to consider the links between law in different sites. If one starts with understanding law as communications, one does not need to reify or prioritise textbook law in one's descriptions of law at a local site. By concentrating on the differentiation represented by systems, and taking the idea of self-referential communications as a basis for identifying different systems, one can look at a particular site and ask oneself: to which system do these actors' communications belong? Police officers who arrest suspects communicate, and those communications are legal, whether or not they are in accordance with textbook statements of the powers of arrest. Without the legal system, and other communications about arrest, arrests could not be communications invested with legal meaning. However, police officers are also capable of applying legal communications to themselves. Thus, if they know that arrests are a result of their commitment to 'canteen culture', and are not the result of applying legal communications to the

---

[15]The 'Ways and Means Act' has other variants such as the 'Barbed Wire Act'. These fictional powers represent complex ideas. For example, they can be used to persuade a suspect to co-operate. The police may rely on the uncertainty or complexity of the law, and a reference to a fictitious law, to encourage the idea that the police 'know the law' while the suspect does not, and should therefore consent to the police's demands.

situation, they can make legal communications (arrests) and at the same time acknowledge that these arrests were illegal. This approach allows us to probe and question the gap. Is there a local understanding of legal communications? Or is there a rival system operating in this area, such that communications which trigger operations in the legal system (arrests) are a result of applying non-legal communications - loyalty to the force, canteen culture, etc. If the former applies, one has an intra-system problem. If the latter applies, one has an inter-system problem.

This distinction points to different kinds of failure. In the first instance given above, if one is committed to the textbook accounts, then one might want to ask how one could alter the local understanding of legal communications. An obvious way, recognising the self-referential nature of systems of communication, is to make more communications, thus seeking to render the local understanding incompatible with the system it is drawn from and refers to. In the second instance one asks, how can one prevent a rival system of communication from operating in the site where one wishes legal communications to operate? In both instances, one would acknowledge that the actors participate in different systems of communication, which leads to intra- and inter-system difficulties.

To show the possible use of this analysis in a social situation, take the example of a recent study on the use by police of their stop and search powers. This study revealed that since the highly publicised MacPherson Inquiry into the death of Stephen Lawrence (The Stephen Lawrence Inquiry, February 1999) stop and search powers were no longer being used disproportionately against Afro-Caribbeans by the Metropolitan Police, but were now being used disproportionately against Asian youths (Fitzgerald, December 1999).[16] The study produced various interpretations and reactions. How should the police respond to such statistical evidence? NACRO (the National Association for the Care and Resettlement of Offenders) claimed that many stops and searches were probably illegal. Others argued that they may have been legal (stops were likely to reveal possession of cannabis) but nevertheless discriminatory and unproductive.[17] These interpretations and reactions point to different approaches to reforming police behaviour. If the police are interpreting their powers (from the perspective of other interpreters of criminal law within the system)

[16]See Nick Hopkins, 'Met stop and search 'now hitting Asians'' *The Guardian* 16 Dec. 1999. The figures in this Report for the Metropolitan Police are not supported by other Home Office research. For the country as a whole the frequency of stop and search powers being used against black people relative to their use against others has increased since the Stephen Lawrence Inquiry (see Richard Ford, 'Blacks are still main target of stop and search' *The Times* 10 Dec. 1999).

[17]Navnit Dholakia, the chairman of NACRO, 'Criminal Behaviour' *The Guardian* 16 Dec. 1999.

correctly, then a message to avoid discrimination is a direction not to use a legal power against a particular community. We do not have a corruption of legality, though we do have discrimination in the willingness of the police to use legal powers to achieve functions such as social control. By contrast, the NACRO claim retains a commitment to an objective meaning of legality, and the failure of the police to live up to this standard. The NACRO response leaves open the question of whether police actors are aware of the illegality of their actions, or interpret them as legal but from a perspective not shared by other sections of the legal system. We are left with a more complex appreciation of the problem. Do we need to influence the police's exercise of discretion, or their understanding of their powers, or their willingness to act outside the law to achieve other ends?[18]

What are the advantages of an autopoietic approach to this sort of problem. It avoids the reification of textbook law, without descending into the unhelpful pluralism of treating all kinds of standards and practices as equally law. One does not have to adopt the unitary and neutral model of law characteristic of positivist jurisprudence, whereby law is associated with a single authoritative meaning (prompting incoherent and unsatisfactory attempts to locate the source of that authority). The unity of law is located in a division of labour. It is the differentiation of coding events as legal/illegal that distinguishes law from other systems of communication. All such communications, taken from and referring to, a self-referential system, are law. Unity is achieved through self-reference, not by claiming to avoid the problems of interpretation.

This approach does not deny that other systems of communication involve normativities. There are micro-standards or appropriate action in every aspect of human behaviour. There are occasions when these micro-standards combine with rhetorical commitments to produce situations in which a person's participation in two systems is incompatible (the doctor who conducts a mercy killing, or the police officer who knowingly carries out an illegal arrest). But the fact that other systems of communication produce order, experiences of right and wrong and even a willingness to challenge law as an ethical standard does not turn those other systems into legal systems. Within modern society, law's monopoly of coding legality remains, not because other systems cannot generate rival positions of right and wrong, but simply because they are not systems for coding legality. It makes sense to claim that a health system is not a legal system, even though doctors may find themselves in conflict with the law. And where such

[18]The limited agenda set out in these autopoietic insights is not meant to be inconsistent with or detract from wider concerns recognising the racial character of policing or the institutional racism endemic in it (Holdaway, 1996; The Stephen Lawrence Inquiry, 1999: ch. 6).

conflicts arise, it makes more sense to analyse how a system of health communications can generate such a conflict, than to simply insist that all norms and standards are equally law. The same arguments apply to the arena of criminal justice. It makes more sense to recognise that legal systems codify social life into legal/illegal, and to recognise that the only system doing this in criminal justice is the state legal system, than to treat all aspects of police behaviour and standards as an undifferentiated form of 'police law'. On the other hand there are also benefits, from a sociological perspective, in treating all legal communications as part of the legal system, which includes many police communications. This may be more informative than holding up a relatively specialised and unknown set of texts (or rather their interpretation by a small highly specialised set of legal personnel) as the 'real' law, and treating all other communications and experiences as deviations from the law.

Reforming the criminal justice system

Reforming criminal justice has been a frustrating career for many radicals. Despite episodic moments when change for the better seems inevitable, there is an overall sense of failure.[19] Reform proposals for increasing suspects' rights may not be enacted or, when enacted, are not enjoyed by suspects. The information generated by empirical studies seems to lie ignored, or produce changes that fail to alter the substantive experience of those from suspect communities. The reform strategy of most legal academics is based on the concept of 'enlightenment'. They seek to produce information on the gap between the values espoused by many of the participants in the processes of criminal justice, such as rights, due process and justice, and the experiences of members of suspect communities. They hope that politicians may be persuaded to introduce measures that close this gap. And typically the closure of this gap is seen in terms of the creation and enforcement of rights. Can autopoiesis offer an alternative or addition to this strategy?

There are dangers in lawyers abandoning their commitment to rights, for one would not wish to lose the ideas of equality that underlie this aspect of legality - the belief that subjects should be treated equally despite their differences. There is, despite the rhetorical appeals of deconstruction, little that is attractive to those who experience the sharp end of policing in

[19]We have argued elsewhere that such episodic moments are likely to be constructed by the media as times in which there is a crisis of public confidence in the criminal justice system. However, these media constructions are unlikely to lead to 'appropriate' legal changes (Nobles and Schiff, 2000: ch. 4).

abandoning the idea of formal equalities in favour of an immediate appreciation of each individual's uniqueness. But the challenge for reforming lawyers is how to translate their demands for rights into communications that could expect to operate upon other actors in the criminal justice system. We have already seen some examples of this. Consider the Judges' Rules.[20] While lawyers may have understood these in terms of suspects' rights, the police could have experienced them through their potential for having evidence excluded at trial, which evidence might have been necessary to secure a conviction.[21] For the police, this is essentially a bureaucratic sanction. The resources devoted to an investigation could be wasted through an unnecessary (and discovered) breach of 'legal' rules. Such sanctions do not call directly for an ethical commitment to suspects' rights but only a commitment to effective and efficient investigations. PACE (the Police and Criminal Evidence Act 1984) and its Codes of Practice represent a further development of this process. Instead of seeking to influence the treatment of suspects in custody by the exclusion of evidence, the police were subjected to a detailed system of recording, assigned particular responsibilities, and encouraged to use standardised interview procedures. This was given a sanctioning force not primarily through the criminal law or the exclusion of evidence, but by its use as a code whose breach could produce disciplinary sanctions. This code has been given further force by the creation of the Police Complaints Authority, who use PACE and its Codes of Practice as a normative code to assess the legitimacy of complaints. While one may describe all of this as a panoply of rights for suspects, it is not rights as a simple corollary of duties. Rather, it is a procedure for the self-management of suspects within a locality. While PACE was opposed by many in the police service for imposing an unworkable bureaucracy, it has proved more effective than the Judges' Rules in terms of standardising what police officers understand as the appropriate treatment of suspects. PACE is not foolproof, and for those who believe that imprisonment is inherently oppressive, the pressures created by custody serve to be legitimated rather than reduced by PACE. But before abandoning or applauding PACE, one needs to question the extent to which police officers can ever be expected to orientate their behaviour solely by reference to legal communications. The ability of autonomous police officers to deny suspects their legal rights may be much

[20]For a full statement of these Rules and accompanying Administrative Directives, see Home Office Circular No. 89/1978, [1964] 1 WLR 152.

[21]In practice this hardly ever occurred, thus limiting the consequences of breaches of the Judges' Rules for the police, unless the evidence was thought to have been 'involuntary'. On excluding evidence for breach of the Judges' Rules see *Prager* [1972] 1 WLR 260, and on involuntary evidence see *Smith* [1959] 2 QB 35.

greater than the ability of managed police officers to avoid bureaucratic practices.[22] As such, developing mechanisms for police officers to be managed (record, audit, etc.) may prove to be a more effective way of translating rights into practice than attempts to generate rights in law that are simply applied (through obedience) by the police. To return to the metaphor of language, we need to find indirect ways to generate rights in other systems; to give the sense of rights to persons who do not communicate in such terms amongst themselves, one needs to combine communications about rights within other systems of communication.

Some of these arguments can be restated in non-autopoietic terms. The police have a bureaucratic 'interest' in successful convictions. The Judges' Rules sought to make this interest work for suspects. Individual policemen have an 'interest' in avoiding disciplinary proceedings, and PACE seeks to utilise that interest to secure compliance with standardised treatment of suspects. Cases like *Samuel*[23] in which the Court of Appeal excluded a confession because the suspect had been refused access to a lawyer, seek to apply both pressures. What if anything could be gained by an autopoietic approach? Well, to return to our introduction to autopoiesis, the crucial addition would be meaning. Autopoiesis does not focus on interests, but on meanings, and locates those meanings in self-referential systems of communication. Interest theories assume that police interests can be identified. From this starting point, pressures can be brought to bear that should result in rational actors making predictable responses. Such analysis may even claim that such pressures and procedures can alter police culture (i.e. alter its perception of its own interests). One can end up with a lot of interesting and conflicting claims for the success and failure of policemen to respond to the pressures to which they are subjected. Autopoiesis prompts the researcher to look for the meaning that actors impose on their actions through their participation in systems of communication, and to track changes in meaning through these same processes. It takes hermeneutics extremely seriously, and does not allow the short cuts represented by interest theory approaches (for example, the objective observer cannot read off the meaning of action from the construction of a matrix of sanctions and rewards).

This approach to reform seems to us less crude than much of what passes for radical legal scholarship for reforming the criminal justice system. If one presumes direct translation of rights occurs, and neglects the manner in which actors constitute themselves through systems of communication, one is left with a schema of actors and their interests.

---

[22]This inference is supported by empirical evidence (Dixon et al., 1990; Bottomley et al., 1991).
[23][1988] QB 615.

Police officers with interests that are alien to suspects' rights must be informed of those rights, and their interests altered to induce greater compliance. The usual formulae for altering interests are twofold: sanctions, or changing the persons who can be police officers in order to find more compliant actors. Autopoiesis accepts that the operation of suspects' legal rights at the site of criminal justice can only be partially direct, whatever legislation declares such rights to be. In addition to legal communications, one needs to examine what systems of communication operate within policing, and seek to utilise whatever in those systems of communication can make best sense of the notion of suspects' rights as understood by reforming lawyers. One needs to take the division of labour represented by autopoietic systems theory seriously. Reforming lawyers need to find out how to make other systems of communication work for them. And to do so, inevitably, without a full understanding of how those systems of communication give meaning to actors who participate more fully than do lawyers. The trick is to try expressions in other languages, to see whether they produce the results you desire. If they do, you have potentially achieved a satisfactory coupling.

Conclusion

To provide an insight into order, but not its content, will not commend itself to those who want to alter the structure and content of law to achieve political reforms. But those who dismiss autopoiesis as sterile or irrelevant to the 'real world' may have missed an opportunity to use a theory that can provide an answer to some of their problems of achieving reforms, and alter the agenda of their politics.[24] Autopoietic insights coalesce into the simple conclusion that the ubiquitous use of the phrase the criminal justice system can be highly misleading. Such use encourages the political desire to integrate and co-ordinate the various institutions, actors and practices of criminal justice. But in doing so, and trying to achieve a working interdependence, what is under-represented are the consequences of separate systems of communication. The counter offered by autopoiesis is that it is instructive to analyse criminal justice as a common site of many

---

[24]A striking example of such a dismissal can be found in Walker (1999: 42): 'The theory of autopoiesis also requires the arid and misleading drawing of 'system' boundaries, which confuses and underplays the impact of, for example, academic and journalistic writing, legal political pressure groups and politician-lawyers … and suggests that mere journalists or politicians cannot inspire reforms appropriate to an alien system (the law)'.

systems of communication. Such analysis may encourage a more appropriate approach to empirical research and law reform.[25]

References

Ashworth, A. (1998), *The Criminal Process: an evaluative study*, 2nd edn., Oxford University Press, New York.

Bentham, J. (1970), *Of Laws in General*, The Athlone Press, London.

Bottomley, K., Coleman, C., Dixon, D., Gill, M. and Wall, D. (1991), *The Impact of PACE: Policing in Northern Ireland*, Centre for Criminology and Criminal Justice, University of Hull.

Carlen, P. (1976), *Magistrates Justice*, Martin Robertson, London.

Choongh, S. (1997), *Policing as Social Discipline*, Clarendon Press, Oxford.

Davies, M., Croall, H., and Tyrer, J. (1998), *Criminal Justice: An Introduction to the Criminal Justice System in England and Wales*, Longman, London.

Dixon, D. (1997), *Law in Policing: Legal Regulation and Police Practices*, Clarendon Press Oxford.

Dixon, D., Coleman, C. and Bottomley, K. (1990), 'Consent and Legal Regulation of Policing', 17 *Journal of Law and Society*, pp.345-362.

Feeney, F. (1985), 'Interdependence as a Working Concept', in D. Moxon, (ed.), *Managing Criminal Justice* (HMSO, London 1985).

Fish, S. (1989), *Doing What Comes Naturally: Change, Rhetoric, and the Practice of Theory In Literary and Legal Studies*, Oxford University Press, Oxford.

Fitzgerald, M. (1999), 'Final Report into Stop and Search' undertaken for the Metropolitan Police (http://www.met.police.uk/police/mps/mps/mis/stop).

Hodgson, J. (1999), 'Legal Theory meets Legal Culture'. Paper presented at the Law & Society Conference, Chicago, May 1999.

Holdaway, S. (1996), *The Racialisation of British Policing*, Macmillan, London.

Lacey, N. (1998), 'Contingency, Coherence, and Conceptualism: Reflections on the Encounter between 'Critique' and 'the Philosophy of the Criminal Law'', in A. Duff (ed.), *Philosophy and the Criminal Law*, Cambridge University Press, Cambridge, ch. 1.

Lacey, N. and Wells, C. (1998), *Reconstructing Criminal Law: critical perspectives on crime and the criminal process*, 2nd edn. Butterworths, London.

Luhmann, N. (1982), *The Differentiation of Society*, Columbia University Press, New York.

Luhmann, N. (1986), 'The autopoeisis of social systems', in F. Geyer and J. van der Zouwen (eds), *Sociocybernetic Paradoxes: observation, control and evolution of self-steering systems*, Sage, London, pp. 172-192.

Luhmann, N. (1992a), 'The Coding of the Legal System', in G. Teubner and A. Febbrajo (eds), *State, Law, and Economy as Autopoietic Systems: regulation and autonomy in a new perspective*, Giuffre, Milan, pp. 145-185.

Luhmann, N. (1992b), 'Operational Closure and Structural Coupling: The Differentiation of the Legal System', 13 *Cardozo Law Review*, pp. 1419-1441.

Luhmann, N. (1998), 'Modernity in Contemporary Society', in N. Luhmann, *Observations on Modernity*, Stanford University Press, Stanford, pp. 1-21.

[25]We wish to thank our LSE colleagues Anne Barron and Mike Redmayne, and Jacqueline Hodgson of Warwick University for commenting critically on an earlier draft of this paper.

McBarnet, D. (1981), *Conviction: law, the state and the construction of justice*, Macmillan, London.

Mingers, J. (1995), 'Luhmann's Autopoietic Society Based on Communications', in *Self Producing Systems: Implications and Applications of Autopoiesis*, Plenum Press, New York, pp. 139-45.

Moxon, D. (ed.) (1985), *Managing Criminal Justice*, HMSO, London.

Nelken, D. (1987), 'Criminal Law and Criminal Justice: Some Notes on Their Irrelation', in I.H. Dennis (ed.), *Criminal Law and Justice*, Sweet & Maxwell, London, pp. 139-175.

Nelken, D. (1996), 'Can there be a Sociology of Legal Meaning?', in D. Nelken (ed.), *Law as Communication,* Dartmouth, Aldershot, pp. 107-128.

Nobles, R. and Schiff, D. (2000), *Understanding Miscarriages of Justice: Law, the Media, and the Inevitability of Crisis*, Oxford University Press, Oxford.

Norrie, A. (1998), ''Simulacra of Morality'? Beyond the Ideal /Actual Antinomies of Criminal Justice', in A. Duff (ed.), *Philosophy and the Criminal Law*, Cambridge University Press, Cambridge, ch. 3.

Pullinger, H. (1985), 'The Criminal Justice System Viewed as a System', in D. Moxon, (ed.), *Managing Criminal Justice*, HMSO, London.

Reiner, R. (1994), 'Policing and the Police' in M. Maguire, R. Morgan and R. Reiner (eds), *The Oxford Handboook of Criminology*, Clarendon Press, Oxford, pp. 705-772.

Rock, P. (1993), *The Social World of an English Crown Court*, Clarendon Press, Oxford.

Sanders, A. and Young, R. (2000), *Criminal Justice*, 2nd edn. Butterworths, London.

Smith, J. C. (1999), *Smith and Hogan Criminal Law*, 9th edn. Butterworths, London.

Teubner, G. (1993), *Law as an Autopoietic System*, Blackwell, Oxford.

The Stephen Lawrence Inquiry, Cm 4261-1, February 1999, TSO, London.

Uglow, S. (1995), *Criminal Justice*, Sweet & Maxwell, London.

Waddington, P. (1999), 'Police (Canteen) Sub-culture: An Appreciation' 39(2) *British Journal of Criminology*, pp. 286-309.

Walker, C. (1999), 'Miscarriages of Justice in Principle and Practice', in C. Walker and K. Starmer (eds), *Miscarriages of Justice*, Blackstone Press, London, ch.2.

Wasik, M., Gibbons, T., and Redmayne, M. (1999), *Criminal Justice: Text and Materials*, Longman, London.

Young, M. (1991), *An Inside Job: Policing and Police Culture in Britain*, Clarendon Press, Oxford.

10 Modernising Justice Inside 'UK PLC': Mimesis, De-differentiation and Colonisation

TIM MURPHY

> Today more than ever, it is unrealistic to expect that nature will help physically or that being will help metaphysically. Society can only help itself with its own operations, that is, with communication. Every critique comes up empty-handed if it proceeds all too hastily with the assumption that we could if we only wanted to, and so it reaches for the rod of moral admonition. It might therefore be wise to begin communication with the communication of ignorance instead of linking communication both inside and outside of organizations to the maintenance of an 'illusion of control'… (Luhmann, 1998: 108).

> In May I was told that there were 52,122 people in my Department. How could I know what they all do each day? How could I take decisions, or reach informed judgements, on relative priorities? I had general advice on every policy issue - but no analysis of how each part of the machine operated, why it operated in that way, and how much it cost. I do not know. Nobody knows. (Heseltine, Sunday Times, 1979, quoted in McSweeney, 1994: 254).

Introduction

Perhaps because most of the law is known today, perhaps also because of certain developments in processes of government and society, much legal reflection or scholarship today focuses on questions of legal and social change. In some versions, this is largely a normative affair; in others a normative focus is connected to practical or technical considerations - 'how to… as well as 'what we ought to…'. How to change the law or to reform it become for legal scholars more important projects than the production of another restatement of what the law is.

Some theories of modern law link closely to such scholarly preoccupations. If one is concerned with the problem of the regulation of genetic engineering, for example, Habermas' theory of law and democracy provides quite a useful carapace for one way 'forward' on the central issues which arise. (Whether the invocation of such theories is anything more than window-dressing, I leave to one side here.)

Other theories are less readily raided for such purposes. Of none, at first sight, is this more true than of the theory of autopoiesis. To be sure, certain crypto-normativities seem to lie buried in Luhmann's theory at various stages of its evolution. The preference for differentiation over de-differentiation, for example, in the theoretical work of the seventies on function systems; the equation of differentiation with possibilisation and the valorisation of the latter; even, in the later work, the demand to abandon the categories of being (Luhmann, 1998: 86-87). However much any theory asserts that it seeks no more than to be adequate to the realities of the situation, can it ever persuade others that it does not have a hidden agenda with which they are free to disagree?

For many, of course, the central problem with Luhmann was its lack of normative moorings. Unlike Habermas, the theory did not seem to be guided by any principle regarding Man. It lacked, in that sense, an anthropology. Just as Foucault's emphasis on self-fashioning seemed so open-ended and unregulated that it could not obviously discriminate between a neo-Nazi self and a liberal tolerant respectful-of-others (let us say Canadian) self, so Luhmann's possibilisation as the multiplication of decisions was not located within any framework which regulated what kinds of decisions could and/or should be made. But in each case the lack of an anthropology had a certain normative subtext attached. At its simplest, this was that human beings or human societies were better off without the incubus of an anthropology which limited freedom by pre-empting answers to the questions of who we are and what we could be. Put differently, both Foucault and Luhmann replaced necessity by contingency in a radical sense, and did so in a way more profoundly integrated into their theoretical projects than we find for example in Unger's rather programmatic proclamations of false necessity.

The contrast with Habermas which results is instructive. Habermas rails against the quasi-naturalisation of systemic dynamics which appears in modernity (his version, in essence, of Weber's 'iron cage' of rationalisation) but insinuates a more profound anthropological naturality of the dynamics or mode of functioning of the intersubjective situation. This analysis may wear the badge of 'postmetaphysical thinking' but it continues to rest upon a certain view of the human condition, however empty and procedural, which is precisely from what Luhmann has sought to detach himself.

The separation between social and psychic systems as distinct autopoietic systems. Without this, much of the theory does not make much sense. On the other hand, this separation introduces new problems for conventional protocols of undertaking empirical analysis and description. Secondly, there is the separation between the autopoietic function systems themselves. This presents the problem of connecting or integrating the systems which the theory separates. The gap between systems is in a sense axiomatic in the theory; the problem or critique of the theory centres on how this gap can be bridged, empirically and/or in theoretical terms. Behind many of the general objections to the theory, especially in Anglo-American milieus, lies its neglect - even disparagement - of 'agency'. Agency means of course many things in many contexts: in accounting, for example, it serves as a mechanism for remodelling the concept of an organisation as a nexus of individual contracts (see eg Sunder, 1997). In modern social theory, it first surfaced against the backdrop of and as a critique of a creeping determinism (rather like the rearguard action fought on behalf of so-called Marxist humanism). It must suffice to observe here, first, that agency theory in accounting provides an undercomplex conceptuality for understanding the systemic features of organisations, though it undeniably provides one possible self-referential scheme which can be used to guide the internal operations of organisations. Secondly, that whatever systems theory is, it is not a determinism but a theory of radical, and in Luhmann's case, famously, double contingency (for this, see Luhmann, 1995: 103-136).

Codes and programmes/frames and themes

When we are operating at the more sociological end of Luhmann's theory, there is a difficulty in knowing exactly how to specify (and not just where to 'locate') the boundaries which provide the theory with its architecture. In the more developed version of the theory, we have the distinction between code (or frame as I sometimes prefer) and programme or theme, and for the most part it is this distinction which I shall use in what follows, taking system to refer to systems of communication which are identifiable primarily by means of the code they use, and so on.

In some earlier work, Luhmann was articulating his discovery of Maturana and Varela while still deploying the Parsons-derived problematic of symbolically generalised (differentiated) media of communication. Thus in the essay 'political theory in the welfare state', which was first published in 1981, we find the following claims:

> Communication media provide the premises for decisions and in this way are able to transfer the binding effect of these. In the political system law and money are used for this on the basis of political power, and for the latter's technical diffusion. Both of these media have important advantages within the context of the political system. They can be used abstractly – ie without a very precise pre-determination of the situations in which they are used concretely. Their long-term effects can be worked out, especially with the help of organisations. And they offer the possibility of a centralisable global use, eg in the form of the enactment of laws for as yet unforeseeable isolated cases or in the form of monetary appropriations. With the help of legislating and financing, a central agency can attain political results – without considering the factual consequences of such measures. *That* such decisions with their binding effect have results can be seen from the extensive evidence of these media. And in political communication the intention that underlay the decision can take the place of the effects. *Which* results occur may remain unknown or become the subject of later political discussions (Luhmann, 1990: 82-83).

As Luhmann goes on to point out (1990: 84-85), both tendencies of the welfare state may lead to overload; the excessive use of money promoting ruinous inflationary tendencies; the excessive use of law overstepping the boundaries of what can be handled adequately by legal means. As he concedes, these are essentially empirical questions for the sociology of law. Of more theoretical interest is the point he then adds about the relationship between media like law and money and a system in the sense of a political or legal system:

> In both domains, in money and law, one may not overlook the fact that the conditions of the possibility of these means ultimately have to be guaranteed outside the political system: in the economic system and in the legal system, and that this imposes constraints on political use (1990: 85).

In *Risk* and *Ecological Communication* (Luhmann, 1993; 1989), the broad emphasis is on how a theme is handled and manipulated and processed by different social systems in the absence of any central mechanism for theme selection, theme definition or system management. What is interesting about these earlier observations is the more complex model which it generates for the political system (or the Welfare State). I sidestep here whether we live in a post-welfare state or a crisis-ridden welfare state; as Luhmann wrote:

> ... a complaint syndrome (critique, crisis, ungovernability, failure) signifies little more than the lack of a theory of society. One complains before understanding....One has to begin from the inadequacy of system-internal modes of perception and communication. And then from this one can inquire whether and how system-internal information processing can be improved (1990: 58).

The second point to make is the size scale scope and complexity of the modern welfare state. We can return to some of the reasons for this below: I wish here merely to flag up a rather general theoretical point. The modern welfare state is constructed as a kind of mirror of society. Every aspect of social life has a section or segment of the state which is 'responsible' for its functioning and malfunctioning in some way or other, which can be looked to for an informed view about that aspect of society's functioning or malfunctioning and which can be expected to develop and promote reforms if reforms are needed, very often, as suggested above, in the shape of spending more money or now allocating more resources or enacting more laws. However, these two solutions to society's problems, neither of which is new, and both of which were in full flow in the late Victorian age, have now been joined by more modern solutions. Malfunctioning in society can now also be addressed by improved delivery of government services, 'improved' now meaning, as we shall shortly see at greater length, more efficiency and more effectiveness, or better value for (the same) money. In other words, this kind of no-hiding-place diffuse responsibility-for-everything aspect of the modern welfare state involves increasingly the development of a set of responses to 'failures' - whether policy, implementation, regulatory or whatever - which look inside the admittedly massive machinery of government itself and redesign relabel reorganise etc the activities of government rather than (as well as sometimes in addition to) spending more money or enacting more laws. Society is supposed to be grateful for all this serious attention to detail, though one suspects that it often looks like a game of musical chairs in the conversation of mankind. In any event, potential overload problems now begin to shift, inside the machinery of government, into possibly excessive exercises in institutional reengineering.

Let me conclude these remarks by highlighting what they do not mean. The suggestion that government is meant to mirror society does not mean government poking its nose in where it should stay out. It does not mean planning in the sense that Hayek (1976) deplored in *The Road to Serfdom*. It certainly does not mean the central control of society by an all-knowing all-seeing disciplinary surveillance state. It means if not the opposite then at least something paradoxical. In order to do anything at all (or at all well, at least) government has to devote more and more time and resources and energy to itself, whether the issue is institutional design as mentioned above, or the implementation of policy, or the use of resources. This paradox means if you like that the welfare of the state often has to stand in for the welfare of society. Elimination of waste (never mind corruption), proper management of resources, coordination of cross-cutting departmental activities, coordination of central and local activities, development of performance indicators, development and application of mechanisms to measure performance – all these loom increasingly large on the agenda of modern governments. And this is not to mention 'compliance' with extra-national standards, inter-governmental cooperation and coordination, etc.

The other general point is complexity alongside scale. It seems to me that Luhmann's general approach is useful here in the simplest sense of looking for a code (or a difference). Leaving to one side the universal tendency for modern governmental apparatuses to fragment (and thereby create internal communication and coordination problems for themselves) in functional terms, the better to mirror society as I have just said, and on the misguided theoretical premise of the separation of state from society, we have a proliferation of codes internal to government, some of which mimic (see Lawson, 1993) or emulate codes which operate in the environment of the political system (eg law and money) and some of which are largely unique to or at least generally thought to be distinctive of government. These are codes like regular/irregular or authorised/not authorised which supposedly make public audit more than and distinct from modern private audit schemes (true and fair/not true and fair),[1] in the public

[1]See discussion in Standing Committee A on the Government Resources and Accounting Bill 1999, 18.01.00, pm part 3 (David Davis and Oliver Letwin).

interest/not… (the regulators' guiding distinction), independent/not independent (or policy/operations), executive agencies, 'governmental' ndpb's (eg the former Legal Aid Board), public/private (eg the privatisations of essentially 'commercial' governmental activities, which do not however cease to resonate within government just because they have been sold off).

Efficiency and effectiveness

Autopoiesis is not automatism. Autopoiesis is a theory about social communication. What impulses trigger such communication, and what attributions as to origin and authority of such communications occur, is contingent. Leadership serves as one such attribution, attaching itself, in retrospect, to some communications which travel along networks of communication. Such attribution is a selection mechanism which makes its own distinctions. Certain messages are flagged as messages from the leadership. What individual members of organisations are said to think (their intentions, wishes, projects, desires and so on) is thematised in social communication within the organisation (as well as outwith it). Nothing guarantees or can guarantee any congruence between these attributions and what the individual 'really' thinks.

Viewed in this way, leadership is only one of among a range of possibilities of attributions which can be attached to messages and communications which circulate within an organisation. Supplementary mechanisms like hierarchy may contribute to sorting these attributions as well as making them, but we should not suppose that there is any simple way in which a command from the top becomes an implementation on the ground. Leaders depend on subordinates, and subordinates can respond to commands – or policy initiatives – in a plurality of ways, which include enthusiasm, indifference and apathy, hostility and so on. These modes of response largely escape the control of the leader, whatever the formal position, and therefore must be regarded as contingent and open-ended in relation to any particular proposal or initiative. From an autopoietic perspective, it is necessary to try to maintain the distinction between psychic and social systems. Motives, inner forces, personality – these commonsensical categories and figures which enable the orchestration of the organising figures of the rhetoric deployed in journalism and the mass media more generally – must be bracketed and problematised via (primarily) the device of attribution. Social communication, that is, has to be thought anonymously before eponymous themes can safely be introduced into the observation. Much of this is registered in the burgeoning discussion papers and policy and planning documents concerned with personnel matters within the Civil Service – diversity and equal opportunities, flexible working, personal development plans, Investors in People kitemarks. These are system-level communications about motivation, incentives and so on.[2] For example, the Court Service proclaims that it is 'wholly committed' to 'supporting, recognising and developing its people. We aim to deliver services and results through well-motivated and committed people. We have continued to work towards achieving recognition as an *Investor in People*. The 1998 Staff Opinion Survey, together with local focus groups and use of the *Business Excellence Model*, contributed to this work'.[3] More generally, the current Minister in charge of Modernisation offers the following in response to the question 'What can we do to train, to re-educate the Civil Service?':

> first of all what we have to do is not only train and educate civil servants but we also want to train and educate ministers … it is a two-way process … Sir Richard Wilson [Cabinet Secretary]… has had meetings with junior ministers and had sessions … we are going to try and have monthly meetings, which is optional for ministers to attend, so that they get a chance to communicate with each other, which is one of the things we never get a chance to do. You talk to people very rarely. So I think there are practical things that the Civil Service is looking at both in terms of training but also in terms of socialisation of both groups. … the White Paper talks about … women, talks about ethnic minorities, talks about secondment, talks about the private sector in and out and the Civil Service in and out of the private sector, a two-way street—I think that is there and it is beginning. Having been in the job a month I have already had a meeting with members of the ethnic communities on how they think more work should be done. I have talked to the ethnic press as to how they think they could help encourage people in. Work is being done with the ethnic minorities that are in the service now as role models and mentors to others. There is a whole host of practical, sensible, commonsense ways of

---

[2]Eg Government Expenditure Plans 1999-2002 Cabinet Office et al, (CM 4221) March 1999 sections 2.121-2.128; also 'Report to the Prime Minister from Sir Richard Wilson, Head of the Home Civil Service: Civil Service Reform', (1999) www.cabinet-office.gov.uk/civilservice-reform.

[3]Annual Report 1998-1999 ch 4 ('Supporting Our People'). For BEM, see Cabinet Office *Next Steps Report 1998* (CM 4273 March 1999) ch 3, esp 10-15.

> trying to get greater diversity and there is, I have to tell you, a great willingness in the Civil Service to move on this and I think it will come in the next couple of years and we will begin to see the results.[4]

At the next stage of analysis, we must move to the level of the differentiation of function systems and of coding and programming, or as I have termed it, framing and thematisation. I prefer the latter terminology because it permits a more flexible operationalisation of the theory without losing its basic insights. In particular, it makes it easier to conceptualise the flow from theme to frame which seems necessary to grasp in terms of the evolution of differentiation and possibilisation. Certain themes can acquire a weight and density that they become, to a greater or lesser extent, a new or differentiated frame (whether or not they do is contingent). Feminism is my favourite example, if only because it has the thematic potential to generate a simple and rather pure coding - male/female. Ethnicity is more complex, of course, but the potential for a time at least is there of unfolding a code in the form of white/non-white.

The function systems theory is in a way a modulation of the older model of separation of powers. Separation of powers theory, however, supposes that differentiation is a matter of dividing up the 'same thing', whereas the function systems theory presupposes and articulates precisely differentiation of this 'same thing' into differently coded operations of social communication. The sociological problem this theory creates for itself is how to conceive the linkages or connections or communications between axiomatically differentiated sub-systems of the social system - and for that matter what is meant by the 'social system' other than the totality of all social communications, as well as perhaps noise.

The core intuition which precedes theoretical formalisation is that while themes may circulate randomly in society - whatever the importance of the role of mass media in this process - differentiated coding means that the frames in which such themes are contained, and the codes through which they are processed, are uncoupled. In this sense, it might be better to rethink structural coupling as 'theme convergence' or 'theme sharing', while recognising that it is impossible to tell if a theme is 'really' shared. Themes suggest the unity of society in the sense that the same theme can be utilised by different sub-systems who thereby can be supposed to be communicating about the same thing. The insight of autopoietic theory is

---

[4]Select Committee on Public Administration, Examination of Witnesses, Tuesday 23 November 1999, question 33

that there is no vantage point from which to guarantee that they are, and that an a priori suspicion is that probably they are not.

The themes with which I am concerned here are efficiency, effectiveness and value for money. As these illustrate, themes are what was once called 'ideology'. They resonate throughout society, even if they seem to 'belong' to (never mind originate in) particular sub-systems rather than others. They align with and yet perhaps problematise in some respects the differentiations proposed by the function systems theory.

Modernising government and VFM

Britain underwent a long and uneven transition from monarchical government to a differentiated structure of politics and administration, or policy and implementation (note: these are non-overlapping distinctions). Through out much of this transition, the theme of 'economy' served as both yardstick and measure of 'efficiency'. The idea of balanced budgets as an ideal to be attained or a constraint within which all such government needed to work was in one sense an echo of the much older idea that the King should 'live off his own', and that Parliamentary taxation was to be voted for 'exceptional' measures like war, in respect of which the resource requirement over-spilled what could reasonably be expected to be provided from the King's 'own'.

By the 20th century, of course, this picture had been irredeemably complicated by the coming of normal and after WW2 mass national taxation and in parallel with it modern conventions of national accounting, as well as the coming of the universal franchise. The burden of taxation shifted from local to national taxes providing resources to be deployed in the achievement of national rather than merely local objectives (Britain may have escaped the worst aspects of pork-barrel politics but did not escape them entirely). In the short term politicians promised popular policies which would get them elected, and then worried about how to find the resources if they were successful in electoral contests only later. But the structure of such a politics has led in due course to a situation in which electors asked to support policies are explicitly represented as a source of the resources to fund these policies, so that an 'economic' calculus is injected into political decision-making and political power-seeking in an explicit way. The more an additional cost to the taxpayer could be attributed to support for a particular policy, the more that policy came to be judged critically in terms of its costs and benefits. One option in these circumstances was to pursue the route of privatisation. This explicitly affirmed the differentiation of government and economy, and held out the promise of the elimination of tax subsidies and public sector trade union power, along with improved service delivery resulting from private management taking charge of public utilities which were at the same time businesses and which needed to be run as such.

Unfortunately, it was easier to see what was wrong than to devise viable commercial schemes which combined business incentives with public service delivery in an acceptable way to managers and shareholders on the one hand and the consumer on the other. There was also the regulation issue, a political sop which has acquired an autopoietic dynamic if ever there was one (here the coding I suppose is 'in/not in the public interest'; any content can fill these slots, and that is also why regulation so conceived has the capacity to become, as it is now, generic, rather than industry- or context-specific).

The nationalised industries and their privatisation was one thing; what about the rest of government? On the one hand politicians still had to preserve the capacity to propose and to propose delivery of policies put before the electorate who chose them. On the other, the old theme of 'economy' - which meant spending as little or as cheaply as possible, and which could hook up to the theme of 'efficiency' such that sometimes they meant the same thing - was now joined by more demanding themes like effectiveness and VFM.

The unifying theme which runs underneath or unites these themes is the avoidance of waste and, as a corollary, accountability - for expenditure and/or performance. Both waste and accountability are, however, extremely open-ended terms from a semantic point of view, and have succeeded in occupying a significant place in the public discourses of the last three centuries without, at the same time, achieving or retaining stable and coherent meanings. (If anything, it is not that their meanings suddenly shifted in this epoch or that but rather that they have acquired a range of new meanings as the world has changed until now each term is utterly overdetermined by meaning.) One consequence is that a term like accountability has different meanings today for lawyers, politicians, administrators, businessmen, journalists, the public and so on. But especially via the mass media these divergent semantic contents feed back into and on each other parasitically. Themes cannot be contained by the principle of differentiation.

Within government, the question has been how to improve effectiveness? How to achieve VFM? First promulgated by ministerial enthusiasts like Michael Heseltine in the early 80s with much brio and few immediate results,[5] we now, 20 years on, are at the point of departments being shifted to resource accounting, which will measure outputs rather than just inputs, and require departments to account for the assets they own or occupy and to do so in a way which shifts waste away from money down the drain to efficient asset management. The principal vehicle unsurprisingly of this has been the Treasury; the National Audit Office (NAO), the Audit Commission, the Public Accounts Committee (PAC) and the Treasury Select Committee, have all been consulted and/or involved in the development of this new system. Since the plan has been to extend these new accounting procedures to all departments, the legal system is not unaffected: both its criminal and civil justice components are implicated in the new accounting procedures and many of the reforms currently achieved or in hand must be understood in this light.

I am not suggesting that all these changes are driven by the desire to implement these new accounting procedures. Rather, the position is that this desire is symptomatic of a continued attempt to find a way of achieving effectiveness and VFM in government and the delivery of public sector services. It is the technology which is currently hoped to deliver what has been sought for so long and with such admitted limited success – accountability through more systematic and professional accounting (see White and Hollingsworth (1999); Daintith and Page (1999: 169-206).

The legal system

This paper opens up the question of the impact of what is often called New Public Management on the direction of the present government's policies for the legal system (see generally Hood, 2000). From the perspective of many lawyers, these policies are seen as undermining many fundamentals of the infrastructure of the legal system. These policies are accused of making much lawyering uneconomic, undermining the professional independence of lawyers, especially barristers, threatening hard-fought-for civil liberties. The very pace and volume of change - and specifically, the volume, velocity and complexity of communication - is itself no doubt alarming to many professionals. The new Rules of Civil Procedure are in a

[5]See eg *Efficiency and Effectiveness in the Civil Service* Cmnd 8616 September 1982.

state of seemingly permanent revision and modification; those who operate in the area of legal services provision for the poor, civil or criminal, are also faced with a steady flow of communications reconfiguring activity in these areas - with more, perhaps much more, to come. My general concern was to think about and observe the other side of this distinction – the point of view of purchasers rather than providers of legal and court services, i.e the government in its welfare role as redistributing tax revenues allocated to it to help the poor or in its consumer protection role as protecting the public in relation to standards of service provision. But development of this perspective really required coming to terms with the simple idea that the Lord Chancellor's Department (LCD) had been forced to become a government department like any other – or like any other department with a significant spending budget relative to the activities for which it was responsible. In the LCD case, this meant, essentially, its role vis-à-vis the provision of legal services to the poor or to the community, the court system and the judiciary.

Initially, I intended to concentrate on the impact of the introduction of resource budgeting and accounting (replacing the traditional cash-based system) on the way a department like the LCD is now having to operate. But I concluded that it was premature to do so, although in the near future this will be worth looking at more closely. In the event I chose to focus on another aspect of the NPM which is further advanced, the so-called Public Service Agreements (PSA's) which departments and in some cases areas of activity have been required to produce. (Interestingly for present purposes, one of the first supra-departmental areas which has been flagged up and produced its own PSA is the criminal justice system, which means, in Whitehall terms, the LCD (the court service, the judges, the magistrates' courts, and, now or shortly, the Legal Services Commission and/or the Criminal Defence Service), the Home Office (police, prisons, the probation service, sentencing policy) and the CPS.

My general conclusion is that we are in the middle of a process which is likely to involve a quite significant reconfiguration of the legal infrastructure and thereby, indirectly, of 'the law' itself (or at least of how the law works). I may be wrong; there is nothing inevitable about any of this: just pressures and counter-pressures, projects, problematisations and preoccupations in relation to which teleological thinking of any kind seems misplaced. Concretely: conventional civil adjudication and old-style case-by-case appeals are being significantly curtailed. Appeals are for the first time becoming legislative in character through being lined up where filtered as important and then heard in groups. The old right of appeal and the resulting haphazard and casuistic consideration of points of law as and when they arose and most of the time more or less on the basis of whichever judges happened to be available is disappearing and may soon be largely gone. On the other hand we will have (who really knows how much?) human rights litigation and appeals as well as the kinds of irritants or disasters waiting to happen which can energise unpredictably any single system or several systems in parallel at any time, unplanned, and sometimes uncontainable (eg Stephen Lawrence).

PSAs and the rest, assets registers, accounts and in the end perhaps resource accounts are screen projections which are created and used and communicated with and about within the empty centre of government. These are the 'macro'-objectifications inside government with and through which society is constructed. One interest which this work throws up is what influence such objectifications and/or schemes of self-reference will have inside the legal system, which has hitherto for the most part managed without them. (It will soon be close to a fiction for many barristers, for example, particularly on the commercial and chancery side, that they are not part of a firm with a corporate identity and all the rest – performance indicators and so on - just as happened years ago with partnerships in the large law firms; similarly, judges are already becoming managers not just of their own case loads, but of other subordinate judges as well.)

In earlier work, I explored the thematic tension and conflict between the individual and the aggregate, and we see this at work here. As I read it, this is like the coming-of -age pains of the legal system, the trauma of a system-in-itself coming to communicate with and about itself as a system-for-itself.

What about justice? is the cry which goes up when the impact of these kinds of changes on the legal system is observed. Suits displacing wigs as the determinants of outcomes? Money and power buying the law? And does not this make nonsense of any claim to the utility of differentiated function systems and autopoiesis? Is not a pernicious dedifferentiation rather what we observe?

This does not mean that differentiation and the theory of the function systems fails because everything collapses into the black hole of money. Given a situation of function systems with differential coding structures, decisions have to be made not only within systems as to matters which properly pertain to them (though we would need to regard this question of domain as open-ended and contestable and contingent) but also with regard to which alien systems to use in the pursuit of internal purposes and objectives. Equally, there are many decisions to be made in situations of no-choice: politicians and governments hauled before the courts, administrators before politicians in public and private settings, businessmen before courts and parliamentary committees, judges before the press, and so on.

Secondly, these objections rather register what I have described elsewhere as the tension and/or gulf between the individual and the aggregate (Murphy, 1997: 154-210).[6] The pressure towards developing uniform formats for departmental accounts is closely linked (or at least this is the hope) to the formulation of PSAs, of performance targets which are couched in quantitative terms, and of aggregate measures which in principle at least will enable evaluation of whether these targets have been met, as in Output and Performance Analyses (OPAs). (I discuss these further below.) These kinds of formulations seek to reconceptualise the activities of the LCD and its agencies in terms of effectiveness - improved turnaround and service delivery times - and efficiency - speed, reduced cost, explicitly and ruthlessly managed process - which combined with cost control (eg criminal barristers' legal aid fees) should produce enhanced VFM. Accountability for the management of justice conceived in these terms (the LCD's aim is justice)[7] clearly involves a shift in thinking if not

---

[6]Cf: '... there has been a move towards more evidence based policy in probation, evidence based service; the development of a pretty tight and prescriptive framework from within the Home Office to reshape the way in which probation delivers its service justified by this being evidence based and research based. There is a great benefit in learning from research and evaluation. In so far as it removes the kind of free will of probation officers to deliver good probation service and turns them into functionaries and part of a machine driven from elsewhere, it will not deliver the required social outcomes. In a service like that the independent mind of the probation officer on the ground and his or her manager running that service is crucially important. Their capacity to analyse risk and assess the risk to the public of individual offenders and to channel offenders towards particular forms of community punishment and community service which follow on from that assessment are absolutely crucial. Nobody can do that, however bright or young, from the Treasury. If we do turn the whole thing into a machine bureaucracy, which is a reasonable fear to have, then it will not lead to the social outcomes. It would be counterproductive and we will see that ultimately'. Professor Sue Richards, Select Committee on Treasury, Minutes of Evidence, 14 April 1999, response to q26.

[7]As stated in both versions of the Department's PSA, which is described in more detail below.

in practice from the traditional idea that a case should take as long as it takes in order for justice to be done.

An alternative view would take as its starting point the fact that what is primarily at issue is the expenditure of public money. This has become a somewhat ambivalent or liminal domain between politics and economy. But it also inevitably affects every area of governmental or governmentally-sponsored (as in purchasing of services from the private sector) activity. Beneath the ebb and flow of political/electoral fortunes lies a longer term problem of the management of this public expenditure. It is and it is not like running a business - hence the ambivalence - and it is liminal because of the significance of public expenditure on the economy as a whole (government purchasing decisions cannot simply be treated as governmental ones, as if they have no wider consequences other than some nebulous public benefit. Public goods are one (debatable) thing; public procurement often quite another. Either government buys its paper clips and uniforms from the private sector or it makes them itself. Either way, political or governmental decisions have direct economic dimensions. This is to say that government is a major player in the economic system; hence the significance of projects to improve public procurement).[8]

What this of course means is that the processes of government participate in or occur in the economy as well as in politics and law. But it does not just mean this: it means also that political and legal decisions have economic dimensions not least with regard to the possibility of making them in the first place.

For government, the question is how to conceptualise itself and its activities, and how to measure them. The current vogue after a long gestation period is for the variables of inputs, outputs and outcomes.

So far as inputs are concerned, recent decades have seen the introduction of cash limits and capping as a response to inflation. The most recent development is the Comprehensive Spending Review (CSR) mechanism introduced in 1997 resulting in the allocation of three year spending budgets in the third year of which a further review was planned. (This was published in July 2000 as SR2000).[9] Under this system most major departments, including the LCD, are allocated a Departmental Expenditure Limit (DEL). Departments can keep and roll over any savings achieved at

---

[8]See *Gershon Review of Civil Procurement in Central Government* (HM Treasury April 1999).

[9]HM Treasury, *Spending Review 2000: New Public Spending Plans 2001-2004, Prudent for a Purpose: Building Opportunity and Security for All* (Cm 4807, July 2000).

least during the DEL period. The main exception is Social Security which is on Annual Managed Expenditure (AME), because its (very substantial) annual expenditure is unusually determined by exogenous factors.[10] Immediately it is significant that the LCD budget, much of which has been consumed by civil and criminal legal aid, has not been treated in the same way – though presumably it could have been. Indeed, this registers quite firmly that the LCD is just one department among others, and not a law unto itself (Stevens 1993 discusses the traditional set-up).[11]

So the focus is supposedly shifting to Outputs and Outcomes. The CSR required all departments to formulate aims and objectives and following this departments have identified a range of performance targets, usually, unsurprisingly, of a quantitative kind, and are developing PSAs which state department-by-department what is to be achieved. All of these indicators are undergoing review and refinement at the time of writing as part of the process of preparing and negotiating the next CSR round.

The PSAs are meant to be part of the Modernising Government process along with many other developments discussed here. They are supposed to be SMART (specific, measurable, achievable, relevant and timed).[12] But on the most 'optimistic' view, they are in the end about managing or reducing the internal complexity of government by flagging certain key indicators against which departments can be assessed, not primarily by Parliament – though it is difficult to see in the medium term how these quantified indicators of performance will be kept from the NAO, the PAC and the Departmental Select Committees – but for Ministers in Departments vis-à-vis the performance of their civil servants, for senior civil servants vis-à-vis their subordinates (with much talk about line management levels having 'ownership' of their targets), for departments in their dealings with executive agencies, and, moving outside departments, to provide some focus for cross-departmental initiatives, and to provide focus for periodic spending reviews conducted by the Treasury, ongoing performance reviews by the key Cabinet committee,[13] and (though to what extent is unclear)

[10]Treasury Pre-Budget Report November 1999, 2.26-2.28.

[11]The change to being an 'ordinary' department was signalled by the appointment in 1997 of the present Permanent Secretary Sir Hayden Phillips. He was not a lawyer but a career civil servant who had worked in the Home Office and significantly the Treasury (see Lawson 1993: 619 on his role in the development of the NHS internal market) and came to the LCD from DCMS, where he had been Permanent Secretary. The appointment required legislation (Supreme Court (Offices) Act 1997).

[12]One wonders which came first - the attributes or the acronym?

[13]Cf Treasury Pre-Budget Report November 1999 2.30-2.31.

overall evaluation of areas of strength and weakness, success and failure by the Cabinet Office and the Prime Minister's 'Office'.

According to the Prime Minister:

> publishing these new agreements is an important step to improving democracy and accountability. PSAs are agreements with you. They show what we as a Government will deliver in return for the investment you have made in public services. Publishing them today is therefore only a start. Our key task will be to make sure that the reforms and programme of modernisation we have set out here are actually put into place. By publishing clear, measurable targets, we are making it possible for everyone to judge whether we meet them. To ensure that you are in the best position to do so, we will report annually on the progress we have made in delivering the public services for the future that we are promising here.[14]

'CM 4181 talks about accountability as between the Government and the citizen…But in real life the accountability will be between the Treasury and the Department' observed Sir Peter Kemp, recalling from his experience with Next Steps that:

> it is incredibly difficult to find meaningful translation from the objectives of government into how you measure it. Public sector is one of the most difficult things in the world. There is no bottom line. You cannot just measure the money. Objectives are confused, they are contradictory, they are very, very difficult to set up.[15]

In the same Select Committee, Colin Talbot observed that ' …it would be very interesting to carry out some serious research on whether or not performance information which has been generated so far after the last seven or eight years, which is quite considerable, has actually been used by anybody'.[16]

---

[14]Tony Blair, Foreword to CM 4181. In all of this there are strong echoes of earlier developments (rhetoric?) in the USA: see, eg, 'Memorandum for Heads of Executive Departments and Agencies: Improving Customer Services' (White House Office of the Press Secretary, 23 March 1995).

[15]Annex to Memorandum to Treasury Select Committee. More generally, the whole area is given perspective in Light 1997.

[16]Professor Colin Talbot, Treasury Committee Minutes of Evidence (14 April 1999) responses to q5. The Government has already recognised that the first round of PSAs involved a certain institutional overstretch: see Andrew Smith 'The Future for Public Service Agreements' (HM Treasury News Release 48/00, 4 April 2000).

Whether or not the new PSA/OPA system 'works' or collapses beneath indifference and bureaucratic overload ('data rich, information poor' as Talbot put it in response to q 34), it seems undeniable that all ministers are in some sense constrained to become, in part, managers or at least to be able to read 'with conviction' an increasingly explicit managerial brief. The development of and switch to Resource Account Budgeting presses in the same direction : a National Assets Register has already been drawn up in preparation for this stage, and departmental plans are going to have to address explicitly not just questions relating to cash and its spending but resources and their utilisation more widely (in the case of the LCD, the resources tied up in court buildings and residences are likely to be the main focus).[17]

The 'modern' theory of accountability in relation to any department is that it is for Parliament and its select committees to hold the department to account. It is in other words a political matter. Increasingly this sits alongside more traditional 'apolitical' accounting - the work of the NAO and the Audit Commission, and the PAC. The PAC makes much of its apolitical character and yet at the same time does not rest its legitimacy on expertise.[18] In Standing Committee A, the Treasury ministers, presumably (or so their opponents on the committee claimed) acting on the clear advice of their civil servants, repeatedly resisted any formal role for the NAO in auditing the outturns of the PSAs on the grounds that this would encroach upon 'policy'.

What results is a system which is effective for matters of probity (White and Hollingsworth, 1999: 130) but which, some argue, is deficient in other ways. First, the NAO contributes to data overload and produces far more material than the PAC can examine; bottlenecks occur in the system of government audit as a result. There is also no reason to suppose that Departments and agencies are avid consumers of their findings. It is also claimed that the present system involves structural delay: 'often PAC reports are published so long after the event in question that those responsible are no longer in the department and cannot be held to account, or brought to answer for their actions.' (White and Hollingsworth 1999: 132). One solution would be for departmentally related select committees rather than the PAC to examine NAO reports, but of course these

[17]National Assets Register November 1997. The LCD's assets are at ch 8.

[18]White and Hollingsworth (1999: 133) describe the NAO as acting as an 'interpreter' for the PAC - 'The NAO is the accounting expert, and members of the PAC are not expected to be qualified accountants'.

committees are 'political' and such a move would confuse audit and policy.[19]

The LCD PSA[20] lists six Objectives (now called Strategic Objectives and now revised with a view to the recently completed second CSR exercise - in the jargon, SR2000).[21] The new ones are:

- *To provide a fair, swift and effective system of justice* which promotes confidence in the rule of law; helps reduce crime, the fear of crime, and the economic consequences of crime; and gives value for money.
- *To improve people's knowledge and understanding of their rights and responsibilities* including how to resolve disputes which affect them, in a way and at a cost proportionate to the issues at stake.
- *To improve the availability of affordable and good quality legal services* so that the law underpins economic success, at home and abroad, and that the use of public funds secures greater social justice and reduces social exclusion.
- *To make civil and family law clearer and more easily enforceable* giving priority to key Government objectives in tackling social and economic issues.
- *To improve the lives of children and help build and sustain strong families* through providing a legal and procedural framework to sustain family relationships and when they do break down to resolve disputes, with the least distress to those affected, especially the most vulnerable.
- *To uphold the independence of the judiciary* especially through the appointment of sufficient judges, magistrates and other judicial post holders of the right calibre to match needs, and through promoting a partnership with the judiciary for delivering justice effectively.[22]

The department is committed to operating 'efficiently and effectively within the available resources' in pursuit of these objectives.

The original PSA set out performance targets, in quantifiable terms wherever possible (eg to halve the time from arrest to sentence for persistent young offenders from 142 days to 71 days; to increase the

---

[19](For the arguments see White and Hollingsworth 1999:134-137). See also Eighth Report of Treasury Select Committee 1997-8.

[20]The full PSA covers all the departments for which the Lord Chancellor is responsible. I limit discussion here to the Lord Chancellor's Department (LCD) itself and one of its executive agencies, the Court Service. I do not discuss the Public Trust Office, or the other areas of LC responsibility: the Northern Ireland Court Service, the Public Record Office and HM Land Registry.

[21]See Departmental Report 2000-2001 to 2001-2002 (April 2000).

[22]Departmental Report Ch 2 para 3.

proportion of mediated as against court-based divorce proceedings from 5% to 20% by 2001-02 for those areas where the Family Law Act is implemented). Further measures and targets are being developed, including measures of cost effectiveness for legal aid. 'Intermediate milestones' (leaving Woolf to one side) include contracting for civil and family legal aid solely with quality-assured providers, and identification, by July 2000, of indicators which will enable the Legal Services Commission to assess and report to the Lord Chancellor on the impact of co-ordinated planning by Community Legal Services Partnerships on delivery of legal services to meet local priority needs.

Both PSAs promise the usual efficiency gains and increased productivity. The Woolf reforms of the civil justice system have produced a particular problem here. The PSA commitment is 'to reduce the unit cost of civil cases in real terms', but these costs and volumes will have to be 're-based' from 1999-2000. This is mainly because the new procedures, in introducing several tracks, and actively promoting settlement before a full hearing of the case, potentially raise the unit cost (which at the same time needs to be clearly identified and monitored so that progress can be assessed) though not the overall cost of cases in the civil justice system. Other efficiency/productivity gains sought include: (1) stability in real terms in the cost of legally-aided criminal defence services by March 2002; (2) reduction in real terms in the unit cost of cases in the Crown Court by an average of 3% per annum ('the baseline for this unit cost will be rebalanced in 2000-01 to take account of the Human Rights Act and the Crime and Disorder Act'); (3) reduction in courtroom over-capacity. There are also targets relating to electronic service delivery, reduction in absence through sickness (a prominent theme in all or most PSAs), reduction of fraud in the legal aid system, and reductions in general procurement expenditure.

The new PSA explicitly embraces the Modernising Government agenda:

> In order to meet effectively the challenge of these objectives the Department itself will have to be transformed. This is not only a matter of proper implementation of the Modernising Government agenda, which it has in common with all other Departments, but in being much more proactive than it has traditionally been, and across a wider canvas. This stretches beyond the Department's two core historic businesses of running the courts and dealing with the judiciary and judicial appointments, to cover several new areas, especially in the markets for legal services (Ch. 2; para 32).

In addition, the LCD is developing through the new Legal Services Commission a range of benchmarking and kitemarking techniques which build upon the existing franchising mechanisms of the soon-to-be-wound-up Legal Aid Board. The idea is that this combined with a shift towards contracting – which has not yet but presumably soon will seek to shift away from hourly rates – will weed out the incompetent and provide a means of demonstrating VFM.

The LCD also features prominently in a number of contexts from the CSR onwards as a participant in a concrete example of joined-up government – criminal justice, though it is not the lead department here (this role falls to the Home Office). Cross-departmental solutions are sought to problems like crime when the relevant agencies are spread across departments and executive agencies and ndpb's. All these initiatives are of course problematic in a different way: whatever linkages can be built at the centre and however much co-ordination can be exhorted from the centre, how do such bureaucratic aspirations transmit into achievement on the ground or at the coalface? This is only one aspect of the more general problem of delivery within a large bureaucratic system.

At present, the CJS has a separate PSA in CM 4181 but was not included as a separate chapter in the OPA White Paper. Although there is now extensive documentation on the costs of the Criminal Justice system – mainly produced from within the Home Office but drawing on data from other departmental and agency sources – the CJS is not a department and originally had no DEL of its own.[23] So far as Criminal Justice in particular is concerned, the *Strategy and Business Plan* notes that:

> A number of joint working initiatives, such as the Trials Issues Group arrangements, are already setting national frameworks for improvement and delivering results through local service level agreements – but *until now, no real attempt has been made to manage the system as a whole.* (emphasis in original).[24]

The Plan articulates the need to develop a 'new performance management approach' for the system, which will require:

- reliable statistical data to set targets, otherwise they will lack credibility as a spur to improvement;

[23]There is now a kind of simulation of a DEL (see SR2000 ch 27) in which the joined-up departments have control of a modest discretionary fund.
[24]CJS *Strategy and Business Plan* (May 1999) 2.2.4.

- consistent and comparable data available across the CJS;
- a review of information requirements, to focus them on need, minimise the burden of data collection and make maximum use of electronic techniques;
- measures for the CJS and each agency and service to be consistent, to show the contribution each is making to overall performance at national and local level;
- any measures that create conflicting or perverse incentives to be removed;
- regular monitoring of performance against targets;
- information on comparative performance to help spread best practice and bring the worst performers up to the level of the best;
- results to be used to inform plans for future years.[25]

The Plan also plans future plans.[26] Annual business plans will be published at the start of each financial year. These will develop the 'strategic vision'. As resource accounting develops, this will include 'a better alignment of resources with the objectives for the criminal justice system'.[27] Annual performance reports will also be produced, the first being scheduled for autumn 2000.[28] A quarterly Report is now being produced, summarising 'business activity' in the criminal justice system. These reports are primarily 'for internal use by senior managers within the Trilateral Departments, police and probation services, and courts. The emphasis is on providing the summary promptly and unambiguously. In some areas, more than one source of data exists and choices have been made between them'.[29] This more 'business-like' framing of the agenda may facilitate the re-framing of old practices. For example, there is the question of what happens to the revenue generated by the operations of the CJS. Thus the Plan states that the Government 'has decided in principle to look at whether some of the money received from fines and other penalties may be re-invested to improve performance against objectives. For example, fines resulting from the use of speed cameras might be used to fund more cameras. Using fines money to improve fine enforcement is another potential area'.[30]

---

[25]Plan, 3.5.2.
[26]Plan, 6.2.
[27]Plan, 6.2.1.
[28]Plan, 6.2.2.
[29]*Criminal Justice Business Quarterly Report* Third Quarter (July – September) 1999.
[30] Plan 4.3.3.

Before the Home Affairs Committee, Lord Irvine himself said explicitly that the changes are about control and about quality. A cynic might say that the rhetoric of quality and more particularly of quality assurance - which is par excellence a bureaucratic rhetoric, systems monitoring systems (Power 1997) - is activated here to cover over the fact that control really means cuts, and that what is really going on in the LCD is one facet of a broader attack by this government on the proud legacy of the Welfare State. I have no way of knowing what is motivating people in the LCD or the Treasury, what the real relationships and balance of power might be between ministers and civil servants, or how sincerely meant any public statement made by a minister or public official might be. There are clear rhetorics for all of these social communications; people know them and work with and within them. Sincerity, good intentions, 'my aim is true' is not the point or is at least pointless as a tool of observation. Indeed, my example of the LCD reforms is an example of something quite different: the relative unimportance of actors and the relative importance of systems. This follows from the simple fact that all of the framework constraints and pressures referred to here have been in the making for 20 years, as both ministers and public officials have come and gone.

A more effective legal system?

Such then are the attempts so far to develop effective and efficient management systems for effective and efficient legal communications (adjudication; decisions deploying the code legal/illegal). Changes in civil procedure, fast track, limits on appeals are all part of the latter, as is substantive law reform. A significant component of the former is the promotion of ADR, ie the idea that a different mode of social communication (which may or may not yet be coded (eg some adaptation of the love code - it could just still be noise)) is to be preferred. Effective management is also supposed to achieve efficient legal communication - discouragement of unnecessary adjournments, more generally of unnecessary delaying tactics by lawyers.

Effective and efficient management of legal communication also involves entrusting more powers to judges on both the criminal and civil side. Instead of being largely passive vessels through which the communications of the lawyers flow with minimal or light touch interference, they are now to manage when, where and what communications occur, including a plan to develop on the criminal side a much expanded decision-making power on the mode of trial.

Although some of this will possibly lead to a reduction in the volumes of legal communications, eg ADR and restrictions on appeals, the general implication is more likely to be an increase in reflexive communication both legal and managerial. At the line management level, one might expect to see more solicitors being appointed as judges, if only because some of them are more likely to possess the new skills on the basis of their professional experience (managing partners for example) than barristers. This is not dedifferentiation but rather the development of reflexive strategies for the most part within an enclosed legal system to monitor, quantify and kitemark/benchmark legal communications. This is to say that these changes will promote a greater self-awareness of the system by and for itself. But it also involves the development of much more sophisticated ways of communicating about the legal system to its 'external' 'stakeholders', and to government in particular.

For the most part the LCD can only influence change and not really manage it directly. It formulates performance targets and promises their achievement because that is the current language of intra-governmental communication; but its main direct levers are financial, and even these are limited in terms of control over or target achievement in respect of the system as a whole. Indeed, the agency and commission or board structure adopted throughout much of government is useful here and no doubt will be even more useful in the future. Legal services will be overseen by the Legal Services Commission, with umbrella organisations below it (CLS, CDS); the courts are under the umbrella of the Court Service. (Magistrates' Courts are since 1992 now the direct responsibility of the LCD (previously the Home Office) though local authorities play a significant role). If targets set for each are not met, heads may roll (as happened in effect with the CPS recently). Heads rolling is a way to buy time for the future, as is an enquiry followed by reorganisation (again see the CPS). (The possibility of splitting the LSC into two, to manage the civil and criminal sides, is already explicitly floated.)

The LCD's contribution to achieving joined-upness in the CJS seems secondary to that of the lead department, the Home Office. One should not, however, rule out organisational change as a solution if targets are not met on this front. The problem with the Narey approach[31] to delivering on joined-upness on the ground, especially so far as the police and the CPS

---

[31]Refs.

and the Courts are concerned, is that aspirations and so on can be formulated in inter-departmental committees but not really followed through on the ground, or implemented more successfully in some locations than others for purely contingent, historical or interpersonal reasons. Similar problems arise in relation to the CLS, which is being formulated in terms reminiscent of the central/local, state/voluntary sector debates of the 1950s and 1960s in relation to the provision of social services (Finlayson 1994: 287-400), except with a much more pronounced role for the commercial sector (ie lawyers in private practice) than was the case in those debates.

From an autopoietic viewpoint, the problems of the LCD are not so very different from that of many other departments: judges judge, teachers teach, doctors doctor and so on. (This perspective does not emerge so starkly in theories preoccupied with either separation of powers or legal autonomy.) Indeed, for government 'as a whole' (not much more of a 'whole' than 'society'), one needs to see differentiation of coding and the institutional fragmentation which accompanies it (though they map only unevenly on to each other) as a constant problem not an achievement which may or may not be under threat.[32] How much technical knowledge do 'policy makers' have or need to have? Is the division between generalists and specialists in departments satisfactory? What about the respective domains of ministers and the Senior Civil Service? (Now there is talk of joint training, seminars for senior ministers and permanent secretaries for example.) A recurrent problem is the relationship between ministers and their officials, or between politics and administration. In the modern world these two activities are extremely closely intertwined; at the same time they cannot be collapsed into each other. Perhaps one can say rather simply that this is because in a liberal multi-party democracy of periodic elections, this is because they operate within different codes, different temporal horizons, different concerns with time-binding. The political operates within the coding popular/unpopular or power/non-power; the administrative within the coding do-able/non-do-able or affordable/non-affordable or even urgent/non/urgent. One can observe considerable co-dependency between these two forms of communication. The precise way in which at the highest levels the political and the administrative is divided is itself no doubt

[32]Discussion of the commitment to produce 'Whole of Government Accounts' (as something more than the old, now superseded Control Total or the Current TME) to be audited by the C & AG - who will not have audited all of the components of the accounts - highlights the problem of what Government-as-a-whole actually is today.

contingent on a comparative basis. But both the division and the intertwining seem almost inescapable in modern societies (and not just democracies).

I have said very little here so far about the law 'itself'. In a sense it is as if most of the issues discussed above are concerned with the modernisation, streamlining, refurbishment of the infrastructure of, inter alia, the judicial system and the delivery of legal services, in the light of the development of standards and policies across government as a whole. To be sure, the LCD's modernising agenda includes law reform, and several objectives are formulated in this area. Similarly, if the 'promotion' or whatever we should call of human rights is part of a modernising agenda, then as we have seen some of the infrastructural refurbishment has been undertaken in the expectation of new pressures arising for the system now that the HRA is onstream. But is there more to be said, or does a commitment to the separation of powers, individual liberty, the independence of the Bench and respect within government for the rule of law (for which see Daintith and Page, 1999: 207-210) mean that once fresh paint is applied it is business as usual inside the courtroom?

It seems inevitable that case management will transform aspects of the mode of functioning of the civil justice system in the direction of efficiency and effectiveness. Related changes flowing from these initiatives may have more widereaching effects, especially so far as the (by now) traditional expectations of common lawyers are concerned. In particular, the attempts to narrow and rationalise the appellate process on the civil side may prove significant.[33] Also alongside this may need to be set the commitment first made by Lord Mackay and reiterated by the present Lord Chancellor that the civil justice system must pay for itself, and that this requirement includes judicial salaries.[34]

Running behind this is the review now beginning of the criminal justice system, with a view among other things to look at case management and streamlining of judicial handling of cases on Woolf lines in this area. Auld's terms of reference are to conduct a 'review into the practices and procedures of, and the rules of evidence applied by, the criminal courts at every level, with a view to ensuring that they deliver justice fairly, by streamlining all their processes, increasing their efficiency and

---

[33]See eg the consultation paper Civil Procedure Rules Part 59: Appeals and CHK on follow - up to responses.

[34]I have not been able to find a public document which clearly measures if this is possible the degree of public subsidy if any which is still present in the civil justice system.

strengthening the effectiveness of their relationships with others across the whole of the criminal justice system, and having regard to the interests of all parties including victims and witnesses, thereby promoting public confidence in the rule of law'.[35]

In this new environment it becomes increasingly unclear what the continued rationale of the present Appellate Committee of the House of Lords is. It is not improbable to anticipate a future in which commercial appeals stop at the level of an Appeal Court and some reconstituted final court of appeal be created for constitutional and human rights matters. The ingenuity of deploying the Privy Council to deal with (hypothetical?) devolution disputes, on the basis that it is an arm of the monarchical rather than the UK parliamentary apparatus and therefore not constitutionally part of a dispute between, say, Edinburgh and Westminster, hardly disguises the rather absurd position of the current arrangements. Similarly not all are persuaded (indeed, is anyone persuaded?) by the honeyed words of Wakeham on the retention of the lawlords as members of the legislative House of Lords.[36]

Mimesis or colonisation?

It can be said that the purity of function systems differentiation obscures the pluralism of communication within so-called systems, and that this is unhelpful or worse when thinking for example about modern law or government. But this obscures the distinction between deciding what is legal or illegal, for example, on the one hand, and the themes which are relevant in making this decision or in rationalising it or in developing a critique of it. Autopoiesis is concerned with the observation of observation; it is not concerned with the choice of themes; it simply presupposes that such choices will and must be made and may or may not be interested in what choices are in fact made. To turn this around, holistic theories which think that society can be reconstructed through the unified pursuit of one single theme or the proclamation of being open to many themes (pluralism) simply fail to take differentiation and coding into account and as a result miss their mark or unfold future presents which are unattainable because they are merely thematic.

[35]The space to watch for the moment is http://www.criminal-courts-review.org.uk.

[36]*A House for the Future: Royal Commission on the Reform of the House of Lords* (Cm 4534, January 2000) ch. 9.

It is also claimed that systems theory loses sight of the very contingency it proclaims. Law, politics, economics are corralled into different hermetically sealed systems when the reality is quite different, such that political transformations can transform the law, and the economy can colonise both. Many interpret the material I have discussed here in this way. I think this involves a misunderstanding. The separation of popularity/power, wealth and justice are contingent and can never be relied upon: buying power or justice is always possible and happens; seeking or taking account of popularity and/or wealth in doing justice happens (think of Lord Denning); and so on. (Historical comparisons provide some perspective here: see Doyle, 1996; Waquet, 1991). But, equally, there is a strongly developed public discourse routed through the mass media in many modern societies that there are clear and firm distinctions here which need to be preserved, defended or strengthened. Preoccupations with political corruption, the funding of political parties, and in a more complicated way the composition of the judiciary are all examples of this. The simple difference between a code and a programme or a frame and a theme enables us to express this, and all the contingency which underpins it and accompanies it, very clearly. To the extent that these conceptual, figurative and communicative distinctions are deeply embedded institutionally in the West, what we in fact see is the difficulty of creating new distinctions, and of escaping from these established ones.

It might make more sense to conceptualise this problem as institutional and/or systemic mimesis or imitation. Although this concept may seem excessively psychological or 'subjective', it is no more confined to such a deployment than some of the phenomenological themes which underscore the theory of the autopoiesis of social systems. What I have in mind here is the distinction between imitation and de-differentiation, and specifically 'mimicking' as Nigel Lawson called it.[37] Resource budgeting, for example, is justified because it is what modern businesses do, and so to be more professional government should do it too. Similarly, the development of business plans, investment plans, and many of the measures and badges of

---

[37]'[Ibbs] .. believed that the route to efficiency in the public sector was to mimic the private sector as closely as possible… I myself considered Treasury control of spending to be very much a second-best form of financial discipline: the discipline of the market place was altogether superior…. But so long as public services existed, insulated from the discipline of the market place, with no 'bottom line' and, indeed, in most cases providing services free at the point of use so there was not even a price mechanism at work, Treasury control was essential. The alternative was no financial discipline at all' (Lawson 1993: 391). This was why Lawson was suspicious of Next Steps agencies.

achievement (IiP, BEM) were referred to above. The focus of this paper – 'UK plc' – might suggest that this traffic is one-way. Of course it is not. As governments mime corporations, so corporations become statesmanlike. But mimesis does not obliterate the gulf between the guiding distinctions which frame the themes which give colour to the formulation of purposes – in power/out of power,[38] profitable/unprofitable.

This chapter has involved observations of operations within the political system – political communication – which have as their thematic content and focus of attention what are effectively environmental problems arising in organisations. As we have seen, these problems are generally articulated by means of two sub-themes – management and motivation – which are supposed to give shape to the distinctly plastic long-term headline themes of economy, efficiency and effectiveness. In the specific case of the legal system, the additional question arises (though not uniquely) which involves the idea of building a 'system' in order to achieve or deliver these thematic goals. At this point, confusion can arise. The project of building a legal 'system' within primarily political communication is essentially concerned with managerial and efficiency questions which occur within an organisational focus: better management of resources deployed by the state in relation to the provision of legal services by the professions and the courts; promotion of the competitiveness of UK legal services by comparison with the quality on offer elsewhere; facilitation of alternatives to traditional legal mechanisms for conflict and dispute resolution in the interests of economy. The distinction between organisation and system is especially important at this point, and the paradox of the current UK position is that building a better managed organisation exposes the law to systemic dedifferentiation.

References

Daintith, T. and Page, A. (1999), *The Executive in the Constitution*, Oxford, University Press, Oxford.

Doyle, W. (1996), *Venality*, Clarendon Press, Oxford.

Finlayson, G. (1994), *Citizen, State, and Social Welfare in Britain 1830-1990*, Clarendon Press, Oxford.

Hood, Ch. (1998), *The Art of the State*, Oxford University Press, Oxford.

Lawson, N. (1993), *The View from No 11*, Corgi Books, London.

[38]For all that it pursued business-as-usual for a full term - including in the LCD - it is this which gave Norman Lamont's phrase 'in government but not in power' such resonance as encapsulating the failure of the Major administration.

Light, P. C. (1997), *The Tides of Reform: Making Government Work 1945-1995*, Yale University Press, New Haven, Conn.

Luhmann, N. (1989), *Ecological Communication*, Polity Press, Cambridge.

Luhmann, N. (1990), *Political Theory in the Welfare State,* de Gruyter, Berlin.

Luhmann, N. (1993), *Risk: A Sociological Theory*, de Gruyter, Berlin.

Luhmann, N. (1995), *Social Systems*, Stanford University Press, Stanford, Ca.

Luhmann, N. (1998), *Observations on Modernity,* Stanford University Press, Stanford, Ca.

McSweeney, B. (1994), 'Management by accounting', in A. G. Hopwood and P. Miller (eds), *Accounting as Social and Institutional Practice*, Cambridge University Press, Cambridge.

Murphy, T. (1997), *The Oldest Social Science?*, Clarendon Press, Oxford.

Power, M. (1997), *The Audit Society*, Oxford University Press, Oxford.

Stevens, R. (1997), *The Independence of the Judiciary,* Oxford University Press, Oxford.

Sunder, S. (1997), *Theory of Accounting and Control*, South-Western College Publishing, Cincinatti, Ohio.

Waquet, J.-C. (1992), *Corruption*, Penn State Press, University Park, PA.

White, F. and Hollingsworth, K. (1999), *Audit, Accountability and Government*, Clarendon Press, Oxford.

11 Abiding the World: Globalism and the Lex Mercatoria

PETER FITZPATRICK

How much can come
And much can go,
And yet abide the world!

(Emily Dickinson,
'There Came a Wind Like a Bugle')

Introduction

Being somewhat agreeable so as then to be thoroughly disagreeable is a not unusual point of departure in the academic essay, but my intention is to be more nuanced about it. Let me, for the sake of agreement, grant at the outset the gist of the theory of legal autopoiesis insofar as it relates to what could be called law's internal constitution. Self-reference, self-production, self-constitution – to borrow the terminology – would seem to be a condition of any existential assertion. What may be less impelling is the quality or force of the 'external relations' of the autopoietic entity (Teubner, 2000a: 1, for the phrase). This is a dimension of some apt turbulence, perturbation, irritation – still borrowing the terminology – within the theory of autopoiesis, but doubtless its own autopoietic quality can accommodate this in some 'paradoxical' way.

Taking a selection of Teubner's formulations as instances of the quality or force of the external, we find that it is decidedly not 'the environment which determined whether or not the system continued and reproduced', but nonetheless there is 'the fact that law is determined to a considerable extent by political influences, economic structures, and social factors'; or there is the fact that 'a self-producing legal system is strongly influenced by social, economic, and political factors' but not, it seems, 'subject to ...

direct influence' (Teubner, 1993: 16, 21). The dissonance here between determination and influence seems to be resolved in the achievement of some 'circular', autopoietic closure, whence 'there has to be a move away from the simple logic of cause and effect towards a logic of 'perturbation'', and towards the terminology of 'influence' (Teubner, 1993: 35). (Perhaps the whole issue could be disposed of when Tuebner proceeds to set that separation in a perspectivist position – the 'interdependence' between law and other things must 'be seen as a problem of how circular, causal processes are subject to external influences' (Teubner, 1993: 35) – but his own position is not perspectivist.)

My purpose here is not to pursue such difficulties into the anfractuous depths of autopoietic theory itself but simply to indicate that the matter of external relations is rightly emphasized by Teubner. However, I hope to show that this emphasis cannot avoid going beyond the dimension of influence and beyond the straitened effects of turbulence, perturbation, or irritation, so much so that the very self-sufficing of the autopoietic entity subsists in a relation of apposition to its externality. The problem of how to begin setting that demonstration was solved by one of the sweeter uses of adversity. A particularly malevolent virus of the non-virtual kind delayed work on this paper beyond the receipt of Gunther Teubner's 'Alienating Justice: On the surplus value of the twelfth camel' (Teuber, 2000a). With it came the added joy of the elusive cue – the Derrida problem. On the first page, Derrida is found observing, at best inadequately, 'the violence of law's self-foundation'. Such an attribution, if a little abrupt, would most probably be accorded the imprimatur of Derridean. On the following page is a contrary attribution which most probably would not. With that attribution 'deconstructive justice' would be taken as the 'roots' of law. Leaving aside the inability of Derrida's 'deconstructive justice' being able to 'root' anything at all, his foundation and his root of law are, in this account, antithetical – and 'foundation' and 'roots' here look like the same thing. It will, however, prove no strain on companionability to agree that law does subsist in this opposition – the opposition between the violence of law's self-foundation and deconstructive justice. I will extract agreement on the point from Derrida also. That will serve to orient the main engagement, which is with the autopoietic quality of the *lex mercatoria* in the claims which Teubner makes for it, claims in which law oscillates in-between its antithetical 'foundation' and 'roots'.

Doing justice

Although it may be to risk tedium, I will now extract the antithetical mainly from a much visited text, Derrida's 'Force of Law' (Derrida, 1992). There Derrida would want to 'make explicit or perhaps produce a difficult and unstable distinction between justice and *droit*, between justice (infinite, incalculable, rebellious to rule and foreign to symmetry ...) and the exercise of justice as law or right, legitimacy or legality, ... calculable, a system of regulated and coded prescriptions' (Derrida, 1992: 22).

Looking in a preliminary way at the justice side of the distinction, we find that for Derrida justice imports an unlimited responsiveness to the singularity of the other. The very particularity or specific finiteness of the other calls for an infinite regard. But the illimitable demand of justice without more, or without less, is impossible and even inexpressible, always beyond attainment and ever 'to come' (Derrida, 1992: 27). To be effective, to be made possible, justice must be given operative force and for this it must, in a sense, be denied. The limitless expanse of justice, that is, must be violently 'cut' into, reduced, and rendered expressible (Derrida, 1992: 24). An obvious contradiction now emerges: justice can only be made just in a way that is unjust.

Turning now, still in a preliminary way, to law, we find that for Derrida law, or more precisely the legal decision, is that which cuts into and assures justice (and less than justice). In this, 'law is the element of calculation' (Derrida, 1992: 16). It imports a stability and regularity. If codifies, prescribes and determines. It lends its intrinsic force and enforceability to justice. It cannot, however, be accounted for in terms of justice. And justice in any case, is unlimiting and cannot account for anything. So, Derrida frequently contrasts justice and the just decision with the legal decision which 'simply consists of applying the law', or in which 'the judge is a calculating machine', or in which 'we placidly apply a good rule to a particular case, to a correct subsumed example, according to a determinate judgement' (Derrida, 1992: 16, 23). Yet, despite Derrida's strangely positivist confirmation that these things 'happen' – an assertion which, as we will now see, is untenable in terms of his own more elaborated argument – he also recognises that matters are more mixed, that law is not 'simply' to be distinguished from justice but must itself integrally be more (Derrida, 1992: 22-3).

Law may be necessary for the enforcement of justice, but that justice which lies ever beyond determination is also necessary for the enforcement of law. A living law, to borrow the phrase, is not containable in some terminal stasis but is incipiently, promiscuously and self-transgressively oriented beyond what it may at any moment be. There is then, 'an ordeal of the undecidable' which is not only anterior to but also inhabits and persists in and beyond the legal decision: 'the undecidable remains caught, lodged, at least as a ghost – but an essential ghost – in every decision, in every event of decision'; and, 'each case is other, each decision is different and requires an absolutely unique interpretation, which no existing coded rule can or ought to guarantee absolutely' (Derrida, 1992: 23, 24). The persistently undecidable in law, its constant 'inadequation' opens law to justice or, put another way, the undecidable brings justice into law (Derrida, 1992: 20). In all, the act of legal decision combines law as the calculable with justice as the incalculable response to the 'absolutely unique' beyond determined calculation, exchange or reciprocity. Justice, in its turn, is effected through law as calculable. Each is necessary for the operation of the other yet each is necessarily distinct from the other. There is a relation of 'difference and ... co-implication' between them (Derrida, 1994: 177).

The distinction between law and justice entails nothing less, and perhaps somewhat more, than the process of Derrida's 'deconstruction', especially in its ability to reveal the unavoidable incompleteness of an entity or to reveal the impossibility of any positing of the entity purely in itself. Deconstruction for Derrida, 'is justice' or situated 'between law and justice' (Derrida, 1992: 15, 21). More elaborately, 'deconstruction takes place in the interval that separates the undeconstructability of justice from the deconstructability of *droit*' (Derrida, 1992: 15). Justice can be called in aid to convey the movement of deconstruction continually beyond all presence (Derrida, 1992: 16). And law could be a figure of determined presence or a figure of its determination. But if these things are so, 'justice' is not the compendious way of describing deconstruction which, rather, 'takes place' between justice and law (Derrida, 1992: 16).

So, justice may 'be' deconstruction but justice operates dependently through law. The 'possibility' of deconstruction, it may be said, relies upon law as presence (cf. Derrida, 1982: 14). And that presence, as Derrida recognises, persists (Derrida, 1977: 248). Its avatars – presences as against presence and laws as opposed to the law – are 'deconstructable'. But ultimately an active, assertive presence is, like justice, a condition of deconstruction and cannot itself be deconstructed. No matter how illimitable, no matter how 'mad' justice or the desire for justice may be

(Derrida, 1992: 25-6), it is held in conjunction with presence (cf. Derrida, 1978). So, 'justice exceeds law and calculation' but law is also seen by Derrida as 'exceeding' justice (Derrida, 1992: 28). We must, Derrida emphasises, calculate and we must negotiate 'the relation between the calculable and the incalculable': 'this requirement does not properly belong either to justice or law. It only belongs to either of these two domains by exceeding one in the direction of the other' (Derrida, 1992: 28). Law, then, as calculation can only 'properly belong' to itself, by exceeding itself 'in the direction of' justice (Derrida, 1992: 28). Calculation, in short, goes to as well as against justice. Or inversely, as we have already seen, justice is operatively integral to law, to the legal decision. The question of how just is the decision, of how far it goes 'in the direction of' justice, is another matter. Law orients the decision in a relation to justice, in an inclination towards the other. Neither illimitable justice nor law – law which is not beholden to anything 'before' it – can be contained in some notion of the just as ideal or as the Good. Justice always sits 'very close to the bad, even to the worst for it can always be re-appropriated by the most perverse calculation' (Derrida, 1992: 28).

As to the 'other' side of the equation, justice exceeding itself in the direction of law, we have also seen that, to have effect, justice depends on law: 'incalculable justice *requires* us to calculate' (Derrida, 1992: 28 - his emphasis). If 'I' am to be in a relation of responsibility to the other, to say nothing of relating to a diversity of others, then justice must be delimited in the act of legal decision. Without a limit, there can be no relation to the other. Giving my-self to the other in the unalloyed demand of justice is inherently unachievable. It could never form or resolve into a relation. Or, in a more apocalyptic vein, once the giving were achieved, there would be a simultaneous dissolution of the very 'I' which was to relate to the other. In all, if law is the place where contained presence impossibly combines with uncontained responsiveness, perhaps deconstruction connects more compendiously with law than with justice.

Law, in summary, becomes the combination of determination with all that is beyond determination. It cannot be simply or solely the principle of calculation, that which cuts into and renders the responsiveness of justice operative. Justice, responsiveness, responsibility – responsability, in the archaic usage – also renders law operative. The legal decision must:

> be both regulated and without regulation: it must conserve the law and also destroy it or suspend it enough to have to reinvent it in each case, rejustify

> it, at least reinvent it in the reaffirmation and the new and free confirmation of its principle (Derrida, 1992: 23).

Again, 'no existing, coded rule can … guarantee absolutely' what will be decided (Derrida, 1992: 23). And what has been decided, judicially or legislatively, cannot stand apart in a determined or determining isolation. The decision cannot 'be' in the world if it seeks merely to affirm or be affirmed in itself - if it has no connection, no relation to anything else. To maintain its 'place' it must ever go beyond its own bounds and relate to such circumstance and possibility as would come to or be brought to it (Derrida, 1977; 1992: 38). Hence, law or the legal decision has constantly to destroy itself to stay itself. It has always to decompose in order to be composed. There is always something 'rotten' in law (Derrida, 1992: 39).

Such a responsiveness 'in' law can never, then, be satisfied in terms of what can be cognitively brought to bear. No decision could ever 'furnish itself with infinite information and the unlimited knowledge of conditions, rules or hypothetical imperatives that could justify it' (Derrida, 1992: 26). Inversely, a determination based on knowledge cannot ever be complete in some final isolated resolution. Even if it could, we, being 'within' knowledge, could never know it to be complete. Something could always come from beyond, something 'more', and reveal our over-confident conclusion to be not so. We could begin to grasp that 'more' in its relation to law by looking at it negatively. If determination were adequate or complete, there would be no place for decision or for judgement. Alternatively, there will always 'in' the legal act be something beyond any particular or possible determination. There will always and at every moment (that is, at every point of impinging difference) be a demand for 'fresh judgement' (Derrida, 1992: 26). It is in the very absence of determination, or in the presence of irresolution, that there is a demand for law and for legal judgement. The responsibility, or the responsability, involved in judgement cannot be accommodated within the determined or the known. There is always 'in' it a 'secret', a mystery, a 'madness' (Derrida, 1992: 26; 1995: 65).

Given this divide in law and its insistence, perhaps enquiry should be diverted. Rather than seeking law in that which simply conforms to either side of the opposition – to its autonomous determination or to its determination by what it is must respond to beyond itself – perhaps we could seek a law which 'is' in-between the opposed dimensions, which 'is' the experienced combination of them, and which has its being because each dimension is inexorable yet unable to 'be' by itself. Thence it would seem that the condition of being in law is always unresolved and calling for incessant decision and judgment. Nonetheless, we may find prospects for resolution in these dimensions being not only opposed but also somehow integral to each other. A complete determination of position and a responsiveness to what is beyond position are antithetical things, but there can be neither enduring position without responsiveness to what is always beyond it nor effective responsiveness without a position from which to respond. In their separation, these dimensions mark the horizon of law, the horizon both as a condition and quality of its contained being, and the horizon opening onto all which lies beyond that being. These dimensions of law are integral to each other. The separate insistence on each would be death carrying with it either a terminal fixity or a dissolving responsiveness to what is beyond. Law, in short, subsists in-between these two dimensions.

Making global

As a prelude to tracing these dimensions constituently within Teubner's account of the *lex mercatoria*, not just by way of reorienting the autopoietic quality discerned in the *lex mercatoria* but also by way of countering its 'global' grounding, I will provide a sketch of globalization, so-called. With its theorists being unable to locate a singular universal content for globalization, depictions of it resort to the list. The effort positively to locate claims to the universal produces the list which enumerates specific qualities whilst intimating an idea of a universal whole encompassing them. Apart from the tautologous – the global being simply affirmed as global – that whole is not given its own content. Perhaps the most invoked quality is an increasing connection or communication between people and places. This is said to be manifested in a 'time-space compression' (Harvey, 1989: 240). Or there is a new 'time-space distanciation' which accompanies the 'intensification of world-wide social relations which link distant locations in such a way that local happenings are shaped by events occurring many miles away and vice versa' (Giddens, 1990: 14, 64). Such things are usually presented as the outcome or effect of more situated items on the list.

To 'cover' these items, I will simply refer to the briefest and yet most compendious of lists and move on immediately to indicate some of the items which tend to be emphasized more than others (see Waters, 1995: 94, 123, 157). At the top of most lists of the situated are things seen in economic terms – the dominance of 'the market', the growth of transnational corporations, the mobility of capital and of labour, the increase in world trade. Next in order of emphasis are 'cultural' factors. These usually celebrate the supposedly tentacular efficacy of new technologies of communication. Then there is 'politics'. This is very much about governing and being governed and, in the literature on globalization, politics is increasingly being subsumed in the label 'governance'. This term is often used to draw or to suggest a convenient distinction between a kind of unitary world government, now seen as an antique aspiration, and supposedly more diverse sets or clusters of governing relations. Politics is most prominent on the lists when it intersects with the economic. The most significant instance of this intersection comes from the so-called Washington consensus reflecting the views and dictates of, mainly, the International Monetary Fund and the International Bank for Reconstruction and Development, the 'World Bank'. As between these institutions, the consensus has of late become strained, but they both continue to focus and give effect to key imperatives of governance in which neo-liberal economic rectitude is prerequisite. Their requirements also extend to the observance of human rights and of the rule of law, and to 'democratization'.

There is, finally, one item on the list which is frequently mentioned in connection with all of the others – whether they be economic, cultural or political – and that is that they are not contained or containable within the sphere of the nation but somehow assume a cohering being beyond it. That is, attributes of the global are monotonously elevated in their being beyond the range of regulation or of the dominating concern of the nation and its state. This is not merely a matter of the dissolution or the displacement of nation in the direction of the global. Power is seen as inhering more and more in other entities 'besides' the nation-state – sub-national and international regions and transnational corporations being the most cited repositories.

Of course, the practical epistemology of all this transcends the specificity and the diversity of the list. Globalization simply and singly is, or is assuredly becoming so. For this we have the authority of new lords of human kind. In a speech to the then rather more self-confident World Trade Organization on May 18 1998, the President of the United States revealed that 'globalization is not a policy choice – it is a fact'. In the same forum and in the same global context, the Prime Minister of Great Britain decreed on the next day that 'whether there should be free trade' is not 'the question now'; free trade is 'an irreversible and irresistible trend'. It may consequently seem a little puzzling as to why these oracles of the global go to such extraordinary lengths to bring about something that either exists already or is inexorable. Nor do their bald pronouncements sit easily with the fragility of 'the global market' and with escalating calls for the regulation of this now less-than-brave new world.

Perceptions contrary to those associated with globalization are almost as well rehearsed and, if one of them predominates, it would be that this supposed globalization is an extraversion of nation. The preponderance of trade and production remains concentrated within national borders and the 'global' lying beyond these is revealed as an extension of national economies. The global market and so-called transnational corporations remain primally connected to national economies and overwhelmingly to a limited number of these, a number which rarely strays or stays beyond North America, Japan and Europe. The global financial market is usually admitted to be an exception, being often hailed as autonomous and beyond the control of nation. Obviously effective as the financial market has been in outflanking particular national economies, it is hugely the emanation of the most powerful nations and it has not been immune to their combined control (see Hirst and Thompson, 1996: 129-36). Quite apart from that, finance is not yet quite everything and nobody seems to be arguing, yet, that a global financial market is sufficient to constitute globalization. There is also a key element of the economy which is seen as becoming less global and that is the permitted mobility of labour across national borders. There are also dimensions of the economy, such as the interests of workers and environmental effects, which are somehow deemed less deserving of effective attention in global terms. Broadly similar observations have been often made about the national dominance of 'global' culture and politics, and these observations are greatly facilitated in the case of politics by explicit provision made for certain countries to control key institutions of 'global governance'.

Perhaps unsurprisingly, there is a marked tendency in these perceptions against globalization to see it as more of the same, a tendency generously accommodated by the observers sympathetic to globalization who describe it as an augmentation of what was already there – as an increase in world trade, an 'acceleration' of contact, an 'intensification' of relations, and so on (Giddens, 1990: 64). If globalization has been initiated in a break with what was, or if there has been a qualitative change emerging out of an 'intensification' of quantity, no one seems to have discovered these things (cf. Robertson, 1990: 20-8; 1992: 183-3). And certainly there are obvious similarities between accounts of globalization and the 'old' ways of talking about imperialism and the expansionary dynamic of capital. The weary discursive legitimations of development and modernization have now been resurrected as quite inviolate in the setting of globalization. Even globalization's supposed inclusion of the local as yet somehow contrary to its general sweep has a counterpart in a large and once influential literature which saw the advance of capitalism as reliant on 'traditional' pockets of production and culture (e.g. Taylor, 1979).

Globalization and these apparent predecessors are not only at one in their claims to an encompassing coverage, they also confront similar challenges to such claims. Just as claims once made for the pervasion of capitalism and occidental imperialism were reduced in the revelation of contrary and potent modes of existence (e.g. Wolf, 1982), so also globalization has been opposed by the vitality of economic relations, of cultural and political assertion, all countering the encompassing claims made for it (e.g. Appelbaum, 1998). These not only deny 'global' coverage but also refuse to be reduced to some site of the 'local' related to that global. Globalization seems, then, not to extend to large parts of the globe. Furthermore, elements of globalization itself, such as the transfer of investment funds to an ever 'developing' world and the resulting pall of debt, keep people apart from its supposedly benificent reach.

Elusive as it still doubtless remains, globalization in this account so far begins to resemble those more venerable occidental occupations of the world in the name of the universal. Denied a positive point of transcendent origin, the modern universal self-constitutes negatively in excluding what is other to itself. Like this universal, globalization seems to make its foundational claim to an encompassing hold only in a relation to what it opposes or excludes. And also like the universal, the exclusion contradicts in its turn the foundational claim to inclusiveness, thus revealing an 'original' ambivalence or irresolution within globalization. The comparable difficulty afflicting the modern universal has been putatively overcome by making the included element exemplary and setting the excluded on an aspirational or evolutionary path towards it. Most accounts of globalization would also deem it to be exemplary, and see it as presently incomplete but in the process of being achieved by bringing in what is for the time being apart from it.

The *Lex Mercatoria*

Let me now turn to that global law which comes with the benefit of refined theoretical analysis by Teubner (1997a; 1997b), the modern manifestation of *lex mercatoria*, which could be rendered as 'mercantile law' but is not as extensive as that would suggest. An initial difficulty is the elusiveness of the *lex mercatoria*, the welter of diverse meanings given to it, the questioning whether it really exists at all. I will return to the difficulty but for now will cling to the confidence of Teubner's conception and to his text:

> In *lex mercatoria* it is the practice of contracting that transcends national boundaries and transforms a merely national law production into a global one - numerous international business transactions, standardized contracts of international professional associations, model contracts of international organizations and investment projects in developing countries. However, as soon as these contracts claim transnational validity, they cut off not only their national roots but their roots in any legal order (Teubner, 1997a: 15).

But such deracination depends on a theoretically impoverised globalism, even if Teubner seeks somewhat to improve the theory.

Teubner's modes of constituting the global and the 'global law' of the *lex mercatoria*, aptly enough resemble general perceptions of globalization. 'Globalization has certainly become a reality today' when there is now 'one world society' dating 'from the historical moment in which communication became worldwide' (Teubner, 1997a: 5-6, 22 n.6). The global law of the *lex mercatoria* can at least aspire to a similarly rounded reality by having regard to its foundation in contract. Teubner is concerned to establish the self-creating or self-validating quality of this law. It does not come particularly from anywhere. It seems to be simply a primal assertion that the contract is law. What supplements and solidifies this primal assertion, what 'conceals' or even overcomes the otherwise 'fatal self-validation', is the emergence out of the contract of such confirming modes as arbitration and the standardization of rules (Teubner, 1997a: 15-17). In a way, this scenario can be taken as unexceptional. Law does self-originate in a primal assertion. There is nothing 'before' it. The problem for Teubner, however, is that he hails this new-created law as global in origin and quality, and seems to be unable to say exactly what *that* is or may ever be.

This is an inability shared with the theorists of globalization, and the impossibility of affirming the global is obliquely recognized by Teubner when he dilutes it into something less assuredly achieved. As with much globalization theory, a once confident condition, a 'one world society', becomes an evanescent process, 'a dynamic ongoing process'; indeed, he now finds that 'an authentic global society' has only 'begun to form' (Teubner, 1997a: 5-6). Dissolution of the once 'one world society' is taken even further. Teubner would emphasize that the 'modern experience' is one 'of a fragmented rather than a uniform globalization'; there is 'a fragmented multitude of diverse global societies' (Teubner, 1997a: 5-6). Global law, in turn, is 'a new 'living law' growing out of fragmented social institutions' and it 'can only be adequately explained by a theory of legal pluralism' (Teubner, 1997a: 4-7). The argument from diversity also is not uncommon in globalization theory. But if the diverse entities are to be in some relation, then each cannot simply be complete unto itself, purely plural. There must be some element or configuring of commonality between them. Teubner somewhat aggravates the problem by insisting on the distinct and self-reproducing nature of the diverse entities (e.g. Teubner, 1997a: 7). He does, however, suggest an ostensible advance on globalization theory when in an expansive theory of autopoiesis the diverse entities are bidden to cohere into an encompassing 'system' which somehow comes from a supposed evolutionary 'shift from territorial to functional differentiation on the world level' (Teubner, 1997a: 16, 23 n.6).

Nonetheless, the global law 'growing out of fragmented social institutions' does not emerge as integral but as itself fragmented:

> While in nation-states - at least in some of them - the legal process has developed a rather high degree of institutional insulation, global laws will probably remain, for the foreseeable future, in a diffuse but close dependency upon their respective specialized social fields (Teubner, 1997a: 8).

Indeed, 'the overriding characteristics of *lex mercatoria*' consist in its being 'a law that grows and changes according to the exigencies of global economic transactions and organizations' (Teubner, 1997a: 19). It is little wonder that, in this overriding and diverse dependency, the 'empire' of 'global laws' approximates to an 'uncoordinated ensemble of many small domains, a patchwork of legal regimes' (Teubner, 1997a: 21). So, in that same 'foreseeable future, the development of this law will follow the 'external' evolution of the economic system but fail to develop an 'internal' evolution of its own' (Teubner, 1997a: 20). For the *lex mercatoria* 'the relative autonomy and independence which historically national legal orders have been able to achieve will probably remain something unknown'

(Teubner, 1997a: 19). This global law, then, is at best yet to be. It is yet to happen beyond the foreseeable future, and what it will be cannot be known until it is. Somewhat more optimistically, 'it can be anticipated that a global economic law discourse will find a dynamic stability of its own and will develop 'eigenvalues' which must be understood in their own right' (Teubner, 1997a: 19). In the meantime, global law as a 'living law' can live but spectrally in its dissipating dependence on other things. In all, global law either disappears in its dependent relations or it fails to appear at all, at least not for the time being.

Following Teubner's pursuit of global law, then, seems to end in nothing; but, more companionably, perhaps something is to be found in this nothingness. There has to be, I have argued, a necessary responsiveness to law. Law could not simply be determinate. Indeed, that quality of determination itself depended on law's being responsive. Yet this argument was also reversed and law's responsiveness seen to depend on a ground of determination, on something 'there' already. Without such a ground to come from and to go to, responsiveness would infinitely dissipate. It could be said, then, that Teubner has identified the responsive dimension of his global law. In an aptly contrary way, however, he also describes global law in terms which are quite determinate and quite different to what is either dependently related or yet to be revealed 'in its own right'. Specifically, the *lex mercatoria* is 'an autonomous non-national body of law' and global law is already 'a legal order in its own right' (Teubner, 1997a: 4, 9).

The lineaments of a global law now appear to be in place but this global law lacks a ground of determination. Apart from the indefinite suggestion of the global as a ground, all that Teubner will say on that score, repeatedly, is that global law is not national and it is not international. But it is these things. Switching to another account of the *lex mercatoria* for a moment, we find Santos encapsulating it as 'a globalized localism' (Santos, 1995: 290). That localism is distinctly national and occidental, and probably becoming more narrowly so with the increasing dominance of the United States and the common law (cf. Santos, 1995: 293). In Teubner's account, however, this situation seems to be redeemable since the *lex mercatoria* is based in contract and, much like the naturalizing of the market in globalization theory, there is a global givenness attributed to contract. As such, it has a 'depoliticized origin' and an 'apolitical character' which only afterwards becomes susceptible to political and national infiltration (Teubner, 1997a: 21-2). A return can now be made to the *mélange* of meaning associated with the *lex mercatoria*. There one finds a persistent division between the celebration of the purely 'spontaneous' and 'unsystematic' responsiveness of the *lex mercatoria* to the customs and practices of business people and a more dourly set emphasis on its being a specific body of rules embedded in national and international legal domains – and in either dimension, the range of relevance has not extended beyond the 'civilized' or some equivalent (see Hatzimihail 2000).

More bluntly, the contract as a legal form is not historically innocent (e.g. Teubner, 2000b: 400-4, 411-12). It was integral to the creation and potent assertion in the modern period of 'rational' occidental law. And the contract as *lex mercatoria* - in its ethos, its contents and modes of enforcement - will overwhelmingly be aligned with occidental law. Furthermore, accounts of the *lex mercatoria* and the sources drawn on in its official application extend its connections with the national beyond the 'private' law of contract into something formed in the same terms as much international law. In these more expansive versions, the *lex mercatoria* incorporates 'general principles of law recognized by commercial nations' or 'by civilized nations'; it will also accommodate the customs or 'practices of the dominant actors' associated with commercial and civilized nations (Santos, 1995: 289-90; cf. Teubner, 1997c: 150, 163-5). The occidental grounding of legal sources like this has for centuries been close to exclusive in international law.

Conclusion

Prior to this account of the *lex mercatoria*, Teubner had coined the oxymoron 'partially autonomous' to encapsulate it (Teubner, 1993: 38). This kind of description, one which caused some turbulence for autopoietic theory more generally, seems to lie in-between Teubner's seeing the *lex mercatoria* as 'an autonomous ... body of law' and as being forever dependent on an 'external' element. Such a radically attenuated autopoiesis lies closer to the analysis offered here. With that analysis, law's 'dependent' responsiveness and its 'autonomous' determinacy could not be separated from each other, neither entirely nor in some calculated proportion. Each suffused the other to its full extent. The responsive cannot be purely beyond and thence be merely inaccessible. It must be positioned in possibility or, put another way, oriented towards determinability. Neither, however, can determinant position be at all irenically set. The assertion of position has always to be made in relation to the infinitely responsive. Position cannot be enduringly stilled in its completion, or in or at any point, or in any severable part. It is, moreover, the absence, the impossibility, of an assured systemic shielding which creates the very demand for law – which iteratively calls for decision or for determination 'for the time being'. It is in the very response to this call, in the making and sustaining of law's constituent separation, that law 'finds itself', ever and integrally tied to its exteriority.

So, if in the demand for yet inevitable failure of resolution law is continually sustained in responsiveness to exteriority, there must nonetheless be a place where responsiveness can be brought into determination. Law comes from and returns to position. One can, then, sympathize with the elevation of some determinant autonomy since law, especially of the occidental variety, does import a separation from and a settling 'for the time being' of an importunate responsiveness. But this cannot be a position which would ever contain law's responsiveness. It must itself be labile and protean to an infinite extent. There is a clear enough price to be paid for the denial of this in law and that price is the constant, reductive effort to ensure that 'the aleatory margin… remains homogeneous with calculation, within the order of the calculable' (Derrida 1989: 55). The resulting content and the particular impelling quality of this reduction is, however, pervaded by the relation to what is beyond.

This chapter extracts from ideas of legal autopoiesis a constituent movement of law in-between determinant position and what was ever beyond position, and that which moved law was the antinomy between these two dimensions combined with their necessity for each other. Even at its most settled, or especially at its most settled, law could not 'be' otherwise than responsive to what was beyond its determinate content 'for the time being', but neither could it dissipate in a pure responsiveness. Law, that is, matched the antinomic qualities of determination and responsiveness and formed when a position was 'taken' in-between them. In occupying this position, law could not repose in some systemic security but was itself a specular version of these antinomic qualities. The relation between these consequent dimensions of law is one of apposition, where apposition would comprehend, as it does, things being proximate and applied to each other along with their being parallel and opposed.

References

Appelbaum, R. P. (1998), 'The Future of Law in a Global Economy', 7 *Social & Legal Studies*, pp. 171-192.

Derrida, J. (1977), 'Limited Inc abc', 2 *Glyph*, pp. 162-254.

Derrida, J. (1978), 'Cogito and the History of Madness', in *Writing and Difference,* Routledge, London.

Derrida, J. (1982), *Margins of Philosophy*, trans. Alan Bass, University of Chicago Press, Chicago.

Derrida, J. (1989), 'Psyche: Inventions of the Other', trans. Catherine Porter, in Waters, L. and Godzich, W. (eds), *Reading de Man Reading*, University of Minnesota Press, Minneapolis.

Derrida, J. (1992), 'Force of Law: The 'Mystical Foundations of Authority',', in D. Cornell et al. (eds.), *Deconstruction and the Possibility of Justice*, Routledge, New York.

Derrida, J. (1994), *Specters of Marx*, Routledge, New York.

Derrida, J. (1995), *The Gift of Death*, University of Chicago Press, Chicago.

Giddens, A. (1990), *The Consequences of Modernity*, Polity Press, Cambridge.

Harvey, D. (1989), *The Condition of Postmodernity*, Blackwell, Oxford.

Hatzimihail, N. (2000), 'The Many Lives – and Faces – of *Lex Mercatoria*: A study of the Genealogy of International Business Law', paper delivered to the Law & Society Association, 2000 Annual Meeting, May 26-29, Miami, Florida.

Hirst, P. and Thompson, G. (1996), *Globalization in Question*, Polity Press, Cambridge.

Robertson, R. (1990), 'Mapping the Global Condition: Globalization as the Central Concept', in M. Featherstone (ed.), *Global Culture: Nationalism, Globalization and Modernity*, Sage, London.

Santos, B. de S. (1995), *Toward a New Common Sense: Law, Science and Politics in the Paradigmatic Transition*, Routledge, New York.

Taylor, J. G. (1979), *From Modernization to Modes of Production: A Critique of the Sociologies of Development and Underdevelopment*, Macmillan, London and Basingstoke.

Teubner, G. (1993), *Law as an Autopoietic System*, Blackwell, Oxford.

Teubner, G. (1997a), 'Global Bukowina: Legal Pluralism in the World Society', in G. Teubner (ed.), *Global Law Without the State*, Dartmouth, Aldershot.

Teubner, G. (1997b), 'The King's Many Bodies: The Self-Destruction of Law's Hierarchy', 31 *Law & Society Review*, pp. 763-787.

Teubner, G. (1997c), 'Breaking Frames: The Global Interplay of Legal and Social Systems', XLV *The American Journal of Comparative Law*, pp. 149-169.

Teubner, G. (2000a), 'Alienating Justice: On the surplus value of the twelfth camel.' in this book, ch. 2.

Teubner, G. (2000b), 'Contracting Worlds: The Many Autonomies of Private Law', 9 *Social & Legal Studies*, pp. 399-417.

Waters, M. (1995), *Globalization*, Routledge, London.

Wolf, R. R. (1982), *Europe and the People Without History*, University of California Press, Berkeley.

12 Beyond the Metaphor of Legal Transplants?: Consequences of Autopoietic Theory for the Study of Cross-Cultural Legal Adaptation

DAVID NELKEN

'Words are but wise men's counters but they are the money of fools'
Thomas Hobbes

Introduction

It would be impossible within the bounds of one paper even to describe, never mind to comment upon, the large and fruitful contributions made by the social theory of autopoiesis which Niklas Luhmann developed in the course of reworking his ideas about the operations of social systems in modern society. Much the same would be true even if we limited ourselves to the way his ideas have been adopted and adapted in legal and social theory by Gunther Teubner and other scholars. The theory has been applied to topics as different as contracts, tort and insurance law, public law, conflicts of law, company law, criminal law, environmental law and family law, as well as to socio-legal and policy topics as various as legal regulation, legal pluralism and the globalization of law. There are few other social theories which are as ambitious (and even some of these, such as the work of Habermas or Foucault, have been in part cannibalised by Autopoietic theorists!). It is hard to think of any other approach which offers so direct a challenge to the theoretically - poor empiricism which dominates much Anglo- American socio-legal commentary on law.

In my own writings in sociology of law I have found the theory of autopoiesis, especially as put to work by Teubner, both provocative and helpful in a wide range of enquiries: how to formulate and reformulate the relation between 'law' and society' (Nelken, 1986; 1987), how to identify what could be meant by 'law's truth' (Nelken, 1990; 1993), how to study law 'as communication' (Nelken, 1996a), how to examine the role of scientific expertise in the law (Nelken, 1998a), and how to establish the limits of legal and sociological reflexivity (Nelken, 1994; 1996b; 1998b). But I have, so far, assumed the theory to be less relevant to those of my studies which have focused rather on interpreting differences in legal culture and explaining processes of legal and social change (e.g. Nelken, 1994; 1995; 1997a; 1997c; 1997d; 2000a). It is therefore of particular interest for me to take this opportunity to examine Teubner's attempt to apply autopoietic theory to this type of problem. I shall be focusing in particular on a recent stimulating paper entitled 'Legal Irritants: Good faith in British Law or How Unifying Law Ends up in New Divergences.' (Teubner, 1998). The paper describes the likely fate of a European Union Directive which seeks to apply the doctrine of 'good faith' throughout the Union. But the purpose of Teubner's article goes well beyond this particular example of legal and judicial law making. His aim is rather to assert more general propositions about the best way of studying legal transfers, offering if you will a new paradigm for such research. And my concern here is with these wider claims.

Teubner's argument is already influential.[1] Nonetheless, it may be thought that to give such extended consideration to one article is to exaggerate its importance. But, apart from the difficulty of doing justice to the full range of such a prolific author within the space of one chapter, this limited focus provides an ideal opportunity to see the potential consequences of the theory as applied to one controversial area of socio-legal endeavour. Nor should the subject of legal transfers be seen as somehow marginal to the central problems addressed by autopoietic theory. On the contrary it offers an excellent theoretical and practical test

[1]Teubner's essay was widely referred to, for example, in both the London (W. G. Hart) and the Cambridge Workshops on Comparative Law (both held in July 2000). In Nelken and Feest's forthcoming collection *Adapting Legal Culture* Teubner's article is cited approvingly in chapters as various as those dealing with the transplanting of product liability law in Japan (Nottage, 2001) or the effects of globalisation on bankruptcy law (Flood, 2001). On the other hand, many of those finding inspiration in Teubner's ideas about the unpredictable effects of 'legal irritation' do not bother very much about the details of his argument. Still less, do they sign on as autopoietic theorists.

of the applicability of its fundamental ideas about the relationship between law and society. The study of legal adaptation and transfer does not only provide us with valuable information about the operation of law under different social conditions. Success in understanding and predicting the effects of cross-cultural legal transfer also serves as a test of the extent to which we have really understood the part played by law 'at home'.

Given that there is little agreement on the appropriate theoretical framework to use for such investigations (Nelken and Feest, 2001) the topic of legal transfers is ripe for colonisation by such an apparently rich and powerful theoretical approach. In this chapter I shall give special attention to the way Teubner handles the issues of law's autonomy as compared to its dependence on its social context and the reasons he advances as to why we should stop talking about legal transplants and begin thinking in terms of what he calls 'legal irritants'. But these issues cannot be taken by themselves. Unlike most historical or sociological descriptions or explanations of particular examples or occasions of legal adaptation, autopoietic theory attempts to incorporate the topic of legal transfer into an all encompassing social theory. As with the other issues to which the theory has been applied the topic of legal transfer thus becomes an occasion for reaffirming the validity of the larger theory through the insights which it makes possible (see Teubner, 1993; 1997a).

But this then raises the series of problems which are at the heart of this essay. Does the issue of cross- cultural legal adaptation offer yet another demonstration of the versatility of autopoietic theory, or does it (also) show that the theory has weaknesses where it comes to explaining the transfer of law from one legal culture to another? Like any sufficiently complex set of ideas, there is no doubt that autopoietic theory can incorporate and make space for most of the important variables which need to be taken into consideration in analysing the effects of legal transfers across different political, economic and social and cultural settings (cf. Friedman, 1996). But how, if at all, does this theory take us further than existing approaches? Does it do so by resolving their difficulties, or showing their weaknesses, or in some other way? What new lines of enquiry does it open up? Are there losses as well as gains? Are Teubner's proposals intended only to influence scholarly reflections or also lawyerly practices? How far is there a parallel between introducing new theories within scholary discussion and overcoming the problems of communication across differentiated subsystems? (Should we expect the transfers of ideas and of laws to have similar consequences?) Teubner does talk at one point about new scholarly arguments 'irritating' older certainties. But it is not clear how far this is just a clever pun, or whether it is actually an integral part of his theory.

Autopoietic theory offers a new theory for new times. In applying it to the problem of legal transfers Teubner seeks to introduce a suggestive metaphor of legal transfer which bridges organic and communicative models of law whilst remaining within the terms of Luhmann's social theory. He attempts to incorporate but also transform the investigation of legal culture in the light of claims about the operation of modern social systems. He also offers to engage in an explanatory exercise which can, at the same time, and in much the same terms, also serve as an intervention in legal scholarship geared to normative and policy goals. In keeping with his long standing approach to legal policy making he warns of the need to avoid the facile alternatives of instrumentalism or deregulation.

The main insights into legal transfers which the theory of legal autopoiesis makes possible have to do with reconceiving them in terms of their effects on what Teubner calls 'law's binding arrangements' to other social subsystems and discourses. The foundational problem for any socio-legal theory of law is the 'fit' between law and society and the main disagreements within the field concern whether this 'fit' should be conceived and explored in institutional, functionalist, structural, hermeneutic or other terms (Nelken, 1986). Autopoietic theory valuably focuses on the changing nature of such 'fit' under the highly differentiated conditions of modern society. On the other hand, it takes less account of the many other ways in which law may or may not 'fit' other current features of the society in which it is found. Law 'belongs' to the past, to a previous social and economic order, to tradition and to history, as much as to the present. It may 'fit' another place, the ideas and ideals of some members of a society and not others, etc. In other respects, as part of society's myths and fictions, law aims at the future, acting as an index of desired social, political and economic change, what society would like to become or should like to become. Many of these matters, as we shall see, are particularly relevant when we come to consider the prospects for cross-cultural transfers.

We shall also need to query whether notions of what is an appropriate 'fit' are, or can ever hope to be, culture- free. Theorists of autopoiesis may not be mainly interested in the goal of exploring cultural variation in the role and rule of law. This is subsidiary to their principal task of trying to establish (and apply) universally applicable propositions about the nature of the 'fit' between law and all modern societies, propositions – and then prescriptions- which are derived from the theoretical resources of

Luhmann's system theory (the theory of autopoiesis as the 'holy grail' of the sociology of law). What needs to be clarified, however, is how far these two goals are compatible. The possibilities and meanings of 'legal instrumentalism', and hence the opportunities for 'post -instrumentalist' theorising, vary widely even amongst European societies!

On my reading, autopoietic theory itself carries (concealed) cultural assumptions about the way law does and should 'fit' society which affect its ability to examine cultural variability. The methods which systems theorists propose for investigating the connections between law and society do not therefore exploit all possibilities for understanding such variation. The difficulty of combining a strategy of interpretative sociology with an analysis based on systems theorising is all the more telling in a theory which purports to be about the creation and reformulation of meaning. It is one thing to warn of probable changes in meaning in the course of transfers from one legal culture to another. It is a further methodological problem to actually 'grasp' such transformations of meaning.

In this commentary I shall first offer a brief outline of Teubner's argument. I shall then go on to discuss three of the many issues which his proposal raises for the student of cross-cultural legal adaptation:

- The relationship between the use of metaphors and the theorising of legal transfers
- The possible role of the concept 'legal culture' within autopoietic theory, and
- The attempt in this adaptation of autopoiesis theory to marry descriptive and normative claims.

Hopefully, this analysis should thereby provide us with a valuable close up of a new and important socio-legal theory at work.

Spreading good faith

Teubner argues that, even as a EU directive, (and no longer merely as a rule of a foreign legal system), the doctrine of 'good faith' in commercial contracts is likely to have very different effects in the UK to those it has in Germany. I will make no attempt to summarise the wealth of detailed evidence Teubner adduces for this proposition. What interests me here are only the bare bones of his argument about legal transfers which are intended to be of more general relevance. In this respect, Teubner identifies two sorts of resistance which the doctrine will face when transferred to the UK. In the first place, common law judges will interpret it according to their own legal style and fashion (which includes a reluctance to use 'general notions'). In addition, attempts to introduce this legal doctrine will prove to have quite different and unpredictable effects when transferred from a 'production regime' based on high trust and high autonomy, such as Germany, where the doctrine is 'at home', to a country such as the UK where the opposite conditions prevail. 'Good faith' will hence become a legal irritant:

'Legal irritants', says Teubner, 'cannot be domesticated; they are not transferred from something alien into something familiar, not adapted to a new cultural context, rather they will unleash an evolutionary dynamic in which the external rule's meaning will be reconstructed and the internal context will undergo fundamental change' (Teubner, 1998: 12).

Whatever problems there are in communicating with the legal side of law's binding arrangements with its local social system are as nothing compared to what he calls the 'social side':

> The transferred rule ... will still be recognisable on the legal side of the binding institution but on the social side the legal impulse, if recognised at all, will create perturbation in the other social system and will trigger there some changes governed by the internal logics of this world of meaning (Teubner, 1998: 28).

Teubner then goes on to explain that once the rule is reformulated in the codes and programmes of the social system involved, it will work back as an irritation to the legal side of the institution thus creating a circular co-evolutionary dynamic in such a way that 'will alter its identity fundamentally'. In sum:

> attempts at institutional transfer seem to produce a double irritation in the new context. They irritate law's binding arrangements to society. Foreign rules are irritants not only in relation to domestic legal discourse itself but also in relation to the social discourse to which law is, under certain circumstances, closely coupled. As legal irritants they force the specific epistemé of domestic law to a reconstitution in the network of its distinctions. As social irritants they provoke the social discourse to which law is closely tied to a reconstruction of its own. Thus they trigger two different series of events whose interaction leads to an evolutionary dynamics.

Given this, Teubner argues,

> the result of such a complex and turbulent process is rarely a convergence of the participating legal orders, but rather the creation of new cleavages in the interdependence of operationally closed social discourses (Teubner, 1998: 31-32).

The idea of 'legal irritation' as a way of theorising legal transfers thus both repeats and extends the solution offered by the theory of legal autopoiesis to the basic problem of law's communication with other discourses as this problem presents itself at 'home'. Once transferred, law, it turns out, is 'doubly removed' from other subsystems.

Does this theory offer an advance on other theories of legal transfer? There is no question of the strengths of this approach in relation to those which Teubner chooses to treat as its competitors. It certainly warns us against those theorists who argue for inevitable convergence. But it would be hard to find sociological theories which assert that it is law itself which produces this convergence rather than, in most cases, merely registering it. Teubner also has little difficulty in disposing of the claims about legal transfers which emerge from Legrand's 'culturalism' and Watson's historical researches. Each of these authors, conveniently for Teubner, adopt extreme positions. Either law and culture are inseparable, so that legal transplants are impossible, or else law and culture are so unconnected that transplants are always possible - though this may often mean that not much else changes in the process of transfer!

Teubner criticises the culturalists because their approach would make it impossible to explain real cases of successful transfer. But Teubner's own theory of legal irritation does not make this exactly easy either! For Teubner, the culturalists are right to draw attention to culture, but they ignore other important sources of incommensurability, especially those emphasised by autopoietic theorists who point to the fractures opened up by functionally differentiated and operationally closed social subsystems and discourses. Watson's position, on the other hand, is disposed of with the argument that law is never that free of social and cultural context. The problem is to define exactly what sort of autonomy it possesses in modern society. However, it should be said that Watson, an expert on Roman law, was not principally interested in developing a theory of 'modern' law. Whilst insisting on the importance of the fact that law is often taken from sources which have little in common with the societies into which it is imported, even Watson does sometimes admit that it can and often does then undergo considerable transformation.

Teubner argues convincingly that we need to get beyond dichotomies which juxtapose cultural dependency and legal insulation or social context and legal autonomy (Teubner, 1998: 17). The problem (for socio-legal theorising) is not *whether* law fits society but finding the best route to capture the way law does and does not 'fit'. But it is not so clear how radical Teubner wants his claims to be. On the one hand, when describing how commercial law does and should 'fit' production regimes, Teubner seems to be well within the tradition of socio- legal studies of 'law in context'. He is critical of assumptions that we can or should expect legal rules or institutions to have the same effects when torn from their original context, and he appears to share the sociological conventional wisdom that the more 'congruent 'or 'compatible' with its new environment, the more likely law is to transfer effectively. But at the same time, Teubner also claims that law is bound by its difference to social discourses. Hence he asserts that (useful) change is best achieved by seeking to ensure that transferred law works as a 'strong irritant' which will trigger reaction just because it does not correspond to current conditions in the society in which it is introduced. Can all these claims be reconciled? Where is the line between paradox and contradiction ?

Legal irritation as a metaphor of legal transfer

For better or worse, Teubner's argument is not set out in terms of the advance it represents over current socio-legal theorising but rather as an attack on the metaphor of legal transplants which, he says, currently shapes academic debate over legal transfers. He begins his paper by stating that the metaphor of legal transplants is misleading and that there is therefore a need for the new metaphor of 'legal irritation', which he uses both as a verb to describe the process of legal transfer and to describe the law or institution being transferred.

This raises a number of intriguing questions whose importance goes well beyond the strengths and weaknesses of Teubner's essay. What can it mean to claim that a metaphor is misleading? Metaphor is defined as 'a figure of speech in which a word or phrase is applied to an object or action that it does not literally denote in order to imply a resemblance' (Chambers Dictionary). Given that there will necessarily also be limits to this resemblance, can any metaphor avoid being misleading, at least in some respects? What exactly is misleading about the metaphor of 'legal transplants' according to Teubner? And how can we be sure that the metaphor of irritants will not also be misleading? How should we choose our metaphors? Do we choose them or do they choose us? (As the factory age gives way to the age of the computer metaphors seem to change accordingly, see e.g. Balkin, 1998.) How far do figures of speech 'work' because of their persuasive powers, because of what they evoke, rather than because of their correspondence to what they purport to describe? If we live by metaphors, do metaphors also bring phenomena into being (Lakoff and Johnson, 1980)? Most important of all, are metaphors part of the stories we tell, or are they part of scientific constructions. And where exactly lies the difference? As far as Teubner's use of metaphor is concerned, what is the relationship between his theorising and his use of metaphorical or other figurative language?

Can we avoid metaphors?

Seeking to identify the appropriate as compared to the misleading implications of these or any other metaphors might seem beside the point. It risks taking them too seriously and encouraging what will be an ultimately sterile enquiry. Surely what matters is the argument behind the metaphor, not the figure of speech? But, as long as we use metaphors, the problem remains how we are to discover the arguments they mobilise. Are metaphors simply a distracting diversion from theorising. Should we do our best therefore to purge our arguments as far as possible of metaphorical language? But is this really desirable? Is it even possible? Is the best we can do, as Teubner argues, to explicitly seek to improve our metaphors?

The effort to avoid metaphorical language entirely in speaking about legal adaptation or any other matter of importance to socio-legal studies seems doomed to failure. It is easy enough to reject talk of transplants in favour of apparently more common sense descriptive terms. But the dangers in using workaday language arise precisely because it makes it too easy to lose sight of the metaphorical qualities intrinsic in all our communications. By seeking to avoid metaphorical language all we may be doing is repacing 'live' metaphors with the 'dead' metaphors with which ordinary language is littered. In these terms, the advantage of both legal transplants and legal irritants is that their very strangeness means that one is less likely to forget that they are metaphors. Better a striking metaphor which calls attention to its artificiality than one which attempts to pass unobserved?

When we speak, for example, of 'borrowing, diffusion and imposition' (Friedman, 2001), or of 'begging, borrowing or stealing' other people's laws (Friedman, 1998), none of these terms denote what actually goes on when laws are transferred. All carry with them from other contexts questionable implications regarding the manner in which legal adaptation takes place, the means by which it is achieved and its likely results. (Can the owner ask for his borrowed legal institution back again? Can the thief be taken to court for theft!) The same applies if we talk of 'import' and 'export', of 'competition', 'borrowing' and 'reception', or of 'transfers' or 'the circulation of legal models', to name only some of the currently popular alternatives.

Friedman himself is not averse to metaphors. In trying to demystify the process of legal transplants he compares the process of legal borrowing to getting clothes 'off the peg', rather than having them made to measure (Friedman, 1998). What he intends to convey here, we may assume, are the advantages of borrowing other people's laws in terms of the gains in time and convenience of not making too much of a fuss about achieving too close 'a fit'. His choice of metaphor also implies that borrowing laws is as normal and unproblematic as buying standardised clothes. Perhaps he also seeks to suggest that few can afford the costs of tailor- made!

These or other implications of Friedman's metaphor would need to be tested in relation to the historical and sociological evidence available. But, if we are to take this metaphor seriously, it is as well to acknowledge that it has these and other implications which are far from obvious. Are laws manufactured like clothes on the basis of abstract and average suitability for all comers? Is this not something which varies by type of law and by time and place? Does it not make all the difference that laws always already belong to somebody else? Certainly it does for those advocating competing approaches to legal adaptation. Asking to copy or borrow clothes which someone else was actually wearing might be a better analogy and would suggest a much more complicated transaction where similarity of shape or need to the original owner of the clothes would be all important. Given these problems could it be the metaphor itself which has been taken 'off the peg'?

By their very nature metaphors are neither true nor false, only more or less useful. The value of metaphors lies in their heuristic possibilities - leading us to think in new and imaginative ways, in the present case, about the processes of legal transfer. But they can also be misleading, as

Teubner argues, by sending us in the wrong direction, and, in the case of mixed metaphors, by sending us at the same time in different directions! We will therefore need to pay attention to the message conveyed by different metaphors regarding for example their implied definitions of adaptation of legal culture or their image of the typical processes of adaptation. Rather than seeking to avoid metaphors, we will have to take them seriously - which, of course, does not mean taking them literally. If, for example, we want to talk about a legal transfer 'failing', we may choose to discuss this in terms of 'rejection' by a society or culture because of its foreignness, or seek to explain it in terms of 'resistance' by those groups who oppose it for reasons of interest or ideals. The terms we use will make a difference. Taking metaphors apart and examining their implications may often be the only way to stopping them running away with the argument, and the best means 'to come to grips' with their power to shape both scholarship and action.

Why choose the irritants metaphor?

Teubner does not argue that we can do away with figurative language. His recommendation is rather that we should switch metaphors. What he likes about the transplants metaphor is that it suggests that there is an organic link between law and society. But there are two respects in which, according to him, it can be misleading. In the first place it suggests that the result of transferring legal rules and institutions is either an outright success or failure, when it is more likely to be more mixed. Talking instead of legal irritants will allow us to get over what he calls 'the false dichotomy of repulsion or interaction which is a result of thinking with this metaphor.' Secondly, it helps us realise that what happens is not that the new rule or institution is transplanted into a new organism but instead that it triggers off a set of new and unexpected events.

Teubner's criticisms by no means exhaust all that can be said either in favour or against the transplants metaphor. Until we have a thorough analysis of this problem it will be difficult to decide whether his irritation metaphor offers the right remedy. Nor, and this is as important, is there any acknowledgement that the chosen metaphor which he proposes to substitute can also be misleading. In this section I shall therefore say something more about the strengths and weaknesses of both transplants and irritants as metaphors.

A major drawback of the transplant metaphor which Teubner does not discuss is the extent to which it is used (and usable) in contradictory ways. For some authors, talking in terms of transplants implies that the rule works as it always did in its originating culture; for others that it succeeds in achieving the same results in its new context. Krygier (1997) argues that the success of the ombudsman in Poland is an example of the possibility of successful transplants to that country. Friedman (1998) comments that the worldwide success of the institution of ombudsman should not be considered as an example of transplant because those who have adopted it may be quite unaware of its origins in Sweden. So does success consist in getting something foreign accepted or in making it not seem foreign? How far are these the same processes? The answer is likely to vary for different examples of transplants. If in some cases the whole point of the legal transplant is to help what exists to survive, in others the hope is that the society on the receiving end will change to become more like the source of the transfer.

Part of the reason for this ambiguity is the difficulty of knowing how far we should expect to find resemblances between legal and other types of transplants. Some scholars do manage to find parallels between the situation of altruistic donors and recipients of medical and of legal transfers (Feldman, 1997). But, in the context of legal transplants, these become very loaded terms. Watson, who strongly promotes the use of the term, delights in showing how far the choice of which legal rules are transferred depends on the accident of which foreign university lawyers attended, chance encounters between scholars, or chains of mistaken interpretations of ancient texts. But medical transplants, by contrast, are typically highly planned affairs, and even botanical transplants are often - though not always - carefully programmed.

There may also actually be more in common between the legal transplant and legal irritation metaphors than Teubner would want to acknowledge. If metaphors direct us where to look, how to look and why to do so, then it could be said that the metaphor of legal irritants, is much like that of legal transplants in that it also directs our gaze mainly to the regulatory problems of trying to use law to change other legal and social orders. Both metaphors leads us naturally to use the language of engineering and pathology, of problems and solutions. Their implicit model of the process of transfer is that of a directed planning process, tending to exclude, on the one hand, the investigation of processes of imposition connected to colonialism, and, on the other, examples of borrowing through imitation. Likewise, Teubner explicitly rejects the 'all or nothing' implications of the transplants metaphor. But he concludes his own analysis of the process of interaction initiated by transferring the doctrine of good faith by arguing that *either* it will not even be an irritant *or* it will become a 'strong irritation' (Teubner, 1998: 28).

These similarities between the transplants and irritation metaphors are thrown into even better relief by comparing them with entirely different ways of conceiving and investigating legal transfers. Some authors have argued that we should enlarge our way of thinking about the process of promoting legal change abroad by placing these efforts in the context of what they call (metaphorically?) 'palace wars'.[2] The focus thus becomes the way competitions for prestige amongst elites, both at home and abroad', produce transformations in national structures for governing the economy' (Dezalay and Garth, 1997: 114). The questions this different approach opens up include: when do 'clientilist' (Eisenstadt and Roniger, 1984) forms of power come to be legalised and why? Garth and Dezalay claim that this depends on the gaining of 'symbolic capital' and on strategies of social mobility. More than might be imagined, educational experiences and prior relationships between professors and students are also important.

Unlike both the transplants and irritants metaphors Dezalay and Garth's approach stresses the extent to which legal transfers have consequences for the *originating* society as well as for the societies to which new laws or procedures are being introduced. In fairness, it should be said that, as compared to the transplant metaphor, Teubner's argument could be more easily extended so as to consider the perturbation effects on legal and social order in the home society, as well as abroad, of 'successfully' having its institutions accepted as appropriate objects for transfer. And he may have had less reason to address this issue in his case study of 'good faith' because he was talking about EU directives rather transnational borrowing. But, even in terms of this case study, a crucial aspect of applying common standards and legal rules throughout the Union (or purporting to do so) is the role it plays as part of the process of constructing the EU and legitimating its central institutions (and perhaps also the German doctrines accepted as a model) 'at home'. The problem of course is to identify what counts as 'home' here. On the other hand, not all of the differences between the metaphors are to the advantage of the irritants metaphor. It

[2]The irritants idea makes it hard - but certainly not impossible- to formulate questions about who is doing the irritating and why. Within the framework of social systems theorising, however the question of human agency is displaced by the blind operations of subsystems.

remains a useful feature of the transplant metaphor as compared to the irritant metaphor that it alludes unmistakably to the perceived 'otherness' of the transferred rule, emphasising the fact that it 'belonged' to another society or culture.

Neither the legal transplant nor the legal irritant metaphor help us to recognise that the need for 'compatibility' between the intermediaries who carry legal transfers is as important as that between the societies of origin and transfer. They suggest little specific about the role of state agencies, of International organisations and NGOs, of bankers and entrepreneurs, of the competition between international and domestic lawyers, elite, marginal lawyers and 'cause lawyers', economists, and accountants. These metaphors do not lead us to examine the informal 'invisible college' and professional networks. An approach to legal transfer using the legal irritants metaphor would have to encompass all of this in terms of its focus on communication between different systems and discourses. It might do so by embracing concepts and levels of analysis belonging to other social scientific studies of regulation (see Paterson and Teubner, 1998). But to remain at all consistent with its Luhmannian heritage it would have to stop well short of Dezalay and Garth's claim that legal transfers show 'the triumph of personal connections' (Dezalay and Garth, 1997).

The metaphor of legal irritants, like that it seeks to displace, thus has both strengths and weaknesses. Its highly original way of conceiving the relationship between law and other social subsystems makes us to rethink what happens when new legal institutions or rules are introduced into different settings. And it has something genuinely new to teach us regarding the difficulties of communication between the economic and political subsystems of society, such as those which dogged the last round of exercises in 'law and development', and which may well doom the present attempts as well. The approach would be fruitful in many other cases beyond Teubner's example of 'good faith' in contract. We could for example, use it to investigate the possible effects of globalising discourses of human rights in stimulating the reworking of Islamic traditions in some Arab cultures.

On the other hand, this approach to legal adaptation may be less helpful for investigating periods of revolutionary and post-revolutionary nation-building, where new legal institutions are formed (e.g. Australia or Canada), where borrowing aims at a radical break (e.g. Japan or Turkey), or where the object of legal transfer is to go back to previous traditions, as with some fundamentalist states or, in different respects, some post-communist regimes. Given that much of the debate about legal transplants concerns transfers from first world nations to economically or politically 'less developed' countries (including those of the 'third world'), a metaphor which presupposes, as Teubner's does, a high level of modern subsystem differentiation in the receiving society will not be appropriate for analysing all times and places. And it is a moot point how far the problems in efforts to promote law and development arise from the unpredictable consequences of sub- system differentiation or rather from excessive 'interference' between the subsystems whose distinctiveness Luhmann's model assumes.

The irritation metaphor, as such, suggests little which is specific about the conditions under which transfers are made, where they are taken from, or why they are introduced. This may in itself not be a bad thing. Different metaphors may be useful for distinguishing different stages in the life of legal transfers; for example the metaphors which are useful for illuminating aspects of the process of *introducing* legal transfers can be quite different from those which help to capture the *outcome* of such processes. Orucu (1994), for example, uses culinary metaphors to distinguish what happens when laws are transferred between societies which have either or both legal or cultural affinity. Her metaphors underline how legal transfers contribute to shaping different patterns of legal pluralism. Indeed, when attempting to describe the outcomes of current processes of trans-national legal transfer, Teubner (1997c) has elsewhere used the colourful expression, 'Legal Bukowina' referring to that multi- cultural part of the dying Austro Hapsburg empire immortalised by Eugene Ehrlich in his arguments about 'living law'.

At the same time, however, the irritation metaphor may sometimes be taken to imply too specific conclusions. Teubner (and even more those who seek to apply his ideas) seem to want to draw from the irritants metaphor pessimistic conclusions concerning the possibility of predicting the eventual outcome of a legal transfer, or a series of transfers. But such an assumption will not always be warranted in advance of empirical research. It may be concluded that any one metaphor is unlikely to enable us to capture all that is important about legal transfers. A given metaphor cannot be good for all purposes. In that sense *any* one metaphor is bound to be misleading.

Metaphors or theories?

The underlying problem in addressing Teubner's idea of legal irritation however, is deciding whether it really is intended to be a metaphor highlighting certain aspects of legal transfers, or whether, instead, it should be treated as a 'term of art' within autopoietic theory, deriving, as it does, directly from Luhmann's writings about the possibility for communication between functionally differentiated social systems (Luhmann, 1995). Could it be both? Teubner frequently makes use of other figurative language, for example speaking (as in the texts quoted previously) of law 'forcing', 'provoking', or 'triggering' different effects. In the course of his essay Teubner also talks of law as an 'infecting virus', and describes how 'courts reject good faith like a contagious disease of alien origin'.

Teubner does in fact call irritants a metaphor and this is a term which does seems heuristically applicable to the area of legal transfers (the dictionary tells us that the term 'irritation' refers to the capacity of being excited to (vital) action by the application of an external stimulus).

But the strong impression remains that the term irritants also has a technical role to play as part of social systems theory, and that its sense has to be compatible, for example, with other terms in the theory such as 'structural coupling', 'perturbation' and 'closure'.[3] What is fundamental is the theory. But can a metaphor be truly heuristic whilst at the same time forming part of a theory which delimits its meaning? Is it not already misleading to assume that a metaphor can denote that to which it refers?

Teubner could try to handle this question by replying that all metaphors belong to, more or less developed, theories.[4] If few are as elaborated or articulated as that of autopoietic theory there are usually at least quite a range of important assumptions being mobilised by any given metaphor. It is interesting, for example, that we find a range of mechanical, organic and discursive metaphors applied to the phenomenon of legal transfers, each of which reflect and advance different approaches to the relation between law

---

3Teubner employs a number of different 'technical metaphors'. Sometimes he uses the expression 'order from noise' as a roughly equivalent idea.

4The use of metaphors can be quite variable. On occasions they represent condensed theoretical hypotheses, at other times they serve mainly as striking images to help make an argumentative point, or summarise an argument which has or will be demonstrated in other ways. According to Lakoff and Johnson (1980: 179) 'it is because many concepts are metaphorical in nature, and because we understand situations in terms of these concepts, that metaphors can be true or false'.

and society. 'Mechanical' metaphors of legal transfer in terms of export, diffusion and imposition (as in the work of Lawrence Friedman) tend to accompany talking about legal transfers using the language of impact and penetration. They reflect a vision of law as a working institution, as an instrument, and as a technique of social engineering. Organic metaphors, on the other hand, speak about grafts, of viruses and contamination, and, of course, of transplants (whether medical or botanical); legal transfers when they succeed, blossom, are fertile and set root. They form part of a functionalist vision of law as an interdependent part of a larger whole. To talk of 'adaptation' for example is to use a metaphor derived from the language of functionalist survival. Finally, discursive metaphors speak about transferring law as a matter of translating and reformulating implicit meanings. They approach law as communication, as narrative and as myth.

The research questions which these approaches open up are understandably different. What is it for a transfer to succeed and how are we to decide? Does this depend on it achieving a given goal, on it helping a given type of social order or system to reproduce itself, or on it conveying 'the same' meaning? Certainly the meaning of 'the same' is likely to be different in all three kinds of metaphor.

Teubner makes some use of all three kinds of metaphor (though without adverting to these differences). Interestingly, however, he sometimes gives the impression that the kind of metaphor used must do more than suggest ways of thinking about law and social change and must also correspond to the nature of the connection being described. Thus at one point in his argument Teubner is tempted to say that a mechanical metaphor might be appropriate to describe the sort of law which is less closely tied to society and (hence) more movable than other sorts of law. Building on the claim that the link between law and other social discourses (or fragments) is looser in some cases and tighter in others, he plays with the idea that this could correspond to the difference (as suggested by the great comparativist Otto Kahn Freund) between law which has a mechanical as compared to an organic connection to society. But he quickly rejects the idea that transferring law could ever be like 'transferring parts of a machine' (Teubner, 1998: 12), acknowledging the culturalists' claim that the legal episteme will affect all types of law. He concludes that there are always two sets of organic links involved in any case of legal transfer, that between law and society in the culture from which the law is taken, and that to which it is being transferred. (We will see in the next section that there may be problems in simply adding the culturalist approach to autopoietic theory.)

Teubner sees his approach as an advance on the transplants metaphor because of the way it allows us to examine the effects of a legal transfer both in terms of the 'transformation of meaning it will undergo' and the way its role will differ once it is reconstructed anew by the legal culture into which it is received. In terms of the categories distinguished here, Teubner's mobilisation of the idea of legal irritants can be seen as an attempt to combine the organic and discursive metaphors. This allows him to maintain his allegiance to Luhmann's social systems theory of the social as a functioning set of communications as well as acknowledge the claims of the culturalists. For much of his article he summarises in organic terms the way the transplant approach would analyse the problems of transferring good faith (e.g. 'the implementation of this 'living law' into the British soil simply would not find its roots in a corresponding economic culture ... the British economic culture does not appear to be a fertile ground on which continental *bona fides* would blossom'). He concludes that 'the legal transplant approach would lead us to expect repulsion, not interaction'.

But, in formulating his own preferred approach, Teubner then switches to a discursive analogy, asking, 'Alternatively what is the narrative that emerges from the irritant metaphor?' (Teubner, 1998: 27). But this does not mean that he is (merely) telling stories. As a follower of Luhmann's theory, he has not and cannot 'take the interpretative turn'. For other proponents of the discursive approach, however, one of the advantages of their approach is that, as compared to the other approaches, it allows us to talk about the way people use, refuse,[5] and in general are moved by metaphors. In this way, we can also put ourselves 'in the frame' and be reflexive about the way scholarly advocacy of certain metaphors can affect that which is being studied.[6] It would have been useful to know more about where Teubner stands on these matters.

Legal culture and the autopoietic idea of law

The issue of reflexivity introduces the wider issue of the notion of legal culture which Teubner presupposes in his study of changes in other people's legal culture. Is legal culture something to be analysed with the

---

[5]For example Borre and Palombara (1998: 15) criticise the transferring of foreign constitutional systems 'as if we were dealing with the importing of wholesale grain or dried skins' (my translation).

[6]See footnote 2.

help of the theory, or is it also something which has shaped the theory itself? Can we still talk of national legal cultures? What of the problems of starting points involved in defining and investigating legal culture? Can this ever be done except from a point of view within some other legal culture? (Nelken, 1995; 1997a; 2000b; 2000c). What if cultures vary in the 'metaphors they live by'?[7]

An important issue for all students of legal transfers is the extent to which the problems encountered are the same as those entailed in any attempt to change a society through law even within a domestic arena. Certainly even such more limited attempts at social engineering face the same problem of law communicating with other discourses. Here too law has to communicate with itself (i.e. with all the loosely interconnected levels and actors this represents) as well as the social sphere or spheres it is supposed to influence or actually does affect. And any given legal institution is also more or less bound up with some fragment of society. There may be as much difference between domestic public and private law (whether defined in legal or social scientific terms), between penal and non - penal law, or between business and family law, as there is between private law in two separate but economically similar societies. So what exactly is the further difficulty of achieving communication between 'foreign' and domestic 'law'? Is this a difference of degree or of kind? Are the terms 'foreign' and 'domestic' ones which belong within a social scientific framework? Do they beg the question of whether differences in the source of law have the same significance for legal, social and scientific discourses?

A further difficulty is whether the relationship between law and culture is assimilable to that between law and the various societal discourses of politics, economics and science. Does autopoietic theory allow us to capture what is special about law facing another culture, or does it simply transform this into another example of discourse differences akin to those entailed in communicating between society's subsystems? Is it a strength of this approach that the difficulty of communicating between legal cultures poses no special problems for a theory which turns all aspects of society into competing and self reproducing world views forms of discourse much like distinct cultures? If we argue, on the contrary, that there are important conceptual differences between these types of problems

[7]Lakoff and Johnson (1980: 180) explain that concepts (and hence also metaphors) arise in the course of interaction between people and their social and material worlds. Hence they are bound to vary between cultures.

it would be a weakness of the theory that the so called 'culturalist' argument is here categorised as (or reduced to?) one of different legal epistemes.

Autopoietic theory, we are told, assumes a *global* culture in which national differences in legal culture have lost importance (King, 1997). The cornerstone of autopoietic theorising is of course that it is no longer possible to talk about 'the totality of society'. We live in an era (or an area?) in which law is attached not to wider cultures but to fractured (and frequently transnational) social elements – 'the fragmented multiplicity of discourses which 'today' constitute society' (Teubner 1998: 21). 'The new ties', between law and society, says Teubner,

> are highly selective. Since contemporary legal rule production is institutionally separate from cultural norm production, large areas of law are only in loose, non systematic contact with social processes (Teubner, 1998).

This should lead us to search for 'culture' in the fragmented subsystems which make up modern society rather than in the idea of national cultures. Can all this be reconciled with the view that differences between national legal cultures or areas of legal culture such as civil and common law systems are still the source of important contrasts in the way law is bound to elements of society?

Teubner's arguments in this paper show him valiantly attempting to do just this. He tells us explicitly that 'globalising processes' have created one world - wide network of legal communications which downgrades the laws of the nation states to mere regional parts of this network which are in close connection with each other. This is the basis of his criticism of a one-sided 'culturalist' approach which would argue that the fate of transfers depends on national legal cultures. 'Transfer of legal institutions is but a direct contact between legal orders within one global discourse and this explains the frequent and relatively easy transfer of legal institutions from one legal order to the other' (Teubner, 1998: 16).

On the other hand, Teubner also admits that 'law still has cultural ties', he insists that 'differences between civil law and common law still have a part to play', and even assumes that 'good faith will reproduce in legal form larger differences of the national cultures involved' (Teubner, 1998: 24).

It is hardly surprising that Teubner recognises the continuing importance of legal culture. It could hardly be otherwise for a leading international scholar who has worked for long periods in cultures as different as the USA, Germany, Italy and the UK! The term he uses (borrowing from Legrand, 1997) is 'legal episteme' - as where he talks about acknowledging the important role played by 'the specific episteme of domestic law'. But Legrand's use of this term is not easily reconciled with the approach to 'legal discourse' found in autopoietic theory. The latter takes law (as compared to other forms of discourse) to be centrally concerned with the distinction between what is legal/illegal. Legrand's approach to legal culture, on the other hand, is more wide ranging - law is seen as an inseparable aspect of a society's myths and narratives. Legrand's passionate insistence that there are important and crucial differences in what each culture takes to be law (Legrand, 2001) also sits uneasily with autopoietic theory's need for a universal definition of law. Teubner is right to argue that the claim that differences are unbridgeable is going too far. But we are still left with the awkwardness of combining an idea of legal culture which aims at universality with one that seeks to stress incommensurability. At best we would have to say that Teubner makes use of Legrand's term whilst denying it almost all its point.

Leaving Legrand aside, how far can legal cultural differences realistically be (re)formulated in terms of autopoietic theory? Seeing legal culture as an 'episteme' makes it similar to other societal discourses (as opposed to seeing legal culture for example as legal behaviour or litigation rates). But autopoietic theory would seem to be unable to recognise differences between legal discourses in different cultures except as differences betwen between law and other social communications. Teubner distinguishes situations in which law is in a looser or tighter relationship with other social discourses. In the former case, law is technical and insulated from its social context but still assimilated via the deep structure of the legal episteme. In the latter, 'legal and social processes are tightly coupled; here legal rules are formulated in ultra - cyclical processes between law and other social discourses which bind them closely together while maintaining at the same time their separation and mutual closure' (Teubner, 1998:18). It is the latter sort of law which meets most resistance because 'transfers will not only be confronted with the idiosyncrasies of the new legal culture, they will have to face resistance which is external to the law'.

It does seem as if here Teubner wants to have it both ways. Legal culture shapes law whether it is loosely or tightly bound to society's fragments. Yet when law is tightly bound to other social discourses, it becomes more difficult to transfer because it now reflects something 'external to the law '! But what does it mean to be 'external' to the law and yet still shaped by legal culture? Is there some echo here of Friedman's distinction between the 'internal legal culture' of legal practitioners and scholars and the 'external legal culture' of other groups in society who bring pressure to bear on the law? Certainly culturalists such as Legrand (or followers of the school of 'law as literature') who view law as inseparable from the larger meaning of society's myths and narratives would have difficulty in speaking of what lies 'outside' the law. And Teubner himself comments wryly at the beginning of his article that the last thing he wants to end up showing is that law has a 'relative autonomy'. One of the most interesting insights of autopoeitic theory is the way it helps us see legal and other discourses each operating and reconstructing other discourses from its own 'internal' point of view (Nelken, 1990/1993). Surely we must rather say that, like the notion of 'contract' itself, 'good faith' exists as a term in law but also within other social discourses. And different legal cultures surely connect these discourses in different ways.

Rather than incorporating Legrand's culturalist approach, the importance which autopoiesis theory gives to social fragmentation under modern conditions is therefore more consistent with other research which shows the need to avoid reifying 'national legal cultures'. Many rules and institutions result from a process of redrawing one's own legal institutions in the light of the other. Law is made sufficiently similar to that in another country in order to be able to make treaties with it; often we only invent or discover domestic law in the moment that new social and technical problems arise which require collaboration with other cultures (see Sherman, 1997). The cross-cultural similarities between law are often stronger than those within law in the same legal culture. As Sherman notes, academic and practising lawyers working in the same area of law in different jurisdictions often find it easier to understand each other than they do lawyers working in different legal areas in the same jurisdiction.

So what is legal culture?

We have argued so far that Teubner makes selective use of Legrand's ideas about legal culture even though the term would rather need a thorough rethinking in terms of autopoietic theory. Such a rethinking would need to touch on a variety of issues because socio-legal thinking is far from any consensus about what is meant by legal culture and the problems there are in studying it (Nelken, 1995; 1997a). Legal culture is taken to refer to a variety of types or number of units - the culture of the local courthouse, that of the nation state, wider cultural entities such as 'Latin legal culture' (Garapon, 1995), or even 'modern legal culture' (Friedman, 1994). It can also, with more difficulty, be applied to so called 'third cultures' of international trade, communication networks and other trans-national processes. There are unresolved questions, amongst others, about how to draw the boundary between political culture and legal culture (Brants and Field, 2000), or between social structure and culture, as explanations of legal culture (Blankenburg, 1997; Nelken, 1997b).

Only somewhat less controversial is the type of topic which is covered by this term. Legal culture points to differences in the way aspects of law are themselves embedded in larger frameworks of social structure and culture which constitute and reveal the place of law in society. These may concern the extent to which law is party or State directed ('bottom up' or 'top down'). It has to do with the number, role and power of courts and legal professions, the role and importance of the judiciary, the nature of legal education and legal training. It concerns ideas of what is meant by 'law' (and what law is 'for'), of where and how it is to be found (types of legal reasoning, the role of case law and precedent, of general clauses as compared to detailed drafting, of the place of 'law' and 'fact'). It can be found in different approaches to regulation, administration and dispute resolution, and what are considered appropriate ways of reaching or of motivating judgement.

There may be important contrasts in the degree to which given controversies are subject to law, the role of other expertises, the part played by 'alternatives to law (including not only arbitration and mediation but the many 'infrastructural' (Blankenburg, 1997) ways of discouraging or resolving disputes), and the role of other religious or ethical norms and the ambit of the 'informal'. Law will have a different (and changing) role and significance in different social arenas, settings, for different groups and classes, and even in different periods. Accompanying and concretising such differences, explaining and attempting to justify them, there are likely to be contrasting attitudes to the role of law, formal and substantive ideas of legitimacy, or the need for public participation as compared to legal autonomy. Hence what is at stake in adapting legal culture may concern both institutions, models and practices as well as philosophies, mentalities and ways of conceiving and categorising methods, problems and solutions.

Processes of legal transfer can involve a wide variety of aspects of law. They may involve one or more elements of foreign institutions or professional organisations and legal and other expertises. What is taken can range from single laws of rules, principles and procedures, to codes, constitutions, or entire legal systems. Transfers may involve very different kinds of law, (it is enough to think of the differences between family law, criminal law, human rights law or commercial law) each of which, it is said, may travel more or less well, and have greater or lesser difficulty in being accepted. Some law may be more univocal, other law more 'chaotic' (Dewar, 1998), in that it aims at a variety of audiences and attempts to straddle a multiplicity of (incompatible) values such as rights and utility or autonomy and community. Some law may be intended to change behaviour in a certain direction, other law only to facilitate choices. In some cases it may be possible to speak of success or failure. In others there may no specified end state of affairs. Law can be valued as a point of reference, as a bargaining lever or a threat. All this is in addition to the differences that arise between transferring technical 'lawyers law' as compared to law which is more closely bound to social practices such as the production regimes examined by Teubner.

The main reason for resorting to the concept of legal culture in this context is because of the way it reminds us that the aspects of law described so far normally come in 'packages' of one sort or another (see e.g. Damaska, 1986, on co-ordinate and hierarchical forms of criminal procedure). Teubner's article is about attempts at harmonisation by a regional legal union such as the EU in the face of the variation which exists amongst modern European countries. But most legal transplant literature, on the other hand, is concerned with countries which represent even greater contrasts, where the relationship between law and society may diverge greatly from that in Europe (see e.g. Galanter, 1989; Lopez-Ayllon, 1995; Rosenne, 1971). Even within Europe, however, there are many differences in legal culture which could be even more relevant to eventual projects of harmonisation by means of EU directives than the differences mentioned in Teubner's article. Garapon describes France as an example of 'Latin Legal culture' which he says 'is always on the verge of inefficiency' (Garapon, 1995). And what is one to say of a country like Italy which combines a highly successful production regime (in the North and Centre) with a civil justice system which is widely acknowledged to be paralysed. In Italy, as in Germany, 'economic action is closely coordinated by business associates and by informal business networks'. But Italian private law - with the exception of extra- judicial arbitration - plays a very restricted role in Italian business governance.

Greater sensitivity to cultural variability in the place which law occupies in different societies may suggest that often what is being transplanted is not so much a particular legal institution or procedure but *the very idea that law is something which does or should 'work'*. The same applies to other aspects of the crucial relationship between law and the economic and political spheres. It is not just that proposing or introducing legal reforms such as mediation or court management in the name of greater working 'efficiency' can form part of political strategies or carry political implications. In many societies questions of legal organisation are political 'all the way down'.

All this suggests that there may be some danger of autopoietic theory being insufficiently reflexive about the extent to which its ideas about legal culture are shaped by the legal culture in which it was created. It may be unsafe to generalise that 'where formerly law was tied to society by its identity with it, ties are now established via difference' (Teubner 1998: 18; which Teubner calls his 'third thesis'). And this idea does not go well together with the argument that commercial law is to be understood as existing in some functional relationship with production regimes. This means that this theory, like other approaches to legal culture (for example Lawrence Friedman's stress on legal culture as reflecting pressure from below) may be less universal than it purports to be. This problem is compounded, as we shall now see, when the theory is then used to craft recommendations for judges and policy makers.

The repercussions of autopoietic theory

For whom and how is autopoietic theory supposed to have consequences? Is the descriptive and explanatory or the normative and policy agenda more important? Can they get in each others' way? Who are the audiences for the findings of autopoietic theorising? How are they expected to respond to them? These questions, important enough in any 'socio- legal' enquiry, are absolutely crucial for a theory which is focused on the difficulties created by the fragmentation of incommensurable discourses. At stake too is the plausibility of Teubner's application of Luhmann's theory. There is some evidence that Luhmann was unhappy with the attempt to insert the theory into juridico-political discourse. Does Teubner see himself as merely developing the implications of Luhmann's theory, or as changing and applying it? It is not clear how far Teubner would be happy to accept the label 'sociological jurisprudence' that some would wish to attach to his adaptation of Luhmann's work. But, in general, the debate is open as to how far sociological insight can be combined with legal reasoning (Nelken, 1998b).

Too often the very practical context and the political implications of debates over legal transfers means that here there is (as has often been remarked) an obvious risk that of social scientific enquiries becoming subordinated to a legally and politically defined agenda. But there also exists the opposite danger that important political questions about whether and how legal transfers should be encouraged can be transformed into technical questions of effectiveness.[8] The relationship here between the descriptive and the normative means that arguments often aim at a curious form of mutual reinforcement. It might be thought that what is impossible does not need to be exorcised. Yet the same authors who argue that legal transfer (especially if it aims at harmonisation) is impossible also warn against the negative consequences of proceeding down this path. Legrand – who thinks legal transplants are impossible - is worried about the dangers of excessive homogenisation. Even Teubner, who believes attempts to produce convergence end in greater divergence makes a strong plea in favour of preserving diversity, urging the need 'to pay utmost respect to the autonomy and diversity of European cultures' (though it is not clear in practice how his theory assists us in doing so given the contemporary conundrum of attempting at the same time to build ever closer union in the European Union).

To whom is autopoietic theory being addressed? Who is being described in statements such as 'European efforts at harmonisation have not yet seriously taken into account the 'varieties of capitalism', the difference of production regimes' (Teubner, 1998: 31). Are scholars or practitioners the main target? There is no reason to assume that there is only one specific audience for the theory. We could say that (like any other socio- legal theorist) Teubner intends his arguments to be considered both by social scientists and practitioners. Thus he will (hopefully) have some influence on the discourse and actions of teachers and students, lawyers and judges, policy makers and regulators. But this – for a follower of autopoietic theory – then leads to some less obvious potential difficulties. According to Teubner's own theoretical assumptions, legal discourses are unable to absorb, except for their own purposes, sociological information

[8]Krygier (1997) suggests that pessisim and optimism of the will have as much to do with this as do historically shaped circumstances.

about production regimes and unable to learn about the effects of their interventions? How will this affect their role as strong irritants?

We could contrast for example the use which would be made of the theory by the policy- maker, trying to achieve certain goals, by the judge, seeking to exercise legal oversight, or by the lawyers trying to make strategic use of the theory on behalf of his or her clients. Is the same message likely to be received and used by all its potential audiences in the same way? According to the theory itself, *could* the *same* message be received by these groups, given that they can at most be an irritation to existing discourses? Will these discourses 'co-evolve' according to the same theoretical principles which apply to law and the discourses with which it is bound? How far can the message of legal autopoiesis be used (and abused) and how does this affect its predictive claims and the normative policy aims associated with the development of the theory?

What are the relevant differences between more theoretical discourses (such as those about autopoiesis) and more practical discourses which need to achieve and justify the closure which allows for decisions to be taken? How much is the discourse about autopoiesis part of the phenomenon of legal culture being explained and how much is it part of what is doing the explaining (Is a journal article part of what Teubner is considering here or marginal to it)? As noted, Teubner talks about his (and other theoretical work) 'irritating' scholarship. Does this mean that scholarship is part of the phenomena of legal transfer which is being discussed, or is this just a throwaway line? What is involved in using autopoiesis theory to make recommendations to lawmakers and others? How, if at all, does its 'truth' depend on it being explicitly taken up? The cross-cultural context of debates about legal transfers adds further complexities. Are the audiences for this sort of theory the same groups in different cultures? Is Teubner's argument applicable to the type of audience found in one jurisdiction more than another? Does he have in mind in particular the theoretical contribution made by law professors to the relatively high level of theorising found in civil law as compared to common law cultures?

Teubner expressly says that he want to reshape the academic debate. In particular, he claims that he is responding to those comparative lawyers and others who use the term legal transplants and who are said to assume that harmonisation is bringing about convergence and functional equivalence. (The fact that his intervention here regards harmonisation and not other examples of legal transfers possibly explains why the competing theories he addresses in this piece did not include more sociological accounts of legal transfer such as those of Dezalay and Garth (1996;

1997).) The main message of this application of autopoietic theory to efforts at harmonisation conducted through EU directives is that such activity is more likely to lead to new divergences than to convergence. The richly interdisciplinary substance of his discussion of what is likely to happen to the good faith doctrine is of great value. But the general point about the unexpected consequences of legal interventions aiming at harmonisation is certainly not 'news'. Whatever many politicians, legal practitioners or bureaucrats may be saying or doing, there are no scholars, certainly no social scientific scholars, who are identified in the text as making the claim that such harmonisation by law is plain sailing. Even within domestic society the unexpected outcome of much socio-legal engineering is by now conventional wisdom.

In fact Teubner himself says of those that he is critiquing that 'they have not been listening enough to the social scientists'. Whether or not he has fairly captured the views of comparativists it certainly would be hard to find social scientists who believe that convergence is produced by law – rather than that law often expresses or consolidates such change – usually following in its wake. But would 'social scientists' agree on much else? And how far can judges and practitioners be expected to 'listen' to the findings of this or any other social scientific theory whilst reproducing their own discourses?

The contribution to explanation

Insofar as Teubner intends his analysis to make a contribution to the task of describing or explaining legal transfers, it must stand or fall by the empirical claims it advances or opens up to investigation.[9] He does offer some defeasible claims about the 'predictable result' of what is likely to happen to the good faith doctrine once it is applied with the situation sensitivity of common law judges (Teubner, 1998: 21). But such assertions are based on his knowledge of different legal cultures and do not in themselves derive from autopoietic theory. Other arguments, such as the need to make sense of law in relation to wider social and economic factors such as 'production regimes', take us back to the truths and truisms of the

[9] Some of those currently signing up for Teubner's theory seem tempted to treat unexpected outcomes of legal transfers as sufficient evidence to confirm the theory, rather than asking if the theory tells us enough about what *sort* of outcomes to expect, when, why and how.

'law in context' approach which the notion of legal transplants, as pioneered by Alan Watson, was intended to put in doubt.

When it comes to the key issues of explaining what is likely to be the wider effects of legal transfers, Teubner's predictions are (understandably?) almost always hedged with conditional statements about possibilities which realise themselves 'rarely', or only 'under certain circumstances'. We are told repeatedly of the difficulty of achieving 'fundamental' change but this risks being a truism. Even his major finding comes near to tautology (and not of the sort which is inseparable from theorising). Teubner brings his paper to an end with the following argument:

> And good faith? It will not even be an irritant[10] to the British production regime if it presents itself (sic) as a bundle of legal duties of mandatory co-operation, German style, imposed on the parties to the contract. The British regime would react with cool indifference.[11] However - and this is my concluding thesis - good faith will become a strong irritation to the market- driven production regime in Britain *if the new context transforms* good faith from a facilitative rule into a prohibitive rule...its effect would be to outlaw certain excesses of economic action (Teubner, 1998: 28, my italics).

But is not the question whether the 'new context' will transform the rule exactly what we want to know? And what is meant here by the term 'context'? Is there not some circularity in the claim that only if a rule becomes mandatory it can have definite effects?

Teubner's article does include some apparently more speculative arguments such as the claim that 'transfer will be effectively excluded without a simultaneous and complimentary change in the other social field' (Teubner, 1998: 22). But, apart from the difficulty in pinning down what all these terms mean, it would seem that all that is being argued here is that everything depends on what else is going on at the same time. But why should this be restricted to simultaneous change? Is it not typically the case that law precedes or more likely follows social developments? If time is all

---

[10]This sentence suggests the importance of examining variation in the way law does and does not act as an irritant. But the important issue of the conditions under which this occurs is not otherwise explored in Teubner's article.

[11]The price to be paid for Teubner's vivid style - as in his reification of the 'British Regime... acting with cool indifference' - is that it is often difficult to work out which would be the best way to test his claims

important, as is suggested also by Teubner's idea of irritants as a trigger which sets off perturbations in the different logics of development of law and of social discourses, then surely it would be best to define transfer as something which happens if at all over the long period? In other recent writing Teubner has in fact stressed the need to distinguish between processes of *ad hoc* contacts, systemic linkages and co-evolution (Paterson and Teubner, 1998).

If the outcome of a legal transfer depends on the future, it is also conditioned by the past. Perhaps because of the way the social systems approach focuses on current differentiation amongst social discourses, less attention tends to be given to the different levels of historically inherited culture. It is a controversial but highly relevant question how much the possibility of legal transfer depends on more recent or more remote legal, social and political history (Krygier, 1997), including the experience of past contacts and 'the history of suspicions' (Mertus, 1998). This may override similarities or differences in 'production regimes' or any other such contemporary functional considerations.

Needless to say there are many other aspects of legal transfers which Teubner's general theory (and not only the metaphor of legal irritants) may not be particularly equipped to highlight. We may wish to distinguish between the likelihood of success in transferring 'strong' and 'weak' law to 'strong' and 'weak' social groups (Cotterrell, 2001). There are likely to be different results in transferring legal institutions, ideas, methods of education alternatives to law and so on. We should not expect legal irritations to apply in the same way to attempts to spread human rights law, intellectual property and products liability law. To understand the likely outcome in all these cases, it may not be sufficient to concentrate only on the quality of law's binding arrangements with society.

Much more needs to be known about the general and particular contexts of a given legal transfer to explain the conditions in which transfers take place and the conditions of their success (Nottage, 2001). Different problems may be posed by the study of processes of social and economic homogenisation, convergence and divergence, the globalisation of law and globalisation by law (Heydebrand, 2001), the creation of ' third cultures' or a trans-national legal order from very different legal cultures ('good faith' comes in here too regarding international commercial law), or the role of state as compared to different elements of society (Jettinghoff, 2001). It would also seem essential to distinguish situations where elites import laws from abroad and where they have them imposed. In his paper Teubner seems relatively uninterested in such differences, moving unselfconsciously between talking about the transfer of legal institutions, the interpretation and application of common EU directives in different jurisdictions, and speaking of 'when a foreign rule is imposed' (Teubner, 1998: 12).

But can success be established from the outside? The question of what constitutes success in legal transfers is something which is fought over and success in persuading or imposing such definitions has major consequences both at home and abroad. Perceived and actual differential outcomes of attempts at legal transfer may have a great deal to do with the way they are presented (and understood) as chosen or imposed. As much as objective differences between one culture and another, what matters is the way such *factors* are turned into *arguments* in favour of certain types of social change or in opposition to them. Such arguments can then become self-fulfilling so as to make a given transfer appear and become a success or a failure. Examples in the context of legal culture include the defence of 'Asian values' or resistance to 'Americanisation' or 'globalisation'. In the present case study Teubner mentions at the outset how some authors claim that the introduction into English law of the doctrine of good faith will work 'practical mischief' whilst others argue that it will 'help infuse healthy communitarian norms' (Teubner, 1998). But we hear nothing more about these protagonists. It is a weakness of his approach that Teubner does not engage with such arguments as *part* of the phenomenon under investigation but rather just uses them as evidence of mistaken ways of grasping the problem.

Whether or not a transfer takes place thus depends on how it is *interpreted* by the receiving culture. Even where a transfer actually helps transform an institution, or even an entire legal culture, it can leave behind a sense of inauthenticity. Some have argued that this is the case for Japan's apparent success in importing a modern legal system even whilst continuing to feel that in some respects it is not truly a modern society (Tanase, 2001). As Cotterrell (2001) rightly emphasises, 'the way law is conceptualised - for example as rules, as ideas embedded in legal culture, as a part of culture in some wider sense, or as an instrument for particular purposes - colours the way that the success (indeed, the very possibility) of legal borrowing is judged'. It is hard to see how cross-cultural research can manage without interpretative understanding when it is so crucial to decide whether legal cultures have similar or different concerns for 'effects' (and for what sort of effects). To make (or break) claims about such matters requires methods of comparative research based on hermeneutic understanding of texts and actions which are rather different from those required for developing the theses of social systems theory. The contents of legal culture (and not just the existence of different legal cultures) may not be accessible through the theory of autopoiesis but, as Teubner himself concedes, they are all important to understanding the process of transfer.

The external observer is, of course, also entitled to make his or her claims about the effects of a legal transfer. But, if determining the aim of legal interventions and policies is difficult enough in the domestic context, it becomes doubly difficult when we come to consider cross – cultural transfers. Teubner relegates this problem to a footnote (1998; 22, n. 47) commenting that it is a 'wider question whether (a borrowed institution) was supposed to work properly'. Perhaps this is the only place it can find in a theory which is so committed to predicting the likely effects of borrowing without reference to the intentions and aims of those promoting, receiving or resisting the transfer.

By contrast, an alternative approach to legal transfers would focus precisely on such competing interests and battles over meaning. Some of those using such an interpretive approach have in fact been led to conclusions which if anything show that the subsystem model of differentiated sub-systems assumed by the theory of autopoiesis can serve as a handicap rather than help advance our understanding of the processes of legal transfer. Garth and Dezalay for example observe that 'the categorical and institutional boundaries ... are more permeable than first appears. Distinctions among family capital, law, business, economics and politics are less rigid and unbreakable than is claimed by professional discourses. The discourses are often only rhetorical arguments – aiming to exclude competitors or to support or contest internal and external hierarchies' (Dezalay and Garth, 1997: 115). The activity of legal transfers is here seen as a matter of market competition and conflict between elites at home and abroad involving the competing expertises of lawyers, accountants, economists, bankers. Do experts in legal autopoiesis also come into this?

... and the normative implications

Whatever may be his explanatory project, Teubner is also interested in showing how autopoietic theory can be used to improve socio-legal engineering. The policy implications of autopoietic theory are explained by Teubner as involving the use of legal transfers to set up a 'strong irritation'. It is not entirely clear, however, what this means or what it entails. Are we being encouraged to protect or to increase diversity through strong irritation? Or is the goal to try to curb unexpected and excessive perturbations by taking more account of social and economic differences in our application of law? Is the main message that of encouraging 'subsidiarity', so as to empower local and sectoral systems and discourses? What if these local systems choose unification in preference to divergence? How do our interventions change the theory's predictions? What would happen if the legal authorities try to pursue harmonisation without heeding Teubner's advice? Would legal irritation not happen anyway – so producing divergence rather than convergence (is it not that which he has been describing?).

When, towards the end of his paper, Teubner does address judges and policy makers directly, the language he uses is unusually hesitant. 'If there is a role for the European legal authorities to play',[12] he says, ' it would be to strengthen the capacity for irritation of the good faith clause instead of neutralising it when they try to enforce its unitarian interpretation' (Teubner, 1998: 31). The message for politicians, legislators and bureaucrats is similarly cautious: 'if there is a lesson to be learnt then it would be a new interpretation of the subsidiary principle' (ibid.). How are we to understand this change of tone to the conditional when turning from his presumed academic readership to practitioners? Is this to be understood as stylistic modesty, natural caution in the world of affairs, or genuine, theoretically – based doubt about the possibility of paradoxical legal engineering without this becoming self-defeating?

Consistent with his wider social theory, Teubner conceives of 'good faith' in autopoietic terms as having the 'role of linking contracts to a variety of different discourses'. Does he assume that judges and practitioners can and should share this way of thinking? Can judges and policy makers be expected to learn about and update themselves on the Luhmann/Teubner theory of autopoiesis? How far can the alleged 'cognitive openness' of the legal system be stretched? Would it be sufficient for them to know only the fundamentals – for example to appreciate the operational limits of their subsystem (and so avoid trying to regulate social life directly)? Scholars are certainly selective in the parts of the theory they appropriate. Can policy makers be allowed more or less

---

[12]The term 'European Legal authorities' is a strange one. It appears to refer to the judges of the European Court or other members of a central administration. But the message Teubner wishes to pass on needs also to be taken on board at least as much by judges in national courts.

license? Certainly it would seem empirically improbable that judges and policy makers could actually apply this or any other social science theory in the course of their operations. Moreover the theory itself would suggest that the operational 'closure' of discourses will forestall this. Elsewhere, Teubner himself has analysed trenchantly what he calls 'hybrid artefacts', terms 'with ambiguous epistemic status and unknown sociological consequences' (Teubner, 1989: 747), which result from attempts by lawyers and judges to import social scientifc ideas.

Insofar as Teubner is appealing to practitioners, policy makers, lawyers and judges, is the term legal irritant really helpful? Why should judges and policy makers give such centrality to the fragmentation of social discourses? Could anybody want or choose to create a legal irritant with unexpected and unpredictable results? Who could or would set out deliberately to introduce 'irritants'? Certainly, those who set out to irritate can hardly expect a good reception! In other words, is this a metaphor we can 'live by' (Lakoff and Johnson, 1980)? Would it be responsible, judicially, or even politically, to declare this as an aim in relation to those whose interests are directly affected by a given decision (as well as those affected more indirectly).

We also need to ask whether it make sense to issue a recommendation to work for strong irritations in all cases indifferently? Must this not vary by case and situation? Could there not be occasions where this would be counterproductive or otherwise inappropriate? Given the complexities of legal and political decision-making and planning, such advice risks over – simplification, and it is hard to see how it would necessarily produce legally, sociologically and politically sound consequences. As far as policy making is concerned, it might be argued that the appropriate route to take must also depend on what is being transferred and on the interests and desires of those sponsoring and receiving the transfer. Success, according to the groups involved in the transferring country, may be, and may be seen to be, different from success from the point of view of those in the country receiving it (Nelken, 2001). Little is said about this, perhaps because Teubner gives so little attention to analysing the arguments used by those promoting or resisting legal transfers. He does take a definite (rhetorical?) stand, however, in favour of what he calls 'the paradox of the unitas multiplex' as against 'all the rhetorics of an ever closer union'.

I have suggested in this commentary that the topic of cross – cultural adaptation of law (admittedly a notoriously difficult subject) illustrates a number of problems with the claims and applicability of autopoietic theory. But I would not wish to be taken to be arguing that the theory is unhelpful for these purposes, or that a way could not be found to deal with many of the points which have been raised. A likely course which could be taken would be to build in information about contrasts in legal culture, and the ideas and practices which concern 'the fit' between law and society, as examples of further differences in law's binding arrangements. And, more than many other approaches, autopoietic theory would appear to be particularly well suited to applying its ideas to itself. After all, a theory about paradox and reflexivity could hardly be uninterested in its own social and cultural embeddedness.

What does seem essential for any theorist engaged in describing, promoting or evaluating legal transfer is to seek such reflexivity both as an intellectual necessity and a political requirement. The metaphor of legal irritants can make it look as if legal transfers are out of anyone's control – except for those willing to learn from autopoiesis theory. But any metaphor we choose to adopt should not be allowed to distract us from asking who seeks or stands to gain from such processes and who only undergo rather than control them.[13] As Teubner rightly reminds us, as compared to past and present practioner proponents of 'law and development', the social science literature is more aware of divergent effects of globalization and the 'exclusion of whole segments of the population from its integrative effects'. The word metaphor itself derives from the Greek 'metaphora', which means 'to transfer'. But it also comes from the Greek 'metapherein' meaning 'to bear'.

References

Balkin, J. (1998) *Cultural Software,* Yale University Press, New Haven.

Blankenburg, E. (1997) 'Civil Litigation Rates as Indicators for Legal Culture', in D. Nelken (ed.) *Comparing Legal Cultures*, Dartmouth, Aldershot, pp. 41-68.

Borre, G. and Palombarini, G. (eds.) (1998) *Il Sistema Sanzionario Penale e le Alternative di Tutela*, Franco Angeli, Milan.

Brants C. and Field, S. (2000) 'Legal Cultures, Political Cultures and Procedural Traditions: Towards a Comparative Interpretation of Covert and Proactive Policing in England and Wales and the Netherlands', in D. Nelken (ed.), *Contrasting Criminal Justice,* Dartmouth, Aldershot, pp. 77-116.

[13]See footnote 2. Schutz (1997: 258-259) rightly argues that the concept of power takes on a distinctive meaning in autopoietic theorising in terms of the relationship between subsystems. But many scholars (myself included) think this makes the problem worse not better.

Cotterrell, R. (2001) 'Is There a Logic of Legal Transplants?', in D. Nelken, and J. Feest (eds), *Adapting Legal Cultures*, Hart, Oxford.

Damaska, M. (1986) *The Faces of Justice and State Authority*, Yale University Press, New Haven.

Dezalay,Y. and Garth, B. (1996) *Dealing in Virtue,* University of Chicago Press, Chicago.

Dezalay,Y. and Garth, B. (1997) 'Law, Lawyers and Social Capital: 'Rule of Law' versus Relational Capitalism', 6 *Social and Legal Studies,* pp. 109-43.

Dewar, J. (1998) 'The Normal Chaos of Family Law', 61 *Modern Law Review*, pp. 467 485.

Eisenstadt, S. and Roniger, L. (1984), *Patrons, Clients and Friends,* Cambridge University Press, Cambridge.

Feldman, E. (1997) 'Patients' Rights, Citizens' Movements and Japanese Legal Culture', in D. Nelken ed. *Comparing Legal Cultures*, Dartmouth, Aldershot, pp. 215-236.

Flood, J. (2001) 'The Vultures fly East: The Creation and Globalization of the Distressed Debt Market', in D. Nelken, and J. Feest (eds), *Adapting Legal Cultures,* Hart, Oxford.

Friedman, L. (1994) 'Is there a Modern Legal Culture?', 7 *Ratio Juris*, pp. 112-131.

Friedman, L. (1998) 'Comments on Applebaum and Nottage', in J. Feest and V. Gessner (eds), *Proceedings of the 2nd Onati Workshop on Changing Legal Cultures*, Onati Institute, Onati, pp. 139-149.

Friedman, L. (2001) 'Some Comments on Roger Cotterrell and Legal Transplants', in D. Nelken, and J. Feest (eds), *Adapting Legal Cultures,* Hart, Oxford.

Galanter, M. (1989) *Law and Society in Modern India,* Oxford University Press, Oxford.

Garapon, A. (1995) 'French Legal Culture and the Shock of 'Globalization', in D. Nelken (ed.), *Social and Legal Studies: Special issue on Legal Culture, Diversity and Globalization,4, 4*, pp. 493-506.

Heydebrand, W. (2001) 'From Globalization of Law to Law under Globalization', in D. Nelken, and J. Feest (eds), *Adapting Legal Cultures,* Hart, Oxford.

Jettinghoff, A. (2001) 'State Formation and Legal Change: On the Impact of International Politics' in D. Nelken, and J. Feest eds. *Adapting Legal Cultures*, Hart, Oxford.

King, M. (1997) 'Comparing Legal Cultures and the Quest for Law's Identity' in D. Nelken (ed.), *Comparing legal Cultures*, Dartmouth, Aldershot.

Krygier, M. (1997) 'Is there Constitutionalism after Communism? Institutional Optimism, Cultural pessimism, and the Rule of Law', 26 *International Journal of Sociology,* pp. 17-47.

Lakoff, G. and Johnson, M. (1980) *Metaphors We Live By,* University of Chicago Press, Chicago.

Legrand,P. (1997) 'Against a European Civil Code', 60 *Modern Law Review,* pp. 44-63.

Legrand, P. (2001) 'What "Legal Transplants?"', in D. Nelken, and J. Feest (eds), *Adapting Legal Cultures,* Hart, Oxford.

Lopez-Ayylon, S. (1995) 'Notes on Mexican Legal Culture', in D. Nelken (ed.), *Social and Legal Studies Special issue on Legal Culture, Diversity and Globalization* 4, 4, pp. 477-492.

Luhmann, N. (1995) *Das Recht der Gesellschaft* , Suhrkamp, Frankfurt.

Mertus, J. (1999) 'The Liberal State vs. the National Soul: Mapping Civil Society Transplants', 8 *Social and Legal Studies,* pp. 121-146.

Nelken, D. (1986) 'Beyond the Study of Law and Society', in *American Bar Foundation Journal,* pp. 323-338.

Nelken, D. (1987) 'Changing Paradigms in the Sociology of Law', in G. Teubner (ed.), *Autopoietic Law: A New Approach to Law and Society,* De Gruyter, Berlin, pp. 191-217.

Nelken, D. (1990) *The Truth about Law's Truth,* European University Institute Law department Working Paper, Florence, Italy, 1990, no. 1.

Nelken, D. (1993) 'The Truth about Law's Truth', in A. Febbrajo and D. Nelken (eds), *European Yearbook of Sociology of Law,* Giuffrè, Milan, pp. 87-163.

Nelken, D. (1994) 'Reflexive Criminology?' in D. Nelken ed. *The Futures of Criminology,* Sage, London, pp. 7-43.

Nelken, D. (1994) 'Whom Can you Trust? The Future of Comparative Criminology', in D. Nelken (ed.), *The Futures of Criminology,* Sage, London, pp. 220-244.

Nelken, D. (1995) 'Disclosing/ Invoking Legal Culture', in D. Nelken (ed.), *Legal Culture, Diversity and Globalisation*: Special issue of 4 *Social and Legal Studies*, pp. 435-453.

Nelken, D. (ed.) (1996a) *Law as Communication*, Dartmouth, Aldershot.

Nelken, D. (1996b) 'Getting the Law 'Out of Context'', 19 *Socio-Legal Newsletter* pp. 12-13.

Nelken, D. (ed.), (1997a) *Comparing Legal Cultures*, Dartmouth, Aldershot.

Nelken, D. (1997b), 'Puzzling out Legal Culture: A Comment on Blankenburg', in D. Nelken (ed.), *Comparing Legal Cultures,* Dartmouth, Aldershot, pp. 58-88.

Nelken, D. (1997c) 'Studying Criminal justice Comparatively', in M. Maguire, R. Morgan and R. Reiner (eds.), *The Oxford Handbook of Criminology,* Oxford, Oxford University Press (*2nd* edition), pp. 559-576.

Nelken, D. (1997d) 'The Globalization of Crime and Criminal Justice: Prospects and Problems', in M. Freeman ed. *Current Legal Problems: Law and Opinion at the end of the 20th Century,* Oxford University Press, Oxford, pp. 251-279.

Nelken, D. (1998a) 'A just measure of science' in M. Freeman. and H. Reece (eds), *Science in Court*, Dartmouth, Aldershot, pp. 11-36.

Nelken, D. (1998b) 'Blinding Insights: The limits of a reflexive sociology of law' 25 *Journal of Law and Society,* pp. 407-426.

Nelken, D. (ed.) (2000a), *Contrasting Criminal Justice,* Dartmouth, Aldershot.

Nelken, D. (ed.) (2000b), 'Just Comparing', in D. Nelken (ed.), *Contrasting Criminal Justice,* Dartmouth, Aldershot, pp. 3-22.

Nelken, D. (2000c) 'Telling Difference: Of Crime and Criminal Justice in Italy', in D. Nelken (ed.), *Contrasting Criminal Justice,* Dartmouth, Aldershot.

Nelken, D. (2001) 'Towards a Sociology of Legal Adaptation', in D. Nelken, and J. Feest (eds), *Adapting Legal Cultures,* Hart, Oxford.

Nelken, D. and Feest, J. (2001) *Adapting Legal Cultures*, Hart, Oxford.

Nottage, L. (2001) 'The Still Birth and Re- Birth of Product Liability in Japan', in D. Nelken, and J. Feest eds. *Adapting Legal Cultures,* Hart, Oxford.

Orucu, E. (1995) 'A Theoretical Framework for Transfrontier Mobility of Law', in R. Jagtenberg, E. Orucu and A. de Roo (eds), *Transfrontier Mobility of Law,* Kluwer, Deventer, p. 4.

Paterson, J. and Teubner, G. (1998) 'Changing Maps: Empirical Legal Autopoiesis', 7 *Social and Legal Studies*, pp. 451-486.

Rosenne, K. S. (1971) 'The Jeito: Brazil's Institutional Bypass of the Formal Legal System and its Development Implications', 19 *American Journal of Comparative Law*, pp. 514-549.

Schutz, A. (1997) 'The Twilight of the Global Polis: On Losing Paradigms, Environing Systems and Observing World Society' in G. Teubner (ed.) *Global Law without a State,* Dartmouth, Aldershot, pp. 257-294.

Sherman, B. (1997) 'Remembering and Forgetting: The Birth of Modern Copyright', in D. Nelken (ed.) *Comparing Legal Cultures,* Dartmouth, Aldershot, pp. 237-266.

Tanase, T. (2001) 'The Empty Space of the Modern in Japanese Law Discourse', in D. Nelken, and J. Feest eds. *Adapting Legal Cultures,* Hart, Oxford.

Teubner, G. (1989) 'How the Law Thinks: Toward a Constructivist Epistemology of Law', 23 *Law and Society Review,* pp. 727-757.

Teubner, G. (1993) *Law as an Autopoietic System,* Blackwell, Oxford.

Teubner, G. (1997a) 'Altera Pars Audiatur: Law in the Collision of Discourses', in R. Rawlings (ed.) *Law, Society and Economy,* Blackwell, Oxford.

Teubner, G. ed. (1997b) *Global Law without a State,* Dartmouth, Aldershot.

Teubner, G. (1997c) 'Global Bukowina: Legal Pluralism in the World Society', in G. Teubner ed. *Global Law without a State,* Dartmouth, Aldershot, pp. 3-38.

Teubner, G. (1998) 'Legal Irritants: Good faith in British Law or How Unifying Law Ends up in New Divergences', 61 *Modern Law Review,* pp. 11-32.